The Sudan was an anomaly in the history of empire. A colony of Egypt, it was administered by Britain as a condominium, and negotiations for its independence were inextricably entangled in the broader fabric of Anglo-Egyptian relations. As an anomaly the Sudan's position in the broader scheme of decolonisation within the British Empire has generally been overlooked by both Commonwealth and African historians. The Sudan's independence has been classed as a part of post-war Anglo-Arab politics of the Middle East, with no special relevance to British policy in Africa. Yet, as these documents show, events in the Sudan did influence the direction and pace of decolonization elsewhere in British Africa. Precedents were set in the Sudan, often against the objections of the Colonial Office. It was through the Sudan, and the Foreign Office, that Britain first committed itself to the right of self-determination for subjects living in an African territory. It was in the Sudan that the idea of self-government was defined to mean a Cabinet composed exclusively of African ministers. It was the Sudan's approach to independence which precipitated the debate within the British government which ultimately led to opening Commonwealth membership to non-white African territories.

Part one, which covers the period between April 1942 and December 1950, begins with the anticipation of the post-war settlement as Sudanese nationalists, British administrators and Foreign Office diplomats each contemplated the impact of the Atlantic Charter on the Sudan. It then documents the shifts in strategies and alliances as different Sudanese political groups allied with either of the codominal governments in their manoeuvres against each other for power in a post-indepencence state. Britain's conversion to the principle of self-determination for a colonial people here came about as a means of preventing Egypt from reasserting its sovereignty over its own colony of the Sudan. This set the tone for the re-negotiation of the Anglo-Egyptian treaty (to be read in conjuction with John Kent's volume on Egypt) and the first stages of Sudanese involvement in the government of their own country. The diplomatic stalemate between Britain and Egypt was paralleled by rapid constitutional and administrative changes in the Sudan.

(continued on back flap)

Sudan

The British Documents on
the End of Empire Project
gratefully acknowledges
the generous assistance of
the Leverhulme Trust.

The Project has
been undertaken
under the auspices
of the British Academy.

BRITISH DOCUMENTS ON THE END OF EMPIRE

General Editor S R Ashton
Project Chairman A N Porter

Series B Volume 5

Sudan

Editor
DOUGLAS H JOHNSON

Part I
1942–1950

Published for the Institute of Commonwealth Studies
in the University of London

London: The Stationery Office

First published 1998

ISBN 0 11 290563 3

British Library Cataloguing in Publication Data
A CIP catalogue record for this book is available from the British Library

If you wish to receive future volumes from the British Documents on the End of Empire project, please write to The Stationery Office, Standing Order Department, PO Box 276, LONDON SW8 5DT, or telephone on 0171 873 8466, quoting classification reference number 040 30 017

Published by The Stationery Office and available from:

The Publications Centre
(mail, telephone and fax orders only)
PO Box 276, London SW8 5DT
General enquiries 0171 873 0011
Telephone orders 0171 873 9090
Fax orders 0171 873 8200

The Stationery Office Bookshops
123 Kingsway, London WC2B 6PQ
0171 430 1671 Fax 0171 831 1326
68–69 Bull Street, Birmingham B4 6AD
0121 236 9696 Fax 0121 236 9699
33 Wine Street, Bristol BS1 2BQ
0117 9264306 Fax 0117 9294515
9–21 Princess Street, Manchester M60 8AS
0161 834 7201 Fax 0161 833 0634
16 Arthur Street, Belfast BT1 4GD
01232 238451 Fax 01232 235401
The Stationery Office Oriel Bookshop
The Friary, Cardiff CF1 4AA
01222 395548 Fax 01222 384347
71 Lothian Road, Edinburgh EH3 9AZ
0131 228 4181 Fax 0131 622 7017

The Stationery Office's Accredited Agents
(see Yellow Pages)

and through good booksellers

Printed in the UK by the Stationery Office

J49357 11/98 C5

Contents

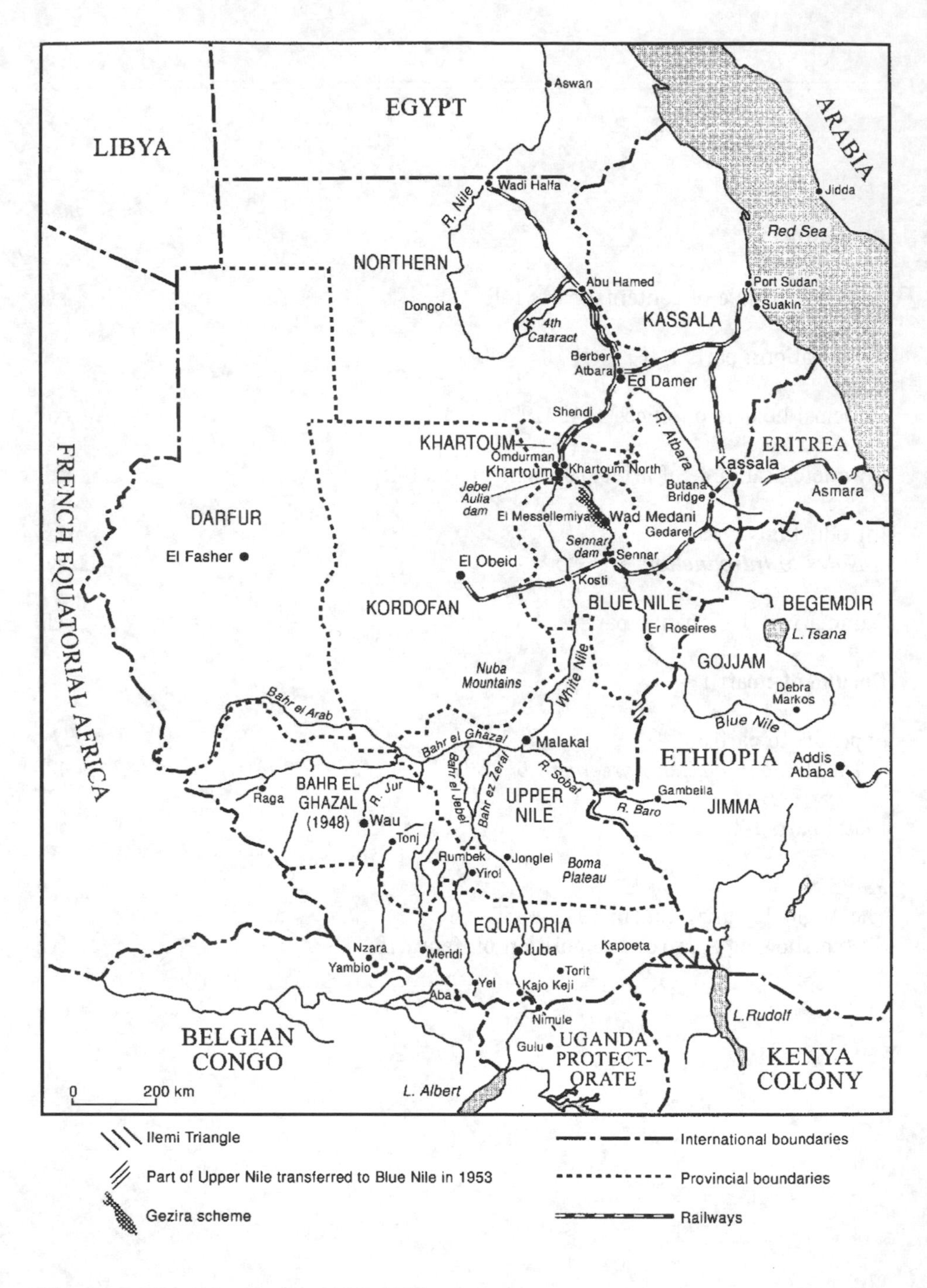

The Anglo-Egyptian Sudan 1942–1955

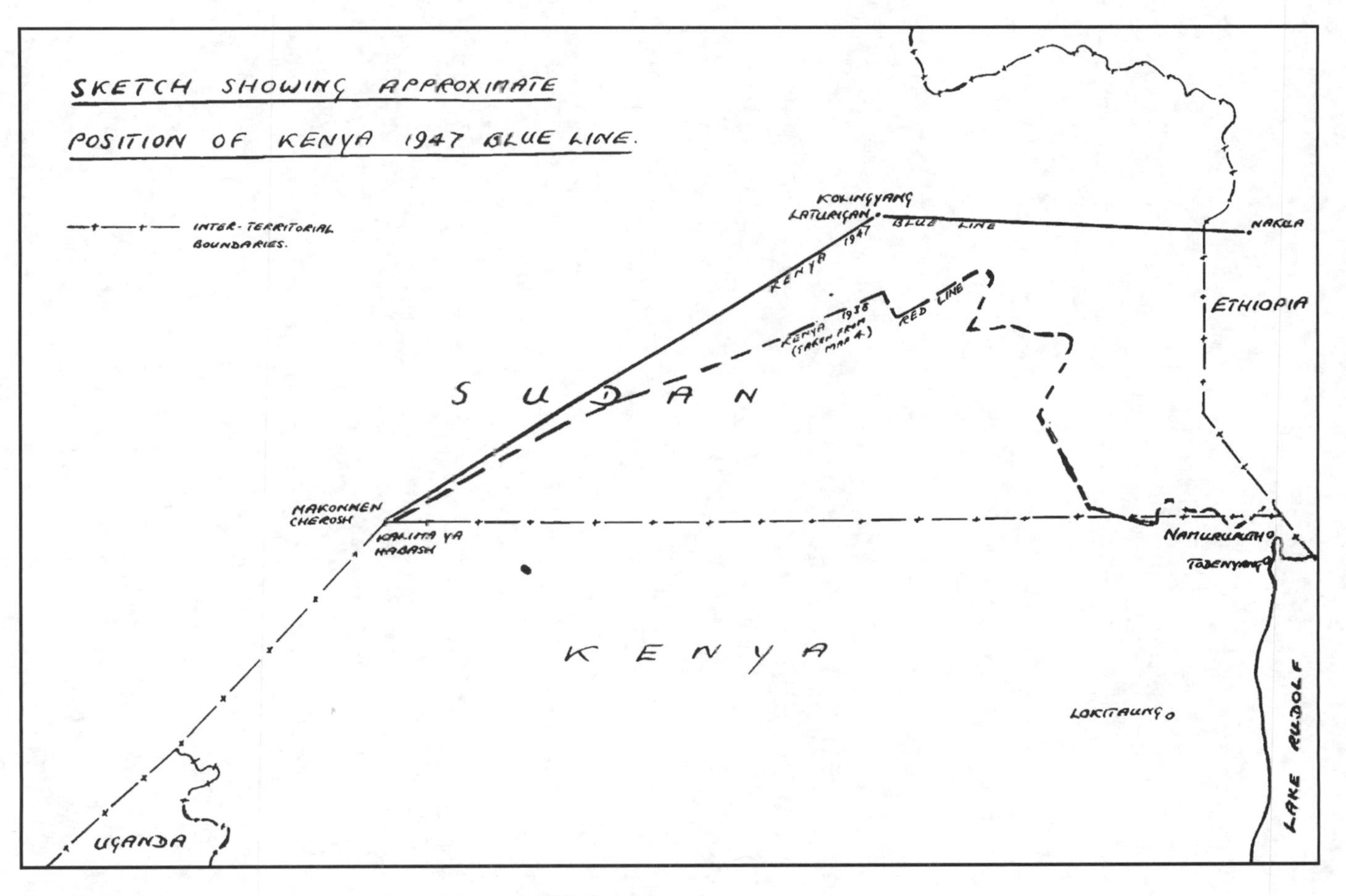

Sketch showing approximate position of Kenya 1947 Blue Line

Foreword

The main purpose of the British Documents on the End of Empire Project (BDEEP) is to publish documents from British official archives on the ending of colonial and associated rule and on the context in which this took place. In 1945, aside from the countries of present-day India, Pakistan, Bangladesh and Burma, Britain had over fifty formal dependencies; by the end of 1965 the total had been almost halved and by 1985 only a handful remained. The ending of Britain's position in these formal dependencies was paralleled by changes in relations with states in an informal empire. The end of empire in the period at least since 1945 involves a change also in the empire as something that was more than the sum of its parts and as such formed an integral part of Britain's domestic affairs and international relations. In publishing official British documents on the end of empire this project is, to a degree, the successor to the two earlier series of published documents concerning the end of British rule in India and Burma which were edited by Professors Mansergh and Tinker respectively.[1] The successful completion of *The transfer of power* and *The struggle for independence*, both of which were based on British records, emphasised the need for similar published collections of documents important to the history of the final stages of Britain's association with other dependencies in Africa, the Middle East, the Caribbean, South-East Asia and the Pacific. In their absence, scholars both from sovereign independent states which emerged from colonial rule, as well as from Britain itself, lack an important tool for understanding and teaching their respective histories. But BDEEP is also set in the much wider context of the efforts made by successive British governments to locate Britain's position in an international order. Here the empire, both in its formal and informal senses, is viewed as an instrument of the domestic, foreign and defence policies of successive British governments. The project is therefore concerned with the ending of colonial rule in individual territories as seen from the British side at one level, and the broader political, economic and strategic considerations involved in that at another.

BDEEP is a sequel, not only to the India and Burma series but also to the still earlier series of published Foreign Office documents which continues as Documents on British Policy Overseas (DBPO). The contemporary volumes in DBPO appear in two parallel series covering the years 1945 to 1955. In certain respects the documents published in the BDEEP volumes will complement those published in DBPO. On issues where there is, or is likely to be, direct overlap, BDEEP will not provide detailed coverage. The most notable examples concern the post-Second World War international settlements in the Far East and the Pacific, and the immediate events of the Suez crisis of 1956.

[1] Nicholas Mansergh *et al*, eds, *Constitutional relations between Britain and India: the transfer of power 1942–47*, 12 vols, (London, 1970–1983); Hugh Tinker, ed, *Constitutional relations between Britain and Burma: the struggle for independence 1944–1948*, 2 vols, (London, 1983–1984).

Despite the similarities, however, BDEEP differs in significant ways from its predecessors in terms both of presentation and content. The project is of greater magnitude than that undertaken by Professor Mansergh for India. Four major differences can be identified. First, the ending of colonial rule within a dependent empire took place over a much longer period of time, extending into the final years of the twentieth century, while having its roots in the Second World War and before. Secondly, the empire consisted of a large number of territories, varying in area, population, wealth and in many other ways, each with its own individual problems, but often with their futures linked to those of neighbouring territories and the growing complexity surrounding the colonial empire. Thirdly, while for India the documentary record for certain matters of high policy could be encapsulated within a relatively straightforward 'country' study, in the case of the colonial empire the documentary record is more diffuse because of the plethora of territories and their scattered location. Finally, the documents relating to the ending of colonial rule are not conveniently located within one leading department of state but rather are to be found in several of them. As the purpose of the project is to publish documents relating to the end of empire from the extensive range and quantity of official British records, private collections and other categories of non-official material are not regarded as principal documentary sources. In BDEEP, selections from non-official material will be used only in exceptional cases to fill gaps where they exist in the available official record.

In recognition of these differences, and also of the fact that the end of empire involves consideration of a range of issues which operated at a much wider level than that normally associated with the ending of colonial rule in a single country, BDEEP is structured in two main series along with a third support series. Series A represents the general volumes in which, for successive British governments, documents relating to the empire as a whole will be published. Series B represents the country or territory volumes and provides territorial studies of how, from a British government perspective, former colonies and dependencies achieved their independence, and countries which were part of an informal empire regained their autonomy. In addition to the two main documentary series, a third series – series C – will be published in the form of handbooks to the records of the former colonial empire which are deposited at the Public Record Office (PRO). The handbooks will be published in two volumes as an integral part of BDEEP and also as PRO guides to the records. They will enable scholars and others wishing to follow the record of the ending of colonial rule and empire to pursue their inquiries beyond the published record provided by the general studies in series A and the country studies in series B. Volume One of the handbooks, a revised and updated version of *The records of the Colonial and Dominions Office* (by R B Pugh) which was first published in 1964, is entitled *Records of the Colonial Office, Dominions Office, Commonwealth Relations Office and Commonwealth Office*. It covers over two hundred years of activity down to 1968 when the Commonwealth Office merged with the Foreign Office to form the Foreign and Commonwealth Office. Volume Two, entitled *Cabinet, Foreign Office, Treasury and other records*, focuses more specifically on twentieth-century departmental records and also includes references to the records of inter-departmental committees, commissions of inquiry and international organisations. These two volumes have been prepared under the direction and supervision of Dr Anne Thurston, honorary research fellow at the Institute of Commonwealth Studies in the University of London.

The criteria which have been used in selecting documents for inclusion in individual volumes will be explained in the introductions written by the specialist editors. These introductions are more substantial and contextual than those in previous series. Each volume will also list the PRO sources which have been searched. However, it may be helpful to outline the more general guiding principles which have been employed. BDEEP editors pursue several lines of inquiry. There is first the end of empire in a broad high policy sense, in which the empire is viewed in terms of Britain's position as a world power, and of the inter-relationship between what derives from this position and developments within the colonial dependencies. Here Britain's relations with the dependencies of the empire are set in the wider context of Britain's relations with the United States, with Europe, and with the Commonwealth and United Nations. The central themes are the political constraints, both domestic and international, to which British governments were subject, the economic requirements of the sterling area, the geopolitical and strategic questions associated with priorities in foreign policy and in defence planning, and the interaction between these various constraints and concerns and the imperatives imposed by developments in colonial territories. Secondly, there is investigation into colonial policy in its strict sense. Here the emphasis is on those areas which were specifically—but not exclusively—the concern of the leading department. In the period before the administrative amalgamations of the 1960s,[2] the leading department of the British government for most of the dependencies was the Colonial Office; for a minority it was either the Dominions Office and its successor, the Commonwealth Relations Office, or the Foreign Office. Colonial policy included questions of economic and social development, questions of governmental institutions and constitutional structures, and administrative questions concerning the future of the civil and public services and of the defence forces in a period of transition from European to indigenous control. Finally there is inquiry into the development of political and social forces within colonies, the response to these and the transfer of governmental authority and of legal sovereignty from Britain to its colonial dependencies as these processes were understood and interpreted by the British government. Here it should be emphasised that the purpose of BDEEP is not to document the history of colony politics or nationalist movements in any particular territory. Given the purpose of the project and the nature of much of the source material, the place of colony politics in BDEEP is conditioned by the extent to which an awareness of local political situations played an overt part in influencing major policy decisions made in Britain.

Although in varying degrees and from different perspectives, elements of these various lines of inquiry appear in both the general and the country series. The aim in both is to concentrate on the British record by selecting documents which illustrate those policy issues which were deemed important by ministers and officials at the time. General volumes do not normally treat in any detail matters which will be fully documented in the country volumes, but some especially significant documents do appear in both series. The process of selection involves an inevitable degree of sifting and subtraction. Issues which in retrospect appear to be of lesser significance or to be

[2] The Colonial Office merged with the Commonwealth Relations Office in 1966 to form the Commonwealth Office. The Commonwealth Office merged with the Foreign Office in 1968 to form the Foreign and Commonwealth Office.

ephemeral have been omitted. The main example concerns the extensive quantity of material devoted to appointments and terms of service – salaries, gradings, allowances, pension rights and compensation – within the colonial and related services. It is equally important to stress certain negative aspects of the official documentary record. Officials in London were sometimes not in a position to address potentially significant issues because the information was not available. Much in this respect depended on the extent of the documentation sent to London by the different colonial administrations. Once the stage of internal self-government had been reached, or where there was a dyarchy, the flow of detailed local information to London began to diminish.

Selection policy has been influenced by one further factor, namely access to the records at the PRO. Unlike the India and Burma series and DBPO, BDEEP is not an official project. In practice this means that while editors have privileged access (in the form of research facilities and requisitioning procedures) to the records at the PRO, they do not have unrestricted access. For files which at the time a volume is in preparation are either subject to extended closures beyond the statutory thirty years, or retained in the originating department under section 3(4) of the Public Records Act of 1958, editors are subject to the same restrictions as all other researchers. Where necessary, volume editors will provide details of potentially significant files or individual documents of which they are aware and which they have not been able to consult.

A thematic arrangement of the documents has been adopted for the general volumes in series A. The country volumes in series B follow a chronological arrangement; in this respect they adopt the same approach as was used in the India and Burma series. For each volume in both series A and B a summary list of the documents included is provided. The headings to BDEEP documents, which have been editorially standardised, present the essential information. Together with the sequence number, the file reference (in the form of the PRO call-up number and any internal pagination or numeration) and the date of the document appear on the first line.[3] The second and subsequent lines record the subject of the document, the type of document (letter, memorandum, telegram etc), the originator (person or persons, committee, department) and the recipient (if any). In headings, a subject entry in single quotation marks denotes the title of a document as it appears in the original. An entry in square brackets denotes a subject indicator devised by the editor. This latter device has been employed in cases where no title is given in the original or where the original title is too unwieldly to reproduce in its entirety. Security classifications and, in the case of telegrams, times of despatch and receipt, have generally been omitted as confusing and needlessly complicating, and are retained only where they are necessary to a full understanding. In the headings to documents and the summary lists, ministers are identified by the name of the office-holder, not the title of the office (ie, Mr Lyttelton, not secretary of state for the colonies).[4] In the same contexts, officials are identified by their initials and surname. In general

---

[3] The PRO call-up number precedes the comma in the references cited. In the case of documents from FO 371, the major Foreign Office political class, the internal numeration refers to the jacket number of the file.

[4] This is an editorial convention, following DBPO practice. Very few memoranda issued in their name were actually written by ministers themselves, but normally drafted by officials.

volumes in series A, ambassadors, governors, high commissioners and other embassy or high commission staff are given in the form 'Sir E Baring (Kenya)'. Footnotes to documents appearing below the rule are editorial; those above the rule, or where no rule is printed, are part of the original document. Each part of a volume provides a select list of which principal offices were held by whom, with a separate series of biographical notes (at the end) for major figures who appear in the documents. Minor figures are identified in editorial footnotes on the occasion of first appearance. Link-notes, written by the volume editor and indented in square brackets between the heading and the beginning of a document, are sometimes used to explain the context of a document. Technical detail or extraneous material has been extracted from a number of documents. In such cases omission dots have been inserted in the text and the document is identified in the heading as an extract. Occasional omission dots have also been used to excise purely mechanical chain-of-command executive instructions, and some redundant internal referencing has been removed, though much of it remains in place, for the benefit of researchers. No substantive material relating to policy-making has been excised from the documents. In general the aim has been to reproduce documents in their entirety. The footnote reference 'not printed' has been used only in cases where a specified enclosure or an annex to a document has not been included. Unless a specific cross-reference or note of explanation is provided, however, it can be assumed that other documents referred to in the text of the documents included have not been reproduced. Each part of a volume has a list of abbreviations occurring in it. A consolidated index for the whole volume appears at the end of each part.

One radical innovation, compared with previous Foreign Office or India and Burma series, is that BDEEP will reproduce many more minutes by ministers and officials.

Crown copyright material is used by permission of the Public Record Office under licence from the Controller of Her Majesty's Stationery Office. All references and dates are given in the form recommended in PRO guidelines.

* * * *

BDEEP has received assistance and support from many quarters. The project was first discussed at a one-day workshop attended by over thirty interested scholars which, supported by a small grant from the Smuts Memorial Fund, was held at Churchill College, Cambridge, in May 1985. At that stage the obstacles looked daunting. It seemed unlikely that public money would be made available along the lines provided for the India and Burma projects. The complexities of the task looked substantial, partly because there was more financial and economic data with which to deal, still more because there were so many more territories to cover. It was not at all clear, moreover, who could take institutional responsibility for the project as the India Office Records had for the earlier ones; and in view of the escalating price of the successive India and Burma volumes, it seemed unlikely that publication in book form would be feasible; for some while a choice was being discussed between microfilm, microfiche and facsimile.

A small group nevertheless undertook to explore matters further, and in a quite remarkable way found itself able to make substantial progress. The British Academy adopted BDEEP as one of its major projects, and thus provided critical support. The Institute of Commonwealth Studies served as a crucial institutional anchor in taking responsibility for the project. The Institute also made office space available, and negotiated an administrative nexus within the University of London. Dr Anne Thurston put at the disposal of the project her unique knowledge of the relevant archival sources; while the keeper of the Public Records undertook to provide all the support that he could. It then proved possible to appoint Professor Michael Crowder as project director on a part-time basis, and he approached the Leverhulme Trust, who made a munificent grant which was to make the whole project viable. Almost all those approached to be volume editors accepted and, after consultation with a number of publishers, Her Majesty's Stationery Office undertook to publish the project in book form. There can be few projects that after so faltering a start found itself quite so blessed.

Formally launched in 1987, BDEEP has been based since its inception at the Institute of Commonwealth Studies. The work of the project is supervised by a Project Committee chaired by Professor Andrew Porter, Rhodes professor of imperial history in the University of London. Professor Porter succeeded Professor Anthony Low, formerly Smuts professor of the history of the British Commonwealth in the University of Cambridge, who retired in November 1994. At the outset Professor Michael Crowder became general editor while holding a visiting professorship in the University of London and a part-time position at Amherst College, Massachusetts. Following his untimely death in 1988, Professor Crowder was replaced as general editor by Professor David Murray, pro vice-chancellor and professor of government at the Open University. Mrs Anita Burdett was appointed as project secretary and research assistant. She was succeeded in September 1989 by Dr Ashton who had previously worked with Professors Mansergh and Tinker during the final stages of the India and Burma series. Dr Ashton replaced Professor Murray as project director and general editor in 1993. When BDEEP was launched in 1987, eight volumes in series A and B were approved by the Project Committee and specialist scholars were commissioned to research and select documents for inclusion in each. Collectively, these eight volumes (three general and five country)[5] represent the first stage of the project which begins with an introductory general volume covering the years between 1925 and 1945 but which concentrates on the period from the Second World War to 1957 when Ghana and Malaya became independent.[6]

It is fitting that the present general editor should begin his acknowledgements with an appreciation of the contributions made by his predecessors. The late Professor Crowder supervised the launch of the project and planned the volumes included in stage one. The volumes already published bear lasting testimony to his resolve and dedication during the project's formative phase. Professor Murray played a no less critical role in establishing a secure financial base for the project and in

---

[5] Series A general volumes: vol 1 *Imperial policy and colonial practice 1925–1945* (published 1996); vol 2 *The Labour government and the end of empire 1945–1951* (published 1992); vol 3 *The Conservative government and the end of empire 1951–1957* (published 1994).

Series B country volumes: vol 1 *Ghana* (published 1992); vol 2 *Sri Lanka* (published 1997); vol 3 *Malaya* (published 1995); vol 4 *Egypt and the defence of the Middle East* (published 1998); vol 5 *Sudan* (published 1998).

[6] Research is currently in progress for a second stage covering the period 1957–1964.

negotiating contracts with the volume editors and HMSO. His invaluable advice and expertise during the early stages of editing are acknowledged with particular gratitude.

The project benefited from an initial pump-priming grant from the British Academy. Thanks are due to the secretary and Board of the Academy for this grant and for the decision of the British Academy to adopt BDEEP as one of its major projects. The Academy made a further award in 1996 which enabled the project to employ a research assistant on a fixed-term contract. The principal funding for the project has been provided by the Leverhulme Trust and the volumes are a tribute to the support provided by the Trustees. A major debt of gratitude is owed to the Trustees. In addition to their generous grant to cover the costs of the first stage, the Trustees agreed to a subsequent request to extend the duration of the grant, and also provided a supplementary grant which enabled the project to secure Dr Ashton's appointment.

Members of the Project Committee, who meet annually at the Institute of Commonwealth Studies, have provided valuable advice and much needed encouragement. Professor Low, the first chairman of the Committee, made a singular contribution, initiating the first exploratory meeting at Cambridge in 1985 and presiding over subsequent developments in his customary constructive but unobtrusive manner. Professor Porter continues in a similar vein and his leadership and experience are much appreciated by the general editor. The director and staff of the Institute of Commonwealth Studies have provided administrative support and the congenial surroundings within which the general editor works. The editors of volumes in stage one have profited considerably from the researches undertaken by Dr Anne Thurston and her assistants during the preparation of the records handbooks. Although BDEEP is not an official project, the general editor wishes to acknowledge the support and co-operation received from the Historical Section of the Cabinet Office and the Records Department of the Foreign and Commonwealth Office. He wishes also to record his appreciation of the spirit of friendly co-operation emanating from the editors of DBPO. Dr Ronald Hyam, editor of the volume in series A on *The Labour government and the end of empire 1945–1951*, played an important role in the compilation of the house-style adopted by BDEEP and his contribution is acknowledged with gratitude. Thanks also are due to The Stationery Office for assuming publishing responsibility and for their expert advice on matters of design and production. Last, but by no means least, the contribution of the keeper of the records and the staff, both curatorial and administrative, at the PRO must be emphasised. Without the facilities and privileges afforded to BDEEP editors at Kew, the project would not be viable.

S R Ashton
Institute of Commonwealth Studies
March 1998

Sudan

Schedule of Contents: Parts I–II

Abbreviations: Parts I–II

A/DC	assistant district commissioner
A–E	Anglo–Egyptian
AIM	Africa Inland Mission
Alex	Alexandria
appt	appointed
Atty-gen	attorney-general
BBC	British Broadcasting Corporation
BDEEP	British Documents on the End of Empire Project
BMEO	British Middle East Office (Nicosia)
CBE	Commander Order of the British Empire
Civ sec	civil secretary (Sudan government)
CMS	Church Missionary Society
CO	Colonial Office
Con	Conservative (Party) (UK)
Congress	Graduates' Congress
CRO	Commonwealth Relations Office
DC	district commissioner
Dept	department
dft	draft
DSO	Distinguished Service Order
educ	educated
EEL	Egyptian embassy, London
EG	Egyptian government
est	established
FO	Foreign Office
FS	financial secretary (Sudan government)
GHQ	General Headquarters

GC	Graduates' Congress (Sudan)
GOC	general officer commanding
gov	governor
gov-gen	governor-general (Sudan government)
govt	government
gp./ grp. undec.	group of characters undecipherable as transmitted (telegram)
H of C Debs	*House of Commons Debates* (Hansard)
HBM	His/Her Britannic Majesty
HE	His Excellency
HM	His/Her Majesty
HMG	His/Her Majesty's Government
IBRD	International Bank for Reconstruction and Development
ICFTU	International Confederation of Free Trade Unions
ILO	International Labour Organisation
KAR	King's African Rifles
KBE	Knight Commander of the Order of the British Empire
Khtm	Khartoum
Kt	Knight Bachelor
LA	Legislative Assembly (Sudan)
Lab	Labour (Party) (UK)
LE (£E)	Egyptian pound, contemporary exchange rate at £1.0.6d
LS	legal secretary (Sudan government)
MBE	Member of the Order of the British Empire
MC	Military Cross
memo	memorandum
MLA	member of legislative assembly (Sudan)
M of S	minister of state (FO)
MP	member of parliament
NBE	National Bank of Egypt
NUP	Nationalist Union Party (Sudan)
NY	New York
OBE	Officer of the Order of the British Empire

OC	Officer Commanding
PDP	People's Democratic Party (Sudan)
PM	prime minister
Pres	president
PRO	Public Record Office
PSC	Public Service Commission
PT	Piastre, unit of currency, 100th of £E1
PWD	Public Works Department (Sudan)
RC	Roman Catholic
RCC	Revolutionary Command Council (Egypt)
RIP	Republican Independence Party (Sudan)
RL	Reservoir level
SA	Sudan agent
SAM	Sayyid Ali al-Mirghani
SAR	Sayyid Abd al-Rahman al-Mahdi
SDF	Sudan Defence Force
Sec	secretary
SIME	Special Intelligence Middle East
S of S	secretary of state
SPA	Sudan Press Agency
SPIS	Sudan Political Intelligence Summary
SPS	Sudan Political Service
SRP	Socialist Republican Party (Sudan)
tel	telegram
UK	United Kingdom
UKTC	United Kingdom Trade Commission(er)
Umma	Umma (Party) (Sudan)
UN(O)	United Nations (Organisation)
UNP	Upper Nile Province
US(A)	United States of America
VFM	Verona Fathers Mission (now Missionari Comboniani)
WAA	Workers' Affairs Association (Sudan)
Wash	Washington, DC

Principal Holders of Offices 1942–1950: Part I

UNITED KINGDOM

1. *Ministers*

(a) *Wartime coalition (10 May 1940–23 May 1945) and Conservative caretaker government (23 May–26 July 1945)*

Prime minister	Mr W L S Churchill (10 May 1940)
Chancellor of Exchequer	Sir Kingsley Wood (12 May 1940) Sir John Anderson (24 Sep 1943)
S of S foreign affairs	Mr R A Eden (22 Dec 1940)

(b) *Labour governments from 26 July 1945 to 17 Dec 1950, the concluding date for part I of this volume*

Prime minister	Mr C R Attlee (26 July 1945)
Lord chancellor	Lord Jowitt (27 July 1945)
S of S foreign affairs	Mr E Bevin (27 July 1945)
S of S colonies	Mr G H Hall (3 Aug 1945) Mr A Creech Jones (4 Oct 1946) Mr J Griffiths (28 Feb 1950)
S of S air	Viscount Stansgate (3 Aug 1945) Mr P J Noel-Baker (4 Oct 1946 & office not in Cabinet)

2. *Junior ministers*

Foreign Office

M of S (not formally attached until 1950)	Mr P J Noel-Baker (3 Aug 1945) Mr H McNeil (4 Oct 1946) Mr K Younger (28 Feb 1950)

Parliamentary under-secretary of state	Mr H McNeil (4 Aug 1945) Mr C P Mayhew (4 Oct 1946) Lord Henderson (7 June 1948) Mr E J Davies (2 Mar 1950)

3. *Civil Servants*

(a) *Foreign Office*

(i) Permanent under-secretary of state	Sir Alexander Cadogan (1 Jan 1938) Sir Orme Sargent (1 Jan 1946) Sir William Strang (1 Feb 1949)
(ii) Superintending under-secretaries of state	Sir Maurice Petersen (Egyptian Dept, 1942–1944) Sir Orme Sargent (Southern Dept, 1945–1946) (Sir) R G Howe (Egyptian Dept, 1946–1947) M R Wright (Egyptian/African Dept, July 1948) R J Bowker (African Dept, 27 Nov 1950)
(iii) Assistant secretary/counsellor, head Egyptian Dept (African Dept from Oct 1948)	P S Scrivener (Mar 1942) D W Lascelles (Apr 1947) G L Clutton (Apr 1948) R Allen (Feb 1950)
(iv) Assistant secretary/counsellor, head of Eastern Dept	C W Baxter (Sept 1944) B A B Burrows (Nov 1947–Dec 1949)
(v) Legal adviser	(Sir) W E Beckett (1945–1953)
(vi) Ambassador to the UN	Sir Alexander Cadogan (1946–1950)
(vii) Sudan agent, London	R C Mayall (1941–1951)

(b) *Colonial Office*

(i) Permanent under-secretary of state	Sir George Gater (1942–1947) Sir Thomas Lloyd (1947–1956)
(ii) Deputy under-secretary of state	Sir Arthur Dawe (1945–1947) Sir Sydney Caine (1947–1948) } joint Sir Charles Jeffries (1947–1956) } joint Sir Hilton Poynton (1948–1959) } joint

(iii) Assistant under-secretary of state	A B Cohen (Africa Division, 1947–1951)
(iv) Select governors	
Gov of Kenya	Sir Philip Mitchell (1944–1952)
Gov of Uganda	Sir John Hall (1944–1952)

SUDAN

1. *Governor-General's Council (1942–1947)*

Governor-general	Major-gen Sir Hubert Huddleston (1940–1947) Sir Robert Howe (1947–1955)
Civil secretary	(Sir) Douglas Newbold (1939–1945) (Sir) James W Robertson (1945–1953)
Financial secretary	F D Rugman (1934–1944) J W E Miller (1944–1948) (Sir) Louis Chick (1948–1953)
Legal secretary	T P Creed (1941–1948) C Cumings (1948–1953)

2. *Advisory Council of the Northern Sudan (1944–1947)*

President	Sir Hubert Huddleston (1944–1947) Sir Robert Howe (1947)
Vice presidents:	(Sir) Douglas Newbold (1944–1945) J W Robertson (1945–1947) T P Creed (1944–1947) J W E Miller (1944–1947)
Honorary members:	Sayyid Sir Ali al-Mirghani Pasha Sayyid Sir Abd al-Rahman al-Mahdi Pasha
Ordinary members:	Shaikh Abu Shamma Abd al-Mahmud Dr Ali Badri Shaikh Ahmad Uthman al-Qadi Abdallah Khalil Yaqub Ali al-Hilu Shaikh Hamid al-Sayyid Abd al-Karim Muhammad Nuh Abdallah E A Turner (chamber of commerce)

Mustafa Abu Ala (chamber of commerce)
Shaikh Babu Uthman Nimr (Kordofan Province)
Shaikh Yahya Ahmad (Kordofan Province)
Khalil Akasha (Kordofan Province)
Shaikh Ibrahim Musa Madibbu (Darfur Province)
Sultan Muhammad Bahr al-Din (Darfur Province)
Hamid al-Sayyid (Darfur Province)
Shaikh Muhammad Muhammad al-Amin al-Tirik (Kassala Province)
Shaikh Abdallah Bakr (Kassala Province)
Hasan Ali Shakalawi (Kassala Province)
Shaikh Ayub Abd al-Majid (Northern Province)
Shaikh Zubair Hamad al-Malik (Northern Province)
Uthman Abd al-Qadir (Northern Province)
Mak Hasan Adlan (Blue Nile Province)
Shaikh Fahal Ibrahim (Blue Nile Province)
Makki Abbas (Blue Nile Province)
Mirghani Hamza (Khartoum Province)
Muhammad Ali Shawqi (Khartoum Province)
Shaikh Surur Muhammad Ramli (Khartoum Province)

3. *Executive Council and Legislative Assembly (1948–1950)*

President (gov-gen)	Sir Robert Howe
Civil secretary	(Sir) James Robertson
Financial secretary	Sir Louis Chick
Legal secretary	Sir Charles Cumings
C-in-C of the SDF	Major-gen Sir Lashmer Whistler (1948) Major-gen Sir Geoffrey Scoones (Sept 1950)
Minister of agriculture & leader of the LA	Abdallah Khalil
Minister of health	Dr Ali Badri (Bedri)
Minister of education	Abd al-Rahman Ali Taha
Under-secretary for irrigation	Abd al-Rahman Abdun (Abdoun)
Under-secretary for economics & trade	Abd al-Majid Ahmad (Abd el Magid Ahmed)
Councillor-without-portfolio	R J Hillard (Sudan Railways)
Councillor-without-portfolio	A Gaitskell (Sudan Plantations Syndicate, 1948–1950)

Councillor-without-portfolio	Muhammad Ahmad Abu Sinn (Sept 1950)
Councillor-without-portfolio	Ibrahim Ahmad (vice-principal Gordon College)
Speaker of LA	Muhammad Salih al-Shinqiti (Shingeiti) (Umma)

EGYPT

1. *Government of Egypt*

Head of State	King Faruq (28 Apr 1936)
Prime minister	Husain Sirri (Sirry) (Independent, 15 Nov 1940) Mustafa al-Nahhas (Nahas) (Wafd, 6 Feb 1942) Ahmad Mahir (Maher) (Saadist, 9 Oct 1944) Mahmud Fahmi al-Nuqrashi (Nokrashi) (Saadist, 25 Feb 1945) Ismail Sidqi (Sidky) (Independent, 7 Feb 1946) Mahmud Fahmi al-Nuqrashi (Nokrashi) (Saadist, 10 Dec 1946) Ibrahim Abd al-Hadi (Abdel Hadi) (Saadist, 28 Dec 1948) Husain Sirri (Sirry) (Independent, 26 July 1949) Mustafa al-Nahhas (Nahas) (Wafd, 12 Jan 1950)
Foreign minster	Mustafa al-Nahhas (6 Feb 1942) Mahmud Fahmi al-Nuqrashi (Nokrashi) (9 Oct 1944) Abd al-Hamid Badawi (7 Mar 1945) Ahmad Lutfi al-Sayyid (17 Feb 1946) Ibrahim Abd al-Hadi (Abdel Hadi) (12 Sept 1946) Mahmud Fahmi al-Nuqrashi (Nokrashi) (10 Dec 1946) Ahmad Muhammad Khashaba (19 Nov 1947) Ibrahim Dassuqi Abaza (28 Dec 1948) Ahmad Muhammad Khashaba (27 Feb 1949) Husain Sirri (Sirry) (26 July 1949) Muhammad Salah al-Din (12 Jan 1950)

Ambassador to Britain	Abd al-Fattah Amr Pasha (1945–1952)

2. *British Embassy*

Ambassador	Lord Killearn (Sir Miles Lampson) (22 Dec 1936) Sir Ronald Campbell (12 Mar 1946) Sir Ralph Stevenson (10 June 1950)
Minister	R J Bowker (Apr 1946) E A Chapman-Andrews (Nov 1947)
Oriental secretary	W A Smart (Apr 1926–Jan 1948) T C Ravensdale (Jan 1948–Jan 1949)
Oriental counsellor	T C Ravensdale (Jan 1949)
Counsellor	R J Bowker (Sept 1945) R L Speaight (Apr 1946) D D Maclean (Nov 1948)

3. *Sudan agent, Cairo*	G E R Sandars (1941–1945) A M Hankin (acting 1945) E C Haselden (1945–1953)

Chronological Table of Principal Events: Parts I & II

1936

Aug	Anthony Eden, S of S for foreign affairs, and Mustafa al-Nahhas, Egyptian PM, conclude A–E Treaty covering the terms of the military alliance between Britain and Egypt and the continuation of the condominium administration in the Sudan. The treaty is to last for a period of twenty years, with the option for renegotiation after ten years

1938

Feb	Graduates' General Congress established

1940

June	Italy declares war on Great Britain
July	Hostilities begin between Italian forces in Ethiopia and the SDF
Oct	Maj-gen Sir Hubert Huddleston appointed gov-gen of the Sudan

1941

Jan	Ethiopia is invaded from the Sudan
May	Italian forces in Ethiopia surrender
Aug	The Atlantic Charter
Oct	Egypt and Sudan put forward proposals for the construction of a dam at Lake Tsana

1942

April	The Graduates' Congress presents its memo calling for self-determination after the war to the Sudan government; Cripps advises Newbold to establish an advisory council in the Northern Sudan
May	Newbold rejects Congress memorandum

1943

June	Robert Howe presents Lake Tsana proposals to Emperor Haile Selassie
Sept	Advisory Councils Ordinance promulgated

1944

May	First session of the Advisory Council for the Northern Sudan

Oct	Formation of Ashiqqa (Full Brothers), Ittihadiyin (Unionist) and Ahrar (Liberal) parties out of factions within the Graduates' Congress
Nov	Graduates' Congress elections
Dec	Huddleston states the Sudan's future Nile waters needs (24 Dec)

1945

Feb	Umma Party founded
Mar	Newbold dies (23 Mar) and James Robertson is appointed civ sec
May	Allied defeat of Germany
July	General election in Britain (25 July), Labour Party victory under Clement Attlee; Ernest Bevin appointed S of S for foreign affairs
Aug	Allied defeat of Japan; Communist Party founded in Sudan
Dec	Egypt demands revision of 1936 A–E Treaty (20 Dec)

1946

Feb	Ismail Sidqi becomes Egyptian PM
Mar	Lord Killearn is replaced by Sir Ronald Campbell as ambassador to Egypt
Mar–Apr	United parties delegation to Cairo
Apr	Huddleston's pledge to the Advisory Council on self-government and self-determination; Sudan Administration Conference convened
Apr–Oct	A–E negotiations
May	Bevin's statement in the House pledging consultation with the Sudanese before any change in the constitutional status of the Sudan (15 May)
Oct	Sidqi-Bevin protocol
Nov	Riots in Khartoum (2 Nov) after Sidqi announces return of Sudan's sovereignty to Egypt; Huddleston flies to London (9 Nov)
Dec	Huddleston returns to Khartoum (6 Dec); Sidqi resigns (9 Dec) and Mahmud Fahmi al-Nuqrashi becomes Egyptian PM
	'Southern Policy' is formally abandoned (Dec 16)

1947

Jan	al-Nuqrashi breaks off negotiations (27 Jan); takes A–E dispute to the UN
Apr	Howe appointed gov-gen of the Sudan
June	Juba Conference
	Draft Constitutional Ordinance submitted to Co-domini
July	Railway strike, ends with recognition of the WAA as the representative of the railway workers

1948

Jan & Mar	Sudan railways strike, leading to the first trade union legislation in the Sudan
June	Constitutional Ordinance promulgated
Dec	Executive Council established and LA opened (15 Dec) following elections
	al-Nuqrashi assassinated by the Muslim Brothers in Cairo (28 Dec); Ibrahim Abd al-Hadi becomes Egyptian PM

1949

Feb	Egyptian proposals concerning the construction of the Lake Tsana and Owen Falls dams
Apr	Marshall Report on local govt in the Sudan
July	Husain Sirri becomes Egyptian PM
Aug	Workers' Congress created
Dec	Informal conversations between Egyptian and Sudan irrigation depts produces agreement on technical memo to be presented to Ethiopia concerning Lake Tsana

1950

Jan	Wafd election victory in Egypt (3 Jan), al-Nahhas becomes PM
Feb	General election in Britain (23 Feb), Labour returned to power
June	Anglo–Egyptian talks resume
Nov	Faruq's speech from the throne (16 Nov) announces intention of abrogating the 1936 A–E Treaty and 1899 Condominium Agreement; Workers' Congress reconstituted as the SWTUF
Dec	LA in Sudan passes a self-govt resolution by 1 vote

1951

Mar	Herbert Morrison appointed S of S for foreign affairs
Apr	Constitutional Amendment Commission appointed
June	Police strike in the Three Towns
	Constitutional Amendment Commission issues its initial report
Aug	US govt begins more active involvement in negotiations between the UK and Egypt
Oct	Egyptian abrogation of the A–E Treaty and the Condominium Agreement (8 Oct); general election in Britain (26 Oct), Conservative Party victory under Winston Churchill; Eden becomes S of S for foreign affairs; twelve members of Constitutional Amendment Commission request UN trusteeship for the Sudan (28 Oct)
Nov	Eden reaffirms policy of self-govt in the Sudan, followed by self-determination (15 Nov)
	Constitutional Amendment Commission dissolved (26 Nov) following the resignation of six of its members
	Socialist Republican Party founded

1952

Jan	Report of the Constitutional Amendment Commission tabled (23 Jan)
	'Black Friday' riots in Cairo (27 Jan); al-Nahhas dismissed and Ali Mahir becomes Egyptian PM
Mar	Ahmad Najib al-Hilali becomes Egyptian PM (2 Mar)
Apr	SWTUF call for a general strike fails
July	Sirri becomes Egyptian PM (2 July); al-Hilali becomes PM (22 July); Free Officers coup in Egypt (23 July); King Faruq abdicates (26 July);

	Muhammad Najib presides as chairman of the RCC and Ali Mahir becomes PM and foreign minister
Sept	Najib becomes PM (7 Sept); agreement between UK and Egypt over Equatorial Nile project (15 Sept)
Oct	NUP formed; Egypt obtains preliminary agreement with northern Sudanese parties over the terms of self-govt legislation in the Sudan
Nov	Egypt presents its note on self-government in the Sudan to HMG (2 Nov)
Dec	Mahmud Fawzi becomes foreign minister (8 Dec)

1953

Jan	Salah Salim's visit to the Sudan; All Parties Agreement signed between the Egyptian govt and the three Northern Sudanese parties (11 Jan)
Feb	Anglo–Egyptian Agreement regulating self-govt and self-determination for the Sudan signed (12 Feb)
Mar	Office of the UKTC established in Khartoum; Self-Govt Statute promulgated (21 Mar); Southern Liberal Party founded
Apr	Election Commission appointed
	Robertson retires as civ sec
May–June	Churchill stands in for Eden as S of S for foreign affairs
June	Lord Salisbury acting S of S for foreign affairs; Najib becomes president of Egypt
Nov	Sudanese elections; visit of NUP leaders and Salah Salim to Southern Sudan
Dec	Results of elections announced, NUP majority in both the House and the Senate

1954

Jan	Formation of the first Sudanese govt with Ismail al-Azhari as PM
	Governor-General's Commission appointed
Feb	Political struggle between Najib and Jamal Abd al-Nasir; Najib deposed but reinstated
Mar	Anti-Najib riots in Khartoum (1 Mar); Parliament opened (10 Mar); Sudanisation Committee begins
Apr	Nasir takes over as chairman of the RCC and PM of Egypt
June	Sudanisation Committee issues its report on the Sudanisation of the administration, police and army
Oct	All Southern conference at Juba (18–21 Oct)
Nov	Nasir takes over as president of Egypt
Dec	Cabinet crisis: al-Azhari dismisses Mirghani Hamza and two other Khatmi ministers

1955

Jan	Mirghani Hamza forms the RIP
Mar	Sir Knox Helm appointed gov-gen of the Sudan
	al-Azhari speaks of NUP's desire for independence (16 Mar); NUP parliamentary party opts for full independence of the Sudan (31 Mar)

Apr	Eden replaces Churchill as PM in UK (6 Apr); Harold Macmillan becomes S of S for foreign affairs
	NUP executive endorses parliamentary party's policy on independence (12 Apr)
May	Southern ministers resign from the NUP and join Liberal party; al-Azhari's government publicly announces abandonment of policy of unity with Egypt; inconclusive talks between Salah Salim and al-Azhari over restarting Nile waters negotiations
	General election in Britain (26 May), Conservatives returned to power
June	Struggle between al-Azhari and Muhamad Nur al-Din for control of the NUP; Nur al-Din dismissed from cabinet.
July	Juba conference called by Southern Liberal Party (6–7 July)
Aug	Sudanisation is completed; mutiny in Torit and disturbances in many parts of Southern Sudan; parliament passes a motion calling for self-determination decided by a plebiscite
Oct	Czech arms deal with Egypt
	HMG informs al-Azhari that it is willing to support a vote for independence in the Sudanese parliament
Nov	Withdrawal of British and Egyptian troops complete (10 Nov); al-Azhari loses vote of confidence in the House of Representatives (10 Nov) but is re-elected PM (14 Nov); Sudan rejects Egypt's proposal over the division of Nile waters to follow the construction of the Aswan High Dam (20 Nov)
Dec	Helm departs on leave (15 Dec); both houses of the Sudanese parliament pass independence resolutions (19 Dec); Selwyn Lloyd becomes S of S for foreign affairs (20 Dec); Egypt refuses to grant Sudan's requests on division of Nile waters (28 Dec)

1956

Jan	Sudanese independence takes effect (1 Jan)

Introduction

The Foreign Office and the Foreign Office documents

This collection of documents illustrates an anomaly in decolonisation. Before Britain fully accepted the twin principles of self-government and self-determination for her own colonial empire, here she became the main international advocate for granting independence to the colony of another country, Egypt, then in the process of disentangling itself from Britain's informal empire in the Middle East. It was an anomaly stemming from the Sudan's unusual position as a territory administered by the Foreign Office, which was more directly exposed than the Colonial Office to the changing international order in the immediate post-war years. The Colonial Office did anticipate changes in the international order at the end of the war, and this was reflected in its thinking on such issues as colonial development and welfare and international accountability in colonial affairs.[1] Yet it was the Foreign Office who first had to contend with the practical realities of anticipated post-war changes: the foreign secretary was confronted by Britain's shrinking role as a world power and the constraints of international opinion, and the Foreign Office was made constantly aware of the decreasing options empire had. Those involved in the daily affairs of administering other African territories often took longer to realise just how the rules of the imperial game had changed. This difference in perception was evident as early as 1946 and was revealed, as we shall see, in the contest between Egyptian sovereignty and Sudanese self-determination. It became even more pronounced in the early 1950s when the Colonial Office, by now set on parallel courses for self-government in the Gold Coast and Nigeria, repeatedly objected to the precedents being set in the Sudan.

The criteria for selection of these documents follow the broad guidelines adopted by other volumes in this series, being confined to those documents produced by, or which came into government departments in London during the course of, official business. Given the limits of publishing space it has not been possible to represent all topics contained in the files (such as compensation schemes for retiring British officials, the technical aspects of grants-in-aid or development projects, local level administrative reports or Sudanese representation on international bodies). Nor has it been possible to cover in extended detail all of the major diplomatic, political, constitutional or administrative issues which do figure in this volume. Given the Sudan's chronological position in the history of the end of empire, the wide variety of its international relations even before independence, and the complexity of its internal politics, an attempt has been made to provide as wide a coverage as possible of topics illustrating not only the process of the transfer of power, but the Sudan's place in the broader trends of decolonisation and the state of the Sudanese nation at independence.

Documents have been chosen to illustrate four broad areas: 1) international diplomacy concerning the Sudan, 2) constitutional and administrative developments within the Sudan, 3) internal Sudanese political developments and 4) inter-departmental matters in the British government. The first covers Anglo–Egyptian negotiations over the future status of the Sudan, Anglo–American debates concerning the Sudan within a broader Middle Eastern policy, the Sudan's relations with its neighbours most affected by the Nile Waters (Egypt, Ethiopia and British East Africa), and the administration of sensitive border areas (Eritrea, Ethiopia and Kenya). The second includes the creation of institutions of self-government and the transition from self-government to independence. The third concerns the emergence of political parties and the entrenchment of sectarianism in the North, the development of a southern political consciousness, relations between Sudanese parties and the Egyptian and British governments, the development of trade unions and labour legislation, electoral and parliamentary politics, and the 1955 mutiny in the South. The fourth refers to policy discussions between Whitehall, the Cairo embassy and the Khartoum government, and debates between the Foreign, Colonial and Commonwealth Relations Offices about the precedents being set in the Sudan.

The restrictions on the availability of sources which have affected most acutely the volume on Middle East defence[2] apply to a lesser extent to this volume. The withholding of a number of files and an even greater number of individual jackets within released files has made it impossible to follow through on some issues and thus give a comprehensive account of policies decided and actions taken.[3] It has not always been possible to gauge the true impact of back bench or extra-parliamentary pressure at crucial stages in the decisions concerning the Sudan's future. The internal deliberations of the governments of Egypt and the Sudan are only partially revealed by Foreign Office documents, though in the case of the latter researchers in the United Kingdom have the advantage of access to collections of the personal papers (including copies of official documents) of a number of British administrators in the Sudan during this time.[4] These restrictions notwithstanding, the documents available in FO 371 come from a wide variety of sources within the Sudan, Egypt, the United Kingdom and the Commonwealth generally. They offer a very full, and at times surprisingly intimate record of the events leading to the Sudan's independence, and the attitudes and ideas which influenced policy. Thus we are able to include not only reports describing events and documents recording how policies were decided and implemented, but more reflective drafts and minutes exploring broader issues and options not taken. The types of documents range from diplomatic telegrams giving the first account of significant events, to minutes providing an overview of a series of documents covering a period of months. These latter are included especially as summaries for lengthy discussions and negotiations such as the Nile Waters, or for extended policy debates which came to nothing, such as the controversy over the recognition of the King of Egypt's title, unexpectedly resolved by the Free Officers' coup in 1952.

As already noted by John Kent, matters concerning Egypt and Britain's informal empire in the Middle East were discussed in greater detail in Cabinet meetings than many other topics concerning the colonial empire.[5] It was through its attachment to Egypt that the internal affairs of the Sudan were brought into far greater prominence in Cabinet discussions than other African territories at this time. The Sudan fell under the responsibility of the foreign secretary, a much more significant political figure in post-war governments than the colonial secretary. The prime minister also frequently became centrally involved. Attlee's collection of Sudan papers was extensive (PREM 8); Churchill's and Eden's even more so (PREM 8, 11). Churchill's copies of telegrams and reports are largely unannotated, aside from a few explosive interjections; Eden's many marginal notes show the continuity of his personal interest in directing Britain's Sudan policy from foreign secretary to prime minister. Other Cabinet members also became involved: Macmillan's first submission on the Sudan was made when he was still minister of housing and local government (308).

Within the Foreign Office the Sudan originally came under the Egyptian Department, and communications from Khartoum were routed through HBM's representative in Cairo. The Egyptian Department became the African Department in October 1948, and Egypt and the Sudan continued to be dealt together by the same official. Only as Sudanese self-government approached in the early 1950s was the Sudan assigned its own 'desk'. The work of the department was supervised by a superintending under-secretary of state within the Foreign Office, and important matters of policy were further vetted by a deputy under-secretary of state or the permanent under-secretary of state. From time to time a minister of state also deputised for the foreign secretary (as McNeil did in London during Bevin's absence in 1946, and as Selwyn Lloyd did for Eden in 1953). The importance of the embassy in Cairo declined during the period covered by these documents. From 1946 on the ambassador's responsibility for the Sudan lapsed and the governor-general communicated directly to the Foreign Office and the foreign secretary; thus increasing the governor-general's importance in subsequent Anglo–Egyptian negotiations, at the same time giving the secretary of state more direct oversight of Sudanese affairs.[6]

Within the Foreign Office there was considerable continuity of Egyptian expertise. Sir Eric Beckett, legal adviser throughout the crucial period of Anglo–Egyptian negotiations in 1946–1953, had helped draft the 1936 treaty. Exchanges between, and the eventual amalgamation of, the foreign and diplomatic services meant that there were a number of officials who saw service in both Cairo and Whitehall (including Bowker, Chapman-Andrews, Riches, Scrivener and Shuckburgh, and two ambassadors, Campbell and Stevenson). A few (Chapman-Andrews and Riches) had even served on diplomatic missions in the Sudan during the war. There was no reciprocal movement between the Sudan Political Service and the Foreign Office, despite the former being supervised by the latter. The Sudan government staffed agencies in Cairo and London, but the Sudan agents acted as liaison officers with the Cairo embassy and Whitehall on a number of largely technical matters and provided supplementary political information. Given the suspicions the Sudan government had of Foreign Office intentions, the Sudan agent also supplied informal 'intelligence' on Whitehall to Khartoum.[7] It was only when self-government and self-determination for the Sudan became the dominant issues that the Foreign Office broke with established tradition and appointed two of its own men (Howe and Helm) as the last governors-general of the Sudan. The opening of the United Kingdom Trade Commissioner's Office in Khartoum in 1953 (set up for political, rather than commercial reasons) allowed the Foreign Office to send personnel with both Egyptian and Whitehall experience to Khartoum (Riches, Morris), leading finally to the appointment of Chapman-Andrews as the first ambassador to the Sudan.

The consequence of all this was that the Foreign Office was not the remote and isolated bureaucracy of the Sudan administrators' imagination. Whitehall had to keep in focus the tripartite demands of Britain's broader strategic interests and its specific commitments to both Egypt and the Sudan. The Cairo embassy often argued

Egypt's case with considerable strength, while Howe, once installed in Khartoum, appeared just as intransigent in the Sudanese interest as his much-decorated predecessor, Major-General Sir Hubert Huddleston. Officials in Whitehall had to balance these competing interests in the increasingly hopeless task of squaring many circles, but collectively they exhibited a surprisingly detailed knowledge of conditions in the Sudan, and their individual comments often showed greater perspective and foresight than those of the Sudan administrators. Despite this most Sudan government officials had a lasting suspicion of and hostility towards the Foreign Office, a suspicion which pervades their private papers and memoirs, and which continues to colour historical writing about this period.

All editing projects are collaborative efforts, but BDEEP has been more so than most. Overall guidance was provided in the early stages by the first two general editors, the late Michael Crowder and David Murray, but the hard task of editing the editors fell to Stephen Ashton, a job he performed (in my case) with tact and, at times, admirable diplomacy. It has been a privilege for me to work in tandem with the other editors of the project, but I have benefited most from the parallel research of and comments from Ronald Hyam, Richard Rathbone and John Kent. We all owe a debt of gratitude to the staff at the PRO for the processing of bulk orders and photocopying, but I owe my personal thanks to Jane Hogan and the special collections staff at the University of Durham Palace Green Library for their quick response to my urgent requests for supplementary material from the university's Sudan archive. I am also grateful to Catherine Lawrence, cartographer at the School of Oriental and African Studies, for the general map of the Sudan reproduced in both parts of this volume.

* * * *

The Anglo–Egyptian condominium

The evolution of the internal administration of the Sudan, and the relationship of its central government at Khartoum to the embassy in Cairo, the Egyptian government and the Foreign Office can be best described in a summary of the condominium from its inception in 1899 to 1946. Britain's occupation of Egypt in the 1880s coincided with the onset of the Mahdiya (1881–1898), the religious rising against Turco–Egyptian rule in the Sudan led by Muhammad Ahmad al-Mahdi ('the Rightly Guided One'). It was at Britain's insistence that Egypt abandoned its African empire (which included the Sudan and parts of the Congo, Uganda, Abyssinia and the Eritrean and Somali coasts). The European scramble for Africa followed immediately upon the collapse of the Egyptian empire, and as European powers began to push their claims into the interior, Britain resurrected the continuation of Egypt's former claim to the Nile valley. The reconquest of the Sudan (1896–1899) was undertaken for Egyptian strategic reasons, largely with Egyptian troops (under British command) and was paid for mainly by Egypt. Britain presented itself as assisting Egypt militarily to regain its territories 'in rebellion', and diplomatically to re-assert its rights to the Sudan against claims of the Abyssinian, French and Belgian empires, even flying the Egyptian, rather than the British flag in the confrontation with the French expedition at Fashoda in 1898 (86). This early symbolic assertion of Egyptian sovereignty was to return to haunt Britain in subsequent negotiations with Egypt (91).

The 1899 Anglo–Egyptian Agreement (appendix, part I) established the co-dominal nature of the administrative structure of the Sudan. Britain claimed the right, by virtue of participating in the reconquest, to administer the Sudan on behalf of Egypt. The governor-general of the Sudan was appointed by the viceroy (later king) of Egypt on the recommendation of the British government. He had the right to legislate by proclamation but was also subordinate to the British agent and consul-general in Cairo, then Lord Cromer.[8] Sovereignty in 1899 was not the issue it later became as Egyptian sovereignty itself was qualified by British occupation. Ultimate sovereignty over the Sudan was left deliberately vague. Egypt (rather than Britain) paid a subvention to the Sudan government, and the administration of the Sudan grew out of the Egyptian army of occupation, with the sirdar (commander-in-chief) of the Egyptian army also serving as governor-general of the Sudan. This arrangement lasted until 1924, nearly half the span of the condominium.

The majority of the pre-1920 administrators of the Sudan were seconded from the Egyptian army, with British officers occupying the senior positions in civil administration, and Egyptian and Sudanese officers drawn from the Egyptian and Sudanese battalions of the Egyptian garrison serving in junior administrative capacities throughout the Sudan. This continued until the crisis of 1924, after which the Egyptian battalions and Egyptian officers were expelled and a new Sudan Defence Force was created independent of the Egyptian army. Being derived from the Egyptian army the SDF retained similar structures, especially in the granting of commissions to Sudanese native officers (unlike East and West Africa). This was to have important implications in the period of decolonisation because it established a Sudanese officer corps: Abdallah Khalil, a leading member of the Umma Party before independence and subsequent prime minister, served in both the Egyptian army and SDF, retiring with the rank of brigadier.

Egypt being a Foreign Office responsibility, the Sudan administration came under Foreign Office supervision, and remained so because of the Sudan's legal status as an Egyptian possession. Not only did the Foreign Office nominate the governor-general, but it recruited the civilian element of the Sudan administration – those on permanent service rather than on contract who were later referred to as the Sudan Political Service. Selection for the Sudan administration was organised on Foreign Office lines: with no entrance exam (unlike the Indian Civil and Colonial Services) much depended on recommendations and the *viva voce*. It was only in the 1920s that the civilian SPS began to outnumber the contract soldiers, and civilians occupied all the highest posts from province governors to the civil secretary. The first civilian governors-general were also appointed in the 1920s, and it was during the 1920s that the balance of power within the central government in Khartoum began to shift away from the governor-general towards the triumvirate of the civil, financial and legal secretaries. A Governor-General's Council had been in existence since 1910, but during the interwar years the council came into its own as more than a mere advisory body and the civil secretary, especially, took a leading role as head of the civil administration.[9]

The crisis in relations between Egypt and Britain following World War One had a profound impact on the Sudan's relation to Egypt. The 1919 nationalist demonstrations in Egypt against the protectorate declared by Britain in 1914 were suppressed (with Huddleston, a future governor-general of the Sudan, taking part in the suppression) (107). Leaders of the main nationalist party, the Wafd, then attempted to negotiate an end to the protectorate, but these negotiations faltered, in part because of the Wafd's insistence on asserting Egyptian sovereignty over the Sudan. In 1922 Britain unilaterally recognised Egypt's independence, subject to reservations over the security of imperial communications, the defence of Egypt, the protection of minorities and foreign interests, and the Sudan. This forced the Sudan's ambiguous position as an Egyptian colony governed by Britain into the forefront of Anglo–Egyptian relations. In 1923 Britain intervened in the drafting of the Egyptian constitution to remove any reference to the King of Egypt being the King of the Sudan. In 1924 talks resumed between the British and Egyptian governments to resolve the reserved points. Egypt, under the newly elected Wafd government of Zaghlul Pasha, hoped for a greater recognition of its rights over the Sudan, while the Sudan government hoped for complete political and military autonomy from Egypt, with the withdrawal of the Egyptian army and Egyptian officials (but not of Egyptian money). London and the high commissioner in Cairo, at different times, attempted to take positions somewhere between these two poles, hoping that Egypt might be persuaded to drop its claims to the Sudan, but continue its subvention, in return for a secure southern frontier and a guaranteed share of the Nile Waters.

The crisis spread to the Sudan through a series of pro-Egyptian demonstrations among Sudanese army units. It came to a head with the assassination of Sir Lee Stack, governor-general of the Sudan, by Egyptian nationalists in Cairo in November 1924. Lord Allenby, British high commissioner, issued an ultimatum to the Egyptian government to pay a fine of half a million pounds, withdraw all military personnel from the Sudan and accept an unlimited increase in the Sudan's share of the Nile Waters. Zaghlul was unable to accept these conditions and resigned. Allenby suspended the 1923 constitution, and the Sudan government began the evacuation of all Egyptian forces from the country, provoking some Sudanese troops to mutiny in their support. The mutiny was quickly put down by British troops in the streets of Khartoum (with Huddleston, once again, in command). British officials in the Sudan hoped that the formal abolition of the condominium would follow, but this was opposed by the Foreign Office and Allenby, both of whom hoped for the creation of a friendlier government in Egypt, and both of whom recognised the continued importance of Egypt's annual subvention to the Sudan.[10]

The expulsion of the Egyptians led to the Sudan being governed as a British colony in practice, but not in law. The Sudanese battalions of the Egyptian army were reorganised as a separate force, with Huddleston as the first *kaid al-amm* (commander-in-chief) and all Sudanese officers receiving their commissions from, and taking an oath of allegiance to the governor-general. Throughout the 1920s the Sudan government aggressively asserted the Sudan's rights to a share of the Nile Waters and increased cotton production. Water became the one regular point of diplomatic contact between the Sudan and Egypt: Egypt's most important presence in the Sudan being the Egyptian Irrigation Department. The completion of the Sennar Dam in 1926 to provide irrigation for the new Gezira scheme south of Khartoum was eventually followed by a Nile Waters agreement negotiated by Britain and Egypt in 1929, allowing Egypt an 11 to 1 share in the Nile Waters, restricting the construction of further irrigation works inside the Sudan and allowing the EID inspection rights. The 1929 Nile Waters Agreement gave the Sudan more than it had previously received, but it upheld 'the principle of the primacy of existing land usage and water needs versus potential use and needs',[11] and was not well received by politically-conscious Sudanese, who of course had not been consulted.[12]

There was no agreement over the status of the Sudan. Four separate attempts between 1927 and 1930 to re-negotiate Anglo–Egyptian relations failed over the demand by successive Egyptian governments to return to the pre-1924 arrangement. Britain's position that Britain and Egypt exercised conjoint sovereignty over the Sudan was consistently rejected by the Wafd party, which was riven by internal splits and unable to form a stable government to press the issue. The Abyssinian crisis of the mid-1930s served as an incentive to both Egypt and Britain to conclude a treaty of alliance in 1936. The Wafd prime minister, Mustafa al-Nahhas,[13] secured a restoration of the 1923 constitution and led a united parties delegation into the negotiations with Anthony Eden, then British foreign secretary, seeking an alliance with Britain and a modification of the 1899 Anglo–Egyptian Agreement to give Egypt an effective share in the administration of the Sudan.

The Sudan government's position in the negotiations was presented by the governor-general, Sir Stewart Symes, supported by the high commissioner, Sir Miles Lampson (later Lord Killearn). He urged Egypt's recognition of a *de jure*, as well as *de facto* autonomous government in the Sudan, exercising conjoint sovereignty under the condominium agreements in the form of a 'mandatory' administration for the welfare of the Sudanese, until such time as the Sudanese had reached 'a higher level of civilisation'. Symes countered the Egyptian proposal to direct involvement in Sudanese administration by announcing that junior public service posts already occupied by some 500 Egyptians would gradually be filled by qualified Sudanese. The Foreign Office accepted Symes' arguments, but qualified them with the acknowledgement that Egypt did have 'legal rights' in the Sudan, however much these were in conflict with 'moral and historical' considerations. In the end the 1936 treaty did not modify the 1899 agreement but did restore something of the pre-1924 position by readmitting a small Egyptian garrison to Khartoum. The principle of the governor-general's autonomy in legislating for Sudan was maintained, requiring him merely to inform both co-domini of legislation after the fact; though in practice he continued to seek and receive HMG's approval through the ambassador before passing legislation (13). The 1929 Nile Waters Agreement was appended to the treaty and remained unchanged. The Sudan's debt to Egypt was in effect written off (it would not be cancelled, nor would it be called in). The question of sovereignty was again left in abeyance (6). The treaty had to be renegotiated at the end of twenty years (1956), but there was a provision for renegotiation after ten years (1946) at either party's request.[14]

The Anglo–Egyptian negotiations between 1923 and 1936 had an impact on the internal administration of the Sudan, despite leaving the terms of the original 1899 agreement unchanged. The Sudan government's attitude to the negotiations not only reflected, but sometimes altered their relationship with different classes and categories of Sudanese leaders. At the time of the re-conquest the newly established Sudan government sought allies among the tribal notables who had formerly allied with the old Turco–Egyptian regime, or who had suffered under the centralised theocratic state of the Mahdiya. Conscious of its position as an 'infidel' government among a Muslim population in the northern part of the country, it was especially keen to build up a rural base of support, bolstered by an 'established' Islam, to guard against the resurgence of potentially anti-government Islamic reformers. Throughout the first two decades of the twentieth century tribal groups were reconstituted around notable families in a hierarchy of shaikhs (high notables), nazirs (leaders of tribes or large tribal sections) and omdas (headmen of towns or groups of villages). These were the men who, through government support, began to acquire rights to labour and land, and who after the adoption of the policy of 'native administration' in 1922, were given formal judicial powers as well. The advent of World War One and the Egyptian nationalist struggle brought about a modification of the government's religious policy. Previously it had favoured the Khatmiya religious order, whose leader, sayyid Ali al-Mirghani, had been a staunch supporter of Egypt throughout the Mahdiya (116 n 7), and had kept a close watch on the activities of the family of the late Mahdi, especially his son sayyid Abd al-Rahman al-Mahdi[15] and his followers, the Ansar. But Mahdiism's anti-Turkish and anti-Egyptian ideology brought it into an alliance with the Sudan government first during the war against Turkey, and again in 1919, countering pro-Egyptian sentiment in the Sudan. The rehabilitation of sayyid Abd al-Rahman and his Ansar sect brought him a profitable livelihood as he secured government contracts for the provision of meat and fuel, and was soon able, along with many other notables and merchants, to invest in the new cotton-growing area of the Gezira scheme. By the end of the 1920s sayyid Abd al-Rahman was financing his inherited mantle of sanctity with profits from big business.[16]

This attempt to build up and rule through a 'gentry' was achieved at the expense of some of the government's earlier allies: the officer corps of the Sudanese battalions and the newly emerging 'effendia', the modern educated class in the lower ranks of the civil service. Both were employed in institutions derived from Egypt. The soldiers were products of the old slave battalions of the nineteenth-century army, families of professional soldiers of slave descent (what British administrators in the 1920s termed 'negroid but detribalised') who formed the nucleus of a new literate native officer class owing their commissions, and their loyalty, to the king of Egypt; but who, because of their servile origin, had few, if any ties with the emergent tribal gentry of the northern provinces. It was only those sons of the gentry and the merchant classes that also entered the civil service via modern education who came into contact with this class on equal terms, with a shared educational background and similar aspirations. In the immediate aftermath of World War One many of the Sudanese effendia looked to Egypt for political inspiration and sympathised with the Wafd's struggle for independence. By 1924 the most active Sudanese nationalist group was the White Flag League, advocating the contradictory platforms of 'Sudan for the Sudanese' and 'the unity of the Nile valley', and whose leader, Ali Abd al-Latif (116 n 9) was the son of former slaves, a graduate of Gordon Memorial College in Khartoum, an ex-officer, and a friend of such Egyptian officers stationed in the Sudan as Muhammad Najib, the future president of Egypt.

The new 'Sudan Question' raised by the 1924 negotiations divided the effendia from the notables, and split the nationalists. Ali Abd al-Latif's slave descent and his strong opposition to the religious notables' collaboration with the British administration (particularly that of the 'two sayyids') alienated the notables and their adherents (even among the effendia) from the nationalist cause. When in 1924 Britain raised, for the first time, the idea that the 'will of the Sudanese people' should be given priority in solving the 'Sudan question', but that this will should be 'delegated', the idea of 'delegation' of the Sudan's rights in the Anglo–Egyptian negotiations was widely accepted. The tribal and religious notables who were seeking, by investment in the Gezira, to become a landed gentry or an agricultural bourgeoisie, were allies of the Sudan government and delegated their rights to Britain. The White Flag League delegated their rights to Egypt (and in particular to the Wafd). But there was an essential conflict between the idea of 'delegation' of the Sudan's rights and the idea of the right of Sudanese to self-determination which was never fully resolved and was one of the causes of the League's ultimate failure. The conflict between the co-dominal powers was played out between contesting groups in the Sudan. The Sudanese nationalists foundered on issues of race and class indigenous to the Sudan, and many repudiated Ali Abd al-Latif and others like him as men of no importance with no right to speak on matters of state politics. The defeat of the mutineers, the suppression of the White Flag League and its leaders, and the expulsion of the Egyptians meant that Sudanese 'nationalism' of the 1930s and 1940s developed along much more restricted lines than those proposed by Ali Abd al-Latif.[17]

The organisation of the rural administration of the Sudan around tribal leaders continued throughout the 1920s and early 1930s, with a further dilution of the influence of old Sudanese officers. In the reorganisation of the SDF the regular battalions of Sudanese were gradually disbanded and replaced by 'irregular' corps of largely locally-recruited territorial units. There was an increase in the number of 'Arab' officers (169), and many non-commissioned officers as well were recruited from the families of tribal notables. Positions vacated by the expelled Egyptian officers were either abolished or filled by younger educated northern Sudanese. One motive for the reliance on native administration was certainly to support the more 'loyal' gentry against the less reliable effendia, but even though educated Sudanese in the civil service felt that they were being marginalised during this period, their social and economic importance in the country was growing. The effendia's disillusionment with Egypt's own imperial attitudes toward the Sudan displayed in the 1929 Nile Waters and 1936 Anglo–Egyptian Treaty negotiations certainly helped in the gradual rapprochement between the educated classes and the government in the late 1930s. After 1936 more minor administrative posts were created for educated Sudanese, and new structures of local government in the municipalities, townships and rural areas began to replace or supplement native administration (7). Educated northern Sudanese organised themselves into the Graduates' Congress in 1938 (1), initially a non-political organisation of secondary school graduates which grew out of the Omdurman and Wad Medani graduates' clubs and literary societies of the post-1924 era. The Graduates' Congress presented itself to the government as a semi-public body interested in social reform and affairs of public interest, and received a sympathetic welcome from an administration which was even then toying with the idea of creating some form of advisory council.[18]

The 'Southern Policy', first enunciated in 1930, was an extension of the principles of native administration to the three southern provinces, whereby tribal systems were massaged into the structures of local administration, each supported by (and supporting) their own forms of customary law. Beyond that there was also a fear of the political consequences of the spread of Islam into non-Muslim areas, the example of Ali Abd al-Latif (though born in Egypt) and other 'detribalised' officers of southern stock being taken as proof of this. There was a genuine concern about the destructive legacy of the slave trade in the South and other slave-taking reservoirs such as the Nuba Mountains, which was reinforced by the discovery of a resurgence of slaving in the late 1920s. To the principles of native administration then universally applied throughout the Sudan were added further restrictions on movements of northern Sudanese into the South and other non-Muslim areas of the North through the Closed Districts Ordinance. Education, which had never received priority in the South, was left in the hands of Christian missionaries. Despite the over-enthusiastic application of these restrictions in the Western District, Bahr al-Ghazal, significant Muslim communities continued to live in the major towns of the South, select northern Sudanese merchants continued to receive permits to trade even in remote areas, and northern Sudanese and Muslim clerical staff, administrative officials and even some police and army officers continued to serve in the southern provinces (one, Ibrahim Badri, later became a prominent nationalist politician). The British 'Bog Barons' of southern administration gained a reputation for eccentric insularity, but there was no separate administrative service for the southern provinces. The majority of British officials serving in the South between 1930 and 1946, including the provincial governors, also saw service in the North. The possibility of merging the Sudan's southern provinces into the administration of the East African colonies was an option which was raised, but it was never seriously pressed on the Colonial Office (11). Symes' modernising reforms served to entrench the social and economic differences between North and South as resources were directed away from the backward regions into the relatively few developed areas of the North.[19]

The preceding summary suggests a number of similarities between the Sudan and Britain's African colonial territories, contrary to the often voiced assumption that the Sudan was governed according to the Foreign Office's 'Middle Eastern axioms'. Despite the Balliol-like image of 'effortless superiority' which the SPS cultivated, and the outward disdain for colonial ways it often expressed, the Sudan administration did look to the Indian and colonial empires for inspiration. The 1899 agreement deliberately excluded the mixed courts and Egyptian law from the Sudan, allowing the government to adapt the Indian civil and penal codes for use in a multi-religious context, just as the governments of the East African colonies did. Native administration as the basis for local government was derived from the principles of indirect rule as practised elsewhere in British Africa. Islamic (sharia) law was relegated mainly to realm of family law, and customary law was given a significant place, even in rural Muslim communities.

Some political developments happened in the Sudan earlier than in West Africa, partly because the Sudan was *not* under the Colonial Office but *was* linked to Egypt. As early as 1925 civil posts vacated by Egyptians were filled by promoting Sudanese, and in 1936 the governor-general managed to get acceptance of the principle of Sudanising *Egyptian* posts. Yet there were similar problems and attitudes. The post-1936 policy of bringing more educated Sudanese into the administration met with the same type of resistance among senior administrators in the Sudan[20] that was provoked by Sir Alan Burns' later reforms in the Gold Coast. The arguments in the Gold Coast concerning the lack of a popular base for the 'small minority' of literate Africans[21] had their antecedents in the Sudan as early as 1924 and were paralleled in 1942 (1, 3). But in both 1936 and 1946 the Sudan government had to drop their reservations in order to build alliances with that 'small minority' to keep Egypt out.

In each significant round of Anglo–Egyptian negotiations Britain progressively redefined the rationale for its presence in the Sudan. In the 1920s it was to provide good government, with 'the will of the Sudanese people' being invoked in support of removing Egyptian influence. In 1936 it was as a 'mandatory' administration with the 'welfare' of the Sudanese in mind, and the claims of Sudanese effendia were advanced over Egyptian claims to greater administrative representation. By 1942 self-government was being advocated as a way of obtaining Sudanese independence from Egypt (3). It was only in 1946, as we shall see, that the Sudan government explicitly declared that Sudanese self-government and self-determination were – and always had been – the objects of British administration, again as a counter to the Egyptian reassertion of its sovereignty over the Sudan.

Anticipating the post-war settlement, May 1942–Dec 1945
The events of World War Two had a direct impact on British relations with both the Sudan and Egypt. The Sudan won a reputation for loyalty to the British war effort through the contribution of its troops in Ethiopia and subsequently in Libya. In contrast Britain never took Egyptian loyalty for granted, and on 4 February 1942 Lampson employed British troops to force King Faruq to invite the anti-monarchist Wafd Party (the co-architects of the 1936 treaty of alliance) to form a government under Mustafa al-Nahhas. Faruq's antipathy towards the Wafd deepened and he would later show great reluctance to invite them to form any post-war government, preferring instead governments of unstable coalitions. The Wafd gained a reputation as a pro-British party, which it would try to shake off in opposition after the war.

By early 1942 there were significant developments in the war which affected the Sudan both directly and indirectly: the removal of the immediate threat to the Sudan's security with the defeat of Italy in Ethiopia, the publication of the Atlantic Charter, and the Cripps mission to India. The Graduates' Congress took the opportunity of Cripps' advertised stop-over in Khartoum on his way to India in April to present the government with a memorandum directly responding to the Atlantic Charter without specifically mentioning it, and calling upon the co-dominal powers to guarantee the Sudan's right to self-determination after the war (1). In the memorandum Congress described itself as representing 'enlightened public opinion' and submitted its proposals as expressing 'faithfully the inclinations and aspirations of this country'. In addition to asking for guarantees for the exercise of the right of self-determination, the memorandum listed a number of specifically northern Sudanese concerns: measures for including Sudanese at all levels of government and for its eventual Sudanisation; removal of restrictions on indigenous economic activity; the establishment of a Sudanese nationality (as opposed to the extension of Egyptian nationality to the Sudan); a halt to immigration not covered by the Anglo–Egyptian Treaty (a reference to West African immigrants); and the reversal of the Southern Policy in regards to permits to trade and the missionary education system.

The reaction of the Sudan government was ambivalent. Many points in the memorandum concerning greater Sudanese involvement in administration had been under consideration since 1936 and were in keeping with the trend of reforms initiated by Symes and enacted by his civil secretaries, Gillan and Newbold. But while the war may have receded from the Sudan's borders, British forces were still under threat in North Africa, and Congress's timing appeared to some officials as nothing less than seditious.[22] Newbold's brusque rejection of the memorandum, his repudiation of Congress's claim to speak on national issues and his instructions to senior administrators not to discuss the memorandum with Sudanese won the approval of both the governor-general and the Foreign Office. Yet all seemed agreed that some form of inclusion of Sudanese in administration and central government was necessary (1, 3). Newbold had written nearly two months before receiving the memorandum: 'I think we must start *now* taking note of the Atlantic Charter' (2). Sir Stafford Cripps subsequently advised him 'we must have a Sudanese Advisory Council and not wait on events'.[23] One effect of the memorandum and subsequent discussions and correspondence with Congress (4, 5) was that it revealed 'the urgent need' for proceeding with plans to bring Sudanese into closer association with the government (7) which Newbold had begun drafting in February (2). It also meant that despite repeated attempts to put Congress in its place over constitutional and political matters (4, 8) the government finally had to accept that it must find ways of engaging Congress and other politically-minded Sudanese in a constructive dialogue about self-government, lest 'the Paradise of the Sudan of the Golden Age may prove a Fool's Paradise' (7, 9).

Historians of decolonisation have argued that the issue of Sudanese self-determination was raised prematurely by external factors before it could arise naturally among the broader population within the Sudan, and even that the very idea of a Sudanese nation originated with British administrators. It could more accurately be said that northern Sudanese nationalist leaders seized on international events to their advantage earlier than African nationalists elsewhere. Thus, at a time when Churchill himself was arguing against the application to India of the right of self-determination enshrined in the Charter, some Sudanese leaders already had grasped the significance of the language of the Charter to their own aspirations. By their actions in 1942 they placed not just a 'closer association' with government, but self-government and self-determination on the post-war agenda.

Newbold redefined British 'trusteeship' as being 'that of a guardian for a ward who will eventually come of age' (7). This was given expression in his directive statement to British administrators (9) outlining the government's 'tutelary' role to lead Congress back from the error of its presumption and 'regain Government's sympathy and confidence'. For all of its recognition of the rising importance of the educated class, older ways of perceiving the Sudanese still governed the approach to Congress. In establishing guidelines for the involvement of civil servants in Congress, administrators were enjoined to seek ways of supporting the older and more moderate generation against the younger 'hot-heads' (7, 9), a common theme in native administration where the position of the shaikhs, chiefs and elders was constantly having to be reinforced against the challenges of the 'young bloods' below. In the plans for an advisory council Huddleston hoped that the 'vacuum' of Sudanese participation in central government would be filled, not by Congress, but by the government's traditional provincial allies routed through province councils (11). Legislation was proposed for new province councils and an Advisory Council for the Northern Sudan in March 1943 and received British government approval (13). Internal criticism of the legislation by British and Sudanese alike was that it was overly cautious (14). The Colonial Office noted that this 'elaborate "pyramid of local Government"' would 'remain extremely paternal', but remarked somewhat wistfully: 'One cannot escape the feeling that the Sudan Government is able to proceed by carefully considered steps without being hustled by pressure of public opinion in the United Kingdom or elsewhere as is the case in many parts of the Colonial Empire.'[24] Pressure of opinion in Egypt and the Sudan was to prove them wrong.

The Foreign Office was already considering the future of the Sudan's sovereignty in light of the Atlantic Charter when documents concerning the Congress memorandum arrived from Cairo. Earlier in May Lampson had advised that al-Nahhas, the newly installed Egyptian prime minister, was under some pressure to raise the treaty issue. Scrivener, head of the Egyptian Department, minuted that the only logical solution to the deferred question of the Sudan's sovereignty in keeping with the spirit of the Charter was to vest sovereignty in the Sudanese themselves through the creation of an assembly of some kind (2), a proposition which his department, on further reflection, judged premature (6). Yet Congress's memorandum, and the reported Egyptian suspicion that Congress was itself inspired by the Sudan government as a means of separating the Sudan from Egypt, suggested to the Egyptian Department that securing the independence of the Sudan from Egypt was a distinct possibility (3). A simple transfer of the Sudan to sole British sovereignty by swapping it for Cyrenaica with Egypt was eventually ruled out as not only counter to the spirit of the Atlantic Charter, but outside the realm of practical politics given the importance of the Nile to Egypt (2, 6, 11, 12). The necessity of courting Sudanese nationalists, however few and unrepresentative, both to prevent them from seeking help from Egypt, and to strengthen Sudanese opposition to incorporation into Egypt, was not lost on Lampson in Cairo (10, 12, 16).

Egypt, therefore, had some reason to see the creation of the Advisory Council of the Northern Sudan as a prelude to separating the Sudan from Egypt (13, 15). By the end of 1943 there were already indications that the Sudan was set to become a major issue in Anglo–Egyptian relations; and here it is interesting to note that it was Beckett at the Foreign Office who predicted the grounds on which the dispute would be raised more accurately than either Newbold in Khartoum or Lampson (now Lord Killearn) in Cairo (15, 16). Yet, for all the Foreign Office's attempt to anticipate the impact of the Atlantic Charter and US policy on the future of British colonial administration generally, and on the co-dominal relations over the Sudan specifically (6, 16), Scrivener identified what would become Britain's weakness in any long-term confrontation with Egypt over the Sudan: 'Apart from the sentimental side of the question, & from the strategic angle, we have really very small *interests* in the Sudan – as opposed to responsibilities' (15). Once the strategic angle changed, as it did in the course of the defence negotiations, all Britain was left with in the Sudan were responsibilities.

The drafting, presentation and rebuff of the 1942 memorandum had repercussions inside the Graduates' Congress, already subject to the strains of the sectarianism which dominated northern Sudanese political life. Disagreements on the form and extent of co-operation with the government over the war led to confrontations within the two-tiered ruling committees of Congress, the Committees of 60 and 15 (1). A more secular group, less conciliatory to the government, called the Ashiqqa (Blood Brothers), formed around the leadership of a mathematics teacher, Ismail al-Azhari. In the Congress elections of 1940 sayyid Abd al-Rahman became involved through his support of Ansar members, and an Ansar-Ashiqqa alliance dominated the Congress executive. A split among the Ansar about the al-Mahdi family's control of the sect became public in 1941 and the alliance began to weaken. It was still in place during the drafting of the 1942 memorandum, with the group of authors including leading Ashiqqa, such as al-Azhari, and leading Ansar, but the Committee of 60 was not fully consulted on the memorandum and not all agreed on its presentation.[25] Newbold's public rebuff of Congress, his more conciliatory private contact with Ibrahim Ahmad which ended in yet another rebuff (1, 4, 5, 8) undermined the position of those in Congress who advocated continued dialogue with the government. The position of the Ashiqqa was strengthened in the executive, and it was they who voiced Congress's initial criticism of the proposed Advisory Council as restrictive and unrepresentative (14). A new alliance between the Ashiqqa and sayyid Ali's Khatmiya sect gave the Ashiqqa the electoral muscle it needed within the crucial Three Towns area (of Khartoum, Khartoum North and Omdurman) in the 1944 Congress elections, returning al-Azhari as president, supported by a strong Ashiqqa-Khatmiya majority on both committees (23).[26]

The 1942 memorandum had distanced Congress from Egypt by insisting on a separate Sudanese nationality and the right of the Sudanese to decide their 'natural' relationship to Egypt (1). But just as the internal politics of the Congress involved the patronage of the leaders of the two main rival religious sects in order to mobilise votes on a large scale, so the prickly response of the Sudan government encouraged the Ashiqqa to look for patronage from the rival co-dominus, Egypt. A visit to Egypt on behalf of Congress by al-Azhari in 1943 led to a final rupture with sayyid Abd al-Rahman, and by 1944 various factions (perhaps too small to be called parties) began to organise around platforms advocating degrees of autonomy or union with Egypt. Full union with Egypt was generally supported by the *muwalladin* (sing. *muwallad*), persons of mixed Egyptian and Sudanese descent, often with family or business ties with Egypt. The Ashiqqa opted for an undefined union, the Ittihadiyyin (Unionists) advocated an independent Sudan as a dominion of Egypt and the Ahrar (Liberals) advocated autonomy within a federation with Egypt (though it soon split between those wishing a closer form of union and those advocating secession). Others, like the Qawmiyyin (Populists) advocated full independence. The Ashiqqa–Khatimiya alliance proved by far the strongest in the 1944 Congress elections, and the other groups of necessity sought (and received) the patronage of sayyid Abd al-Rahman and the Ansar (23, 30). The Ashiqqa victory led to the formation of the pro-independence, 'Sudan for the Sudanese' Umma (Nation) Party under sayyid Abd al-Rahman's patronage in January 1945 (30). This established the political pattern for the next few years: sayyid Abd al-Rahman and his Umma Party and other independents were virtually to concede Congress to the Ashiqqa and Khatmiya but took their places in the official bodies set up by government – the Advisory Council and later the Legislative Assembly – which the Ashiqqa and Khatmiya boycotted.

Sudanese political positions at this time were marked by ambivalence. At the beginning of 1944 Ibrahim Ahmad was taking a decidedly gradualist line towards independence, and clearly saw the advantages of the condominium in that the Sudanese needed both Egypt and Britain to serve as checks against each other (18). Sayyid Abd al-Rahman tried to exploit the Sudan's position under the Foreign Office by making the novel claim that this made the Sudan an ally, rather than a subject of Britain, an argument which would be repeated by the Umma Party shortly after is foundation (20, 30). But sayyid Abd al-Rahman's scarcely concealed monarchical ambitions were already proving a hindrance to the pro-independence cause, creating concern among some of his allies (18) and driving others into the Egyptian camp (26, 30). His tepid disclaimer in May 1945 failed to convince many

(33); in fact it is clear that he harboured royal hopes as late as 1953 (312). When the Umma Party was founded in January 1945 it suffered from too close an association with sayyid Abd al-Rahman, his family and his *daira* (estate or business), as well as from a public perception that it was pro-government. This was to prove a lasting dilemma for the government. 'Our main difficulty', the civil secretary noted, 'is that although we cannot openly say so, the Umma party, whatever its motive, is on our side, and ... we do not want it discouraged' (30). At the same time the government found sayyid Ali taciturn and evasive, given to Delphic statements or no comment at all (18). The difficulty of engaging sayyid Ali directly in political negotiations was to be another of the government's lasting dilemmas. By the end of 1945 the battle lines were clearly drawn between the Khatmiya and Ansar not only in the Congress, but in the province and local councils (46), sayyid Ali having declared unambiguously 'that the real issue in this struggle was S.A.R.'s ambitions and not union with Egypt'.[27]

1945 saw changes in both the governments of the Sudan and Britain. Newbold suddenly and unexpectedly died in March, to be replaced by James Robertson as civil secretary. In Britain the general election of July brought in a new Labour government with Bevin as foreign secretary. Neither of these changes produced immediate alterations in policy. Robertson continued to follow Newbold's line on self-government and dealings with Congress (36, 44). 1945 was also the last year in which Congress acted as the main forum for political discussion among educated and northern Sudanese. The elections for the 1946 committees firmly established the grip of Ansar-Khatmiya sectarianism on northern Sudanese politics (42). The Umma and other pro-independence parties' boycott left Congress entirely under the control of the Khatmiya-backed Ashiqqa, with al-Azhari now referring to Congress as 'a party' (43).

At the beginning of the year the other parties within Congress had been willing to oppose al-Azhari's growing closeness to Egypt (26), but with a strong Ashiqqa majority al-Azhari obtained Congress's endorsement for a resolution calling for an independent Sudanese government in union with Egypt under the Egyptian Crown (30, 34). Al-Azhari attempted to broaden the base of this agreement through the formation of a special 'United Parties Committee', which issued a statement of common goals concerning the steps to be taken to establish a democratic and independent Sudanese government in union with Egypt and alliance with Britain. The form of union was deliberately left undefined, and outside Congress the parties reserved their positions concerning the degree of union they would accept (35, 36, 42, 43). What did emerge was that despite the Ashiqqa's organisational strength over the Umma in Congress elections, the Umma's clearer position on independence commanded more solid support among its members than the vaguer terms of union with Egypt commanded among the disparate factions which constituted the Ashiqqa (42). What is of significance for events in the following year was that a proposal for union under the Egyptian Crown had been raised and debated within the northern Sudan, and some consensus reached.

Up until now all political activity had been confined to the northern Sudan (mainly within the Three Towns and the larger provincial capitals), and revolved around northern Sudanese political concerns. But the structural weakness of the Sudan as a nation, the division between the northern, mainly Muslim provinces and the non-Muslim southern provinces was never far beneath the surface and was a factor in the calculations of the Foreign Office, the Egyptian and Sudanese governments and northern politicians from the very start. Congress's proposal that the co-dominal powers commit themselves to granting the Sudan self-determination within its present boundaries (1) was viewed with scepticism by the Foreign Office who were reluctant 'to perpetuate a union which in later times might be found impracticable' (6); reservations which were heartily endorsed by Huddleston (11). Accelerated educational and economic development within the South were seen as necessary, whether or not the southern provinces remained in the Sudan or were separated off from it (11, 15). Though the need for accelerated development to make up for years of neglect was acknowledged in 1942, there were no practical demonstrations of this realisation by 1944 (19). Northern Sudanese and Egyptians alike were sensitive to administrative measures that seemed to entrench the division between the two parts of the country, and this was a criticism levelled by northern Sudanese and the Egyptian government at the proposals for an Advisory Council for the Northern Sudan (14, 17, 38). The Sudan government adopted an evolutionary line of defence, leaving open the option for the South either to form an advisory council of its own or take part in the Advisory Council in Khartoum when it had reached an equivalent stage of development as the North (21, 38).

The divergent views on the South were clearly stated at this early stage. To the British the division between Northern and Southern Sudan, being racial and historical, was natural (6, 11, 21, 38). To the Egyptian government and many northern Sudanese the division was entirely artificial (17, 26, 38). But the version of Sudanese nationalism which al-Azhari proclaimed, based as it was on 'bonds of religion, language, blood, education and the Nile' (35), while linking the North to Egypt contained within it an important contradiction, which was that the ties of religion, language and blood (as calculated by Arab patrilines) were absent between northern and southern Sudanese. It was the nationalist contention that a common religion, language, education (and eventually blood) were being spread to the South in the nineteenth century before being halted by the British. The nationalist version of a shared Sudanese past which al-Azhari proclaimed, linking Arab and African Sudanese since the time of the Funj Sultanate (38) was partly true, but it is unfortunate that the examples of common endeavour he listed were all based on the institution of slavery and evoked a very ambiguous legacy. Northern nationalists admitted they knew little about the South (38), and it is for this reason that they tended to exaggerate the influence of the Christian missionaries, whose schools taught in vernacular languages and English (both being used in administration),[28] but whose efforts had produced very few converts; the importance of these converts being that they constituted the southern counterpart to the northern 'effendia'.[29] However much the motives of altruism and political calculation may have been mixed in northern attitudes towards the South at this time, al-Azhari's address to Congress in January 1945 spoke to another important consideration, 'above all, the economic need of the North for the South' (26). Here, as in many of his early memoranda to the government, he criticised the administration for its record of uneven development throughout the country.

Development, in all of its facets, became a political issue in the post-war agenda, not only between the Sudanese intelligentsia and the Sudan government, but between the Sudan and co-dominal governments. It was in education that the disadvantage of the Sudan's position outside the Colonial Office became immediately apparent, in that the Sudan was not eligible for Colonial Development Fund grants (19, 22). Here Sudanese were able to compare themselves with other parts of British Africa, to their disadvantage. It was, however, eligible for Egyptian grants, and the Sudan government felt keenly that this imbalance would have internal political ramifications. As Britain depended on US support for sterling the Treasury was doubly hesitant to 'play the Lady Bountiful with foreign currency', and it resisted the Sudan's request for a £1 million grant to endow Gordon College (then being raised to the status of a university college) (22). Huddleston's inept attempt to circumvent the Treasury through the 'Old Boy Network', by appealing directly to the chancellor, whom he had known in India, produced a curt refusal (28) (and also revealed to the Foreign Office Huddleston's lack of tactical finesse in political matters, having 'enabled the Treasury to put a second refusal on record in advance of our own communication').[30] A different line of attack was tried, arguing for a commitment from HMG to development for the Sudan similar to that made for the colonies, as being entirely consistent with US interest in 'the general welfare' (28). Huddleston, who had to do his pleading through Killearn, repeatedly argued for some public disclosure of HMG's intentions with a development-related gesture of goodwill to counter growing Egyptian propaganda (22, 32). Encouraged by the Foreign Office in September 1945 he presented his arguments (some of which followed the language of (28) very closely) for the political need for a £5 million development grant (37). This general proposal was followed by a request to associate Gordon College with the Inter-University Council for Higher Education in the Colonies (48).

Any long-term development would have to come from inside the Sudan, and any plans for expanded agricultural output to meet the post-war expectation for increased social services ultimately came back to the Nile (24). Sudan's share of the Nile Waters was governed by the 1929 Nile Waters Agreement, but plans for increasing the discharge of the Nile had been under discussion in the EID since before World War One. The integrated system of proposed regulators at strategic points throughout the Nile valley which emerged from these discussions has become known as the Century Storage Scheme: in its final form it aimed to increase overyear storage using the East African lakes and Lake Tsana in Ethiopia as reservoirs, and to improve flow with a grand canal circumventing the sudd (central swamps) in the southern Sudan.[31] An earlier agreement with the Ethiopian government to construct a dam on the Blue Nile at its source on Lake Tsana, mainly for the benefit of Egypt and the Sudan, was interrupted by the Italian occupation of Ethiopia, and both Egypt and the Sudan were eager for the reactivation of this proposal after Italy's defeat (27). Diplomatic obstacles posed by the Ethiopian government, however, meant that by the end of 1944 the Sudan had to consider reopening Nile Waters talks with Egypt in order to readjust its share of water (24, 27). Egypt, in the meantime, indicated its desire to resurrect the Jonglei Canal scheme (the sudd diversion canal) which, in its original proposal, benefited mainly Egypt (29). The Foreign Office subsequently advised the Sudan government in April 1945 that its case for renegotiating the Nile Waters Agreement was doubtful, and in so far as this would lead to additional friction with Egypt (who were already preparing to renegotiate the 1936 treaty the following year), they should place their hopes on an agreement over Lake Tsana as the best way of meeting their needs (32). The Sudan hoped to do this in such a way as to gain control over the Lake Tsana dam and become the chief beneficiary of the project (27, 39). Egypt then approached Uganda over the issue of constructing a barrage and reservoir at Lake Albert, as part of the Jonglei Canal scheme (41). By now it was clear that Egypt was just as eager as the Sudan to push on with development schemes increasing the Nile discharge, and that it fully intended to retain control over these projects and the subsequent division of water shares as part of its own post-war settlement. Huddleston found Killearn's suggestion that Britain could use its physical control of the Nile Waters as a 'trump card' in coming negotiations over the Sudan's future unhelpful, not to mention unrealistic (25, 31). At the beginning of 1946 Huddleston proposed a general review of the Nile Waters question as soon as possible, covering the allocation of water as well as the three proposed major engineering schemes of the Jonglei Canal and the dams at Lakes Albert and Tsana (45).

The first warning that Egypt intended to renegotiate the Anglo–Egyptian treaty in 1946, with the aim of getting British forces to withdraw from Egypt and extending its control over Sudan, came in January 1944,[32] and al-Nahhas' personal attitude towards such renegotiations was confirmed in a meeting with al-Azhari (34). Some Sudanese feared that their future would be decided over their heads at the San Francisco meeting of the United Nations in 1945, prompting the Sudan government to ask for public assurances to be made concerning future consultations (30). A statement to the Advisory Council promising to consult that body about any future changes was approved in September, issued in November and explicitly defined to include 'other representative bodies' such as Congress (40, 44, 47).

The Anglo–Egyptian treaty negotiations and the Sudan protocol, Jan 1946–Mar 1947

Egypt gave official notice of its demand for the revision of the 1936 treaty on 20 December 1945 (47). The Foreign Office, the embassy and the Sudan government had already formulated preliminary positions in anticipation of this demand. The Foreign Office saw developments both inside and outside the Sudan as leading to the Sudan's ultimate autonomy from Egypt. The embassy under Killearn viewed the Sudan more abstractly, as a 'trump card' in the game with Egypt, and Killearn continued to exclude Huddleston from matters 'of higher policy'. Bevin's replacement of Killearn with Campbell in March 1946, which led to the lapse of the ambassador's responsibilities over the Sudan, gave the governor-general a greater role in the forthcoming negotiations and direct access to the foreign secretary, even if at the expense of regular communication with the embassy.[33] The embassy's pre-occupation with 'higher policy' was not shared by the Sudan government. Newbold showed an awareness of how the changing global situation affected the internal relations of the empire (7), but his observation that many of his British colleagues in the Sudan did not yet realise how delicate the international situation was and 'how fast the outside world is moving in new political ideas' (15) was to be echoed by Foreign Office and embassy officials frequently throughout the ensuing decade. The Sudan government's commitment to a self-governing Sudan in the distant future did not yet extend to full independence (11, 36, 49). Within a year Britain's policy would explicitly foresee independence as the desired outcome of self-government, and this came about as the logical extension of the principle of consultation with the Sudanese during the Anglo–Egyptian negotiations.

There were two facets to this principle of consultation: administrative and diplomatic. The principle was established as a direct result of Newbold's discussions with Congress in the aftermath of their memorandum (2, 5), and expressly included the Advisory Council (11, 15, 40). Bevin incorporated it in his first memorandum on the treaty negotiations in January 1946, and hoped to use the necessity of consultation as a means of deferring the question of the Sudan's sovereignty altogether (47). Consultation requires some body to consult, and the establishment of the Advisory Council became only the first step in a new policy leading to Sudanisation. In a reversal of what might be the expected roles, it was the Foreign Office who began to urge upon the Sudan government a faster pace of administrative Sudanisation, while the Sudan government pressed the British government for a clear diplomatic commitment to consulting the Sudanese on their future constitutional status.

Robertson's Sudanisation proposal envisaged merely a reduction of British political staff in the northern provinces by more than half over a twenty year period (49). Bowker at the embassy declared that such gradual dilution was out of the question 'in present world conditions'; Scrivener agreed, adding 'we cannot go on keeping Egyptians out of the Political Service *unless* we can put Sudanese in' (49, 52). Campbell urged Khartoum to draft and publicise a 'bold plan' of Sudanisation, lest the Sudanese 'throw in their lot with the Egyptians simply in order to get rid of the British'; Bevin minuted, 'action is needed immediately' (57). Huddleston, however, expressed reservations about the possibility of an accelerated programme (60), but saw as a matter of greater urgency the establishment of a mechanism for internal consultation over the constitutional issues connected with the treaty (51).

Bevin was inclined to agree with the Sudan government's desire (against embassy opposition) to hold such consultations before agreement had been reached on the defence sections of the treaty, but he also urged Huddleston to widen his intended consultations to include the Southern Sudan, a recommendation which came from the Sudan Agent in London, R C Mayall, a former DC in a southern province (56, 53). Huddleston responded by pressing the foreign secretary to make a categorical statement concerning British policy in the Sudan as a way of countering increased Egyptian propaganda, and provided the first draft of such a statement. Bevin thus announced in the House of Commons on 26 March 1946 HMG's support for the establishment of self-government 'as a first step towards eventual independence', and a commitment that no change to the status of the Sudan would be made without consulting the Sudanese (54). Next (within days of arguing with Campbell against accelerating Sudanisation) Huddleston made his own statement to the Advisory Council (approved by the Foreign Office) in which he linked the ultimate goal of independence for the Sudan to a new programme of rapid Sudanisation, announced the convening of a broadly representative committee to make recommendations for Sudanisation, and predicted a fully self-governing Sudan in twenty years (58, 60, 61).[34]

Egyptian-based propaganda in the Sudan during the early part of 1946 came from unofficial as well as official sectors and included the first appearance of the Muslim Brothers (Ikhwan al-Muslimin) (46, 50), an organisation which was to have little impact on the direction of the Sudanese independence movement, but was to become a major political force in the Northern Sudan by the end of the century. Emissaries of the Egyptian government encouraged a revival of the United Parties declaration (43), and in March and April a 'United Parties' delegation, having agreed on a modified formula (which reserved to the Sudanese the right to choose what form of union they might have with Egypt), went to Egypt under al-Azhari's chairmanship. Bevin's statement in March, followed by Huddleston's in April were contrasted uncomfortably with Egyptian government insistence that the delegation accept the principle of the unity of the Nile valley under the Egyptian Crown, and eventually the delegation dissolved itself in disagreement (60, 61).[35]

Fear of the extension of Egyptian political control was also felt in the matter of Nile Waters, this time the Ugandan government objecting to Egyptian proposals for the Lake Albert reservoir on political, economic and environmental grounds (55). Reminded by the Foreign Office of existing obligations under the 1929 Nile Waters Agreement, Uganda adopted a line the Sudan took on the Jonglei Canal (29), and insisted on a full socio-economic and hydrological survey before any decision could be taken (62, 63).

Despite the political instability and change of governments in Egypt some continuity in the Egyptian negotiating position was maintained, given an earlier all-party declaration on the subject and the fact that so many leading members of the government and opposition had been members of the 1936 treaty delegation (including Sidqi, al-Nuqrashi and al-Nahhas, three of the prime ministers who would be involved in the negotiations of 1946–1952). Bevin's commitments as foreign secretary meant that he would not be directly involved in negotiations until the very end of 1946. Throughout 1946 his attention was taken up by the peace treaties being negotiated in Paris, defence matters in the Mediterranean and Middle East, the Palestine conference in London, and the Council of Ministers and UN, quite apart from the Labour government's domestic nationalisation programme. Bevin was in Paris in April to May, June to July, August to September and September to October. He left for the meetings of the Council of Ministers and the UN at Lake Success on 27 October, immediately upon the conclusion of his talks with Ismail Sidqi, the Egyptian prime minister.[36] It was Lord Stansgate, the secretary of state for air, who led the UK delegation to Egypt in April 1946.[37]

In keeping with previous Cabinet decisions, it was decided in June to deal with the Sudan under a separate protocol, with Britain proposing a formal commission structure to consult the Sudanese and decide their future. By July it was realised that there was considerable opposition to this in Egypt and that the entire treaty could be lost over the issue of the Sudan (64, 65). Stansgate felt that his own room for manoeuvre over the Sudan was prejudiced by the line the UK had adopted on defence issues (65), and on 1 August the Cabinet (minus Bevin, who was in Paris) agreed with Stansgate's proposal to compromise on some of the defence matters and reaffirmed their determination to resist any implication of recognising Egyptian sovereignty over the Sudan (66, 69). It was Bevin's refusal to accept the Egyptian draft of article 2 of the defence treaty which prolonged negotiations at this stage (129).[38]

By August it was becoming clear that Britain's refusal to recognise Egyptian claims to sovereignty over the Sudan was going to be difficult to sustain. It was already understood that unqualified recognition of Egyptian sovereignty would lead to trouble in the Sudan, but Egypt's historical and legal justification was strong and, since there was no internationally agreed definition of sovereignty, it could make an uncomfortable case if presented to the UN. Stansgate warned that there would be a need for a compromise formula, but that if negotiations were going to break down (as it appeared they would) it was far better for Britain's standing in world opinion for them to break down over an Egyptian denial of the Sudan's right to self-determination than over the finer points of the defence treaty (67, 68, 70). Deadlock over the defence clauses in August provoked King Faruq's intervention and his official request for inclusion of a reference to the unity of the Nile valley under the Egyptian crown in the Sudan protocol (72).[39]

The problem which Bevin and the UK government faced was one of a changed international climate of opinion, not a change in international law. Bevin had been adamant before negotiations began that 'the future of the Sudan belongs neither to this country nor to Egypt, but to the Sudanese themselves...' (47). When Sidqi asserted 'there could be no doubt whatever regarding the sovereignty of the Egyptian crown over the Sudan. ... There could be no question whatever of asking the Sudanese their own opinion of sovereignty which was ... already in the King's, i.e. King of Darfour Senaar and Kordofan...', resurrecting the old titles of the conquered territories to which the Egyptian viceroy had been granted title by the Ottoman sultan, his sovereign overlord at the time, he was in fact pressing a claim which the British government had never formally disputed and was on record as having asserted.[40] Confronted with the Egyptian position Bevin could only reiterate that 'in dealing with any Colonial or Quasi-Colonial problem' the attitudes of the US and the UN had to be taken into consideration, and that 'to recognise Egyptian sovereignty with the Sudan ... would be regarded as a retrograde step' (74).

Warnings that a substantial section of Sudanese public opinion would be hostile to any acknowledgement of Egyptian sovereignty came from both Huddleston (in Britain) (73, 77) and the Umma Party (71, 82). A triangular correspondence between Stansgate in Egypt, the Foreign Office, and Bevin in Paris (73–80) began to push the question of sovereignty away from the old dispute about whether sovereignty resided solely in Egypt or was shared between Britain and Egypt (2, 6, 77) and toward a new position which qualified any reference to Egyptian sovereignty by a recognition of the Sudanese right to choose their own future from a variety of options. Bevin wanted to avoid recognising Egyptian sovereignty at all and wished to leave open a genuine choice between full independence for the Sudan and union with Egypt (75, 76). It was at Bevin's insistence, against Stansgate's warnings about the likely Egyptian reaction, that the redrafted protocol presented to Egypt in September adopted a formula which did not prejudice claims to sovereignty, but made an explicit commitment to the Sudanese deciding their own future. The Egyptian rejection of this draft came on 28 September, much as Stansgate had warned, with Egypt conceding the right of the Sudanese to self-government, yet insisting not only that Egypt should take part in Sudanese administration, but that the UK must recognise Egyptian sovereignty (81).

In October, after Stansgate's return to the UK, divisions were beginning to appear in the Egyptian coalition government, especially within its treaty delegation. Sidqi was eager to win some form of treaty and backtracked on his demand for a share in the administration of the Sudan, saying that he would concede that if Britain would concede 'symbolic' sovereignty (83, 87). It was not just the desire to get an agreement on article 2 which led Bevin to drop his insistence on avoiding all reference to Egyptian claims of sovereignty.[41] By October both Stansgate and Bevin doubted the validity of Britain's former position of preventing Egypt from exercising sovereignty over the Sudan (84). In this they received unexpected support from Sir Reginald Wingate, former governor-general of the Sudan and high commissioner for Egypt, who was of the opinion that Egyptian sovereignty over the Sudan was 'undoubted' but advised (in Machiavellian terms) that 'it is far better to give Egypt a status in the Sudan openly if we wish ourselves to retain our paramount interest there' (86). The attempt was resumed to produce a draft which would give qualified recognition to Egyptian sovereignty by making a distinction between sovereignty and administration (84), despite the Sudan government's fear that any admission of Egyptian sovereignty would swing the political balance in the Sudan away from Britain and towards Egypt (85).

Sidqi came to London for personal meetings with Bevin between 18 and 25 October. He failed to persuade coalition and opposition leaders to come as members of his delegation; thus casting doubts on his ability to ratify any resulting treaty, and restricting him to presenting his 'personal view' in what were later described as 'conversations'. Sidqi's initial position was that sovereignty was 'an emblem of unity', that recognition of Egyptian sovereignty would not alter the 1899 agreement and would not give Egypt a greater share in administration. When Bevin pushed Sidqi to concede the Sudan's right to 'secede' Sidqi was evasive, agreeing only that 'nothing on paper could prejudice the right of independence', but suggesting that it was unnecessary to confirm this in the treaty as it was already enshrined in the UN charter. It was only in the third meeting that Sidqi shifted from the language of sovereignty to 'a legitimate union between Egypt and the Sudan' and conceded that the Sudanese could determine their own future (87–89).

The British delegation included Stansgate and Campbell (from the original negotiating team), and Howe, then superintending under-secretary of state for the Egyptian Department. Both Huddleston and Robertson were present in London, arguing that the Sudan's status was altered by the very fact of HMG admitting 'what they had never admitted before' (85). During a break in the negotiations Bevin reported back to the Cabinet commending a draft protocol which would prejudice neither the current Sudan administration nor 'the ultimate freedom of the inhabitants', acknowledging at the same time the likelihood of political tension in the Sudan over any reference to Egyptian sovereignty in the treaty. By this time, however, the lord chancellor had given his advice on the weakness of the UK case in international law, asserting that all actions during and immediately after the 're-conquest' of the Sudan in 1898 restored sovereignty to what it had been before the Egyptian evacuation in 1885. 'Juridical sovereignty' rested exclusively with one power (Egypt), even though the administration was shared by two. This left Britain with very little leeway.[42] The alternative proposed by the chancellor of the Exchequer, Hugh Dalton, of partitioning the country and retaining the South under exclusive British rule was overruled by Attlee (90, 91).

Britain's dilemma was that its insistence on a public acknowledgement that the present régime in the Sudan be left unchanged was countered by Egypt's that this also meant acknowledging Egypt's existing sovereignty. In the light of the lord chancellor's advice Britain had to agree. 1946 was not 1922 or 1924: Britain could no longer expect to act on its own unilateral understanding of international law with impunity. The final formula reached in the last two sessions between the delegations avoided the words 'sovereignty', 'self-determination' or 'independence'. Diplomatic circumlocutions were used instead, referring to both 'unity between the Sudan and Egypt under the common Crown of Egypt' and 'the right' of the Sudanese 'to choose the future status of the Sudan' (92, 93). Ostensibly it left the *de jure* state of the condominium and the *de facto* administration of the Sudan unchanged, while affirming a Sudanese right to change their status. But 'unity under a common Crown' and the right 'to choose the future status' qualified each other almost to the point of nullification and opened the protocol to counter interpretations.

Sidqi still had to get the treaty ratified in the face of Wafd opposition and uncertain coalition allies. For this reason the terms of the treaty, including the Sudan protocol, were not made public. Sidqi's own interpretation, reported in the Egyptian press, that he had secured sovereignty over the Sudan caused an immediate reaction in the pro-independence population of the Sudan, and made it impossible, as far as the government there were concerned, to explain the nuances of the protocol and stress its 'undoubted' long-term advantages. Huddleston feared an outbreak of violence, asked for and received a reinforcement to the British garrison in Khartoum, but the disorders were few and small and confined to the Three Towns. A new 'Independence Front' was formed, but political alignments within the Sudan remained the same. Convinced that a break-down of trust between the government and the effendia and widespread risings in the western provinces were likely, whatever the outcome of the treaty negotiations, Huddleston requested permission to return to London to explain the situation more fully (94–98).

The confrontation which now developed between Huddleston and HMG (100–111) was the product, in part, of the Sudan administration's long-standing distrust of the Foreign Office, compounded by the isolation from contact with the wider empire which attachment to the Foreign Office had fostered. The near 'messianic' fervour with which Huddleston pursued his case, and the irritation which Bevin, Attlee, McNeil and Sargent all expressed in private can be traced to one grand misunderstanding. Members of the SPS were convinced that Whitehall was going to do a deal with Egypt and literally sell the Sudan down the river in exchange for a treaty.[43] Huddleston therefore did not approach the members of the Labour government on the understanding of a shared commitment to self-determination within the empire, dating back to Labour's interpretation of the Atlantic Charter. Bevin and his colleagues in government and the Foreign Office resented accusations of betrayal and were frustrated at their inability either to persuade Huddleston of their commitment to self-determination for the Sudan, or convince him that changed world conditions had altered the way in which Britain could conduct its imperial relations (100, 101). The Sudan government's dire predictions of the imminent breakdown of law and order (102), which in the end were unfulfilled (112), did nothing to improve trust between London and Khartoum. Previous Sudan governments – perhaps genuinely nervous of the precedent of Gordon's fate – had played the security card before, most recently in 1924 when pressing London to detach the Sudan entirely from Egypt. The fact that persuasion ultimately did help to contain disturbances in the capital only reinforced Whitehall's suspicion that Khartoum was once again scare-mongering.

Huddleston's desperation was evident in the tone of his communications with Attlee and McNeil, and was based in part on his consciousness of Wingate's fate as high commissioner in the aftermath of the Zaghlul riots in Egypt in 1919 (102, 105–107, 109, 110). Bevin, being in the USA at the time, was not part of this direct confrontation, but he shared Attlee's view that sooner or later the Sudanese were bound to realise the importance of the commitment to self-determination enshrined in the protocol, whatever their immediate reaction to Sidqi's partial interpretation (103, 104).[44] The Cabinet readily accepted Huddleston's argument that some further measures were necessary to reassure the Sudanese of this, at the same time that they rejected his more extreme demand to abandon the protocol altogether (108, 111, 115). There was still hope that the treaty would be ratified, but Sidqi faced opposition first within his own delegation and was attempting to win them over with an interpretation of the protocol which denied that the Sudan's right to determine its future status extended to full independence (99). Bevin and the Foreign Office were manoeuvring to commit Sidqi in public to language he had used in private, hoping that Britain's interpretation of the protocol would become a matter of public record once the treaty as a whole was ratified (111, 113, 118). Bevin refused to allow Huddleston to go beyond that language and insisted that the word 'independence' rather than 'secession' or 'separation' be used in any public statements (115). After quibbling over the value of a statement confirming a right to independence Huddleston returned to Khartoum and issued the agreed statement on 7 December (121).

By this time it was clear that Sidqi was unable to get either his own delegation or the Senate to agree to the treaty. Ironically, given Huddleston's objections to the language of the protocol, the Egyptian opposition rejected it precisely because they placed the same interpretation on it as did the British government (113, 118). Bevin's insistence that independence be publicly acknowledged as an option, even if along with the other options of some form of union with Egypt, was seen by some (especially Stansgate) as the ultimate stumbling block to treaty ratification (118, 120). Sidqi's resignation on 9 December was not immediately attributed to this, but rather to Faruq's decision that Sidqi was too compromised to be able to reach agreement with Britain over the treaty (119).

Huddleston's visit did have an impact on the British and Sudan governments' relations with the pro-independence groups in the Sudan. Huddleston was moved to accelerate even faster plans for the Sudanisation of administrative *and* political institutions, having now completely cast off his earlier reluctance (109, 115). The first demonstration of this new resolve was to announce the appointment of a Sudanese grand *qadi* (canonical judge) to replace the Egyptian *qadi*, the most senior Egyptian then in post in the Sudan, on the expiry of his term (though this had, in fact, been agreed with the Umma Party prior to Huddleston's departure for London) (123, 124). More importantly, the British government agreed to a visit by sayyid Abd al-Rahman and the Independence Front (sayyid Ali declined a similar invitation). This allowed both the government and sayyid Abd al-Rahman to take the measure of each other, with mixed results. Attlee took the opportunity to emphasise that 'the reality' had not changed and that sayyid Abd al-Rahman and like-minded Sudanese could get both self-government and self-determination through close collaboration with the Sudan government (114). Sayyid Abd al-Rahman played his part alternating between declarations of loyalty to Britain and reassertions of Sudanese sovereignty. He pressed for a personal 'guarantee' which he could take back to the Sudan, and finally presented his demand for self-government now and independence in ten years (114, 117). He and his British supporters put forward exaggerated claims about sayyid Abd al-Rahman's popularity (116), but only Stansgate, now marginal to the negotiations, expressed open scepticism (120, 129). Given the Sudan government's inconsistency, at one time claiming that sayyid Abd al-Rahman and the independents represented the majority in the country (102), and then reporting that the majority of the rural population wished to be ruled by the British and not sayyid Abd al-

Rahman and the town-based politicians (112), Stansgate had reason to raise these doubts.

Sidqi was replaced by al-Nuqrashi in December 1946. The new prime minister immediately proclaimed his firm commitment to the permanent unity of Egypt and the Sudan and lodged protests about Huddleston's public statements and appointment of a new grand *qadi* (122–124). The actions agreed between the British and Sudan governments to reassure Sudanese pro-independence opinion helped to harden his attitude, but given the internal political opposition to Sidqi's treaty al-Nuqrashi could scarcely retreat from Sidqi's line to be more accommodating to Britain. As al-Nuqrashi became more insistent about the permanent unity between the two countries, Bevin became more adamant that he and HMG could not defy the spirit of the UN Charter and deny the Sudanese a free choice (125, 127). On 3 March 1947 al-Nuqrashi broke off negotiations and announced he would take his case to the Security Council of the UN (130).

The breakdown in negotiations had been imminent since al-Nuqrashi's first statement, but before it came various departments were able to take stock of where Britain's position lay. Stansgate, now completely outside the negotiating process, persisted in the belief that al-Nuqrashi was really in favour of a treaty and rehearsed the arguments for a more conciliatory approach to Egyptian claims (129). Campbell, however, took a much harder line on Egypt. The outcome of the negotiations had been such as to make Britain's commitment to Sudanese self-determination and possible independence – and not the defence of the Middle East – the main principle at stake. To yield on that 'is not only a question of our losing the Sudan as a military base or passage; but our position in other parts of the Orient and Africa might be greatly affected' (126). The controversy over the Sudan's future status also contributed to a restatement of British thinking about the future of colonial territories generally. Earlier in the year the Sudan government had been ambivalent about independence, arguing that this was not automatically implied by self-government (71). Sidqi had argued the same (99), as had the UK in the drafting of the UN Charter. In the case of the Sudan, however, Britain accepted that self-government and the political aspirations of the people would mean 'that the real meaning of the Charter' was that the Sudan 'should become independent' (128).

Coinciding with the breakdown in negotiations came the appointment of a new governor-general, a change which had been under consideration since January 1946. Huddleston expressed his own views about the political qualities his successor would need, and already the Foreign Office contemplated someone, possibly from the Foreign Office itself, who could 'goad the Sudan Political Service to more rapid progress in Sudanisation' (59). Huddleston originally stated a preference for leaving in July 1946, but in the context of the Anglo–Egyptian negotiations then under way this did not appear to the Foreign Office, or to other members of the Sudan government, as an opportune time for a replacement, and Huddleston agreed to stay on until March 1947.[45] In the aftermath of the Sidqi–Bevin protocol Huddleston appeared both to his subordinates in Khartoum and to his superiors in London on the verge of resignation and was persuaded to stay on (102, 105, 108). But Huddleston's behaviour convinced the Foreign Office that they needed 'a new type of British official whose job will be to advise and assist Sudanese in the administration of their own affairs', and that the process should begin with the appointment of Huddleston's successor in the spring (101). Stansgate's suggestions that a man acceptable to King Faruq be appointed was not welcomed (129). The appointment of Howe, as a man with diplomatic and political skills, fully conversant in the subtleties of Anglo–Egyptian relations, to replace Huddleston in March 1947 was thus the culmination of a process which had begun, at Huddleston's initiation, over a year before. Nevertheless, the state of mind in Khartoum at the time was such that Howe's appointment was interpreted as a punishment to Huddleston for 'standing up' to Bevin.[46] Howe's preliminary appreciation of the Sudan's place in Anglo–Egyptian relations prior to his departure for Cairo and Khartoum was an indication of the strength of his own commitment to Sudanese self-determination (131).

Preparations for self-government, Apr 1947–Dec 1950

Egypt made her complaint about the treaty to the Security Council in 1947, but the UN declined to become involved and referred the dispute back to the treaty partners for resolution (140). Blocked on the sovereignty issue Egypt pursued her aim of liquidating the condominium and asserting control over the Sudan through the issue of internal constitutional and administrative reforms.

The adoption of the principle of Sudanisation of various levels of government, and even the acceleration of Sudanisation in order to limit Egyptian interference in administration, was confirmed with acceptance of the recommendations of the Administrative Conference in 1947 (133, 138). Egypt's unexpected and novel objection that the constitutional reforms did not go far enough in the direction of self-government camouflaged its more serious intent of transferring the legislative power from the governor-general to the co-domini, and replacing the condominium with a self-governing Sudan under the Egyptian Crown (139, 141, 144, 155). The Sudan government and the Foreign Office attempted to meet specific criticisms by re-drafting its ordinances to make the forthcoming Legislative Assembly more truly representative and give it more than consultative powers, while safeguarding the governor-general's executive position (144, 145, 147–151, 153). Against Egyptian objections that the new ordinance enlarged the governor-general's powers, and gave him a power to make constitutional changes which were not his, the Foreign Office attempted to obtain Egyptian consent by offering them places on the new Executive Council (the 'Campbell-Khashaba agreement'). By now the Palestinian crisis intervened: al-Nuqrashi's personal opposition to compromise over the Sudan and the Egyptian foreign minister's preoccupation with the impending Arab–Israeli war meant that Britain received no reply to its concessions and finally gave permission to the governor-general to promulgate the constitutional ordinance on his own authority, an act of doubtful legality. The ordinance became law on 19 June 1948 (154–157, 160–162).

Elections for the Legislative Assembly began in September 1948, and the assembly opened on 23 December. Both before the enactment of the new legislation and after the first meeting of the assembly sayyid Abd al-Rahman sought to persuade the government to support Umma Party activities in the rural areas and sayyid Abd al-Rahman himself nationally (135, 170). Sayyid Abd al-Rahman's very open alliance with the government was a qualified blessing. Not only had many Khatmiya boycotted the elections in protest (165, 176), but the government's apparent support for sayyid Abd al-Rahman only confirmed Egyptian suspicions (167). The Sudan government therefore continued to woo the extra-parliamentary opposition, while trying not to alienate sayyid Abd al-Rahman himself. The Legislative Assembly which convened in December 1948, and the Executive Council which was drawn from it, was not solidly Umma. There was still room for non-sectarian formations, representing a range of social groups from the rural areas and towns. One, the 'Black Bloc', attempted to rally the old 'Sudanese' population of Omdurman and the Three Towns, who had been increasingly marginalised by the Arabisation of Sudanese nationalism since the 1920s, and it was still possible to speculate in 1948 that such a parliamentary formation might offer a political bridge between parts of the North and the South (169).

It had been realised by early 1947 that something had to be done about the southern Sudan. Sayyid Abd al-Rahman's unguarded private comments about southerners had disturbed Stansgate (116, 129), but there were others in the Sudan lobby in Britain who, being aware of similar widespread prejudice in the North, expressed their own fears of the consequences of a forced amalgamation of the two regions. As late as April 1947 the Foreign Office was still willing to consider the prospect of a separate self-determination for the South (132), but this option was already being ruled out in the Sudan. The Sudan Administration Conference recommended in its first report that the southern provinces be fully incorporated into the new administrative and legislative structures of the country. No southern Sudanese had been included in the deliberations of the conference and Robertson convened a meeting in Juba with a few select southerners from the civil and tribal administrations, along with the British governors of the southern provinces and a few northern Sudanese to discuss the conference's recommendations. Given the importance to national unity retroactively attributed to the 1947 Juba conference one must note that it was Robertson alone who took the decision to adopt the Administration Conference's proposals for the South.[47] No record of the Juba conference was forwarded to the Foreign Office, who were informed of this momentous decision only in the report of the civil secretary's own recommendations (134).

Howe's first impressions of the South were very unfavourable and he expressed a determination to effect more rapid social and economic development (136). Despite the appointment of southern members to the Legislative Assembly, the creation of southern province councils, the expansion of education and the first attempts at internal economic development in the South which followed, by 1950 there had been little noticeable impact on southern and northern attitudes towards each other, and it was reported that northern acceptance of southerners on equal terms was still predicated on Arabisation (188). Howe's resistance to Umma Party calls for immediate self-government at the end of 1950 was based in a large part on his own anxiety over the fate of the South under a northern Sudanese government at that time (200).

There were other organisational developments of political importance outside the arena of permitted electoral politics. The July–August 1947 railway workers' strike ended with the creation of what was in effect the first Sudanese trade union (the WAA) and a recognition by the Sudan government of a need for labour legislation. Further strikes in 1948 and 1949 attracted support from workers in other sectors, though the general public was more ambivalent (152, 153). The Trades Union Ordinance passed by the Legislative Assembly was the object of a one-day protest on 15 March 1949, which was linked to the Khatmiya extra-parliamentary opposition, but which also raised the spectre of communist infiltration (173). By May 1949 the government reached an agreement with a 'moderate' delegation of the WWA (179), and in early 1950 Donald McLean's reassurance that there were no Russian-trained agents being infiltrated via Egypt could be taken as conclusively settling that matter – either way (185). In November 1950 forty-eight trade unions organised themselves into the new Federation of Sudanese Trade Unions, electing Muhammad al-Sayyid Salam and al-Shafi Ahmad al-Shaikh, both communist trade unionists, as its first president and secretary.[48]

During the presentation of the Egyptian case at the UN in September–October 1947 the Umma Party deferred to the Foreign Office and were on the whole satisfied with the outcome of the Security Council debate and the swift moves towards establishing the Legislative Assembly which followed (137, 140). In the Legislative Assembly, and in other matters concerning the Sudan's future, the Umma Party continued to align itself with the Sudan government and with Britain (176). Opposition leaders began to reconsider their alliance with Egypt, in light of Egypt's failure at the UN (140), but they found fruitful areas of collaboration in criticising the Sudan government's administrative performance concerning the welfare of the Sudanese people, as in the 1949 famine in the eastern Sudan (183). With no organised opposition in the assembly the Umma Party increased its pressure on the government in late 1949 and early 1950 to scrap the condominium and set a definite date for full self-government. Howe resisted this by pointing to the absence of Khatmiyya participation in the assembly as evidence that it was not fully representative of the Sudan; and he was able to rely on ministers and the country and southern MLAs to support the government against specific criticism (184, 187). This was to last only while Anglo–Egyptian negotiations remained dormant. When, on 16 November 1950, Faruq announced to the Egyptian parliament in his speech from the throne the intention of his government to abrogate both the 1936 treaty and the 1899 agreement, pro-independence sentiment in the assembly hardened (196). The Umma Party tabled a self-government motion for debate in December. Despite Egyptian objections that such a motion was outside the jurisdiction of the Sudan government, and despite the debate coinciding with resumed discussions between Bevin and the Egyptian foreign minister, Howe allowed it to proceed. There was intense lobbying of MLAs by sayyid Abd al-Rahman himself. A much milder amendment to the motion proposed by Robertson was voted down, but in the end the Umma motion itself was passed by only one vote, against country and southern member opposition. This narrow victory was interpreted by the government as evidence of the Umma Party's overall weakness, even in an assembly it was said to dominate. The motion was ignored, but the episode opened the way for further discussions between the government and the Umma Party about bringing the Khatmiya into the assembly, and establishing specific safeguards for the South during any future period of self-government (198, 200, 202).

During this period, when treaty negotiations between the UK and Egypt were either dormant or desultory, the Nile Waters negotiations became the main focus of Anglo–Egyptian discussions on the Sudan, though also complicated by the issue of sovereignty. Britain had attempted to reassure Egypt over the Sudan during the 1946–1947 negotiations by offering to guarantee Egypt's legitimate interests in the Nile Waters, but this was no simple matter, with other governments now involved in the complex set of technical and political discussions. The Lake Tsana dam being seen as critical for both Egypt and the Sudan's immediate needs it was now considered 'legally essential' for Britain to participate in talks with Ethiopia, but such talks were postponed because of al-Nuqrashi's policy of non-co-operation with Britain (142). Egyptian and Sudanese technical discussions were successfully concluded in March 1948, but when Egypt delayed ratification Bevin suggested that Britain should deal unilaterally with Ethiopia. The Foreign Office was further concerned that, since they would ultimately have to disappoint Ethiopia on its post-war territorial ambitions, it was best to secure the Lake Tsana agreement before Haile Selassie could use it as a bargaining counter. Howe objected that such an unilateral approach would breach earlier Nile Waters agreements, but Campbell argued that by offering Egypt a new guarantee on their future water supplies, this might improve the negotiating atmosphere over the Sudan question. Howe was appalled at any suggestion linking the Nile Waters with the constitutional ordinance, fearing that if 'water is brought into the political field I feel the Sudan may lose on both counts'.[49]

The Ugandan government and the Colonial Office also began to fear that, with the double complications of the Egyptian attitude towards the Sudan and Ethiopia's use of the Lake Tsana project in its bargaining for ex-Italian colonies, final agreement over the Owen Falls dam would be delayed indefinitely. They argued for the separation of the Equatorial Nile projects from other Nile Waters issues. Since both the Sudan and the Foreign Office were convinced that the Sudan's position would be prejudiced unless all questions of the Nile Waters were treated together, a conflict of interests developed between the Sudan and Uganda. The Foreign Office argued that as Uganda could go ahead with any one of its three alternative plans for a dam whatever Egypt decided, it had nothing to lose if the Equatorial Nile scheme continued to be linked to that of Lake Tsana in preliminary negotiations (163, 166).

The unanswered question was whether Egypt's self-interest would allow it to go ahead with negotiations over these projects regardless of the other Sudan issues, or whether political considerations would lead them to subordinate Nile development to the stalled Anglo–Egyptian treaty negotiations.[50] The real obstacle to progress on both the Blue and White Nile plans was not the terms of the 1929 Nile Waters Agreement, but the Sudan question (166). Bevin was lobbied by both Creech Jones, on behalf of Uganda, and Howe, on behalf of the Sudan, to push forward Nile talks with Egypt,[51] but events surrounding the Arab-Israeli war, including the assassination of al-Nuqrashi, convinced Campbell that the time was not propitious to raising such matters (171).

An approach on the Owen Falls dam was made in January 1949, and the Egyptian response at first seemed entirely in line with British thinking, not only in wishing to proceed with both the Equatorial Nile and Lake Tsana schemes, but in separating Nile Waters issues from other political and constitutional questions (172). This was not to last. In this favourable climate it was felt that Egypt should be informed of the Sudan's need to share in the water produced by the White and Blue Nile schemes, which raised the further question of the Sudan's representation in talks at either the technical or political level with Ethiopia (174, 177, 178). On 30–31 May 1949 Britain and Egypt exchanged notes agreeing to technical discussions between Egypt and the Sudan over all these projects (178, 181). Encouraged by this Bevin proposed to the Egyptian foreign minister on 1 June that all the territories of the Nile Valley should be joined in a co-ordinated plan for social and economic development; a proposal which struck the Colonial Office as 'a characteristic piece of F.O. nonsense' they vowed to kill off.[52] They need not have worried: by July 1949 Egypt made it plain that it wished to exclude both the Sudan *and* Britain from talks with Ethiopia over Lake Tsana, in an apparent bid to wring an admission of Egypt's sovereignty over the Sudan from Britain (181, 186, 189). But Egypt's needs were such that it was in no position to out-wait Britain over the Nile. By September 1950 Egypt was again indicating its desire to push ahead with the Lake Tsana project as well as the construction of a new dam at the fourth cataract (inside the Sudan), and raising the storage level of the Sennar dam (192).

The Nile Waters were not the only complex set of diplomatic negotiations involving the Sudan and Egypt's claims to territorial sovereignty. The Sudan's long eastern border with Eritrea, Ethiopia and Kenya cut through the territory of many peoples, so that not only were there permanent settlements of the same people on either side of the border, but the borders were constantly being crossed by pastoralists in search of grazing and traders in pursuit of both legitimate and illegitimate trade. Throughout much of the first half of the condominium the Sudan government had put forward proposals to rationalise its borders and bring various remote territories under closer administration.[53] The trading enclave at Gambela leased by the Sudan from Ethiopia at the beginning of the century did not extend the Sudan's control over Ethiopian Nuer and Anuak, but these peoples had been brought briefly under British military administration following the defeat of Italy in Ethiopia, and the Sudan government hoped that a post-war settlement could be arranged whereby the entire Baro salient could be ceded to the Sudan in exchange for some less desirable border territory further south. The Kenyan government objected to allowing Ethiopia into that part of the Ilemi Triangle inside the south-eastern corner of the Sudan which was already under Kenyan administration, but in 1947 it was willing to strengthen its hold over the Triangle by co-operating in offering Ethiopia parcels of Sudanese and Kenyan territory in exchange for transferring the Baro salient to the Sudan; a series of exchanges which the Foreign Office doubted Egypt would sanction (143).

The fate of Eritrea, then under British military administration, presented Britain and the Sudan with a different set of problems.[54] Britain's main interest in the future of Italy's ex-colonies lay in securing its position in Cyrenaica and in avoiding jeopardising the Lake Tsana and Equatorial Nile schemes by antagonising Ethiopia. It was the US, not Britain or the Sudan government, who proposed in 1948 the partition of Eritrea and the transfer of its western province permanently to the Sudan. This was received very sceptically by the Foreign Office, British administrators in the Sudan and Sudanese members of the Executive Council. Not only did the Foreign Office fear that the proposal would give Egypt the opportunity of reviving the Sudan question in the UN, it raised the further constitutional question of whether the governor-general could annex a new province on his own authority. Campbell saw this (incorrectly, as it turned out) as another deplorable example of Khartoum exerting its autonomy from the embassy and objected to what he saw as the Sudan government's tendency to act like the government of an independent state in external affairs (175). The proposal to partition Eritrea never had strong support in the UN and was blocked in the General Assembly, but as late as 1953 it was reported that a bloc of Muslim Beja in Western Eritrea, opposed to incorporation into Ethiopia, were seriously considering forming a secessionist movement with the Beja of Kassala Province in the Sudan.[55]

Because Egypt had been largely preoccupied with the Palestine crisis, the 1948 Arab-Israeli war and its aftermath, the treaty issue remained dormant until 1950. The uncertainty over Britain's bases in the region generated by the Palestinian crisis in 1947–1948 increased the Sudan's strategic value to Britain (albeit only temporarily), and strengthened Howe's hand in resisting embassy pressure to compromise on constitutional reform in the Sudan as an avenue for re-opening treaty negotiations generally (138, 146). Bevin, while anxious to secure an agreement over the defence clauses with Egypt before the expiration of the Palestine Mandate in May 1948, agreed that there was no question of returning to the formula of the Sidqi–Bevin protocol, or of delaying constitutional reforms in the Sudan in order to entice Egypt back to the treaty negotiations (150). Egypt's refusal to give assent to any of the drafts of the constitutional ordinance was not allowed to delay elections to the assembly or appointments to the Executive Council (167, 168, 182). The Sudan government and the embassy increasingly diverged on issues which the Sudan chose to regard as purely domestic matters, but which the embassy saw as affecting Anglo–Egyptian relations. By mid-1949 the obvious tension between the embassy and the Sudan government was causing the Foreign Office some alarm (167, 180).

In 1950 the embassy saw what they hoped were signs of a more amenable attitude towards the Sudan in the Egyptian government. Britain's new ambassador, Sir Ralph Stevenson, discussed ways in which the condominium could be revived and made to work with Hamid Zaki, the Egyptian minister of state for foreign affairs (190), but found that Muhammad Salah al-Din, the foreign minister, spoke only of bringing the condominium to an end (191). The divergence of opinion within the Egyptian government enabled Howe to argue against offering Egypt any concessions on the Sudan (193, 194), but even the embassy accepted that it was out of the question to imply recognition of Egyptian sovereignty or agree to either increasing Egyptian, or reducing British, involvement in Sudanese administration (190, 195). The glimmer of hope the embassy professed to see was snuffed out by Faruq's announcement of his intention to abrogate the 1936 treaty and 1899 Condominium agreement (196). The embassy's complaint that the Sudan government already tended to regard the condominium at an end, and that Howe was emphasising his responsibilities towards the Sudanese people at the expense of his duty to *both* co-domini, received little sympathy at the Foreign Office (197). This was the context in which talks between the British and Egyptian foreign ministers resumed in December 1950, where the differences separating the two governments were restated. The crux of the disagreement was that Egypt claimed that all developments towards self-government since 1947 had been at the expense of Egypt's sovereign rights over the Sudan. Britain countered by stating that Egypt had, by its intransigence over the question of sovereignty, removed itself from having any positive role in those developments. Both governments claimed, but could not yet prove, that they were supported by the majority opinion in the Sudan (199). Egypt, being unable to halt the progress towards self-government, was prepared to try to do so through abrogation.

The abrogation crisis, Jan 1951–July 1952

The Foreign Office prepared its legal line of defence in anticipation of unilateral abrogation, claiming that it would regard the condominium as still in force up until 1956 (201). The embassy saw no hope of a settlement on defence questions without a prior agreement on the Sudan and restated its 'Cairo doctrine', proposing as a basis for negotiation a set of general principles recognising the interdependence of Egypt and the Sudan (203). The Sudan government, concerned about the scale of Egyptian propaganda and the growing determination by the Sudanese political classes to take part in decisions affecting their future (202), rejected Cairo's formula not only because it overlooked the possibility of Sudanese independence, but because it continued to politicise the Nile Waters (204). Stevenson attempted to remind the Foreign Office of its responsibilities towards Egypt, but his arguments served only to remind the Foreign Office of Bevin's 1946 commitment to the Sudan's 'eventual independence' (205).

Egypt's restatement in April 1951 of its insistence that Anglo–Egyptian negotiations proceed upon the basis of the unity of Egypt and the Sudan under the Egyptian crown convinced the Foreign Office that it would get agreement on neither the Sudan nor the defence questions but, since it could not sacrifice the interests of the Sudanese for the sake of a defence treaty, preferred to break over the Sudan issue.[56] To this end it authorised Stevenson in June to present the Egyptian government with a re-drafted set of principles, in which neither Egyptian sovereignty nor Sudanese independence were mentioned, but the Sudanese right to self-determination was implicit (208). Discussions between Stevenson and Salah al-Din in July revealed just how far apart the two governments were on the Sudan, with Egypt disputing the very basis of British administration there (213). Britain, while willing to consider further concessions on defence, could see no room for similar flexibility over the Sudan, and began preparing for the breakdown of negotiations (215).

It was at this point that the United States began to express concern about Britain's likely failure to secure a treaty of alliance with Egypt. At the time of the Sidqi–Bevin negotiations in 1946 Britain had assumed that US policy towards Egypt and the Sudan would be guided by anti-colonial principles, and this had been a factor in Bevin's early commitment to Sudanese self-determination (74). In fact the US government expressed no official opinion about the Sudan before 1951, by which time its policy was guided more by the geo-political considerations of the Middle East than by principle of extending democracy to the colonial world. The State Department under both Acheson and Dulles exerted increasing pressure on the Foreign Office to secure a defence agreement with Egypt.[57] In 1951 the embassies of both countries in Egypt agreed that internal politics made it unlikely that a Wafd government would give way on the Sudan but hoped that they might be induced to do so if presented with more favourable terms for alliance (216). In talks between Morrison (Bevin's replacement as secretary of state) and Acheson in Washington a formula was drafted for neutralising the Sudan question by introducing international bodies to oversee specific aspects of constitutional progress and Nile Waters development; despite the Cairo embassy's scepticism of Egypt accepting the latter when it was first suggested by Howe earlier in the year (204, 205). In the end the State Department judged that these proposals, too, would not satisfy Egypt and reverted to their original stance that the US had no substantive position on the Sudan; an attitude which the Foreign Office characterised as a 'tendency to stick their heads in the sand' (217, 218).

A political breakthrough was achieved in the Sudan when the majority of the unionists were persuaded to participate in the Constitutional Amendment Commission, which both the Sudan government and the Foreign Office hoped would produce recommendations leading to a greatly expanded legislature (207). The Commission's initial recommendations revealed a growing militancy among the Sudanese political class in that they proposed a decrease in the governor-general's responsibility for administration and a limitation of his legislative role (212).

There were signs of increased militancy in the labour movement as well. The Trade Union Federation had mixed results in organising general strikes in April and May, but the most serious disturbance was that of the police strike, or mutiny, in the capital between 8 and 13 June 1951 (209–211). The Sudan government used the occasion of the mutiny to detain some communist pamphleteers, but it avoided a general witch-hunt within the trade unions, prefering to distinguish between ideological communists and a larger group of 'revolutionaries' found especially among those affected by the recent rise in the cost of living (214). The government attempted to address questions of wages and the cost of living through a cost of living sliding scale agreement and a commission on unclassified staff wages but faced renewed strikes over wages in February and March 1952. Strikes organised around political issues, however, attracted little support from the majority of union members (245).

The pace of political and constitutional discussion was dramatically altered by Egypt's abrogation of both the 1936 treaty and the 1899 agreement on 8 October 1951. Britain responded by reaffirming its adherence to both as the basis of administration in the Sudan (219). Sudanese reaction (other than the Ashiqqa) welcomed the abolition of the condominium as a prelude to immediate self-government and an acceleration towards self-determination. The Constitutional Amendment Commission, then still in session, began discussing proposals for placing the Sudan under either a UN or an international commission, a suggestion which the Foreign Office first dismissed as 'obviously rubbish' (220–222). The Colonial Office was opposed to the idea of any such commission (235), but the Foreign Office subsequently drew a distinction between a UN commission, which gave Russia and its allies scope for interference, and an international commission answerable to both co-domini (232). Howe responded to Sudanese expectations by attempting to commit both the Sudan and British governments to holding elections for a new assembly under a new constitution in 1952, even setting a date for self-determination if possible (220, 222).

By this time Britain itself had a new government, with the election of the Conservatives on 26 October. This was to have no appreciable impact on the direction of Britain's Sudan policy. Despite Churchill's attempt to slow down the pace towards self-government the Cabinet endorsed Eden's first statement on the Sudan,[58] which broadly followed the outlines of Howe's suggestion and was immediately welcomed by Morrison as an endorsement of the previous Labour government's own policy (223). Eden's statement strengthened the position of those Sudanese members of the Legislative Assembly and the Constitutional Amendment Commission who opposed replacing the condominium with an international commission, and after this idea failed to be endorsed by the majority in either body the Constitutional Amendment Commission was dissolved (225).

Two major problems continued to worry the Sudan government: the fact that the sectarian nature of the northern political parties was preventing the formulation of a national consensus on the country's future constitutional structure; and the continuing gulf between Northern and Southern Sudan.

The formation of the Socialist Republican Party as a non-sectarian alliance of mainly country members of the Legislative Assembly was widely heralded by the Sudan government as a positive development in articulating Sudanese nationalist opinion, freed from the Ansar-Khatmiya conflict (226). It was denounced as a government creation, especially by the Umma Party who stood to lose the most. The Foreign Office, too, suspected official encouragement.[59] The party was initially promoted as a possible coalition of the rural North and the South, but solutions to the North-South divide were not to be so simple.

Despite some progress in local government reforms, training schemes and the expansion of education in the South, economic progress had been slower and by early 1952 there was still a marked social and political gap between northerners and southerners (206, 207, 240). Throughout 1951 both the Foreign Office and the Sudan government were committed to maintaining some sort of constitutional safeguards for the South, allowing for the retention of British administrative staff later than elsewhere in the Sudan (218); this was one advantage that Howe foresaw of Commonwealth membership, as it might allow for the appointment of a British high commissioner as a trustee for the South while the rest of the country became self-governing (222). But with abrogation spurring Khartoum to accelerate its pace towards self-government southern anxiety increased, especially after the northern majority in the Legislative Assembly voted down the proposal for a southern minister of southern affairs (241). The earlier prediction by the governor of Bahr al-Ghazal Province, that 'any rapid plunge' into self-government would provoke a crisis in the South (206) was about to be realised.

Just as abrogation accelerated constitutional and political developments in the Sudan, so these, too, were to have wider international implications, affecting not only Britain's negotiating position with Egypt and its relations with the US over its Middle Eastern policy, but provoking a debate within the branches of the British government about future relations within the colonial empire and the Commonwealth.

The Sudan government committed itself to a rapid realisation of self-government with elections to be held in 1952, a schedule delayed by the constitutional requirements for notification of the co-domini (241). The proposed speed towards self-government and the authority reserved by statute for Sudanese ministers within an all-Sudanese Cabinet far exceeded anything contemplated elsewhere in Britain's African territories (231, 241). In its own response to the Sudan's constitutional proposals the Foreign Office was naturally concerned with such issues as the transfer of interim sovereignty to an international commission, the balance of authority between the governor-general and the Sudanese Cabinet, the schedule and exact means of self-determination, and the availability of 'enough suitable Sudanese' to fill the executive and legislative branches of government (239). The terms of the draft constitution alarmed the Colonial Office because of its implications for its West African territories (234). In particular they were concerned about the precedent established by the proposed creation of an all-Sudanese Cabinet with no *ex-officio* British ministers and the affirmation of the right to self-determination. Discussions held between the Foreign, Colonial and Commonwealth Relations Offices in 1952 attempted to find ways of limiting the potential impact of such precedents on the colonial empire by formulating the argument that such provisions were unique to the Sudanese by virtue of previous specific commitments, and not generally applicable to the colonies.[60] Yet even here the Colonial Office began to realise that a failure of the UK to deliver these pledges to the Sudanese could have a detrimental impact on trust in other territories, especially the Gold Coast and Nigeria (235).

The prospect of early Sudanese self-determination now forced the departments of government to debate seriously the issue of expanding membership of the Commonwealth to non-settler African territories. Howe first proposed the idea of the Sudan entering the Commonwealth as a response to Egypt's abrogation of the treaty in November 1951 (222). The immediate reaction of the Foreign and Commonwealth Relations Offices was that support for such a proposal would risk South Africa leaving the Commonwealth (226, 229). In suggesting the possibility of a two-tiered membership, with something short of dominion status for the less important territories, the Colonial Office tried to separate the developments in the Sudan from the rest of the empire (229). There were others in the government who wished to push the issue on behalf of the Sudan. Dodds-Parker, then a back bench MP (later to be parliamentary under-secretary in the Foreign and Commonwealth Relations Offices), put forward the case for Sudanese membership of the Commonwealth and, noting that many colonial territories were watching closely HMG's arrangements for the Sudan, urged an examination of the implications of such membership for the rest of the empire (230). It was an issue which received increasing attention throughout 1952 and into 1953.

In the meantime there were internal and external pressures to try to renew dialogue with Egypt. Late in 1951 Stevenson in Cairo touched on the need to secure the minimum co-operation from Egypt in order to operate the bases in the Canal Zone, and felt that some lip-service to the Sidqi–Bevin formula, acknowledging the legality of Egyptian claims to sovereignty over the Sudan, was needed (224). Howe argued against any such concessions, and the Foreign Office, with some regret, agreed (227). Egypt's very Anglophile ambassador in London, Amr Pasha, privately voiced his own pessimism about the growing militancy of Egypt's policy towards Britain (228). Early in 1952 Eden proposed that Britain might suggest that it would not oppose Faruq's title as King of Egypt and the Sudan in return for a defence agreement, the continuation of the administration in the Sudan, and Egypt's acceptance of self-determination for the Sudan. Realising that Egypt was unlikely to accept all this, his next (but equally unpalatable) proposal was that Egypt should agree to allow the future Sudanese parliament to decide the sovereignty issue (233, 236).

The US State Department now shifted out of its position of sympathetic non-interference and began to press the Foreign Office to come up with a 'new idea' for Anglo–Egyptian rapprochement. Following the premise that without recognition of Faruq's title there would be no defence agreement US proposals, too, tried to combine qualified recognition of the King's titles with some form of international supervision of Sudanese self-government and self-determination, whereby the Sudanese would make the final decision over sovereignty either through a plebiscite or a constitutional assembly. The Foreign Office insisted that the Sudanese must be able to decide their final status before they decided on a constitution (232, 242, 243). A formula of recognition of the King's title in exchange for Egyptian recognition of the Sudan's right to self-determination was finally agreed in April 1952, which the US was to put directly to Faruq with their backing (244, 247). Any such recognition of the King's title, however, was vigorously opposed by members of the SPS, whose neutrality on the future of the Sudan was doubted not only by the State Department, but by many in the Foreign Office (237, 238). But the SPS were not alone. It was also clear to the government that a substantial segment of British public opinion (certainly among the Conservative government's own back benchers) would not tolerate a betrayal of the Sudan either (243).

With both the US and the UK insisting that the Sudanese must be consulted on their future Egypt's prime minister, al-Hilali, invited sayyid Abd al-Rahman to send a delegation from the Umma Party to Cairo in May 1952. Acheson appeared to hope that this unofficial delegation could be persuaded to accept the King's title (247). Various Sudanese in Khartoum feared that some personal deal might be struck on behalf of sayyid Abd al-Rahman (246).[61] Eden was concerned that a wide-ranging agreement between Egypt and the Umma might accelerate constitutional developments 'so much that the Southerners felt that their interests were being prejudiced', necessitating UK intervention (248). In the end the delegation was unwilling to exchange sovereignty for self-determination and returned to Khartoum only days before the fall of al-Hilali's government and just weeks before the Free Officers' Coup of 23 July overthrew Faruq and changed the political landscape of Anglo–Egyptian relations (248, 249).

The all parties agreement and the Anglo–Egyptian agreement, Sept 1952–Mar 1953
It was not immediately apparent how Faruq's abdication might improve the atmosphere for negotiations. Khartoum was eager to get elections underway for a new parliament, but the change in Egyptian government had delayed the presentation of the draft self-government statue to the two co-domini. By September it appeared that the new government wished to reach an agreement on the Sudan before constitutional provisions were brought into force, and this seemed to open the way for disentangling the Sudan and defence issues. In September Eden instructed Stevenson to place before Najib, the chairman of the RCC, new proposals for an international commission to supervise Sudanese elections (250). The Sudan sub-committee of the RCC, led by Major Salah Salim, indicated in its first meeting with the ambassador that Egypt was willing to concede the Sudan's right to self-determination (251).[62] Najib further accepted the need to consult with Sudanese political leaders and deferred responding to Eden's proposals before he had done so, leaving Eden to announce HMG's own consent to the self-government statute on 22 October 1952, before having received Egypt's agreement (252, 253).

The invitation to representatives from the main political parties to meet with Najib in Cairo in October at first sight looked like a significant advance on the position of previous Egyptian governments, but Khartoum warned that Britain might be outflanked by direct discussions between the parties (not fully representative of the whole Sudan) and the Egyptians (252). These worries proved well-founded when Najib announced an agreement with the Umma Party on 30 October, which accepted self-government and provided for a transitional period in which the dual administration of the condominium would be liquidated to create a 'free and neutral atmosphere' for self-determination (255, 256). There were parallel, if slightly different, agreements with other parties including the SRP and the newly formed NUP, a coalition of unionist parties brought together at Najib and Salah Salim's insistence.

British reactions were mixed. All agreed that Egyptian acceptance of the Sudan's right of self-determination was a major breakthrough; they differed on the price to be paid to achieve this. Stevenson urged acceptance (256). Howe argued against the transfer of the governor-general's powers to a commission, and he pointed to the discrepancies between Egypt's agreements with each of the three parties to argue that the Sudanese remained unconsulted on this new change of status, and that only a newly elected Sudanese parliament would be competent to accept or amend the proposals (255, 257). In the discussions which followed between Stevenson and Najib these were the two most difficult points of contention.

Both Najib and Salah Salim appeared to be sympathetic to a revision of the articles concerning the South, but claimed that these provisions had been forced on them at the insistence of the Umma Party and the NUP – but more particularly the Umma – and they could not back down on them (257, 260, 268).[63] The Foreign Office insisted that the governor-general's reserved powers in article 100 of the draft statute must not be completely subordinated to the commission, arguing that the removal of safeguards risked making the whole question of a united Sudan a 'burning issue' in the election (261, 264).

By the end of 1952 Anglo–Egyptian discussions were once again deadlocked. At issue were the governor-general's reserved powers for the South, his subordination to his commission, the conditions for terminating the transitional self-governing period, and the Sudanese parliament's power to approve changes to the agreement prior to ratification. The Cairo embassy urged that Britain accept the restrictions on the governor-general's powers or risk the break down of negotiations with 'extremely serious consequences' in the Sudan and a 'disastrous effect' on the Middle East (263). In December Eden proposed to the Cabinet that the only issues on which Britain must stand firm, at the risk of breaking off negotiations, were adequate safeguards for the South and a flexible period for Sudanisation of the administration (271).

Khartoum, the Cairo embassy and the Foreign Office struggled over a redrafted compromise article 102 on the governor-general's power to call a constitutional emergency, with Khartoum hoping to reinforce the governor-general's autonomy from the commission (275). The embassy objected to a further mention of the South in this article (as the main provisions were contained in article 100, where the governor-general was empowered to secure fair and equitable treatment for the peoples of the southern provinces) and warned that this aspect of Khartoum's draft would jeopardise the compromise already reached with Egypt (278). Howe was warned by the Foreign Office that a stand could be made over the explicit safeguards stated in article 100, but not over article 102. He gave his reluctant concurrence as long as article 100 was retained (280, 281).

In the meantime an approach was made directly to sayyid Abd al-Rahman to try to persuade him to make a public declaration accepting the governor-general's reserved powers for the South, reminding him that it was only because of the inclusion of this guarantee in the draft self-government statute that southern members of the Legislative Assembly had agreed to co-operate in a unitary constitution for the country (265). The British found sayyid Abd al-Rahman evasive on the subject, and the Umma Party particularly adamant against any special status for the South (272, 276).

Southern opposition to the Egyptian agreements with the northern parties was becoming more vocal and organised. A political committee was formed in Juba to denounce the northern parties' unilateral abandonment of the self-government statute agreed in the Legislative Assembly, and an underground organisation emerged to arrange protests and meetings in various towns (269, 274). One governor of a southern province drew direct comparisons with Britain's colonial experiences in Palestine and Ireland and warned of the long-term damage of coercing the South into an unsafeguarded union with the North. 'They will hate the North still. They will hate us the more' (267). Other expatriates in the South were also becoming anxious about the future. Fearing restrictions on church activity under a Muslim majority government the Catholic church petitioned for the removal of restrictions on proselytising in the South, which was refused by the Sudan government (266). The irony of Egyptian and northern Sudanese opposition to Britain's policy over the South was not lost on the Foreign Office. 'Far from tending to split the South off, the inclusion of such safeguards is probably the only hope of maintaining a united Sudan', minuted Allen, 'and the Egyptians want a united Sudan, so that the whole plum can eventually fall into their lap'.[64]

Salah Salim came to the Sudan in December in order to shore up the agreements with the northern parties and to tour the South, ostensibly to consult southern opinion. His tour of the southern provinces caused considerable outrage among the British administrators and the majority of politically active southerners. Salah ignored significant groups of leaders assembled to voice their opposition to the agreement and collected signatures from chiefs and others to show support for the Egyptian government's position (277, 290).[65]

The first hint of a new agreement between the Egyptian government and the two main northern parties, which contained a pledge by the Umma and NUP to boycott the elections should Britain insist on retaining safeguards for the South and extending Sudanisation until after self-determination, was published by a Sudanese journalist on the first day of 1953 (279). Salah Salim revealed a new agreement which included the SRP as well as the small Watan (National) Party on 10 January (283). It was clear that Britain had been outbid by Egypt, and that an agreement on anything but Egypt's terms was now virtually out of the question (285). The Foreign Office, who already had entertained doubts of the political acumen of the SPS, were now convinced that the Sudan government had become dangerously out of touch with Sudanese politicians (285).[66] Churchill, then in Jamaica, grumbled: 'We seem to have been ill served by our agents in the Sudan' and offered to return early before a final decision was made, declaring 'what happens here will set the pace for us all over Africa and the Middle East'.[67] The Cabinet still hoped for some compromise with Egypt over the governor-general's special responsibilities for the South and appointed a committee including the foreign, Commonwealth and colonial secretaries to deal urgently with the question (286).

Whatever Egypt's real intentions towards the South, it soon became evident that it was in the North, among the government's former allies, that the greatest opposition lay. Howe complained that 'the South have been contemptuously overridden' and doubted that it was now possible to obtain any of the safeguards which would satisfy southern political opinion (284). Willie Morris, in charge of the Sudan desk in the Foreign Office, shrewdly observed that it was the northern politicians who wanted to get the British out of the South (285). This appeared confirmed by sayyid Abd al-Rahman's belated response to the secretary of state's personal message to him when, shifting responsibility for the terms of the All Parties' Agreement to Egypt and the other parties, he declared 'the Southerners would have to accept [it] in their best interests' (289). This lack of inclination to compromise with southern aspirations boded ill for the future, especially set against the warning of the Southern Sudan Political Emergency Committee that 'unless Northerners compromise with us, it will be very difficult to establish a government, which assures equality of treatment to all . . .' (291).

But pressure to accept the *fait accompli* over the South was growing. Stevenson argued that Britain's 'duty to keep faith with the country as a whole' meant that there was 'no question' but that they should 'accept a compromise on the South acceptable to Egypt and the Sudanese politicians ... even at the risk of trouble in the South' (287). The Cabinet committee on the Sudan, while agreeing that a firm stance must be taken with Egypt in general, questioned whether it was worth risking a breakdown in negotiations if the Sudanese themselves were willing to compromise with Egypt. The only hope of getting the Sudanese politicians back on Britain's side lay in arguing that the Sudanese parliament should have the final word on the governor-general's powers and the pace of Sudanisation (292). With pressure mounting on the British base in the Canal Zone, and Howe urging an immediate break in Anglo–Egyptian talks, the Cabinet contemplated reinforcing the Sudan garrison (293). But Stevenson managed to negotiate a slight compromise with Egypt over article 100 (deleting a specific reference to the South, but extending the governor-general's reserved powers to all provinces, 'subject to the advice of his Commission'), and giving the governor-general some power of delay over Sudanisation (294). Howe was pressed by the Foreign Office to agree, and gave his reluctant assent (295, 296). Having won over Howe, Eden next had to win over Churchill, who raised objections to the draft agreement in Cabinet. These objections were withdrawn only after Eden secured the support of an influential group of back benchers (297),[68] and on 12 February the Anglo–Egyptian Agreement on self-government and self-determination for the Sudan was signed (appendix to part 2).

Throughout all of this the Foreign Office had had to contend with reservations from the Colonial Office as well. The Colonial Office objected to Eden's statement to the House on October 1952 welcoming progress to 'government by an all-Sudanese Cabinet, responsible through an all-Sudanese parliament to the Sudanese People' (253). This 'was just about the most awkward imaginable' statement that could have been made from the Colonial Office's view, implying, as it did, that the forms of government applying to the Gold Coast and other colonial territories fell short of 'self-government' (254). In discussing the terms of Egypt's note the Colonial Office objected strenuously to the possible inclusion of an Indian on the proposed international commission, as this would possibly encourage the Indian government in presenting themselves as the 'protectors of colonial peoples'. They objected equally to the notion of a fixed timetable for self-determination, and of Sudanisation as a requirement for self-determination (258, 282). These criticisms were reiterated during the course of Anglo–Egyptian negotiations in December 1952 because, 'however much we may disclaim the comparability of the Sudan with the more advanced Colonial territories, people in the latter, especially the African Ministers in the Gold Coast and Nigeria, will ask us why administrative machinery accepted in the Sudan cannot likewise be adopted in their territories' (270). The Foreign Office, while trying to accommodate some of the Colonial Office's objections to specific terminology, could only fall back on the argument of the special nature of the Sudan's circumstances (270, 282, 288).

Eden raised another potential problem when, addressing the Cabinet in December, he suggested that should the Sudan choose independence, it would be free to apply for membership of the Commonwealth (271). This went further than his comment the previous month when he was non-committal to an enquiry from the Sudan Party concerning eventual Commonwealth membership.[69] The issue being raised, it had to be considered. The Commonwealth Relations Office produced a paper which concluded that the question of the Sudan's admission to the Commonwealth be deferred until such time as a more detailed position paper concerning Commonwealth membership of more important colonial territories, the Gold Coast in particular, could be drafted (273).[70] Having argued vigorously against the pace of the Sudan's progress towards self-government and self-determination, the Colonial Office appeared to be much more favourable to the idea of the Sudan joining the Commonwealth than either the Foreign or Commonwealth Relations Offices.[71] Ultimately the Foreign Office decided that any appearance of pressing for Sudanese membership would be misrepresented by Egypt, and possibly misunderstood in the Sudan as an attempt to maintain British control over the country; for this reason no active measures were taken to encourage the Sudanese to apply (298, 299, 304, 318).

The Foreign Office was particularly anxious about the political mood in the Sudan in the aftermath of the Anglo–Egyptian Agreement. On visiting the Sudan Morris warned of the dangers of a mutiny among police in the South, or of a military coup eventually in the North (300). He also commented on the political naïveté of British administrators in the Sudan who believed 'fervently rather than rationally' that HMG had sacrificed the Sudan's interests, but who also believed that British control of the civil administration could continue almost indefinitely beyond self-determination, showing 'a serious misjudgement of the way dependent peoples behave'. It was this misapprehension which had enabled the Egyptians to make effective propaganda that the British had no serious intention of transferring power. The question of the South, he warned, was still the one issue which had the potential to unite the independents with the unionists and Egyptians against Britain, and it was important to avoid any controversy until southern representatives could get into parliament and make their opinions heard (301). This was easier said than done. In the South there was reported to be widespread resentment at the unilateral action of the northern parties in making agreements without consulting the South's political leaders. The main anxiety about the new agreement was the Sudanisation clause; for it was well understood that 'Southernisation' of the South's administration would be impossible in three years. Demands were already being made for a pan-southern conference to be convened. One British assessment of the South's impact in the future parliament anticipated that the self-interest of individual politicians would undermine southern unity (302).

Elections and self-government, Mar 1953–Feb 1954

The politicians in the government and the mandarins in the Foreign Office emerged from the Anglo–Egyptian negotiations in a far more combative mood than the administrators in the Sudan. Eden immediately drafted for Howe a broad outline of the propaganda measures which must be undertaken to counter Egypt's advantageous position in the new transition period leading to self-determination. It was clear that the morale of the British civil servants in the Sudan had to be bolstered by addressing such practical matters as pensions and future employment in other government departments (such as the Foreign Office) following Sudanisation, and quite considerable efforts were expended over the next few months to offer convincing reassurances to prevent an exodus of British officials from the Sudan which would dilute British influence further (298, 299, 303, 306).[72] But Howe was at first sceptical that British prestige and influence could be maintained: 'Our arms and armour have been struck from us' he lamented (303). Such despondency, coupled with what appeared to be political naïveté, was frustrating to those who took the broader, if more distant view from London. The Foreign Office had already been disillusioned by Khartoum's maladroit handling of Salah Salim's visit (277). Sir Lawrence Grafftey-Smith, HMG's man on the governor-general's commission, was immediately struck by the SPS's neglect of basic politics.[73] In March the minister of state for foreign affairs, Selwyn Lloyd, visited the Sudan and Egypt in order to take political soundings more directly, and to encourage both British officials and their allies to stand up to the Egyptians (307).

Selwyn Lloyd returned from this visit with a much clearer picture of the political realities of the Sudan. It was still anticipated that no single party would obtain an overall majority in the future parliament, but it was also evident that the SRP was weaker than the Sudan government had presented it, and that a policy built around an expectation that the first Sudanese government would be formed from a pro-independence Umma–SRP coalition was beginning to look unrealistic (306). It was also clear that the as far as the South was concerned there was a very great discrepancy between what the northern parties were willing to say to reassure the British and what they actually did to reassure southerners (305). Selwyn Lloyd defined British objectives in the Sudan as ensuring that the Sudan chose independence, that the South got 'a fair deal', and that the transfer of power 'should take place with dignity and goodwill' (306).

The elections were the key to achieving these aims. Even before the final text of the 1953 treaty had been agreed the Foreign Office had turned its attention to the Electoral Commission, preferring an Indian commissioner to a Pakistani on the grounds that the complexity of Indian constituencies bore some comparison to the Sudan, and that Indian elections had been freer of corruption than in Pakistan (259). They also looked to the precedent of Libyan elections for ways in which the Electoral Commission could be set up to the advantage of the UK without relying on British officials (262). Selwyn Lloyd had personally encouraged the pro-independence parties during his March visit to the Sudan, even advising southern leaders to form their own party (305). But combating Egypt's vigorous propaganda campaign was the government's main concern, and the delay of elections until autumn 1953 appeared to give Egypt an advantage. Selwyn Lloyd's personal protest to Najib about propaganda having had no effect (304), he proposed the opening of a Trade Commission and Information Office in Khartoum with its own 'information' budget, as well as harnessing the services of the BBC and the British Council in the pursuit of British objectives (307). Macmillan, though only minister of housing and local government, took a personal interest in the elections, claiming they 'will, in effect, decide the future of the Sudan, and to a large extent of British prestige in Africa and the Middle East' (308).

Churchill pressed Howe to take a more active role in countering Egyptian propaganda, a role Howe resisted as inconsistent with his being an agent of both co-domini.[74] The mood of the SPS now appeared to be more buoyant than at first thought, but Derek Riches, the first UK trade commissioner, judged that they were effectively leaderless following the retirement of their most senior members, including Robertson (316). Decisions in the Electoral Commission were not going Britain's way, with the reduction of the number of indirect constituencies in both the North and South, where it was thought that tribal leaders would have greater influence on the voting of their people (310). More direct action was needed.

Britain placed its hope in the strength of the pro-independence parties, but more particularly the Umma. Since the All Parties' Agreement it was no longer possible to take the tactical alliance with the Umma for granted (309). Egypt was also wooing the Umma over the Nile Waters. Salah Salim had already accepted the need for a revised Nile Waters agreement in the event of the Sudan opting for full independence (250), and in the summer of 1953 the Egyptian government and the Umma Party worked their way towards a 'gentleman's agreement' in which the Sudan would receive favourable terms in the new engineering schemes designed to increase the flow of water for both countries (314, 317). The opportunity for Britain to intervene more directly in the Umma electoral strategy came through sayyid Abd al-Rahman's perpetual need for money.

Sayyid Abd al-Rahman was known to be in debt at a time when cotton prices had dropped. In May he approached Riches, as the conduit to the Foreign Office, with a proposal that the British government should arrange to buy his cotton above the market price to enable him to finance the pro-independence campaign. The Foreign Office was reluctant to subsidise sayyid Abd al-Rahman but entered into negotiations with him and his son, Siddiq, on the conditions to be met whereby some assistance could be given. The Foreign Office was at this point contemplating a 'grand remonstrance' to expose the extent of Egyptian propaganda, bribery and corruption in the Sudan, and it now looked possible to co-ordinate this with action from the Umma Party. The original terms proposed were that the Umma were to repudiate their earlier agreement with Egypt, form an independence front with the SRP, and commit themselves to maintaining British administrators in the southern Sudan beyond the three year transitional period (311). These points were put by Selwyn Lloyd in person to sayyid Abd al-Rahman on the latter's visit to London for the coronation of Elizabeth II, in a meeting where the minister of state also expressed a personal (as opposed to official) preference for a monarchical form of government in the Sudan. The precise nature of the assistance which Britain offered in exchange has still not been revealed, as those passages concerned have been obliterated from the documents released (312). A written agreement was initialled by Siddiq on his cotton-selling visit to Britain in July, the main qualifications being that the Umma would make an effort to reach an understanding with the SRP, and that they would support the retention of British administrators in the South should the majority of southern MPs so desire (314). On 8 August the Umma Party denounced Egypt for breaching its own undertaking not to finance propaganda in the Sudan. Britain gave its 'practical assistance', but despite this the Umma and SRP were unable to agree on a common election strategy and spent most of the period preceding the elections in arguing with each other (319).

There was some indication, however, that whatever the relative strengths of the Khatmiya and Ansar as political organisations, pro-independence opinion was crossing the NUP–Umma divide. In an unusually frank interview before the elections, sayyid Ali al-Mirghani declared himself in favour of Sudanese independence and then, taking a leaf out of sayyid Abd al-Rahman's book, asked for a government subsidy to the Khatmiya (315).

As elections were put back from October to November British officials in Khartoum admitted that they really had no idea of the likely outcome. It was only at the end of October that observers began to get a glimpse of the real strength of the NUP, and the negligible showing of the SRP (320). The surge in votes for the NUP which resulted in the party's majority in the House of Representatives followed the cementing of the NUP–Khatmiya alliance and a corresponding ambiguity of what was meant by 'unity' with Egypt (320, 321).

In the post-mortem following the elections Britain identified the Umma's greatest weakness as its unwillingness to go beyond a sectarian line, in effect, failing to become a truly national party (323). The NUP, on the other hand, had been moving to a more nationalist, i.e. a more independent stand throughout the election and it looked set to seek greater autonomy from Egypt during the period of self-government. Recognising that the one point on which Egypt and the NUP fully agreed was rapid Sudanisation and the swift departure of the British, HMG now saw the best strategy for securing Sudanese independence lay in a quick endorsement of the election and support to the NUP government (324–326).

A subtle shift in UK policy towards the Sudan was necessitated by the NUP victory, but even when anticipating a pro-independence majority before the elections the Foreign Office had recognised the likely need to accelerate the transition period to achieve self-determination in less than three years (318). Riches, in a rapid and partial pre-election tour of the South, also cast doubt on the predictions of disorder coming from the 'old hands' in a report which laid the foundations for the argument to abandon 'a sort of "Polish" unimplementable guarantee to the Southerners' (313). The Foreign Office was thus already willing to accept accelerated Sudanisation under an NUP government, though in its instructions to Howe it also emphasised the importance of retaining the friendship of the Umma while trying to influence the NUP government through official advice (327). Howe was altogether more sceptical about being able to exert influence without power, but he expressed a strong commitment to working with the NUP government even at the expense of alienating the Umma, who were already blaming Britain for their misfortunes (331).

Early discussions between the new prime minister, al-Azhari, and Luce as constitutional affairs adviser, indicated areas of concern as well as hope for British policy. Al-Azhari expressed a strong view that the political attitudes of tribal leaders, especially in the West and South, were influenced by British administrators, and that political differences between Sudanese would decrease once the British left. Rapid Sudanisation was clearly going to be a high priority. But he also showed an unwillingness to allow 'union' with Egypt to become domination. He referred to the alliance with Egypt as tactical in order to remove the British: 'the old idea of unity was dead as a political force', he reassured Luce (332).

Sudanisation, mutiny and independence, Mar 1954–Oct 1956

The year 1953 had brought irreversible changes to the Sudan. 'When it opened', Riches wrote in his annual review, 'the Sudan was governed, as it had been for decades, by an oligarchy of officials of British nationality in contact with, rather than under the control of, Her Majesty's Government. ... When it ended, a Senate and House of Representatives composed solely of Sudanese had been constituted ... it is the passing of the direct power of the British oligarchy rather than the particular politics of the Sudanese who are for the time being inheriting it that marks the end of an era. ... The Sudanese will remember with gratitude that there used to be a well-meaning and even benevolent British Administration. But they will only do this if we get out gracefully as and when the Sudanese want us to go'.[75]

The establishment of a Sudanese government had immediate consequences on the administration of the Sudan's borders. The Governor-General's Office informed Kenya in January that it could not bind any future Sudan government to the agreements concerning the Ilemi Triangle, and that it would be up to the Kenyan government to make what arrangements it could with the Sudanese after the transfer of power (328). Later that year the government of Ethiopia announced its intention to terminate the lease on the Gambela enclave after British officials had been Sudanised. They proclaimed their intention to do this in 'a decent and orderly manner', but they categorically refused to negotiate with the Sudanese ministers on the subject (371).

The first test of the ability of the Governor-General's Office to work with the new Sudanese government came with the dispute over the composition of the Governor-General's Commission, which prior to the elections had one Umma and one NUP member, but whose membership could be varied by parliament. In January it appeared that the NUP was planning to replace Ibrahim Ahmad, the Umma member, with one of their own; thus producing a pro-Egyptian majority on the commission (329). HMG contemplated a variety of measures to forestall this, and the Cabinet authorised instructions to Howe to threaten al-Azhari with a constitutional emergency should the balance of the commission be disturbed. Plans were begun to reinforce the governor-general's authority with troops flown from the Canal Zone (335, 340). Howe disagreed sharply with the Cabinet over strategy. He argued that a constitutional emergency could be called only to avert the imminent breakdown of public order, and he was not convinced that the threatened alteration to the commission was sufficient provocation (341).

On the likely threat to order there was some disagreement. Najib's arrival in Khartoum on 1 March 1954 for the official opening of the Sudanese parliament provoked a serious riot around the palace by Umma supporters, in which several persons (including police) were killed, and which was subsequently described as a battle between the Ansar and the predominantly Khatmi police. Selwyn Lloyd, who was also visiting Khartoum at the time, was a witness to this disturbance. Both the NUP government and the Umma Party, in their own ways, tried to place the blame for the riots on the British. In the aftermath of the disturbances sayyid Abd al-Rahman urged the British to abandon the 1953 agreement and declare the Sudan independent. Britain risked sharpening of the sectarian divide within the northern Sudan by imposing a constitutional emergency (333, 334, 336, 338).

Howe seemed to have reached an understanding with al-Azhari to defer the question of membership of the commission when the Umma insisted on pressing the issue in parliament. Al-Azhari split the opposition by nominating a failed southern NUP candidate, Siricio Iro, obtaining southern support in this vote (347). The Sudan's first consitutional crisis was averted rather than resolved.

The Umma Party, having seen what political confusion could be caused by extra-parliamentary means, continued to press the British government on several occasions to renounce the 1953 agreement, re-establish direct control, and declare Sudanese independence (335, 353). Sayyid Abd al-Rahman renewed his requests for money, which were all refused (330, 355). The Foreign Office and HMG were now even more convinced that the only hope of achieving Sudanese independence was through loyal co-operation with the NUP government and rapid Sudanisation as a means of reducing anti-British feeling among Egypt's Sudanese allies (338, 353, 357). Finding Al-Azhari more approachable in the aftermath of the constitutional crisis than before it, and the Umma opposition inept in parliament (351), the Governor-General's Office made the conscious decision to switch their hopes from the Umma to the NUP (358). The Umma Party's requests for assistance were met with repeated advice to broaden their own political base to include non-Ansar, to commit themselves to opposition through constitutional means and try to improve their parliamentary performance (348, 353, 357).

The Governor-General's Office argued for financial aid to the Sudan as one element of its more positive approach to the NUP government (358), but in this the Sudan's position outside the Commonwealth told against it. With the Sudan's relatively healthy sterling reserve (of £12 million), and the UK government's decision to confine as much as possible of its overseas investment to the Commonwealth, Howe's request for a £5 million development loan was rejected (322). Britain was more supportive of the idea of the Sudan becoming a full member of the sterling area, making formal what was an informal arrangement, and also giving support to the eventual separation of the Sudanese from the Egyptian currency (388).

Sudanisation became the real testing ground of whether Britain's tactics would succeed. The British member of the Sudanisation Committee, R R Burnett, was instructed by Selwyn Lloyd to ensure that Sudanisation was 'as expeditious and orderly as possible', that British officials be treated fairly, and that he resist any attempt by the committee to expand its remit to include posts unrelated to self-determination (344). Burnett found himself outvoted by the Egyptian and three Sudanese members of the commission (two of the latter being NUP appointees). Sudanisation of the senior ranks of the police was agreed without controversy (337), but the committee recommended a far more rapid and comprehensive Sudanisation of the army and the administration than Britain found comfortable (339, 342, 343). The committee's decision to Sudanise the judiciary was contested by both Britain and the governor-general and led to the temporary withdrawal of the British member. Howe proposed to delay implementation of the committee's recommendation by referring it to the co-domini (345, 346, 349, 350). The committee continued to recommend the Sudanisation of other departments, including education (360). Relations between British officials and the Sudan government deteriorated throughout much of 1954, as those whose posts were first Sudanised left, and by the time the committee was contemplating Sudanising the technical departments Burnett had already concluded that for the sake of Britain's future relations with the Sudan the sooner Sudanisation was completed the better (359).

When the Sudanisation Committee completed its recommendations by the beginning of 1955 it was expected that it would take a full year to implement them. The voluntary retirement of non-Sudanised British staff, taking advantage of the generous compensation scheme Howe had negotiated with al-Azhari's government, meant that far more replacements had to be found than originally anticipated. The pace of departure of officials accelerated, so that by August 1955, when the committee reported that its task was completed, only 200 British staff out of a previous total of 1200 remained in the country (375, 391).

There was some indication that Britain's acquiescence on accelerated Sudanisation, along with the Anglo–Egyptian defence agreement in October 1954, was helping to moderate the anti-British attitude of many within the NUP (365, 370). There was also evidence that Egypt was becoming worried about the solidifying of the pro-independence feeling within the Sudan. In October 1954 both Nasir and Salah Salim openly voiced their concern about political instability in the Sudan to British officials in Cairo, urging support for a policy of 'co-ordination' (rather than full union) between Egypt and the Sudan (364, 366). At the time the pro-Egyptian wing of the NUP appeared to be on the ascendant within the Sudanese Cabinet (365, 367), but there were cracks opening in the NUP coalition. Nasir's dismissal of Najib provoked vocal anti-Egyptian protests within the NUP itself, forcing a confrontation in the Cabinet which ended with the dismissal of Mirghani Hamza and two other non-Ashiqqa Khatmi ministers in December 1954 (374). Howe argued forcefully against any diplomatic re-examination of British objectives in the Sudan, whatever the improvement in Anglo–Egyptian relations, lest this strengthen the pro-Egyptian faction in the government. The Sudan's best hope for the future lay in full independence, he stated, and that independence would be more secure if it could be achieved under an NUP government (372). The Foreign Office agreed (373).

One further consequence of accelerated Sudanisation was that it brought forward Howe's own resignation. Howe felt that the departure of the British governor-general would remove the last focus of Egyptian and Sudanese anti-British sentiment and help increase the momentum towards full independence (352). The Foreign Office came out against the idea of a neutral replacement, arguing that the governor-general still had the right to be informed, to 'guide, encourage and warn' and could influence events 'even if only to a minor degree' (354). By November 1954 it was still anticipated that the full process of self-determination might not be concluded until spring 1957. Given that time-table, and Howe's eagerness to leave, it was decided that a British successor should be installed as soon as possible (368). The improvement in Anglo–Egyptian relations following the October 1954 agreement enabled Britain to obtain Egyptian approval for the appointment of the last British governor-general of the Sudan, Sir Knox Helm, a career diplomat with extensive Middle Eastern experience who had been Britain's minister to Tel Aviv after the 1948 Arab-Israeli war and more recently Britain's ambassador to Turkey. His views were decidedly anti-Egyptian. Instructed not to upset the political balance in the Sudan by becoming a focus for overt anti-Egyptian feeling, he took up his appointment in Khartoum in March 1955 (377).

The political climate in the Sudan had changed between Howe's resignation in November 1954 and his departure in March 1955. The scheduled withdrawal of British officials and Howe's own resignation helped to persuade many in the NUP that the British really were willing to quit the Sudan, and there were many in the party openly advocating complete independence (381, 391). In his valedictory message to Churchill, Howe noted that pro-independence sentiment now crossed party lines, and he urged a public policy supporting a free choice in self-determination, which he now saw as coming earlier rather than later (378).

Relations with the NUP government continued to improve. The Sudanese minister of social affairs showed himself amenable to advice from both the home government and the TUC against introducing repressive anti-communist legislation as part of the government's labour policy (376). Finally on 31 March 1955 the NUP parliamentary party came out publicly for total independence for a Sudanese republic, a policy which was formally endorsed by the party executive on 12 April (381).

These developments were not welcomed by Egypt, and Salah Salim had tried to convince Helm on his way to Khartoum of the inherent political instability of the Sudan (379). One of Egypt's particular concerns was getting the Sudan to agree to the construction of the Aswan High Dam. The first issue on which al-Azhari expressed a marked independence from Egypt was the Sudan's share of Nile Waters (332). The advent of self-government in the Sudan had altered Ethiopia's attitude towards negotiations over the Lake Tsana scheme, and by mid-1954 it was clear that Ethiopia would not consent to any project designed for the sole benefit of Egypt and the Sudan (356). The removal of the Lake Tsana option increased the importance of joint Egyptian–Sudanese projects. The points of contention over the Aswan dam were the calculation of evaporation at the dam in the division of shares of extra water and the compensation for those Sudanese living along the Nile near the international border who would be displaced by the construction of the dam. Egypt was offering the Sudan a very much smaller share of water than the Sudanese thought fair (372). Talks between the Egyptians and Sudanese were suspended early in 1955, and Britain was putting discrete pressure on the International Bank to withhold a loan to Egypt for the construction of the dam until a satisfactory agreement had been reached between Egypt and the Sudan.[76] Egypt attempted to enlist Helm's assistance to persuade the Sudanese government to moderate their demands, giving a Nile Waters agreement a higher priority than union between the two countries (379). But the politics of self-determination were never fully disentangled from the politics of the Nile. Egypt's offer of a 50–50 share of new water in May 1955 was interpreted in the Sudan as a quid-pro-quo for a pro-union vote in self-determination (385). Al-Azhari's reported intention in July to reject this offer was seen by the embassy in Cairo as a fresh provocation to Egypt. 'There is little doubt in my mind', wrote F R H Murray, minister and *chargé d'affaires*, 'that this news, when and if it reaches the Egyptians, must increase their propensity to consider wild and dangerous policies in regard to the Sudan and to render them more impenetrable to the counsels of moderation and good behaviour'.[77]

An increase in Egyptian political activity in the Sudan was reported as a direct result of the suspension of Nile Waters talks and the NUP's support for an independent republic. There was still a sizeable pro-Egyptian 'fifth column' in the NUP, headed by the party's vice-president, Muhammad Nur al-Din, which was inhibiting al-Azhari from pushing ahead with independence. Of more serious concern was new Egyptian support for southern Sudanese separatism (382).

The political crisis in the South had been growing since the announcement of the Sudanisation plans in 1954. The NUP maintained a majority in parliament in part by winning some southern members to their side. Southerners voting as a bloc had the potential to make the difference between a government majority and a government defeat. The NUP (and Salah Salim) had made a number of promises of preferential treatment for southerners in Sudanisation which were now clearly not going to be fulfilled, and even southern ministers in the NUP government began complaining of a northern invasion of the South as newly-appointed officials arrived in their posts (362). In the autumn of 1954 Buth Diu, the most influential leader of the southern Liberal Party, organised a pan-southern conference in Juba (361). Al-Azhari's response was to announce minor alterations in southern pay scales and promotions (363). The conference took place in October and included representatives from throughout the three southern provinces, southern members of the NUP and southerners living in Khartoum, making it the first truly representative meeting of southern political opinion ever held. It resolved to support Sudanese independence under a presidential (as opposed to monarchical) government, but it also supported proposals for a federal system. The conference proclaimed the South's right to its own self-determination, and stated that complete independence of the South was the only acceptable alternative to federation with the North (369).

Southerners became even more vocal in April 1955, when several southern members of the NUP, prior to leaving the party, denounced their own government's southern policy and came out in favour of federation (380). In the same month it was reported that the Egyptians were now bribing southern MPs to support a constitutional link with Egypt. Even Siricio Iro, who had been placed on the Governor-General's Commission as an NUP man, left the party and was identified as Egypt's main agent in the Sudan (381, 382).

Helm's one visit to the South was made in May. He was impressed by the northern Sudanese administrators he found there, thought the southerners on the whole were lazy and educated Southerners 'cut off from their environment'. Already suspicious of Egypt he was alarmed by the evidence presented to him by the three provincial governors of the extent of Egyptian bribery and propaganda through the EID, and predicted that the South would 'go the way of the Egyptians' unless something was done (383).

Throughout the early summer more reports came from northern officials in the South of widespread Egyptian political propaganda. Al-Azhari and other members of the NUP did not see it as their responsibility to curb such activities, and the governor-general came under pressure to invoke a constitutional emergency in order to crackdown on Egyptian agents. 'It is a reflection of the basic political immaturity of these people', Grafftey-Smith reported, 'that their hopes are always set on some miraculous intervention from outside' (384, 385). Talk of federalism was on the increase, and another all-southern conference was held in Juba in July (385, 396).

The attention of politicians in Khartoum was focused elsewhere. With the conversion of the NUP to the cause of independence there were moves in parliament 'to eliminate self-determination' (381). The Umma Party, which had been willing to tear up the 1953 agreement after failing in the elections, now proposed to dispense with the self-determination process 'on the ground that the whole country is agreed upon independence'. Failing that, they wished to replace elections to a constituent assembly with a plebiscite on independence (382). The idea for a plebiscite had been floated before and at different times had been advocated by the Umma, al-Azhari and the Egyptians (191, 213). Al-Azhari was at first resistant to the idea of a plebiscite (384), but in July sayyid Ali al-Mirghani lent his support to the idea, even if it meant asking the Egyptians to agree to an amendment of the Self-Government Statute (387).

The process for self-determination began when the Sudanisation Committee reported on 2 August 1955 that its task was completed (391). A self-determination motion was debated in the House of Representatives on 16 August, in which the possibility of a plebiscite was mentioned (390), and both houses of parliament passed the resolution unanimously. The two sayyids now publicly supported the call for a plebiscite and Britain's new ambassador to Cairo, Sir Humphrey Trevelyan, was authorised to inform Salah Salim that Britain would accept a plebiscite if the majority of Sudanese so wished.[78]

By this time events in the South were forcing themselves on the attention of Khartoum, Cairo and London, nearly derailing the whole process of Sudanese independence. The British diplomatic team now responsible for keeping self-determination on track were mainly new to their positions. Macmillan had been foreign secretary since only April, Trevelyan had just taken up his post earlier that August, and Helm, who had been governor-general since March, was in Britain on leave. It fell to William Luce, constitutional affairs adviser, acting governor-general, and a former deputy governor of Equatoria Province, to make the first assessments of the disturbances and authorise the initial response.

Civil unrest in western Equatoria, centred at Yambio and the small industrial complex of Nzara, had occurred in July and was being publicised in Cairo by southern Sudanese politicians and Salah Salim. What was more serious was that on 6 August evidence was uncovered of a plot to mutiny among southern soldiers based at Torit, the headquarters of the Equatorial Corps (389). Despite this advance warning a mutiny did break out in Torit on 18 August, and the first information was sent to London and Cairo by Luce (392). Luce did not declare a constitutional emergency, but proclaimed instead a state of emergency in the three southern provinces under the Defence of the Sudan Ordinance; thus allowing al-Azhari's government to deal with the emergency without reference to the Governor-General's Commission or the co-domini. He urged the immediate transfer of northern Sudanese troops south via RAF transport planes to prevent the Egyptians from sending their own troops ostensibly to protect their irrigation personnel (393).

The first meeting between Trevelyan and Salah Salim concerning the mutiny took place on 21 August, three days after the first official news of events in Torit reached either the Foreign Office or the embassy.[79] Over the next two days Salah pressed for joint Anglo–Egyptian military intervention to restore order in the South, proposals which Trevelyan resisted (394, 395).[80] Helm, on his way back to Khartoum, was given clear instructions by the Foreign Office to avoid the use of co-dominal troops in restoring order (397, 402).

Reports came in of the containment of further disturbances in Upper Nile and Bahr al-Ghazal, but of general support for the rising among civilians throughout Equatoria. Opinions differed about the instigation and extent of the revolt. Northern Sudanese generally attributed the mutiny solely to Egyptian agitation (396). This was a view initially shared by Helm, who accused Egypt of being the principal immediate cause of the trouble in the South either with the intention of deliberately breaking up the Sudan, or (more likely) having started something which then got out of hand (400). Luce, one of the few British administrators to have held senior positions in both the North and the South, was of a different opinion. The mutiny was 'symptomatic of the major internal political problem of the Sudan i.e. the relationship between the North and the South', which could be settled only by the Sudanese themselves and would require a fundamental reappraisal by the North of its attitude towards the South (396). The immediate problem in Khartoum was 'to get Azhari and his Ministers to understand that this is anything more than a mutiny of troops'. Given the obvious pro-British sentiment of so many in the South, British advice, even if based on a more intimate knowledge of the region, was suspect to the new Sudan government (398). Helm modified his own view once he returned to Khartoum. There was no doubt, he now concluded, that the entire South had been behind the revolt. The Egyptians had worked upon southern dread of the North, 'but it is probably doubtful whether even without Egyptian injections the South would have remained quiet indefinitely' (405).

Together Luce, Helm and al-Azhari worked for the surrender of the mutineers, and Luce went to Torit to negotiate and observe the surrender. In the end very few mutineers came in, the majority fleeing to the bush or crossing into Uganda (405, 406). The influx of refugees into Uganda now brought Uganda and the Colonial Office directly into discussions about the Sudan's immediate future.

With fugitive mutineers, civilian refugees, missionaries and even fleeing northern Sudanese officers of the SDF crossing the border, Uganda was in a unique position to accumulate information about the situation inside Equatoria Province, which it forwarded to the Colonial Office for transmission to Khartoum, via the Foreign Office. Cohen, the governor of Uganda, recognised the undesirability of re-deploying co-dominal troops in the South and argued for Belgian observers, administrators and even troops to be sent to the South as neutrals best equipped to restore administration (401). One CMS missionary coming from western Equatoria expressed concern that should northern Sudanese troops see the extent of the popular participation in the rising, reprisals would be inevitable. He pressed for the renewal of British or Anglo–Egyptian administration in the South (409). The Foreign Office rejected all such proposals: Macmillan minuted that Cohen 'must be rather lacking in judgment', and the Foreign Office dismissed the missionary proposal as really 'dreadful stuff' (409). Neither the Foreign Office nor Helm dissented to any significant degree from the Ugandan government's appreciation of the causes of the rising, but they did disagree (Helm in particular) over the role of Egyptian instigation (418) and the prospect of restoring settled administration without external intervention (427). The Colonial Office did not press the point, but kept in reserve the possibility that they might, at some future point, press the prime minister to re-establish direct British control over the South (411).

The size of the influx into Uganda of mutineers and civilians created new long-term problems between Uganda and the Sudan. Given the close relations that existed across the border between many Sudanese and Ugandan peoples, and the political nature of the refugee influx, Cohen did not feel that he could automatically extradite the mutineers and refugees back to the Sudan under previous colonial legislation regarding fugitives. New legislation was drafted to meet with the new situation – the precursor of many similar refugee movements in post-independence Eastern Africa (399, 403).

Uganda's response to the refugee crisis, fully endorsed by the Colonial Office, caused considerable strain between Khartoum, London and Entebbe (404, 426, 427). The Governor-General's Office was particularly concerned that Uganda's actions were being interpreted by the Sudanese as a British plot to side with the mutineers (426, 427). While the instinct of many in the Foreign Office was to give full support to Khartoum's demands for extradition, there were others who saw broader international implications in the politics between two incipient independent African states. Sir Harold Caccia, pointing to possible asylum claims from potential risings in Eastern Europe (particularly Poland) asked 'what would be the effect of this in Africa now? And elsewhere as a precedent in the future?' From general principles he argued that Britain could not force wholesale extraditions. Added to that were the specific facts of Britain's own role in the current political set up in the Sudan. 'Is it, indeed, justice to look at this revolt in isolation and approach the problem with the idea that we must "try to find some method of returning these men to the Sudanese authorities"?' Macmillan recorded that he was 'shaken' by Caccia's arguments (417).

Despite his robust defence of the Sudanese government against Uganda's doubts, Helm was far from optimistic in his dealings with al-Azhari in the immediate aftermath of the mutiny. He found al-Azhari uncommunicative, complacent and detached from the details of reasserting administrative control in the South, despite his direct responsibility as minister of the interior (412, 416, 419).

The immediate effect of the Torit mutiny was to accelerate the process towards independence, leading eventually to a circumvention of the self-determination procedures agreed in the 1953 Self-Government Statute. The question to be resolved was whether this could best be done through a plebiscite or a direct declaration of independence.

Helm was one of the first to argue against a plebiscite as too difficult to implement in the wake of the Torit mutiny (400). At the same time that the mutiny was being suppressed the Foreign Office and the Egyptian government agreed in advance to accept a plebiscite should the Sudanese parliament vote in favour of one, which they did at the end of August (408). But support for a declaration of independence for the Sudan came from a variety of corners. Nasir was reported to be contemplating unilateral recognition of Sudanese independence as a means of salvaging some of Egypt's influence in view of the backlash against its Sudan policy after the Torit mutiny (410, 413). The Colonial Office, for its part, supported a unilateral declaration of independence by Britain for the opposite reason: to forestall the advance of Egyptian influence towards East Africa (411). Helm urged the Foreign Office to persuade Egypt to participate in a joint recognition of independence and the drafting of a new constitution by parliament, to be accomplished 'while the south is still quiet' (414).[81] On this last point Helm was at odds with the Foreign Office, who were then of the view that the parliament had no mandate to settle constitutional issues (408). But the real pressure for rapid British withdrawal continued to come from Helm. 'For me the moral is crystal clear', he stated in September, 'namely that the sooner we can get out of these almost unlimited commitments, without accompanying powers, the better' (416).

Nasir now began to resist British pressure to accelerate self-determination, in September arguing against altering the self-determination procedures (415) and in October accepting a plebiscite but not a declaration of independence (420). The Czech arms deal of October removed Britain's last inhibition against offending Egypt over the Sudan, and Macmillan instructed Helm to inform al-Azhari that Britain was willing immediately to recognise Sudanese independence (421).

Helm was already on record claiming that 'from every point of view I can see nothing but advantages in H.M. Government divesting themselves of their Condominium responsibilities and liabilities at the earliest possible moment. If they cannot do so in agreement with Egypt then I suggest that other means should be found' (421). Predictably, the embassy in Cairo argued against unilateral action, citing the possible repudiation of the Suez Canal base agreement in retaliation, but the Foreign Office on the whole, and Macmillan in particular, saw the initiative over the Sudan as a way of showing Nasir that Britain would not 'accept tamely a defeat of the kind he has administered us' with the Czech arms deal (422). The only concession to Cairo was the instruction to Helm to inform al-Azhari that HMG would respond to an initiative from the Sudanese parliament (423, 424). Britain's desire to extract itself from the Sudan in the aftermath of the southern disturbances now appeared to override earlier commitments to constitutional procedures. The Foreign Office had apparently forgotten its own warning back in 1953 that a declaration of independence, even by a large majority of both houses of parliament, would be likely to create discontent among minorities and pave the way for civil war (318).

Al-Azhari was informed on 12 October 1955 of the United Kingdom's willingness to agree to an independence resolution passed by parliament (425). He at first saw no need for a hurried resolution, and it was Helm who had to press him. His hesitation seemed to stem from disagreements within his own party and the demand by the opposition that a coalition 'national' government should supervise the drafting of the constitution (428, 429). When the southern representatives of the Liberal Party declared that it was not prepared to discuss the Sudan's future in parliament, the Foreign Office was dismayed that this boycott would undermine their justification for cutting short self-determination (432).

By now Nasir had been informed by his own sources in Khartoum of the manoeuvres towards a declaration of independence. His main fear seemed to be that independence would still leave a British governor-general in office until a constitution had been adopted, and that independence under the present parliament would leave al-Azhari in power for some time to come (430, 431).[82]

Al-Azhari's position was not so secure as it looked from Cairo. In November sayyid Ali al-Mirghani agreed to withdraw his support from al-Azhari, which led to a no-confidence motion being passed in parliament. But sayyid Ali changed his mind, the vote was reversed, and al-Azhari just survived (434).[83]

In the midst of parliamentary deadlock in the Sudan, renewed concern for a fair deal for the South was expressed in both houses of parliament in Britain. Luce reassured the Foreign Office that the question of the South could not be settled independently of the constitutional questions for the entire country. Since a plebiscite would address only the issue of independence from Egypt, whose outcome was now considered a foregone conclusion, and not the internal constitutional structure of the Sudan, it was far better, he declared, to get past the formula for independence and on to the real issues confronting the country. A national government, which he felt likely to replace the NUP government, would be bound to treat the South generously (435).

It was precisely to avoid the creation of a national government that al-Azhari finally tabled the independence motions, and then only after Helm had returned to Britain on Christmas leave (439). The wording of the resolutions agreed between government, opposition and the Governor-General's Office requested the governor-general to ask the co-domini to recognise Sudanese independence forthwith. A constituent assembly would be set up after independence and, in response the demands from the Liberal Party, federation for the South would be given 'serious consideration'.[84] Al-Azhari sent a personal emissary to Cairo who obtained Nasir's agreement. The motions were passed by the House on 19 December and the Senate of 22 December, but a date for independence (1 January 1956) was not decided until 27 December. Helm was requested not to return to the Sudan for the independence ceremonies (436, 437, 439). 'Thus the way was opened for the Sudan to become independent without bloodshed or disaster but with a haste which might well cause legal and administrative chaos', reported the UK trade commissioner, and 'the Sudan will need friends and friendly advice' (439).

Friends were needed not least on the outstanding dispute with Egypt over the Nile Waters. The Sudan insisted that Egypt bear the cost of the evaporation loss at Aswan and the Sudan be given a larger share of the balance of the unused Nile flow. Egypt was pressing Britain to mediate, but the Sudanese showed no signs of wanting mediation (433) and on 20 November officially rejected Egypt's formula. Before al-Azhari announced his intention to table the independence motions Egypt had already indicated that they would not approach the Sudanese further as they did not think they could get anything from al-Azhari.[85] An Anglo–American offer to finance the construction of the dam in December was made conditional on a resolution to the Egyptian–Sudanese dispute.[86] On 28 December, the day after a decision was reached on the date of the Sudan's independence, Egypt informed the Sudan that it would grant none of their requests for a revised share of the Nile Waters, rescind all its previous offers and hold strictly to the provisions of the 1929 agreement (438).

An epilogue of sorts to the transfer of power in the Sudan was offered in October 1956 with the publication of the Cotran Commission report on the previous year's disturbances. There was an ironic reversal of roles in the Foreign Office commentary. Sir Edwin Chapman-Andrews had played a minor role in setting Britain's policy towards Sudanese independence from posts in Cairo and Whitehall in the 1940s (59, 146, 148, 156, 160, 172, 176). He was now in Khartoum, as Britain's first ambassador to Khartoum. Writing just as the Suez crisis was beginning he reviewed Britain's administrative record in the Sudan and accepted as justified some of the criticisms of that administration the report contained. In Whitehall now, commenting on this report 'from the field' was J S R Duncan, a former DC from a southern province and assistant constitutional affairs adviser in Khartoum at the time of the mutiny. A vocal critic himself of the 'zoo' mentality of the old Southern Policy, but also a publicist of the condominium's achievements,[87] here his defence of the administration's record is restrained. 'At bedrock', he concluded, 'it is an unhappy accident which placed two such deeply different peoples within a common frontier and, in my view, trouble was inevitable … the gap could only have been narrowed. It could never have been closed' (440).

Notes to Introduction

1 BDEEP series A, vol 1, S R Ashton & S E Stockwell, eds, *Imperial policy and colonial practice 1925–1945* in 2 parts (London, 1996).

2 BDEEP series B, vol 4, John Kent, ed, *Egypt and the defence of the Middle East* in 3 parts (London, 1998).

3 Even when documents were released at the project's request (as in 312) sensitive portions were blotted out.

4 The main collection being in the Sudan Archive in the University of Durham (see Bibliography 2).

5 John Kent, *op cit,* part I, p xxxvii.

6 This change in responsibility meant that the consular files of the embassy contained in FO 141, which proved of such value to John Kent's Egypt volume, cease to be of any real use to us just when the issue of the Sudan becomes a matter of major contention between Egypt and the Britain.

7 Reports from the Sudan agent in London to the civil secretary in Khartoum can be found in Sir James Robertson's papers in the Sudan Archive, University of Durham, and are cited in G Balfour-Paul, *The end of empire in the Middle East: Britain's relinquishment of power in her last three Arab dependencies* (Cambridge, 1991).

8 The agent and consul-general became the high commissioner on the proclamation of a British protectorate over Egypt in 1914, and ambassador to Egypt, assuming the duties of high commissioner for the Sudan, on the signing of the 1936 Anglo–Egyptian treaty.

9 For a comprehensive description of the evolution of the early administration in the Sudan see M W Daly, *Empire on the Nile: the Anglo–Egyptian Sudan, 1898–1934* (Cambridge, 1986).

10 For accounts of Anglo–Egyptian negotiations before 1924, and for the crisis in the Sudan, see Hassan Ahmed Ibrahim, *The 1936 Anglo–Egyptian treaty* (Khartoum, 1976) pp 13–16; Gabriel Giet Jal, *The Sudan question in the Anglo–Egyptian treaty of 1936* (Juba, 1989) pp 8–13; Mohamed Omer Beshir, *Revolution and nationalism in the Sudan* (London, 1974); and Daly, *Empire on the Nile*, pp 298–315.

11 J Waterbury, *Hydropolitics of the Nile valley* (Syracuse, 1979) p 67.

12 Muddathir Abd al-Rahim, *Imperialism and nationalism in the Sudan* (Oxford, 1969) p 114.

13 There is no agreement on the proper transliteration of Arabic words into English, and the documents published here are inconsistent in the variety of systems adopted. I have chosen a modified modern literary transliteration, minus diacritical marks, for use in the introduction, notes and editorial apparatus (except the bibliography).

14 Hassan Ahmed Ibrahim, *The 1936 Anglo–Egyptian treaty*; Jal, *The Sudan question in the Anglo–Egyptian treaty of 1936*. For an extract from the text of the 1936 Anglo–Egyptian Treaty, see John Kent, *op cit,* appendix 1 (reproduced in all three parts).

15 'Sayyid' is an honorific title. As rivals sayyid Ali and sayyid Abd al-Rahman were known as 'the two sayyids'. In official circles they were known by their initials, 'SAM' and 'SAR'.

16 T Niblock, *Class and power in Sudan: the dynamics of Sudanese politics, 1898–1985* (London, 1987).

17 Yoshiko Kurita, 'The concept of nationalism in the White Flag League movement', in Mahasin Abdel Gadir Hag el Safi, ed, *The nationalist movement in the Sudan* (Khartoum, 1989).

18 Niblock, *Class and power in Sudan*, chapter 4; M W Daly, *Imperial Sudan: the Anglo–Egyptian condominium, 1934–56* (Cambridge, 1991) chapter 2; Mohamed Omer Beshir, *Revolution and nationalism in the Sudan*.

19 R O Collins, *Shadows in the grass: Britain in the southern Sudan 1918–1956* (New Haven, 1983); Daly, *Empire on the Nile*, chapter 10; Daly, *Imperial Sudan*, chapter 2.

20 Transcript of an interview with Sir Angus Gillan, Rhodes House, Oxford, MSS Afr. s. 1715 (103); Daly, *Imperial Sudan*, p 45.

21 BDEEP series B, vol 1, Richard Rathbone, ed, *Ghana*, pp xxxviii ff.

22 F M Deng & M W Daly, *Bonds of silk: the human factor in the British administration of the Sudan* (East Lansing, 1989) pp 72–75.

23 Newbold's diary, quoted in K D D Henderson, *The making of the modern Sudan: the life and letters of Sir Douglas Newbold* (London, 1953) p 542.

24 CO 822/108/21, minutes by C G Eastwood and D C Watherson, 29 Oct and 3 Nov 1943.

25 FO 371/80358, no 5, Civil Secretary's Office, 'Note on the Graduates' General Congress as a back ground to its potential danger to public security', 28 Feb 1950.

26 Mohamed Omer Beshir, *Revolution and nationalism in the Sudan*, pp 156–164; Daly, *Imperial Sudan*, pp 155–163.

27 FO 371/45972, no 552, SPIS No 45, Dec 1944, para 358.

28 The Sudan administration used vernacular languages in native administration throughout the country, which in the North was usually (but not universally) Arabic. English was used at the higher levels of administration throughout the Sudan until well after independence. It was only after the 6 Day War in 1967 that Sudan finally replaced English with Arabic as the language of instruction in all of its secondary schools.

29 Various statistics have been given for the number of Christians and Muslims in the South at the time of independence, but as the first fully national census of 1955–1956 gives no figures for religious affiliation, these remain estimates only.

30 FO 371/45973, no 890, minute by Scrivener, 10 Mar 1945.

31 An analysis of the hydropolitics of Nile control is to be found in Waterbury, *Hydropolitics of the Nile valley*. Details of proposals pertaining to the Sudan can be found in R O Collins, *The waters of the Nile: hydropolitics and the Jonglei canal 1900–1988* (Oxford, 1990).

32 FO 371/41326, no 414, despatch no 75 from Killearn to Eden, 23 Jan 1944.

33 Balfour-Paul, *The end of empire in the Middle East*, pp 3, 25; Daly, *Imperial Sudan*, pp 249–250.

34 Robertson also reports that embassy pressure on him at this time helped to persuade him of the need to accelerate Sudanisation. See 201 and Sir J Robertson, *Transition in Africa: from direct rule to independence* (London & Khartoum, 1974 & 1975) p 94.

35 FO 371/53328, nos 2622 & 3511, SPIS nos 56 & 57, Jan–Apr 1946 & May–June 1946.

36 A Bullock, *Ernest Bevin foreign secretary, 1945–1951* (London, 1983) chapters 6–8.

37 John Kent, *op cit*, part I, for the context and coverage of the defence negotiations.

38 Ibid, 69.

39 FO 371/53310, no 3639, FO tel no 68, 26 Aug 1946; see also John Kent, *op cit*, part I, p xlix.

40 PREM 8/1388/1, Cairo tel no 33, 25 July 1946.

41 John Kent, *op cit*, part I, p xlix.

42 Sir Pierson Dixon, Bevin's private secretary, noted in his diary: 'There is no doubt that sovereignty has continuously been Egypt's. ... Our ancestors landed us in the soup when they failed to make Queen Victoria the co-sovereign, as they easily could have done,' cited in Balfour-Paul, *The end of empire in the Middle East*, p 203.

43 The conviction lingered beyond 1946 and has been expressed in such Sudan memoirs as Robertson's *Transition in Africa* (pp 95–96), Sir G Bell's *Shadows on the sand* (London, 1983) pp 169–170, and G Thomas, ed, *Last of the proconsuls: letters of Sir James Robertson* (London, 1994) p 17. Robertson's memoirs are inaccurate on a number of crucial points. He claims that on 7 October Huddleston and he were first informed of 'the still secret Bevin-Sidky Protocol', and reproduces the text of the final version as the one he was shown then. In fact, Bevin and Sidqi had yet to hold their private talks, and the text Robertson and Huddleston were shown on 8 October was a consultation draft which was later presented to Sidqi after their approval (85). Robertson later claims that he and the other two secretaries threatened in the letter presented to Huddleston in November that 'we did not think that we could possibly remain in the Sudan to force a Treaty' on the Sudanese (p 97), but no such implied resignation threat appears in the letter (102). Balfour-Paul, an ex-SPS man who later consulted the FO papers, recognised that the hostility of the SPS towards Bevin was unwarranted and concluded that 'Bevin himself was at no stage prepared to "sell the Sudan for his treaty"'. Balfour-Paul, *The end of empire in the Middle East*, p 29. Douglas Dodds-Parker, who was part of a group of ex-SPS Conservative MPs who lobbied Bevin on behalf of the Sudan in 1946, greatly admired Bevin for his commitment to the Sudan's right to self-determination (Sir Douglas Dodds-Parker, personal communication, 1996).

44 In this they were ultimately proven right, as even Robertson recorded in his diary early in December. Robertson, *Transition in Africa*, p 98.

45 FO 141/1095, Robertson to Bowker, 8 May 1946; FO 371/53391: no 2203, Cairo tel no 894, 18 May 1946; no 3425, Huddleston to Howe and Huddleston to Bevin, 6 Aug 1946, Bevin to Huddleston, 16 Aug 1946.

46 Robertson, in both his published and private papers, was one of the main authors of the position that Huddleston was the real architect of Sudanese statehood, secured in the face of Foreign Office opposition, for which he paid the price: see Robertson, *Transition in Africa*, p 101; P Woodward, *Condominium and Sudanese nationalism* (London, 1979), pp 55–59; Balfour-Paul, *The end of empire in the Middle East*, pp 30, 204 n 29; and W Travis Hanes III, 'Sir Hubert Huddleston and the independence of Sudan', *Journal of Imperial and Commonwealth History* vol 20 (1992) pp 248–249, 264–265, 267, 269. As a matter of record it was Bevin who proposed a peerage for Huddleston on retirement, Attlee who vetoed this proposal. FO 371/63043: no 1326, Moscow tel no 72, 14 Mar 1947; no 1753, Bevin to Attlee, 9 May 1947; no 1467, Rowan to Sargent, 31 Mar 1947.

47 Robertson later wrote: 'I looked upon the conference solely as a means of finding out the capabilities of the Southerners, and it was therefore quite inaccurate for some people to say later that at the Juba conference the Southern representatives agreed to come in with the North. No decisions could be made at the conference, since members had received no mandate from their peoples. ... The only decision resulting from the conference was taken by myself'. Robertson, *Transition in Africa*, p 107.

48 FO 371/90108, no 1, SPIS no 8, Nov–Dec 1950, para 89.

49 FO 371/69303: no 2352, minute by G L McDermott on Lake Tsana, 15 Mar 1948 and FO tel no 99 to Addis Ababa, 2 Apr 1948; no 2497, Howe tel no 87 to FO, 9 Apr 1948; no 2628, Campbell despatch no 468 to FO, 16 Apr 1948; no 2819, Howe tel no 102 to FO, 25 Apr 1948.

50 FO 371/69233, no 7022, minute by G L Clutton, 16 Oct 1948.

51 FO 371/69233, no 8253, Creech Jones to Bevin, 21 Dec 1948; FO 371/73613, no 704, Howe tel no 21 to FO, 27 Jan 1949.

52 BDEEP series A, vol 2, Ronald Hyam, ed, *The Labour government and the end of empire 1945–1951*, part II, 131.

53 For border relations in the south-east prior to the Abyssinian crisis see P P Garretson, 'Vicious cycles: ivory, slaves, and arms on the new Maji frontier', and D H Johnson, 'On the Nilotic frontier: imperial Ethiopia in the southern Sudan, 1898–1936', both in D Donham and W James, eds, *The southern marches of imperial Ethiopia: essays in history and social anthropology* (Cambridge, 1986).

54 Ronald Hyam, *op cit*, part III, 304–306, 311, 316–318.

55 FO 371/102712, no 141, E B Boothby to D M H Riches, 16 Oct 1953.

56 Ronald Hyam, *op cit*, part I, 34–35.

57 See eg John Kent, *op cit*, part I, pp lxii–lxiii.

58 BDEEP Series A, Volume 3, David Goldsworthy, ed, *The Conservative government and the end of empire 1951–1957*, part II, 254, 255.

59 Robertson denied in his memoirs any direct involvement in setting up the SRP (Robertson, *Transition in Africa*, p 151). Confidentially he admitted to the FO that 'We did to some extent encourage its establishment as a party aiming at independence, but non-Mahdist ...' (FO 371/96910, no 308, Robertson, 'S.A.R'S. memorandum to Mr. Eden', 7 Oct 1952). He confessed closer involvement to one of his Sudan correspondents, Graham Thomas, who has described the SRP as 'inspired by Civil Secretary's Political section', and quotes a 1953 letter from Robertson stating, 'I agree with you that as things have worked out the SRP may have been a mistake. The idea was to try and build up a non-Mahdist party supporting Independence—because I felt very sure that there were many Sudanese who did not want to be associated with SAR & co, but were equally not pro-Egyptian—and without some central party there was no way in which they could express their opinion. However it certainly doesn't seem to have worked'. Thomas, ed, *Last of the proconsuls*, p 39.

60 David Goldsworthy, *op cit*, part II, 256, 257, 265.

61 It was reported that even some of sayyid Abd al-Rahman's own followers were disturbed by his sending this delegation to Egypt. FO 371/96906, no 178, tel no 169 from Robertson to FO, 29 June 1952.

62 Husain Zulfakar Sabri later wrote that Egyptian policy changed following his contacts with the independence parties in Khartoum as envoy of the RCC during the month of August 1952, and that it was

he who recommended that Egypt should grant self-determination immediately. H Z Sabry, *Sovereignty for Sudan* (London, 1982), pp 29, 51, 55–67, 73–75.

63 Prior to going to Cairo for meetings with the Egyptians sayyid Abd al-Rahman presented a memorandum to Eden which requested the deletion of the governor-general's reserved powers for the South and public service. FO 371/96910, no 308, J W Robertson, 'S.A.R'S. memorandum to Mr. Eden', 7 Oct 1952. Muhammad Ahmad Mahjub also subsequently claimed that he and the Independence Front delegates were largely responsible for the text of the Egyptian note. M A Mahgoub, *Democracy on trial* (London, 1974), pp 51–52.

64 FO 371/96917, no 580, minute by R Allen, 23 Dec 1952.

65 According to Sabri, Salah's rudeness to the British was calculated. The signatures he gathered, often on random scraps of paper, were taken as genuine expressions of political support in Cairo. Sabry, *op cit*, pp 109–110, 116, 127.

66 With good reason. Compare Robertson's description of SRP's positions on the South and Sudanisation (276) with Sabri's account of the SRP during his negotiations with the northern parties, where the idea of an international commission and a three year transition period during which the administration would be completely Sudanised were first proposed by SRP politicians. Sabry, *op cit*, pp 61–66.

67 John Kent, *op cit*, part II, 356; and David Goldsworthy, *op cit*, part II, 35.

68 Eden later wrote that 'this was one of the rare occasions when I differed from Sir Winston Churchill on a matter of foreign policy'. Eden accepted that the agreement was less than he wished, but it was sufficiently important that 'I should have had to resign if I had not got my way'. A Eden, *Memoirs: full circle* (London, 1960), pp 246–247.

69 David Goldsworthy, *op cit*, part II, 258.

70 Such a paper was presented to cabinet in April 1953. See David Goldsworthy, *op cit*, part II, 178, 260 n 3.

71 W A Morris commented that 'The Foreign Office seem to be moved by the desire to get shot of the Sudan, in the interests of easy relationships with Egypt, and the C.R.O. by fear of anything which is going to cause awkwardness with Dr. Malan', and worried about the possible effect on West African territories if the arguments for the Sudan's exclusion were made public. W L Gorell Barns minuted: 'It seems to me that FO underrate both the strategic importance of the Sudan and ... the degree of psychological influence which members of the Commonwealth can exercise on a country's behaviour ...'. See David Goldsworthy, *op cit*, part II, 259 n 4.

72 Details of compensation schemes for British officials then serving in the Sudan can be found in FO 371/102767–71.

73 FO 371/102757 no 417, Grafftey Smith to Allen, 15 Mar 1953.

74 PREM 11/544, FO tels no 513 & 533, 10 & 16 April 1953.

75 FO 371/108311, no 2, Riches despatch no 10 to Eden, 22 Jan 1954, 'Sudan: Annual Review for 1953'.

76 FO 371/113730, nos 14 & 15, R W Bailey to T E Bromley, 16 Feb 1955 and Bromley, 'Brief for Lord Reading. Nile Waters', 18 Feb 1955.

77 FO 371/113735, no 121, F R H Murray to C A E Shuckburgh, 29 July 1955.

78 FO 371/113783, nos 23–25, Adams tels no 139 & 140, 16 Aug 1955, and Luce tel no 202, 16 Aug 1955. FO 371/113784, no 27, FO tels no 1676 & 1685, 18 & 19 Aug 1955.

79 Compare this with Trevelyan's later account that Salah Salim came to him with news before the governor-general had received it. Trevelyan's memoirs refer to the meeting on 22 August reported in 395. Helm had still not returned to Khartoum by this time. H Trevelyan, *The Middle East in revolution* (London, 1970), p 18.

80 Nutting claims that Salah Salim's proposal horrified Nasir as 'it would strike at the very fundamentals of his policy to invite Britain to prolong her military presence in the Sudan by so much as twenty-four

hours'. Salah was made the scapegoat for the failure of Egypt's policy in the Sudan and dismissed. A Nutting, *Nassser* (London & NY, 1972), p 113.

81 The anti-colonialist Labour MP Fenner Brockway also argued that the Sudanese parliament be allowed to reach 'a decision on the issue of the Sudan's future international status without the cost and delay of a plebiscite or further general election'. FO 371/113617, no 186, 'Text of parliamentary question by Mr. Fenner Brockway for reply on Oct 31 [1955]'.

82 According to Nutting's account of these events (which, on the whole, is better corroborated by the official record than many other published memoirs of this period), 'the net result of this unfortunate piece of double-dealing by Whitehall was to deepen still further Nasser's inherent distrust of British policies and methods'. Nutting, *op cit*, pp 114–115.

83 Nasir commented that during this crisis £6000 was the going rate for buying a Sudanese MP's allegience, and that al-Azhari still had at his disposal the remains of earlier Egyptian disbursements. FO 371/113626, no 410, Trevelyan to Schuckburgh, 15 Dec 1955 (to which Schuckburgh added his own marginal note, 'Nasser has a sense of humour—it is partly this which endears him to so many visitors'). In later years Nasser told both Trevelyan and Nutting that his Sudan experience 'taught him that bribery was a bad method of conducting policy because the people who took bribes were interested in the money and not in the policy'. Nutting, *op cit*, p 113.

84 A number of southern MPs were then under investigation for their possible role in the disturbances (Woodward, *op cit*, p 155). It was later alleged that for this reason they voted with the government and the northern Sudanese majority for independence without pressing for greater constitutional guarantees for the South. O Albino, *The Sudan: a southern viewpoint* (London, 1970), pp 38–39.

85 FO 371/113740, no 327, Trevelyan tel no 1918, 14 Dec 1955.

86 FO 371/113741, no 346, FO tel no 480, 20 Dec 1955; and FO 371/119059, no 2, FO tel no 540, 30 Dec 1955.

87 J S R Duncan, *The Sudan: a record of achievement* (Edinburgh, 1952).

Summary of Documents: Part I

Chapter 1
Anticipating the post-war settlement, May 1942–Jan 1946

Chapter 2

The Anglo–Egyptian treaty negotiations and the Sudan protocol, Jan 1946–Mar 1947

Chapter 3

Preparations for self-government, Apr 1947–Dec 1950

1 FO 371/31587, no 2664 22 May 1942
[Sudanese Graduates' Congress]: despatch no 536 from Sir M Lampson to Mr Eden. *Enclosures*: despatches from Sir H Huddleston

I have the honour to transmit herewith a copy of a despatch from the Governor-General of the Sudan, together with its enclosures, regarding the Sudan Graduates' Congress.

2. The oriental counsellor[1] has informed Nahas Pasha verbally through Amin Pasha Osman of the contents of item (1) of the memorandum submitted by the Sudanese Graduates' Congress and of the sense of the first paragraph of the reply sent to them by the civil secretary. At the same time, he mentioned to Amin Pasha the appointment by the congress of the Cairo Committee, to which reference is made in paragraph 2 of the despatch, and warned him that it would be advisable that the Egyptian Government Departments should refuse to have any official contacts with the members of the committee. He suggested that these irresponsible activities of the congress might prove as embarrassing to the Egyptians as to ourselves.

3. It is of interest to observe that leading Egyptians in the Sudan regarded the memorandum as a document drawn up under British inspiration with a view to eliminating Egypt's connexion with the Sudan. This view is also held in political circles in Egypt.

Enclosure 1 to 1: despatch from Sir H Huddleston to Sir M Lampson, 12 May 1942

I have the honour to enclose for your Excellency's information copies of a letter addressed to me by the president of the Sudanese Graduates' Congress on the 3rd April last and of a reply which has been sent to him by my civil secretary. The genesis of the Sudan Graduates' Congress was described in our despatch No. 98 of the 5th July, 1938.

2. To assist your Excellency in obtaining a correct appreciation of the position of this congress as the first conscious expression of a nascent Sudanese nationalism, I am also enclosing a short memorandum on its past history and that of the movement it claims to represent.

It will be seen that on more than one occasion the saner and more balanced members have allowed themselves to be rushed by younger extremists into an act which they had subsequent reason to regret. The letter enclosed is the greatest and, save for the appointment of the Cairo Committee mentioned in the memorandum, the latest of these errors.

3. The passage of Sir Stafford Cripps through the Sudan on his way to India and the possibility of his casting a benevolent eye upon Sudanese aspirations on his return journey were the acknowledged reasons for the decision to "put the Sudan's case before the Government." The vigorous and successful part played by the Sudan Defence Force and Sudanese ancillary services, both military and civil, in the campaign against Italian East Africa and the subsequent further expansion of the Sudan Defence Force in Imperial interests, *e.g.*, the garrisoning of Eritrea and other

[1] Sir W Smart, oriental secretary (later counsellor) at the embassy in Cairo, 1926–1945.

projected uses, have also accelerated the already growing speculations of the educated Sudanese about the Sudan's share in the promises of the Atlantic Charter.

4. The drafters of the letter ignore the long years of India's painful progress to her present status; nor can they claim to represent the whole of the educated class, itself a small, if powerful, because the only self-conscious, section of general public opinion. From information so far at my disposal it is clear that many sections even of the educated class, whether members of the congress or not, have been alarmed and indignant at the tone and content of the letter. There can be little doubt that were there any effective method of mobilising the general opinion of the backbone of the country—the tribal leaders and their people, the merchant class and the older and more stable executive officials—it would be found to be in robust condemnation of the document. It is also noteworthy that the letter was viewed unfavourably by the leading Egyptians in the Sudan, who regarded it as further proof of their suspicion that the congress was a Government-inspired movement designed to counteract Egyptian plans for the ultimate fusion of the Sudan with Egypt. To allay these suspicions the congress felt it necessary on their own volition to call upon the Egyptian Grand Kadi and Inspector-General of Irrigation[2] and to give a reassuring explanation of the contents and purpose of their letter. The drafters have been scared by their own boldness and it is to be hoped that a period of sanity will supervene. Yet the letter is itself evidence of the evolution of a genuine Sudanese nationalist feeling which must be taken more and more into consideration by the Sudan Government in its domestic policy (even though the Government does not accept this particular body as the legitimate mouthpiece of Sudanese nationalism) and which must be recognised by His Majesty's Government as the preponderating factor under the treaty in post-war negotiations with Egypt.

5. As for the immediate future, I enclose a copy of a directive which my civil secretary has addressed to all Governors and heads of departments. In brief, my attitude is that the onus is now on the congress to show evidence of its good faith by taking practical steps to put its house in order; and that, in such an event, the Sudan Government would not, if approached, withhold its advice.

6. I may perhaps not unsuitably close this despatch by quoting a recent remark of the Sudan's leading personality, El Sayed Sir Abdel Rahman-el-Mahdi Pasha—"After this war Egypt will claim the reward of her loyalty and her services. The loyalty of the Sudan has been greater than Egypt's, her services more direct. Do not again therefore reward Egypt at our expense, and do not forget that we also will claim our recompense."

Enclosure 2 to 1: letter from Ibrahim Ahmad to Sir H Huddleston, 3 Apr 1942

The Graduates' Congress has the honour to submit to your Excellency, in your capacity of representative of both the Government of His Majesty King George VI and of the Government of His Majesty King Farouk I, the following memorandum which expresses the desire of the Sudanese people at the present time:—

---

[2] Sheikh Hasan Mamun, grand qadi of the Sudan, 1941–1947; Abd al-Razik abd al-Qadir Bey, inspector-general of the Egyptian Irrigation Department in the Sudan, 1941–1943.

The world developments and the events of the present war have inspired the nations with a strong desire to assure humanitarian justice and the freedom of peoples; this has been expressed in the statements of British politicians and recorded in the agreements of democratic leaders.

The Sudanese people, as one of the peoples who have co-operated with the British Empire since the outbreak of the war, is fully cognisant of its rights as a nation seeking life, after years spent under an orderly Government. The congress, which represents enlightened public opinion, and which is itself one of the "ripe fruits" of the condominium, feels its great responsibilities towards its country and all its countrymen.

The congress, therefore, submits this memorandum, hoping that it will meet with the consideration it deserves and expecting that it will be welcome. The congress is confident that this memorandum expresses faithfully the inclinations and aspirations of this country:—

(1) The issue, on the first possible opportunity, by the British and Egyptian Governments, of a joint declaration, granting the Sudan, in its geographical boundaries, the right of self-determination, directly after this war; this right to be safeguarded by guarantees assuring full liberty of expression in connexion therewith; as well as guarantees assuring the Sudanese the right of determining their natural rights with Egypt in a special agreement between the Egyptian and Sudanese nations.

(2) The formation of a representative body of Sudanese to approve the budget and the ordinances.

(3) The formation of a Higher Educational Council, composed of a Sudanese majority, and the devoting of a minimum of 12 per cent. of the budget for education.

(4) The separation of the judiciary from the Executive.

(5) The abolition of ordinances on closed areas, and the lifting of restrictions placed on trade and on the movements of the Sudanese within the Sudan.

(6) The promulgation of legislation defining Sudanese nationality.

(7) The stopping of immigration, except within the limits agreed upon in the Anglo–Egyptian Treaty.

(8) The termination of the Sudan Plantations Syndicate contract at its expiration.

(9) The carrying out of the principle of the welfare of the Sudanese and their priority to Government posts as follows:—

(a) By giving the Sudanese an opportunity to share effectively in ruling the country; this is to be attained by the appointment of Sudanese in posts of political responsibility, in all the main branches of the Government.

(b) By limiting the appointments to Government posts to Sudanese.

As regards posts for which it is necessary to appoint non-Sudanese, they shall be filled with persons serving on definite term contracts; in the meantime Sudanese to be trained to fill the posts at the expiration of the contract.

(10) The Sudanese to be enabled to exploit the commercial, agricultural and industrial resources of the country.

(11) The promulgation of an ordinance imposing on companies and commercial firms the obligation of reserving a reasonable proportion of their posts for the Sudanese.

(12) The cancellation of subventions to missionary schools and the unification of syllabus in the Northern and Southern Sudan.

These are the requests which, if answered, we consider will satisfy the desires of the Sudanese at the present time. The congress looks forward to your help and hope to be fortunate enough to receive a reply indicating that these requests have been approved of and are being carried out.

Enclosure 3 to 1: letter from D Newbold to Ibrahim Ahmad, 29 Apr 1942

I am directed by his Excellency the Governor-General to inform you that he has read your memorandum dated the 3rd April, 1942. He observes that many of your requests directly concern the status and Constitution of the Sudan. This Constitution, based on the Condominium Agreement of 1899 and the Anglo–Egyptian Treaty of 1936 and implemented by the appropriate legislation, cannot be altered save by a joint act of the Condominium Powers. The Sudan Government is not prepared to discuss its revision with any body of persons. If, however, the Condominium Powers at any time decide to review the agreement or treaty, the Sudan Government would hope to consult responsible Sudanese opinion. The Government, however, can make no promises to any body of persons in the name of the Condominium Powers or in its own.

You will further recollect that Sir A. Gillan,[3] in his letter dated the 22nd May, 1938, to the president of the Graduates' Congress stated that he would be prepared to receive communications from the congress on such matters as came within its purview, and he noted that the congress did not claim to represent the views of any but its own members. I must also ask you to re-read my letter to you dated the 30th October, 1940, and particularly paragraph 11,[4] in which I stated that in claiming to represent all the Sudanese and in attempting to turn itself into a political national body, the Graduates' Congress not only could not retain the co-operation of Government but could not hope for continuance of recognition. By the very act of submitting the memorandum which is the subject of this letter, and by its wording, the congress has fallen into both these errors against which I warned it and has accordingly forfeited the confidence of Government. There can be no restoration of that confidence until the congress has so reorganised the direction of its affairs that the Government can rely on having its wishes respected and its warnings observed.

For the above reasons his Excellency finds himself unable to accept your memorandum, which is therefore returned to you herewith.

His Excellency desires me to add that he and his advisers are fully aware of the needs of the Sudan and of the natural and legitimate desire of the enlightened Sudanese for an increasing participation in the Government and development of their country. To this end the Sudan Government is constantly studying and carrying out plans for the closer association of the Sudanese with the direction of their affairs and for the general welfare and orderly development of this country and its people.

---

[3] Sir Angus Gillan, civil secretary, 1934–1939. For civil secretary to honorary secretary, Graduates' Congress, 22 May 1938 see National Records Office, Khartoum, Misc 1/98/1540, quoted in A A M Abu Hasabu, *Factional conflict in the Sudanese nationalist movement 1918–1948* (Khartoum, 1985) pp 86–87.

[4] Sir K D D Henderson, *The making of the modern Sudan: the life and letters of Sir Douglas Newbold, KBE* (London, 1953) p 538.

The congress, however, must realise that it is the duty and business of the Sudan Government alone, having paramount regard to is tutelary obligations to the people of the Sudan, and in consultation if need be with the Governments of the two partners in the condominium, to decide the pace at which this association and this development shall proceed. It is the earnest wish of the Government that the educated classes of the country should show themselves fitted and able to take their proper share in the administration of internal affairs, but any advance to such a position must be most seriously embarrassed and delayed unless the congress realise clearly once and for all that the Government must and will insist that the congress confine itself to the internal and domestic affairs of the Sudan and renounce any claim, real or implied, to be the mouthpiece of the whole country.

In conclusion his Excellency desires me to say that he deeply regrets that you should have seen fit to take so hasty a step as the submission of this memorandum.

Enclosure 4 to 1: memorandum on Sudanese nationalism and the Graduates' Congress

The first expression of Sudanese nationalism was the violent Egyptian-inspired movement of 1919–24. The failure of this movement led to a re-orientation of national feeling under the slogan—"The Sudan for the Sudanese."

The new nationalism aimed at autonomous development by peaceful means and in co-operation with the Sudan Government. The Graduates' Congress is its first organised expression.

2. The growing political consciousness of the educated Sudanese was sharply stimulated by the conclusion of the Anglo–Egyptian Treaty in 1936. Sudanese Nationalists, while accepting the treaty, resented the fact that it had been concluded without any reference to the Sudanese themselves. They also resented the appearance of the Egyptians in the new guise of equal partners with the British, demanding not independence for Egypt and the Sudan as one entity, but equal rights with the British over the Sudan. They felt that it was up to them to show the condominium partners that the Sudan was no longer a passive body whose destiny could be shaped without reference to its own wishes. It was necessary to establish the existence of a corporate Sudanese national consciousness before the treaty came up for re-consideration after a period of twenty-five years and to form an organisation to be the focus and expression of this national feeling within the framework of the treaty and under the aegis of the Sudan Government.

Since the welfare of the Sudanese was declared in the treaty to be the principal aim of the Condominium Government, the educated Sudanese felt they were entitled to share in its implementation.

3. The first concrete idea of calling a general meeting of graduates of schools above elementary standard in order to elect a representative body was mooted in the summer of 1937 and the first meeting of congress, on the 12th February, 1938, was attended by just over 1,000 graduates (roughly one-fifth of the entire educated class). These elected a body of sixty to form a sort of parliament, and the sixty in turn elected an executive committee of fifteen. The aims of the congress as defined at its first meeting were:—

(i) To formulate and express a collective point of view representing graduate opinion.

(ii) To promote a national consciousness by combating partisanship and tribalism.
(iii) To lay the foundation of sound national life by carrying out a programme of social reform.

The first act of the new congress was to send a copy of its constitution to the Governor of Khartoum. The second, after lengthy deliberations and not without some trepidation, was the despatch of a letter to the civil secretary, on the 2nd May, 1938, in which it was stated that the graduates were prompted by a sense of duty towards their country and by a desire to co-operate with the Government, "in such ways as may be opened to them" in furthering its welfare.

They defined their duties as being concerned with:—

(i) Social reform and other internal matters lying outside the orbit of official Government concern.
(ii) Matters of public interest lying within the scope of Government policy.

They promised friendly co-operation and obedience to the law in the former sphere and expressed the hope that the Government would give consideration to their views and suggestions in the latter. They denied any claim to a position "prejudicial to that of important elements in the country," but claimed a peculiar position "as its only educated element." They expressed the hope that the Government would abandon its habit of taking the advice of individual educated Sudanese and instead consult them as a separate body.

The civil secretary, in reply, noted their desires with sympathy, and promised careful consideration of any communications which he might receive from congress, on the definite understanding that "the congress was neither seeking formal recognition as a political body nor claiming to represent the views of any but its own members, but wished to be regarded as a semi-public organisation interested in philanthropic and public affairs." He also pointed out that the inclusion in its membership of a number of Government officials must preclude participation in any line of action likely to bring it into conflict with Government policy or with constitutional authority.

4. The first public act of the new congress was to prove typical of future mistakes. It became involved, by pressure of extremist opinion amongst the younger Sudanese officials, in a controversy which arose in the summer of 1938 over the issue of revised regulations governing leave and Government cadres. Notes were submitted to the civil secretary, who replied that "in no circumstances could the Government allow such matters (*i.e.*, the contractual relationship between itself and its officials) to be the subject of negotiation or discussion with the Graduates' Congress." At the same time measures were being taken, through the proper channels, to investigate the causes of complaint. This reply had a markedly depressing effect on the Committee of Fifteen, who took the view that the position of Sudanese in Government service was a matter of public interest, and not merely of contractual relationship, and that if this was to be the Government's attitude towards their submissions, congress might as well disband. However, the agitation died down and congress busied itself for some time with its own internal organisation.

5. The annual general meeting of 1939 showed a considerable drop in attendance and subscribing membership, and the younger extremists began to agitate for bolder

action and younger representation on the committee. They were successful only in persuading it to send a stupid telegram to the Governor-General over a personal incident between the Sheikh of the Ulema and a British official in Omdurman.

In April of that year the Committee of Fifteen submitted to the civil secretary a well-worded and reasonable memorandum containing recommendations for the reform of the Omdurman Maahad. Although this action was marred by the simultaneous publication of the memorandum in the vernacular press, it was generally regarded as the most concrete and useful thing congress had achieved to date, and the Government indicated its appreciation.

A second memorandum, on education in the Sudan, was presented later in the year and was acknowledged by the civil secretary as "a constructive contribution to a problem vitally affecting the Sudan."

Shortly afterwards the Committee of Fifteen accepted an informal Government invitation to nominate four persons to co-operate with nominated British officials in the foundation of the Sudan Cultural Centre.

6. On the outbreak of war with Germany congress addressed a message of loyalty to the Governor-General and issued an appeal to the Sudanese people urging support of the Government and of the Allied cause.

The extremists, however, were still restive at the Government's refusal to acknowledge the principle of collective consultation. They tried again, still unsuccessfully, to secure the election of an extremist committee in 1940, and the general feeling of lack of achievement to date caused a further drop in membership.

The annual general meeting rejected proposals that:—

(i) Congress members should ask for the substitution of the word "Sudanese" for the tribal designation in their service dossiers; and
(ii) Individual consultation of congress members should be banned.

7. The visit of the Egyptian Prime Minister, Ali Maher Pasha, in February 1940 was made an opportunity for demonstrating congress solidarity at a tea-party in the Sudan Schools Club. The president delivered a carefully worded speech, in which he made it clear that the Sudanese did not regard themselves as Egyptians, but as a separate and autonomous entity that wished to develop along its own lines in co-operation and friendship with Egypt.

This meeting won congress a renewed prestige in the Sudan and convinced Egyptian opinion that it was the embryo of a genuine Sudanese Nationalist movement in which Egypt must take a sympathetic interest.

It had the further effect of encouraging congress to use its Egyptian relations as a useful tactical means of obtaining great recognition from the Sudan Government. A request for financial assistance for various social projects addressed to "The Egyptian People through Ali Maher Pasha," and handed to Ali Maher before his departure, earned a severe reprimand from the civil secretary, who intimated that if congress continued to listen to its extremist element the Government might have to demand the withdrawal of its serving officials from membership and possibly dissolve congress altogether. In spite of this the congress maintained contact with Ali Maher by an exchange of telegrams on various occasions, suitable and otherwise.

8. This rebuff was followed by an improvement in relations, and when Italy declared war on the Allies three senior members of the Committee of Fifteen were included in the assembly of notables and leaders summoned to hear the Governor-

General read his proclamation on the 11th June. Elated by this recognition, the congress asked permission to broadcast a message from Omdurman, addressed to "The People of the Sudan." Permission was granted on condition that it should be addressed, not to The People of the Sudan, but to "Members and Friends of Congress." This was received badly; and as an indirect result the extremists later secured the defeat of the Committee of Fifteen for having agreed to co-operate with the Broadcasting Service in preparing its cultural programmes without specific recognition of the corporate entity of the congress. The new committee tried to impose a ban on any congress member broadcasting in his private capacity. It sponsored a suggestion in the press that no congress member should volunteer for national service without congress permission. It urged the inclusion of other classes of the community in order to make the congress truly national, and the adoption of a National Anthem and a National Flag. These activities culminated in the sending of a farewell telegram to Sir Stewart Symes[5] "in the name of the whole country."

In a letter dated the 30th October, 1940, the civil secretary drew attention to these breaches of the understanding on which Congress had been founded and announced the withdrawal of Government sympathy. This resulted in apologies, protestations of goodwill and promises of future good behaviour. Nevertheless, at the annual meeting in January 1941 the president[6] boasted of having removed the grievances of certain students, settled a labour dispute and intervened with the Government on behalf of dismissed railway workers—on all of which issues he had, in fact, been severely reprimanded. He further added that he and the committee had succeeded in removing the "misapprehensions" apparent in the civil secretary's letter of the 30th October, 1940—a statement far removed from the truth.

Fortunately, the new committee contained a fair proportion of senior and moderate graduates, who soon gave earnest of a desire to improve relations with the Government. It abandoned the obstructive attitude of its predecessor over broadcasting and launched an education day scheme, by which it hoped to win pubic approval without incurring Government hostility. It continued, however, to flirt with Egypt.

9. During 1941 the number of subscribing members rose to the record figure of 1,390. The new president for 1942, Ibrahim Ahmed, was, however, a better and abler man that [sic] his predecessor and showed a welcome readiness to co-operate and to take advice.

The programme for the New Year ranged over a wide field from education, village reform and co-operative societies, to the problem of the Southern Sudan and the question of Sudanese nationality.

The education day scheme has been a considerable success and is regarded by the Sudan Government as the kind of effort into which congress energies should most desirably be canalised. All possible assistance has been given.

10. It was therefore the more disturbing that this comparatively moderate committee with its enlightened president should have been stampeded into addressing to the Governor-General a letter containing extravagant and ill-considered claims for immediate Sudanese autonomy after the war. Although as is usual, considerable fear of the consequences has supervened since the letter had been sent, and at least one of the drafters was prompt with verbal assurances that it did not mean what it said, nevertheless, in the interval between the receipt of the

[5] Sir Stewart Symes, governor-general of the Sudan, 1934–1940.

[6] Ismail al-Azhari.

letter and the issue of a reply congress has again blundered by instituting a branch committee in Cairo without previous consultation with the Sudan Government. A warning letter on this subject has been addressed to the president and a copy is attached to this memorandum.

Extract from circular note by D Newbold to all governors and all heads of department, 2 May 1942[7]

... 3. The following is for your guidance should your Mamurs, Sheikhs, Notables, Effendia (whether members of Congress or not) and others refer either to the Memorandum or to the future of the Congress:

(i) You should decline to discuss the contents of the Memorandum in any way whatever. Even those of the 12 points which by themselves might have been unobjectionable are contaminated so long as they are associated with the Memorandum and as such are not for discussion. His Excellency has given his reply, the Memorandum has been returned and the matter is closed.

(ii) The Government's attitude towards Congress is that they have deliberately and after due warning forfeited its confidence. The onus is now on them to show their good faith by so amending their Constitution and reorganising their machinery that the repetition of such an incident will be impossible. To do this in such a way as to restore the confidence of the Government they would have to convince the Government

(a) that they are dropping any claim to be the mouthpiece of the whole country;

(b) that they are ensuring that their future communications to the Government will represent the considered views of the majority of their members, and not merely of a caucus or Committee;

(c) that they intend to confine themselves in their representations to the Government to internal administrative and social issues, except where those issues have been the subject of specific agreements with other Governments;

(iii) Should they show a genuine desire to put their house in order on these lines the Government would not refuse to give them reasonable help and advice during the process.

[7] This document was included in those forwarded by Lampson, but was not printed and circulated along with the preceding set of enclosures.

2 FO 371/31587, no 2664 26 May 1942

'The Sudan': minute by P S Scrivener to Sir M Peterson on the Anglo–Egyptian treaty[1]

The treaty consecrates present arrangements for administering the Sudan while reserving the question of sovereignty for the future. This shelving of the essential question has clearly been necessary heretofore, since we were not prepared to recognise Egyptian sovereignty, and they were not prepared to recognise ours, while the Sudanese were in an entirely "pre-national" stage. When negotiations were first

[1] This minute, originally drafted in the anticipation that the newly installed Wafd government would shortly raise the treaty issue, was copied from FO 371/31571, no 2192 and added to the other documents on the Sudanese Graduates' Congress in jacket 2664 (see Scrivener's minute, 3).

mooted the Sudan had been recovered for little more than a quarter of a century. It has now been under civilised administration for nearer half a century, and, though the growth is slow, the beginnings of national feeling are clearly perceptible. A possible solution would be to exchange Egyptian sovereignty over Cyrenaica for exclusive British sovereignty over the Sudan, but if we are to live up to the spirit of the Atlantic Charter, this would be a retrograde step. It would equally be a retrograde step for Egypt to claim sole sovereignty over the Sudan and it would be very unwelcome to the Sudanese. In fact we can adopt the Egyptians' slogan as our own for the future "complete independence for Egypt and the Sudan" (which in Egyptian eyes meant Egyptian domination of the Sudan). The logical solution of the problem is to vest sovereignty in the Sudanese themselves. For the time being (probably for another generation at least) they will be unable to exercise it, and must therefore continue to rely on British (and Egyptian) guidance, while Egyptian rights in the Nile must continue to be guaranteed.

The obvious practical difficulty in the way of such a solution is to discover some person or body in whom Sudanese sovereignty can be vested. At present there would appear to be none. There are two "Popes" (the Mahdi and Sayid Ali Morghani) but no lay potentate and no body or assembly of any kind. It does not, however, follow that none could be found or created.

The Sudan Government have at present a very progressive Civil Secretary,[2] who on February 9th wrote as follows:—

> "I think we must start *now* taking note of the Atlantic Charter. Intelligentsia here and elsewhere will naturally want to cash in on it and the vernacular press in Khartoum and W. Africa is already doing so. So is India. We must start now clarifying and intensifying our plans for (1) local government in towns, which is far behind tribal local government (2) Sudanese dilution of the British cadre which means the proper use and after-care of Higher School graduates and (3) Sudanese association with central government. I am preparing a note on all this and will send you a copy. I'm sure its [sic] wrong to retard education or self-government in colonies, because of the war. Its [sic] the worst kind of propaganda: rather we should accelerate it. Plain acts and facts carry the day with the educated classes who distrust vague post-dated pledges. We are still in the Golden Age in the Sudan with no communal problems (as India) no racial problems (as Palestine) no settlers (as Kenya) no poor whites (as S. Africa) no slums or trades unions (as W. Indies). Our only distraction is external, i.e. Egypt, and as Sudanese self-government grows, the danger of Egyptian penetration should recede. So we should act while we still have time and not wait for internal or external pressures."[3]

If we took the initiative in asking for the revision of the Sudanese clauses of the treaty, I think we should frighten Nahas off pretty effectively, but it is a big step and calls for very mature consideration.

I should like to go into the matter with Mr. Mayall (Sudan Government Office) who is a member of the Political Service of many years' standing and a former Governor of the Gezira.

---

[2]D Newbold.

[3]D Newbold to R C Mayall, 9 Feb 1942, in K D D Henderson, *The making of the modern Sudan: the life and letters of Sir Douglas Newbold, KBE* (London, 1953) p 233. See also 7.

3 FO 371/31587, no 2664 12–13 June 1942

[Sudanese self-government]: minutes by D S Laskey[1] and P S Scrivener [Extract]

Self-government for the Sudan must be our long-term aim, though it will probably not be attainable for one or more generations. Congress, for all its shortcomings, does more or less represent the class from which the country's future rulers will have to be drawn, but it is clear that they are as yet quite unqualified for such responsibility. It is of course true that people cannot be taught a sense of responsibility unless they are first given responsibility, but the Sudan Gov. are well aware of this and have never shrunk from delegating authority and entrusting powers to the Sudanese, if necessary on an experimental basis, as soon as they think is justified.

One of the biggest steps towards self-government will be to obtain independence for the Sudan from Egypt and this need not wait until the Sudanese are ready for autonomy. The possibility of including it in the post-war settlement is already under consideration but no detailed plans can be made until the end of the war and the circumstances that will then exist are more clearly in sight. . . .[2]

D.S.L.
12.6.42

This is a very interesting development. I heard of it first of all from Mr Mayall, with whom I have discussed (privately) a recent minute I wrote on the Sudan question (copy at back).[3] When I wrote that minute I was unaware of these developments.

It seems to me that the Sudan Govt have handled the Congress very wisely. They have, on occasions, given them proper encouragement; they have been studiously polite: but have reacted with uncompromising firmness to attempts to arrogate to Congress a position to which it has no right to pretend.

The attitude of Egyptian political circles is very significant. . . .

P.S.
13.6.42

---

[1]Then second secretary in the FO.
[2]Marginal note by Scrivener: 'No: but we can start thinking about it—& are doing so.' [3]See 2.

4 FO 371/31587, no 4288 17 July 1942

[Sudanese Graduates' Congress]: letter from D Newbold to Ibrahim Ahmad

I should like to record that we had a conversation yesterday about the subject matter of the letters exchanged between the Government and the Graduates' Congress. I hope that the present position is now clear to you and that you will be able to make it equally clear to your Committee.

I explained to you why the Government wrote these two letters and that it meant what it said, and that these letters stand. At the same time, besides explaining the reasons for the Government's attitude, I took the opportunity to emphasise that the Government is not actuated by any hostility to the educated classes, and I write you this letter to reassure you and your Committee of this. The increase of the Sudanese share in Government and the giving of greater responsibilities to Sudanese are still fundamental points of Government policy. Active steps are in fact being taken for their further application, but I wish to record that, while announcements of Government policy are and will continue to be made from time to time, it is obviously right that they should be made to the public of the Sudan rather than to a particular section. I have also said that the Government is always anxious to maintain constant contact with responsible Sudanese opinion, whether it be through the administrative or religious leaders of the people, or senior Sudanese Government officials, or the Executive Committee of the Graduates' Congress (which, I know, represents a considerable body of educated opinion), or other representative bodies. The contact is in fact kept by a combination of all of these.

At the same time, I have explained to you the Government's objections to Government servants indulging in public political controversy, and the reasons why Congress cannot be recognised as a political body. Until such time as adequate machinery exists for the official representation of Sudanese opinion in matters of policy, there is no objection, as I have said, to Sudanese leaders of opinion and responsible Government officials, whether members of Congress or not, making known to Government their views on matters of policy by personal approach or private delegation. But it is essential for the efficiency and reputation of Government that such communication should be strictly private and confidential. I have also reminded you that the *private* and reasonable discussion of political matters by Government servants is not and never has been prohibited in this country, provided it does not impair or prejudice their capacity loyally to carry out approved Government policy.

5 FO 371/31587, no 4388 — 23 July 1942

[Sudanese Graduates' Congress]: letter (reply) Ibrahim Ahmad to D Newbold

I thank you for your letter of 17th July, 1942,[1] and the Congress is glad to express its satisfaction at the friendly spirit that characterised your conversation with its representatives on the 16th July, 1942, in which you assured them that the Government was sympathetic to the hopes and aspirations of Congress.

We are also glad to refer to what was said in your conversation and in the conversations that took place between the Deputy Civil Secretary, Mr. Penney,[2] and the President of the Congress, to the effect that the tendencies and wishes of the Government were not in conflict with the hopes of the Congress for the progress of the Sudan and its future. This was suggested in those conversations by the following:—

---

[1] See 4.

[2] J C Penney, Sudan government service 1925–1945; director of public security and commissioner of prisons, civil secretary's office, 1937–1942; commissioner of police and prisons, civil secretary's office, 1942–1945.

The consultation of the Sudanese when the Anglo–Egyptian Treaty is reconsidered.

Increasing the Sudanese share of responsibility in the administration of their country's public affairs by endeavouring to set up a representative advisory Sudanese body, and by increasing the number of responsible Sudanese posts in the Government.

Since the realisation of the demands embodied in its Memorandum was one of the aspirations of the Congress, the Congress has pleasure in expressing its gratification, since it sees from the aggregate of conversations and letters that followed it—although they were not free from certain differences of opinion—that the Government is concerned to realise some of our wishes. We shall therefore await with interest such practical steps as will accompany the Government's good intentions in the execution of the policy which the Government affirmed that it was pursuing.

The Congress hopes, however—seeing that you have expressed the Government's sincere wish that contact should continue between it and the Congress—that this contact will lead to complete understanding on all its demands, as it also hopes that it will be given the opportunity, at the proper time and before the details have been settled, to express its opinion on the important matters which we learned from our conversations were now under consideration.

In conclusion we hope that future steps by the Government and the Congress will help to build up and strengthen a spirit of real understanding based on a sound realisation of the intentions of the Government and the wishes of the Sudanese.

6 FO 371/31587, no 3736 1 Sept 1942

'The Sudan': memorandum by the Egyptian Department, FO, on the Anglo–Egyptian treaty

1. The position of the Sudan under the Anglo–Egyptian Treaty of the 26th August, 1936, is regulated by Article 11, which runs as follows:—

Article 11

1. While reserving liberty to conclude new conventions in future, modifying the agreements of the 19th January and the 10th July, 1899, the High Contracting Parties agree that the administration of the Sudan shall continue to be that resulting from the said agreements. The Governor-General shall continue to exercise on the joint behalf of the High Contracting Parties the powers conferred upon him by the said agreements.

The High Contracting Parties agree that the primary aim of their administration in the Sudan must be the welfare of the Sudanese.

Nothing in this article prejudices the question of sovereignty over the Sudan.

2. Appointments and promotions of officials in the Sudan will in consequence remain vested in the Governor-General, who, in making new appointments to posts for which qualified Sudanese are not available, will select suitable candidates of British and Egyptian nationality.

3. In addition to Sudanese troops, both British and Egyptian troops shall be placed at the disposal of the Governor-General for the defence of the Sudan.

4. Egyptian immigration into the Sudan shall be unrestricted except for reasons of public order and health.

5. There shall be no discrimination in the Sudan between British subjects and Egyptian nationals in matters of commerce, immigration or the possession of property.

6. The High Contracting Parties are agreed on the provisions set out in the Annex to this Article as regards the method by which international conventions are to be made applicable to the Sudan.

2. The Department have been considering, in consequence of a rather diffident attempt by Nahas Pasha to raise the Sudan question, whether any advance on the state of affairs consecrated by this article is likely to be possible at the end of the war, and it may be worth while to place on record the conclusions which they have reached.

3. In the analysis of the Anglo–Egyptian Treaty contained in the "British Year Book of International Law" 1937, the following footnote appears on the question of Sovereignty over the Sudan:—

> "This has been a subject of dispute, Egypt contending that sovereignty over the Sudan remained vested wholly in Egypt, whose territory it originally was and in whose name it was recovered, and that the condominium agreements only provided for a method of administration leaving the sovereignty untouched. The United Kingdom contends that sovereignty cannot be divorced from administration in this way but lies where the responsibility for administration is situated, and that since this was shared, so was the sovereignty. The question is largely academic when the method of administration is agreed, and turns as much upon differences of view as to the criteria for sovereignty under international law as upon divergencies as to the position with regard to the Sudan itself."

4. The only method of dealing, hitherto, with this intractable question of sovereignty over the Sudan has been the unconstructive one of shelving it. But in fact no other solution was possible. His Majesty's Government were not prepared to recognise Egyptian sovereignty since, to quote Lord Cromer, it is "essential that British influence should in practice be paramount in the Sudan, in order that the Egyptians should not have conferred on them a 'bastard freedom' to repeat the misgovernment of the past". Moreover, any such admission of Egyptian sovereignty would tend to prejudice a policy of ultimate Sudanese independence (see paragraph 9 below). Equally, the Egyptians, with their cry of "complete independence for Egypt and the Sudan" (as a combined entity) were not prepared to recognise British sovereignty. The Sudanese themselves were (and are) in an entirely "pre-national" stage and quite incapable of exercising sovereignty, in any modern sense, on their own account.

5. Our conclusion is that although the intentions of His Majesty's Government and the Egyptian Government as regards the future can be restated with greater precision and in a more satisfactory fashion, it will not be possible for many years to establish a new regime.

6. One suggestion which has been put forward is that Egypt should be given sovereignty over Cyrenaica in return for the recognition of exclusive British sovereignty over the Sudan. This is at first sight an attractive arrangement, and it would be welcomed by almost the entire *tribal* Sudan (insofar as it conveyed any sense of change at all beyond the removal from the picture of a rather shadowy King of Egypt) and by a considerable proportion of the intelligentsia. But whether such a bargain could be struck or not depends—apart from Egypt's willingness to accept it—on the future colonial policy which will ultimately be worked out by the United Nations—and more particularly H.M. Govt. and the U.S. Govt.—in the light of the Atlantic Charter. And it would be calculated to focus, and to give an undesirable impetus to, more extreme national movements within the Sudan itself. The formation of one such movement is, and has been for some years, an accomplished fact. The so-called "Graduates Congress" recently summoned the authorities concerned to grant the Sudan "self-determination" at the end of the war, (and was snubbed by the Sudan Government who very properly decline to recognise any generally representative status in a body which only represents a fraction of the urban intelligentsia). This event is a portent, the meaning of which is perfectly plain.[1]

7. The handing over of the Sudan to Egypt remains as inacceptable as ever, and we are therefore left (assuming the rejection of the idea of sole British sovereignty) with the possibilities of the Sudan as an independent country.

8. There are two decisive reasons why the Sudan cannot be left to its own devices at present:—

(a) It is not yet sufficiently advanced in political development or education to stand alone in the modern world. It is still necessary to find a synthesis between the intelligentsia and the tribal leaders, to create a national consciousness, and to associate the best elements thus thrown up more closely with the Government of the country. To these tasks the Sudan Government is very much alive, and it is addressing itself to them in a thoroughly progressive spirit, but their completion cannot be expected in any immediate future.

(b) The cleavage (which is bound to become more and more marked) between the Northern and Southern Sudan. To the profound racial difference between the two parts of the country has now been added as deep a cleavage in religion and lines of development. In the southern (pagan) areas, the inhabitants are being educated by

[1] J E Coulson (then acting first secretary in the FO) minuted on 3 Sept: 'The suggestion that we might hand over Cyrenaica to Egypt in return for exclusive rights in the Sudan has something to commend it, but I rather fear that the woolly idealists, who will be our chief critics whatever post-war settlement is reached, would be very disturbed by this sort of political barter which might appear purely opportunist.' Scrivener replied on 5 Sept: 'I think that the immediate dangers foreseen by Mr Coulson are rather more apparent than real. It would be useful at some stage to have an opinion whether the "idealists" are likely to prevail, or not ...' Sir M Peterson (superintending under-secretary of state for the Egyptian Dept) minuted on 6 Sept, '... I don't altogether like your para. 6. So far as we've got in consideration of post-war arrangements, in the Pacific, and elsewhere, is that we are all agreed that the object to work for—the lowest common denominator as it were between U.S. policy and our own—is to secure independent British administration of our colonial territories subject to international supervision (but not international control). From this point of view I don't think that undivided British sovereignty over the Sudan would be a breach of the Atlantic Charter. Or do you mean that the taking over of Cyrenaica by Egypt would be a breach? If so, haven't we got to find *some* solution for Cyrenaica?'. Scrivener replied: 'No. I think this is the solution for Cyrenaica in *any* case' (FO 371/31587, no 3736).

missionary bodies and are thus being Christianised, while in the northern areas the population has been and will be Moslem, with a Moslem system of education. In the north, Arabic is and will remain the *lingua franca*; in the south, it will be English. Were the Sudan now to be established as an independent country, the primitive south would be overwhelmed—and indeed more or less enslaved—by the more sophisticated Arab north whose predatory instincts, if held completely in check by the present regime, are by no means yet dead. Clearly such a development could not be contemplated by His Majesty's Government. In the realm of speculation it seems likely that in the fullness of time the Sudan will split in two. The north may well become an independent Arab state, and the south may join the British East African system, certain parts of which it will shortly begin to resemble.

9. The only concrete suggestion which we can put forward at the moment is that, if and when the Anglo–Egyptian treaty comes under review, a provision on the following lines should be inserted after sub-paragraph 1 of the present Article 11:—

> "The High Contracting Parties declare that it is their common intention that, as soon as circumstances permit, the Sudan shall become a fully independent state, exercising full rights of sovereignty; and that the administration of the Sudan, exercised as provided in the preceding paragraph, shall be directed towards the fulfilment of this aim."[2]

10. The Egyptians may profoundly dislike this suggestion. In the recent past they have blocked proposals tending to treat the Sudan as a kind of state so that, in connexion with the representation of the Sudan at international conferences (Article 11 (6)) it became necessary to consider treating the Sudan as a joint colony for the purpose of carrying out the Annex to this article. But it is difficult to see what really convincing *long-term* arguments the Egyptians can adduce against the new clause suggested above.

---

[2]Coulson minuted on 3 Sept: 'Unless we are pressed very hard, it might be somewhat dangerous to volunteer the declaration suggested in paragraph 9, in view of the linguistic and religious split between the two halves of the Sudan. Such a declaration might unnecessarily tend to perpetuate a union which in later times might be found impracticable' (FO 371/31587, no 3736).

7 FO 371/31587, no 4388 10 Sept 1942

'Note on further association of Sudanese with local and central government in the Sudan': note by D Newbold on devolution to the Governor-General's Council

[In his response to Lampson Sir A Cadogan commented that the following note reached broadly the same conclusions as the FO and he 'unhesitatingly' accepted the civil secretary's proposals for Sudanisation (Cadogan to Lampson, 2 Nov 1942). Newbold's note was passed on to the CO for their information. Scrivener minuted, 29 Oct: '... the Civil Secretary's note on Sudanisation ... contains an acute—indeed a brilliant—appreciation of the whole situation. I should like to see this document printed & placed in the hands of the C.O. *and* the Americans, but it would require a little preliminary editing—not that that need present any difficulty. I would further observe that the cleavage between the Northern & Southern Sudan to which attention is drawn in J3736[1] emerges clearly in these papers, & not least from the fact that most of Mr. Newbold's recommendations are, in terms, only applicable to the northern provinces—but this by the way'. It was decided, however, not to include any mention of developments in the Sudan in the statement by the secretary of state for colonies on the Empire, 'since the Sudan is not an integral part of the Empire (but a dominion of ourselves & Egypt jointly) and a terrible commotion would ensue in Cairo if such a thing happened. But it is a pity that we can't!' (minute by Scrivener, 28 Nov 1942, FO 371/31587, no 4388).]

1. During the five years immediately before the present war the Northern Sudan was moving out of what may be called the "Arcadian Period" of comparatively simple administration into a period of accelerated economic and educational development, accompanied by social and political problems of greater complexity. Factors contributing to this were:—

(i) the rising prosperity of the country after the economic depression of 1931.

(ii) the adoption of the Substitution Grade for Sudanese in 1935, designed for posts where Sudanese replace British staff of Division I, and rising to a salary maximum of £E.800. (N.B. Nearly 40 Sudanese have been promoted to S. grades to-date.)

(iii) the signing of the Anglo–Egyptian Treaty of 1936 with its emphasis on the Welfare of the Sudanese and on the prior claims of Sudanese to fill any posts in the Sudan Government for which they may be qualified.

(iv) the passing of the three Local Government Ordinances in 1937, covering Rural Areas, Townships and Municipalities.

(v) the publication in 1937 of the educational proposals of the de la Warr Commission.[2]

(vi) the formation of the Sudan Graduates' Congress in 1938.

2. During the first two years of war, the distractions of threatened and actual invasion, and the mobilisation of the Sudan's manpower and resources, followed by the Sudan's vigorous partnership in the Imperial conquest of the Italian East African Empire, diverted the minds of nearly all British officials and of most of the educated Sudanese from the political development of the Sudan. The Graduates' Congress, it is true, founded originally as a sort of Union of Educated Sudanese, with a programme ostensibly social and cultural, took on a stronger nationalist and political colour during 1940, but did not, until recently, embark on any definite political agitation or submit formally any wide political demands.

In the Provinces Local Government, rural and urban, moved along its statutory paths, at a reasonably fast tempo in the case of what is called 'Native Administration' (tribal federations, native courts, N.A. Budgets etc.) and at a regrettably slower pace in towns and municipalities. In early 1940 I tried to hasten the latter in a circular to Governors of the 6 Northern Provinces (CS/SCR/1.D.9 of 22/3/40) but the entry of Italy into the war shortly afterwards, and the depletion of political staff through war releases, prevented any substantial results. Moreover replies to the circular showed that it was by no means realised in several provinces that urban local government was in a sadly backward state.

---

[1] See 6, para 8(b).

[2] *Higher Education in East Africa: Report of the Commission appointed by the Secretary of State for the Colonies, September 1937* (Col No 142, 1937) [De La Warr Commission].

3. A strong stimulus, however, to political thinking in the Sudan was applied, in the winter of 1941 and spring of 1942, by,

(i) the promulgation of the Atlantic Charter in August 1941 with the consequent commentaries in the world's press and broadcasts, and the adherence to the Charter by the 26 Allied Nations proclaimed in January 1942.
(ii) Sir Stafford Cripps' spectacular mission to India, the effect of which was heightened by his passage through the Sudan, both going and returning, and the brief interview given by him on 15.4.42 to the two Editors of the Vernacular Press in which he said:—"We are all looking to the future. The Sudan is playing its part in the war effort very well, and this will gain it a place in the new era which we all hope to see in the world when we have finished with the evil forces. There are a lot of things to be done: and we must perhaps do them more quickly than we have in the past".

4. It was obvious that the Sudan, like other African dependencies, could not be oblivious to progressive trends of thought and declarations in Great Britain and the United States, and in February 1942 I began to study further lines of advance in associating the Sudanese (and especially the educated Sudanese) with local and central Government, and had begun to draft proposals when three things intervened to delay them:—

(i) large increases in the establishment and commitments of the Sudan Defence Force, and in the Sudan's obligations to develop still further our Lines of Communications to Middle East by air, river, road, and rail, threw more urgent war work on my office, and I had little spare time for political problems.
(ii) the fall of Malaya and Burma engendered a number of articles in the British, American, and Dominion Press, which were highly critical of British colonial administration in those areas and in general. These articles led to others, which, after the first reaction from defeat, became more objective in analysis of past, and proposals for future, policy, and also to a series of valuable debates in the Houses of Lords and Commons. I thought it right to secure these documents (Hansard, press-cuttings etc.) by air-bag through the London Office, and to sift and summarise them, before completing this memorandum.
(iii) the Graduates' Congress suddenly submitted on April 3rd 1942 their manifesto with its 12 demands, headed by a claim for the Sudanese to exercise self-determination after the war. This led to a rebuff by the Government, a second memorandum by the Congress, a further formal reply by Government, and several interviews and subsidiary letters.[3] A certain political agitation in Khartoum and some ill-advised speeches and "electioneering" in the Provinces accompanied this sequence of events, and raised, in an acute form, not only the undesirability of public servants (who form the great majority of the Graduates' Congress) actively participating in political controversy, but the whole question of relations between Government and the educated classes. It was manifestly impossible to study administrative and political reforms calmly, or to obtain objective British and Sudanese advice, while this Congress sandstorm was blowing and fogging the basic issue, which still lies before us, of how to meet adequately the legitimate and

[3] See 1, 4, 5, 8.

reasonable aspirations of the enlightened Sudanese, both in the towns and in the countryside, and including the more progressive tribal leaders and merchants as well as the mainly official class known as "effendia".

5. The six months' delay, however, in presenting the proposals outlined below, has actually been valuable not only because we now have a mass of evidence of the future trend of British colonial policy from trusteeship to partnership, but also because the episode of the Congress manifesto and succeeding exchanges has thrown into clearer relief the urgent need to get a closer relationship between British and Sudanese officials, to give clearer proofs of our devolutionary aims, and to conceive our trusteeship as that of a guardian for a ward who will eventually come of age. This need is genuine and should not be denied or obscured by the extravagant and ill-considered demands of a section of the educated Sudanese. Individual Sudanese officials or groups who overstep the political mark can be dealt with disciplinarily. The Congress itself has received a damaging rebuff. The Administrative Regulations limiting political activities of public servants have been reaffirmed (they are by no means ungenerous). The Vernacular Press has been warned that, while objective criticism is welcomed, and censorship is sparingly exercised, liberty does not mean licence. But any general policy of repression or even of slowing down of partnership, causing the educated classes as a whole to suffer for the follies or vanities of young hot-heads, would indeed be visiting the sins of sons upon their fathers; the Sudan Government is a powerful autocracy, independent of the Colonial Office, untrammelled by an electorate, or by any unofficial representation on its Council, or by an influential Press, but no colonial Government can conduct for long a progressive or happy administration without the co-operation of the educated classes; to deny or delay their effective participation in the various branches of government means that disgruntlement turns into despair, and despair into revolt, of which the end is Amritsar. It therefore behoves the Government to study closely and keep well abreast of progressive opinion both in responsible circles in England and in enlightened Sudanese society here. Recent events in India, Syria, and Iraq do not pass unnoticed by the Sudanese.

6. The articles and debates referred to in paragraph 4 (ii) are numerous and impressive. I have listed and summarised the most relevant in the Appendix to this Note.[4]

The main thread running through these articles and debates is the aim of converting 'trusteeship' into 'partnership', and a noticeable point is that these progressive sentiments are not put forward by people or newspapers normally described as 'left-wing idealists' or 'humanitarian cranks'. They come from Colonial Ministers and ex-Ministers, ex-Governors, and the leading journals, general and professional. They all agree that more concrete plans must be made for association of Africans with the administration, education and solvency of their countries, that Englishmen must get on more even terms with educated Africans, that colour bar policies, explicit or implicit, are anachronistic and dangerous, that Indirect Rule must not become frozen, and that good government is no lasting substitute for self-government. This consensus of opinion to examine our colonial conscience is

---

[4] Not printed.

something more than what Macaulay termed "The British Public in one of its periodical fits of morality".

7. It may be argued that, granted all this, the Sudan is at War, has been invaded once and may be invaded again: and that War-time is no time for far-reaching schemes of political or administrative development and we should await the piping times of peace.

But, firstly, the times of peace will not be so piping. There will be a psychological malaise among British officials, a reaction from war-effort, an exodus on long leave, a spate of retirements with consequent changes in higher posts, an influx of raw recruits, a restlessness among Sudanese for the removal of economic restrictions (which may well have to be kept on awhile) and a probable distraction of the Central Government on to external affairs (future of Eritrea, Lake Tsana, increased attention from Egypt, pan-Arabism, winding up of Imperial finance questions). We should begin now to lay the foundations of a full Sudanese share in the Government not only to honour local and Imperial pledges, but also to present a united front to the outside world. Internal trouble will only weaken our ability to deal with external affairs.

Secondly, it is surely wise to take time (and budgets) by the forelock and plan 'dilution' and other progressive reforms on the Government's initiative, as matters of pre-declared policy rather than be pushed, or appear to be pushed, into them by pressure from without or blackmail from below. The examples of India, Burma, and Ireland are always before us. In spite of Congress and periodic Egyptian claims there is probably no other dependency which is in so favourable a position to go ahead with a liberal policy of "Sudanisation". We have not the distractions of white settlers (Kenya) racial and community feuds (Palestine and India) poor whites (South Africa) industrial problems (Rhodesia and W. Indies) and so we should lay our foundations while the going is good. Our very immunity from these distractions is a snare: the temptation to linger in what the author of the Forsyte Saga wistfully called "the gilt-edged period" is almost overwhelming, especially to those of us, who have served in the contented countryside. But it is a temptation which must be resisted or The Paradise of the Sudan of the Golden Age may prove a Fool's Paradise.

8. The submissions that I wish to put before Council are not, at the moment, detailed: they are, simply, a request that Council should agree with the need for closer association of the Sudanese with Government, as argued above, and set the ball rolling, as far as war conditions allow, by the following resolutions:

(i) that the system of executive Town Councils, already begun, be extended, and that financial devolution be an integral part of the system.

(ii) that a system of advisory Province Councils for the northern Provinces of Blue Nile, Darfur, Kassala, Kordofan, and Northern be considered. N.B. Khartoum Province already has a joint Municipal Council for the Three Towns.

(iii) that a small Special Committee be instructed to investigate the expediency of forming a central Advisory Council for the Northern Sudan, and, if found feasible, to make recommendations about its composition, terms of reference, and approximate date of creation.

(iv) that Heads of Departments be asked to consider and report on the greater use of Sudanese as members of departmental and inter-departmental committees.

(v) that the Establishments Committee be instructed to review the progress of 'dilution' since the signing of the Anglo–Egyptian Treaty and to make specific recommendations, where desirable, for its acceleration.

(vi) that a special senior Political Officer be temporarily appointed attached to but not an integral part of the Civil Secretary's Office, as special officer in charge of Sudanese relations with terms of reference to be approved by the Governor-General.

8 FO 371/31587, no 4388 19 Sept 1942
[Sudanese Graduates' Congress]: letter (reply) from D Newbold to Ibrahim Ahmad

I acknowledge receipt of your personal letter to me dated July 23rd[1] but not received till August 24th. I regret delay in reply which has been due to press of work.

The renewed reference in your letter to the "demands" embodied in your Memorandum of April 3rd[2] to His Excellency the Governor-General seems to show a misunderstanding of the position which my letters of April 29th[3] and June 16th made clear and which I explained fully in my subsequent interview with you and your two colleagues, an interview which I felt to be of great advantage to us both.

In that interview I gave you an assurance, which I repeated in my letter of July 17th,[4] that Government has no hostility towards the educated Sudanese and that it has under continual and active consideration measures designed to increase the association of Sudanese with Government. But I also gave you some advice about the attitude and activities of the Graduates' Congress. I referred especially to the apparently indiscriminate canvassing for new members, without due regard to their educational qualifications, which the Government considers to be contrary to the rules of the Graduates' Congress, and to the unjustified claim of the Graduates' Congress to represent the whole Sudan, a claim which is not accepted by the Government and denied by very many Sudanese, educated and uneducated.

I am sorry to see in your letter nothing to indicate any intention on the part of the Graduates' Congress to examine those aspects of its activities and organisation to which I referred in my conversation and which I consider contrary to the expressed desire of the Graduates' Congress "to co-operate with the Government in such ways as may be opened to them, in furthering the country's welfare". I hope however that this omission does not mean that the Graduates' Congress intends to refuse all advice or criticism, although your letter, while stressing the obligations of Government, omits all mention of the obligations of the Graduates' Congress and of public servants, on which I laid emphasis in my interview.

Proofs of the Government's intention to associate the Sudanese in an ever-increasing degree in the Government of the country have been given and are being given:—

(a) by the recent advances in local self-government

(b) by the continued appointment of Sudanese to fill posts held by British, Egyptian, and Syrian officials.

---

[1] See 5.

[2] See 1, enclosure 2.

[3] See *ibid*, enclosure 3.

[4] See 4.

(c) by the appointment of a British official of considerable experience and seniority, whose special duty it will be to make and maintain contact with responsible Sudanese opinion in all sections of the community.

I am confident that all enlightened Sudanese will see in the above measures tangible proofs of the earnest intention of the Government to execute its policy and I hope that the Graduates' Congress will realise its own responsibility and make a serious effort to co-operate both in the restoration of good relations and in the execution of Government policy.

As the Government is fully aware of the aspirations of the educated classes and has made its own policy and attitude clear, there is no need for further letters, but rather for closer personal relations, and I therefore consider this correspondence closed.

9 FO 371/315887, no 4388 21 Sept 1942
'The Graduate's [sic] Congress directive statement': note by D Newbold

[In a circular letter to all governors and heads of department, dated 22 Sept 1942 (included in the same folder), Newbold wrote: 'The Government is steadily pursuing its plans for increased dilution and consultation.... In the civil as in the military sphere it is of the first importance to maintain contact with friend and foe, whether actual or potential. We do not yet know whether we shall get co-operation or opposition from the Graduates' Congress; but in either case contact must be maintained. The choice lies with them. It is for us to help them to choose aright.' The following directive statement was issued as a guideline to all British officials on how to deal with the Congress and its members. E A Chapman-Andrews[1] of the FO minuted, 27 Oct: '... The educated Sudanese, the "Effendia" have in the past been looked at rather askance by the British administrative officers, country folk and tribesmen alike. This is to stop so far as British officers are concerned' (FO 371/315887, no 4388).]

I. *Introduction*

(i) From the recent correspondence between this office and the Graduates' Congress, copies of which have been circulated to Governors and Heads of Departments, it is clear that the Congress has made a deliberate attempt to assume a definitely political role.

(ii) The fact must be faced that the Congress, so long as it exists, will inevitably interest itself in public affairs or "politics". To expect it to confine itself to matters of purely social interest is to refuse to face realities. The dividing line between public affairs and social activities is always difficult to define.

(iii) To admit that the Congress is certain to interest itself in public affairs is not to admit that it may be allowed to become a political body in the sense of an opposition party.

(iv) We must therefore clarify our attitude towards it in our own minds and at the same time convince the Congress that we mean what we say.

(v) Our task is to guide the Congress so that it may become a useful focus for the constitutional expansion of thought of a particular class—what form it would take is

[1] Then consul in the FO, having recently returned from the Sudan where he had served as political liaison officer to the Emperor Haile Selassie, 1941–1942.

as yet undefined and is not for discussion with the Sudanese at this stage. Unless we do this we may find ourselves faced by the alternatives of a policy of appeasement on the one hand, or of suppression on the other, neither of which does the Government intend to adopt unless forced to do so. Appeasement means a sequence of blackmail and premature concessions, and would bewilder the non-Congress body of enlightened Sudanese: suppression would create a sense of frustration, clashes, and probably "martyrs", and might drive the movement underground and into the arms of Egypt.

(vi) The point has been reached when it is for Congress to prove by their actions whether they wish to regain and retain Government's sympathy and confidence or not. If they honestly wish to do so and to co-operate with the Government, they will need help and advice, and we must be ready and willing to give it.

II. *Directive*

In furtherance of these aims, the following directive is issued:—

(i) *Constitutional expression of views*

Members of Congress should be made to understand that Government has no objection to their presenting their considered views on public affairs, subject to certain provisos:—

(a) that if they have any doubt about the propriety of the subject or the method of presentation, they seek advice from a responsible British official;

(b) that, having presented their views or recommendations, they are prepared to abide by the result and not to oppose declared policy by agitation or other means;

(c) that they eschew exhibitionism and their present publicity methods of press propaganda;

(d) that they do not arrogate to themselves the Government's function of redressing wrongs through its petition system and courts of justice by championing isolated personal causes.

(ii) *Co-operation with the more responsible elements*

(a) The recent deplorable actions of Congress (due largely to pressure from the less responsible members of the Committee of LX), the extravagant demands of their ill-timed manifesto, their self-advertisement in the Vernacular Press and the general tone of the latter due largely to Congress influence, their unwarranted claim to represent the country as a whole and their efforts to increase indiscriminately the membership of Congress—contrary to their constitution—with the object of making it a more representative body, have no doubt alienated the sympathy of many British officials. It must, however, be remembered that a very large proportion of the members are genuinely anxious to co-operate with Government.

(b) It is important to make contact with them and to strengthen their hands against the more vocal but less responsible hot-heads.

(c) They must be persuaded of the need to rehabilitate Congress as a respectable movement in the eyes of the Government and of the more responsible members of the community.

(d) We must make them realise that we are interested in them and their views, that we want to understand and appreciate their outlook and that we are prepared to tell them frankly when and why we disagree with them. They will take almost anything individually, if they know the motive is sincere. If every British official made himself a safety-valve, the total pressure harmlessly released would be enormous.

(iii) *Attitude towards the less responsible elements*

(a) It is desirable that we should maintain contact with the less responsible elements, but it is undesirable to increase their self-importance by granting indiscriminate personal interviews. Personal interest in them and occasional sympathetic discussion of their more reasonable aspirations are more likely to prove efficacious than simply to disregard them or to treat them as a mere nuisance.

(b) Efforts should be made to win the cooperation and loyalty which the Sudanese are usually more ready to give to the individual than to such impersonal entities as "the Service" or "the Government".

(c) If mutual confidence can be established, there is at least a prospect that they may adopt a more friendly and co-operative attitude towards the Government's efforts for the advancement of the Sudanese.

(iv) *Government officials and politics*

(a) Most of the members of Congress are Government officials and, since we admit that Congress will inevitably continue to interest itself in politics, we have to face the danger of a political Civil Service.

(b) It is a choice of evils. We must either allow them to continue to be members of Congress and do all we can to keep them on the rails, or forbid them to be members and face the awkwardness at this juncture of a large number of resignations and the consequent dangers of secret societies and sedition. (A small number of resignations from Government of the more irreconcilable Congressmen might be a good thing and have a salutary effect).

(c) The Government has in fact recognised by implication that Sudanese officials are by nature prone to interest themselves in public affairs. The 1938 amendment to Chapter IV of Administrative Regulations and Explanatory Note (attached) define the extent to which they may do so.

(d) His Excellency has directed that at present these Administrative Regulations shall be applied as follows:—

(1) Any Government official may be a member of Congress.

(2) Judges and Registrars of the Civil Courts and Kadis and Legal Assistants of the Sharia Courts, Sub-Inspectors (Administrative), Mamurs, Sub-Mamurs and Police Officers may not become, nor continue to be, members of the Committee of XV or the Committee of LX of the Graduates' Congress, or of standing executive branch committees in the Provinces. There is no objection to their being members of a Committee whose sole function is to deal with educational or cultural matters.

(e) Other Government officials may continue to act as members of Congress Committees, provided such activities do not interfere with their duties or impair their position as public servants.

(v) *Closer association of the Sudanese in the work of government*
Much of the intelligentsia's distrust of Government's motives and intentions is due to the fact that they see so little of the work done in committee and conference. They have to carry out decisions affecting the welfare of their country with no idea of the work that has gone to their making. Suitable senior Sudanese should be admitted to committees and conferences at every possible opportunity. (A special circular is being issued to Governors and Heads of Departments on this). Their closer association with the mills of policy should go far to dispel the atmosphere of mystery with which we are apt to surround ourselves.

(vi) *Congress and local government leaders*
(a) If tribal or local government leaders want advice as to whether to join the Congress, your line should be that the Government would view with disfavour their joining any organisation likely to distract them from their local duties and interests or to impair their impartiality. Their hands are full with the important job of laying the foundations of sound local Government and they should stick to realities and the job in hand.
(b) To those who are already members and want your advice you should again emphasise the importance of their duties as an integral part of the Government and add that they should maintain an attitude of impartial aloofness, decline for the present to serve on any local Congress Committee or join in any public meetings, and discourage indiscriminate canvassing of members.

(vii) *Non-Congress elements*
The majority of the educated classes are not members of the Congress, and among this majority is a large and important body of reputable and loyal officials and notables. The interests and opinions of these men, who are not always vocal, are apt to be obscured or neglected (especially in the Three Towns, less so in the Provinces) by our preoccupation with the Congress. In our efforts to secure a better understanding with the Congress, it is most important that we should not make the mistake of letting this large body of non-Congress elements feel neglected—particularly the Sub-Inspectors, Mamurs, Police Officers, senior Departmental officials, Sheikhs, Notables and merchants. A right balance must be struck between them and members of Congress in representation on Committees, in consultations and informal contacts. They should be told that the Government's letters to Congress stand as a clear statement of its attitude towards them, and you can tell them candidly the line which Government has adopted towards Congress. They are an unorganised body and the Government must rely mainly on provincial and departmental authorities to keep in touch with them and make them feel that they and their views *are* of concern to Government. We have no intention whatever of throwing our friends to the wolves, nor of failing to apply proper disciplinary measures to any official where necessary.

III. *Conclusion*
(i) In order to carry out successfully the above directives, we must rid our minds by deliberate effort of any feeling of hostility towards Congress or the intelligentsia in general.
(ii) The response to the directive from this office calling for a sympathetic attitude

of mind to the Congress Education Day scheme was admirable. It was instantly recognised and appreciated by Congress. If it can succeed on the minor issue, it can succeed also on the major.

(iii) One or two members of the Government cannot hope to achieve all this alone: the effort must be universal and as consistent as possible.

10 FO 371/31587, no 4388 11 Oct 1942
[Sudanese Graduates' Congress]: letter from Sir M Lampson to Sir A Cadogan[1] [Extract]

... The position as it emerges from all this is briefly that the Graduates' Congress is beginning to emphasize even more than hitherto its claim to represent in the political sphere educated Sudanese opinion, and that the Sudan Government, while frowning on any improper exercise of the Congress's functions, are fully conscious from this and other symptoms that something is stirring and that they must make up their minds how to deal with it and begin to set on foot certain preliminary measures almost at once.

My first reaction to all this is that it is, by and large, wholesome. Our bogey until recently has been an attempt to Egyptianise the Sudan. We have had to counter this by various means, some of them rather devious, during the last few years. The present Government have not shown any very special inclination to extend Egyptian influence in the Sudan (except perhaps for Nahas' rather indefinite statement recorded in my telegram No. 1543 of 11th June and some ill-judged newspaper reports about activities connected with the Sudan alleged, without any foundation, to have been undertaken by various Ministries here), but it is likely that when they have exhausted the possibilities of gaining popular support by xenophobic legislation here, they may easily turn to penetration into the Sudan as a further vote-catching device. In many ways our best answer to this is an increase in Sudanese popular feeling. I remember with some glee having made Makram[2] admit to me at the time of the Treaty negotiations that "The Sudan for the Sudanese" was a thesis impossible to attack. This somewhat unwilling but inevitable admission on his part subsequently took definite shape in the Treaty. The Egyptians, though clearly believing it was a mere phrase, really did not like seeing it enshrined in the Treaty, but I put it there all right!

Now it is becoming a live issue and a very normal and natural one, but I am sure the Egyptians will not at all like it. There is, however, always the possibility that in their usual way of finding any stick good enough to beat us with they might come to make use of it if we give them the chance. It seems to me that we should be giving them this chance if we disappointed Sudanese aspirations to such an extent as to lead the Sudanese to apply for help to the more extreme elements in Egypt. That is a definite danger but it is one of which the Sudan Government appear to be fully aware and which they are evidently trying to avert. As I see it we must encourage this effort

---

[1] Lampson forwarded documents 4, 5, 7–9 with this letter to Cadogan.

[2] Makram Ubayd, Wafdist politician, ally of Mustafa al-Nahhas, minister of finance and member of the Egyptian delegation in the 1936 Anglo–Egyptian treaty negotiations.

of the Sudan Government to get on terms with the Sudanese national movement and try to guide it and keep it on sound lines. Up to date they seem to be handling the matter liberally and wisely.

I may have given the impression in these comments that I am looking at the matter from a rather parochial angle. I would emphasize that, as I have said, these are my first reactions and are intended to deal with the immediate problems likely to arise here. I fully realise that the wider issues of Sudanese nationalism are of greater ultimate importance and interest. Fortunately they seem to require the same treatment as I have advocated from the local point of view. The way in which nationalist movements have gone wrong on us in so many places which we control has surely been largely due to the fact that at a given moment the Government—sometimes of course with very good reason—became impatient of the nationalist movement and lost or abandoned all day-to-day control over it. It is far more difficult and laborious to maintain continual contact with inept and undisciplined politicians of the kind which come to the surface in the early days of these movements and to guide them as it were from within, rather than to alternate between repression and concessions given against one's better judgment and merely because one has not the force or the will to carry repression to its logical conclusion.

Both the Sudan Authorities and we ourselves would naturally welcome any preliminary comments of yours on this. I am expecting a visit from Huddleston towards the end of next month and no doubt we shall have talks about it. I shall naturally keep you informed of any developments of interest.

11 FO 371/31587, no 5145 18 Nov 1942

[Future of the Sudan]: letter from Sir H Huddleston to Sir M Lampson

Rugman has shown me the papers attached to your letter to him, No.1275/4/42 of 12th October, 1942. To begin with I agree generally with the appreciation of the situation here given in your letter of October 11th to Sir Alexander Cadogan.[1] However troublesome an "increase in Sudanese popular feeling" may become, it is certainly preferable to increased Egyptian penetration and, indeed, is the only legitimate counter thereto.

I am also grateful for your commendation of the way we are trying to handle the Sudanese national movement and keep it under some sort of unrepressive control.

Our immediate difficulty in this respect is to tide over the interim period which may be a year, or two or three, before we can get some respectable Sudanese Advisory Council in the saddle. Town, District and Province Councils are comparatively easy to set up and they are a proof of our good intentions as regards Anglo–Sudanese partnership, but the eyes of the intelligentsia are naturally glued on the Central Government, where there is admittedly a Sudanese vacuum. Nature abhors a vacuum, and into it the Graduates' Congress has rashly stepped. We have pushed them out politely, but the vacuum must be filled and until it is filled by a representative body of enlightened Sudanese, fed probably by delegates from the

---

[1] See 10.

Province Councils and a few nominated notables from the capital, we can only say 'Trespassers will be prosecuted', and get on with certain cognate measures, e.g. (i) accelerated dilution of British posts in Departments by Sudanese (ii) development of our Post-Secondary Schools, (which are going through various teething troubles) and (iii) the greater use of Sudanese on the various Central Government Committees and Boards which are almost entirely composed of British officials. Active steps are actually being taken in these three directions which I can explain to you in Cairo, and which Shone can discuss with my Secretaries here.

So much for our immediate internal policy. As regards the status of the Sudan and its future, this, of course, bristles with difficulties, of which the main are the inherent anomalies of the Condominium, and the cleavage between the Northern and Southern Sudan.

As regards the former the suggestion that Egypt should receive Cyrenaica in exchange for her 'rights' in the Sudan is ingenious and attractive, and, if Egypt could be induced to accept the exchange, we should be only too glad. But I fear the historic connexion with the Sudan and the dependence of Egypt on the Nile waters make their agreement most unlikely.[2]

Incidentally, prior to an agreement being reached on this issue between the Co-Domini, responsible Sudanese opinion should be consulted, as a qualified pledge was made, with my authority, in the Civil Secretary's reply of April 29th, 1942 to the manifesto of April 3rd, 1942 submitted by the Graduates' Congress. The relevant sentence reads:—"If the Condominium Powers at any time decide to review the Agreement or Treaty, the Sudan Government would hope to consult responsible Sudanese opinion. The Government, however, can make no promises to any body of persons in the name of the Condominium Powers or in its own".[3]

Although this was only a qualified pledge, I think we should be bound to consult leading Sudanese (and this is where we need a Sudanese Advisory Council) over any alteration in the status of the Sudan.[4] There was a good deal of feeling among the educated Sudanese at the time of the 1936 Treaty that they should have an opportunity to express their views, and world events and the growth of 'nationalism' have since intensified that feeling. What their views would be on a complete political separation from Egypt, I cannot precisely say, except that the majority of the country would probably welcome it, while the educated minority would want safeguards for future independence and possibly some sort of cultural and commercial Treaty with Egypt. They are ready to see the Sudan as a sister to Egypt, but not as a daughter. They would distrust a purely Colonial status under British rule, unless some sort of Colonial charter on partnership lines had by that time been evolved.

The second problem, that of the Southern Sudan, is a separate and real difficulty, and I am glad that the Foreign Office Memorandum[5] has stated it so realistically. Our obvious duty to the Southern Sudanese is to push ahead with their development, especially in the sphere of education, as fast as we can, so that if they are ultimately left under the control of a Government largely or wholly recruited from the Arab and Moslem North, they can at least stand up for themselves as a large progressive and cohesive minority. Similarly, if they are to be absorbed into East Africa, we must push on their development, both educational and economic, so that their degree of

---

[2] See discussion in 1, 2 and 6.

[3] See 2.

[4] Marginal note by Cadogan: 'I agree'

[5] See 6.

civilisation and self-sufficiency comes somewhat nearer to that of Uganda. It is at present far behind and we cannot ask Uganda to take over a white elephant.

The only gleam in the Southern darkness, therefore, is that a policy of faster development is equally suitable, whether the Southern Provinces remain linked to Khartoum or are hived off to East Africa. I may say that this development will still be a very slow business especially in the big Nilotic Dinka-Nuer belt.

As regards the suggested declaration in paragraph 9 of the Foreign Office Memorandum, there is no doubt that this would please the educated Sudanese enormously, although it might well raise qualms in the minds of the older sheikhs and merchants, and the village elders. Moreover, it is in accord with recent statements about the future of the Colonies in the British Houses of Parliament and Lord Hailey's remarks in the Colonial debate in the House of Lords, which I attach,[6] are very apposite. Nevertheless, I think it goes too far. We do not know what the attitude towards small nations will be after the war, and even if the Sudan could find, within a measurable period, sufficient capable Sudanese to run a harmonious popular and fairly efficient Government, which would also continue to be solvent, there are the questions of defence and foreign relations. The trend of world opinion seems to be away from small and weak sovereign nations and towards some form of confederation.

These declarations, if not carefully worded, are apt to come home to roost, and even if carefully worded, frequently lead to accelerated and exaggerated demands. I do not see how the Sudan can become "a fully independent state exercising full rights of sovereignty" for many years (I hesitate to name a term) and its future may well lie either in Dominion status in the British Commonwealth or in autonomous membership (with or without its Southern Provinces) of a Near Eastern Federation (Egypt, Arabia, Palestine, Syria, and Iraq). My present opinion is that an early declaration would be inopportune.

---

[6] Not printed.

12 FO 371/31587, no 5145 1 Dec 1942

[Future of the Sudan]: letter from Sir M Lampson to Sir A Cadogan

With reference to my letter 1275/3/42 of 11th October and Scrivener's letter to Shone J 3736/1528/16 of 10th September, I enclose a copy of a letter from Huddleston about the future administration and status of the Sudan.[1] I discussed the question with Huddleston during his recent visit here and he has since seen this letter in draft and agrees with it.

I agree generally with Huddleston's letter. The exchange of Cyrenaica for the Sudan is, in our joint view, quite outside the sphere of practical politics. The Egyptians would no doubt like to have Cyrenaica or at least a part of it up to Bardia to which they sometimes advance a claim based on proposals alleged to have been made in Kitchener's time, but they are not seriously interested in it and would certainly not regard it as in any sense comparable to the loss of their interest in the Sudan. The Sudan has for Egypt practical, historical and sentimental associations which will

---

[1] See 11.

I surmise never be eradicated. Their share in the control of the Sudan is regarded as an important guarantee for the safety of their supply of Nile water. These general considerations are reinforced by the present ideas of increasing the supply of water eventually by the Lake Tsana scheme and by the proposed canal through the sudd.[2] I do not believe any Egyptian Government could ever agree to give up its claim to share in the control of the Sudan in return for any territorial concession however large.

If this exchange is excluded, what are we left with? At present, during the war, I feel fairly confident that we can, without too much difficulty, damp down any Egyptian movement towards greater control over the Sudan or towards raising questions of sovereignty with regard to it. I would have no hesitation in refusing point blank to listen to any agitation of this kind. If we make our position clear in this way in the face of any talk or agitation, it will be in the Government's interest to damp it down, as they can perfectly well do with their powers of censorship and état de siège.

After the war we ought to be in a position to continue to take a strong line if we wish to do so. There will inevitably be a period of ebullition on the part of the "young" nations of the Middle East which, in Egypt, is likely to include a certain amount of irredentist feeling with regard to the Sudan. After the last war we did not use our military position to deal with movements of this kind with a strong hand. This time we shall have even greater preoccupations elsewhere than we had last time, but I sincerely hope that we shall not lose our grip in the same way.

It will be much easier to avoid making concessions to Egyptian agitation about the Sudan against our better judgment, particularly with the state of feeling likely to be prevailing at home, if we have a Sudanese national movement to oppose to Egyptian pressure. Huddleston's letter shows that the Sudan [Government] are fully conscious of the importance of not repressing the beginnings of a Sudanese national movement however tiresome this may be to the administration, and I am sure that he will take every opportunity of moving towards the vitally important next stage of associating Sudanese with the administration at the centre. This being so the longer we can put off a show-down with the Egyptians the stronger will be our position. The question in so far as Egypt is concerned is at present dormant and I trust we can keep it so at least until the end of the war. The position which will arise then must for the present remain a question mark, both as regards the feeling of British public opinion and as regards the progress which will by then have been made in "Sudanisation". In these circumstances I do not feel able to comment usefully at the moment on any detailed proposal for a new statement of the relationships of Great Britain, Egypt and the Sudan.

---

[2]For a summary of Nile Waters proposals at this date, see 27.

13 FO 371/35576, no 1773 — 10 Apr 1943

[Advisory Council for the Northern Sudan]: despatch no 343 from Sir M Lampson to Mr Eden. *Enclosure*: despatch from Sir H Huddleston (21 Mar 1943)

With reference to my despatch No. 185 of the 18th February, I have the honour to transmit herewith a copy of a despatch from the Governor-General of the Sudan containing his Excellency's proposals for the creation of a General Advisory Council for the Northern Sudan and of Province Councils.

2. The draft legislation enclosed in Sir H. Huddleston's despatch marks a most important step forward in the political development of the Sudan. A Central Advisory Council for the Northern Sudan would meet the need which has for some time now been felt for the creation of a central organ of Sudanese opinion which would enable the Administration to be informed more authoritatively of the needs and feelings of the population and would gradually train the Sudanese up to the level at which they can themselves contribute to the central administration of their country. Many recent signs of awakening political consciousness, such as the activities of the Sudanese Graduates' Congress, have shown that a demand for greater Sudanese participation in the administration is beginning to arise. The remarkable success of the various forms of local government which have been entrusted to Sudanese in different parts of the country shows equally clearly that the Sudanese are capable of assuming a fuller measure of political responsibility. It is certainly wise to introduce measures of the kind proposed before the demand grows too insistent and before political agitation has begun to make it more difficult for enlightened Sudanese to co-operate with the Government.

3. The moment seems also to be well chosen, having regard to more general considerations. The disturbing effects of the war have to a considerable extent receded from the Sudan, and the political ferment which is thought by some observers to be likely to follow the general cessation of hostilities, and of which certain incipient signs are perhaps visible in other Middle East and Arab countries, has not yet begun to spread into the Sudan. The Sudan will be in a much better condition to meet it if measures of the kind now proposed are passed now.

4. The proposed council is confined at present to the Northern Sudan because this area is so much more advanced in every way than the south. The racial and other differences between the two areas make it perfectly feasible to deal with the north as a separate unit for this purpose.

5. I strongly recommend that I may be authorised to inform Sir H. Huddleston that His Majesty's Government approve the draft legislation enclosed in his despatch and the immediate implementation of his proposals.

6. On the assumption that my recommendation is approved, it remains to consider Egyptian reactions to the action proposed. There is always a tendency among those of extreme opinion in Egypt to suggest that measures tending to give greater autonomy to the Sudanese are inspired by us mainly with a view to detaching the Sudan from Egypt and keeping it under our own influence. The enemy propaganda mentioned in the last paragraph of Sir H. Huddleston's despatch might perhaps render it more likely that suspicions of this kind will be entertained with regard to the measures now proposed, even though those Egyptians who can regard the question with any objectivity must approve proposals which represent so important a step in the path of political development which they themselves have followed. But in fact these considerations are not altogether relevant. Whatever the feelings of the Egyptians who consider these proposals, it would not be possible for them in practice to voice objections to any measures giving greater political responsibility to the Sudanese, as this would inevitably alienate Sudanese opinion from them. It may be assumed, therefore, that the Egyptian Government and

Egyptian opinion will have to acquiesce in these measures, quite apart from any pressure which we might put on them. I have carefully considered whether as a matter of tactics it is better to treat this legislation in regard to the Egyptian Government in exactly the same way as ordinary legislation passed from time to time in the Sudan, or whether some special arrangement should be made to associate the Egyptian Government with it, and I have come to the conclusion that the first of these courses is definitely right. The first Condominium Agreement of 1899 gives the Governor-General power to make by proclamation any laws, orders and regulations "for the good government of the Sudan." There is nothing to show that he must obtain the consent of either of the Condominium Powers before making any such laws. Indeed, on the contrary it is only laid down that he should notify them to the British and Egyptian authorities. The practice is that the approval of His Majesty's Ambassador at Cairo and High Commissioner for the Sudan is obtained by the Governor-General before ordinances are passed into law. But this is a private arrangement of which the Egyptian Government are not, so far as I know, aware. The Egyptian Government are never consulted before an ordinance is passed, but are informed of it by the Sudan Government immediately after it is passed. I am sure it is far best in the present case to follow this normal routine procedure, and I therefore propose that, as soon as you inform me that His Majesty's Government approve the proposed legislation, the relative ordinances and regulations should be issued by the Governor-General, and notification be sent to the Egyptian Government in the usual way.

7. The Sudan Government are most anxious not to lose any time in putting these proposals into effect and I fully share their feelings on this point. I therefore request that you will be good enough to inform me by telegram of the instructions of His Majesty's Government both as regards the Sudan Government's proposals and as regards the manner of presenting them to the Egyptian Government.

8. I am sending a copy of this despatch to Sir H. Huddleston and the Minister of State.

Enclosure to 13: despatch from Sir H Huddleston to Sir M Lampson, 21 Mar 1943

I have the honour to refer to the correspondence between your Excellency and Sir Alexander Cadogan, and between your Excellency and myself, which arose out of my despatch No. 82 dated the 7th October, 1942, forwarding a note by my civil secretary dated the 10th September, 1942, on the closer association of the Sudanese with the local and central Government of the Sudan.

From this correspondence I was encouraged to think that the implementation of the specific measures recommended in paragraph 8 of the note of the 10th September, 1942, was likely to enjoy the support both of your Excellency and His Majesty's Government.

2. Acting upon this, I approved the formation of the Special Committee recommended in paragraph 8 (iii) of the note and charged them with the task of investigating the expediency of forming an Advisory Council for the Northern Sudan, and, if found feasible, to make recommendation as to its composition, terms of reference and approximate date of creation. The committee, a strong one which

included five members of my Council and the Governors of the two largest provinces, duly presented their report. Their recommendations, which I accepted in principle, were on my instructions embodied by my legal secretary in preliminary draft legislation.

3. This draft legislation consists of three documents, viz.: The Advisory Councils Ordinance, 1943; the Advisory Council for the Northern Sudan Order, 1943; and the Local Government (Province Councils) Ordinance, 1943. Copies of all three documents are attached.(1)

The draft Local Government (Province Councils) Ordinance, though local and provincial in character, should be regarded as an integral part of the whole since its provisions are closely interlocked with and complementary to those of the Advisory Councils Ordinance. Furthermore, it completes the pyramid based on the many rural and urban local Government bodies existing or coming to birth throughout the Northern Sudan and leading up through the Province Councils by a direct and logical sequence to the Advisory Council.

4. Being aware that this provisional body of legislation represents a political development of far-reaching import which may well ultimately affect the Constitution of the Sudan, I considered it proper and convenient to invite my Council in the first instance to consider it purely in draft legislative form and then, if agreed, to forward it in the same form for consideration and approval in principle by your Excellency and His Majesty's Government.

My Council accordingly took note of the draft legislation at their 508th Meeting and approved its submission to your Excellency in its present form.

5. I should therefore be glad of an assurance that this draft legislation is not inconsistent with the general policy of His Majesty's Government in relation to the wide trends of political development both within the British Commonwealth of Nations and elsewhere. On the receipt of such an assurance my Council would at once proceed to pass the legislation subject to such amendments in detail as it may consider desirable. This would be followed by the preparation and approval of suitable regulations governing the proceedings of the Advisory Council for the Northern Sudan and by the promulgation of orders setting up Province Councils in such provinces as are ready for them.

6. I think it right to inform your Excellency that, as was inevitable, rumours have begun to circulate in the Sudan regarding the establishment of some form of Central Advisory Council and it can only be a matter of time before these rumours reach Egypt. Furthermore, as your Excellency is no doubt aware, the Axis Propaganda Service has already launched a campaign misrepresenting and exaggerating the functions of a newly-formed departmental Advisory Committee on purely local government affairs and affecting to see in the establishment of this departmental committee a perfidious step towards the severance of the connexion between Egypt and the Sudan. I suggest, therefore, to your Excellency that it has become necessary to consider whether and, if so, to what extent and in what manner the Egyptian Government should be informed at this stage of the present proposal.

(1) Not printed.

14 FO 371/35576, no 4998 8 Nov 1943

[Advisory Council for the Northern Sudan]: letter from F D Rugman (acting governor-general) to T A Shone[1]

I am now in a position to inform you of the first reactions of Sudan public opinion, British as well as Sudanese, to the Advisory Council Legislation which was submitted under cover of my despatch No.61 dated the 17th August 1943. It was perhaps regrettably inevitable that public interest should concentrate on the Central Advisory Council to the exclusion of the equally important institution of partly executive province councils, the coping stones of the whole local government system.

2. The most universal criticism voiced by some British as well as most Sudanese is against the large number of safeguards which are regarded as redundant and uncalled for in a council which is purely advisory and are interpreted as being intended to stifle all criticism and the free discussion of any important or controversial subject. Similarly the seemingly cumbersome machinery by which private members may ask for a matter of policy to be explained is regarded as being an effective barrier against the introduction of any burning problem of the day.

These criticisms are regarded as being of a genuinely constructive nature and the possibility of taking measures to meet them at least in part and after the formation of the Council is under consideration.

3. Less responsible criticism has followed the expected lines, suspecting and condemning an implied intention of separating the Northern from the Southern Sudan, reflecting the refusal of the educated class to recognise the right of "rural elements" from the provinces to a majority or even an equality of representation, and resenting the lack of legislative powers. I am enclosing a copy of a summary of press criticism made at the end of September.

4. Since then the Graduates' Congress has submitted a Memorandum arguing first in general terms that a Council with even partial executive or legislative powers has been proved in practice to be more efficient and effective than a purely advisory body, and condemning the whole Southern policy of the Sudan Government as apparently reflected in the legislation. It goes on to complain that the number of members is far too small in proportion to the population, and that representatives are nominated and not elected by popular vote. It attacks the restrictive provisions which are to be found in Clauses 9, 10, 15, 20, 21(2) and 22 of the Order setting up an Advisory Council for the Northern Sudan, and it concludes that the Council in view of these safeguards cannot be expected even to carry out the advisory duties for which it was instituted.

The Congress Committee later passed by a small majority a resolution boycotting the Council and forbidding its members to accept nomination on pain of expulsion, but I have reason to believe that this was the work of a clique which has not the support of the majority of members and that it is likely to be repealed. I consider it unlikely that any Sudanese who is invited to accept nomination will decline to do so.

5. Informed and moderate opinion throughout the country may be said to welcome the Council as a substantial step forward but to be disappointed at the safeguards and to share in greater or less degree the criticisms set out in paragraph 2

---

[1] Counsellor with the local rank of minister plenipotentiary at the embassy in Cairo, 1940–1944.

above. This section of opinion is prepared to admit that the success of the Council will largely depend upon the selection of suitable members and the manner in which it will in practice be called upon to work. Moderate reaction may in fact be better described as apprehension rather than criticism, and I have every reason to suppose that if the necessary action is taken to remove this apprehension either by partial amendment or by liberal interpretation or both, public opinion will be prepared to await with benevolent interest the practical results of the legislation.

15 FO 371/35576, no 4986 24 Nov 1943

[Sudanese political development]: letter from D Newbold to G E R Sandars on Egypt and the status of the Sudan.[1] *Minutes* by W E Beckett and P S Scrivener

As you are only too well aware, there are indications that we may be moving towards another crisis with Egypt over the Sudan, a crisis which looks like developing as soon as the war is over (probably as an offshoot of the peace settlement tussle), and which may prove to be the final show-down. On the one hand, we keep hearing reports from Egypt that Nahas intends to raise the whole Sudan question after the war, and personally I think there are very strong reasons for believing that he (or indeed any Egyptian Government that finds itself in office at the end of the war) will do so. The Egyptians are now convinced that, under the protection of the Treaty, the Sudan Government is encouraging a separatist Sudanese movement inimical to Egypt's interests, and that unless they do something about it quickly they may lose the Sudan for good. The moment for them to act will naturally be immediately after the war, and the grounds on which they will raise the Sudan question, will, I imagine be that (i) the Treaty is not working satisfactorily and (ii) that the time has come to offer the Sudanese a clearer and more secure basis for their development than an unreal and thorny partnership between two ill-assorted mandatories vaguely guaranteeing their welfare but unable to co-operate effectively to that end. On the other hand, the Sudanese, conscious of having made a notable contribution in men and material to the British war effort, and established their identity and name in the Empire and the world as a recognisable semi-autonomous entity, are staking a claim to a higher political status after the war than they have hitherto enjoyed under the Condominium, and they definitely expect to get 'something' out of H.M.G. and the Atlantic Charter as a reward for what they have done. These aspirations, which are not unreasonable under modern conditions, may have to be met in some way or another, but it is almost certain that anything we here or H.M.G. may propose to that end (e.g. a Sudanese Nationality law, some Sudanese seats on H.E.'s Council, a conversion of the Advisory Council into a Legislative Council) will be considered by the Egyptians as prejudicial to their position in the Sudan.

The most salient feature in this situation, as I see it, is that the wishes of the Sudanese themselves will, for the first time in the history of the Anglo–Egyptian tug-of-war over the Sudan, be one of the decisive factors. Sudanese political consciousness has developed considerably since the conclusion of the

[1] This copy was forwarded to the FO on 28 Nov 1943 by R C Mayall.

Anglo–Egyptian Treaty, and with an Advisory Council in being and the Atlantic Charter in the background, it will be impossible for the Condominium partners, separately or jointly, to modify the status of the Sudan or make any new decisions about its future without some formal consultation of the wishes of its people. A promise has in fact been given that responsible opinion would be consulted in this eventuality. The Egyptians are doubtless aware of this, and may be clever enough to stake their whole case on a direct appeal to the Sudanese. They have come to know the Sudanese much better since 1936 than they had ever known them before. They now know that any Egyptian claim of sovereignty over the Sudan deriving from rights of conquest is highly offensive to the Sudanese. Some of them have even come to realise, at last, that Sudanese nationalism is not a British invention, and that the Sudanese really wish to preserve and develop an autonomous identity. It is certain therefore that the Sudan question this time will not be raised merely in the form of a bilateral argument with the British Government about Egyptian rights in the Sudan, but rather in the form of proposals to be put to the Sudanese. Nor are indications lacking as to what line these proposals will follow. Nahas's recent speech gives a clear pointer. His declaration that in the eyes of Egypt the Sudanese and Egyptians are the sons of one nation having equal rights and obligations is in fact tantamount to an implied offer of equal citizenship. Again when Ali El Bereir[2] was here last winter, he gave it out that if the Sudan was united to Egypt, the Egyptians would respect the Sudanese desire to preserve their own identity and would allow them a large measure of autonomy; and the same idea, I am told, was expressed by Prince Omar Toussoun[3] to Mohammed Khalifa Sherif,[4] the Prince suggesting that there would be no objection to the Sudan having its own local government under a Sudanese 'Wali' representing the Egyptian Crown.

I may have slightly exaggerated the danger, but this is how matters look to me at this end, and some sort of infiltration, propaganda, etc. is the least that we can expect. *I should be very grateful for any views you may have to offer from your angle, and for any indication that may come your way, now or later, as to the intentions of the Egyptian Government, or how and when they are likely to make a move in this direction. We must have some warning.*[5]

I don't think it is realised by the majority of British officials here (a) how delicate the situation may become, (b) how fast the outside world is moving in new political ideas, (c) how difficult it will be to adopt a non-possumus attitude over political advance after the war to the Sudanese, when Egypt may be dangling a deed of partnership like a yellow carrot in front of their nose, when the British have exercised pressure on the French to unloose their grip in Syria, and when new constitutions may be visible in Libya, W. Africa, Ceylon, Philippines and perhaps Malaya. We must be ready to regard the Advisory Council, not as the end of a series of devolutionary measures, but as the *first* of a series of real steps towards self-

[2] Ali Birair, a Sudanese living in Egypt was a strong advocate of Egyptian claims to the Sudan. He later attempted to stand for the Egyptian Chamber of Deputies in December 1944, but withdrew his candidacy following British protests to the Egyptian government.

[3] Prince Umar Tusun (1872–1944), a great-grandson of Muhammad Ali, was an advocate of the retrocession of the Sudan to Egypt, and the author of several historical studies of Egypt's involvement in the Sudan (see R H Hill, *A biographical dictionary of the Sudan* (London, 1967), p 365).

[4] Muhammed Khalifa Sharif, nephew and business partner of SAR.

[5] Underlined by FO.

government, and the pace of those steps will be dictated not by the Sudan Government or even, probably the British Government, but by world opinion and world events and especially events in Egypt and the Arab States of the Middle East, and that pace certainly will be faster than most people here realise.

Minutes on 15

Most of what is said in these letters seems to me to be very sound. I should have thought we could take it as very nearly certain that the future of the Sudan will become a burning issue before long. I must say I do not think that the grounds on which the Egyptian Government will raise the Sudan question will be the grounds specified in (1) and (ii) in the first paragraph of Mr. Newbold's letter. These grounds seem to me far too measured and judicial and not sufficiently popular for the Egyptian Government. I should have thought the Egyptian Government would put their case on the grounds (a) Egyptian sovereignty over the Sudan (which they always assert, though we say that it is only half sovereignty), (b) that the Sudanese are Arab and Moslem brothers (conveniently forgetting of course all the southern part of the Sudan which is neither of these things). Further, I cannot resist a feeling that the Arab and Moslem brotherhood line will have some appeal in the Sudan especially if it is combined with offers of local autonomy as well as having a tremendous appeal to the Arab world in general. So far as I can see the practical alternatives before us would seem to be a continuation of the con-Dominium [sic] with increased Sudanese self-government, and to divide the Sudan so that the southern and non-Arab part becomes a purely British responsibility and the northern and Arab part goes to Egypt with some guarantees of local autonomy, etc. (I don't suppose that we should like this course). Anyway, if the Advisory Council is to come into being before the future of the Sudan is settled, it will obviously be important that it is constituted in such a manner as to be purely representative of the Sudan and not merely of the Arab and Moslem part of it. . . .

W.E.B.
17.12.43

As regards Mr. Beckett's second alternative, I agree that it is distasteful—but if such are the wishes of the Sudanese Arabs, freely expressed, it will be difficult to avoid it. Apart from the sentimental side of the question, & from the strategic angle, we have really very small *interests* in the Sudan—as opposed to responsibilities.

P.S.
17.12.43

16 FO 371/41363, no 264 29 Dec 1943

[Sudanese political development]: letter from Lord Killearn to Sir A Cadogan

I enclose a copy of a private letter from Newbold in Khartoum to the Sudan Agent here about the future of relations between Egypt and the Sudan.[1] Newbold has

[1] See 15.

agreed to my sending you a copy of this letter provided that its private and unofficial character is fully understood.

My general impression is that Newbold credits the Egyptian Government with more definite ideas on policy than they in fact yet have. It is worth recalling that the Opposition representatives, in their recent communication to the "Big Three", talked in the traditional Egyptian style of Egyptian rights in the Sudan but said nothing about Sudanese rights. Newbold appears to attribute too precise a sense to Nahas' declaration that in the eyes of Egypt the Sudanese and the Egyptians are the sons of one nation, having equal rights of citizenship. This is the sort of thing that Egyptian politicians have been saying for decades.

When the time comes for Egypt to formulate her claims in the Sudan, she will have to make her action conform to the Atlantic Charter in theory at any rate, and this would involve asking the Sudanese what they think about it. It seems, therefore, that our policy must be to offer the Sudanese a more hopeful prospect than Egypt can do, in other words, that we should endeavour to associate the Sudanese more and more in the administration of the Sudan and at the same time endeavour to promote Anglo–Sudanese economic development. If in this way numerous educated elements are absorbed into administrative and economic jobs and they see that they are making a good thing out of the British connection, there is less chance that the "yellow carrot" of the Egyptians will prove much of an attraction.

With reference to the penultimate paragraph of Newbold's letter, one of the Sudan Agent's informants claims to have learnt from Abdel Hakk, the present Minister of Wakfs,[2] that a Wafdist committee is to examine the whole question of Egypt's post-war claims, including that of the Sudan. It may, however, be difficult for us to get early information of the intentions of the Egyptian Government as regards the Sudan. They are likely to keep pretty quiet about it, particularly as they are afraid of offending us at a moment when their continuance in office depends on our support.

If the Egyptians come to shaping their policy to take account of Sudanese aspirations, it seems that their support for these aspirations can only be dangerous to us, (as Egyptian support was dangerous to the French in the Lebanon), if Sudanese aspirations are being blocked by us. If we keep reasonable pace with genuine Sudanese political feeling or do not apply too great a retarding influence, any Egyptian campaign in favour of greater Sudanese independence would be tilting at windmills. In so far as Egyptian action was effective in the Lebanon, this was so only because the French had flagrantly repressed a spontaneous Lebanese movement towards greater independence. I surmise it will be a long time yet before any such movement in the Sudan can be said to exist and the Egyptians have the further difficulty in this case that it is dangerous for them to propagate among the Sudanese ideas of independence as such, as this may easily lead to a desire for greater independence from Egypt as well as from Great Britain.

It is perhaps worth noticing that so far as I know no attempts have been made by the Egyptian Government to consult the Sudanese about Arab unity, though I think there was just a reference to it in one of Nahas' earlier conversations—I think with Nuri? This may be because the Egyptian Government regard themselves as speaking for both Egypt and the Sudan in this matter, but it suggests that the Egyptian

---

[2] *Waqf*, Islamic endowment. The ministry of Waqfs (or *Awqaf*) disbursed funds in support of religious projects, and regulated Islamic trusts.

Government do not yet wish to cash in on the new Sudanese autonomous aspirations and probably are still thinking in terms of a return of the Sudan into an Egyptian state.

In spite of the fact that Newbold is perhaps crediting the Egyptians with a too definite line of policy, it seems most desirable that the Sudan Government should continue to pursue the policy which he advocates, namely, that they should not sit back now and think they can leave Sudanese political development to look after itself for another period, but that they should continually look for new means of associating the Sudanese with the Government of the country and giving them opportunities for developing a healthy sense of standing on their own feet. In short should lead rather than be led.

You will remember we specifically included the phrase about the Sudan in the Treaty to forestall any Egyptian attempt to "Egyptianise" it. It looks as though the phrase was likely to prove helpful and useful.

I am sending a copy of this letter to Huddleston.

17 FO 371/41363, no 2121 1 Jan 1944

[Unity of the Sudan]: despatch from Mustafa al-Nahhas to Sir H Huddleston [Extract]

... 2. *The division of the Sudan*

The Sudan Government has carried out a very vital change in the administration. Some of its proceedings lead one to believe that it is intended to divide the Sudan into two parts: a Northern and a Southern one. You have appointed an Advisory Council to the Northern Division. At the same time you have given extensive authority in Administrative and Legal matters to the Tribal Chiefs. You should not have undertaken these steps at all without the previous knowledge and agreement of the two Governments—the Egyptian and British—and in particular of the Egyptian Government. This action may be interpreted to mean that the object is to divide the Sudan into two parts, keeping the Southern Division isolated to be a pasture land for the Christian Missionary Societies. Your Excellency is well aware of the nervous tension of Mohammedans throughout the Nile Valley which will result from such a step—since it will raise religious problems, the raising of which is neither wise nor to any one's interest. What lends colour to the above interpretation is the information which has reached me that you prevent the people from the North to enter the Southern Zone, and vice versa. This is very odd arrangement in the Administration. ...

18 FO 371/41363, no 713 12 Jan 1944

[Future of the Sudan]: note by E S Atiyah[1] of a conversation with Ibrahim Ahmad on 7 Jan 1944 [Extract]

... 3. He then opened the subject of the future of the Sudan and expressed concern over the intensification of Egyptian propaganda and the new line it was taking. I

[1] Edward S Atiyah, Lebanese employed in the intelligence and public security departments of the civil secretary's office, 1930–1941; public relations officer, press and publicity section, civil secretary's office, 1942–1945.

asked him what his own opinion was on the future of the Sudan and what he thought were the views of the majority of the educated Sudanese. His reply was extremely candid and interesting; indeed, I was quite surprised at his frankness. He said there was, as yet, no clear homogeneous opinion in the Sudan concerning the future but many conflicting desires and views. The most conspicuous feature in the Sudan was Sayed Abd el Rahman el Mahdi's policy and personal ambitions. The Sayed, supported and encouraged by Mohammed Khalifa Sherif, was pursuing too impetuous and blatant a line. His separatist attitude towards Egypt gave the impression that he hoped to become King of an independent Sudan. Ibrahim went on to say that he did not approve of this policy of the Sayed's and that he had advised him very frankly against it. Kingship without real independence would be, in his opinion, a bad thing for the Sudan as for any other country, because the King, in such a situation, would be, or at least appear to be, as a mere tool in the hands of the ruling power, a facade behind which the real rulers would exercise their power without responsibility. The Sudan at the present stage of its development could not possibly become really independent. Any independence granted to it would be a sham. Therefore, Ibrahim did not want either independence or a King for his country for the time being, and he believed that this would be the attitude of the majority of the educated Sudanese.

4. The Sudan, he went on, was still in need of guidance and training for self-government. He was convinced that it was only from England that the Sudan could have the help she needed. The British were good administrators and he wished them to remain here for a considerable time to come to train the Sudanese in administration and gradually hand over the government to them. But, on the other hand, he did not wish to see the British remain in the Sudan without the Egyptians. He did not wish to see the Condominium dissolved and the Egyptian share in it completely abolished, because, much as he admired the British as administrators and desired their help, he did not trust them sufficiently to be willing to place the Sudan entirely at their mercy. The Sudan was a small and weak country and if Great Britain obtained exclusive control over it, the Sudanese would have no safeguards against exploitation. The Egyptians were very bad administrators, their morals were corrupt and the Sudan could not benefit directly from their presence, but their partnership in the Condominium constituted a check on the British, and, he believed, this check was very beneficial to the Sudan. Besides, the Sudanese had many things in common with the Egyptians and it was to their advantage to maintain friendly mutual relations with Egypt. In his opinion it was undesirable that the Sudan should prejudice these good relations by demanding the dissolution of the Condominium in favour of Great Britain. If they did that, they would make an enemy of Egypt and that would certainly be to their disadvantage. Ibrahim therefore believed that the best thing for the Sudan for the time being was to remain under the Condominium as at present working, i.e. a Condominium in which Egypt's share was nominal and real control and administration in the hands of the British. Within this frame-work the Sudanese should press for quicker training in the arts of self-government and a steadily increasing share in the management of their own affairs until, at some day in the future, they were ready to stand entirely alone and have complete self-government. Then they could choose what external connection to have with Britain, Egypt and the Arab world. . . .

19 FO 371/41363, no 1099 [Mar 1944]

[Condition of the country]: note by P S Scrivener on his tour of the Sudan (23 Feb–1 Mar 1944) [Extract]

To anyone who has not visited the Sudan recently the proofs of awakened national consciousness are impressive. The ambitions of Sudanese nationalism may be expressed crudely and with a doctrinaire disregard for inconvenient facts (we[1] heard examples of this) but, hitherto at any rate, the Sudanese concerned seem to have succeeded (thanks no doubt to the way in which they have been handled) in preserving a certain sense of humour which enables discussion to proceed without rancour. What interested us more particularly was the vigorous questioning by the Sudanese of the tangible advantages of condominium status. The Sudanese have clearly made themselves thoroughly familiar with the different funds etc., which are in existence for promoting various aspects of Colonial development, more particularly in the field of education; and they regard themselves as being at a serious disadvantage in that, despite their efforts in the war, the Foreign Office has no equivalent sources of bounty at its disposal. Indeed they did not hesitate to ask what we proposed to do about it. The political implications, or possible implications, of being assimilated to British Colonies for charitable purposes (if one may so describe it) did not appear to worry the Sudanese in the least: and whatever complications may be present in the situation, confidence in the ultimate virtue of our intentions towards them does not seem to be lacking. But they all want us to force the pace, as witness the view expressed recently by the Civil Secretary that it must continue to be His Majesty's Government and not Egypt who hold and exercise the initiative in the matter of Sudanese political progress. (The Sudanese would love a five year plan all worked out in advance.)

The foregoing remarks lead directly to the main difficulty which, as explained to us personally by the Governor-General, confronts the execution of a forward political policy, viz., the dearth of fully educated Sudanese to take over technical and administrative posts, and the virtual impossibility under present conditions of producing an educated class in sufficient numbers.

The Sudan started with nothing in the nature of an upper or cultured class anywhere. In the early days of the condominium educational progress was bound to be slow, but when it became desirable—on account of the development of an indigenous nationalist movement—to give a marked extension to higher education, the whole programme was restricted and thrown out of gear by the war with its crop of administrative and man-power difficulties, and the virtual interruption which it imposed on the technical training and higher education of Sudanese abroad.

However, despite these handicaps the Sudanese (on the authority of a private report, which I was allowed to see, by Mr. Cox[2] on his recent visit there) are in the van of Colonial educational progress, and it is hoped that the forthcoming visit of the Asquith Commission[3] will enable them to develop plans for the future. Under these

---

[1] Scrivener was accompanied by C H Johnston, 2nd secretary at the embassy in Cairo.

[2] C W M Cox, fellow of New College, Oxford, seconded to Sudan as director of education, 1937–1939; member of governor-general's council, 1938–1939.

[3] Sir Cyril Asquith's commission on higher education in the colonies, set up by the CO in 1943, was instructed to take into account evidence from the Sudan. The Asquith Commission Report was published in 1945 (Cmd 6647, June 1945).

conditions it seems very desirable that His Majesty's Government should consider what assistance (apart from the advice of the Asquith Committee) can be given to the Sudan Government to enable them to recover lost ground in the educational field. The question is of future political importance and I propose shortly to put forward proposals (which would, however, unduly lengthen this report).

The second point which struck us was the feeling that too little was known in the outside world about what the Sudan had done and was doing, not only as regards active campaigning but also as regards cotton production, economy in consumption of supplies, anti-inflation measures and so forth. This feeling was coupled with the hope that some concession in the matter of the supply of consumer goods would now be made to the Sudan in recognition of the sacrifices willingly accepted in the more critical years. Criticisms on this score were voiced by such varied elements as the Head of the Sudan Plantations Syndicate and a member of Congress (who, I should imagine, were not accustomed to seeing eye to eye on any conceivable subject whatever)....

A third point which Sir D. Newbold was good enough to discuss with us at some length is the Southern Sudan, the alleged neglect of which by the Sudan Government has been a subject of criticism both by the Egyptians and also by Congress. Broadly speaking the intentions of the Sudan Government (which have not yet, I think, been crystallised into a definite policy) are to re-divide the present Equatorial Province into its two former components, Mongalla and Bahr-el-Ghazal,[4] and to launch as soon as possible a major educational drive with the object of placing the inhabitants on a footing where progress on the lines of that recently initiated in the north will become possible. This plan does not embrace the Upper Nile Province where the nature of the country and the racial peculiarities of its inhabitants are *sui generis* and call for special and less ambitious measures. It may be observed in parenthesis that the policy hitherto followed by the Sudan Government of making the missionary societies the agents of their educational policy in the south is beginning to prove unsatisfactory owing to the inability of the societies to deliver the goods above a certain standard. It looks as though sooner or *later* the societies may be relegated to a purely secondary position; and a certain amount of friction may be generated in the process.

[4] Mongalla and Bahr al-Ghazal provinces were amalgamated in 1936 to form Equatoria Province as part of Symes' drive for economy in administration. They were redivided in 1948, with Equatoria retaining the western-most districts along the Congolese and French Equatorial borders, previously administered by Bahr al-Ghazal.

20 FO 371/41363, no 1418 5 Mar 1944
[SAR and SAM]: note by E S Atiyah of P S Scrivener's interviews with Sayyid Abd al-Rahman al-Mahdi and Sayyid Ali al-Mirghani [Extract]

Mr. Scrivener called on S.A.R. at his Abbasia house in Omdurman at 9.15 a.m. on Saturday, 26th February.

After the usual courtesies, the Sayed passed on to the subject of the war, expressing his great admiration of the heroism displayed by the British people in 1940 and 1941, and his gratification at the now sure prospect of an Allied victory.

This prospect, he said, was naturally beginning to focus people's attention all over the world on what was going to happen after the war. The Sudanese, like every other people who had fought on the Allied side, had their aspirations and hoped to see them realised through the victory of Britain and the United Nations. The Sudanese could have taken the view, which indeed was held by Sir Stewart Symes the then Governor-General, that the defence of the Sudan was the concern of the British and Condominium Governments, and that no obligation rested on them to participate actively in it, but they did not. They elected to regard the war as *their* war and to engage in it actively side by side with British, first in the defence of their country against the common enemy, and then further afield. They did this in the conviction that they would be able to realise their national aspirations through a British victory and at the hands of the British people and Government, in whose fairness and justice the experience of 45 years encouraged them to put their trust. The Sayed thought that the British people would be pleased to know that he, the son of Mahdi who was their enemy sixty years ago, was now, as the result of the just and beneficial administration of the British in the Sudan, their staunchest friend and ally, and believed that only through co-operation with Britain could the Sudan realise its destiny.

The Sayed went on to say that the fact that the Sudan was not a colony, but a territory coming under the Foreign Office and enjoying the status of a special connection with Britain, had been one of the factors that made the Sudanese decide to regard the war as theirs and to engage actively in it. They felt that in doing so they would be acting rather as the "allies" than as the subjects of Britain.

The British and the Sudan Governments, the Sayed continued, had for a long time adopted the principle of 'the Sudan for the Sudanese' as the basis of the present régime in the Sudan. By proclaiming this principle the British repudiated any intention on their part of annexing the Sudan as a colony, a repudiation which was very reassuring to the Sudanese. Unfortunately, however, there was another quarter from which the Sudanese felt threatened and they wanted the principle of the 'Sudan for the Sudanese' to apply vis-à-vis that quarter too. The Sudan Government had recently taken several propitious and well-timed steps in the direction of self-government for the Sudanese. The Sudanese wished this policy to continue and hoped through it to rise after the war to a higher status than that accorded to them in the Anglo–Egyptian Treaty of 1936. When that Treaty was concluded the Condominium partners considered that the Sudanese people were not politically mature enough to be consulted about the future of their country, and therefore contented themselves with including in the Treaty a unilateral declaration affirming that the object of the Condominium Government must be the welfare of the Sudanese. This declaration was accepted by the Sudanese at the time as a pledge of good faith on the part of the Condominium partners, but the world had moved forward considerably since the conclusion of the Treaty and the Sudanese felt today, particularly in view of the part they had played in the war, that that welfare clause had ceased to be an adequate recognition of their rights and status. Despite the Condominium Agreement and the Zaafaran Treaty,[1] the Egyptians had refused to take any part in the defence of the Sudan. The Sudanese could not help feeling that this refusal made a difference to the Egyptian position in the Sudan.

---

[1] i.e. the 1936 Anglo–Egyptian agreement (negotiations for which began in the Zaafaran palace in Cairo).

Mr. Scrivener replied that while he had no authority to discuss such important and far-reaching questions, he was greatly interested to hear the Sayed's views on them and very grateful to the Sayed for expressing these views to him. At the same time he pointed out that the Treaty of 1936 covered other questions than the Sudan and had been of great benefit to Britain in the war, in that it ensured her a military base in Egypt of the utmost importance for the defence of the whole Middle East, including the Sudan. He added that the Egyptians had carried out their obligations under the Treaty to the full. The Sayed agreed, but countered by saying that Egypt had benefited from the Treaty as much as Britain, and that in any case it would be unjust to reward one party at the expense of the other. If the British felt that they owed Egypt something for the help she had given them in the war, the Sudanese had nothing to say to that, provided they were not made to pay the price. They had helped Britain in a more positive way than Egypt and expected Britain to reward them by a greater recognition of their national aspirations. . . .

The interview with Sayed Ali took place at 12.30 p.m. I had warned Mr. Scrivener not to expect any expression of interesting views from him, predicting that the Sayed would only talk about the weather and the war. In the event I was only 50% right. The Sayed talked only about the weather dealing with the subject, as Mr. Scrivener commented on leaving, "pretty thoroughly".

21 FO 371/41363, no 2121 18 May 1944

[Unity of the Sudan]: despatch (reply)[1] from Sir H Huddleston to Mustafa al-Nahhas [Extract]

... *The division of the Sudan*

(i) Any division of the Sudan which exists does not arise from the Advisory Council or from any other administrative arrangement carried out by the Sudan Government, but from the natural, historic and tribal composition of the country. The six northern provinces are predominantly Arab in origin and culture, and the two southern provinces are inhabited by peoples akin racially to the tribes of central Africa and largely pagan.

The people of the two Southern Provinces have not yet reached a stage of development in which they can usefully take part in the Advisory Council which I have recently set up, but nothing has been done which will prevent them doing so when they reach that stage.

(ii) I cannot agree that the steps taken to establish local self-government in the Sudan or to set up an Advisory Council should have been submitted for the prior approval of the Government of Egypt. Article IV of the 1899 Agreement contains no such provision.

This development is merely the most recent step in a series of legislative enactments which have become law since 1922, when an Ordinance giving judicial powers to Nomad Sheikhs was first introduced.[2] This was followed by several other ordinances:—a Village Courts Ordinance in 1925, Powers of Sheikhs Ordinances in

[1] Reply to 17.

[2] The Powers of Nomad Sheikhs Ordinance, 1922.

1927 and 1928, a Chiefs Courts Ordinance in 1931, a Native Courts Ordinance in 1932 and finally a corpus of three Local Government Ordinances passed in 1937 covering Municipalities, Townships and Rural Areas.

All these ordinances were, in accordance with the Condominium Agreement, notified to the British and Egyptian Governments at the time and have excited no previous comment.

Local Government progress is normal in civilised countries and the steps so far taken to associate the Sudanese with the local administration of rural and urban areas, and more recently with the central government of their country have been welcomed by the Sudanese, and are, in my opinion, fully in accordance with the intention of the High Contracting Parties in the Treaty of 1936, where it was agreed by them that the primary aim of their administration in the Sudan must be the welfare of the Sudanese.

(iii) There have been Christian Missionary Societies in the Southern Sudan for over a century and they were first admitted there by the former Egyptian Government. Since the reoccupation of the Sudan the Sudan Government has seen no reason to reject their generous and devoted efforts in the humanitarian aim of improving the education and health of the primitive tribes of Upper Nile and Equatoria Provinces. The missionary societies have no monopoly of education as is implied in Your Excellency's memorandum. Government education of a secular type is being introduced and will increase especially in the higher branches as funds and staff become available. Government hospitals and dispensaries are already widespread. Moreover such Moslem communities as exist in the South have their own mosques and undisturbed facilities for Arabic and Islamic teaching.

(iv) There is no legislation to prevent people from the Northern Sudan going to the South, or southerners coming to the North. There are at the present time hundreds of Southern Sudanese in the north, where they come in search of work, and even enlist in northern units of the Sudan Defence Force. The Closed Districts Order of 1942 [sic, 1924] (Amended in 1925) reads:—"The districts set forth ... shall be closed districts to the extent that no person other than a native of the Sudan shall enter or remain therein unless he is the holder of a permit." This order, which has been applied to large areas in the Northern and western Sudan as well as to the two southern provinces, is designed to prevent unscrupulous foreigners from exploiting the simple inhabitants of these regions; and all traders entering such "closed" districts are compelled to obtain a special permit to trade therein. ...

22 FO 371/45973, no 99 — 7 Dec 1944

[Education grant]: despatch no 128 from Sir H Huddleston to Lord Killearn on the proposed gift to the Gordon Memorial College

[In July 1944 the FO forwarded to the Treasury a request from the Sudan government for £1,000,000 to endow Gordon College. This was rejected by the Treasury secretary on the grounds of 'our extremely difficult position as regards external finance', and 'the difficulty of convincing the Americans of the gravity of our problem if we continued to spend abroad as freely as we had in the past.' He went on to say: 'The essence of the present proposal, as I understand it, is that, for political reasons, we should make a spectacular gesture of munificence. I am afraid that ... we are no longer in a position in which we can play the Lady Bountiful with foreign currency, and, while I have no criticism of your objective, I fear that the Treasury view of your present proposal must be that on general financial grounds the suggested grant would be most inopportune' (Hopkins to Cadogan, 10 Aug 1944, FO 371/45973, no 1318). In renewing the request and forwarding Huddleston's despatch to the FO, Killearn (22 Dec 1944) argued that the Sudan's claim to financial assistance for higher education from HMG was equal to those of the colonies, and 'the responsibility of His Majesty's Government no less real'. In addition to this there was competition from Egypt which was aimed at increasing Egyptian interest and intervention in Sudanese affairs. Sir O Sargent's minute to the Treasury of 3 Feb 1945, urging Huddleston's claim for an education grant, further noted that the grant would be spent within the sterling area, '... if the Sudan is not a British Colony still less is it a foreign country' (FO 371/45973, no 99).]

I have the honour to refer to correspondence received under cover of Embassy Despatch No.238 dated August 3rd 1944, and to our conversation regarding the attitude adopted by His Majesty's Government to the proposed gift of £.1,000,000 to the Gordon Memorial College.

2. I fully realise the difficulties which lie in the way of His Majesty's Government making such a gift, the vast expenditure which has occurred during the war and which still continues, the commitments which are obligatory on the British taxpayer, and the necessity for avoiding all non-productive external expenditure.

The Sudan's plea is prompted by an urgent political need for some such gesture, and justified by the country's contribution to the British War Effort. These arguments have already been advanced at some length in my Despatch No.77 dated the 10th June, 1944, but in the circumstances I feel it is necessary to restate and amplify them.

3. The Egyptian Government has recently opened a Secondary School in Khartoum at an estimated capital cost of £E.250,000, and has asked for permission to build a hospital on a similar scale. There is evidence that Egyptian funds have been, and are being, freely expended in the Sudan on propaganda. Sudanese wishing for higher education in Cairo are normally admitted to schools and universities free and it is estimated that in 1943 there were 158 students being educated there in this way at the expense of the Egyptian Government.

The Sudanese as a whole do not wish to be administered by Egypt, and remember earlier Egyptian rule with distaste, but an increasing minority of the educated class is attracted by the glitter of Egypt's gold, and there can be little doubt that a few have already been dazzled by it.

4. As I explained in my previous Despatch, the benefits of the British connection are less tangible, and, although the middle and lower classes are apparently content with the present administration, numbers of well-disposed persons are disappointed by the failure of the British Government to interest itself in the Sudan except where its own security or profit is concerned. They are fully aware of the existence and purpose of the Colonial Development fund, and there have also been frequent references in the Vernacular Press to the Sudan's ineligibility to benefit from the British people's determination to assist their colonies on the way to progress.

The following extract from a News Letter produced by a leading local journalist is quoted as a recent example of such comment:—

> "Condominium Development Fund. The British have their four years' plan, and the Egyptian have a five years' one. Both governments have shown their willingness to spend as much as they can for Post-War reconstruction and social reforms. The British have gone further and founded a special Colonial

> Development Fund, of which the Sudan, which fought with them, shall have no share! The principal aim of the High Contracting powers is our welfare. Can I say they are bound to find a Condominium Development Fund? To achieve that welfare means waging a vigorous campaign against ignorance, hunger and disease. The Sudan Budget, standing at about £E.6,000,000 more than half of which goes in salaries, pensions and gratuities, cannot withstand financing that campaign. It becomes necessary that the two Governments should find the necessary money. Is that too much for these 'so few' who have rarely been owed so much by so many? We do not think it is."

This attitude was remarked on by Mr. Scrivener when commenting on his visit to the Sudan last winter.[1] While stressing "the vigorous advantages of condominium status" he also remarked:—

> "The Sudanese have clearly made themselves thoroughly familiar with the different funds etc., which are in existence for promoting various aspects of Colonial development, more particularly in the field of education; and they regard themselves as being at a serious disadvantage in that, despite their efforts in the war, the Foreign Office has no equivalent sources of bounty at its disposal. Indeed they did not hesitate to ask what we proposed to do about it."

5. Should the British interest in the Sudan prove in the eyes of the Sudanese to be so weak that His Majesty's Government will not grant them assistance similar to that given to British Colonial territories it seems likely that the Sudanese will be driven against their wiser counsels to look to Egypt for the capital required for their future progress. The British attitude is to them impossible to understand, in that while they read daily of grants to Nigeria, Kenya, Uganda, and other African territories, they are told that the Sudan is ineligible, and that the British cannot afford to give to them what they give to others.

They point out that the Sudan was considered eligible to send its young men to fight the Italians in East Africa and the Germans in North Africa and to garrison the Italian Colonies of Eritrea, Libya and Tripoli on behalf of His Majesty's Government and that within the past war years its products have been sold to the British Army and to the British Ministry of Supply at Sudan prices, which are well known to be the lowest in the Middle East and therefore must represent a most substantial saving to the British taxpayer.

6. There exists now a great opportunity to win the sympathy and co-operation of the Sudanese by a gesture of this kind, and an equal danger that if it is not made in the near future the chance will be lost, possibly never to return, and Egyptian influence will have freer scope to spread than ever before. Egypt is prepared to spend money for this purpose and her pressure is growing.

7. To assess British strategic interests in the Sudan vis-à-vis the Middle East and the route to the Far East is not within my competence, but should not be lost sight of in considering this proposal. A greater factor in my mind is the moral obligation laid upon us to maintain the present predominantly British régime in the Sudan with its willing co-operation between the Government and the governed, until the Sudanese

---

[1] See 19.

have reached a stage of political development in which they will be able to decide their own future. Failure to retain their confidence may result in jeopardising the patient and successful work of 45 years, and the surrender of a virile and friendly people to a corrupt and inefficient Government before they can stand upon their own feet.

23 FO 371/45972, no 97 12 Dec 1944

[Sudan Graduates' Congress elections]: report from SPIS no 44 for November [Extract]

[The Graduates' Congress elections in November 1944 marked the emergence of sectarian involvement in nationalist politics. Shortly after the elections, in which a Mirghanist (Khatmiya)-sponsored majority was elected, SAM openly declared that his intervention was necessary to prevent SAR from capturing the Congress, as he had already captured the Advisory Council, and that the real issue was SAR's monarchical ambitions, not union with Egypt (see SPIS no 45, para 358 in FO 371/45972, no 552).]

Local affairs

356. *The Congress elections*

The Congress Annual General Meeting was held on 27.11.44 at the Graduates' Club, Omdurman. As expected, it dwarfed all previous meetings in size and its quality was in the necessary inverse proportion. The number of registered members stood at 9,400 (cf. 1,300 in 1943 and 1,800 in 1942) on the day of the elections. Admission cards had been issued for 5,864 of them, but the number of members who actually attended and voted was 4,667 (cf. 966 in 1943 and 1,230 in 1942).

In spite of its size, the excitement that had prevailed during the election campaign and the importance of the ostensible issues over which the election was being contested, the meeting itself was not only quiet but extremely perfunctory and lasted barely an hour, the reason being that everything had been decided beforehand and that the purpose of the meeting was not to discuss any controversial views but merely to record the results of bloc party voting. By election day the whole campaign had clearly resolved itself into a struggle on the old sectarian basis between Mahdists and Mirghanists, and practically all the groups that had formed themselves as professedly independent bodies were definitely ranged under the Ansar or Khatmy banner. This result had become inevitable from the moment that the two sects decided to throw their numerical weight into the elections, for no independent group could, in these circumstances, hope for any success if it did not enjoy the backing of the one side or the other. The Mirghanists had been supporting the Ashigga throughout the year, and when members of the rival groups (Qawam'yia, Ahrar and a section of the Ittihadiyin) realised how effective this support was going to be they had no choice but to ally themselves openly with the Ansar and depend on the Mahdist bloc vote.

The only thing worthy of note in the proceedings that preceded the voting was the President's annual speech—an admirable pronouncement by Ibrahim Ahmed—which for courage, wisdom and moral tone would have done credit to any statesman in any country, and in which he particularly warned his hearers of the danger of misapplying democratic procedure in a backward country like the Sudan.

This danger was only too apparent in the elections that followed, for the majority of the voters certainly did not belong to the educated class (they were mostly ignorant Tariqa followers, workers, artisans and small tradesmen, cultivators from the Khartoum Deims[1] and the Khartoum North rural areas) and it was obvious that the various safeguards devised to prevent cheating had failed and that effective checking at the gate was impossible.

The results were a sweeping victory for the Ashigga and the Mirghanists who obtained 36 seats out of the 60 and secured the election of their leader Azhari by a majority of nearly 1,500 votes over Ibrahim Ahmed, the top scorer on the other side. . . .

The Ashigga won (a) because the Mirghanists are a majority in the Three Towns, particularly in the Deims of Khartoum and the rural areas of Khartoum North, (b) because the Ansar did not enter the field in earnest till a short time before the elections and until the end were in a divided mind as to whether they should ally themselves with any of the existing groups or not, whereas the Mirghanists had been solidly supporting the Ashigga throughout the year, (c) because, quite apart from sectarian support, they were a better organised and more united party than any of their opponents and had behind them the bulk of the younger graduates.

The result has a multiple significance. On the face of it it is a verdict in favour of Egypt and this is how the local Egyptians have interpreted it and how it will be represented by the Egyptian papers and politicians. More concretely it is a slap in the face to Sayed Abdel Rahman and his suspected monarchical ambitions. Lastly it is an indication of an anti-British and anti-Government spirit among the majority of the younger effendia, for in so far as the results are the expression of a political opinion independent of sectarian motives they are more anti-British than positively pro-Egyptian. What binds the Ashigga together is their emotional hostility to the Sudan Government and not any unanimous love for Egypt, and they are certainly not agreed among themselves on the degree of 'Union' they want with Egypt.

The older and more responsible graduates are genuinely and profoundly alarmed at what has happened and at the prospect of the results likely to follow from it if nothing is done to prevent them in time. They see that they are losing control over Congress, that the body they formed to represent educated opinion on a non-sectarian basis has now fallen into the hands of irresponsible persons and become a battleground for the two religious parties. The more sensible graduates, whether they incline to S.A.R. or S.A.M., deplore this development which means the submergence of Corporate graduate identity in the old struggle between the sects, and that political leadership by the religious heads will again dominate the country and divest the Graduates of any independence they may have acquired in recent years.

So much for the general and long-range dangers—implied in these election results. There is as well an immediate and specific danger—that the Ashigga may decide to pass a resolution in favour of Union with Egypt. Opinions on the likelihood of their taking some such step differ widely. Some believe that they intend and will try to do it; that the Egyptians expect it of them and will press for it in order that they

[1] The 'deims' were working class quarters or shanty-towns on the outskirts of Omdurman and Khartoum.

should have a counter-blast in advance to any expression of Sudanese national aspirations that might come from the Advisory Council, a verdict which they could present at the Peace Conference. An article that appeared recently in El-Musawar lends colour to this opinion. On the other hand, others do not believe that there is any real danger of their doing this. Their reasons are: (a) that they are not sufficiently agreed on the form of association they wish to have with Egypt, and that, in their opinion, many of them do not desire union at all, (b) that even if they were agreed on Union they would not dare to proclaim their desire in a formal resolution, from fear both of the Government and the Sudanese public at large, (c) that Sayed Ali whose responsibility for the victory of the Ashigga was now a matter of common knowledge, however much he might deny it if taxed with it to his face, would probably decline to sanction such a step. ...

24 FO 371/46081, no 643 24 Dec 1944

[Nile Waters]: despatch no 132 from Sir H Huddleston to Lord Killearn

I have the honour to address Your Excellency on the amount of Nile water at present available to the Sudan for irrigation and storage and of the need to secure, with the agreement of the Egyptian Government, additional quantities.

2. The need for these additional supplies is no new or unforeseen development. It was stated in Sir Stewart Symes' despatch No. 79 of the 6th May, 1939. It was pointed out in my own despatch No.39 of the 22nd June, 1941 when the question of the project at Lake Tsana was reopened for the first time since the war: and again in despatch No.32 of the 25th May 1943 on the same subject. But the march of events and the requirements of post-war planning now make the need for a settlement more urgent.

3. The immediate post-war period will be marked in the Sudan by an urgent demand for expansion of the social services; for more schools and teachers: for more hospitals, clinics and dispensaries; and for a general raising of the standard of sanitation and health measures and for their expansion. To meet these reasonable and in many cases essential claims, and at the same time maintain financial equilibrium, additional revenue must be found by a widening of the productive capacity of the country. To raise the existing level of taxation would not of itself be sufficient and is in any case in my view impractical. Nor would such a course satisfy the need to find a livelihood for men, who by their experience in war have learned a higher standard of living than can be maintained by pastorals with occasional rain cultivation. An expansion of productive capacity in the Sudan must largely be agricultural and from the physical circumstances of the country must mainly depend on perennial irrigation. Time is running short for the execution of the works, necessary to such expansion, but before they are begun it is essential to know that water will be available at the proper time.

4. In 1939 the balance of unallotted water (including the January allowance) in the Sennar reservoir was 165 million cubic metres out of a total of 922 millions. To-day this balance has shrunk to some 50 million, a margin which will be readily and

rapidly absorbed. The question that follows [is] of how and from where further storage supplies are to be found.

5. The project at Lake Tsana on the Blue Nile, constructed and operated on the terms envisaged by the Sudan–Egyptian agreement of 1935, constitutes both technically and financially the best and easiest [source?] of the Sudan's needs. But recent despatches indicate little prospect of immediate or fruitful negotiations with the Ethiopian Government.[1] Moreover the Egyptian Government's attitude is presumably still that expressed in its Aide-Memoire of November 1938 as follows:—

> "The Royal Egyptian Government do not consider that so far as their own interests are concerned the immediate construction of such a work (i.e. Tsana regulator) is in any way necessary to their programme of agricultural expansion for the next fifteen years."

Therefore it seems that the Sudan can no more look for an early achievement of this project than in 1939, when any chances of its fulfilment had been set back by Italy's invasion and occupation of Ethiopia.

6. At that time Sir Stewart Symes deemed it necessary to seek an alternative but temporary satisfaction of the Sudan's needs by putting forward a claim for the type of review of the relative storage positions of the two countries which had been contemplated in paragraph 83 of the Nile Waters Agreement (1929). It was argued by Mr. Robertson,[2] the then Irrigation Adviser of the Sudan Government, that any lag in irrigational development in the Sudan, resulting from delay in the execution of the Lake Tsana project, should and could be made good by Egypt from the surplus storage which had accumulated as a result of works executed by her since the conclusion of the Nile Waters Agreement of 1929, and of which that Agreement had taken no account. Thus the Nile Waters Agreement had envisaged the Sennar and Jebel Auliya reservoirs as parallel schemes forming the first stage in the development of Nile storage for both the Sudan and Egypt.

Expressed in volumes these stages represented

781 million cubic metres at Sennar as the Sudan's share, and
2000 million cubic metres from Jebel Auliya at Aswan as Egypt's share.

The second raising of Aswan together with Jebel Auliya has given to Egypt 4400 million cubic metres (or 4800 million if the Aswan reservoir is raised from R.L. 121 to R.L. 122 as the present structure permits).

The technical arguments and data supporting this claim were contained in two papers by Mr. Robertson entitled "The respective shares of Egypt and the Sudan in the Waters of the Nile" dated 16th March, 1939, and "Review of the Tsana 1935 Agreement" dated 26th March 1939. Copies of these papers were annexed to Sir Stewart Symes' despatch No.79 of the 6th May, 1939.

7. With the consent of His Britannic Majesty's Government Sir Stewart Symes made a direct approach to the Egyptian Government. I attach as annex to this despatch copies of the notes of his conversations with the Egyptian Ministers and of the Aide-Memoire left by him in the hands of the Prime Minister. I would draw Your

[1] For a summary of negotiations with Ethiopia up to this date, see 27.

[2] A N M Robertson, director of irrigation (Sudan government), 1934–1937; irrigation adviser, 1937–1940.

Excellency's attention to the Prime Minister's remarks as reported therein, that as a result of his visit to the Sudan he might be able to make a formal announcement on the water question which would be reassuring to the Sudanese. In the event no such pronouncement was in fact made and owing to the course of the war no further progress has been made in the matter. But at the time of that visit the then Minister of Works in discussion expressed the view that Egypt could not be expected to give up part of her storage water merely on the ground that Lake Tsana was not yet available for the Sudan.[3]

8. It is unlikely that Egypt's response to any renewal of such a claim will be favourable or prompt. Evidence of their probable attitude can be found in their constant refusal since 1939 to consider any advancement of the date on which the Gezira canal may begin to draw on the natural flow of the river, and in their rejection in 1942 of a request to permit a temporary lift of 30 centimetres at Sennar during September. Further evidence of this lack of regard for Sudan interests may be seen in the withdrawal of Aswan water in 1943 and 1944 to such extent as completely to interrupt communications on the Shellal reach. Expansion of agricultural areas to meet temporary war-time needs is likely to be claimed as a permanent peace-time necessity. Lastly I need not remind Your Excellency of the way in which the Egyptian press always reacts to any issue on Nile Waters.

9. On the other hand the Sudan's claim is no new one nor one of which Egypt has not been well aware. Egypt must know full well that her present position relative to that of the Sudan is out of line with the Nile Waters Agreement. That a revision of that agreement would be necessary was foreseen by its creators and was admitted by the Egyptian Prime Minister when accepting the recommendations in these words:

> "It is realised that the development of the Sudan requires a quantity of the Nile water greater than that which has been so far utilised by the Sudan. As Your Excellency is aware the Egyptian Government has always been anxious to encourage such development and will therefore continue that policy and be willing to agree with His Majesty's Government upon such increase of the quantity as does not infringe Egypt's natural and historical rights in the waters of the Nile and its requirements of agricultural extension".

10. The Sudanese are now conscious, as they never formerly were, that the present restrictions to their agricultural expansion lie in the terms of the Nile Waters Agreement and will continue only if Egypt is unwilling to recognise their legitimate claims. The need for a revision of the Agreement has now been twice spontaneously raised during this year by members of the Advisory Council of the Northern Sudan, besides previous allusions in the vernacular press, and Sudanese restiveness over this question is likely to increase.

---

[3] Not printed. 'Notes of conversation on 23rd November 1939 with Hussein Pasha Sirri (minister of finance) and Abdel Kawi Bey Ahmed (minister of works)'; 'Note of conversation with Ali Pasha Maher (prime minister), Hussein Pasha Sirry (minister of finance) and Abdel Kawi Ahmed (minister of public works) on 28th November 1939'; 'A note on Nile water questions at issue between Egypt and the Anglo–Egyptian Sudan (November 1939)'; and 'Aide memoir, November 1939'.

11. In all these circumstances I consider that the question can no longer be held in abeyance, and that the position should now be fully examined.

12. The Sudan objective during such examination would as in 1939 be to secure, for use until the full supply of water from Lake Tsana can be made available, the lesser supply which would result from agreement that the Sudan should:—

(a) Advance the July water date as provided in paragraph 13 of the Lake Tsana Agreement.
(b) Raise the reservoir level at Sennar to provide the extra volume of 150 million cubic metres approximately which was agreed upon in paragraph 15 of the Lake Tsana Agreement.
(c) Withdraw an extra 500 million cubic metres from the Blue Nile during the period January to April as an alternative to the arrangement contemplated in paragraph 9 of the Lake Tsana Agreement.

13. I am advised that the first and second of these three steps could be taken without harmful effect on the supply of water to Egypt. This is not so as regards the third step, but it may alternatively be possible to negotiate for the allotment of 500 million cubic metres to the Sudan from the first additional storage made available, the Sudan of course paying a proportional share of the cost. Agreement by Egypt to this allotment could reasonably be balanced by the Sudan's consent to the inception of any further Egyptian projects on the White Nile or on the main Nile. This negotiation might also focus Egyptian attention on the desirability of giving the Lake Tsana scheme priority over other developments.

14. The extra supplies of water which would be obtained by the first two of the steps proposed would allow for as much development by the Sudan as is likely to be practicable during the next ten years by increase of gravity irrigation in the Gezira area and of pumping on the White Nile. It is worth noting that these increases are needed to ensure the livelihood of people whose lands are now flooded by water stored for Egypt in the Jebel Auliya reservoir. The larger supply to be obtained from the third step is necessary, if development, especially in the Gezira, is to proceed along the lines of the second stage contemplated when the 1929 Nile Waters Agreement was made. Agreement to the third step should therefore, I consider, be included in the immediate objective, but it will not be necessary to press that it should be acted upon so immediately as the first two.

15. I therefore request that the Egyptian Government—who recently both in respect of Lake Tsana, and of the river Baro, have shown their interest in safeguarding their own rights in the Nile Waters should, subject to Your Excellency's views, now be reminded of the claim made by the Sudan Government in 1939, and should formally be asked to consent to an early examination of the present water storage position in detail and by technical experts authorized by each Government for the purpose.

16. If the consent of the Egyptian Government is secured, I shall seek again to employ Mr. MacGregor to negotiate on behalf of the Sudan Government, as his intimate knowledge of the problem is unrivalled and as he is experienced in negotiation with the Egyptians.

25 FO 141/1013, no 22 7 Feb 1945

[Anglo–Egyptian relations]: despatch no 44 from Lord Killearn to Sir H Huddleston on British interests in the Sudan and the possibility of using the Nile Waters as a means of resisting Egyptian pressure[1]

[Extract]

The recent series of minor crises in Anglo–Egyptian relations relative to the Sudan question … suggests that the present moment may be opportune for an attempt to clarify our ideas and intentions in regard to the future of the Sudan. …

3. I take it that our objectives in the Sudan are, primarily, to maintain our predominant position in a strategically important area, and, secondarily, to carry out in the Sudan our traditional policy of guiding a backward people by gradual stages towards self-government, with the definite intention that when they reach that stage they will be willing to maintain particularly close relations with us; and to ensure for them a good administration meanwhile. All the objectives seem to me, in the light of experience, to postulate that Egyptian influence in the Sudan should be kept at a minimum. Egyptian influence competing with ours might well be inconsistent with our strategic interests and interfere with the orderly movement towards a self-governing Sudan bound by close ties to us. It can hardly be questioned that effective Egyptian participation in the administration would seriously lower its efficiency. If this is, as I believe, a correct estimate, it follows logically that we have every ground, strategic, sociological and administrative, for resisting Egyptian political claims in regard to the Sudan. Our record in the Sudan, contrasted with the state of the country before the Mahdi's rebellion and with the probable performance of any even partly Egyptian administration there, should give us a strong case before world opinion in resisting Egyptian claims.

4. The Sudan question and the present tendency in Egypt to force the issue for internal political reasons thus contain the elements of a serious clash between British and Egyptian policy at no distant date. It is presumably in our interest to do all we reasonably can to avoid such a clash. To that end I submit that generally speaking we should, while resisting strongly any serious Egyptian attempt to intervene in Sudan affairs, continue to do our best to avoid provoking Egyptian interest or anxiety regarding the Sudan. For example we should maintain the condominium facade by consulting the Egyptian Government as and when possible keeping them informed in formal questions, and avoid giving the impression that we intend to use our position in the Sudan to the detriment of Egypt.

5. Should the Sudan issue nevertheless come to a head, it has always seemed to me that we hold in our hands the trump card of our physical control of the Nile waters. Perhaps it may even be opportune to consider now what use could be made of this instrument if driven to it.

6. The terms of Lord Lloyd's[2] letter of 7th May, 1929 to the then Egyptian Prime Minister are unequivocal. Writing in confirmation of the Nile Waters Agreement, Lord Lloyd stated therein that His Majesty's Government in the United Kingdom regarded the safeguarding of the natural and historical rights of Egypt in the waters

---

[1] A copy of this letter was forwarded to the FO and is also found in FO 371/45984, no 722.

[2] High commissioner for Egypt and the Sudan, 1925–1929.

of the Nile as a fundamental principle of British policy, and he conveyed to Mohamed Mahmoud Pasha the most positive assurances that this principle and the detailed provisions of the Nile Waters Agreement would be observed at all times and under any conditions that might arise. It is clear that His Majesty's Government are thus committed to safeguarding Egyptian rights in the Nile under any conditions, that is to say no matter how great may be the desire and need of the Sudan for extra water at any given time. As I pointed out in my despatch No.699 of 31st July, 1941, the water of the Nile is such an integral part of the life of every Egyptian that any suspicion that we or any outside influence were trying to get undue control of it would most effectively be used as propaganda to rally feeling against us in almost all classes of the population. We must naturally make every reasonable effort to avoid giving grounds for such agitation by disposing of Nile water without the agreement of the Egyptian Government or, even more, contrary to their interests. These considerations still apply, and in normal circumstances they should continue to guide our policy. Any disregard of Egypt's vital interest in the Nile waters would increase Egyptian opposition to our semi-exclusive control of the Sudan, and any British interference in the Sudan with Egypt's water supply would greatly strengthen the movement here for the reunion of Egypt and the Sudan. I understand that our inclusion of the Nile waters in the demands presented to the Egyptian Government by Lord Allenby after the murder of the Sirdar created a feeling of uneasiness in Egypt which eventually we felt it in our interest to allay by the signature of the Nile Waters Agreement.

7. The present despatch is not meant to challenge the validity of our existing policy so long as Anglo–Egyptian relations continue normal. What I have rather in mind is the consideration in advance of a potential situation where for some reason it might be necessary to bring heavy pressure to bear on the Egyptian Government, and of the possibility that in such a case, the restriction, real or threatened, of Egypt's water supply could in fact be used as a decisive sanction. It would, for instance, be a sovereign act by His Majesty's Government of a less drastic nature than a resort to war. Such a sovereign act would not be precluded by the contractual obligations referred to above, any more than our treaty obligations with Italy prevented the application of sanctions against her in 1933–1936. Similarly I am advised that a treaty of perpetual friendship has seldom prevented two nations from going to war. The suspension of the water supply would create violent hostility to Egypt, but ex hypothesi such hostility would have existed before it had been necessary to proceed to such a drastic sanction.

8. We have in fact the whip hand over Egypt, should we ever be forced to use it.

9. I should be glad to learn Your Excellency's reactions to the ideas discussed in this despatch, of which a copy is being forwarded to the Foreign Office.

26 FO 371/45972, no 837 12 Feb 1945

[Sudan Graduates' Congress programme]: report from SPIS no 46 for January [Extract]

. . . *Local affairs*

365. *Congress*

The Committee of Sixty met on 12.1.45 to consider the programme for the year drawn up by the XV. The programme, which was presented by the President, Ismail

El Azhari in a speech which lasted one hour, consisted of the following items:—

National Affairs.

1. Congress Memorandum.
2. Explaining the ultimate position of the Sudan.
3. Southern Sudan.
4. Definition of the Sudan war effort.
5. Study of post-war schemes.

Education.

Education Fund.

(a) Revenue.
(b) Expenditure.

1. Establishment of schools and religious institutions.
2. Aids for the establishment of schools and religious institutions.
3. Grants-in-aid for existing schools and institutions.
4. Scholarships for students:—
   (a) Beit Es Sudan (Sudan House) in Cairo.
   (b) Educational missions outside the Sudan.
   (c) Teachers' training.
5. Industrial development through the Piastre Orphanage.
6. Anti-illiteracy measures through grants-in-aid for night schools.
7. Public Library.
8. Establishment of a high council to supervise national education.

Economic Affairs.

1. Gezira Scheme.
2. Endeavours to establish commercial corporations.
3. Exhibitions of local industries.
4. Study of the proposal for a Sudan Bank.

Social Affairs.

1. Taking steps to establish a maternity hospital.
2. Care and encouragement of sports.
3. Labour Day.
4. Visits to the villages.

Culture.

1. Support for the preservation of the Koran.
2. Encouragement of authorship and publication.
3. Study of the history of the Sudan.
4. Prizes for students.
5. Encouragement of Literary Festival.
6. Support of Literary Societies and giving lectures.

Propaganda.

1. The Congress paper, and the question of purchasing a printing press.
2. Furthering relations with the Arab countries.
3. Propaganda for the Sudan abroad.
4. Contact with distinguished visitors to the Sudan.
5. "Congress hymn."

On paper it looks a very ambitious programme, as comprehensive and far-reaching as any put forward by a new Government in the speech from the Throne. The first three items imply political issues of the first importance. In introducing the item dealing with the future status of the Sudan, the President after quoting the Atlantic Charter and emphasising the right of small nations to determine their fate and shape their own form of government, went on to say that the Committee intended to make careful study of this vital matter and that it was hoped that "by the grace of God it may be able to arrive at a resolution suitably expressing the hopes and aspirations of the country".

With regard to the item dealing with the Sudan's war effort, the President after affirming that the Sudan had made its contribution to the war effort voluntarily and from conviction and belief in the justice of the Democratic cause went on to explain that the object behind the proposal to draw up an exact account of what the Sudan had done in the war was that "like other nations we should share in the fruits of victory to the extent that we have contributed towards it".

On the question of the South, the President harped on the usual theme—the essential unity of the Sudan, the regrettable isolation of the South, the need for co-ordinated development in both parts of the country and, above all, the economic need of the North for the South.

An outstanding feature of the debate that took place on the programme was that the 24 opposition members were able to make their presence felt to a much greater degree than had been expected. With the support of a number of Ashigga they succeeded in introducing an important amendment into the programme, viz: the inclusion, right at the beginning, of the Congress Memorandum of 1942. The Memorandum, it will be remembered, contained a demand for Sudanese nationality, and the object of the opposition in pressing for its inclusion in the programme was to tie down Azhari and his party to this demand and so make it impossible for them to pursue a policy of fusion with Egypt. Azhari resisted the amendment on the grounds that since the substance of the Memorandum was contained in the various items of the programme its inclusion as an item by itself would be superfluous, but enough of the Ashigga sided with the opposition to carry the motion for its inclusion.

The result of the debate, favourably commented on in the press as showing that the opposition can effectively voice its views, has increased the already evident willingness of the Moderates to acquiesce for the time being in the results at this year's elections; and the general tendency to condemn and challenge the present Congress, which was noticeable for a few days after the elections, has died down.

The Ashigga are now reported to be negotiating with the Ittihadiyin and Ahrar for a formula acceptable to all of them concerning relations with Egypt. They are said to repudiate fusion and profess their willingness to accept the Ittihadiyin's Dominion status conception. If agreement is reached (which is doubtful) the formula will be put up to the Sixty in the form of a resolution expressing Congress' attitude towards Egypt—and there will be a large majority behind it. . . .

27 FO 371/46081, no 709 13 Feb 1945

'Lake Tsana: the present position': memorandum by Research Department, FO, on the Nile Waters

Formal engagements still in force

The rights in relation to Lake Tsana which His Majesty's Government enjoy by Treaty are defined in Article 3 of the Anglo–Ethiopian Treaty of 1902, by the terms of which the Emperor undertook:—

> "not to construct, or allow to be constructed, any work across the Blue Nile, Lake Tsana or the Sobat which would arrest the flow of their waters into the Nile except in agreement with His Britannic Majesty's Government and the Government of the Sudan."

2. The interest of Egypt in all plans for regulating the flow of the Nile was given formal recognition by His Majesty's Government in the exchange of letters which constituted the Nile Waters Agreement of 1929. Lord Lloyd's letter to the Egyptian Prime Minister on that occasion contained the following assurance:—

> "In conclusion, I would remind your Excellency that His Majesty's Government in the United Kingdom have already acknowledged the natural and historical rights of Egypt in the waters of the Nile. I am to state that His Majesty's Government in the United Kingdom regard the safeguarding of those rights as a fundamental principle of British policy, and to convey to your Excellency the most positive assurances that this principle .... will be observed at all times and under any conditions that may arise."

Abortive Negotiations, 1902–35

3. The two texts quoted above appear to be the only formal undertakings conferring rights or imposing obligations on His Majesty's Government at the present time. Agreements with Italy, both before and after the Italian occupation of Ethiopia, will be ignored in this paper as irrelevant to the existing situation. But the long history of discussions with the Ethiopian Government before 1935 cannot be entirely omitted, since reference will no doubt be made to it during future negotiations.

4. It is possible, for instance, that the last has not been heard of Ethiopian claims based upon an offer made in 1907 to the Emperor Menelik, "in consideration .... of Article 3 of the Treaty," of £10,000 annually so long as friendly relations continued. This arrangement, though accepted in principle, was never signed owing to difficulties raised by Menelik over the form of our note. His Majesty's Government therefore consider this offer to have lapsed, and a demand put forward by the Ethiopian Government in 1930 for payment of arrears amounting to £230,000 was rejected. But the Ethiopian Government have not at any time admitted the invalidity of their claim, which they again raised in 1933.

5. The Treaty of 1902 conferred on His Majesty's Government and the Government of the Sudan no more than a veto on the construction of works to control the outflow from Lake Tsana. Later, between 1914 and 1927, attempts were made to secure an agreement by which His Majesty's Government would themselves

construct and operate a regulator across the head waters of the Blue Nile at their outlet from the Lake. It proved impossible to reach agreement on these lines, and we gradually acquiesced in the Ethiopian demand for a larger degree of control over the projected enterprise. In an exchange of letters with the present Emperor of Ethiopia in 1924, Mr. Ramsay MacDonald agreed to the building of the dam by engineers responsible to the Ethiopian Government, provided that His Majesty's Government were satisfied of the competence of the engineer chosen for the work. In 1928 His Majesty's Government again agreed that the construction of the dam should be arranged for by the Ethiopians themselves, subject both to the condition laid down four years earlier and to guarantees that the dam would be constructed and operated in such a way as to secure the full benefit of the waters of Lake Tsana to Egypt and the Sudan.

6. Meanwhile, in 1927, an approach had been made by the Ethiopian Government to the J. G. White Engineering Corporation of New York. In December 1928 the present Emperor was informed that His Majesty's Government would raise no objection to negotiations between the Ethiopian Government and the J. G. White Corporation, on the understanding that they would be given an opportunity of satisfying themselves that the project would be executed with due regard for economy as well as on sound engineering lines, and also that the plans for operating the dam were in accordance with their requirements.

7. After the completion of surveys carried out by the J. G. White Corporation in 1930–34, the Ethiopian Government issued invitations to the Governments of Egypt and the Sudan to send representatives to a conference at Addis Ababa in April 1935. This conference was postponed, and, as a result of the Italian invasion of Ethiopia, never met. The last development before the Italo–Ethiopian war was a preliminary conference in Cairo between representatives of Egypt and the Sudan, who on the 20th May signed an agreement providing for both the distribution of the water and the allocation of the cost. They also drafted joint instructions to the delegates who were to represent the two countries at the proposed conference in Addis Ababa.

8. It was agreed at the Cairo Conference that the designs of the J. G. White Engineering Corporation were "generally satisfactory," and that the execution of the work should be undertaken "as soon as possible." The expenditure, both for construction and for operation, would be borne in the first instance by Egypt, the Sudan's share being recovered in accordance with an agreed procedure. The Sudan, participating initially to the extent of 10 per cent., would have the option of gradually increasing her share, by virtue of an escalator clause, up to a maximum of 50 per cent.

9. The joint instructions drafted for the delegates who were to conduct the anticipated negotiations with the Ethiopian Government were based upon the assumption that it would probably be necessary to adopt the more expensive of the alternative plans offered by the J. G. White Corporation. The cheaper alternative would involve raising the level of the Lake, and it was expected that, although the central Government might find this acceptable, it would be opposed by the local chiefs and ecclesiastical authorities. The offer to be made to the Ethiopian Government in return for the adoption of the low-level scheme was to consist of: (1) the construction and maintenance, at the expense of Egypt and the Sudan, of an all-weather road from Addis Ababa to the Lake; (2) a cash payment of £30,000 on signature of the agreement; and (3) a rental of £10,000 annually from the year in

which the works were completed. On the question of operation and maintenance, the delegates were to be instructed that "an arrangement which might prove satisfactory to all parties would be for the J. G. White Engineering Corporation to take control of the works after completion for a period of, say, ten years. By that time .... it should be possible .... to make some new arrangement if desired." It was noted, however, that the Ethiopian Government would probably desire to have at least a partial control, or the appearance of it, over the works. (The Ethiopians had, in fact, insisted on this during the discussions which took place in 1930–31.)

Attitude of the interested parties after the liberation of Ethiopia

10. *Ethiopia*.—Before 1930 the Ethiopian Government viewed proposals for the Tsana reservoir with suspicion, and countered them by procrastination. In this year their attitude changed as a result of acute financial embarrassment, and in 1935 they again pressed for an early agreement, this time with the additional motive of providing His Majesty's Government with a material interest in the independence and integrity of Ethiopia. A further attraction to the central Government in Addis Ababa was the prospect of strengthening its authority in the troublesome regions of Gojjam and Begemdir by means of the projected road from the capital to the Lake. Since the liberation of Ethiopia in 1941, the second and third of these motives have no longer operated: the Italian menace has, it may be assumed, been finally removed; and the Italians constructed a good motor road between Addis Ababa and the Lake, by way of Debra Markos, which, though its condition has deteriorated, could doubtless be put in good order at a comparatively small cost. The Emperor is still short of money, but, if he has hopes of a substantial loan from the United States, this consideration may not affect his attitude to the Tsana project in the immediate future. A new factor in the situation is the control by British military authorities of ex-Italian territories—in particular the Tigrinia-speaking region of Eritrea and the harbours of Massawa and Assab—to which the Ethiopian Government lay claim. The Emperor may well consider that, in any discussion of the future of these territories, Lake Tsana might be his most useful bargaining counter.

11. *The Sudan*.—The Government of the Sudan, whose interest in the project had waned in the years 1931–35 owing to the effects of the economic crisis, are now more anxious than at any previous time to press on with the control of the Blue Nile. They point out that, whereas in 1935 the balance of unused storage water in the Sennar reservoir was 236 million cubic metres, it has now shrunk to 70 million, so that the Sudan is likely to need its half-share of the Tsana water at an earlier date than was supposed at the Cairo Conference in 1935. Egypt, on the other hand, already has enough water to permit of considerable agricultural expansion. (The Egyptian Government estimated in 1938 that the Tsana regulator would not be essential to their programme of development for the next fifteen years.) The Government of the Sudan are therefore apprehensive lest the primary responsibility of Egypt for financing the project, as provided in the 1935 agreement, should lead to delay in its execution. The Governor-General has therefore suggested, in a despatch of the 23rd November, 1943, to Lord Killearn, that "the Sudan Government .... might reasonably stipulate that the Tsana works, if financed by Egypt, should be completed within a definite period from the date of the grant of the concession." They would prefer, indeed, to invert the 1935 agreement, "assuming primary responsibility themselves and selling water to Egypt instead of buying it from her;

but the Governor-General, in the despatch already quoted, conceded that there seemed to be little prospect of securing this advantage.

12. *Egypt.*—The Egyptian attitude appears to have undergone less change since 1935. The Prime Minister (Nahas Pasha), writing to Lord Killearn on the subject on the 26th September, 1943, took the 1935 agreement as his starting point, and affirmed the desire of his Government to resume the interrupted negotiations without delay. It appeared, however, from one phrase in this communication—"L'Egypte est disposée à construire *et à diriger* ce réservoir"—that the Egyptian Government might be contemplating an extension of the rights conferred on them by the 1935 agreement.

13. *The J. G. White Engineering Corporation.*—The President of the Corporation has informed Viscount Halifax, in a letter of the 29th February, 1944, that "we are still interested in the fortunes of the Lake Tsana project, which at some future time may be revived by your Government; and we desire to report to you that to this effect we have so advised his Excellency the Ethiopian Minister" in Washington. Mr. Dunn added that he was reporting this resumption of contact in accordance with the policy adopted by the Corporation since the beginning of their interest in Lake Tsana, when they had committed themselves "to taking no step without prior consultation with and approval of the British authorities."

Developments since 1941

14. Shortly after the liberation of Ethiopia, the Governments of Egypt and the Sudan each put forward suggestions for a fresh approach to the Emperor on the question of Lake Tsana. The former wished to participate in negotiations, and the latter proposed that the concession should be granted directly to the Sudan.

15. On the 30th October, 1941, a plan of action was drawn up at a meeting in the Foreign Office attended by the Financial Secretary to the Sudan Government and Mr. McGregor. It was agreed that the best procedure would be for His Majesty's Government to conduct the negotiations with the Emperor, assisted by Sudanese and Egyptian consultants. They would propose as a basis for negotiations that the Sudan Government should construct the dam, providing the finance in the first instance, and should operate it (with Egyptian observers present). The water would be shared equally by Egypt and the Sudan, who would settle by direct negotiation the final division of the costs between them. In addition to the considerations mentioned in paragraph 11 above, it was argued on behalf of Sudanese administration of the concession that the Egyptian Government, with an eye to political penetration in the Sudan, might at some future time seek to extend such rights as Egypt obtained at Tsana over the Sennar dam and the Gezira Irrigation Scheme.

16. The next question to be considered was that of the *quid pro quo* to be offered to the Emperor when the request for a concession was made. The alternatives seemed to be: (a) financial payments, including rent in perpetuity, not for the water itself but for the land on which the works were constructed and for the exercise of the various rights necessary to their operation; or (b) territorial compensation, which could probably not be offered until such time as the fate of the ex-Italian colonies was determined by the United Nations. The Government of the Sudan wish to avoid a continuing financial obligation, though this would have at least the advantage of providing the Ethiopian Government with a permanent profit from the existence of the concession and so diminishing the possibility of agitation for its

abrogation. A third possibility was that compensation might be held to have been paid already in the shape of British and Sudanese assistance in the restoration of the Emperor to his throne. It was eventually decided that the initial approach should be made on this basis, by His Majesty's Minister in Addis Ababa. If, as seems probable, the Emperor was unresponsive, the ground would at least have been cleared for an offer of territorial compensation in place of the financial inducements which had figured in all earlier negotiations.

17. Mr. Howe accordingly introduced the subject at an audience with the Emperor on the 10th June, 1943, and left with him a memorandum containing suggestions for an agreement in principle on the following lines: (1) the grant of an area in the region of Lake Tsana on which His Majesty's Government would be free to construct and operate hydraulic works, together with the free use of roads to the Lake from the Sudan and from the interior of Ethiopia, and right of access to the area by air (an airfield and a marine landing place being constructed at the expense of His Majesty's Government); (2) "His Majesty's Government and the Sudan Government would regard the free grant of the facilities required at Lake Tsana as a fitting and practical expression of gratitude for the restoration of the Ethiopian Empire to His Imperial Majesty by British and Sudanese troops."

18. Four days after this audience the Egyptian Prime Minister was informed that, as part of a general settlement between His Majesty's Government and the Ethiopian Government, the Emperor was being asked "to give his approval in principle to the construction of works at the outlet of Lake Tsana." Amin Osman Pasha, through whom this communication was made, "presumed that the Egyptian Government would be brought in at some stage." In the Egyptian Prime Minister's subsequent letter to Lord Killearn, referred to in paragraph 12 above, there was a reference to the necessity of renewing negotiations "between the British and Egyptian Governments on the one hand, and the Ethiopian Government on the other." (It has been pointed out that the Egyptian Government's desire to be a party to any agreement on Lake Tsana may be due in part to the fact that otherwise we should be in a position to modify it without their consent.)

19. Reverting on the 12th August to the memorandum which Mr. Howe had handed to him two months earlier, the Emperor observed that "there were certain things Great Britain required from Ethiopia while Ethiopia needed certain things from us." There were difficulties in the way of a firm and lasting agreement between the two countries and His Majesty proposed to go to London himself "to clear away these misunderstandings." The Emperor was dissuaded, however, from pursuing this suggestion, and the issue of Lake Tsana has not since been raised on either side.

28 FO 371/45973, no 1318 5–16 Mar 1945

'Sudan': minutes by P S Scrivener, P M Broadmead[1] and Sir R I Campbell on the failure of the Treasury to support the education grant to the Sudan

[Shortly before the FO forwarded his request for an education grant for the Sudan to the Treasury (see 22), Huddleston had written directly to the chancellor, on the grounds that

[1] Head of North American Dept, 1944–1945.

they had known each other in India when Sir J Anderson was governor of Bengal. Huddleston advanced the argument that the Sudan was 'practically' a part of the British Empire, but had Egypt to turn to if Britain failed it. Anderson replied that aside from 'adequate Treasury reasons' for refusing, the grant would be misinterpreted by the USA (Huddleston to Anderson, 10 Dec 1944 and Anderson to Huddleston, 22 Jan 1945, FO 371/45973, nos 651 & 890). B A B Burrows,[2] writing from the embassy in Cairo, forwarded copies of the exchange to the FO, and suggested applying for a general development grant, rather than confining the request to education: 'The suggestion would be that a grant for development purposes might lead either to a demand for imports of plant and machinery from the United Kingdom or to a general rise in the standard of living in the Sudan which would in turn increase the importance of the Sudan as a general market for British goods. Education would no doubt be included in any such development scheme, but the difference would be that it would no longer form the primary or sole object of the grant. The needs of the Sudan for development and help are as great as those of the Colonies and as the Sudan is in the sterling area the foreign exchange problem is the same' (Burrows to Scrivener, 24 Feb 1945, FO 371/45973, no 890). In commenting on the correspondence from Cairo and forwarding the following minute, Scrivener noted on 10 Mar 1945: 'This is all right as far as it goes, but I don't think it goes far enough; and in any event it is in my opinion useless to go on arguing with The Treasury at the "official level" any more. They will simply go on saying "No." Rather different tactics (having in fact much the same objective) are suggested in the minute attached' (FO 371/45973, no 890).]

The attitude adopted by the Treasury on the question dealt with in this file makes it, in my opinion, essential to consider the policy to be followed by His Majesty's Government in regard to the whole question of future development in the Sudan.

Since the time of the negotiation of the Anglo–Egyptian Treaty, Sudanese nationalism has, for the first time since the reconquest, become a factor with which the Sudan Government have had to reckon. It owes its existence to the policy of devolution practised by the Sudan Government, and to the emergence of an intelligensia [sic] in the few large centres of population. This intelligensia [sic] is still very small, and is by no means representative of the country as a whole; but it is politically minded and highly articulate. What it says today the tribal Sudan (in the north at any rate) will probably say tomorrow. The development of the nationalist movement coupled with the fostering of native institutions by the Sudan Government in recent years have led to the establishment of the Advisory Council for the Northern Sudan, which marks the beginning of representative government in the Sudan.

Sudanese nationalism has shown itself in its relations with the Sudan Government to be of an extremely enquiring turn of mind; and one of the questions which it asks most frequently is "What are His Majesty's Government going to do for the Sudan on the lines of what they are doing for their Colonial Empire?" The colonial policy of His Majesty's Government has been very closely studied, and no part of it more closely than the Colonial Development Acts, for the benefit of which the Sudan is not, of course, eligible and for which it could not be made eligible except by declaring it to be a British colony, and thus tearing up the agreements of 1899 *and* the Anglo–Egyptian treaty. It should also be mentioned by way of a conclusion to this general preface that the Sudanese intelligensia [sic] have become the main conductor along which Egyptian influence flows into the Sudan. That influence is not as yet considerable, but it is being actively fostered and could in certain circumstances become powerful.

[2] Acting first secretary at the embassy in Cairo.

With these considerations in mind the Sudan Government decided a year ago to ask His Majesty's Government to give—as a symbolic gesture—a sum of £1,000,000 to endow the new Gordon College, that foundation having been raised from the status of a secondary school to that of a University College, the ostensible object of the gift being the recognition of the services rendered by the Sudan in the present war. It has never been pretended that the Sudan in its present financial situation could not provide the money itself; the objective of the proposal was exclusively political, viz. to mark the continued interests of His Majesty's Government in the Sudan no less than in the territories directly eligible for British bounty, and to answer the reproach that the Sudan, in British eyes, was no longer an object of British interest and solicitude. The purpose of the proposed gift was extremely well chosen, since the first act of this country after the reconquest in 1898 was to raise a fund to endow the original Gordon College; and a similar gesture at the present time could have been impressed on Sudanese minds with overwhelming effect.

The proposal was accordingly put to the Treasury officially and semi-officially (Annexes A and B)[3] on the general lines of the foregoing. The result is shown in the document which forms Annex C. The Treasury rejected the proposal as "inopportune" since "we are no longer in a position in which we can play the Lady Bountiful with foreign currency."

Since in fact the Treasury were at that moment in the process of going violently into reverse, we left the matter alone for the time being, until the movement had been completed and the road (ahead or astern) had become clearer.

Early this year the Governor-General and Lord Killearn returned to the charge. In writing to the Treasury again (Annex D) we contested the economic justification of the Treasury's earlier attitude; and emphasised, in the light of further developments in our colonial policy—such as the voting of £120,000,000 over the next ten years for development and research—the sheer impossibility of explaining to the Sudanese, as things were, our lack of visible interest in their country.

The result of this was even worse than before. The Treasury this time pleaded (a) American opinion and (b) penury (Annexes E and F). I do not propose in this paper to contest the Treasury's arguments because when they said "I can't" they obviously meant "I won't, whatever you may say or however sound your case is". (The effect of their letter on the Sudan Government has been to give the impression—so tendencious [sic] is it—that Egypt is about to leave the sterling area and to drag the Sudan along with her.)

In putting to the Treasury the Gordon College proposal we had intended to rest content with it, and not to raise for the time being the broad question of future development in the Sudan. But I submit that we must now face this issue in its entirety. In essence it is simple:—"Are we to accept in respect of the Sudan a responsibility analogous to that which we accept in respect of a British colony—although it is not one—or are we not?" If we are, then what is right for the colonial Empire becomes right for the Sudan, and since it has been recognised by the Cabinet and by Parliament that to fulfil our imperial responsibilities we must make, over a period of years, substantial financial grants to the dependent Empire, the Treasury must withdraw their veto on similar grants to the Sudan and consider ways and

[3] Annexes not printed.

means of implementing a policy of financial backing for that country. If we are not, we proclaim that we regard the Sudan as a foreign country (which incidentally, we are apparently not prepared to treat as favourably as Abyssinia).

On the first hypothesis what is our justification, vis-à-vis Egyptian and world opinion, of our assimilation of the Sudan to the colonial Empire? The key, I think, can be found in Article 11 of the Anglo–Egyptian Treaty which states that "The High Contracting Parties agree that the primary aim of their administration in the Sudan must be the welfare of the Sudanese." If the Governor-General of the Sudan, who exercises "on the joint behalf of the High Contracting Parties the powers conferred on him by the (1899) agreements", decides to apply, in the interests of the welfare of the Sudanese, for financial assistance to the Party which has just initiated a large development scheme to promote the welfare of its own colonial territories, surely the action is perfectly defensible? *Theoretically* the Governor-General is equally entitled to appeal to Egypt, and should Egypt spontaneously offer assistance to the Sudanese it would be difficult if not impossible to stop her. But, in any case, there is no need to publicise the matter. All that we require is an undertaking that the Treasury will give sympathetic consideration to any requests that may be received from the Sudan Government through His Majesty's Ambassador in Egypt and the Foreign Office for assistance which shall not exceed £X over the next ten years (the sum to be fixed as a result of detailed discussion), in the development of the Sudan on the lines approved in the case of the Colonial Empire. Everything should then be plain sailing. We shall continue our task of leading the Sudan to self-government; and of preventing Egypt from pre-judging, by agitation or intrigue, the decision which the Sudan will one day be equipped to take regarding her future destiny. And it should here be remarked that the financial assistance required may be relatively unsubstantial. The financial position of the Sudan is satisfactory. It is the *principle* that is important.

On the second hypothesis, a very different prospect appears. If we decline to give the Sudan that support which, by our acts, we have recognised as essential to the development of colonial territory, can we any longer seek to dissuade the Sudanese from turning to Egypt, and can we raise any objection if Egypt takes over our responsibilities? The answer, it seems to me, is in the negative. That being so, we must recognise that we should be turning our backs on the last half-century (very nearly) of great achievement in the Sudan, and should be committing something uncommonly like a breach of trust. No doubt we can continue to administer the country efficiently but, [it may be questioned whether the Sudan Government Service would have, to an Englishman, the same meaning as it used to have; and whether any Englishman of the necessary calibre would accept appointment as Governor General under such humiliating conditions.][4] nowadays, just and efficient administration is evidently not by itself enough—the recent evolution of our colonial policy is there to prove it. [His Majesty's Government should surely reflect very earnestly before finding themselves placed in this position by a wave of defeatism in the Treasury. And I should mention that The King himself might not be indifferent to this issue having regard to the keen interest which his father took in Sudanese affairs. It is also perhaps relevant to remark that the Delegation of M.P.'s which recently visited Africa did not fail to note Sudanese inquisitiveness on this subject.]

---

[4] The two sections in brackets in this para were written and then crossed out.

Fortunately, there is, so far as one can estimate at present, no very great urgency about this matter. We have missed a magnificent opportunity both of emphasising the value of the British connexion, and of marking our appreciation of the Sudan war effort, but Sudanese disillusionment is not yet in a dangerous phase. The Governor General is due to come home on leave this summer and I think our next step, if this minute be generally approved, is to send a copy of it to Lord Killearn and to ask him, if he concurs, to suggest that Sir H. Huddleston be invited to re-examine the matter with his Council in the light of the foregoing considerations and to prepare a restatement of the whole case on the broadest basis for discussion with the Secretary of State on his arrival and for submission to the Cabinet if necessary.

P.S.S.
5.3.45

As regards American public opinion I should rather doubt whether they make much distinction in their minds between the status of the Sudan & of the Colonies. In any case, however, educational projects are the sort of thing that appeal to the American mind. . . .

P.M.B.
15.3.45

Sir A. Cadogan

It seems clear to me that H.M.G. can in their own minds assimilate the Sudan to a British colony to the extent of our share in the condominium, and of the responsibility for which we claim, in the interests of the Sudanese people. . . .

As for the Treasury's fear of American disapproval, which presumably is based on consciousness of the aid which we are getting from the United States Government in 'Stage II' and which we expect from them in 'Stage III',[5] I very much doubt whether there is great danger in this, for the reasons which Mr. Broadmead gives in his minute of March 15th. American interest in the work of the Anglo–American Caribbean Commission can be cited in support of his opinion. Moreover, American assistance to us is grounded in self-interest and the effect which the general welfare can have on that interest, and their view that an economically revived United Kingdom is necessary for both the general and (therefore) United States welfare. It is not based on generosity to the United Kingdom for its own sake. Hence expenditure on promoting the welfare of the dependent people of the Sudan and not on some purely United Kingdom object which could be regarded as a luxury, would not, I think, affect in a manner dangerous to us the United States Government's estimate of where the American interest lies, and would not, I should have thought, be ill received by them, especially since we have apparently been able to 'get away with' the expenditure entailed by the Colonial Development Act.

R.I.C.
16.3.45

---

[5] US aid to the UK during the war was divided into stages: Stage II represented the period until Japan's defeat, and Stage III was the post-war reconstruction period.

29 FO 371/46024, no 1346 27 Mar 1945

[Nile waters: Jonglei canal] letter from Secretariat, Khartoum to Chancery, Cairo. Annex: despatch from F D Rugman to Muhammad Ali al-Alfi,[1] 'Jonglei canal scheme' (17 July 1940)

[A canal diverting water around the central swamps of the Upper Nile to increase the flow of water northward was first suggested in 1904, but no detailed proposals were made by the Egyptian Irrigation Department until the 1930s. No serious attempt had been made to assess the possible impact of such a canal on the livelihood of the people of the region until a local DC[2] made his own survey of the proposed canal line through his district and submitted a report in May, 1940, coinciding with Italy's declaration of war against Britain. Part of his report was incorporated into the Sudan government's response to the canal proposals (reprinted here), but all discussion of the scheme was shelved for the duration of the war. The objections raised in 1940 led to the formation of the Jonglei investigation team after the war.]

The Egyptian Government, through their Inspector-General of Irrigation here, have asked for the initiation of technical consultations on the Sudd project now called the Jonglei Canal Scheme. The Inspector-General suggests that if these consultations on the technical aspects of the scheme were initiated now with our Irrigation Department, time might be saved in the later discussions of the administrative and other questions which will arise. He also informs us that the scheme has been accepted in its general form by the Minister of Works as the official scheme to be carried to the constructional stage in due course.

2. The Jonglei Scheme was raised in 1938/39, when the Sudan Government's general views were sought. The matter was reported to you by Khartoum despatch No.101 of 5th July 1938, of which I attach a copy for ease of reference.[3] The Inspector-General was told in 1940 how we proposed to tackle our study of the matter; a copy of the relevant letter is also attached. The Inspector-General however agreed that during the War nothing would be done.

3. Adequate study of the question will mean a call on a considerable staff to form a survey team. Whether it will be possible for us to do this or to find irrigation staff to go into the purely technical side is not yet clear.

4. The purpose of this letter is to warn you that the matter has been raised, and to assure you that if we eventually have to tell the Egyptian Government that we cannot at the moment find staff we shall let you know before such an answer is given.

Annex to 29

I have the honour to refer to this Office letter No. FDK/798-1 of 18.12.39 on the subject of the Jonglei Canal Scheme.

2. As foreshadowed in my letter of 5.7.1938 the preliminary study of this complex problem has taken a considerable time and it is clear that at the present stage the

---

[1] Inspector general of irrigation, Egyptian Irrigation Department, Khartoum, 1939–1941.

[2] J Winder, assistant district commissioner, Zeraf district, 1939–1942; later Jonglei investigation team, 1946–1948; deputy governor, Upper Nile Province, 1948–1951; and governor, Upper Nile Province, 1953–1955.

[3] Not printed.

data available is insufficiently precise to enable any final view or commitment to be taken by the Sudan Government in regard to the project.

Generally speaking it would appear that up to the present the subject has been studied essentially from the hydrological and engineering points of view and, whilst it is only natural that the aspects of the situation should command priority of examination, much additional information will be required before any clear view can be obtained as to the effect of the scheme on local interests.

3. These interests may conveniently be classified under the headings of irrigation, navigation and roads, and administration and the following observations are submitted, without commitment, with a view to providing, so far as is at present possible, a broad indication of the nature and extent of the local problems involved.

(a) *Irrigation*

In paragraph 13 of the report of December 1936 of the Director-General Southern Nile reference is made to the question of untimely water. Additional water during either the timely or untimely season will increase the flood discharge in the White Nile from the Zeraf mouth northwards but no data are available as to the extent to which flooding of the riverain lands will be increased, and as to the effect on local (e.g. agricultural sanitary) interests. Cross drainage is another factor, upon which further information is required but preliminary investigation suggests the probability that drainage requirements will be considerably greater than is indicated in paragraph 24 of the Director-General's report. It will also be necessary to obtain an estimate of the effect of regulation at Lake Albert on the river levels South of Bor.

(b) *Navigation and roads*

In paragraph 12 of his report the Director-General states that a precise estimate of navigation difficulties can be made when the scheme is in operation. Under existing conditions the Bahr el Gebel is superior to the Bahr el Zeraf as a navigable waterway but there is some apprehension that with the scheme in operation the former will deteriorate to an extent that makes it necessary that the Sudan Government should have a statement of the Ministry's anticipations in this connection. Before a definite opinion can be expressed on the possibility of routing shipping through the Zeraf and the canal it will be necessary to ascertain the permissible speed for navigating the canal, the arrangements for controlling and passing craft and the best point of entry from the Zeraf into the canal. With the existing towage arrangements of steamers of the Sudan Railways locks 250 feet long and 65 feet in width would be required, but, if navigation of the Zeraf and canal proves to be practicable it might be possible, though costly, to change the method of working by introducing self-propelled cargo barges either alone or with other barges in tow.

Any conditions of navigation rendering Shambe unsuitable as a port would have serious repercussions upon the trade of Equatoria Province. The average tonnage handled by steamer services at Shambe is approximately 1,000 tons per annum.

If Shambe were rendered useless as a port some alternative outlet for this trade would have to be provided and this would involve extensive and expensive remodelling of the road system in this area.

As regards Upper Nile Province roads it would appear that such part of the existing road system for the Zeraf District as is not put out of action by the scheme may be rendered useless because centres of administration will be cut off from it by flooded areas.

(c) *Administration*

It is under this heading that the greatest difficulties are foreseen. The existence and mode of living of the local tribes are completely dependent upon the regime of the Upper Nile swamps. The chief characteristics of the areas and peoples likely to be affected by the Scheme are indicated in the attached extracts from a report by a former Governor, Upper Nile Province.[4] Recent enquiry has shewn that there has been very little change since it was written and it is emphasised that a full appreciation of the unique conditions therein described is the first essential step towards understanding the numerous administrative problems involved.

It is apparent that any scheme for the purpose of improving the water supply from the Upper Nile will materially alter the existing regime within the Upper valley of the Nile and that these alterations will directly affect tribal and other local interests.

It will be necessary to ensure that dislocation and damage are minimised to the greatest extent possible and that modifications of existing conditions are introduced very gradually. A primary consideration would be to avoid, as far as possible, the disturbance of existing channels within the Sudd region.

Observations of the seasonal migration of game animals shows that in certain years large areas dependent upon rain-produced conditions fail to support animal life. The effect of lack of food for man or beast for even a brief period which exceeds their powers of endurance is as disastrous as a prolonged period. Substituted conditions must therefore, not only be permanent but must also be within easy reach of any group driven out of their normal habitat by local failure of supplies or disease.

The extent of the damage to local interests in this region will be dependent largely upon the final alignment adopted for the canal and upon the date at which the Lake Albert Reservoir comes into operation.

From the point of view of local interests it would appear that the minimum of damage could be obtained by aligning the canal outside the main swamp areas and outside the important grazing, fishing and agricultural areas, and by combining the operation of the canal by suitable control from Lake Albert.

3. From the considerations above described it is clear that much additional information is required to enable the Sudan Government to offer any final comments on the Jonglei project and the immediate question is as to how this information can best be supplied. The technical data has taken some twenty odd years to attain a stage of formulation and it will be readily understood that the re-actions upon the important interests directly concerned cannot be estimated without adequate time, study and expenditure. Tribal, irrigation and economic surveys of the areas concerned will be required and the questions of land and river communications, and the probable effect of the scheme on local fauna and flora will require examination.

The cost and time involved in such surveys cannot, on present data, be estimated but it will be readily appreciated that, under the physical conditions of the Upper Nile

---

[4] Not included with this copy, but see C A Willis, *et al, The Upper Nile province handbook: a report on peoples and government in the southern Sudan, 1931* (Oxford, 1995), appendix 2.

area, any form of field survey is lengthy and difficult undertaking. The cost may be considerable but it would appear to be conditioned by the amount of information and facilities which can be afforded by your staff. Before committing the Sudan Government to any expenditure of this nature I should be grateful to receive an assurance that it will be refunded by the Egyptian Government and some indication of the time factors involved. I note that the project has not yet been officially adopted by the Ministry of Public Works and I should be glad to know whether it may be assumed that no action by the Sudan Government will be necessary in the matter during the period of the present war.

In the meantime however I would suggest that technical consultations be engaged in, without commitment, between your local representatives and those of the Governors, Upper Nile and Equatoria Provinces, the Sudan Irrigation Department and the Sudan Railways.

It is, I think you will agree, quite clear that the information required with regard to the effects on local interests of the Jonglei Scheme can only satisfactorily be obtained through the close co-operation of all concerned. I need hardly add that I should be pleased to discuss this matter with you at any time.

30 FO 141/1024, no 3 8 Apr 1945

[Umma Party]: letter from J W Robertson to C E Fouracres[1] on the foundation of the Umma Party. Appendices: "A" (2) constitution of the Nation Party, 14 Feb 1945; "B" (1) letter from Abdallah Khalil[2] to Sir H Huddleston, 19 Mar 1945

1. We included a brief account of the new UMMA party in the January issue of the S.P.I.S. which you have, and gave some further details in the issue for February, but as there have been critical allusions to it recently in the Egyptian Press, and as it seems likely that a good deal of capital will be made both here and in Cairo out of its alleged connection with the Sudan Government, I think that you and the Embassy should have some further information.

2. The party is a revival in a new form of a group which in about 1926, centering round the then Editor of the Hadara (the late Hussein Khalifa Sherif),[3] adopted as its slogan "the Sudan for the Sudanese". This group was thrown up as part of the direct reaction to the Egyptian fiasco in 1924. It was a moderate pro-Government party, though Government had no hand in its appearance. It was not an active party, and indeed in those years, when Egypt and all things Egyptian were thoroughly discredited, there was no need for any active or organised opposition to Egyptian

---

[1] C E Fouracres: SPS 1922–1949; assistant Sudan agent, Cairo, 1939–1949.

[2] Secretary general, Umma Party.

[3] *Al-Hadara* (*Hadarat al-Sudan*), the Sudan's first independent Arabic newspaper, was founded in 1920 by sayyids Ali al-Mirghani, Abd al-Rahman al-Mahdi, and Sharif Yusuf al-Hindi, with the blessing of the government. It was in part a reaction to the Egyptian nationalist rising of 1919, and adopted a mainly pro-government, anti-Egyptian line, contending that Britain should continue its administration of the country until such time as the Sudan was capable of governing itself. Its first editor, Husain Sharif, was a relative of sayyid Abd al-Rahman and a founding member of the Sudanese Union Society, a moderate nationalist group.

claims. With the death of Hussein Khalifa Sherif in 1929 the original "Sudan for the Sudanese" group broke up but the group slogan remained as the political motto of a number of individual officials and officers, and reappeared again some years later as the inspiration of a group of young intellectuals—known as the Fagr group—headed by the late Abdalla Mohammed Arafat.[4] Arafat had taken a prominent part in the 1924 disturbances, had no illusions about Egypt and aimed at founding the national aspirations of the Sudanese on a constructive patriotic basis, before the reviving interest of the Egyptian propagandist again succeeded in leading them astray.

3. With Arafat's death the Fagr group (and its organ the Fagr magazine) disappeared, and the political objectives of the intelligentsia were temporarily lost sight of in the prosecution of local internal rivalries eventually reappearing in the rather nebulous ideas which were embodied in the Congress Memorandum of 1942. The latter day history of the Congress is well known to you—its most sinister feature being the appearance once again towards the end of 1944 of a new pro-Egyptian party (the Ashiqqa) which under the leadership of Ismail el Azhari fought and won the 1944 Congress elections on a "union with Egypt" programme. There were admittedly other influences which contributed to the Ashiqqa's success. Azhari and Co., made deliberate use of sectarian (Mirghanist) support to capture the Congress Executive Committees, but at the same time they were and are undoubtedly playing a pro-Egyptian hand to an extent which has seriously alarmed moderate "patriotic" opinion, which aims in the first place at some form of local autonomy unencumbered by premature commitments to either Condominium partner. The Umma party is the organised expression of this alarm. I have gone into all this at some length because I think it important to underline the fact that the Umma is not a Government creation; it is an automatic response to the new Egyptian threat.

4. Unfortunately the clarity of the main issue—"separatism" versus some form of union with Egypt—is being hopelessly obscured by the old Mahdist/Mirghanist rivalry. Both Sayeds took a hand in the recent (November 1944) Congress elections. Both of them roped in to the polls numbers of illiterate adherents who were in fact ineligible to vote and had almost certainly no views about Egypt one way or the other. In the event the Azhari-Ashiqqa-Mirghanist party won, their victory being largely due to the success of their propaganda which threatened the voters, if they failed to support them, with the return of the Mahdia, and Sayed Abd El-Rahman as King of the Sudan. The folly of some of Sayed Abd El-Rahman's own followers, who had themselves been propagating the "kingship" idea, contributed very largely to the Mahdist defeat. The failure of Sayed Abdel Rahman to make any attempt to deny this idea, and his own royal manner of living lend support to this propaganda. To say, therefore, that the Umma party was started as a reaction to the Ashiqqa political programme, is only half the truth. Its inspiration was Mahdist.

5. The late Civil Secretary[5] saw this coming last August. He was afraid that Sayed Abd El-Rahman's separatist and "royalist" ambitions would drive the Mirghanists into the Egyptian camp; that Sayed Ali would go to any lengths to counter his rival's rather blatant campaign to "cash in" on Sudanese self-government, and that the

---

[4] Arafat Muhammad Abdallah (d. 1937), a graduate of Gordon College and a postal clerk who fled to Egypt after the failure of the 1924 revolt. He returned to the Sudan in 1930 and founded the *al-Fajr* ('The Dawn') literary magazine in 1934.

[5] Sir D Newbold.

result of it all would be the emergence of a definite Union with Egypt party. He hoped that we should be able to persuade the more longsighted Sudanese to damp down the Sayeds' rivalries and to form some sort of united front which would devote its immediate energies to the practical realisation of our internal self-government programme, without prejudice to the eventual political issue. These hopes were defeated by the intransigence of the Sayeds. We were, moreover, not in a position to exert any effective pressure on either party. We could not, in view of our Treaty obligations, openly comment on the folly of Mirghanist flirting with Egypt, nor could we go too far in debunking Sayed Abd El-Rahman, who did and does command the allegiance of a large body of influential Sudanese.

6. The stage is now set for a two party contest—the Ashiqqa and the Umma. The latter began to take definite shape soon after the 1944 elections were over. On February 18th, 1945, Abdallah Bey Khalil, the party Secretary, submitted to the Civil Secretary, through Governor Khartoum, the application attached as Appendix "A".[6] The Governor approved this application as referring to a "club" under Section 165 of the Local Government (Municipalities) Regulations 1938. (We do not recognise political "parties" as such.) The party then proceeded to register itself as a private company for the purpose of producing a newspaper to be called "The Umma", and to serve as the party organ. Difficulties in securing a competent editor have delayed the paper's appearance but appear now to have been overcome. It is said that in order to deprive the opposition of one of their main weapons of criticism, Sayed Abd El-Rahman will publish in the first issue of the paper a repudiation of the idea that he aims at kingship. How categorical his self-denying message will be, or whether it will appear at all, we do not yet know.

7. After the first flush of their election victory the Ashiqqa party remained temporarily inactive—possibly because they were a bit alarmed at the extent to which they had committed themselves to their Egyptian supporters and (it is believed) paymasters. They had undertaken to produce a Resolution on their Union with Egypt programme which could be made use of in Cairo but hesitated to take the decisive step. This hesitation was resolved by the publication in the local Press of the programme of the Umma party; a special meeting of Congress was convened; and the Ashiqqa Resolution (Union with Egypt, in the form of two independent Governments under the single Egyptian Crown) was duly published here on April 6th.

8. Meanwhile there has been a certain amount of canvassing for both Ashiqqa and Umma parties in the provincial north. How these campaigns will go remains to be seen. The Umma party suffers from two disadvantages. Its Mahdist origins damn it in the eyes of many tribal leaders and educated "moderates"; and, having adopted as its programme what is in effect the Government's policy regarding the gradual transfer of the administration to Sudanese hands, it has laid itself open to the obvious charge of being a Government party. As regards both of these disadvantages the promoters of the party have mainly themselves to blame. They hold their meeting in, and are largely financed and staffed by, the Mahdist Daira and they have selected as their main propagandists persons like Mohammed Khalifa Sherif and Mohammed Ali Shawqi,[7] notorious Mahdist partisans. They are, more-

---

[6] Not printed.

[7] Muhammed Ali Shawqi, assistant registrar general (1942–1948) and member of the Advisory Council for the Northern Sudan; later to be under-secretary of justice, 1948–1953.

over, themselves widely proclaiming that they have Government support. The fact that the Government had encouraged the formation of a new independent newspaper with a non-sectarian rural bias which had been named "El Umma" before the party was constituted appeared to confirm the Government connection with the party.

9. It is important that we should make it quite clear to the public at large that this claim is untrue and we are taking steps to circulate Governors and others in this sense, and to warn off the promoters of the Umma party themselves. Many of its more moderate members are fully conscious of the embarrassment of the Mahdist connection and would be glad to see persons like Mohammed Khalifa Sherif removed from active participation. It has already been suggested to Sayed Abd El-Rahman that he should be delegated to his White Nile pump scheme and directed to stay there, but nothing has been done nor is likely to be done. Sheikh Ahmed Othman El-Qadi's[8] activities on the other hand—he is one of the main Umma propagandists—can be, and if necessary will be, restrained. All we can do for the time being is to challenge any suggestion that the Umma party is our party, damp down any extravagant propaganda, and watch developments (particularly Egyptian developments), intervening only in the activities of either party if they seem likely to prejudice good order and good government or to lead to a definite breach of the peace.

10. Our main difficulty, as you will have gathered, is that although we cannot openly say so, the Umma party, whatever its motive, is on our side, and that however much we disapprove its tactical errors, we do not want it discouraged. If we so neglect or mishandle it as to lose its support we may find ourselves a trifle friendless when the inevitable show down occurs. We can do nothing to encourage it here. There is, however, one way in which the Embassy might indirectly help us. The members of the Umma party and a good many other moderates who belong to no party are very disturbed in their minds over the San Francisco Conference. They have misread or misinterpreted various articles which have appeared in the Egyptian and world Press and have submitted a letter to His Excellency of which I attach a copy with the answer, as Appendix "B".[9] They believe that San Francisco will settle the future of the Sudan and that the Egyptian and British Governments have already put their heads together and "agreed" what that future is to be. We have assured them that the San Francisco Conference is not concerned with, and will not deal with, their future. This, they say, is all very well but they want something more. They want an assurance that, in the course of discussions on subjects which are on the Agenda, no Egyptian delegate will be allowed to claim directly or indirectly that he represents also the Sudan. The EL NIL article in the Local Vernacular Press Summary No.325 gives their attitude. Presumably no such claim would be allowed, but may we say so? The point may seem to be a small one but an assurance of the kind suggested would do a great deal to clear a political atmosphere here in Khartoum which is getting definitely cloudy.

---

[8] Ahmad Uthman al-Qadi, former editor of *al-Hadara*; at this time superintendent of Arabic publications and a member of the Advisory Council for the Northern Sudan.

[9] B(2), Robertson's reply not printed.

Appendix "A" (2) to 30

(1) Name:	This party shall be called the Nation Party.
(2) The principle:	The Sudan for the Sudanese.
(3) The purpose:	To work for the realisation of the independence of the Sudan with its geographical boundaries intact, and maintaining friendly relations with Egypt and Great Britain.
(4) Membership:	Membership of this party is open to every Sudanese above the age of eighteen years of age [sic], who embraces the principle of the party and works for its realisation.
(5) Headquarters of the party:	The headquarters of the party shall be the town of Omdurman.
(6) Annual general meeting:	An annual general meeting shall be held in [the Muslim month of] Rabie—for all members and shall discuss:— (a) A review of the previous year. (b) Consideration of members' suggestions.
(7) Administration of the party:	The party shall have a body selected from its members to form its Council.
(8) Finance of the party:	The finances of the party shall be derived from the following:— (a) Membership fees amounting to 5 PT. per member to to be paid once in life. (b) Subscriptions. (c) Donations.
(9) Rules of procedure:	The Council shall make with the consent of the annual general meeting rules of procedure for the conduct of meetings, regulation of finance matters, and the explanation of what matters the Constitution might have left unexplained, provided that explanation does not conflict with the spirit of the Constitution.
(10) Amendment to the Constitution:	The Constitution shall not be amended unless with the agreement of the annual general meeting.

Appendix "B" (1) to 30

The Sudanese nation which has enjoyed freedom and independence during these last centuries, except for a period not exceeding sixty years after which it regained freedom and independence when the present Administration took over, an administration which has from the start declared is intention to serve, and in fact striven to champion, the cause of this nation and so bring about its uplift to a stage where it could take over the reins of Government and run its own affairs—this nation takes the opportunity of recognising the debt of gratitude owed to the two Condominium governments, on whose behalf Your Excellency is administering this country, and to the Sudan Government for their many sided efforts, which are appreciated and noted with gratitude. It is through those efforts that the nation has reached a stage of progress which would enable it to demand the political rights which have been held in trust for it. If we compare this nation with other Middle East nations, we find that it has achieved a stage of political, cultural and military maturity which would warrant the demand for its natural right which is the independence of the Sudan within its entire geographical boundaries.

The Sudan's declaration of war on 11.6.40 against the Axis powers and its participation in the war with its troops, the giving of its means of communications and its resources and its efforts towards winning the war, have enhanced that natural right. Its troops are still in East and North Africa with other Allied troops doing their duty. Perhaps the first victory in this war won by the Allies was the one in which Sudanese troops took part for the first time. We recall with pride what those troops achieved alone, in preventing the huge Italian armies in East Africa from attacking the Nile Valley and so connecting up with other Italian troops in North Africa.

The Atlantic Charter, and the declarations made by the responsible spokesmen of the Allied Democracies that have followed it have emphasised for all nations their right to self-determination. The San Francisco Conference will meet shortly with the intention of safeguarding international peace and security, of maintaining cordial relations between the nations, of realising international co-operation in solving the international, economic, social or other of humanity's problems, and of finding a central machinery for co-ordinating nations' dealings with each other. Naturally the Sudan has not been invited to that Conference in spite of its having declared war at a time when the enemy's strength was at its zenith and the Allies were not fully prepared, and when no one could have imagined that the price of a chair (at that conference) was declaration of war against the enemy however late it was done. In that critical time the Sudan believed in the justice of the Allied cause and declared war voluntarily to support that cause, and events have realised what it had hoped for.

As the Sudan is to have no representative at that Conference, the Nation Party wishes to demand that this country be accorded its right in attending the conference, on the same footing as other nations who declared war and participated in it.

The Sudan is neither a British nor an Egyptian Colony. Its participation in this war justifies that it should at least demand its full sovereignty which has been held in trust for it, so that it is not deprived of that freedom against whose enemies it waged a war, whose effectiveness has been recognised in the whole world.

The Sudanese nation, which believed in the Allied cause and supported it, wishes to place its confidence in the Sudan Government and in the United Nations, with whom it fought for the restoration of freedom to those from whom it has been temporarily taken away, in order that the Sudan should not be deprived of its freedom or of the realisation of its aims—this nation wishes to approach Y.E. with this Note asking that steps be taken towards this country's representation at this Conference, and as the agent of both H.B.M. and of the King of Egypt, Y.E. will support that demand with testimony as to this country's eligibility.

We are waiting for Y.E.'s reply supporting our aims and accepting our demands.

With our due respects and regard.

31 FO 371/46081, no 1575 12 Apr 1945
[Anglo–Egyptian relations]: despatch no 55 (reply) from Sir H Huddleston to Lord Killearn

I have the honour to refer to Your Excellency's despatch No.44 dated 7th February, 1945.[1]

2. Strategic considerations apart, our attitude to Egypt in the event of a serious Anglo–Egyptian dispute on the Sudan question must, I submit, depend primarily on the view we take of our obligations to the Sudanese and of the objectives of our administration in the Sudan. I will refer later to Your Excellency's ideas as to the form coercive action might take should coercive action be necessary.

3. With Your Excellency's summary of our objectives in this country and with Your Excellency's opinion that as far as possible we should maintain the Condominium facade I fully agree. The realisation of our objectives will depend on our success in resisting the political claims of Egypt, and in creating in the Sudan a willingness, on achieving self-government, to maintain those close relations with us to which Your Excellency refers, and in the meantime to turn a deaf ear to the Egyptian agitator. This willingness will have to be carefully cultivated. The general attitude of the educated Sudanese, even of the Congress group which is still hesitating to commit itself openly to an active pro-Egypt programme is, on the whole, one of suspended judgment. There are at the same time in certain quarters observable inclinations in the direction of one or other of the Condominium partners—inclinations which we cannot afford to neglect. It is in our immediate interest to discourage the one and to stimulate the other. The Egyptian propaganda machine is already actively in the field, and Your Excellency is already fully aware of the various methods employed: propaganda through the Economic Expert's office, large expenditure on the Egyptian Secondary School, a proposed Egyptian hospital, infiltration into our quarantine service, and financial support of the pro-Egyptian elements. His Majesty's Government aims and intentions remain undisclosed though Sir Douglas Newbold in a broadcast address early in 1944, and I myself at the opening of the Advisory Council for the Northern Sudan later in the same year, referred to the goal of local self-government.

4. We shall, I believe, have great difficulty in retaining the support of such Sudanese opinion as is today disposed to align itself behind us, unless His Majesty's Government is prepared to indicate soon by some definite gesture of goodwill that their interest in the Sudan is constructive and continuous and not merely opportunist and casual. At the moment the loyalty of the Sudanese is being gradually eroded by our silence, which is interpreted as indifference, and by the concessions we make to our vocal partner. The re-penetration of the Sudan by Egyptian political ideas and Egyptian agents has already begun. It can be checked to a limited extent by preventive or restrictive action, but it can only be positively countered by the growth of an active pro-British sentiment founded firmly on self-interest and mutual understanding. My recent attempts with Your Excellency's assistance to obtain the gift of an endowment to the Gordon Memorial College from the British Government have unfortunately achieved no success yet, and an opportunity has been missed.

---

[1] See 25.

Furthermore active pro-British propaganda in which British officials of the Condominium Government cannot play an active part might well be intensified by the British Council which at the moment has no representative or activity in the Sudan—and I suggest that the British Council should be pressed to open an active branch in Khartoum as soon as possible.

5. It is always difficult to assess with any degree of accuracy the strength of the emotional pull which Egyptian influences would exert in the Sudan at a time of political ferment. The emotional forces which inspire demonstration and riot are only fully released when a crisis has actually arisen. It is all the more important therefore that we should do what we can now—before the period of tension sets in—to secure the sympathy and self-interest of those of our potential supporters who are capable of taking a realistic view of political alternatives. This action, as I have already ventured to suggest, might take the form of some immediate gesture of good will, to be followed, as soon as a clash became inevitable and the Condominium facade need be maintained no longer, by a clear pronouncement by His Majesty's Government of its intentions for the future of the country.

6. To turn to Your Excellency's suggestion that in the event of a serious dispute with Egypt our physical control of the Nile waters might be used as an instrument of persuasion—I venture to think that there are serious objections to such a course. From a purely practical point whereas it would be physically possible to divert the summer waters of the Nile to a considerable extent to the detriment of Egypt, the diversion would take time. New canalisation, dams and other works would have to be undertaken to render it effective and the time lag alone between the threatened sanction and its enforcement would rob it of all coercive value. During the intervening period the situation, if it had not improved would have inevitably so deteriorated as to necessitate the application of military or naval sanctions of a more immediately forceful kind. I feel, moreover, that in a dispute of which the Sudan is the subject it might be more appropriate to apply sanctions other than those in which the Sudan itself is involved.

7. As Your Excellency is aware, I am intending to go to the United Kingdom this summer, and I propose, if Your Excellency agrees to discuss the Sudan question generally at the Foreign Office, while I am at home.

32 FO 371/46081, no 643 23 Apr 1945

[Nile Waters] letter from Sir R Campbell to Lord Killearn

In your despatch No. 213 of the 4th February you enclosed a copy of a despatch[1] from Huddleston on the subject of additional supplies of Nile water for the Sudan, and requested authority to approach the Egyptian Government with a view to the early discussion of those proposals by technical experts, the intention of the Sudan Government being to employ MacGregor in that capacity. In our telegram No.370 I told you that MacGregor had simultaneously handed us a paper explaining certain aspects of the Nile Waters Agreement 1925/29, and suggested that, as there was some doubt whether the conclusions drawn by the Sudan Government from the water

[1] See 24.

negotiations were correct, it would be desirable to consult MacGregor fully on the whole issue as raised in 1939 and now. The agreement of the Sudan Government to this suggestion was conveyed in your telegram No. 645.

MacGregor has now made a detailed examination of the whole correspondence, and has most kindly embodied his conclusions in the memorandum of which copies are enclosed together with copies of his paper mentioned in paragraph 1.[2] These conclusions are, broadly, that except for the proposal to raise the reservoir level at Sennar by 1.0 metre the case advanced by the Sudan Government will not bear critical examination in the light of the Nile Waters Agreement 1925/29; and that, since this proposal is by itself inadequate for the purpose in view, we should now concentrate our efforts on securing the Tsana concession for the Sudan with a minimum of delay. MacGregor's memorandum in fact confirms the misgivings expressed in my private telegram, and makes it clear, with the authority of the actual technical negotiator of the Nile Waters Agreement, that the Sudan Government, in 1939, were, to put it mildly, imperfectly advised.

The following points seem to call for special emphasis:—

(1) The Sudan Government should henceforth base themselves solely on the Nile Waters Agreement, and dismiss as irrelevant such treatises as Nile Control and the report of the old Nile Projects Commission which, as MacGregor shows, provide more and better ammunition for the Egyptian than for the Sudan negotiator.

(2) The Sudan attitude towards the water agreement as described in paragraph 10 of Huddleston's despatch is in fact ill-founded and is unfortunate politically since there are already sufficient potential causes of friction between the Sudan and Egypt without introducing major—and in fact superfluous ones such as this.

(3) Though this does not arise directly out of the document it looks as though a return should be made to the system whereby Sudan had an Irrigation Adviser who was in close touch not only with all the central departments at Khartoum but also with the Egyptian Ministry of Public Works and with the Foreign Office, and was thus able to survey the field comprehensively.

MacGregor's recommendations about Lake Tsana will require further study which we are about to give to them. We shall then write to you again, after consulting Bob Howe who had just arrived in this country. You will also receive very shortly MacGregor's comments on Murdoch Macdonald's[3] "Report on the proposed third heightening of the Aswan Dam for the flood protection of Egypt" of which, I understand, Macdonald has sent copies to the Embassy.

For the moment I suggest that you should send both MacGregor's reports to Huddleston (with as much of this letter as you think it appropriate to pass on) and suggest that, when they have been fully digested, the question—of which we fully appreciate the great importance from the Sudan's point of view—should be discussed further with MacGregor in London by Huddleston and his advisers when they visit the United Kingdom. By that time we should have completed the necessary readjustment of our ideas about the Lake Tsana project.

---

[2]Not printed. R M MacGregor, former irrigation adviser to the Sudan government (in charge of the Irrigation Department, 1924–1934), retained in 1945 by the Sudan government as a special irrigation consultant (see 24 and 27).

[3]Sir Murdoch Macdonald: adviser, Egyptian ministry of public works, 1912–1921; MP (Lib) for Inverness, 1922–1951; senior partner in the engineering firm of Sir Murdoch Macdonald and partners.

33 FO 371/45972, no 1998 May 1945

[SAR]: report from SPIS no 48 for March–April, on SAR's disclaimer of monarchical ambitions [Extract]

El Sayed Sir Abdel Rahman el Mahdi Pasha

The Sayed's long expected disclaimer of royal ambitions fizzled out in a mild and rather unconvincing interview with the Editor of the NIL,[1] published on April 17th, in which he merely announced that in taking an interest in the Umma party he was not actuated by any personal ambition, being quite happy and contented with his existing circumstances; he was solely concerned with the country's good, and would take an equal interest in any similar movement which had that objective in view. It will take more than an indirect disclaimer of this kind to displace the conviction in the minds of his opponents that he aims at the restoration of a Mahdist 'dynasty'.

---

[1] The Ansar sect newspaper.

34 FO 141/1013, no 71 8 June 1945

[Ismail al-Azhari and Mustafa al-Nahhas]: letter from A M Hankin to J W Robertson reporting a meeting in Cairo

[Ismail al-Azhari went to Egypt in June and July 1945 in order to gauge the reaction of Egyptian politicians to the Congress' declaration in favour of an independent Sudan under the Egyptian crown (see 30), and to find out what assistance might be obtainable from various Egyptian parties ('Note on the activities of Ismail el Azhari in Cairo', FO 371/45984, no 2076). Throughout his visit to Cairo the embassy monitored and reported on many of his meetings and conversations.]

On June 6th Ismail el Azhari was received by Nahas Pasha in the latter's house. The following is a summary of the conversation as described later by Azhari to a friend.

(2) Azhari described at length the objects of the Congress, which he summed up as aiming at future unity with Egypt, with a common foreign policy and Army and under one crown; internal administration only being reserved for the Sudanese. He referred to British fears in the Sudan which he claimed had led them to create the Umma Party to fight unity with Egypt, but assured Nahas that this party was doomed to failure.

(3) Nahas told Azhari that his attitude towards the Sudan is well known, and that he would never agree to its separation from Egypt. He said it was the first subject on the Wafd's programme for discussion when the Treaty modification with Great Britain is considered. He said that no future settlement of the Egypt–Sudan question could be arrived at unless the Wafd participated in the negotiations, as the Wafd continue to be the majority party in Egypt and he was convinced that it would resume government before any negotiations took place.

(4) Azhari asked Nahas to allow the Wafdist press to support Congress. Nahas replied he would do so when censorship was removed. Azhari said that Sayed Abdel Rahman opposed unity with Egypt and supported the Umma Party with influence and money and that Sayed Ali Mirghani at present assisted Congress. He said, however, that Sayed Ali might alter his policy in future because Congress was unwilling to shelter behind the influence of any Tarika leaders.

35 FO 371/45986, no. 3152 23 Aug 1945

[Congress' demand for the independence of the Sudan and union with Egypt]: letter from Ismail al-Azhari to Mr Attlee and Sidqi Pasha

[On his return from Egypt al-Azhari sent this demand for independence to the civil secretary, for transmission to the British and Egyptian prime ministers. Robertson rejected Congress's claim to represent the views of the Sudanese people and refused to transmit the letter to the prime ministers (J W Robertson to Ismail al-Azhari, 1 Sept 1945, FO 371/45986, no 3152), at the same time he relayed the exchange of correspondence to the FO.]

The Graduates' General Congress—the only body representing enlightened public opinion in the Sudan, a body towards which the various national view points in the country converge, and in which the Sudanese nation places its full confidence—has the honour, in fulfilment of its duty towards its country, to present this note in which it expresses our national aspirations and demands at this delicate juncture, when final victory has been achieved and a new day has dawned in the world for all nations, great and small, giving them an opportunity to solve their existing and impending problems, and to set up a just world organisation which will secure to humanity its rights, to the various countries their liberty, and to individuals the happiness and welfare they hope for, in an era of a permanent and stable peace.

The Sudan's share has not been insignificant and she has shouldered a burden exceeding her capacity, so as to take her place with those who fought for the cause of justice and democracy in order that the world struggle should be brought to a happy conclusion, a conclusion which has been reached earlier than expected by the collapse of Japan, the last fortress of tyranny. The great leaders of democracy and of the British Empire have recognised her valuable services and sacrifices and have praised them.

In his proclamation to the people of the Sudan on the occasion of V.J. Day His Excellency the Acting Governor-General referred to the Sudan's efforts in the following terms:—

> "The Sudan can look back with pride on the part she has played in this war. She has acted throughout with the courage, the orderliness and the obedience for which Sir Stewart Symes called in 1940. She has never doubted the path to Victory. In 1940 her forces stood valiantly, with their British and Indian comrades, in the path of the invader and then pressed forward with them to share in the glorious victories in Abyssinia and in North Africa. Always they have brought honour to the Sudan by their valour and their discipline. At home the Sudan assisted in the vital taks of guarding the African lines of communication and gave unswerving support to the military forces who used her soil. Her citizens made many generous contributions to the effort of war, and endured steadfastly the restrictions and shortages which are the inevitable accompaniment of war. Her cultivators worked with faithful persistence. Her merchants have loyally obeyed the demands made upon them. Her officials have shouldered without complaint new and heavy burdens. Her wartime economy has won praise outside the borders of the Sudan. This is indeed a proud record and let us remember it with full hearts in these days of rejoicing."

This is a part of the Sudan's contribution towards the war effort, and the triumph of the cause of democracy and right. It is the right of her sons, after those efforts, to expect that their demands will find from Your Excellency the acceptance and consideration they merit; they also have the right to hope that your government's [sic] will accede to them in the spirit of justice and equity they deserve.

1. For about half a century the Sudan has remained under the present condominium rule, and it has never [been] thought by any one that the present regime should be the final status of the country. It will certainly never [be] consider[ed] as such by the Sudanese. Though we recognise the services rendered by the present regime, in the organisation of the Administration and the establishment of security and justice, the development of the country, however, from the economic, educational and social aspects has been carried out at a slow pace which does not correspond in any way to the real needs of the country, to the ambitions of the Sudanese and to their aptitude for progress. This becomes evident if a comparison is drawn between the development of the Norther[n] part of the Valley (Egypt) and that of its Southern part (the Sudan), although both parties are gifts of the Nile. While prosperity and opulence are found in the lower Valley, misery and harships [sic] are then [sic] lot of the upper part. While education and guidance are found there, ignorance and backwardness are spread here. Even the small share of progress which is the lot of the Sudan has not been equally spread over all parts of the country. The South is still in a primitive condition which can hardly be imagined in the twentieth century. The same conditions also prevail in many eastern and western parts, and have led to the establishment of diffirent [sic] systems of administration, legislation and education in the country. The small share of progress which we have enjoyed has created a deep gab [sic] between the various parts of one country, and our development has thus been partial and lame. All this has taken place under the Condominium rule, which has lasted long enough to have been able to raise the standard of the Sudan and of its institutions to the level of other advanced countries in the world.

2. The situation of the Sudan has created a general feeling throughout the country that rapid action should be taken with a view to putting and end to the present policy, and changing the present abnormal temporary status into a natural one that would secure to the country a steady advance corresponding to its people's aptitude and to its real needs. As a result of this universal feeling the Graduates' General Congress was formed in 1938 and began, since its inception, to study local conditions and to explore the wishes of the Sudanese. In April 1942 it submitted its note in which it expressed the country's aspirations and demands. A copy of this note is attached, together with the correspondence exchanged with the Sudan Government in this connection.[1]

3. Since the first and most important article in the above mentioned note refers to the Sudan's right of self-determination, the Congress has, during its Sessions of the last four years, explored the country's wishes as to the final form of the Sudan's status, which could secure the country's aspirations and guaranteed [sic] its rights.

In April 1945 the Congress General Committee passed the following resolution as regards the country's status: "The formation of a democratic Sudanese Government in a union with Egypt, under the Egyptian Crown".

---

[1] See 1.

In asking for the formation of a democratic Sudanese Government, we realise that the act of ruling is divided into two parts, administrative and technical. As regards the administration, it can be carried out through the good services of the Omda, Sheikh, Nazir, Mamur, the Sudanese O.D. the Sudanese Governor, and the Sudanese Minister.

The technical side however required additional qualifications which may not be adequately available in the Sudan now. This difficulty can be surmounted however through the assistance of British and Egyptian advisers and experts, who could help, to the extent needed, in educational, financial, judicial, agricultural and medical matters, as well as in other services of public utility where competent Sudanese are not available, until missions of Sudanese students have been sent to England, Egypt and other European and American countries, to complete their studies. In stating the above, we have in mind countries of an equal approaching standard, like Ethiopia, the Yemen, Iraq, etc which aim at the same objective and are already on the path which we intend to follow.

Our inclination towards the idea of a union, and the selection of Egypt to be the second partner in that union, appear to us as a natural trend dictated by the many vital and close links which derive their strength from our common history and from the union of interests, in addition to the bonds of religion, language, blood, education and the Nile, that vital and great link which confirms the unity of its valley in the same way as it unites its banks. Our relation with Egypt will guarantee a just distribution of the Nile Waters, as well as the co-ordination of the two countries [sic] economies. There is no doubt that stable prosperous conditions and economic tranquillity will act in support of the great British Empire in a stronger manner than at any time in the past.

In addition we feel that the era of small states has gone, since they are unable to resist alone the world turmoil they have theyrefore [sic] to constitute themselves into groups and federations in order to face the new world order and to play an important part in the new world that was born on Victory Day.

Our inclination twoards [sic] Egypt is natural and through Egypt our trend is directed towards the Arab and Islamic countries with which we are linked with sacred bonds which will guarantee the harmony and the strength required for the expected union.

In order to realise the economic, cultural and social needs of the Sudan we consider that the Sudan should form a union with Egypt, under the Egyptian crown, while its administration is to be taken over by a Sudanese Government in flesh and blood. This is the only way in which the Sudan can benefit materially and morally and can complete what it lacks in education and finance, the latter will enable the country to exploit its resources to the fullest extent, so that the whole of the Nile Valley, the North as well as the South, the East and the West, should progress.

4. Your Excellencies

This solution of the Sudan question will help to establish stable conditions to develop the country economically; it will also assist the country to progress, while its economy will continue to be linked with that of the Great British Empire. We feel more strongly every day that we shall not be able completely to face future curcumstances [sic] or to develop our country in a way which will enable it to gain a suitable place in the new world organisation, without the aid of Great Britain. We also feel that a spirit of affection and confidence must always govern our relations with Great Britain as is now the case.

5. Your Excellencies

We are neither intriguing against the existing Condominium rule nor are we acting in a revolutionary way. The time of terrorism has gone, with the extermination of the Axis. But we are asking for a natural right, necessitated by our right to live and in order to live freely in our own country under a regime whihc [sic], we feel, will conform to our interests and wishes and will realise our national aims and aspirations. That regime is:— "The formation of a Democratic Sudanese Government in a union with Egypt under the Egyptian Crown".

What prompts us to present this note is our deep feeling that these demands are just and that the present time is suitable for their realisation and attainment. We are encouraged in this line by the present ideas prevailing as to the future organisation of the world and by the formation of a Labour Government in the Great Britain, since the principles of the Labour Party conforms [sic] to the spirit of these demands and will help their realisation.

6. Your Excellencies

We present these demands to two Democratic rulers, in a democratic manner. We present them in the name of the Graduates' General Congress—the body which enjoys the confidence of the whole country, represents the enlightened class, and under whose banner all parties in the country are grouped. We present them in the name of our dear Country, the Sudan, which has contributed, in the fight of democracy against fascism, with the blood of its sons, with its economic resources and with its moral support.

We do not forget, and history will certainly remember it, that the stand made by the S.D.F. in the face of the Axis Forces, in the Eastern Sudan together with the loyalty shown by the Civilian population in the Sudan were the beginning of the turning of the scales in favour of the Allies. This stand was followed by the defeat of the Axis at Keren in Abyssinia, at Alamein, in Italy, and then in Berlin and Japan.

7. Your Excellencies

Since the Sudanese have the first claim in the determination of their country's fute [sic] status, we now present these demands, requesting with insistance [sic] that the two Governments of Great Britain and Egypt should issue forthwith a statement approving these wishes of ours, and that rapid action should be taken with a view to carrying them out.

In the name of Justice, equity, fraternity and equality, for whose cause Democracy has fought, the Graduates' General Congress asks for "the formation of a democratic Sudanese Government in union with Egypt under the Egyptian Crown".

God may guide us to success.

Amen.

36 FO 371/45985, no 2977 25 Aug 1945

[Sudanese political aims]: letter from J W Robertson to E C Haselden. *Enclosure:* draft report of the United Parties Committee to the Executive Committee of the Graduates' Congress

1. I am sending you herewith two copies of a Report about to be submitted to the Executive Committee of the Graduates' General Congress by a committee called the

United Parties Committee, which is said to represent the various political parties in the Sudan; and of the conclusions come to by the United Committee. We have obtained these documents secretly.

2. It is expected that they will soon be dealt with by the Executive Committee, and no doubt something will appear in the Sudan Vernacular Press about it, and reference may be made in the Egyptian papers. You should therefore hand a copy to the Embassy, with a copy of this letter. I am sending two copies also to the London Office and asking the Controller[1] to show them to Mr. Scrivener unofficially.

3. This report and its conclusions need not be given too much emphasis; they are not very extreme, and they seem to show that the committee members do not expect that their aims can be attained in the very immediate future.

4. If the "requests" (a word which I prefer to the translation "demands") are sent to us in the near future, clearly (a) will be a matter for discussion at any revision of the 1936 Treaty, and it will be interesting to see what line Egypt takes up regarding a "free democratic Sudan". Personally I have always assumed that the Sudan Government was working towards a self governing Sudan, tied in some way as far as the North is concerned to the Arab Middle East, in connection (whether by alliance or something else) with the British Commonwealth.

5. With regard to (b) the Sudan Government could hardly undertake to execute recommendations of which it did not approve, but I think we might meet this request part of the way by allowing a committee with Sudanese representation to give us suggestions for further Sudanisation, though the Congress is not generally representative and we could not accept its nominees. The main drawback at the moment of course is lack of qualified Sudanese.

6. I do not know what is meant by (c) – maybe wartime restrictions on the press and the closed District Ordinance. We are now considering the abolition of as much war time legislation as possible without weakening our economic controls. I believe the ordinary Sudani is as free in all material ways, as the citizen of any country, from fear, want, religious persecution, and interference with his spoken or written word.

I believe therefore that there is not much to worry us at the moment in this.

Enclosure to 36

In response to the wish expressed by a number of our compatriots and in consideration of the present world conditions which impose upon the educated classes the necessity of uniting their opinion and rallying round the Congress, the various parties have deemed it necessary to form a Committee, composed of three representatives of each party, with Abdel Maged Ahmed[2] as Secretary, to consider:–

(1) the possible unification of the various parties' principles concerning the political future of the Sudan;

---

[1] R C Mayall.

[2] Abd al-Majid Ahmad, Ahrar (Liberal Party) member of Graduates' Congress Committee of 60, an employee of the War Supply Dept., who had earlier refused an invitation to sit on the Advisory Council for the Northern Sudan, but was later to sit on the Executive Council as under-secretary for economics and trade.

(2) the discussion of the first step which should be taken in connection with the realization of the country's national demands, in the light of any eventual agreement reached by the Parties.

The Committee held six meetings, the first on 15.5.45 and the last on 19.6.45. A sub-Committee was entrusted with the task of examining a few details which it was not possible for the main Committee to discuss in full Session. The Committee was therefore able to consider the various view points and, as far as possible, to reconcile them, and was careful in so doing not to interfere with the Congress's decisions and to work for the country's general interest, the latter being the highest objective towards which the efforts of all parties are sincerely directed. Since the decision taken by the coalition Front (representing the Ashigga, the Ittihadiyeen, and the Ahrar-Ittihadiyeen) was the point of divergence between this Front and the other parties, the Committee decided to examine this decision and find out the reasons which had led to their opposition, with the hope of reaching a solution acceptable to all of them.

Discussions have led to the following results:—

(1) All parties agree to work for the formation of a free democratic Sudanese Government.

(2) All parties agree to the principle of union with Egypt, and are perfectly convinced that the formation of such a Union is a necessity dictated by the historic, cultural and economic relations between the two countries and will serve the Sudan's interests more than Egypt's interests.

The Committee however discussed neither the sort of union which was to be formed nor the time within which it should take place; but it unanimously agreed that a reference to the principle of union with Egypt was inevitable when submitting a demand regarding the sort of Sudanese Government acceptable, provided that the said union did not in any way affect the "autonomy" of the Government or limit its powers to act in the interests of the country.

The coalition Front (Ashigga, Ittihadiyeen, Ahrar-Ittihadiyeen) insisted on defining the union as one under the Egyptian Crown. The Umma representatives made the reservations that although it did not oppose the principle of a union with Egypt, the approved principles of their party made no reference to a union with Egypt or any other country; the Party would therefore restrict their activities to working for the formation of a free democratic Sudanese Government only, but would not oppose the other parties' activities in this connection.

In compliance with the foregoing conclusions, and with due regard to the above definitions and reservations the parties' representatives have undertaken that their parties should work jointly, through the Congress, for the formation of a free democratic Sudanese Government that will accept the principle of union with Egypt. It is admitted that this agreement does not prevent the Umma Party from working separately, independently of the Congress, provided its activity does not conflict with the spirit of the decision agreed upon by the Parties. Thus the desired unity will be realised and the work for the attainment of the common aim will be facilitated.

The Committee then discussed the demands which were to be submitted to the Congress, so that the latter should work for their achievement, with the help of the Sudan Government, before the present world-wide opportunities had passed. The Committee divided its discussions into two parts:—

Part I
To demand the publication of a statement by the two Condominium Powers, defining the political future of the Sudan and specifying the aim pursued by the two States.

Part II
To ask the Sudan Government to expedite the means whereby the Sudanese are enabled to reach the desired goal, so that this goal should be attained as soon as possible.

After discussion the Committee considered that the Congress should present the following demands, in the way it deems fit, to the Authorities concerned at the suitable time.

Part I. The present political status of the Sudan is abnormal; it does not tranquillise the Sudanese about their future, not does it conform to the basic principle laid down by the United Nations for the construction of the new world. The Sudan is not a colony, and its sons would not agree, at the present stage, that it should be one. On the other hand the Sudan is not free and cannot join the ranks of free states and cooperate with them in performing its mission, in a way which secures happiness to the Sudanese.

With the termination of resistance in Europe and the unconditional surrender of Nazi Germany the United Nations have won a decisive victory on the enemies of humanity, of equality and of progress. The nations which are today rejoicing over this victory should however remember that this was not the result of their efforts alone, but of combined efforts in which all nations have shared. The effort made by small nations is not in any way inferior to those made by others. The Sudan which has sacrificed both men and money and whose efforts have been recognised by all the United Nations, stands today like the runner who wins a race and then looks around expecting the prize he deserves. The prize which the Sudan expects is nothing short of full freedom; freedom of choosing the sort of government it accepts, a government which secures happiness and welfare of the Sudanese; freedom in choosing the means whereby the Sudanese can reach the stage of governing themselves and joining the ranks of free nations.

It is therefore not strange that the Sudanese should ask the two Condominium powers to recognise this right and to issue a statement clearly defining their aims in the Sudan. Since the Anglo–Egyptian Treaty provides for the possibility of reconsidering the Sudan question ten years after the signature of the Treaty which elapses in 1946, the Committee of United Parties considers that the time is suitable for the reconsideration of the Sudan question and the issue of a joint declaration by the two Condominium Powers that their aim is to work for the establishment, as soon as possible, of a free democratic Sudanese Government with a union with Egypt and an alliance with Great Britain. This is the basic demand which, in the opinion of the Committee of the United Parties, should be presented now, by the Congress before the present opportunity has passed—this being the determination of the future of the world following the wars and the lapse of a period of ten years since the signature of the Anglo–Egyptian Treaty.

Part II. The Sudan Government, as recently stated by the Civil Secretary, is working for the establishment of self-Government in this country, through the Sudanisation of the administration at the slow paces announced in the last Session of the Advisory Council, and through the gradual devolution of larger powers to Municipal, Rural and Provincial Councils and to the Advisory Council. The Government also declared that the constitutional bodies which could advise it were the Province Councils and the Advisory Council. This is excellent and does not conflict with the high objective aimed at by the educated Sudanese. But the Sudanese cannot agree that this (? self-government) should be the ultimate aim of the Sudan Government and also cannot agree upon the slow procedure laid down by the Government for the attainment of that modest aim. We have expressed in Part I our demands concerning the "aim", and it remains to set out the procedure which, in our opinion, should be followed by the Sudan Government for the attainment of that aim.

The Committee considers that in order to quailfy the Sudanese for the attainment of the proposed aim, it is necessary to proceed, at a quicker pace, with the Government of all aspects of progress, whether educational or economic. The Committee however considers that it should limit its recommendations to certain specific aspects which, in its opinion, should be given priority, since they have the way for all others. The Committee also realises that all other aspects of progress have been examined by the Congress on several occasions and are being taken care of, in accordance with the Congress annual programme.

Since the Government is now studying the scheme for the Sudanisation of the administration, the Committee feels that the present time is suitable for the submission to [? of] practical suggestions which would ensure that [? the] execution of the scheme in the shortest possible period. The most efficient means, in the Committee's opinion, is that the Congress should ask the Sudan Government to appoint a Committee formed of an equal number of Government representatives, and of representatives of the educated class provided the latter are nominated by the Congress. The said Committee would be entrusted with the duty of examining the Sudanisation scheme and submitting its recommendations to the Government for their execution. The Government, on its part, should undertake to accept the Committee's recommendations.

The second demand which, in the opinion of the United Parties Committee, the Congress should present to the Government, is the complete release of restrictions on public freedom, such as the freedom of the press, the freedom of writing and publishing, the freedom of movements within the frame of general regulations; the Government should also be asked to amend all special regulations restricting these liberties. Without this release this country will not be able to follow the path of progress, and realise its legal national aspirations.

Signature of the Parties' representatives.

Conclusion

The decisions of the United Front, as registered in the Official minutes, can be summarised as follows:—

(1) They (the various parties) should all work, under the standard of the Congress, for the formation of a free democratic Sudanese Government, with the admission of the principle of a Union with Egypt.

(2) Every party is at liberty to direct its activities according to the principles laid down by it, provided these activities do not conflict with the text or the spirit of the

general formula agreed upon by the parties, as specified in paragraph one above. Due consideration is given to the reservation made by the Umma Party not to undertake to work for a union with Egypt or any other country, but not to oppose such activities. Due consideration is also given to the explanation made by the coalition Parties (Ashigga, Ittihadiyeen, Ahrar-Ittihadiyeen) that Union for them means a union under the Egyptian Crown.

(3) They should ask the Graduates' Congress to endeavour to realise the demands specified hereafter by all peaceful and legal means which the Congress thinks suitable, the help of the Sudan Government should, as far as possible, be sought for the realisation of these demands.

These demands are:—

(a) The issue of a joint declaration by the two Condominium Powers, stating that their aim is to work for the formation as soon as possible of a free democratic Sudanese Government, with a union with Egypt and an alliance with Great Britain.

(b) to ask for the formation of a joint Committee, composed of an equal number of representatives of the Sudan Government and of the Sudanese educated class—the latter to be nominated by the Congress—with a view to laying down a scheme for the Sudanisation of the administration in the shortest possible period, provided the Government gives this Committee all necessary facilities to carry out its mission and undertakes to execute its recommendations.

(c) to ask for the lifting of restrictions on public freedoms such as the freedom of the Press, of gathering, of movement, within the frame of the law; to ask for an amendment of the existing special ordinances restricting these liberties.

(Sgd.) Abdel Maged Ahmed
Secretary

37 FO 371/45985, no 3088 11–12 Sept 1945
'Financial aid for the Sudan' and 'The future of the Sudan': memoranda by Sir H Huddleston

[In September 1945 Huddleston visited London for consultation. These two memos were produced in London prior to a meeting at the FO. Following the meeting Howe summarized Huddleston's arguments on the political need for a £5 million development grant to the Sudan in the following terms: 'Any refusal by H.M.G. at this moment to support financially the schemes of development which the Sudan have in mind would be incomprehensible to the Sudanese people in the face of the establishment of a fund of £120 million for Colonial development. It would be interpreted by the Sudanese that we had no longer any interest in their welfare. To the Treasury's argument that we just could not afford such munificent schemes at this present crisis in our national finances, the governor-general proposed that the sum of £5 million could be obtained by taking off slices from the allocations for each of the Colonies' (minute by Howe, 18 Sept 1945, FO 371/45986, no 3150).]

Financial aid for the Sudan

Correspondence on this subject between the Governor-General, H.M's Ambassador in Cairo, the Foreign Office and the Treasury ended in the Treasury refusing to meet the Sudan's request for a grant to endow the new Gordon College, and in the Foreign Office reserving the right to re-open the matter during the Governor-General's visit to the U.K. in 1945.[1]

In putting up the proposal, the Governor-General emphasised that it was based not on financial but on political grounds. These latter were set forth at length in two despatches and are again mentioned in a note on the Future of the Sudan.

While the political arguments in favour of the grant are no less strong now than they were—indeed the end of the war is an additional reason for an early gesture in recognition of the Sudan's war effort—a new factor has arisen lately in the shape of the first concrete proposals for a Five-Years Plan of economic, social and educational development. These proposals constitute a reasonable and, in the main, essential programme of development, much of which is overdue on account of lack of funds in the past and on account of the six years of war.

They follow very closely the lines of development which are being undertaken in the Colonies and which are being financed under the Colonial Development and Welfare Fund. The proposals will require a capital expenditure in the neighbourhood of £11,000,000; they by no means exhaust the possibilities of reasonable development and demands for capital expenditure over the next few years will without doubt be considerably in excess of this figure, but this represents the minimum sum which should be spent over the next five years if the Sudan is not to fall sadly behind the British Colonies in the welfare of its people and the development of its resources.

It has been admitted that the present financial position of the Sudan is strong but its reserves have been built up only during the last decade and recurrent expenditure has now caught up with ordinary revenue and fresh increments to the Sudan's reserves are unlikely until fresh sources of revenue are developed—moreover expansion of the social services can only safely go forward if such additional revenue is found. It would not be possible for the Sudan to meet from its own reserves more than about half of the capital expenditure required without imperilling its financial stability, particularly in view of the uncertainty which faces the cotton industry.

It is therefore now recommended that H.M.G. should make a grant of the order of £5,000,000 sterling to the Sudan in aid of their programme of development.

Such a grant would serve the triple purpose of:—

(a) recognising the Sudan's contribution to the war effort,

(b) proving to the Sudanese Great Britain's real interest in their country and thereby strengthening her position vis-à-vis Egypt,

(c) enabling the Sudan Government to undertake economic, social and educational development on a scale comparable with that which H.M.G. are financing in the colonies.

To produce the maximum effect in all these directions, it would be desirable for the grant to be made in one instalment at an early date, but if this were not convenient to H.M.G., it could be spread over the next five or ten years.

It is hardly necessary to argue the vital part which the improvement of facilities for education, particularly higher education, must play in developing a policy of eventual self-rule for backward territories and in any programme of economic and social

---

[1] See 22 and 28.

development. If such arguments are needed they are set out in full in the recent Report of the Commission on Higher Education in the Colonies and are summed up in the words:

> "In the stage preparatory to self-government universities have an important part to play; indeed they may be said to be indispensable. To them we must look for the production of men and women with the standards of public service and capacity for leadership which self-rule requires."[2]

If self-government is the eventual aim of H.M.G's policy in the Sudan, H.M.G. cannot escape the obligation of helping to equip the Sudanese with the essential powers of intellect and character and with an economy and social services which will enable them to stand on their own feet and to maintain the welfare of the people at a reasonable level.

A generous act of this nature would, of course, be profitable to H.M.G., not only in the political field; for development in the Sudan will raise the standard of living of the Sudanese and will increase the demand for imported goods. It has always been the policy of the Sudan to buy to the greatest possible extent in the British market and there is every reason to suppose that this policy will continue.

The future of the Sudan

There are three reasons which make it important in the view of the Sudan Government that H.M.G. should as soon as possible decide upon and publish a clear and long term policy for the future of the Sudan.

1. The Sudanese are becoming more and more politically conscious and ambitious: they are growing towards nationhood and they are becoming increasingly interested in their future. This process has been greatly accelerated by the war. They are fully aware of the creditable part the Sudan has played in the war and they now expect their reward.
2. Egypt is demanding her reward for the help she has given the United Nations in the war and one of her foremost aims is the old one of union of the Sudan with Egypt.
3. Revision of the Anglo–Egyptian Treaty, by mutual consent, can first come up in 1946. Egypt has already made it clear that she wants revision and will no doubt formally request it when the time comes. One of the main points on which she will ask for revision will be the Sudan question, hitherto reserved.

To take the first point in greater detail. The Sudan Government has deliberately encouraged Sudanese nationalism both in conformity with its obligations as trustee for the Sudanese and as a defence against Egyptian aspirations in the Sudan. The Government, with the blessing of the Foreign Office, has publicly committed itself to the goal of self-government for the Sudanese and is implementing this policy by:—

(a) progressive Sudanisation in all branches of the Civil Service,
(b) the development of Sudanese local government,
(c) the creation of an Advisory Council for the Northern Sudan, which is a Sudanese body to advise the Governor-General.

---

[2] *Report of the Commission on Higher Education in the Colonies, 1944–1955* (Cmd 6647, 1945) [Asquith Commission].

The ideas of the Sudan Government and of the educated Sudanese on the proper speed at which the policy should be developed not unnaturally differ—the former is guided by what it considers to be to the benefit of the Sudanese as a whole, the latter by their claim to speak for all Sudanese and by their impatience to assume the responsibilities and the powers of government. They wish to advance at the speed of the fastest, not of the slowest nor even of the average. Although the educated class numbers only five or six thousand out of a total population of six or seven millions, this is an attitude which the Government cannot afford to ignore nor condemn as entirely unreasonable. This class can argue that if it has been right for a handful of "superior" foreigners to govern the country for the past 45 years, is it not right for a handful of "superior" Sudanese to do so now that they exist? They are at least of the country. That the handful is as small as it is they say is the fault of the Government's educational policy in the past: the "superior" Sudanese cannot be expected to wait indefinitely while the Government tries to correct its mistake.

Like most young people, the Educated Sudanese, though often unsure of themselves, are full of apparent self-confidence and are impatient of paternal restrictions. Their pride is easily hurt and they are quick to resent criticism of their abilities. It makes no impression to tell them that they do not represent the Sudanese, that they are over-hasty and that they are not yet fit to govern—they ask how they will ever be fit to govern if they are not given the chance to try. It is impossible to tell them, however true, that their rule would be less honest and disinterested than ours and that the ordinary Sudanese may well be less well off than they are now—for this will always be true to some extent and if it were a reason for delaying the achievement of self-government, we might as well abandon that goal altogether.

If the British appear to be delaying the achievement of self-government unduly, however worthy their motives, the educated Sudanese will turn increasingly to the Egyptians in the hope that they will grant it sooner and that they will also provide greater material aid in the development of the country. The Sudan cannot from its own resources provide all the funds required for reasonable economic, social and educational development and Egypt is able and would be only too ready, for political reasons, to help.

If Britain wishes to retain her position in the Sudan, she must state clearly that her policy is the achievement of self-government as soon as is reasonably possible, and she must provide material aid as earnest of her real interest in the future of the country.

The second and third points can best be considered together.

In September, 1944, the Ambassador in Cairo, on the authority of the Foreign Office, read "unofficially" to Nahas Pasha the then Prime Minister, and later to King Farouk, a statement in which were the following passages:—

> "There have lately been numerous indications in the press and elsewhere that in certain Egyptian circles the time is now considered to have come when sweeping changes in relations between Egypt and the Sudan should be actively studied. The advocates of such a policy evidently do not take into account the essential fact that the Anglo–Egyptian Treaty has imposed on Great Britain and Egypt alike trusteeship for the Sudanese and their education towards self-government."

> "The Egyptian Government should be under no illusion as regards H.M.G's intentions to fulfil strictly and conscientiously the obligations which they have assumed in respect of the Sudan under the Anglo–Egyptian Treaty. H.M.G. will tolerate no alteration of the situation established by the Anglo–Egyptian Treaty until such time as the Sudanese have reached a stage of development when they can speak authoritatively for themselves. Any attempt by Egypt to modify the existing situation by arbitrary methods can only result in Egypt's total elimination from the Sudan except in so far as the obligations of H.M.G. under the Nile Waters Agreement are concerned."

In the Foreign Office Brief on Egypt and the Sudan to the British Delegation at the San Francisco Conference it was stated that the old Egyptian political programme of "complete independence" is still being preached and that it includes the union of Egypt and the Sudan.

> "It is claimed that this programme is in accordance with the Atlantic Charter. Whether this be the case or not (and it is highly doubtful in the case of the union of Egypt and the Sudan) it is divorced from all reality, since, to give only the more obvious reasons—the Sudan is itself attaining nationhood, and must be left free to work out its own destiny, which may or may not involve union with Egypt—probably not."
>
> "For the union of Egypt and the Sudan to be realised would involve the revision of the Anglo–Egyptian Treaty."
>
> "The attitude of H.M.G. on this question is simple, viz: – there is no provision in the Anglo–Egyptian Treaty for revision to take place before December 1946, and then only by mutual consent. When revision does come to be discussed H.M.G. may well have important demands of their own to put forward in the light of changes in the world situation since 1936."

While the Sudan question was reserved in the Anglo–Egyptian Treaty, Article II of the Treaty provided that the primary aim of the joint Anglo–Egyptian administration in the Sudan must be the welfare of the Sudanese.

The statements quoted above provide a definite interpretation of this clause and one which supports the policy adopted by the Sudan Government, but if this represents the firm of policy of H.M.G. the Egyptians have not been told of it officially and the Sudanese know nothing of it. They know the policy and aims of the Sudan Government, and in the main approve them, but they also know that the last word lies with H.M.G. and that they, with the agreement of the Egyptian Government, could change the policy at any time by a change in the interpretation of Article II.

The Ambassador in February 1945, described British objectives in the Sudan as being "primarily to maintain our predominant position in a strategically important area, and secondarily to carry out in the Sudan our traditional policy of guiding a backward people by gradual stages towards self-government, with the definite intention that when they have reached that stage they will be willing to maintain particularly close relations with us: and to ensure for them a good administration meanwhile."[3] This accurately describes the Sudan Government's views, and all these objectives "in the light of experience postulate that Egyptian influence in the Sudan should be kept at a minimum."

There is obviously much of all this which cannot be said publicly by H.M.G. without provoking a major crisis with Egypt, but is H.M.G. prepared to record in some form or other their interpretation as given above of Article II? The policy of educating the Sudanese up to self-government is regarded in Egypt as a policy directed towards the eventual complete separation of the Sudan from Egypt and probably its inclusion in the British Commonwealth, and therefore as being in direct conflict with their policy of union. Public statements of its policy by the Sudan Government have at once aroused the deep suspicions of the Egyptians and a public declaration by H.M.G. would probably create a minor crisis.

It seems therefore to come to a choice between H.M.G. provoking the crisis first by making such a declaration or waiting for Egypt to provoke the crisis by formally demanding union through a revision of the Treaty.

The easy way out is for H.M.G. to shelve the whole problem until 1956 by refusing to consider revision of the Treaty, or by trying to frighten the Egyptians out of their request for revision by threats of counter requirements in a new Treaty.

But, and this is the most important point to the Sudan Government, by continuing to keep the Sudanese in the dark as to their eventual intentions, H.M.G. may prejudice beyond recovery their chances of gaining their basic objectives in the Sudan. Like most people, the Sudanese want the best of both worlds: having become a self-governing nation, they would like to establish close relations with both Egypt and Great Britain and to enjoy the advantages of both connections. There can be little doubt that they would value a strong British connection very highly but they will not wait indefinitely for the promise of it. As they find, as they undoubtedly will, that it becomes increasingly difficult to keep on the right side of both Condominium Powers, they would be only human if they turn rapidly to the Egyptian connection before they prejudice their position with Egypt by prolonged acquiescence in the British policy of excluding Egyptian influence from the Sudan. There is already a tendency in this direction amongst certain sections of the politically-minded and uncertainty as to H.M.G's intentions is partly the reason for it.

The Sudan, by the nature of things, has and always will have certain close ties with Egypt, geographical, racial, lingual, religious and economic, and to this extent Great Britain starts with a handicap in the competition for the Sudan's favour.

The British connection, if it is to hold the Sudanese, must mean more than training them for self-government and in the meantime providing them with a good, predominantly British administration. They regard these as the bare minimum of our obligations towards them. Their fulfilment will not arouse feelings of lasting gratitude towards us. In fact, the later stages of the process are likely to assume the superficial aspect of an increasingly ambitious and vocal educated Sudanese class struggling for independence against a reactionary and over-cautious "foreign" Government. The final curtain will fall on the "victory" of the Sudanese in their fight

---

[3] See 25.

for freedom from foreign domination. This is not the foundation on which "particularly close relations" are built.

45 years of British administration have not turned the Sudanese into African Englishmen, nor will another 20 years of it. Their form of self-government and standards of public life will be fundamentally oriental and their national outlook will be Arab and Middle Eastern. The ties of common origin, common outlook and tradition, which play so large a part in binding together the British Commonwealth, cannot influence the Sudanese nation of the future.

Political concessions, however generous, will not be sufficient basis for lasting friendship: what appears to the governing power to be a concession is to the ruled merely the granting, usually belated, of a right.

To be effective, in the absence of spiritual ties, the friendship must be built on the more solid basis of material aid. The benefits of the British connection must be real and practical and visible to all Sudanese—and that means, first and foremost, spending money in aid of economic, social and educational development.

If it is agreed that the case for a declaration of policy has been made out, it remains to consider the way in which this can best be done. A unilateral statement by H.M.G. would no doubt be undesirable and it is suggested that there are two possible alternative courses:—

(i) That H.M.G. should agree to revision of the Anglo–Egyptian Treaty in 1946 with the definite object, so far as the Sudan question is concerned, of including in the new Treaty a provision that training of the Sudanese for self-government is the primary object of Anglo–Egyptian administration in the Sudan and that having attained self-government, the Sudanese should decide their own future status vis-à-vis Great Britain and Egypt.

(ii) That if revision of the Treaty is not desired by H.M.G., Egypt should be asked to agree to a joint statement by the Condominium Powers on the above lines, as an interpretation of Article II of the existing Treaty. In the face of the Atlantic Charter, which she herself has invoked, and of the resolutions of the San Francisco Conference on trusteeship in backward territories, it would be difficult for Egypt to refuse such a request.

In either case it is suggested, as a preliminary step, that the matter should be discussed first by Province Councils and subsequently by the Advisory Council for the Northern Sudan on a basis to be agreed beforehand between H.M.G. and Egypt.

The difficult problem of the sovereignty and nationality of the Sudan would presumably be shelved automatically by the provision that the Sudanese shall eventually decide their own fate, and consideration of the equally difficult problem of the future of the Southern Sudan would also be postponed until that region has developed sufficiently to have some say in its own future.

In the meantime, Great Britain should without delay set about strengthening her position in the Sudan by giving financial aid and by improving cultural relations through, for example, the establishment of a branch of the British Council in Khartoum.

38 FO 371/45986, no 3128 15 Sept 1945

[Southern Sudan]: letter from R L Speaight[1] to P S Scrivener explaining why a statement on the Southern Sudan would be undesirable. *Enclosures:* letter from Civil Secretary's Office, Khartoum to the Chancery, Cairo (3 Sept 1945), forwarding supporting documents [Extract]

With reference to our despatch No. 1174 of 21st August, I enclose a copy of a letter from Khartoum Secretariat about the Southern Sudan.

We agree with Khartoum in so far as the lack of a public statement on our policy in regard to the Southern Sudan is liable to create the same suspicion here as in the Northern Sudan. We are, however, bound to weigh against that consideration the undesirability of any move on our side which might gratuitously stir up extra interest here in this vexed question. The whole problem of the future of the Sudan is bound to come up soon when the Treaty is being revised, and from the Egyptian point of view it seems better to hold up until then any reassuring statement which we may have to make about our intentions in regard to the South. Meanwhile we feel that there is no point in going to meet trouble half way.

I am sending a copy of this letter to Khartoum.

Enclosure to 38

In the enclosure to your printed despatch No.320 Lord Killearn suggested to the Secretary of State that the problems of the Southern Sudan which we set out in our despatch No.89 might be discussed with the Governor-General in the United Kingdom. As you know the Civil Secretary will join His Excellency in the United Kingdom within the next few days, and we very much hope that such discussions will be held. Robertson is therefore taking with him copies of this letter and of the enclosures.

The point is that we feel that the discussions will be of particular value on one point—whether a public statement cannot now be made of the policy. Our present secrecy gives rise to exaggerated suspicions in the Northern Sudan, and our silence or reticence on the subject to some extent prejudices the all-important good relations we hope to maintain with responsible Northern Sudanese.

We should therefore very much like such a statement to be made but we fully realise it will have to meet various Imperial and Egyptian considerations with which we are not primarily concerned. From our point of view, it must be uncompromising on essentials—that responsibility to the Southerners is ours not that of the Northern Sudanese, and that we are best fitted to decide what is best for them,—but we hope that it need not go back on anything so far made public by us nor be avoidably upsetting to Northern Sudanese opinion. The enclosures therefore comprise, briefly, the recent public statements made by us on our policy for the South, and some representative indications of Northern Sudanese opinion. . . .

[1] First secretary in the embassy in Cairo, 1945–1947.

Extract from a memorandum from Ismail al-Azhari to Sir H Huddleston, 6 Oct 1943, giving the views of the Graduates' Congress on the legislation concerning an Advisory Council for the Northern Sudan

... The Advisory Council Ordinance contains a principle which confirms our fears and doubts, i.e. the exclusion of the South from this Council whether in its constitution or with regard to the subjects to be referred to it. We used to approve of the application of different systems of administration in Local Government, because every area has its own problems and nobody can solve the problems of any area better than its own sons. But we cannot understand nor accept the application of this principle to the Central Government.

It is obvious that the sphere of the Central Government covers in particular all legislation which concerns the development of the whole country and its general progress in the fields of education, health, agriculture, trade and industry as well as defence. We had believed that the Central Government with which the Sudanese were to be associated, included the administration of the whole Sudan. The Advisory Council to be formed at the top of the pyramid should therefore cover the whole Sudan. It is not an essential condition for the unity of a country that all its parts should be on the same level or progress. Nor in fact is this principle applied to what is called the "North" when the Juba [sic, Nuba] Mountains which is [sic] included in the sphere of the Council resembles the "South", and the policy of the South is applied to it.[2]

The principle of separation might be approved if there exist hostilities or dissensions which might result in the disturbance of public security. But, praise be to God, we have neither seen nor heard of fighting in the streets of large towns between the sons of the North and those of the South, as happens in Indian towns between the different sections of the Indian population. In fact the sons of both the Northern and Southern Sudan have participated, since the Fung era, in the army and in the administration of the country; and Sudanese troops under the Turkish regime were mostly southerners of whom there were leaders whose names have been recorded in history. During the Mahdia Jihadiya warriors enjoyed a special renown. One of the greatest leaders in the Mahdia is Hamdan Abu 'Anga, a southerner in whose army enlisted Northern leaders and soldiers, who were proud of his leadership.[3] With them, he defeated Abyssinian forces and conquered Gondar. We need not go back to the distant or near past. There is the famous case of the Sudan Defence Force to-day and we are all proud of the services it has rendered in the cause of Democracy. Its fine qualities on the battlefield have been officially recognised. Did we ever discriminate between Northerners and Southerners in its ranks? Did we ever ask when an S.D.F. division had displayed valour, whether its men were mostly Northerners or Southerners? Heaven knows we did not.

Here, Your Excellency, we apologise for a digression. We have come to

---

[2] The Nuba Mountains, also subject to the Closed Districts Ordinance, were contained within Kordofan, a northern province.

[3] The non-Muslim peoples conscripted into the armies of the Kingdom of Sennar (sixteenth to early nineteenth century), the Turco-Egyptian empire (1821–1885) and the Mahdiya (1882–1898) were all slaves. Hamdan Abu Anja (d. 1889) was a Bandala, a group of former slaves who continued to owe service to their Baggara Arab former masters. A personal client of the Khalifa Abdallahi, he was placed in command of the riflemen (*jihadiya*); thus ensuring the Khalifa's control over the only permanent body of soldiers in the Mahdist state.

apprehensions of a policy which has so far been carried out without legislation, but has now been given a legislative form. In this digression we will take up the question of South in its entirely. The present Government has now lasted 45 years during which we admit that the North has made substantial progress in many walks of life, though not to the degree hoped for. We would have liked to see a similar, even greater, progress made in the South. Neighbouring countries, like the Congo and Uganda, have seen the light of civilisation, while the mentality and the ways of production and living of our brothers, the Southerners, have remained as they were, in spite of the fact that the possibilities of progress in their area exceed those of many Northern areas.

This policy for the South which has now been disclosed in order to be confirmed by the new legislation, has existed in fact since the beginning. All sorts of obstacles are placed in the way of those wishing to enter the South. There are also the regulations which prevent Southerners from emigration to the North; the official encouragement of, and monopoly given to certain missionary bodies, and the placing of obstacles in the way of, nay even the complete prevention of the spreading of Islam; the great effort made to create among Southerners a lingua franca written in Latin letters, whereas Arabic will spread among the people of the South as soon as the door between the North and the South is opened. If these missionaries had enlightened the Southerners and raised their standard to the level of Northerners, we would not have objected to their presence and would have looked upon them as servants of humanity and civilisation. But unfortunately they have done nothing of this sort. On the contrary, the various missionaries working there threaten to create religious differences similar to those to which Europe succumbed in the Middle Ages. The seeds of religious antagonism have been sown in Equatorial Africa in general, and in the Southern Sudan in particular.

We are not selfish people who aspire to positions and power for ourselves. But we are a people who feel the responsibility of paving the way and laying the foundation for the coming generations, and we want this Valley to maintain the spirit of united consciousness in religion and language which, as Your Excellency knows, are among the factors of real nationalism. There are nations which suffered before us from these differences which time could not remove. Is it compatible with the spirit of humanity that these differences should be deliberately created among us? To read what is written by Julian Huxley in his book 'Africa View' on the divergence between the different missionary bodies, and their effects on the poor African peoples, is enough to make one's flesh creep in anticipation of these results in our "South" in the future.

Since the old Egyptian regime, the South has formed part of the Sudan, and remained so in the Mahdia. Emir 'Arabi Dafa' all [sic][4] was, as Your Excellency knows, the last Governor of this region. After the Reconquest of the Sudan, the South remained as an integral part of the country from the administrative point of view. So recent history confirms the unity of the Sudan. From the economical point of view the Northern and Southern Sudan form one country. A look at the map shows clearly that the Nile Valley is an economic unity, since there are no natural barriers. The variations of climate and rainfall in the Sudan make the production of various crops contribute to the economic soundness of the whole country. One of the

[4] Arabi Dafa Allah (d. *c.* 1916), last Mahdist governor of Equatoria, 1890–1898, whose troops are remembered locally for carrying out a number of atrocities against the rural population.

great mistakes made in the Treaty of Versailles, was the division of the Austro–Hungarian Empire into sections differing in language and nationality, but economically inter-dependent. If the makers of the Treaty of Versailles were aiming at weakening the Austro–Hungarian Empire, militarily and politically, is there any justification for weakening the economic unity of the Sudan? It is certain that the political separation of the Southern and Northern Sudan will lead at the end to the economic separation of the country, and vice versa, as the political unity is one of the greatest bonds of economic unity.

Slavery was a crime against humanity which had before us been committed by Europe and America. It has completely vanished in our country, and none of us think of reviving it. On the contrary we call for the abolition of any sort of slavery, even in its simplest form, such as the control of thought, let alone the control of the body. There are no ambiguities in our society which justify any fear in this direction. We therefore beg Your Excellency to remove the existing barriers between the Northern and Southern Sudan, and let those who are in fact brothers have the right of intercourse. We also beg Your Excellency to adopt a quick constructive and educational policy, with a view to reducing or removing the cultural differences between the two parts of the country.

We wish to see money from the Central Treasury spent generously on the development of the South. None of us would like to see his fellow-countrymen naked any longer. . . .

Extract from a broadcast on the Advisory Council for the Northern Sudan by Sir D Newbold, 14 Jan 1944

. . . I should like to meet another apprehension, and that is the fear that behind the Advisory Councils Ordinance there is hidden a secret policy to split the Sudan in two and cut off the Southern Provinces from the North. No such decision has been reached nor is the Sudan Government empowered on its own to make such a decision. The reasons for confining this Council to the six Northern Provinces are much simpler. They are practical and not political reasons and have been explained both in the Explanatory Note attached to the Laws and in a simple Note in Arabic of which over 1000 copies were circulated about two months ago. We are not prejudging the future status of the Southern Sudan. It is simply that the Southern Sudanese have not yet, for historic and natural reasons, reached a degree of enlightenment and cohesion which enables them to send competent representatives to a Council of this kind. Nor are there any Northern Sudanese who can fairly claim to be able conscientiously to represent the Southern peoples. We must look facts in the face. The same difficulty applies in a lesser degree to the Nuba Mountains districts, but owing to their closer connections with the North and the fact that they are an integral part of Kordofan Province we have thought it necessary, in spite of some differences of language and outlook and social life, to arrange for their representation on the Kordofan Province Council and I have just been to El Obeid to discuss the method with the Province Authorities. It is not easy but not insuperable. It has been suggested that District Commissioners or even Missionaries might be nominated as Southern Representatives. A District Commissioner might with difficulty represent the Nuba Mountains but the diversity of tribes and customs and languages and the distances in the Southern Provinces are such that almost each district would have to have a separate representative and it is Government's aim that this Council should be a predominantly Sudanese assembly.

We have carefully drafted the Ordinance so that later on, when our plans for accelerating the educational and economic development of the South have matured, it can either join up with the Northern Council or have a separate Council of its own. It is interesting that in several Southern areas native Local Government is developing well....

Extract from a note of a conversation between Sir D Newbold, Ibrahim Ahmed, Abdel [sic] El Magid and Ahmad El Shingeiti in Omdurman on 22 Oct 1943

... *Southern Sudan*

Ibrahim Ahmed said missions had done good work, but were bad educationally, or at least results were terribly slow. Shingeiti said Northern Educated Sudanese knew nothing of South and felt cut off. We discussed question of Arabic (no one really raised religion) and economic development. They suggested a few boys should come to Gordon College (Secondary) from South. I told them, as regards future of South, that in its present primitive state it was idle to prophecy [sic] its future, that it needed development and education (which latter I admitted was backward) whatever its future. If we (Education Department) took over education from missions, it would be much bigger drain on Northern Funds *and staff*, and one wouldn't find Northern teachers to learn Southern vernaculars as long-resident missionaries do. We did not feel Arabic and English could be taught in addition to a group-language or vernacular. I agreed that the question was complicated and delicate, but I took the opportunity to point out that no frontiers in or round the Sudan can be regarded as sacrosanct eternally, and that the happiness and prosperity of the people was more important than territorial inviolacy, e.g. *if* it is legitimate to consider, or press for the Anuak of the Baro Salient to be transferred from Abyssinia to Sudan to their Nilotic brethren in U.N.P. or for the Beni Amer of Agordat District, or Habab etc. of Keren and Nacfa District (which together would mean transfer of over half Eritrea to Sudan) surely it is not an outrage to suppose that it *might* later make for the happiness of the Latuka, Acholi, Lango etc. of Equatoria to be transferred to Uganda later on, with whom they have common language, customs and religion. (Similarly would the Sudanese consider that the Congolese intelligentsia of, say, Stanleyville and Leopoldville, if any, were outraged by the transfer of a large block of tribes West of Juba from Belgian Congo to Sudan in 19?[5]

N.B. I didn't ask this question, but I mentioned that two-thirds Zande lived in the Congo and only one-third in the Sudan.) I hastened to assure the effendia that no negotiations of any sort were in train for any transfer to Uganda, I only wished to point out that Southern Sudanese interests might be separate and frontiers were not eternal. Mr. Owen[6] said economic considerations were valid and I said Yes; these point North for some of the Southern Sudan and South for others....

---

[5] 1910, when the Lado Enclave reverted to Anglo–Egyptian rule, following the death of King Leopold I of Belgium.

[6] T R H Owen, then deputy gov Bahr al-Ghazal sub-province.

39 FO 371/46081, no 3317 18 Sept 1945

'Nile waters and the Sudan': minutes by W N Allan[1] of a meeting held at Wellington House, London.

[While Huddleston was in London a meeting was also arranged between Sudan government personnel to discuss the Sudan's future Nile waters projects. In addition to the governor general the meeting included the J W E Miller (financial secretary), R M MacGregor (irrigation adviser), W N Allan (director of irrigation) and W H Luce (private secretary to Huddleston).]

1. The purpose of the meeting was to consider the line of action to be taken in the light of Despatch No. 132 of 24.12.44. from Khartoum to Cairo,[2] and subsequent correspondence, and in particular of a note, which had been prepared as the result of technical discussions between Messrs. Macgregor and Allan (see copy attached).[3] The main points of this note were:—

(i) A definite forecast of the ultimate needs of the Sudan in water for the full development of irrigation, totalling 7.1 milliards of m3 annually.
(ii) The recommendation that when the question of further water supplies is taken up with Egypt, a final settlement should be aimed at, on the lines of this forecast.

It was pointed out by Mr. Macgregor that the forecast proposed that the Sudan should participate in the Jonglei Scheme, to the extent of 500 million m3 of water, in addition to her ultimate share of 50% in the Lake Tana Project; this was a proposal not previously contemplated in such a form, the corollary to which would be that the Sudan Irrigation Department should take an active part in the engineering development of the Jonglei Scheme.

2. It was noted that the line of action as regards the concession for Lake Tana had already been agreed upon in July, 1945, and that preliminary approaches to Ethiopia would be made when circumstances permitted, Egypt being informed of these after they had been begun. The aim of reaching a final settlement with Egypt on the wider issue would remain the same whether or not the Tana concession was obtained in the near future. It was necessary to consider when and how this question should be opened with Egypt. After discussion, it was agreed:—

(i) That it was not essential to do so immediately since the more urgent question of the Tana concession was already in train.
(ii) That before going further, it was necessary that the forecast of the Sudan's final water needs should be considered by Council. To this end, the Sudan Irrigation Department would submit a comprehensive note setting out the forecast and its implications as regards development in the Sudan.
(iii) That following on (ii) Egypt should be informed of the Sudan's desire for a review of the water question on a suitable occasion. It might be found opportune to do this when Egypt was brought in over the Tana negotiations, or at the time of discussions with her on the Jonglei Project. Further, on Mr. Macgregor's suggestion it was agreed that since the Gezira Scheme had now been in operation

---

[1] Director of irrigation, Sudan, 1944–1945; irrigation consultant (Sudan Agency, London) from 1946.
[2] See 24.
[3] Not printed.

for 20 years, the time was ripe for a review of the results and statistics of irrigation in the Sudan. This would suitably include the forecast of the Sudan's future requirements of water, the publication of which would indicate the Sudan's objective, and in itself provide an occasion for raising the water question with Egypt with a view to a final settlement.

3. It was agreed that in view of the points set out in paragraph 3, it was not at present necessary to have further discussions with the Foreign Office, which might in any case be difficult to arrange. It was to be expected that when Council had considered the forecast of final requirements, the matter would be re-opened in a despatch.

40 FO 371/45986, no 3119 24 Sept 1945

[Anglo–Egyptian treaty]: draft statement to the Advisory Council for the Northern Sudan on consultation prior to any change in the Sudan's constitutional position, forwarded by W H Luce to P S Scrivener

[On 3 Sept 1945 five members of the Advisory Council, including Abdallah Khalil and Muhammad Ali Shawqi, submitted a question concerning self-determination to the secretary of the council, asking whether the opinions of members of council would be sought before any new constitutional arrangements for the Sudan were made (tel no 19 from acting governor-general to HMB ambassador Cairo, 5 Sept 1945, FO 371/45986, no 3119). The following statement was drafted by Huddleston in London and forwarded by W H Luce (his private secretary) to Scrivener (24 Sept 1945, FO 371/45986, no 3119). It was approved by the embassy in Cairo on 6 Oct 1945, and by the FO on 9 Oct 1945 (FO 371/45986, no 3119).]

"Should the question of the future status of the Sudan be raised by the condominium powers in any revision of the Anglo–Egyptian treaty, it would be the intention of the Sudan Government that the Advisory Council for the Northern Sudan should be consulted in order that its views should be at the disposal of the Sudan Government for transmission to the powers. It is the opinion of the Sudan Government that the views of the Sudanese people should be obtained through constitutional channels in a matter of such vital importance to their future well being."

41 FO 371/46024, no 4281 17 Nov 1945

[Nile Waters: Jonglei canal]: despatch no 129 from Sir H Huddleston to Lord Killearn[1]

[The construction of a regulator dam at Lake Albert in Uganda in conjunction with a sudd diversion canal in the Sudan was proposed as early as 1904,[2] and plans for both remained linked throughout the 1920s and 1930s. The resurrection of the Jonglei canal scheme (see 29) coincided with difficulties over negotiations with Ethiopia for a dam on Lake Tsana (see 24 and 27), and the Egyptian government put forward a proposal for a greatly expanded dam project at Lake Albert.]

---

[1] Forwarded by Killearn to Bevin on 10 Dec 1945.

[2] Sir W Garstin, "Report upon the basin of the Upper Nile", Egypt No 2 (1904), pp 147–148.

I have the honour to refer to Cairo despatch No. 352 dated 14th September, 1945, transmitting for my information a copy of Cairo despatch No. 1270 of the same date to the Foreign Office together with copy of a Note from the Royal Egyptian Ministry of Foreign Affairs regarding the construction of a barrage and a reservoir at Lake Albert.

2. It is observed that the Egyptian Government is desirous of having the views of the Government of Uganda upon this subject together with some indication of the conditions under which their agreement to it might be forthcoming. Presumably the views of the Government of the Belgian Congo are also being sought. But except for a reference which is assumed to be to the Nile Waters Agreement (Cmd. 3348) there is nothing in the Note itself to suggest appreciation of the close and vital interest of the Sudan in this matter.

3. The Memorandum attached to the Note referred to above gives some indication of the main lines and general effects of the project, but it provides no basis for technical or administrative opinions except that it appears to be acceptable in principle.

4. Your Excellency will be aware that proposals for the Jonglei Scheme in the Upper Nile Province have been passed by Egypt to the Sudan for study. The investigation of these by the Sudan Government has already been initiated. Now Lake Albert is included in the category of proposals whose execution can no longer be considered as a remote possibility.

5. It is necessary to bear in mind, that from an irrigation point of view, the Lake Albert and Jonglei Projects are inter-related if the full benefit is to be obtained from the works. On the one hand, to store water in Lake Albert and release it into the present channels would only result in increasing the losses in the Sudd swamps. On the other hand, the full benefit of the Jonglei Canal by itself could only be expected in good years; in low years when the water as most needed, the benefit would be seriously reduced.

6. The Sudan as an interested party in the use of Nile Waters, is closely concerned in all features of the combined project in as much as they affect the total supplies of water available for sharing between Egypt and the Sudan, and it recognises, with Egypt, that the final requirements of both countries can only be met if the fullest possible development of storage and conservation works is carried out in the most effective manner. Therefore, both countries are concerned to see that each work proposed is planned so as to fit into a co-ordinated scheme and thus contribute most effectively to the development of the Nile Basin as a whole.

7. I am advised that, so far as can be judged at the present stage, the Lake Albert and the Jonglei Schemes will affect local conditions on the Nile throughout its length in the Sudan. On the reaches from Malakal downstream as far as Halfa, conditions are likely to be improved on the whole, in that the levels during the low river season will be raised, thus facilitating both navigation and irrigation by pumps and sagias.[3] The levels at high flood will probably be little affected. From Nimule to Malakal the effects of the combined project will depend on the alignment and design finally settled upon for the Jonglei Canal, and also on the detailed provisions of the "Working Arrangements" for the operation of the Albert Reservoir. These "Working

[3] Water wheels used in river bank irrigation.

Arrangements" would determine just how and when the extra water would be passed down. The combined project will almost certainly have to be developed in stages; in any case the ultimate effects in the Sudan cannot be forecast in advance with any great degree of certainty. The Sudan should not be expected to agree beforehand to a final "Blueprint", without preserving the right to ask for modifications both of designs of works, and of the terms of the "Working Arrangements", at any stage of development, in the light of actual experience.

8. In the view of the Sudan Government, as a partner in Nile Waters, it is essential to consider the Lake Albert and Jonglei Projects as complementary schemes. As has been indicated in paragraph 4 of this despatch, the Sudan Government has begun to study the proposals of the Egyptian Government as regards the Jonglei Scheme. Similar definite proposals for the Lake Albert Project are necessary. The Jonglei investigations will occupy two to three working seasons, and the whole process is certain to be lengthy. It is therefore all the more necessary that the planning should start on the right lines and that the Sudan should be made aware as soon as possible of the intentions of the Egyptian Government as regards the Lake Albert Scheme in order that the technical authorities of both countries may consider the details and implications of the two Projects as a combined scheme.

9. I feel sure that Your Excellency will endorse these considerations and I should be glad if you would bring them to the notice of his Majesty's Government in order that they may be taken into account when instructions are given as to the reply to be returned to the Egyptian Note.

42 FO 371/45986, no 4163 26 Nov 1945

[Sudan Graduates' Congress elections]: letter from J C Penney to E C Haselden[1]

In response to your personal letter to Robertson dated November 16th I have today sent you as requested three further copies of the Congress letter (and enclosure) dated October 13th [sic: 15th], the receipt of which we have acknowledged, but to which we have not yet replied.[2]

2. The first step to be taken in dealing with these papers was to clear up one or two obscurities in the letter and enclosure themselves. Neither the Civil Secretary nor His Excellency could properly consider them until they were quite certain what they meant. In particular (apart from the comparatively minor question of what the signatories to the United Parties Committee's 'wathiqa' or charter meant when they demanded the removal of restrictions on 'public freedoms') it was not clear whether they had seen and approved the Congress President's covering letter before its despatch, and whether they accepted his definition of the expression 'union' to mean 'union under the Egyptian Crown' as correctly interpreting their own wishes. Enquiries into these points were postponed until after the Advisory Council Meeting, so as to defeat any possible suggestion that 'conversations with Congress' were proceeding behind the back of Councillors on matters on which they themselves had

---

[1] This letter was forwarded to the FO from the Sudan Agent, London, 5 Dec 1945.

[2] See 43, annex.

intimated a desire to be enlightened by the Sudan Government at the coming meeting. It was felt further that if we answered the letter before the holding of the Congress elections on November 16th, our reply, whatever its tenour [sic], might be made use of by the Ashiqqa as an electioneering instrument. If our reply were conciliatory it would be waved in the face of voters as indicating Government support or sympathy; if unfavourable it would help El Azhari to boost himself as a political martyr and to rally votes against an arbitrary alien government. There was the further point that it was conceivable, though unlikely, that as a result of the elections the control of Congress might pass from Ashiqqa to other hands and that it would be a tactical error to 'deal' with a party that might shortly be out of power.

3. With the Advisory Council out of the way (and a satisfactory reaction, at least from the Umma party and their associates to the Civil Secretary's reply to the question on consultation)[3] local interest was focussed on the Congress elections. Before 'zero' day there was a good deal of lobbying and jockeying behind the starting line. The Ashiqqa party had clearly the best chance of victory, because of the overall majority of Mirghanist adherents in the population of the Three Towns and the Rural Districts of Khartoum Province; of the superior organisation and unity of the party itself and the solid support of the younger graduates; and of the lateness and indecision of the Opposition in entering the lists. The Umma party (with their Qawmiyin and Ahrar supporters) fully aware of their handicaps, were first inclined to attempt to bargain in with their opponents for an agreed number of seats in the 1946 Congress Committees. Later, meeting with no success, and feeling that time was getting short and that they were daily losing ground (the Ashiqqa electioneering agents were conducting an intensive canvass with the all-out support, both in the Three Towns and in the provinces, of the Khatmia Khulafa)[4] they demanded as a condition of their entering the elections the setting up of a neutral Committee, composed of representatives of all parties, to see that they were regularly carried through. (They believed, rightly or wrongly, that the ballot boxes which were, of course, in Ashiqqa charge, were already filled, a week before election day, with Ashiqqa voting papers). Their demand, which they advertised in the Press, being refused, their H.Q. Committee decided to boycott the elections, and an announcement to that effect was duly published in the Umma newspaper. The announcement included a statement that the Umma, Qawmiyin, and Ahrar parties, though they still adhered to the terms of the United Parties Committee's charter, withdrew, in so far as the coming session of the Congress was concerned, the 'delegation' which they had therein given to the Committee of 1945. By taking the boycott line, the three parties, of which the Umma party was the moving spirit, hoped, apart from saving themselves from an inevitable defeat, to make it clear to the world that the Congress of 1946, whatever it might have been before, was a single party (Ashiqqa) organisation and that it could no longer rightfully call itself the Graduates [sic] Congress, when a large and influential body of graduates demonstrably stood outside it and dis-associated themselves, through their boycott gesture, from any of its future pronouncements. By the time the boycott was

[3] See 40.

[4] *Khulafa*, pl. of *khalifa*, successor or deputy; here used as a term of office in the hierarchy of the Khatmiya order.

declared El Azhari had no doubts about his party's coming success (he went so far as to telegraph to some of his provincial recruiting agencies, instructing them to suspend their activities, as he had already enough voters assembled in and around Omdurman to ensure his victory) but at the same time he made several attempts to counter the Umma's plan to secure the isolation of himself and his supporters in an All Ashiqqa 1946 Committee by offering Committee seats to some of the younger Umma members. One or two of these seemed at first inclined to disregard the boycott instructions of their H.Q. Committee, but in the event the Umma party stood firm and his efforts failed.

4. On November 16th accordingly the Ashiqqa party went solidly to the Graduates Club to vote. They appeared this year to be very highly organised. A series of printed lists, each containing fifteen names was distributed to the paraded voters. All they had to do was to put them into the ballot boxes. The majority of the lists were printed on white paper and contained only selected Ashiqqa names, El Azhari's name figuring on every list, the other names being varied to give an appearance of choice to the voters. To create further an illusion of competition the white Ashiqqa lists were interspersed with a few lists of 'independent' candidates—Ashiqqa partisans so camouflaged for the occasion—these lists being printed on blue paper, so as to be readily distinguishable. The elections were perfectly orderly and there were no incidents. According to police reports the majority of the voters were small merchants and artisans.

5. Of some 10,000 Congress members, about 5470 paid their subscriptions for 1945. Of these 3524 attended the elections and 3512 actually voted. Before the voting commenced El Azhari delivered his presidential address, in which he stressed that the aim of the Congress was 'a democratic Sudanese government in union with Egypt and under the Egyptian Crown'. Apart from this reference, the speech, which was a good deal shorter than usual, reviewed the activities of the Congress during the past year and was of little consequence. Many telegrams were read out from well-wishers in the Sudan. There was a telegram also from Ali Maher Pasha; and a telephone message from Ali Bereir.[5] The reference to the Egyptian Crown was warmly applauded.

The counting of the votes resulted in the election of a Committee of LX containing 43 Ashiqqa and 17 'Independents'. El Azhari topped the poll with over 3000 votes. His Ashiqqa companions' scores ranged from 1200 to 900, and the 60th member—an Independent—scored 50. The all-Ashiqqa LX then proceeded to elect an all-Ashiqqa XV, with El Azhari as President and Mahmud el Fudali[6] as Secretary.

Two facts stood out clearly from last year's Congress elections. This year, further illustrated by the Umma boycott, they stand out more clearly than ever—that the Congress has ceased to represent the educated classes, and that our political rivalries have resolved themselves into the old sectarian strife between Mahdists and Mirghanists. Congress has now become a movement representing the Ashiqqa/Mirghanist interest only—a movement with which a large number of the more able and more level headed of the educated Sudanese refuse to be associated.

6. Shortly before the elections there was some talk of a split in the Khatmia

---

[5] See 15, note 2.

[6] Mahmud al-Fadli, a teacher at the Ahlia School, member of the Ashiqqa, and assistant secretary of the Graduates' General Congress.

ranks. Yehia el Fudali, Sheikh Omar Ishaq and Sheikh Ahmed el Sid el Fil (the latter backed by Dardiri Mohamed Othman) were reported to be in disagreement over the terms of the Ashiqqa connection. In fact the Khatmia seems today to be as solid as ever but there is no doubt that El Azhari for a time was a bit worried over the possibility of losing some of his Mirghanist backers. Whatever we think of the political sincerity of the two Holy Men, the Umma party has at least got a political programme to which the majority of its thinking members can subscribe on political grounds. The Mirghanist support of the Egyptian Crown formula of the Ashiqqa, on the other hand, is to a far greater extent dictated by sectarian feeling and by the opportunity presented by the current situation of exploiting the Mahdist bogey. El Azhari himself realises the comparative weakness of his 'political' position. The Congress/Ashiqqa combine is founded on what appears to be a common formula, demanding 'union under the Egyptian Crown', but whereas El Azhari seems to be playing with the idea of absorption into the Egyptian Kingdom, Yehia el Fudali—the Ashiqqa No. 2—assures me that his party regards 'absorption' as impracticable and 'utterly undesirable'. El Azhari has therefore somehow to reconcile his commitments as President of Congress with his commitments as Leader of the Ashiqqa, and however competent he may be as a double-dealer, he may be finding it difficult to do so. In any case his political backing has not the comparative solidity which unites the educated elements in the Umma party and its associates. It is for this reason that the support of the Khatmia 'other ranks' is of such importance to him. It is mainly the sectarian cement which holds his racket together.

7. Another feature of the elections may be of interest. All the opponents of the Ashiqqa were not Ansar. Some of the Ittihadiyin and of the Qawmiyin are reported from Omdurman to be neither Mahdist nor Mirghanist. Some of our best intelligentsia are non-sectarian. They are not afraid of the Mahdist wolf; at the same time they object to the corrupt practices of the Ashiqqa; to their reference to the Egyptian Crown; and to their premature dabbling in external politics. It is possible (though I think unlikely) that these folk, if sympathetically handled, might emerge as the nucleus of a middle party with a true non-sectarian constructive policy, with aims approximating to those of the Umma party programme.

8. The situation is still pretty confused. A few days ago I initiated on C.S's instructions the enquiries (vide para. 1) designed to clear up the apparent contradiction between the Congress letter and its enclosure on the 'union' issue. The signatories to the charter (or pact)—of whom I saw one representing each party—explained to me in the course of a general conversation that the six parties, considering that the interests of the country could best be served by some sort of coalition front, had after lengthy discussion, arrived through their representatives at a joint statement (the pact in question) which represented the furthest they were prepared to go together. As signatories to the pact they bound themselves so far but no further. They were all agreed that some form of union or association with Egypt (the expression 'ittihad' as they used it in the pact was left deliberately undefined; it did not mean 'absorption' nor did it necessarily mean a political union as opposed to a cultural or economic union), and some form of relationship with Great Britain would at some date (and here again they deliberately refrained from being specific) be both natural and desirable. Whatever interpretations the several parties to which they belonged might subsequently put, or might already have put, upon the word 'union', they were agreed *as* signatories, to leave those interpretations unstated, in

order to be able to present a common front on the general question. The pact meant what it said and no more. The Umma representative intervened to say that he wanted it to be clearly understood that it was the intention of his party to postpone *all* consideration of the union question until the appropriate time, which was not now. The Ittihadi member on the other hand said that his party had already decided on the form of union, which as a party, it intended to advocate. In short the various representatives reserved to themselves, as party members, the right to endorse their several party programmes.

They had all agreed to forward their pact via the Congress Committee of 1945. They had not seen the covering letter until it was published in the Press. As signatories of the pact, they did not accept, and were in no way bound by, the Congress President's interpretation of the word 'union'. Nor as signatories did they endorse Congress' claim to represent the people of the Sudan. Congress was a party—a distinct party—like any other party and its interpretations were only binding on itself. Other parties might subsequently agree or disagree with those interpretations; as signatories of the pact they had in no way committed themselves to more than the bare statement which the pact embodied.

9. Whether this distinction between 'signatory' and 'party member' can have any practical meaning I don't yet know. The United Parties Committee (which is now tending to call itself the 'United Front') may have a future, or it may be squeezed by circumstances out of existence. In the meantime the Ittihadiyin who boycotted the elections because 'they thought that a coalition front could best serve the country's interests', have announced in the Press that, now that the elections are over, and while still adhering to the United Parties pact, they will continue to support the Congress—the pact and the Congress' recent resolution, i.e. El Azhari's speech about union under the Egyptian Crown, being in their opinion not inconsistent with each other. Perhaps, at your distance, all this is clearer to you than it is to me.

10. The important thing now is the action contemplated by the Umma and Ashiqqa parties arising out of the result of the elections. (The reply to the Congress' October letter is now under consideration; it can hardly fail to take notice of recent developments). The Umma party will almost certainly (if they have any tactical sense) hammer away in their papers and elsewhere on the 'isolation' theme. They have in fact already begun. There are no indications as yet of any move on the part of individual Umma adherents to resign their Congress membership, but there *is* talk of breaking away and founding a new Graduates' association. 'We do not mean', says the Umma newspaper, 'that the Congress should be closed down; but that a body truly representative of the Graduates should be formed as a substitute—a body which might find its nucleus in the present United Front Committee'. The intention is that membership of the new association shall be strictly limited to those to whom the label 'graduate' can fairly be applied and that the association itself should exist quite independently of the Umma party (which aims at a membership of all classes). It would attempt to earn recognition as a body free from sectarian influence or partisanship. The Umma party has also already published a protest against the further handling by the 'unrepresentative' 1946 Congress Committee of the Congress Education Fund.

11. It seems likely therefore that the Ashiqqa/Mirghanist combination will be up against considerable opposition, and their counter efforts (as I have already suggested) may take an Islamic as well as a purely political line.

El Azhari is already in touch with the Ikhwan el Muslimin, agents of which are now in the Sudan paving the way for the opening of a Sudan Branch. With an Ikhwan stimulus and a Mirghanist organisation to propagate the Society's doctrines, we should be confronted (whoever our supporters might be—and the Ikhwan Society has already come in for unfavourable criticism in the non-Mirghanist papers) with an awkward and potentially dangerous situation. The extent of the 'danger' would be largely determined by the amount of energy Egyptian politicians were prepared to devote to the Wadi el Nil independence game. If they really meant to create trouble, they would have, in the politico-religious organisation of the Ashiqqa/Mirghanist group, what is potentially a very effective instrument.

43 FO 141/1013, no 134 8 Dec 1945

[Sudan Graduates' General Congress]: despatch no 134 from Sir H Huddleston to Lord Killearn. *Annex:* translation of an Arabic letter letter from Ismail al-Azhari to Huddleston (15 Oct 1945)

I have the honour to submit to Your Excellency the following report on recent developments regarding the Graduates' General Congress.

2. On October 15th I received a letter signed by Ismail Eff. el Azhari, President of the Sudan Graduates' General Congress, transmitting to me a three-point Agreement signed by representatives of the political parties in Omdurman. I attach a copy of this letter and of the Agreement to this despatch.

In view of the impending session of the Advisory Council for the Northern Sudan on November 3rd, and of the holding of the elections to the 1946 Committees of the Graduates' General Congress on November 16th, it was considered tactically inadvisable to reply to this letter until these events had passed. Its receipt in the meantime was formally and non-committally acknowledged.

3. When the Advisory Council session was over and the elections had been held, a member of my Civil Secretariat got in touch with the signatories to the Agreement, with a view to elucidating the meaning of certain phrases used therein, and in particular of the expression 'union' which appeared in the first of the three heads of the Agreement.[1] At the meeting which ensued (on November 19th) it was clearly established, in the course of a general discussion, that the various party signatories did not all subscribe to the interpretation placed on the word 'union' by the writer of the covering letter, which, they said, they had not approved, and had not even seen until its subsequent publication in the local vernacular Press. Their own interpretations (which they had deliberately left unstated in order to achieve some semblance of a common front) varied from complete amalgamation with Egypt in the case of the Ashiqqa party to a shadowy cultural, economic, and linguistic association in the case of the Umma. The Umma party representative was particularly insistent that the eventual form a union with Egypt might take could not be determined until the Sudanese people had achieved, through the progressive practice of responsible self government, the maturity and experience which would

---

[1] See 42.

entitle them to decide for themselves what their political future should be, and until, having attained an independent status, they could negotiate with Egypt on equal terms.

4. The Graduates' Congress elections duly took place on November 16th. Held, as they were to be, under the auspices of the Ashiqqa-controlled 1945 Committee, which had already on a previous occasion given proof of its skill in the manipulation of votes, the Umma party and its associates were convinced that they had little hope of success, and a request for the appointment of a neutral committee to manage the elections being rejected, they decided not to enter the lists.

Their boycott was designed in the first place to save themselves from an inevitable defeat, and in the second to establish finally and decisively the falsity of the Congress' claim in its present form and under its present direction, to be a representative Graduate body. In the event only members of the Ashiqqa party recorded their votes. About 3500 of them went to the poll, which resulted in the election of an all-Ashiqqa Committee of LX, and in due course of an all-Ashiqqa Executive Committee of XV, with Ismail el Azhari as the 1946 President.

5. The reaction of the opposition parties to the election results has not yet clearly declared itself. Individual members have as yet shown no signs of resigning their Congress membership, and so far the Umma party has confined itself to an announcement in the local Press disassociating itself from the joint party Agreement (referred to above), in so far as its preamble delegated to Congress the authority to present to the Sudan Government on its behalf the views which it embodied. They are, however, considering further steps. They have in mind, in the first place, to challenge the right of the Congress, as at present constituted, to administer the Education Day Fund—a fund inaugurated by the Congress in its early days when it could claim to be truly representative of the graduate class and they have already made unofficial enquiries as to the legal position. Whether a formal application for an injunction to restrain the 1946 Congress Committee from continuing to act as trustees of the Fund will be made or not is still uncertain. They design, in the second place, to attempt to build up a new and independent Graduates association. These projects are still in the discussion stage. Their promoters are, characteristically, awaiting some indication of the Government's attitude to the post-election political situation, before taking any definite action.

The Ashiqqa party for the time being appears to be resting on its laurels. There are, certain signs of dissension within the party over the form of its political programme, but, to whatever internal regroupings this may lead, the party will, outwardly at least, remain solidly opposed to the Umma and its associates on the Mirghanist-Mahdist issue.

6. The Ashiqqa and Umma parties, although they may number by the thousand their registered adherents, do not occupy the whole of the field. There is a strong educated (but hitherto unvocal) element which welcomed with enthusiasm the appearance of the Graduates' General Congress in 1938, as the first native inspired representative institution, and which is now disappointed and distressed that a body, in which their hopes and aspirations were so confidently centred, should have become merely the playground of sectarian partisans. They feel that the Mirghanist-Mahdist rivalry, in splitting the Congress in two, has done an ill-service to the educated classes and to the Sudan itself. Whether the holders of this view will ever feel strong enough to denounce publicly the sectarian strangle-hold remains to be

seen. It is unlikely, but the possibility exists. The Congress as a non-political body had considerable usefulness in voicing the opinions and hopes of the graduate class. It provided a vehicle for the expression of their unformulated desire to assist in their country's development, and its present collapse as a representative body may leave, therefore a gap to be filled. The possibilities of such a situation are receiving attention.

7. Too much significance should not be attached to the recent Ashiqqa success in the Congress elections. It should not, in other words, be interpreted as an all out victory for a party with a pro-Egyptian political programme. There are strong opposition forces. The Ashiqqa party itself is composed very largely of followers of El Sayed Sir Ali el Mirghani Pasha, whose adherence is secured by considerations which are primarily sectarian. They support the Ashiqqa because it is in opposition to the Umma party, the majority of whose members are followers of El Sayed Sir Abdel Rahman el Mahdi Pasha, the party's patron. Both parties have enlisted thousands of members throughout the country on the sectarian ticket alone, but the Congress elections being held in Omdurman, which is predominantly Mirghanist, the Ashiqqa were able to bring to the poll a number of supporters out of all proportion to their total strength throughout the country. The Umma party is credibly reported to have some 100,000 registered members, but the majority of these are resident in the Gezira, the White Nile, and Kordofan and cannot therefore be readily made available to vote.

Future moves of the two main opposition groups are difficult to foresee, and there is likely to be a good deal of uncertainty; of reorientation of parties and individuals; and even of recasting political programmes before the position clarifies.

8. Only a formal acknowledgment of receipt has been sent to the President of the Congress of his letter of October 15th, and next steps are under consideration.

I have not formally reported these developments to Your Excellency before now as the situation has been confused, but the Civil Secretary has kept the Sudan Agent informed from time to time so that Your Excellency's Chancery should not be unsighted.

A copy of my reply to the letter from the President will be sent for Your Excellency's information in due course.

Annex to 43

I have received your letter of the 1st September 1945,[2] in which you say that you do not intend to transmit the Congress Memorandum to the Authorities concerned, and in which you state the reasons which in your opinion justify this procedure. In holding this view you are denying the free expression of their aspirations to a nation whose great sacrifices and fortitude during the darkest hours of the war entitle it to be listened to by those to whose hands it has entrusted its hopes and future destiny,—a nation which fully expects that its aspirations will receive the sympathy of those who have borne the honour of its trusteeship. We cannot understand the reasons which prevented the transmission of this Memorandum, knowing that in

[2] See 35, note.

sending it to the Authorities concerned the Sudan Government would incur no liability nor infringe its responsibility and terms of office. On the contrary we believe that the Government's duty towards the country not only requires it to pass on what is submitted to it, but imposes on it an obligation to take the initiative, formulating the country's demands and sending them on even without being asked to do so.

The Government is no doubt aware of the opinions in the minds of the Sudanese, especially at such a critical moment, and in the face of the general anxiety which exists about the future of this country. The Government is fully acquainted with the opinion which the Sudanese have formed in respect of the future status of the Sudan, namely "the formation of a Sudanese Democratic Government united with Egypt under the Egyptian Crown". It is surprising to find the Sudan Government announcing that it does not intend to put forward the Congress Memorandum because it does not consider that the Congress is competent to represent Sudanese public opinion. What institution other than the Congress should enjoy this right? Moreover the Sudan Government draws our attention to Governor Khartoum's letter of 16th May, 1945, in which he had to rely for the material for his answer on rumours spread about the last elections, and to declare that the Congress Committee and the Council of Sixty could not represent the Graduates, thus ignoring the arguments conveyed to him in our previous memorandum dated April 3rd 1945. By taking up this attitude the Sudan Government ignores the most elementary principles of democratic and parliamentary procedure, known and observed throughout the whole world. A party which emerges as the outcome of elections held in accordance with these principles has always been recognised as a duly elected responsible majority. The Sudan Government ignores all this, and goes on to describe the resolution passed by the Congress Council of Sixty—a Council freely elected in a General Assembly composed of all parties—as being merely the opinion of one section of the Congress despite the fact that the Government is fully aware that the resolution represents the considered opinion of the Graduates' General Congress.

The allegation that the Congress is not entitled to speak on behalf of the Sudan is very strange. If it means anything it proves that the Sudan Government is determined that no opinion from the Sudan is to be heard. Otherwise what is the institution, if any, which the Sudan Government considers as the one entitled to this right? Surely the Congress constitutes the only popular national body in the country and its membership includes the pick of the cultured and thinking classes scattered throughout the whole country, and above all it conducts its activities in accordance with true democratic principles. It is the Congress which has won the hearts of the Sudanese. Even those to whom it cannot extend its membership look to it with satisfaction and confidence.

Your Excellency, in view of the above the Congress indubitably speaks in the name of the Sudan and demands the realisation of its legitimate rights to self-determination. The Congress is thus entitled to submit the demands of the Sudan because it knows better than anyone else what will bring well-being to its inhabitants. In as much as the Congress enjoys the confidence and the sympathy of all classes and as it is looked upon with reverence and respect by the whole Sudanese nation, it has the first right to formulate and put forward the national demands. It is unnatural on the other hand to entrust the responsibility of expressing the views of a people to individuals or groups which have been appointed by Government. Such individuals or groups can never be capable of the expression of unbiased opinion or of voicing exactly the national aspirations and demands which are folded in the hearts and mixed with the blood of a country's sons. These nominated individuals are naturally and largely influenced by considerations of their official position, and it will be clear to Your Excellency also that the Sudan Government itself is neither entitled nor empowered to determine national aspirations because it also is created by appointment. The Congress, Your Excellency, is the only national institution which, in speaking for the people of the Sudan, does not derive its entitlement from the Sudan Government. It derives it on the contrary from the true national consciousness and from the support of the whole Sudanese people. This is the natural and true entitlement borne out by the acceptance by the Sudanese of Congress' activities, an acceptance which is accorded freely and without compulsion and is the outcome of the feelings of true love and trust which the Congress inspires. The Sudanese nation regards Congress as a sacred institution to which it goes on pilgrimage every year. Every year the Congress members who have the necessary qualifications elect a Council of Sixty and an Executive Committee to conduct the business of Congress and to speak in its name. The Sudanese nation has not stopped here but has organised in all towns and in all the larger villages sub committees to act as its eyes and hands and to advise it on all major issues—to spot the disease and prescribe the remedy.

The Graduates' General Congress has said the Sudan word and there is nothing more to say—a word which is supported by the provincial sub-committees and was formed in the best way to secure the happiness and tranquility of the country. The Sudan word is this:—

> "the formation of a Sudanese democratic Government in a union with Egypt, under the Egyptian crown".

Since 1942 when the Graduates' Congress set itself up as the exponent of the country's political rights, in view of the magnificent part played by the Sudanese in the cause of the Democracies, it was the only institution in the country which continued to study the question of the political status of the Sudan, and no other body or bodies claiming to speak on behalf of the Sudan had begun to act independently. All parties moreover which exist today are working within the framework of the Congress and consider themselves to be parts of an inseparable whole.

In submitting its memorandum in the name of the Sudan the Congress meant to convey the aspirations of the Sudanese nation and to exercise a national right to express the Sudanese claim to self-determination. This step was amplified by the support of all the Sudanese so that the demands put forward became in fact the final word of the whole nation. There is therefore no reason to suppose, Your Excellency, that in speaking in the name of the Sudanese for the realisation of the country's legitimate aspirations the Congress has not the right to represent the Sudan.

Your Excellency refers to the Governor, Khartoum's letter in which he denies the eligibility of both the Congress Council of Sixty and its executive committee. This denial has been received with astonishment. Surely the Governor not being himself a member of congress is not competent to utter such a denunciation. The constitution and bye-laws give this right to the members only. We therefore seize this opportunity of expressing our condemnation of the procedure adopted by Governor Khartoum, and of his action in putting an end to the correspondence between us without producing any proof that we were in the wrong. Procedure of this kind, Your Excellency will agree, is contrary to the most elementary principles of true democracy. We still maintain our original assertion that as no member of congress submitted a protest in the proper manner against the last elections we were and are entitled to consider that the results of these elections were legitimate. We enclose herewith a copy of the correspondence exchanged between the Congress and Governor Khartoum[3]—a correspondence which reveals that the spirit in which it was conducted was contrary to democratic principles. Such was the policy which, we had hoped, would never have animated the procedure of the Sudan Government and especially in the capital city.

Your Excellency's statement that the Congress resolution merely represents the opinion of one party in the congress is also strange, especially as it emanates from a Government which draws its inspiration from the oldest democracy in the world. Such a statement is not at all in conformity with the principles followed and respected by the democratic nations at the head of which Great Britain stands. The resolution surely is not that of one party only; it is the decision of the Council of Sixty and therefore it constitutes a decision of congress itself.

The Congress is the legitimate channel for expressing the opinions of the country, and though it adopts the views of the party which holds the majority of seats, as happens also in the case of British Parliamentary institutions, the decisions of the Executive Committee are not to be considered as those of one party only because it has had to study the opinions of all sections of the community before formulating and forwarding those decisions for approval by the Council of Sixty. If they are passed by the latter body they then become the decisions of congress itself. If this course were not followed the whole structure would lose its democratic character and fall to the ground.

This Your Excellency is what has been done by the Congress committee in all loyalty and straight-forwardness to arrive at an opinion as regards the future status of the Sudan. The committee has reviewed the opinions held by all parties represented in Congress and after full consideration and discussion the Executive has found that the following formula satisfies the principles of all parties:—

> "the formation of a democratic Sudanese Government in union with Egypt under the Egyptian crown".

This formula was presented to the Council of Sixty which confirmed and approved it. Thus it became the resolution of Congress as regards the future status of the Sudan.

This proves that this resolution does not represent the viewpoint of one party only, but it is a resolution taken by Congress which includes all parties and which represents their different views. In addition, all parties in the Sudan—Ashigga, Ittihadiyin, Umma, Ahrar Ittihadiyin, Qawmiyin and Ahrar have come to an agreement and submitted on 3.10.45 a note to Congress consisting of the following points:—

1. The establishment of a free, democratic Sudanese Government in union with Egypt and alliance with Great Britain.
2. A request that the Government should approve the establishment of a committee equally composed of representatives of the Condominium governments and rep-

---

[3] Not printed.

resentatives of the enlightened Sudanese, the latter to be appointed by Congress, to draw up a scheme whereby the Sudanese will take over the administration of their country in the shortest possible time; and that the Government should offer all facilities to the Committee and undertake to enforce its recommendations.

3. A request that restrictions on the freedom of the Press, movement, public meetings and trade should be revised within the limits of the law and in accordance with democratic principles. All special legislation at present in force which restricts these freedoms should be amended.

Attached is a copy of the note submitted to Congress signed by representatives of all parties.[4]

This shows Your Excellency that the decision arrived at by all parties agrees in principle with the resolution of Congress submitted in its note to the Condominium Governments.

Thus all sections unanimously request "the establishment of a free democratic Sudanese Government in union with Egypt and alliance with Great Britain". The parties omitted to define the word "union", but congress after considering all aspects of the matter decided that it should be a union with Egypt under the Egyptian crown.

Your Excellency, when congress addressed its note to the Prime Ministers of Great Britain and Egypt it did not expect the Sudan Government to express its views on the advisability of transmitting it or otherwise. Its obvious duty was to forward the note to the Condominium Powers on whose behalf it administers the country, with such comments as it might think it necessary to make. We never realised that the trusteeship exercised by the Sudan Government could empower it to extinguish the natural right of the individual in the Twentieth Century to express his opinions to whomsoever he likes.

The Congress, Your Excellency, has expressed the real view of the Sudanese—a view unprejudiced by any influence, appointment, or authority—the product of natural feeling and true realisation of the people's aspirations. The Sudan Government should not therefore allow the present opportunity to pass when the future status of all nations is being debated in the conferences now working for an everlasting peace and in an atmosphere of equality, justice and brotherhood.

The Congress while realising that it could have submitted its note direct to the Condominium government has preferred to follow the proper procedure by sending it through the Sudan Government as an intermediary. It sincerely hopes that the Sudan Government will reconsider its attitude towards the note and submit it to the authorities concerned.

---

[4] See 36, enclosure.

44 FO 371/53249, no 336 23 Dec 1945

[Sudan Graduates' Congress]: letter (reply) from J W Robertson to Ismail al-Azhari

I regret that owing to pressure of work it has been impossible before now to reply to your letter of October 15th. 1945 addressed to His Excellency the Governor-General, except by my former formal acknowledgment of October 18th.

I have been instructed to say that consideration has now been given to your letter and its enclosure—the All Party Declaration—; and first of all I am directed to remind you of the attitude of the Sudan Government towards the claim of the Graduates' General Congress to be the sole and authoritative mouthpiece of the people of the Sudan. It has already been fully and clearly stated on several occasions in correspondence between us, that the Government does not recognise the Congress as entitled to speak for the people of the Sudan as a whole, and I must also point out that the claim of your committee to represent the educated classes, and in particular to interpret the All Party Declaration enclosed with your letter under reply, has according to my information been challenged recently by elements of the educated classes themselves.

At the same time, however, I would draw your attention to the answer which in my capacity as Chairman of the Advisory Council for the Northern Sudan I gave to a question asked by five members of that Council at the last session of the Council in November.[1] After formally declaring the intention of the Sudan Government to consult the Council, should the future of the Sudan be under discussion at any revision of the Anglo–Egyptian Treaty, I went on to say that the Government would also give such weight as they deserved to the opinions of other representative bodies.

I can assure you, therefore, that it is the intention of the Government when the time comes to ascertain as far as possible the sentiments of all sections of the community, including those of the Graduates' General Congress, and of other representative bodies. Provided such opinions are legitimately presented and are not vitiated by unjustifiable claims as to the extent of their representation, they will be given due weight at the appropriate time.

Meanwhile I beg to inform you that your letter, and the specific recommendations of the United Parties as presented in the Joint Declaration enclosed with your letter, have been filed for future reference.

---

[1] See 40 and 42.

45 FO 371/53371, no 630 — 3 Jan 1946

[Sudan's Nile waters needs]: despatch no 2 from Sir H Huddleston to Lord Killearn

I have the honour to refer to my despatch No. 132 of the 24th December, 1944,[1] in which I addressed your Excellency on the need of the Sudan to secure, with the agreement of Egypt, additional supplies of water from the Nile for the extension of her irrigation. In that despatch I requested that the Egyptian Government should be reminded of the claim made by the Sudan Government in 1939, and should be asked to consent to an early examination of the present water storage position in detail, by technical experts authorised by each Government for the purpose. If this consent were secured, it was proposed to seek the services of Mr. R. M. MacGregor to negotiate on behalf of the Sudan Government.

2. Mr. MacGregor was asked by the Secretary of State to give his views on my

---

[1] See 24.

despatch and on the whole question of the Nile Waters. Following on consideration of the memoranda which he prepared, the matter was discussed with him and with representatives of His Majesty's Government, while I was in London during the summer of 1945.

3. The Lake Tsana project, with regard to which an agreement already exists between Egypt and the Sudan, was considered at a meeting held on the 31st July, 1945, those present being myself, Mr. MacGregor, Mr. Howe, British Minister at Addis Ababa, and Mr. Scrivener of the Foreign Office, with Mr. Mayall of the Sudan Government London Office. The conclusion then reached was that action should be taken, as soon as circumstances permitted, to re-open with the Government of Ethiopia the question of obtaining a concession for the construction and operation of storage works on the lake.

4. Subsequently, on the 18th September, 1945, I and my advisers discussed with Mr. MacGregor the wider problem of the whole future development of irrigation in the Sudan, in relation to the needs of Egypt as at present known, and to the remaining balance of unused water in the river, both that now available and that which might be provided by future projects.[2] We had before us a preliminary forecast of the ultimate needs of the Sudan in Nile Waters, which had been prepared jointly by Mr. MacGregor and my Director of Irrigation. The interim conclusions reached on this occasion have since been fully studied by my advisers in Khartum, in all their aspects and implications.

5. I am now able to state my considered opinions on this wider question, as follows:—

(i) The present surplus of water in the Nile as a whole, and the possibilities of future development of storage and conservation works, are definitely limited. The surplus will diminish year by year as irrigation is extended in both countries.

(ii) Additional supplies of water for the extension of irrigation in the Sudan can only be obtained as the result of a review of the present position in the light of the Nile Waters Agreement, and a settlement leading to the allocation of further volumes to the Sudan. If and when this is initiated the aim should be if possible to reach a settlement which, so far as the Sudan is concerned, would be final, and not just a further instalment.

Reasons for this are:—

(a) Egypt has already formulated and published fairly definite forecasts of her final requirements, and it is right and proper that the Sudan should do the same.

(b) The occurrence of a very low year would quicken Egypt's anxieties about water, and intensify the difficulties of a settlement.

(c) On broad grounds of policy, such a question should not remain unsettled any longer than is necessary.

(iii) In the light of the above considerations, of the terms and spirit of the Nile Waters Agreement, of the fact that the Sudan, unlike Egypt, is not wholly dependent upon irrigation, and of the areas which may be deemed reasonably suitable for irrigation, the Sudan's requirements for full development of irrigation

---

[2] See 39.

on sound and economical lines would be met by a total annual provision of water some 70 per cent. greater than that to which she is now entitled. This would be supplied partly from the natural discharges of the river during the season of surplus, and partly from storage and conservation works, including Lake Tsana, for use in the period of shortage.

(iv) In relation to the forecasts already published by Egypt of the quantities of water required for her full and final development, this provision for the Sudan seems to be a fair and equitable objective, at which the Sudan might aim.

6. The Nile Commission of 1925 foresaw (report, paragraph 89) that the position would have to be reviewed at some future date, and the passage of twenty years seems to provide reasonable grounds for undertaking such a review. It is important that this should be regarded and referred to as a review of the water position in the light of the Nile Waters Agreement, rather than as a review of the agreement itself. The latter might be held to connote a reopening of the whole question, including the present entitlements of the Sudan and the safeguards of Egypt, and this is not desirable from either party's point of view. What is to be visualised is an additional set of entitlements with corresponding safeguards, rather than modifications of those now in force. In view of possible discussions with Egypt, I think it well to lay some stress on this point.

7. Closely bound up with the whole question of Nile Waters are the projects for the Jonglei Canal, through the Sudd area, and for the Lake Albert Dam and Reservoir. Some general views on these have been given in my despatch No. 129 of the 17th November, 1945,[3] showing how closely the Sudan is concerned in these inter-related schemes, both as a partner in the water resources of the Nile Basin and as regards the conditions which will result throughout the length of the river from Nimule to Wadi Halfa. Cultivation on the river-side slopes, irrigation by pumps and sagias, so important in the Northern Sudan, and also navigation, will all be affected. Full account must be taken of these schemes, in all their aspects and implications, in any examination of the Nile Waters position in the light of the Nile Waters Agreement.

8. The Egyptian Irrigation Service in the Sudan is making preliminary surveys and investigations on the Main Nile between Abu Hamed and Halfa in the northern province. It is understood that their objective is to find a suitable site for a dam and reservoir of large size, as a further development of the utilisation of the Nile waters for Egypt's own benefit. Such a project would concern the Sudan not only in its local effects, but also generally as a partner in Nile Waters. From the Sudan's point of view this project would possess, and probably in still greater measure, the disadvantages that attached to the second raising of Aswan from the point of view of the Lake Tsana project, which were dealt with in correspondence leading up to Lord Lloyd's note to Mohamed Mahmud Pasha dated the 26th July, 1928. There is, however, no need to go into this point unless and until some definite proposals emerge from the present studies.

9. The urgency of the Sudan's need for more water was stressed in my despatch No. 132. A definite programme of irrigation development over the next five years has now been prepared, and it is clear that the Sudan's present resources are likely to be

[3] See 41.

used up completely by 1951. As regards Egypt, it is known that in 1943 and 1944 her increased production of crops involved the use of the whole of her present resources of stored water in Aswan and Jebel Aulia Reservoirs. It can only be assumed that the urgency of her present need for more water is comparable with that of the Sudan.

The logical conclusion appears to be that a review of the position under the Nile Waters Agreement at an early date is equally desirable in the interests of both countries, if their immediate needs are to be met without undue delay, and if the future development of the remaining water resources of the Nile Basin is to be planned on the most effective lines.

10. In present circumstances the form and occasion of an approach to Egypt on this subject will clearly need to be considered very carefully. As foreshadowed in my former despatch, I have engaged Mr. MacGregor as expert consultant, with a view to his acting as technical representative of the Sudan in any discussions and negotiations which may be arranged. Subject to your Excellency's views, I would propose that Mr. MacGregor should visit the Sudan in the course of the next few months, and after refreshing on the spot his already intimate knowledge of the whole question, should be authorised to renew his former official contacts with the technical experts of the Ministry of Public Works. These talks could appropriately be concerned in the first place with the specific problems of the Jonglei and Lake Albert schemes. If negotiations for the Lake Tsana concession should have been opened with the Government of Ethiopia, this question might also be discussed. In the light of the results of these preliminary talks, I suggest it may be possible to decide on the best line of approach to the wider question of an examination of the water position.

11. The objectives set out in paragraph 12 of my despatch No. 132 were on the limited scale necessary to meet the more immediate needs of the Sudan, pending the completion of the Lake Tsana scheme. They may be now replaced by, and are embraced in, the following more comprehensive statement of her aims:—

(i) To bring the Lake Tsana scheme to fruition at the earliest possible date, and to secure the share in the water provided thereby which was allotted to the Sudan under the agreement of 1935.

(ii) To reach a clear understanding with Egypt as to the lines on which the Lake Albert and Jonglei schemes are to be developed, and as to the Sudan's interests in them.

(iii) Following on a general technical review of the Nile Water position, to reach a further settlement with Egypt which would provide for the systematic development of the remaining resources of the Nile Basin in such a way as to meet the full needs of both countries.

(iv) Failing such a general settlement, as is indicated in (iii) above, to obtain Egypt's agreement to additional supplies of water for the Sudan, both from the river in the period of surplus, and from conservation works for use in the period of shortage, sufficient to meet her needs when her existing resources have been fully utilised. This I have already predicted in paragraph 8 above as likely to occur by 1951.

12. To sum up, I would propose, subject to your Excellency's views, that Mr. MacGregor, after visiting the Sudan, should renew his official contacts with the technical experts of the Ministry of Public Works and that there should follow a formal request for the consent of the Egyptian Government to a review of the water

position in the light of the Nile Waters Agreement, on the first occasion considered suitable. If negotiations for the Lake Tsana Concession should be opened with the Government of Ethiopia in the near future, the notification of these to the Egyptian Government should provide a suitable opportunity. But whatever the position as regards Lake Tsana, I consider that the request for a review of the water position in the light of the Nile Waters Agreement should be made as soon as possible.

46 FO 371/53328, no 527 17 Jan 1946
[SAM and SAR]: report from SPIS no 55 for December 1945 [Extract]

The holy men

440. Sayed Ali el Mirghani still maintains in local politics the position he took up some time ago. When pressed to explain the Khatmia support of the pro-Egyptian party, he insists that he has no personal political interest. As a religious leader he holds, he says, a mandate from all Mirghanists to guide them on religious issues and to speak on their behalf. Where political or economic issues are concerned he holds no such mandate, nor would his conscience permit him to intervene. Here every Khatmi must think and speak for himself, as an individual guided by his own intelligence. In so far as he personally was concerned, it was thought unwise to focus the attention on a distant political horizon when the foreground was occupied by a dangerous enemy. He was as determined as ever to resist the Mahdist menace. The Khatmia were not a political organisation and had only entered local politics two years ago, when the Mahdist capture of the Advisory Council made it imperative for them in the interests of the country to intervene actively to prevent Sayed Abdel Rahman from dominating also the Graduates [sic] Congress—the only native institution capable of putting up an organised resistance to Mahdist ambitions. Great Britain and Russia fought together as allies to defeat Germany, but no intelligent man would pretend that Great Britain's cooperation with Russia in war in any way committed her, once the immediate common danger had been surmounted, to the support or propagation of the Communist political creed. The Khatmia and Ashiqqa were similarly united in face of an immediate common peril. . . .

441. *Sayed Abdel Rahman El Mahdi Pasha*

Sayed Abdel Rahman divided his time during the month between Khartoum and the Blue Nile Province. He attended the Medani races, visiting on the way the headquarters of the Halawin Khut where a large gathering was reported. Further afield he has recently betrayed a new interest in Darfur, making gifts of money to the ex-Emir of Zalingei, and to the Maahad[1] and Mahdist Zawia[2] in Fasher. The Governor envisages a possible application for a Mulid tent.[3]

The Sayed has taken considerable trouble, in the course of a number of conversations with District Commissioner Kosti, District Commissioner Omdurman and others, to emphasise the danger of Ashiqqa machinations, and of their determined drive to capture Local and Provincial Councils, and to publicise and

---

[1] An Islamic institute.

[2] Small mosque complex belonging to a religious order.

[3] Tent set up during the celebration of the prophet Muhammad's birthday.

exploit their successes in the pro-Egyptian political interest. The internal situation was, he said, rapidly deteriorating, and he was particularly concerned with the appearance on the scene of the Ikhwan el Muslimin, whose dangerous doctrines, preaching as they did the unification of spiritual and temporal rule, might appeal to Moslem fanatics—even to his own less sophisticated followers. We were faced with the definite prospect of a period of unrest, fostered by this dangerous two-pronged Egypto-Islamic propaganda, and culminating, perhaps, in actual breaches of the peace of a serious kind. In the purely political field, the immediate danger was that the Khatmia, still exploiting the Mahdist bogey, might so confuse the fundamental political issues (which were in themselves quite simple) as to open the door wide to the Egyptian politician and to the home-bred pro-Egyptian agitator. He was prepared, in the interests of the Sudan, if we thought it would help to stabilise the situation, publicly to deny his alleged dynastic ambitions if Sayed Ali would deny with equal publicity his attachment to the Egyptian Crown. Meanwhile sectarian antagonism is still at the root of our troubles. . . .

47 PREM 8/1388/1, CP(46)17 18 Jan 1946

'Revision of the Anglo–Egyptian treaty of 1936': Cabinet memorandum by Mr Bevin. *Annexes* [Extract]

[In submitting this memorandum to the Cabinet, Bevin stated that Egyptian sovereignty over the Sudan could not be conceded as 'we must continue to refuse to abandon our responsibilities towards the Sudanese peoples'. The Cabinet then approved a reply to the Egyptian government in terms of the following memorandum (CM 7(46)5, 22 Jan 1946).]

I circulate herewith, for the information of my colleagues (Annex A), a translation of a Note, received from the Egyptian Government on the 20th December, which contains the anticipated demand for the revision of the Anglo–Egyptian Treaty of 1936, and more particularly for the withdrawal of British forces from Egypt in time of peace. I recommend that a reply agreeing in general terms to a review of our present arrangements should be sent, and attach a draft (Annex B)[1] for concurrence.

I should explain that the principles of those articles of the present treaty which are of the greatest importance from our point of view, viz., those establishing the alliance and providing for very extended facilities to our forces in time of war, are automatically renewable *in any revision of the treaty*. (Article 16 of the Treaty.) We should, of course, insist on this renewal as a point of departure. The remaining articles deal with the military facilities afforded us by Egypt in time of peace, the Sudan, and various political questions of a general nature. A number of these articles (notably those relating to the League of Nations) are in any event out of date and since the whole Treaty of 1936 is based on the League of Nations and the Covenant, it cannot be contested that some revision is necessary and is called for now. . . .

As regards the Sudan which, like the question of peacetime facilities for our troops, constitutes a major difficulty (and offers little scope for compromise), His Majesty's Governments have repeatedly refused to abandon their responsibilities towards the Sudanese peoples, amongst whom the idea of nationhood has already

---

[1] Annex B not printed.

taken shape. It is out of the question for His Majesty's Government to accede to the request which will probably be made of them, viz., to recognise *sole* Egyptian sovereignty over the Sudanese. They must, I submit, maintain firmly the standpoint that the future of the Sudan belongs neither to this country nor to Egypt, but to the Sudanese themselves, whose own wishes must be taken in account in any new arrangements which may be devised. Our further tactics must depend on Egyptian reactions to this standpoint. . . .

The general lines of the instructions which I would propose to issue to Lord Killearn are annexed as Annex C.

Annex A to 47: Note from the Egyptian government, 20 Dec 1945

"The Egyptian Government, certain they are interpreting a unanimous national sentiment, consider that the manifest interests of Anglo–Egyptian friendship and alliance demand that the two parties should revise, in the light of recent events and of their experience, the arrangements which govern their mutual relations at the present time.

2. It is certain that the Treaty of 1936 was concluded in the midst of an international crisis at a moment when the spectre of war was already appearing, and it is to these circumstances that it clearly owes its present form. . . .

5. If Egypt accepted the Treaty with all that it implied in the way of restrictions on her independence, it was because she knew that they were of a transitory character and were destined to disappear at the same time as the circumstances and events by reason of which they had been agreed to. . . .

11. Therefore, now that the circumstances which determined the particular character of the Treaty of 1936 have changed, it has become necessary to revise it in order to bring it into harmony with the new international situation; its clauses which detract from the independence and the dignity of Egypt no longer correspond to present conditions. . . .

15. . . . in view of the unanimous urge of the Egyptian people and their ardent desire to see their relations with Great Britain established on the basis of an alliance and a friendship which will no longer be inspired by past prejudices or out-of-date doctrines, the Egyptian Government express their confidence that these views will be shared by their Ally, and that the British Government will take steps to fix an early date for an Egyptian delegation to proceed to London to negotiate with them the revision of the Treaty of 1936.

16. It goes without saying that the negotiations will include the question of the Sudan and will be inspired by the interests and aspirations of the Sudanese."

Annex C to 45: Memorandum

I suggest below the lines on which the preliminary conversations with the Egyptian Government might be conducted. . . .

3. *The Sudan*

His Majesty's Government take note that the Egyptian Government, in discussing the future of the Sudan, will base themselves on the interests and the aspirations of the Sudanese. The standpoint of His Majesty's Government is similar, and they need only refer in this connexion to the Charter of the United Nations which defines the trusteeship system (to which the present administration of the Sudan offers some analogy) as designed to promote the political, economic, social and educational advancement of the inhabitants . . . and their progressive development towards self-government or independence as may be appropriate to . . . the freely expressed wishes of the peoples concerned.

The safety of Egypt's southern frontier is a joint Anglo–Egyptian interest as is also free access to the trade and commerce of the Sudan. Apart from this His Majesty's Government have no objectives in the Sudan save the continued welfare of the inhabitants and the safeguarding and continuity, so long as it is needed, of the great task of administration which has been performed for almost half a century by a number of His Majesty's subjects. Political progress has been rapid in the Sudan in recent years, and it has been necessary to devise constitutional machinery to enable native opinion to be consulted. As the Egyptian Government are aware, the Governor-General, at the last meeting on the 8th November of the Advisory Council for the Northern Sudan, declared that:—

> "Should the question of the future status of the Sudan be raised by the Condominium Powers in any revision of the Anglo–Egyptian treaty, it would be the intention of the Sudan Government that the Advisory Council for the Northern Sudan should be consulted in order that its views should be at the disposal of the Sudan Government for transmission to the Powers. It is the opinion of the Sudan Government that the views of the Sudanese people should be obtained through constitutional channels in a matter of such vital importance to their future well-being."[2]

His Majesty's Government consider, therefore, that any discussion of the modification of Article 11 of the 1936 Treaty should be postponed until the Sudanese people have been consulted and have made known their own wishes. The procedure by which this consultation can best take place is being examined by the Governor-General, who will be available to discuss it with the Egyptian Government if required. But His Majesty's Government again wish to emphasise that the facts of the situation and modern international doctrine render academic, in their opinion, any prior discussion of the vexed question of sovereignty over the Sudan.

[2] See 40.

48 FO 371/53381, no 432 — 29 Jan 1946

[Education]: letter from R C Mayall to P S Scrivener on the association of Gordon Memorial College with the Inter-University Council for Higher Education in the Colonies [Extract]

[One of the recommendations of the Asquith Commission Report on higher education in the colonies (Cmd 6647, June 1945) was the creation of an Inter-University Council for the colonial empire. It was tentatively proposed to contain a reference to the Sudan in the draft Inter-University Council constitution and terms of reference (K W Blaxter[1] (CO) to

[1] Then assistant secretary and head of the CO Social Services Dept.

Scrivener, 19 Jan 1946, FO 371/53381, no 262). Beckett advised caution in a minute on 22 Jan 1946 and proposed that the relevant paragraph 'ought to begin with a clear statement in the sense that although the Anglo–Egyptian Sudan is in no sense a colony of the U.K. but a territory administered under a condominium between the U.K. and Egypt, the Governor-General has expressed a view that much practical help could be given to education in the Sudan if this Council would as a special measure perform the same functions in relation to development of higher education there, and that is has been thought that this request of the Governor-General should be met' (FO 371/53381, no 262). Following consultation with the Sudan government on the matter the council's terms of reference were redrafted to meet these objections.]

I refer to the letter from Blaxter of the Colonial Office to you, No. 12041/12/45 of the 19th January, on the subject of the participation of the Gordon Memorial College in the Inter-University Council for Higher Education in the Colonies, and to the telephone conversation which we had last Saturday morning.

As I mentioned to you on Saturday, I had cabled out to the Civil Secretary in Khartoum on the 21st January, asking him to give me authority to approach you on the subject, with a request to the effect that the Gordon Memorial College wished to be associated with this Council from its inception.

I have now received from Robertson a telegram, a copy of which I enclose herewith.[2] You will note from the contents of this telegram that I am authorised to ask you to be kind enough to make, on behalf of the Gordon Memorial College, a request to the Colonial Office for this association. In this connection I append herewith an extract from the minutes of the Third Meeting of the Gordon Memorial College Council in Khartoum which shows the desire of the Council for this association:—

> ... *'The College Board, having carefully considered the Report of the Commission on Higher Education in the Colonies, recommends to the Council that the Gordon Memorial College should seek the connection with London University as recommended by the Commission, and that representation of the College on the Inter-University Council should be welcomed as and when it may be possible to arrange it.
>
> 'The Board considers that the College is likely to get from this connection benefits which it could not otherwise hope for. At the same time, it considers that it should be made clear that the connection is a temporary one made only with the object of enabling the College to achieve independence as a Sudanese University. We consider that every care should be taken to safeguard the Sudanese character of the College, and that the necessary adaptations to local needs should be maintained both in academic and in other matters.
>
> 'The Board has considered, as an alternative to the proposed connection with London, a similar connection with a university of the Near East. But it recommends the connection with London University because its academic standard is much higher than that of any Near Eastern university, and because of the many facilities which will be provided by the Inter-University Council. At the same time, the Board considers it of great importance that this connection should not impair the closest possible relations with Universities of the Near East, from which also the College can receive much benefit.'*

---

[2] Not printed.

I realise that Robertson, in the opening sentence of his telegram, is correct in stating that since the Gordon Memorial College is an autonomous body, application for association could be made by it to the Inter-University Council without reference to the Sudan Government. Since, however, this latter Council is under the aegis of the Colonial Office, I do not think it would be correct for me to make the request direct to the Council, and especially so since I understand that the Council is not yet actually in being. . . .

* The sub-paragraphs of the minute referring to the proposed association of the Gordon Memorial College with London University are not strictly relevant to the present request for the association of the Gordon Memorial College with the Inter-University Council for Higher Education, but are included in the extract in order to give you a complete picture of the present position.

49 FO 371/53329, no 865 18 Feb 1946

[Sudanisation]: despatch no 241 from R J Bowker[1] to Mr Bevin. *Enclosure*: note by J W Robertson for the Governor-General's Council (23 Dec 1945)

With reference to paragraph 7 of the minutes[2] enclosed in my despatch No. 100 of January 21st, I have the honour to transmit herewith a copy of a note by the Civil Secretary to the Sudan Government, on Sudanisation on the Sudan Political Service, in the form in which the note was approved by the Governor General's Council on 30th December, 1945.

2. I agree with the policy set out in this note so far as it is based on the principle of developing local government by Sudanese and avoiding the imposition of a numerous Sudanese bureaucracy on the country. In present world conditions, however, having regard to the influence of the United Nations Organisation, and the urge for complete independence which is particularly strong in the Arab world, I doubt whether it will be possible to carry out a very gradual programme of Sudanisation on the 20-years basis proposed in this note or to exclude the Sudanese from holding responsible posts in the political administration of their country during this period. It seems difficult to believe, for instance, that it will be possible for 20 years to prevent Egyptians infiltrating into the Sudan Political Service, with results which would be far more harmful to the Sudan than any that could arise from the appointment of Sudanese to the same posts. Experience in other countries, such as Ethiopia, Iraq, and Egypt itself, has shown a strong inherent tendency to prefer inefficient government by fellow-countrymen to good government by foreigners. This is probably also the feeling of the Sudanese. In present circumstances they must feel that whatever happens as regards the development of local government, it is the District Commissioners and Governors who really have all the power. I suggest, therefore, with some diffidence

[1] Minister, Cairo embassy, Sept 1945; counsellor, April 1946; chargé d'affaires, 1946–1947.

[2] 'Minutes of the 539th meeting of [the Governor-General's] Council' (FO 371/53329, no 389), recorded that the council approved an alteration to the wording of the recommendations in paragraph 11 of the civil secretary's draft note.

that the Sudan Government might be well advised to try at a very early date the experiment of appointing Sudanese to responsible political posts and even a Sudanese Governor. The plan explained in the paper within would proceed, but meanwhile something material would have been done to meet the growing demands of the Sudanese. At the came time the wind would be taken out of the sails of the Egyptian propogandists [sic] who are now increasingly active in the Sudan.

3. I am sending a copy of this despatch to the Governor General of the Sudan.

Enclosure to 49

1. At its 532nd meeting held on the 17th March 1945, Council reaffirmed the policy of Dilution on which they had embarked and urged upon Governors and Heads of Departments the need to press steadily ahead, without waiting for the detailed plans which will later be submitted by the Establishments Committee for Council's approval. Inquiries and consultation with Governors have led me to the conclusion that dilution in the Political Service raises problems different from those arising in other Departments of the Government, and Council's direction is now sought on the line to be followed.

2. Sudanisation of the technical services is usually a process of straight-forward substitution of British by technically qualified Sudanese officials but with the rare exceptions to which I refer below in paragraph 5, a Sudanese cannot be a satisfactory Political Officer among his own people. The functions of Governors and District Commissioners are essentially detached and unbiassed [sic] and the Political Service is unanimously agreed that it would be wrong to attempt to impose Political Officers from among the Sudanese over their own countrymen and that the future of Sudanese administrative officers must, therefore, be in an administrative and not in a political capacity. Their view is that a bureaucracy recruited mainly from the Three Towns and the River would be alien to the great bulk of the Sudan and less sympathetic than the existing British bureaucracy. This view undoubtedly has some foundation.

3. The future structure of local government in the Sudan on which the day-to-day life of the population will intimately depend is bound up closely with the future of the British Political Service and with the Sudanisation of that Service. Sudanisation in the Political Service will affect the whole future structure of the Governmental machine in the country. The development of local government and the assumption of responsibility by local government authorities of much of the general administration of both urban and rural areas, necessitates the employment of competent executive agents who, like the town clerks in English local government councils, should be responsible for execution of the orders and policy of the councils and for supervising and managing their services and paid staff. Such agents will in fact be doing much of the administrative and executive work now being carried out by District Commissioners and Mamurs on behalf of the central government, and as their numbers increase so will the duties of District Commissioners and Mamurs as central government officials decrease.

4. The common British practice is for such executive staff (though they belong to a national association of local government officers) to be recruited from the open market, but in the Sudan the bulk of the best men are already in Government

service, and if the local councils are to be staffed efficiently and our young administrative officers are to play their part in the future of their country, they must be transferred from central government to local government employment as the transfer of responsibility to local councils proceeds. Simultaneously with this process the functions of the British Political Staff will become more advisory and political and less executive and administrative and the numbers needed will correspondingly decrease. It is not my view that they should be replaced in this advisory capacity by Sudanese.

5. The rate of development of local government will, of course, vary in different parts of the Sudan and the need for District Commissioners and Mamurs in the more backward areas performing their old functions, political and administrative, will probably continue for a long time. In such areas until local government takes over there will be a case on grounds of political expediency for replacing a small number of British Political officers by Sudanese for a limited period of time, if suitable men are available, but I do not visualise such replacement being permanent except perhaps in a few exceptional cases.

6. There will, I hope, in the coming years be a steady growth of local Government by rural and district councils in the rural areas and I foresee a possible total of 25 to 30 such units covering ultimately most of the Northern Sudan. I foresee also about 10 to 12 independent town and municipal councils and perhaps 20 town committees which will form an integral part of the rural district councils, but some of which may attain independent status later. I do not in this submission attempt to define the future relation of province councils to this organisation.

7. One of the main duties of British District Commissioners will be as chairman in these councils during the early stages and subsequently as advisers when the chairmanship is taken over by Sudanese. At the same time their executive and administrative functions will be taken over by executive agents employed and paid by the councils and drawn generally from the ranks of Sudanese District Commissioners and Mamurs. Only in a few places for example in Khartoum, may it be necessary to have British executive agents for a considerable time to come.

8. The full implementation of this policy over a period of 20 years in the six Northern Provinces cannot be exactly foreseen yet, but from preliminary recommendations received from Governors, which are still under consideration, I think that in that period it may be possible to reduce the British Political staff in the Provinces from 72 to 30 and replace them by an approximately equal number of Sudanese in Division I in local government service, or in a few cases by straight substitution in the Political Service.

9. I have not attempted to bring within the scope of this review the two Southern Provinces which now contain 46 posts for British Political officers. It is quite impossible to prophesy the rate at which Southern indigenous institutions will develop and it is certain that if the approved Government policy for economic and educational expansion is to be properly carried out there is little possibility of reducing the British Political staff in these provinces during the next 15 to 20 years.

10. I have also not tried to state here the details of the dilution plan. The training of Sudanese in local government methods, the terms of service, and transfer of Sudanese from central to local government service, and the appointment of local government supervisory staff at Province Headquarters during the early stages, are all under consideration, and will be taken up shortly with the Financial Secretary.

11. I ask, however, for Council's approval of the principles underlying this proposal, i.e.:—

(a) the Political Service should gradually be reduced in numbers as the functions of local government are effectively taken over by local councils.
(b) the Sudanese Administrative officer cadre should in the main be absorbed into local Government, as Town Clerks, Clerks to Municipalities, and executive officials of Rural District Councils and should not except in a few areas take the place of the Political Service.
(c) the Southern Sudan should continue to be administered by British Political officers, until the Southern Sudanese have evolved a local self-government of their own, when a similar process to that described in (a) and (b) above should be aimed at.

50 FO 371/53251, no 1324 20 Feb 1946

[Ikhwan al-Muslimin (Muslim Brothers)]: circular letter from J W Robertson to all governors and the commissioner of Port Sudan. *Enclosure* 'D': confidential background report on 'el ikhwan el muslimin'

1. As a result of the recent visit to the Sudan of the young Egyptian lawyer Gemal el Din el Sanhuri, during which in a number of our larger towns he addressed local audiences on the doctrines of the Egyptian Ikhwan el Muslimin, Governors must expect to receive applications for their consent to the formation of branches of the Cairo Society, or, alternatively, of local societies on the Ikhwan el Muslimin model. An application of the latter type has already been addressed to Governor Northern Province in respect of Atbara, and there are indications that other Governors may shortly be approached (if applications have not been already received) in respect of such places as Omdurman, Port Sudan, Kassala, Wad Medani and El Obeid.

2. I have given the matter the most careful consideration and have decided that such applications should be dealt with as follows. I fully realise that a society of the Ikhwan el Muslimin type is a potential source of embarrassment, in that its members, under internal or external pressure, may later be tempted into the political field, but the primary consideration, upon which you have to decide whether to accord or refuse your consent to the formation of a proposed society, must be the terms of the Constitution or Rules deposited with you by the applicants. If the aims and objectives of the society as therein defined are plainly and unexceptionably 'religious', you have no alternative but to accord your consent. To refuse consent would be to play gratuitously into the hands of our critics and opponents.

3. In the case of Atbara, the applicant, one Kemal Eff. Bedri, has deposited with the Governor Northern Province a constitution which is based on the constitution of the Egyptian Society, and proposes to use the Egyptian name and call his society the Ikhwan el Muslimin of Atbara. An English translation of this constitution (enclosure 'A')[1] is attached to this letter for your information. You will see that the rules are

---

[1] Enclosures 'A'—'C' not printed.

strictly religious. Indeed every undesirable or political reference in the Egyptian constitution upon which they are based, has been carefully excluded.

4. Governor Northern Province in giving his consent to the formation of this society, has been instructed to make it clear to the promoters that he could not (and would not) give his consent to the formation of any society whose constitution was to be the full constitution of the Ikhwan el Muslimin in Cairo (a short summary of which is attached marked 'B'), because he could not, as an official of the (Condominium) Sudan Government approve the 'national objective'[2]—i.e. the political objective—of that Society as described in Section 2(e) of Chapter II thereof, nor could he approve the provisions of Chapter VI (vide attachment 'C') which require the complete subservience of local branches of the Society to the parent body in Egypt.

5. He is, in fact, only giving his consent, to the formation of a local 'religious' society, whose unexceptionable 'religious' rules have been laid before him—a Sudanese Society, quite independent of the Egyptian Ikhwan el Muslimin, to which he recognises no affiliation.

6. As regards the proposed name of the Atbara society, the Governor Northern Province has been directed to press strongly on the promoter the suggestion that, if he wishes to preserve its non-political character, he should consider very seriously the desirability, in order to stress the difference between its constitution and that of the Egyptian Ikhwan, of giving it a different name. Whilst leaving the final decision to Kemal Eff. Bedri, he will point out that whatever the basic religious inspiration of the Ikhwan el Muslimin may be, they have latterly been closely associated with political agitation. They have fallen foul of more than one Egyptian Government; their leaders have on more than one occasion been arrested and detained as disturbers of the peace; and they show every sign of being prepared to play a prominent part in the troublous times now ahead. He will impress upon him that the use by the Atbara Society of the Cairo name must inevitably suggest affiliation to the Cairo Society, and give rise to misunderstandings which can only be a source of embarrassment to himself and his associates.

7. You should deal similarly with any applications of the like kind which may be addressed to you. I enclose (as attachment 'D') a summary of the Ikhwan el Muslimin's political history. A good deal of this e.g. the detail of the Society's organisation and its possible possession of arms, is confidential, but in illustrating its political character to would-be organisers of similar societies in your province, and warning them of the embarrassments and dangers of affiliation, you may quote any of the public demonstrations and disturbances (e.g. at the time of the recent crisis in the Levant) in which it has played a prominent part.

8. Should any society of the Ikhwan type in your province, having obtained your consent to its formation as a purely religious body either under the name of Ikhwan el Muslimin or under a name of its own, subsequently indulge in political activities in contravention of the constitution deposited with you, you should refer the matter to me, with a full report, for consideration of the question of your withdrawing your consent and shutting it down.

---

[2] The 'national objective' is stated to include 'the liberation of the Nile Valley, the entire Arab world and the Islamic nation in all its parts, from the sovereignty of the foreigner and the aiding of Islamic minorities everywhere in the attainment of their rights.'

Enclosure 'D' to 50

1. The history of the Ikhwan el Muslimin has been summarised at various dates by Defence Security and other Intelligence organisations in Cairo. Briefly it is as follows. Founded in 1930 by Sheikh Hassan el Banna,[3] an undoubted enthusiast for the Moslem way of life, the aims and objects of the Society have gradually assumed a militant political character. Its creed, in its essence a revivalist one, which attributes the debasement of Eastern ethical values to the disastrous influence of Western materialism, and the decay of the Egyptian governmental system to the impact of foreign ideas and foreign culture, inevitably assumed the character of a call for the application of the principles of Islam to practical politics, Islam, it insists, does not tolerate the domination of the Moslem world by peoples of other religions, and it is the task of the Ikhwan to rid Egypt of foreign influences in both economic and political spheres. El Banna's sincerity was unquestioned in the early days of the movement, but as the power and influence of the Society grew during the war years, the character of their founder underwent a change and from a religious leader, he developed, though fortunately lacking in the true courage of the fanatic, into a clever and unscrupulous politician, whose followers were to devote their energies to the creation of a body of anti-foreign feeling sufficiently powerful to support them irresistibly in their demand for "Egyptian independence".

2. The movement was originally organised on social, educational and charitable lines; funds were forthcoming from the most respectable Moslem cricles [sic]; and all sorts of schemes (scouts, sporting clubs, schools, clinics, cooperative societies) were envisaged, but a comparative failure to put these theoretical schemes on a practical basis constituted at this time one of the Society's fundamental weaknesses and reduced the attraction of its appeal. In its later years the movement underwent several reorganisations. At one time, using the Nazi and Fascist systems, which he had carefully studied, as a model, El Banna formed within the Ikhwan the 'Gawala' (or Rovers) and 'Katāi'b',[4] specially trained and trusted groups of adherents who corresponded respectively to the Brown Shirts and Black Shirts of the Hitler organisation. Each Branch had its own Katiba, composed of its most enthusiastic and reliable members, and El Banna had his own special Katiba bodyguard. Certain elements of the Katāi'b were also reported to have been formed into a suicide squad.

3. This Nazi organisation was, however, short-lived and by the middle of 1944 the Ikhwan were believed to have been reorganised on the following lines. The Branches, estimated at over a thousand, were grouped into Shubas, or Districts, each Shuba being controlled by a President and eleven Councillors. The Shubas were arranged in turn in a series of seventeen zones, each possessing its own administrative body of four officials, this decentralisation providing against the disruption or handicapping of the movement's activities through the closing of meeting places or the arrest of leading members. The whole association was directed by a supreme Committee presided over by El Banna. A number of Sub-Committees at H.Q. controlled the activities of the Gawala and of the workers and students (from

---

[3] Hasan al-Banna (1906–1949), founder and leader of Muslim Brotherhood in Egypt, 1929; assassinated in February 1949, probably on the orders of the Egyptian government.

[4] 'Squadrons' (sing, *katiba*).

whom the Society's membership was largely drawn, along with some of the more educated elements of the lower middle class); organised propaganda, cultural and religious teaching; and dealt with other administrative matters.

4. The organisation described in the previous paragraph is believed to be still the organisation today (end of 1945). The Gawala bands have been provided with semi-military training and parade at least once a week. Certain sections are reported to have been issued with firearms and to have been given some preliminary training in their use. (There are in Egypt a large number of arms, obtained in the main from abandoned dumps in the Western Desert, which could be brought into use, should feeling be sufficiently aroused. The existence of these arms makes the Ikhwan a potential danger which cannot be discounted). The weakness of the movement however still lies in its leadership. El Banna is not only the undisputed leader but the only outstanding personality. The society is believed by the Security authorities in Cairo to be entirely dependent on him, and although he may be dangerous (if his nerve holds) because of the power he can wield, the dependence of the Brotherhood on his leadership may yet be the cause of its downfall. Should he be for any reason removed, the Ikhwan *might* crumble away. The membership of the Society has been variously estimated at from 100,000 to 500,000.

5. In a note of this kind the activities of the Ikhwan during recent years can only be very shortly summarised. The Society entered the political arena during the time of the Palestine troubles (1936–1939) when it played a prominent part in anti-British agitation. In 1940 El Banna was associating with Ali Maher and with the anti-British group of which he was the head. He was receiving, also, protection and help from the Palace. In 1941 members of the Ikhwan became less guarded in their anti-British pronouncements; reports were received of attempts at sabotage, collection of information about British troop movements etc., and at the instance of the British authorities El Banna and his Vice President (Ahmed el Sukkari) were arrested in October of that year and interned. He was released in November by the then Egyptian Premier (Hussein Sirri) who took fright at the possibility of agitation in protest against his internment. El Banna, however, appeared to have been frightened too and for some time was more cautious in his public declarations.

6. The subsequent war history of the Ikhwan is one of initial opposition to the British-installed successor of Hussein Sirri (Nahas Pasha); of the subsequent striking of a bargain between El Banna (under the threat of reinternment) and the Wafdist Premier (who was loath to leave such a promising instrument for agitation unattached)—a bargain which was severely criticised at the time by the Society's rank and file and caused a temporary split which seriously affected its activities; of El Banna's gradual success in convincing his subordinates that his bargain, which left him unmolested, was a wise piece of purely tactical opportunism; of the intensification of the Society's build-up in the shelter of Wafdist non-interference; of his breach of the bargain which led in January 1943 to a ban being placed on all Ikhwan meetings, a ban which they attributed to British intervention; of the removal of this ban in May of the same year as the result of a further 'understanding' between the Society and the Wafd; of the caution which it displayed at the time of the El Alamein crisis, in spite of its undoubted Fifth Column and pro-German sympathies; and of its (comparative) latter day quiescence since the fall of the Nahas Ministry and the installation of Nokrashi Pasha. The December 1944 demonstrations in Cairo (over the discussion by the Advisory Council in Khartoum of the Sudanese

nationality question) were traced to Wafdist/Ikhwan instigation, but they were firmly dealt with by the Government, and so far as any overt activity was concerned, the Society seemed, temporarily at least, to be biding its time.

In the summer of 1945, however, its activities recommenced. Members of the Ikhwan joined in anti-French demonstrations in Egypt over the crisis in Syria and the Lebanon, and in October 1945 the Society's growing importance in politics was emphasised by further action. Early in that month a well attended mass meeting passed a number of resolutions supporting the extremist claims of the Arab countries, and according to Cairo reports the Society is now gradually growing strong enough to be independent of the Wafd or of other political parties. Its President, Sheikh Hassan el Banna, 'is feeling his way to influence in national affairs'.

51 FO 371/53250, no 1195 11 Mar 1946

[Consultation with the Sudanese on their future]: despatch no 354 from R J Bowker to Mr Bevin. *Enclosure*: despatch no 31 from Sir H Huddleston to Lord Killearn, 23 Feb 1946

With reference to your telegram No. 25 Saving of 25th January, I have the honour to transmit herewith a copy of a despatch from the Governor-General of the Sudan, regarding the method by which the views of the Sudanese should be obtained in connection with the Treaty negotiations and their effect on the future of the Sudan.

2. I agree generally with the draft memorandum, subject to one criticism of detail, namely, that the last sentence but two in paragraph 2, regarding the proportion of Sudanese in the Central Government service, is somewhat misleading having regard to the sentence which immediately follows it.

3. It is inevitable that the questions asked in the memorandum will be regarded by Egyptians as being to some extent in the nature of leading questions, and that the process of consultation should be considered by Egyptians as artificial. Any consultation of a primitive country is bound to be somewhat unreal and this fundamental difficulty is inherent in the present proposals. The unreality of consultation is all the greater in that it will be restricted to the Northern provinces, but this again is inevitable, as it will be quite impossible to institute any serious consultation of the tribesmen of the Southern Sudan. Obviously consultation must be directed by the Sudan Government as proposed, since the alternative would be consultation by less direct methods from the Egyptian side. Nevertheless, I consider that the British control over the means of consultation should be kept as far as possible in the background for purposes of publicity, and I assume that the estimates of popular opinion in the provinces which, as suggested in the last sentence of paragraph 4 of the enclosed despatch, would be obtained from Provincial Governors, should be for the use of the Sudan Government, and not for production as evidence of the results of consultation. The evidence of British Provincial Governors, however careful and objective, would not be regarded by Egyptians as accurately reflecting Sudanese opinion. This argument could also be applied by Egyptians to most of the existing constitutional channels in the Sudan which are at present more or less under British influence, but it would apply more effectively to the evidence of British officials.

4. As regards timing, Lord Killearn proposed in paragraph 5 of his telegram to the Foreign Office No. 146 of 31st January that the Sudan issue should not be raised in the Treaty negotiations until the military question had been settled. It would clearly be undesirable to start consulting the Sudanese on Treaty revision as it affects the Sudan if the negotiations are subsequently to break down on the evacuation question without touching on the Sudan at all. I therefore consider that consultation of the Sudanese should not begin until there is a good prospect of a favourable outcome to the negotiations over the military question.

5. May I please be informed by telegraph if you agree?

6. I am sending a copy of this despatch to the Governor-General of the Sudan.

Enclosure to 51

As I informed Lord Killearn in my telegram No. 9 of February 1st, I have been considering methods of consulting the Sudanese so that their views about the future of the Sudan may be available at a later stage of the negotiations. I understand from Embassy telegram No. 12 of January 30th, 1946, that the Sudan will be discussed during the present negotiations, but at a later phase when the question of the evacuation of British Troops has been disposed of.

2. On this assumption, I consider that arrangements for the consultation of the Sudanese should be agreed upon as soon as possible, and I have had the attached memorandum prepared for submission to the various bodies which I propose should be consulted. In my opinion it would be impossible for these bodies to be consulted without guidance of this sort being given.

It will take time to convene the Province and Advisory Councils and it is therefore doubly essential to settle the preliminaries so that when the time for consultation comes the members of these bodies can at once be made aware of the issues on which their views are required.

3. With the approval of His Majesty's Ambassador and of His Majesty's Government,[1] and as quoted in Foreign Office Saving telegram No. 25, I have informed the Advisory Council for the Northern Sudan that they will be consulted in this matter, and in my opinion if such consultation is to be really valuable, it is essential that the representatives of the Province Councils in the Advisory Council should have the advantage of knowing the view of their parent councils. The Province Councils are composed of tribal leaders, merchants, and others, partly elected by Town Councils and by Rural District bodies and partly nominated to secure a representation of all interests. I propose, therefore, that the Memorandum should first be debated in the Province Councils, and that it should then be considered by the Advisory Council for the Northern Sudan.

4. As you are aware, the Graduates' General Congress, a body composed partly of politically minded persons, resident almost entirely in Omdurman, and claiming to be the most representative body in the Sudan, has already made two declarations as a result of which it has recently split up into a number of parties, of which the Umma and Ashigga are the largest. The Congress has always boycotted the Advisory Council

[1] See 40.

for the Northern Sudan, and it therefore has not been possible for it to be represented upon it. The Sudan Government would be open to criticism, however, if they did not obtain the views of these parties composed of the politically minded younger members of the educated classes, and I should propose to ask them and the Congress Committee whether they wished to submit their views on the Memorandum or whether their previous declarations were to be taken as their final statement. The influence in the country of Sayed Sir Ali el Mirghani Pasha and Sayed Sir Abdel Rahman el Mahdi Pasha, is still very great; these religious leaders are Honorary Members of the Advisory Council, and would therefore also be asked for their views. The Chamber of Commerce in Khartoum elects two representatives to the Advisory Council for the Northern Sudan and should similarly be asked to consider the memorandum. Provincial Governors would also be asked to estimate popular opinion in their Provinces, and the likely results of any change.

5. On receipt of the replies to the Memorandum and after the Advisory Council had held its debate, I should propose to convey the views collected in this way to you for the information of the Condominium powers. I should be grateful if you would let me know as soon as possible whether the procedure proposed is approved and whether you have any comments on the draft Memorandum.

ANNEXURE

Memorandum on the future of the Sudan, to be submitted to representative bodies in the Sudan

1. As you are aware, the question of the Sudan's future government is to be discussed in the present negotiations between Great Britain and Egypt. The Sudan Government have already announced that they intend to obtain the opinions of the Sudanese, through constitutional channels regarding their future, before the Condominium powers come to any decision on this subject, so intimately concerned with the well-being of the country.

2. The Sudan is at present administered by a Government which was set up by the British and Egyptian Governments in 1899. The aims of this Government were defined in the 1936 Anglo–Egyptian Treaty as being to work for the welfare of the Sudanese, though in fact this policy has been followed since 1898. The Sudan Government have interpreted this definition by working towards local self-government and in pursuit of this aim have recently set up Municipal, Town and Rural District Councils, in addition to the other local administrations which have existed for some time under the authority of tribal leaders. The Government have furthermore in the last few years established Province Councils and an Advisory Council with the avowed aim of associating the Sudanese more closely with the administration of the country. With similar intentions the Government have trained Sudanese for central government service until at the beginning of 1946 out of approximately 6000 posts in Divisions I and II, 78% are held by Sudanese. 81 of these posts are in Division I which contains approximately 800 posts. The Sudan Government have stated that they have imposed no limit to the scale of post to which a Sudanese may attain when qualified for it.

Schemes of Educational, Medical, and Economic development have been pushed ahead, and the progress achieved in the period since 1898 when no school, hospital or wealth existed in the country has been remarkable. The budget for 1946 is balanced at a figure of over seven and a half million pounds, compared with Revenue of £E. 126,596 and Expenditure of £E. 230,238 in 1899; a vast irrigation scheme has been created in the Gezira area, schools of all grades up to the post-secondary level have been established; hospitals and dispensaries are widespread throughout the country. Law and order has been firmly established, and general freedom of movement, thought and speech has developed. A plan for further economic, educational and general expansion is at the moment being worked out.

The Sudan Government have repeatedly declared their aim for the Sudan to be gradual evolution to complete internal self-government.

3. In considering the question now being put to the Sudanese it will be necessary for you to distinguish between immediate and long-term policy, for these are not necessarily the same. There can be little doubt that the Sudan as a whole still requires a considerable time to develop into a homogeneous entity, and to attain that degree of cohesion and unity required before it can stand firmly on its own feet. For this intervening period it needs guidance and assistance, and in considering the present situation it is essential to consider separately and distinctly:—

(a) the final objective to be aimed at, and
(b) the constitution and organisation to be maintained during the immediate training period, and especially the question of who is to guide and train the Sudanese.

4. Your views as to the ultimate objective should be given. The possibilities seem to be as follows:—

(a) a completely independent Sudan which is able to enter into relations with other independent states on a basis of equality and to control its own affairs;
(b) a Sudan completely incorporated into the Egyptian State like an Egyptian Province and subject to the laws of Egypt;
(c) a self-governing Sudan joined in some form of union with Egypt under the Egyptian Crown (either with or without an alliance with Great Britain);
(d) a self-governing Sudan in some form of association with the British Commonwealth of Nations, such as that of Canada, Australia or New Zealand.

5. The possible alternatives for the immediate future may be summarised as follows:—

(a) the progressive development of the present policy adopted by the Condominium Government of creating a self-governing and economically self-dependent Sudan and of replacing non-Sudanese officials by Sudanese in all ranks of the Government service as Sudanese become qualified to fill their posts;
(b) the continuation of the present regime but subject to a substitution of a considerable number of Egyptians for British in all ranks of the Government service. Attention should be given to the difficulties which might arise from a personnel drawn from different nationalities in the higher ranks of Government;
(c) substitution of Egypt for Great Britain as the predominant partner in the Condominium Government with a concomitant substitution of Egyptians for British in the higher posts of the Government for which Sudanese are still not yet qualified.

6. This note has been written as objectively as possible without any discussion of the merits or demerits of any particular solution, it being thought outside the function of the Sudan Government to point out these. It is incumbent upon the bodies to whom these questions are being put to consider the matter objectively and calmly, viewing the welfare and future prosperity and happiness of the people of the Sudan as a whole, not giving undue weight to personal or private considerations and in full consciousness of the responsibility laid upon them. Attention should be paid too to the immediate advantages and disadvantages of any change at a time when schemes of development are being initiated and when modification of the present regime might delay their implementation.

52 FO 371/53329, no 865 18 Mar 1946
[Sudanisation]: letter (reply) from P S Scrivener to R J Bowker

We have read with great interest your despatch No.241 of 18th February, and enclosures in regard to the question of the "Sudanisation" of the Sudan political service.[1]

I may say at once that we fully share your view in the light of the ever-mounting volume of evidence that the Middle East countries are determined to have indigenous (and doubtless inefficient) administrations at the earliest possible moment. We feel that the Civil Secretary's note is unassailable if viewed exclusively from the angle of correct British administrative theory (and we also feel that your suggestion of a Sudanese Provincial Governor at an early date may go rather too far the other way). But the fact remains,—and here we are on our own ground—that, as you say, we cannot go on keeping Egyptians out of the Political Service *unless* we can put in Sudanese. The practical choice, in fact, "in present world conditions" as you rightly express it, is between the fairly rapid introduction of British-trained Sudanese and some loss of artistic perfection, and an influx of Egyptian-trained Egyptians, with the rapid disappearance of all artistry whatsoever. We hope therefore that in the light of your remarks and ours, which are made in no carping spirit, the Sudan Government will give the matter some further consideration. An extra copy of this letter is attached for transmission, if you agree, to Khartoum.

[1] See 49.

53 FO 371/53250, no 1195 25 Mar 1946
[Consultation of Southern Sudanese]: letter from R C Mayall to P S Scrivener [Extract]

[Mayall, then Sudan agent in London, had served in the Upper Nile Province, a southern province, in 1922–1923. This is the first comment on the future of the Southern Sudan from a British official with any experience of the South to enter FO correspondence on the treaty negotiations.]

With reference to my conversation with Howe and yourself this morning on the subject of the contents of Khartoum despatch No. 31 dated 23rd February,[1] I have

[1] See 51.

now had an opportunity of studying carefully the despatch and the annexure thereto.

2. My own *private and personal* view is that the Governor-General, in asking for the approval of His Majesty's Ambassador in Cairo and of His Majesty's Government in London that he should be empowered to consult the Sudanese at an early date as to the future well-being of the country, had in mind the *whole* Sudan, i.e., the eight Provinces including the two Southern Provinces.[2] I base this view on the words in line 4 of paragraph 3 of the annexure, where it is emphatically stated that "there can be little doubt the Sudan *as a whole* still requires. . . ." etc.

3. As regards the method of consultation, I fully realise and appreciate the doubts which Howe and you yourself have as to whether or not the Governor-General, when he wrote the despatch, had in mind the method of consultation to be used to obtain the views of the population of the two Southern Provinces. I can fully appreciate that H.M.G. would find it impossible to agree to the step proposed by His Excellency the Governor-General unless they were certain that their obligations under the United Nations Charter were completely fulfilled.

4. I am, however, of the opinion that there should be no difficulty in obtaining some measure of opinion from the population of the two Southern Provinces. You will note from paragraphs 3 and 4 of the despatch that the Governor-General intends to consult the Advisory Council for the Northern Sudan, Province Councils, the Graduates' General Congress, the two Sayeds, the Chamber of Commerce in Khartoum, *and the Provincial Governors*. I would therefore suggest that His Excellency the Governor-General may have had in mind that, with a view to carrying out the obligations of the Condominium powers under the United Nations Charter, he would obtain the popular opinion of the two Southern Provinces as regards the future of their areas, through the medium of the Provincial Governors. Although the two Southern Provinces are not represented on the Northern Advisory Council—nor do I think it would be wise to suggest that for an *ad hoc* meeting of the Council at which this matter was to be discussed, representatives from these two Provinces should be present—there should be no insuperable difficulty in the two Southern Governors summoning *ad hoc* and informal Provincial Councils composed of District Commissioners and the Chiefs of the Tribes in the two Provinces. I submit that such consultation would be likely to result in as true a picture of general popular opinion as would result from the use of the more constitutional machinery in the case of the six Northern Provinces and the various Sectional interests.[3]

5. I suggest, as a personal opinion, that paragraph 4 of the annexure is incomplete. I would add that there should be a further alternative (which is, incidentally, that of the all-Party resolution) "a self-governing Sudan joined in some form of *association* with Egypt, but not under the Egyptian Crown". I would not, however, suggest including such an additional alternative of an independent or dominion status under the Anglo–Egyptian joint guarantee and safeguard.[4] Such an

[2] Mongalla and Bahr al-Ghazal provinces had been amalgamated into a single Equatorial Province in 1936, and were to be re-divided into Equatoria and Bahr al-Ghazal provinces in 1948.

[3] Scrivener's marginal note: "I agree".

[4] Scrivener's marginal note: "Caveat only against adopting an idea of Sir S. Symes!", the former governor-general who had recently written on the future of the Sudan in the *Times* of 13 Mar 1946.

objective, to my mind, would satisfy none of the three parties, i.e., the Sudanese, Egyptians, British, concerned in the present problem.

6. I have one further comment to make. I showed Howe and yourself the interchange of letters between Bowker and His Excellency the Governor-General on this subject; I understood that you were not in possession of these papers. May I be presumptious [sic] enough, in this private letter, to differ from the opinion not only of the Minister in Cairo but of my own Governor-General? I personally feel, and feel strongly, that the time has come when consultation with the Sudanese should be begun and I cannot help feeling that if permission for this consultation is not given at a very early date, further incidents such as those of the recent demonstration by Gordon Memorial College students, and the despatch by the Graduates' Congress of a delegation to Cairo, may be followed by events and incidents of a more serious nature. I hope and trust that I am being an alarmist over this and that the Declaration to be made to-morrow in the House of Commons by the Foreign Secretary will quieten the position in Khartoum, but to anyone like myself who still has vivid memories of 1924 in the Sudan it is difficult to believe that the Sudan Government can act too early if peace and public security in the country are to be maintained. . . .

54 *H of C Debs,* vol 421, col 217 26 Mar 1946

[Sudanese self-determination]: statement by Mr Bevin on HMG's policy

[Following an exchange between Huddleston and Killearn concerning the increase of Egyptian propaganda efforts in the Sudan, Huddleston expressed his concern that there was confusion among the Sudanese about Britain's policy towards the country's future. He claimed that the government's silence was being interpreted as consenting to the recent Egyptian government announcement that their aim was to incorporate the Sudan into Egypt. He urgently requested that Bevin issue a formal statement reiterating the British government's commitment to self-government in the Sudan (tel no 25, 12 Feb 1946, Huddleston to Killearn, FO 371/53250, no 1112). The following statement follows closely the language Huddleston proposed.]

His Majesty's Government look forward to the day when the Sudanese will be able finally to decide their political future for themselves. It is not proposed by His Majesty's Government to influence their eventual decision in any way. His Majesty's Government have no object in the Sudan other than the true welfare of the Sudanese, and this principle has likewise been proclaimed by the Egyptian Government in the Anglo–Egyptian Treaty of 1936. The welfare of the Sudanese cannot be secured unless a stable and disinterested administration is maintained in the Sudan. The objects of such an administration must be to establish organs of self-government as a first step towards eventual independence, to accelerate the process of appointing Sudanese to higher Government posts in consultation with Sudanese representatives, and to raise the capacity of the mass of the people to effective citizenship. These are the objects of the present Sudan Government, and His Majesty's Government fully support them. In the meantime, His Majesty's Government consider that no change should be made in the status of the Sudan as a result of treaty revision until the Sudanese have been consulted through constitutional channels.

55 FO 371/53371, no 1658 27 Mar 1946

[Nile Waters: Lake Albert reservoir]: inward telegram no 211 from Sir J Hall[1] to Mr Hall[2] objecting to plans for the construction of a dam at Lake Albert

[The Egyptian Irrigation Department's proposal to meet Egypt's anticipated water needs by increasing the flow of the Nile through the construction of the Jonglei Canal and a dam near Lake Albert had already provoked strong comment from the Sudan government (see 41 and 45). The Sudan's irrigation adviser, MacGregor, noted that Egypt's plans to enlarge Lake Albert by fifty per cent implied the submerging of more than a thousand square miles of territory in both Uganda and the Belgian Congo, an area which seemed likely to contain 'some features of importance and value.' He also noted that the Egyptians had not clearly indicated the potential site for such a dam, and concluded: 'It does not seem quite reasonable that the Governments of Uganda and the Belgian Congo should be approached with a suggestion to submerge 1000 square miles of their territory so long as the Egyptian Government, as promoter of the scheme, are themselves unable to come to a final decision on this obviously vital point. It would be fair to expect them to advance their ideas for the dam to the point of a definite design and a definite site, before the other two Governments are asked to consider the problems that would arise from submergence of this very large area, so much in excess of anything previously considered' ('Note by Mr. MacGregor (19.10.45)', FO 371/46024, no 3149). Writing in defence of the Egyptian proposals, Bowker commented that the area in question 'relates largely to sleeping-sickness country and game reserves—all very thinly inhabited; and that there would be some positive advantage to Uganda, where the greater part lies, for purposes of development of fishing' (Bowker to Scrivener, 31 Dec 1945, FO 371/53371, no 159). The Egyptian proposals were forwarded to the governor of Uganda via the CO for comment.]

Your telegram Saving No. 388 of the 12th December, 1945. Construction of Lake Albert Reservoir.

2. The proposals of the Egyptian Government have now been considered in as full detail as is possible, having regard to the absence of a fully detailed survey of the effects of the flooding contemplated.

3. The implications of a dam of the size contemplated in the Nimule area are that over 1,000 square miles of territory would be flooded, most of which lies in this Protectorate.

4. After detailed consultation with my advisers, I feel bound to reply that I am strongly opposed to the construction of any dam of any size by the Egyptian Government, in or near this Protectorate. This view has the full and unanimous support of my advisers. My reasons are as follows:—

(a) It is felt that the probable aim of the Egyptian Government is to control completely the headwaters of the Nile, and that if the request for permission to construct a dam at Nimule were granted, other demands would follow, and control of the water would gradually lead to demands for a greater measure of political control, which might well extend to the whole of the area surrounding the Victoria Nile.

(b) While there is at present no land hunger in the area which would be submerged, with an increasing population and improvements in education and social services, and the consequent demand for a higher standard of living, a

---

[1] Governor of Uganda, 1944–1952.

[2] S of S for the colonies, 1945–1946.

greater cash return from land will be required, which will entail extended cultivation.

(c) With the increasing political consciousness of the people of Uganda, the question of land is becoming of more and more importance, and the submergence of such a large area would undoubtedly cause such great dissatisfaction as to render the project politically impracticable.

(d) The scheme would give the Egyptian Government the right of control over the waters of Lake Albert and Lake Kioga and would make it impossible for this Government to embark upon any large scale irrigation project which might involve the divergence of water from those lakes.

(e) There are indications of the presence of oil near Lake Albert, production of which would be impossible commercially if the area were inundated.

(f) The tribes living on the Semliki flats own approximately 10,000 head of cattle, and there is no suitable grazing land to which they could be moved.

(g) There would be very considerable movement of game and consequently danger from the tsetse fly they would carry with them while the size of the Game Reserve would be much reduced.

(h) The danger of human trypanosomiasis would be enhanced by an increase in the area under water owing to the greater incidence of the *palpalis* fly.

(i) The valuable salt industry at Kibiro would be lost.

(j) Lake services would be seriously disturbed and present port facilities at Butiaba would be entirely lost. The gradual rise in the level of Lake Albert over a period of ten years would entail the provision of improvised port facilities during the whole of that period, and owing to the variation in the level of the water depending upon the amount which Egypt drew off in good or bad years, it would be necessary for tidal port installations to be provided ultimately.

(k) A dam at Nimule would entail the flooding of the area near the Albert Nile, and would consequently dispossess numbers of the Madi tribe for whom no other land could be found.

(l) The effects of the dam on the hydrography and climate of the Protectorate cannot at present be gauged.

56 FO 371/53250, no 1195 28 Mar 1946

[Consultation of Sudanese]: outward telegram (reply) no 588 from Mr Bevin to R J Bowker

[This reply to despatches from Huddleston and Bowker on consultation with the Sudanese incorporates a number of points raised by R C Mayall (see 53).]

Your despatch No. 354.[1]

I approve generally so far as the six Northern Provinces are concerned; but it seems to me essential that *ad hoc* machinery should also be devised for consulting the two southern provinces, and I should be glad if Governor-General would consider this point and telegraph his recommendations.

[1] See 51.

2. I agree with criticism in paragraph 2 of your despatch: and I consider (paragraph 5 of Governor-General's despatch) that views collected should also be conveyed to the Egyptian Prime Minister. While it is difficult for us (paragraph 4 of your despatch) to dispute from here your conclusion that consultations with Sudanese should be deferred until there is a prospect of a favourable outcome of Egyptian negotiations, is there not something to be said for giving Sudanese politicians some local interest, in the form of proposed consultation, to distract their minds from less convenient activities such as present visits to Egypt? It is also perhaps for consideration (c.f. recent all-party resolution) whether Sudanese should not be given additional choice of "a self-governing Sudan in some form of association with Egypt, but not under the Egyptian Crown".

57 FO 371/53251, no 1634 13 Apr 1946

[Sudanisation]: outward telegram no 65 from Sir R Campbell to Sir H Huddleston, commenting on J W Robertson's principles for Sudanisation

[Bevin minuted on his copy, 'Action is needed immediately'.]

Mr. Robertson has explained the principles on which Sudan Government plans for Sudanisation are based, namely:—[1]

(1) promotion of Sudanese who are competent to take on more responsible jobs (such men are limited in number) and
(2) building up of locally selected administration in the provinces (rather than imposition on the country of a Sudanese bureaucracy from towns) and eventual transformation of British administrative officials into advisers.

2. I fully appreciate the wisdom of these principles. The main difficulty at present seems to be that they and the plans based on them are insufficiently known to the politically conscious Sudanese and that the pace is too mild to satisfy them. The latter are anxious to know just when they will be able to take over the administration of the country, and the present danger is that unless they are given an answer to their question which they consider reasonably satisfactory they may throw in their lot with the Egyptians simply in order to get rid of the British. For this reason it seems to me most necessary that the Sudan Government should reluctantly accept the certainty of a lowered standard of efficiency and at once proceed to work out a detached and bold plan of Sudanisation giving the stages in the year in which the process will operate. Such a plan no doubt will take a little time to prepare but I think it essential that an announcement should be made at once (to Adviserory [sic] Council next week) that the plan is in preparation and some indication given of its probable scope.

3. I appreciate the desire that any plan should be based upon the principles referred to in paragraph 1 above. Neverhtless [sic] at the present critical moment with things moving so fast it seems to us at this end important that the plan should be made as impressive as possible and that it may be worth while taking certain risks

[1] See 49, enclosure.

as regards the efficiency and reaction of the British officials in order to hold the main position. If the interests of British political and other staff are prejudiced thereby it is essential that they should receive adequate guarantees from His Majesty's Government as regards future employment and pension.

4. At the same time, I would recommend the appointment of an experienced publicity officer on the staff of the Public Relations Office whose business it would be to put out carefully prepared material to the Arabic Press about progress in Sudanisation already made, and plans for future and about general policy of the Sudan Government.

58 FO 371/53252, no 1743 17 Apr 1946

[Future of the Sudan]: address delivered by Sir H Huddleston at the opening session of the Advisory Council for the Northern Sudan

[Extract]

. . . Before we proceed to the Agenda with which this Council has been specifically called to deal I feel it is due to you that I should make reference to the Political situation. Some of your number have asked for an opportunity to be given you now for a formal debate on the future status of the Sudan. This request has been most carefully considered by me and by my advisers and I have decided that the time for a formal debate has not yet come. Both His Majesty's Government and the Egyptian Government have announced their readiness to discuss the revision of the Treaty and have appointed their representatives for the purpose but those representatives have only just assembled and preliminary conversations have only just begun. I assure you once again that the question of your future will not be decided without your advice. Since we last met the Condominium Governments have both endorsed my assurance. Egyptian Government spokesmen have said that the aspirations and hopes of the Sudanese will be considered in any settlement. The British Government, through their Secretary of State for Foreign Affairs, Mr. Bevin, have categorically stated that they consider that no change should be made until the advice of the Sudanese has been sought through constitutional channels such as this Council. When the time comes, therefore, this Council will be summoned to give its views.

I would, at this time, draw your attention to two other phrases in Mr. Bevin's speech.[1] He referred to the objects of the Sudan Government as being to build up the organs of self-Government with the aim of eventual independence and to accelerate the transfer of responsible posts to Sudanese in consultation with Sudanese representatives. I wish to take this opportunity of declaring again that these are fundamental objects of the Sudan Government policy and to announce to you the following methods of attaining them more quickly, which I intend to put into practice at once.

With regard to the former, I propose to call a conference forthwith, at the close of this session under the chairmanship of the Civil Secretary, to study the next steps in associating the Sudanese more closely with the Administration of their country. The

---

[1] See 54.

recommendations of this conference will be laid before you at your next session for full discussion and consideration.

Secondly, as regards accelerated Sudanisation you will perhaps have noticed in the public press that I have set up a joint British and Sudanese Committee of Civil Servants to enquire into the present plans for Sudanisation and to make recommendations as to how they may be accelerated. I hope that this Committee will prepare a scheme in carefully defined stages, designed to show the expected progress of Sudanisation. This Committee or a similar body will remain in existence and meet at regular intervals to review progress. I have recently discussed the question with many Heads of Government Departments and have urged them to speed up the process without waiting for the Committee to submit their plans.

I wish definitely to deny any suggestions that the Sudan Government is unsympathetic to Sudanese aspirations. The Government is aiming at a free independent Sudan which will be able as soon as that independence has been achieved to define for itself its relations with Great Britain and Egypt. There is much to be done; hard thinking and hard work lies ahead; but with good will and a cessation of political upheavals I see no reason why even in the short space of the next five years a great advance should not be made; and in the ensuing five when our educational developments have gained a further impetus, progress should be sufficiently rapid to satisfy everybody except our most extreme critics.

I feel confident that in twenty years' time the Sudanese will be governing their own country assisted and advised by a certain number of non-Sudanese specialists and technicians. These dates, of course, are only estimates but when we meet again to discuss the views of the Conference which I have just announced to you, I hope that a more definite timetable can be given. . . .

59 FO 371/53391, no 1169 12 Apr 1946

[Selection of governor-general]: letter from Sir R Campbell to R G Howe on the qualities needed in the next governor-general of the Sudan. *Minutes* by P S Scrivener and E A Chapman-Andrews

Please refer to Foreign Office telegram No. 647 asking for the final views of the Governor General of the Sudan and myself about his successor. Sir E. Bridges has suggested the names of four soldiers from whom to choose Huddleston's successor. They are Generals Gammell, Scobie, Macready and Templer.[1] Macready is the only

[1] Lt-Gen Sir James Gammell, chief of staff to supreme allied commander, Mediterranean Theatre, 1944; representative of British Chiefs of Staff with USSR and head of British Military Mission in Moscow, 1945; retired 1946.

Lt-Gen Sir Ronald Scobie, general officer commanding (GOC), Torbruk fortress, 1941; GOC, Malta, 1942; chief of general staff, Middle East, 1943; GOC, Greece, 1944–1946; retired 1947.

Lt-Gen Sir Gordon Macready, chief of British Military Mission to Egyptian army, 1938; assistant chief of imperial general staff, 1940–1942; chief of British Army Staff, Washington, 1942; retired 1946; served subsequently on Control Commission in Moscow.

Lt-Gen Sir Gerard Templer, served in Middle East in two world wars; director, Military Intelligence, War Office, 1946–1948; vice-chief of imperial general staff, 1948–1951; general officer commanding-in-chief, Eastern Command, 1950–1952; high commissioner and director of operations, Malaya, 1952–1954; chief of imperial general staff, 1955–1958.

one I know but from what I hear of the others I myself would put them in the following order—Scobie, Templer, Macready, Gammell, bracketing Templer and Macready. The foregoing is on the assumption that a soldier is to be appointed and is not intended to exclude the possibilities of other soldiers being suggested as candidates.

I had some discussion with Huddleston on April 13th. His views are as follows:—The Governor General should be a comparatively young man nearer forty-five than fifty. He should be energetic and his job would be largely to spur the officials to progressive action and ideas. He considers this is more important than the possession of administrative experience or ability on the ground that the machine pretty well turns itself. He attaches great importance to a man who, from his contacts and position in the United Kingdom, could keep the Sudan "on the map" in high quarters in London. For this reason, therefore, the candidate in the Governor General's opinion must be sufficiently well known and *répandu* to have easy and natural access to and gain the ear of such circles. He doubts therefore that a *run of the mill* good Civil Servant or Colonial Office Governor would meet the case. He is not convinced that a soldier is required or is necessarily the best choice. He would exclude neither a sailor nor an airman nor a civilian. He thinks that among Foreign Service officers might be found the kind of man he is looking for.[2] But he feels strongly that, in view of the importance of continuity, the candidate should be prepared to spend a long period and finish out his public career in the Sudan which means that he should not regard the post as a stepping stone, that he should be comparatively young (because he should not stay in the Sudan beyond sixty) and that he should have a sense of mission.

Huddleston comments that the four above-mentioned soldiers are the suggestions of Sir E. Bridges[3] and that the Military Secretary might have other names to suggest. But he is most anxious to avoid the risk of anyone being appointed mainly from the point of view of finding a post for a deserving officer.

If Huddleston's criteria, which seem eminently sensible and even desirable, are accepted, names which occur to me from my limited acquaintance in the United Kingdom as worth considering are Ian Jacob[4] or Roger Makins.[5] But you will be able to think of many others, no doubt.

I am sending a copy of this letter strictly personally to Huddleston.

Minutes on 59

The Governor General is, quite frankly, being a little *exigeant*. One would indeed need a 'sense of mission' to take this job on at the age of 45 with the prospect of remaining to age 60 (as opposed to entering the Sudan service at 22 with the prospect of a pension at 48) and, maybe, of being summarily displaced by a Sudanese! It would be

---

[2] Marginal note by Scrivener: 'Fancy that!'

[3] Cabinet secretary, 1938–1946.

[4] Lt-Gen Sir Ian Jacob, served in Egypt, 1936–1938; military assistant seceretary to War Cabinet, 1939–1946; retired 1946; subsequently director-general of BBC, 1952–1960.

[5] Serving in the FO from 1928, Makins was an assistant under-secretary of state in 1947 and deputy under-secretary of state, 1948–1952. He was UK ambassador in Washington, 1952–1956.

deceiving a candidate to suggest that he will have any 'mission' other than that of transferring power to Sudanese who are probably ill-developed to exercise them, with the added complication that British influence in Egypt will (in view of recent developments) tend to be a steadily diminishing factor. And, *par desous* [sic, dessus] *le marché* the candidate must be able to gain the ear of 'high quarters in London' whatever they may be. All in all, it strikes me that it is in political, rather [than] in service or civil service circles, that we must continue to search, that is if we are to continue it and not go for General Scobie, who is the favourite at the moment. But would Mr. Chapman-Andrews kindly say whether he knows of a suitable Foreign Service candidate, with an urge to leave diplomacy for 'Sudanisation'?

P.S.
27.4.46

On the point whether a member of the Foreign Service can be made available for this post my feeling is that our own needs are so great at the present time that we cannot spare a really good man and nothing less would fill the bill.[6] . . . I must say I share the Governor-General's misgivings about having a soldier in this post at present. You want someone who can command the respect of the Sudanese, however, and who can goad the Sudan Political Service to more rapid progress towards Sudanisation. . . .

E.A.C.A.
27.4.46

[6] Marginal note by Scrivener: 'I agree'.

60 FO 371/53252, no 1824 22 Apr 1946

[Future of the Sudan]: despatch no 546 from Sir R Campbell to Mr Bevin, relaying Sir H Huddleston's views on the treaty revision, consultation of the Sudanese, and Sudanisation

With reference to my telegram No. 702, I have the honour to submit a record of my discussions with the Governor General of the Sudan at Wadi Halfa on April 13th. The record has been arranged to show the main subjects touched upon in the conversations.

2. *Treaty revision*
The Governor General said that the clause about the Sudan in the British draft of the new Treaty was ideal from the point of view of the Sudan Government. The Sudanese would, however, be disappointed because it contained no provision for consultation of them. It was true that your statement in the House of Commons,[1] that the Sudanese would be consulted before there was any change in their status, implied that if, as was suggested in the British draft Treaty, there was to be no change in the status of the Sudan, then there was no need for consultation. The Sudanese mind was however not logical enough to appreciate this point.

3. This led to a discussion of the best means by which any *consultation of the Sudanese* should be carried out. The Governor General admitted that any enquiry by the Sudan Government alone would be suspect to the Egyptians and he said that the

[1] See 54.

Sudan Government would not object to an enquiry by a Commission from outside the Sudan, perhaps something on the lines of the Mandatory Commission which visited Iraq and which consisted of Lord Lugard, a Belgian, a Turk and one other member. Such a Commission would not be able to do its job inside three months and for climatic reasons it would be best for it to wait until October. Sir H. Huddleston thought that in general the Sudanese would be content if they had free access to the Commission when it came.

4. I said that the Egyptians would probably agree that consultation must necessarily take time but they would want an Egyptian member on the Commission. The Governor General did not demur.

5. The Governor General said that, in his view, Sidky Pasha was not really interested in the Sudan problem which, in all cases, was brought forward for political purposes by the opposition. Egypt's prime interest in the Sudan was in the Nile Waters, and from this point of view the present arrangement suited them well, since without the internal security provided by the Sudan Government the Egyptians would be unable to work their water schemes in the Sudan. The Governor General agreed that we must do what we could to help the Egyptian Government to reach an acceptable solution over the Sudan.

6. It was agreed that the procedure for consultation would have to be worked out in concert with the Egyptian Government.

7. I then put the case for accelerated *Sudanisation* as explained in my telegrams Nos. 65[2] to Khartoum and 662 to you.

The Governor General recognised the force of these arguments, but dwelt at some length on the practical difficulties of Sudanisation at the higher levels, which were as follows:—

(a) There existed Sudanese who could "hold down" responsible jobs, but in present circumstances this was not enough; the Sudan Government had just embarked on an important development scheme and there were few or no Sudanese capable of carrying out the additional functions which this demanded, including the training of junior officials for the expansion involved in the Government's activities.

(b) Putting in Sudanese who were not up to the job of development would mean throwing more work on the already overworked British staff. In fact, the Sudan Government's development schemes had been based on the assumption that it would be necessary to increase the British staff. These schemes would be proportionately held up by Sudanisation.

(c) As the Sudan Government had already pointed out, drastic Sudanisation would undermine the faith of the British personnel. The effect on them of appointments made for political reasons and not on grounds of efficiency would be serious, in fact they would be like the effects of the same policy if applied to the Foreign Service, as was emphasized by Mr. McNeil in his speech in the recent debate on the Foreign Service.[3]

(d) Moreover, as already pointed out, the Sudan Government did not want to create a Sudanese bureaucracy, but wished to proceed more slowly by strengthening the local authorities.

---

[2] See 57.

[3] Marginal note by Bevin: 'Rot'.

(e) Another point already made by the Sudan Government was that to promote the good young Sudanese officials, who certainly existed, over the heads of more senior Sudanese, would do more harm than good and would create widespread grievances among the section of the population now most attached to the Sudan Government.

(f) Another point which might not be appreciated was that the Sudan Government were under a great disadvantage in so far as all enterprise in the Sudan is run or sponsored by the Government. The Sudanese tended to grumble, seeing the vast budget of the Sudan Government and the large number of foreign experts employed. What they did not appreciate was that, owing to this arrangement, they had been saved from the very much worse evil of foreign concession-hunters.

(g) Another serious difficulty was the educational one. The Sudanese were most interested in what would be done in the next five years. This was however just the most difficult period during which the Sudan Government would be shortest of teachers. The training of teachers was a long business and education was a field in which it was supremely difficult to meet suddenly increased demands. The Sudan Government's teachers' training college at Bakht er Ruda had in fact only been started in 1930. The Sudan was suffering now from the errors of the educational policy of the 1920s, when higher education had been at a discount owing to the fear of creating a number of "failed B.As.". Moreover, it was most desirable that Sudanese destined for responsible positions should do a course of study in the United Kingdom, but for this it was necessary to reach a high educational level first. Another serious limiting factor was the need to learn classical Arabic. The Sudan Government had however a large educational programme on hand.

8. Generally speaking, the Governor General felt that the Sudan Government had gone as quickly as possible. Three Sudanese members had recently been taken on to the Sudan Government's Sudanisation Committee. The trouble was that the Sudan Government's measures were unspectacular and that no committee could produce results at once.

9. I took note of these points, but urged that the Sudan Government would, all the same, be able to come out very soon with a phased programme of Sudanisation.

10. The Governor General said that he hoped the Sudanese Delegation in Cairo would soon be split by its internal feuds.[4] The Delegation was already ceasing to be news in the Sudan. I emphasised how important it was in my view to cut the ground from under their feet by showing, through Sudanisation and by other means, that the Sudan Government really was in a hurry to bring the Sudan to the point of self-government. The Governor General expressed the view of the Sudan Government that serious and moderate educated opinion in the Sudan would not be impressed by the Delegation. The Delegation themselves would never be satisfied by any proposals which the Sudan Government could introduce. The point was to carry moderate educated opinion with the Government.

11. I am very grateful to Sir H. Huddleston, to whom I am sending a copy of this despatch, for having made possible this most valuable exchange of views.

[4] A Sudanese United Front delegation, led by Ismail al-Azhari, was then in Cairo meeting with various Egyptian politicians. It had issued two declarations insisting on the right of the Sudanese to be represented at the treaty negotiations, the second qualifying the first after adverse reaction in Egypt (see despatch no 533 from Campbell to Bevin, 18 Apr 1946, FO 371/53252, no 1816).

61 FO 371/53252, no 1743 23 Apr 1946

[Political situation in the Sudan]: circular letter by J W Robertson to all governors and heads of departments

The political situation seems to have eased a little as far as can be judged. This is due to two things:—

(a) His Excellency's declaration to the Advisory Council on 17.4.46 with its estimated date for self-Government, and its expressed aim of eventual independence.
(b) The realisation by the United Parties deputation in Cairo that the Egyptians do not wish to give the Sudanese self-Government or independence.

The pressure put upon them by the Egyptians to withdraw their declaration of Sudanese aims has shewn the Egyptians in their true light.[1] A number of the deputation have returned to the Sudan, and it may well be that most of them will turn to the Sudan Government, and try to co-operate with us in hope of accelerating the period quoted in His Excellency's speech.

His Excellency stated that the joint Committee set up to enquire into the Sudanisation programme would be required to produce detailed plans in defined stages and His Excellency has also called a conference to enquire into methods of associating the Sudanese more closely in the Government of their country. The conference is a representative one, and includes British Officials, Members of the Advisory Council, other leading Sudanese officials and non-officials, and representatives of the Congress and the Political parties.

The first meeting will take place on Wednesday April 24th. under my Chairmanship. I have heard no reports yet of how this conference has been greeted by Sudanese opinion generally, but members of the Advisory Council seemed to welcome the proposal. I imagine we shall deal with the following:—

(a) the future development of the Advisory Council—its powers and size, representation, elections etc.,
(b) similarly with Province Councils,
(c) the composition of central Government Boards and committees,
(d) the establishment of consultative and advisory boards, representing the staff in departments.

The Sudan Government has had its well-established Sudanisation policy and the British Government has in the past supported the aims and intentions of this policy and its proposed pace. Recently, however, the Cairo Embassy and Foreign Office have pressed the Sudan Government strongly to accelerate the process, chiefly on the grounds that too much insistence on Western standards and high performance would drive the Sudanese intelligentsia towards Egypt, and that unless a much more rapid pace was adopted, it would be impossible to keep out Egyptian officials and influence. His Excellency has now received an assurance from the Foreign Office that

---

[1] See 60, note 4. By 20 April the delegation had split over the issue of Sudan's independence from Egypt and the appropriate response to be made to Huddleston's address to the Advisory Council (see 58) (inward telegram no 186 (saving) from Campbell to FO, 12 May 1946, FO 371/53252, no 2176).

in implementing a bold policy of Sudanisation, he is carrying out the wishes of His Majesty's Government. You should make this known confidentially to British officials, who may seem worried by the present policy of Sudanisation.

In all this political hotch-potch the position of the South has not yet been defined, and it is probable that some statement of the Sudan Government's views on the future of the South will have to be given soon. The policy on which we have been working, and which has the approval of the British Government is as follows:—

> "Our obvious duty is to push ahead as fast as we can with their (i.e. the Southern Sudanese) economic and educational development on African and Negroid lines, and not upon the Middle Eastern and Arab lines of progress which are suitable for the northern Sudan. It is only by economic and educational development that these people can be equipped to stand up for themselves in the future, whether their lot be eventually cast with the Northern Sudan or with East Africa (or partly with each). In the former event they would have to resist as a large progressive and cohesive minority the still instinctively predatory attitude of the more sophisticated Arab north, and in the latter they would have great strides to take to catch up with the more rapidly advancing territories of East Africa."[2]

To me the South seems daily to become more tied up economically and socially with the North. More Southerners are coming North, and more Northerners are taking an interest in the South. We have also the nationalistic feeling of the Northern Sudanese to cope with. So the solution of this problem will be no easy one.

---

[2] This was a restatement of the 1930 Southern Policy, issued by J W Robertson in an internal despatch on 4 Aug 1945.

62 FO 371/53371, no 1658 — 30 Apr 1946

[Nile Waters: Lake Albert dam]: letter (reply) from P S Scrivener to A B Cohen (CO), drawing attention to international treaty obligations regarding the possible construction of a dam in Uganda

Thank you for your letter No. 40146/46 of the 9th April transmitting a copy of a saving telegram dated the 27th March from the Governor of Uganda concerning the Lake Albert Reservoir scheme.[1]

While we fully appreciate the Governor's reasons for opposing the construction of a dam in or near the Protectorate, we consider, and hope you will agree, that the international aspect of this problem makes it quite impossible for us to present a flat *non-possumus* to the Egyptian Government. For the last quarter of a century the construction of at least a major work at Lake Albert has been a more or less accepted plan. Moreover we would point out that paragraph 4 (v) of the Nile Waters Agreement of 1929 (Treaty series No. 17 (1929) q.v.) provides that, "His Majesty's Government in the United Kingdom shall use their good offices so that the carrying out of surveys, measurements, studies *and works* of the nature mentioned in the two preceding

---

[1] See 55.

paragraphs is facilitated by the Governments of these regions under British-influence". Again in regard to the Governor's point (d), paragraph 4(ii) of the agreement makes "irrigation or power works or measures" on the Nile or on the lakes from which it flows expressly subject to the "previous agreement of the Egyptian Government". In fact it looks as if the Governor had ignored the agreement altogether.

But this is not to maintain that the Governor's objections are not of sufficient validity to make some modification of the present scheme essential and we consider in the circumstances that His Majesty's Ambassador in Cairo should inform the Egyptian Government officially that a scheme at Lake Albert in the scale at present contemplated raises internal political, social and economic issues of a very serious order for the Government of Uganda, who as we anticipated are unable to take a final decision on the questions propounded by the Egyptian Government without further information and detailed discussions. His Majesty's Government suggest, therefore, that a conference attended by representatives of Egypt, the Sudan, Uganda and the Belgian Congo should be convened as soon as possible, and that all the relevant data should be prepared for submission to this conference.

May we have your views urgently on this proposal?

I am sending copies of the correspondence, unofficially at this stage, to the Embassy in Cairo.

63 FO 371/53371, no 2170 15 May 1946

[Nile waters: Lake Albert dam]: letter (reply) from A B Cohen to P S Scrivener on the need to obtain further data on the area under consideration for the proposed dam site

Please refer to correspondence ending with my letter of the 3rd May about the Lake Albert scheme.

The Governor of Uganda has now replied to our telegram No. 148[1] of which a copy was sent to you. It is clear that he is very much concerned about the project which, he feels, overlooks the interests of the people of Uganda, which we are of course under solemn obligations to protect. He does not dissent from the view that, from the point of view of tactics, the Egyptian Government should not be met with a blank refusal but he is very much opposed to a conference in the near future.

There are a number of points which require to be weighed. In the first place, as MacGregor pointed out in his memorandum (a copy of which was enclosed with your letter of the 13th November to Footman[2]), it is hardly reasonable to expect the Uganda Government to consider the proposal until the Egyptian Government have advanced their ideas in a more definite form to enable all the implications of the project to be examined. Moreover there does not exist even a remotely accurate survey from which the limits of the area likely to be inundated could he gauged. In the absence of statistical data it is quite impossible to make any reliable estimate of

---

[1] In which the contents of 62 were summarised.

[2] C W F Footman, Colonial Service, East Africa, from 1930; seconded to EAG conference, 1942; to CO, 1943.

the probable effects, (social, economical, hydrological and climatic) of the proposed inundation. In short the whole scheme needs consideration by an expert in hydrology and irrigation and the Government of Uganda would be at a very serious disadvantage if it were asked to partake in a conference without expert guidance.

The Uganda Government is indeed in no position as yet to take part in a conference such as has been suggested and the Governor thinks it essential that this should be deferred, so that he may have time to collect essential *data* and to obtain the expert advice. In our view his request is a reasonable one and, bearing in mind the issues at stake for Uganda, we do feel that the Uganda Government should have adequate time and facilities to examine the whole question.

The Governor has suggested that the Egyptian Government should be informed that if they will set out their project in more definite form on the lines suggested above, the Uganda Government will forthwith examine the project from the point of view of the possibility of devising measures to safeguard local interests (vide article (iv) of the 1929 Agreement). For this purpose it will be necessary to assemble special technical staff and for the project to be studied in all its aspects. He further suggests that when this preliminary study has been completed and the economic, social and hydrological *data* collected a technical commission consisting of representatives of Egypt, the Sudan, Belgian Congo and Uganda (and possibly also Kenya and Tanganyika) should be appointed to report on the project.

It is clear that the Governor has given a great deal of thought and attention to the matter. He has personally visited some of the area likely to be affected and we feel that his suggestions and warnings should be heeded. Accordingly we must strongly support the Governor's views and express the hope that any communication which it may now be proposed to make to the Egyptian Government may be couched on the lines which he has suggested. We are the more strongly in favour of this view because we feel that if consideration of the project can be deferred for a period it will be possible for the Governor to obtain the expert advice without which it is virtually impossible to see where a scheme of this magnitude is leading.

Perhaps it might be useful if we could have a word about this either by telephone, or Footman or I could come over and see you.

64 PREM 8/1388/1 July 1946

'Anglo–Egyptian treaty negotiations, position on 4th July 1946': note by Lord Stansgate to Mr Attlee. *Appendix* 'C' [Extract]
***Minutes* by T L Rowan[1] and Attlee**

[By June 5 it was decided to deal with the Sudan in a separate protocol, as this wish of the Egyptian government also coincided with the desires of HMG (CP(46)219, 5 June 1946, 'Revision of Anglo–Egyptian treaty. Memorandum by the Secretary of state for foreign affairs'). Discussions of a preliminary draft of the protocol were held between Campbell and Sidqi (inward telegram no 1121 from Campbell to FO, 20 June 1946, PREM 8/1388/1). Stansgate left this note with Attlee prior to his return to Egypt to resume negotiations.]

---

[1] One of the Attlee's private secretaries.

It may be useful before leaving to resume the Anglo–Egyptian Treaty Negotiations to review the position on the main points outstanding. . . .

(c) *The Sudan*
In a draft Protocol on the Sudan, which we have communicated to the Egyptian Delegation, we have proposed to set up a Joint Anglo–Egyptian Commission to make recommendations on the future of Sudan in full consultation with the Sudanese peoples, and we have stated as basic principles of our policy that we intend to aim at self government for the Sudanese and to let them decide, when they reach this stage, on their relationship with Egypt. This theoretically is a reasonably unassailable position, but in view of the strength of feeling on the subject of Egyptian sovereignty which has not only always manifested itself in previous Treaty negotiations but is known to exist today, it is doubtful if we can hope to secure the acceptance of our proposals without considerable difficulty. . . .

Appendix 'C' to 64

. . . In past Treaty negotiations with the Egyptians, the question of sovereignty over the Sudan has always been a thorny one. The Egyptians have always claimed sole sovereignty; we have never admitted it. No agreement on the point has ever been reached; the best we have ever been able to do is to agree to shelve the issue. In the 1930 negotiations for example which broke down on the Sudan question, it is noteworthy that a direct claim by Mr. Henderson[2] to joint sovereignty provoked the 'loudest protestations to date' from the Egyptians and that, in winding up the negotiations, Nahas Pasha said 'The Sudan was sacred to Egypt and Egypt was sovereign there'.

On the other hand, in modern conditions, our policy of insisting that the Sudanese peoples themselves must determine their relationship with Egypt, including the question of sovereignty, seems quite unassailable and this, combined with the fact that Sidky Pasha seems genuinely anxious to conclude a Treaty, may enable us to get round this awkward question once more with a protocol on the lines of our own draft. Sidky's willingness to postpone a direct conflict on the issue may be indicated by his recent suggestion to H.M. Minister that, in place of a Joint Commission, a purely Egyptian fact finding commission should visit the Sudan in the first instance. This is a suggestion to which we presumably cannot agree.

There is a possibility, however, that the pressure of public opinion may make it impossible for the Egyptians to conclude a Treaty of Alliance with us without, at the same time, negotiating a settlement of the Sudan question satisfactory to themselves. In other words we may have to choose between receding on the Sudan issue or not having a Treaty of Alliance. This however can only be faced when the time comes.[3]

---

[2] A Henderson (Lab), S of S for foreign affairs, 1929–1931.

[3] The last two sentences are marked in the margin by a blue pencilled 'X'.

Minutes on 64

P.M.
This is no doubt a very obvious point, but the phrasing of the last sentences of the Appendix on the Sudan is very loose. Is not the position that if there is a breakdown, then the existing treaty continues. One knows all the objections to this, but the passage now reads as though we have no alternative open if the Egyptians wish to force us into doing what we consider wrong about the Sudan. But as I see it we have an alternative—though perhaps not a very happy one.

T.L.R.
[nd]

Yes literally, but practically the alternative is no use.

C.R.A.
5.7.46.

65 PREM 8/1388/1 23 July 1946

[Anglo–Egyptian treaty negotiations: the Sudan protocol]: inward telegram no 33 from Lord Stansgate to Mr Attlee,[1] reporting Sidqi Pasha's initial reaction to the British draft of the Sudan protocol [Extract]

[Prior to leaving London it had been agreed that Stansgate would leave discussion of the Sudan protocol until after agreement had been reached on the treaty articles and the evacuation protocol. On resumption of talks the Egyptian delegation presented its own draft of the protocol but agreed to leave it for later discussion (inward telegram no 1 from Stansgate to Attlee, 10 July 1946, PREM 8/1388/1).]

... 7. The Sudanese protocol. We then passed to a consideration of a Sudanese protocol which Lufti [sic][2] had clearly been determined to raise. I suggested that assuming that it were agreed that negotiations should take place surely a short statement to this effect would satisfy all parties. They said they had waited long for our comment on their draft. We said we had not yet had your final instructions but we could say at once as the Ambassador had already explained to Sidki Pasha that reference to Egyptian sovereignty presented serious difficulty. Lufti [sic] and Sidki Pasha then went into a long explanation of Egyptian thesis that there could be no doubt whatever regarding the sovereignty of the Egyptian Crown over the Sudan. This they said they could document with papers knee deep. When asked what they meant by consulting the Sudanese they said that they had no desire to make any profit out of Sudan, in fact Egypt had already spent vastly in money and treasure on the Sudan. All they wanted to do was to find out how the Sudan wished administration to be carried out and what were in fact the practical steps which would be taken to accelerate their progress. There could however be no question whatever of asking the Sudanese their opinion on question of sovereignty which was

[1] Bevin was then in Paris attending the peace conference, and was kept informed about the progress of negotiations through the FO.
[2] Ahmad Lufti al-sayyid, Egyptian foreign minister.

[gp. undec: ?in fact] already in the King's, i.e. King of Darfour Senaar and Kordofan [?gp. omitted]. We suggested that from everyone's point of view it seemed advisable not to raise this question specifically but leave it as it had been left. They said that there was only one basis on which they could carry on negotiations and that was the basis of fact as they saw it. There would be no difference in the actual situation. We should continue to administer the country. They both emphasised the embarrassing position they would be in, if they had to tell their colleagues that no agreement had yet been reached on a protocol dealing with the Sudan. They emphasised that from their point of view the points of importance in the treaty were evacuation of troops and unity of the Nile Valley. I asked Lufti [sic] what precisely was meant by unity of the Nile Valley and he replied Egyptian sovereignty of course.

8. Conclusion. . . . The question of the Sudan . . . is largely a question of national emotion and amour propre; further complicated by personal desires of the King. This is the first time that this problem has been seriously discussed and it is difficult to estimate the chances of the Egyptians agreeing to a compromise. Whatever these chances are they are at the moment unfortunately prejudiced by general despondency and diminution of goodwill which has resulted from the line we have taken on other main treaty issues.

9. The very firm stand we have taken upset Sidki Pasha and Lufti [sic] who described it as a serious step backward in the negotiations. Sidki Pasha is seeing his delegation on Saturday and his account to them of this interview may precipitate a critical situation. It is therefore urgently necessary that we should at the earliest possible moment decide what line we intend to pursue. . . . We recommend therefore that we should be authorised:— . . .

(c) to endeavour to obtain Egyptian agreement to our Sudan protocol. We fully realise that His Majesty's Government cannot agree to the present Egyptian demands regarding the Sudan as set out in their protocol. . . .

66 PREM 8/1388/1, CM 76(46)7 — 1 Aug 1946

[Anglo–Egyptian treaty negotiations: the Sudan Protocol]: Cabinet decision to resist Egyptian claims to sovereignty over the Sudan [Extract]

The Cabinet were informed that . . . the Chiefs of Staff consider it essential that a firm stand should be made on the question of the Sudan.

The Prime Minister . . . agreed that a firm stand should be made with regard to the Sudan. It would, of course, be open to the Egyptian Government to make a unilateral declaration on this matter, but we should resist the inclusion in the protocol of any words admitting the sovereignty of the Egyptian Crown over the Sudan. . . .

The Cabinet:—

Agreed that the British Delegation . . . should resist the inclusion in the Sudan protocol of any provision implying recognition of Egyptian sovereignty over the Sudan.

67 FO 371/5325, no 3385 1 Aug 1946

[Anglo–Egyptian treaty negotiations: the Sudan protocol]: inward telegram no 43 from Lord Stansgate to Mr Attlee, listing options for resolving the issue of Egyptian claims to sovereignty over the Sudan

As you know question of the Sudan protocol is now being pressed by the Egyptians and the issue must be faced that in the near future even if we reach a satisfactory compromise on other points in the dispute on the Treaty and on the evacuation protocol it will probably reach a major obstacle to the completion of our task.

2. The objects we are seeking to secure in the Sudan as defined by the Foreign Secretary in his statement on March 21st [sic 26th][1] are, firstly true welfare of Sudan which we have always insisted can only be secured by maintaining the existing stable and [grp. undec.] administration; and secondly gradual build up towards eventual self government. We are also pledged to agree to no change in status of the Sudan as a result of these negotiations until the Sudanese have been consulted through constitutional channels.

3. This position is entirely in line with the letter of United Nations Charter and the Egyptians would find it difficult to justify before the world a rupture of the Treaty negotiations by contesting it.

4. The major difficulty will I think arise on their claim to specifically recognise Egyptian sovereignty over the Sudan, a claim which they have sustained through all past treaty negotiations and which the present delegation is publicly and by the terms of the Senate resolution committed to sustain in the present negotiations.

5. The Prime Minister in a recent conversation with the Ambassador after a long discourse on sovereignty was prepared to admit that Egypt is not qualified for and does not wish for a larger share in the government of the Sudan. He said too that they have no wish to draw profit from the country. But he and his delegation do press with extreme fervour and conviction for recognition of Egyptian sovereignty even though such recognition would, they say, in no way affect the present position. The King is of course behind the delegation in their claim and it is not one on which he would welcome a compromise.

6. I can conceive a situation arising therefore in which the Egyptians would agree to our basic principles as stated in paragraph 2 and to the appointment of commission which we have suggested as the best machinery for consulting the Sudanese themselves but would break on the sole question of recognition of the sovereignty. They might, even though they would do it most reluctantly, and I personally think it doubtful (see my telegram No. 39), admit that the Sudan should have an ultimate right of secession. Vital issue would then be confined to recognition of Egyptian sovereignty in the interim period until the Sudanese are able to decide.

7. The difficulties about the unqualified recognition of Egyptian sovereignty are:—

(a) It prejudices an issue which ought to be decided ultimately by the Sudanese themselves:

---

[1] See 54.

(b) This fact would be seized on by the Sudanese and almost certainly cause trouble in the Sudan. It would undoubtedly be strongly resented by all the UMMA party whose avowed aim is to establish an independent Sudan which will then herself decide on her relationship with Egypt and Great Britain. It would probably also be resented by some of the Ashigga party, who are not entirely satisfied with the whole hog Egyptian policy of their leaders. The rest of the Ashigga would no doubt accept recognition of Egyptian sovereignty which has already been publicly affirmed by Azhari since UMMA party broke away from the Delegation. Their reason for accepting is probably that they hope it will provide them with a lever for getting us out of the Sudan.
(c) It might be regarded by the Sudanese as an indication of declining British influence and would therefore increase the difficulties of administration.
(d) In spite of assurances in paragraph 5 of the above it might well prove to be the thin edge of the wedge for attempts by Egyptians to increase their influence in and their share in the administration of the Sudan.
(e) It would be difficult to defend at home.

On the other hand it must be admitted we have not since 1922 publicly recognised Egypt's sovereignty. There is considerable legal and historical justification for the Egyptian claim which juridically might be awkward if the issue were referred to U.N.O.

8. There seem to be only three solutions:—

(a) A protocol on the lines of our existing draft i.e. agreement set [grp. undec.] in your telegram and meanwhile to maintain existing arrangements based on Article 11 of 1936 Treaty.
(b) A simple deferment of the issue by agreeing to enter on subsequent negotiations at an unspecified date and meanwhile to maintain the existing arrangements. Such a bare agreement to shelve the issue would no doubt disappoint the Sudanese who are expecting the Treaty to include some indication of their advancement [grp. undec.] self-government or at least a re-affirmation of our intention to consult them about their future.

If this position emerged therefore it would no doubt be necessary for the Sudan Government to give assurances that there was no intention of delaying the withdrawing of machinery recently set up for Sudanisation and the association of Sudanese with the administration.

In either of these solutions the question of sovereignty would remain as dealt with in Article 11 of 1936 Treaty, i.e. the agreement would be without prejudice to the question of sovereignty "and on (sic ? in) the present form this will not satisfy Egypt.

(c) The incorporation into either (a) or (b) above of some gesture in the direction of Egypt's sovereignty. If Egyptian delegation as is possible are determined to break on this question it will be necessary to decide whether we can in the last resort agree to any compromise.

You will no doubt wish to consult the Governor-General on this point and I hesitate to make any suggestions. I wonder, however, whether the Governor-General would regard the position of the Sudan Government as compromised if we accepted some such phraseology as "pending the adoption of any new arrangements resulting from a commission or resulting from subsequent negotiations (as the case may be) Egyptian sovereignty over Sudan as at present existing remains unimpaired".

9. I will telegraph further as Sudan question develops in more detail.

It may be useful to you, however, to have this advance summary of the position.

68 PREM 8/1388/1 2 Aug 1946

[Anglo–Egyptian treaty negotiations: the Sudan protocol]: inward telegram no 44 from Lord Stansgate to Mr Attlee, on the Egyptian counter-proposals concerning the Sudan

Egyptian note delivered yesterday and sent to you by last night's air bag.

I do not propose to comment on the note of the Egyptian delegation which in its recapitulation presents various points of the negotiations in an unobjective manner and lends itself to justifiable criticism. I propose to limit myself to what appears to me the essential features of the position created by this note.

2. If His Majesty's Government are not prepared to accept Article 2 of the Egyptian draft treaty unmodified and to compromise on the period of evacuation it is clear from the note that there is no possibility at present of continuing the negotiations.

3. If His Majesty's Government are prepared to accept Article 2 of the Egyptian draft treaty and to compromise on the period of evacuation we think it should be possible to continue the negotiations on that basis and on the basis of a clarification of the Egyptian delegation's claims as detailed in its note. The claim for Egyptian sovereignty is strongest for it might be difficult to convince international opinion and any international juridical body that the Sudan was *not* under Egyptian sovereignty.

4. However the delegation's note goes beyond the claim of sovereignty. The penultimate paragraph on page 6 states that Egypt has "all the rights without any exception" on the Sudan. The second paragraph on page 7 refuses to admit our right to invoke interests of Sudanese to contest "*Unity of the Nile Valley*". The following paragraph states that it is in the interests of the Sudan to "be part of an organised state" i.e. Egypt. The following paragraph claims that Egypt is the country to which the Sudan must attach themselves since it offers them the advantages of a state having a "modern administrative organisation". These passages would be taken by any honest unsophisticated reader to suggest that the Sudan must be not only under sovereignty of Egypt but also part of administrative machine of Egypt and that the Sudanese have no right to object to this administrative unity.

5. No doubt once we began to discuss these claims Egyptian negotiators would try to attenuate these implications and perhaps suggest the administrative rôle of Egypt would be allowed to develop (? gp. omitted) local self-government. It would appear from the note however that this is not the real objective of the Egyptians, for they then propose to substitute Egyptian domination for British control in order to preclude the eventuality of an independent Sudan which they regard as dangerous to Egyptian interests particularly in the matter of water and (gp. undec. ? irrigation). Anyhow the phraseology used in this note would seem clearly to deny the Sudan the right of secession and all independence. It would be to our interest in our discussions

with the Egyptian delegation to put them into the position of denying the right of self-determination to the Sudan as, in the event of a breakdown of negotiations, we would be on the best possible wicket before international opinion and before United Nations Organisation.

6. The possibility need not be excluded that these discussions might lead the Egyptians to accept some face-saving formula regarding sovereignty in view of the fact that they had got their way as regards Article 2 and the evacuation. However the influence of King Farouk who is particularly keen on this sovereignty issue will no doubt make it difficult for Egyptian negotiators to agree to a formula which would not compromise our present administrative position in the Sudan.

7. You will no doubt think it necessary to consult the Governor General regarding the views which I have expressed in this telegram.

8. Sidki Pasha has gone to his country estate and returns to Alexandria on Monday. I have told him and the press that the Egyptian note has been forwarded to you. I would be grateful for earliest direction as to what line I am now to take.

69 PREM 8/1388/1 4 Aug 1946

[Anglo–Egyptian treaty negotiations: the Sudan protocol]: outward telegram no 30 (reply) from Mr Attlee to Lord Stansgate [Extract]

. . . We seem to be placed in the position, that, unless we give way on all points to the Egyptians, we get no Treaty. His Majesty's Government cannot conscientiously give way all round. They consider that Sidky should be faced bluntly with the outstanding feature of these negotiations, namely, the fact that since they started we have met the Egyptians on practically every issue they have raised, whereas their own response to our requests has been both slight and grudging. . . .

6. On the question of the Sudan the Cabinet stands absolutely firm. His Majesty's Government cannot compromise on this. Nor can I see anything in your No. 44[1] received since the Cabinet met which adduces any new argument in support of the Egyptian demand. The Egyptian Government can of course make a unilateral declaration on this matter; but we can accept no form of words in the protocol which admit the sovereignty of the Egyptian Crown.

[1] See 68.

70 FO 371/53254, no 3385 10 Aug 1946

[Anglo–Egyptian treaty negotiations: the Sudan protocol]: outward telegram no 43 (reply) from Mr Attlee to Lord Stansgate, on the legal issue of sovereignty

I am most grateful for the review of the Sudan problem in your telegram No. 43. It is clear from your telegram No. 44[1] and from Egyptian note that the comparative caution displayed by Sidky Pasha over this issue (paragraph 5 of your telegram No.

[1] See 68.

39) is not shared by the Delegation, whose extravagances, now that they have apparently leaked out (your telegram No. 45) may nevertheless produce a useful reaction in the Sudan itself. I do not like the formula suggested in the last sentence of paragraph 8 of your telegram No. 43[2] and my view is confirmed by the Legal Adviser.

2. The answer to the Egyptian thesis on sovereignty is given briefly in the Foreign Office minutes of which a copy was taken by you to Egypt, but a slight elaboration may be useful to you:—

(1) The question of sovereignty in relation to the Sudan is legal and theoretical. Differences of opinion on questions of sovereignty in unusual cases do not usually turn on the actual position of the territory in question, but on what the *criteria* of sovereignty are. Though sovereignty is an every-day term in international law, international lawyers seldom agree exactly on the definition of sovereignty itself. In particular there is a School A which regards the sovereign as being the owner of the ultimate title as opposed to the owner of the immediate rights of administration and a School B which holds that the sovereign is the person internationally responsible at the moment. Thus in the case of a leased territory, some lawyers hold that the sovereign is the lessor, and others that he is the lessee; yet there is no difference as to the actual position of the leased territory. In the case of the Sudan School B holds that the sovereignty is divided because the administration is divided. On the view of School A the position is more complicated and depends on

(a) Whether Egypt ever lost sovereignty over the Sudan before 1890 and
(b) If so whether the re-conquest is to be regarded as an operation to re-establish Egyptian sovereignty or to establish a new position of joint sovereignty.

(2) In the treaty under negotiation, the United Kingdom are not concerned in theoretical questions, and refuse to commit themselves to any statement in the treaty about sovereignty over the Sudan which would inevitably be misunderstood and create more political difficulties than it would solve.

(3) Consequently they are not prepared to do more than in 1936 viz. to say that nothing in the new treaty prejudices the question of sovereignty; a formula which, so far as the United Kingdom is concerned, neither admits nor denies Egyptian sovereignty and enables the Egyptians if they so desire, to say *outside the treaty* that they consider themselves the sovereigns.

(4) Our task is to deal with practical matters viz. what should be put in the treaty about the future of the Sudan, a matter of practical interest to the Sudan as well as to the United Kingdom and Egypt. We stand by our policy that the governing factors must be

(a) the interests of the Sudanese and
(b) the wishes of the Sudanese,

and are proposing machinery for ascertaining what are the wishes, and perhaps also the interests, of the Sudanese, with a view to forming a basis on which the interests of the Sudanese shall ultimately be decided.

3. Finally I might restate the last paragraph of CP(46)17 of January 18th:—[3]

---

[2] See 67.

[3] See 47.

"His Majesty's Government consider, therefore, that any discussion of the modification of Article 11 of the 1936 treaty should be postponed until the Sudanese have been consulted and have made known their own wishes. The procedure by which this consultation can best take place is being examined by the Governor General, who will be available to discuss it with the Egyptian Government if required. But His Majesty's Government again wish to emphasise that the facts of the situation and modern international doctrine render academic, in their opinion, any prior discussion of the vexed question of sovereignty over the Sudan".

4. We have not yet thought it necessary to consult the Governor General, but we are in touch with his staff who are being kept informed.

71 FO 371/53254, no 3525 10 Aug 1946

[Umma Party demand for independence for the Sudan]: despatch no 927 from Sir R Campbell to Mr Bevin. *Annexe:* letter from Abdallah Bey Khalil[1] to Mr Attlee and Sidqi Pasha (19 July 1946) [Extract]

[As early as May the Umma Party had asked for clarifications to Huddleston's April address to the Advisory Council (see 58), requesting a reassurance that reference to 'the Sudan' included both Northern and Southern Sudan, a reduction in the twenty year period for achieving self-government, and a pronouncement that 'Self Governing Sudan'meant a 'fully independent Sudan with complete Sovereignty'. They also proposed that the Advisory Council become a general council for the entire country, and that the Sudan Administration Conference be transformed into 'the Sudan Independence Conference' ('Note by the Umma Party to the Sudan Government', 9 May 1948, FO 371/53257, no 4075). The civil secretary (letter from Robertson to secretary, Abdallah Khalil, 14 July 1946, FO 371/53257, no 4075) eventually reassured them on the matter of maintaining the Sudan within its geographical limits, conceded that the twenty year period could be shortened (or extended), depending on the availability of competent and experienced Sudanese, but insisted that 'self-government' did not equal independence. He left the creation of a general council for the whole Sudan to the Administration Conference to decide and rejected the proposal to transform the conference into an independence convention. Abdallah Khalil's letter to the British and Egyptian prime minister's followed his receipt of the civil secretary's response.]

I have the honour to transmit to you herewith in original a letter addressed to the Prime Ministers of the United Kingdom and Egypt by the Secretary of the Sudanese Umma Party, together with a translation.

2. It will be seen that the theme of the letter is the Sudanese right, for reasons both of history and of the standard of civilisation the Sudan has now attained, to complete independence of the condominium. The letter of course shows no gratitude for the part played by ourselves in bringing the Sudan to the level which she has now reached; this need be no surprise to us. But the letter is useful as evidence that an affirmation of Egyptian sovereignty at this moment, as proposed by the Egyptian Government, would be bitterly resented by many Sudanese, and if the occasion arises I propose to refer to it in this connection in discussion with the Egyptian delegation. I am also suggesting to the Sudan Government that the Secretary of the Umma party might be encouraged to give the letter some publicity not only in the Sudan but in

[1] Secretary general, Umma Party.

Egypt as a counterblast to the repeated pronouncements by the leader of the Sudanese delegation in Egypt in favour of the unity of the Nile Valley.

3. I would venture to suggest that the Acting Governor-General might be authorised to send the Secretary of the Umma party a simple acknowledgement. . . .

Annexe to 71

We claim that we, the Sudanese, have a legal and moral right to independence. From the dawn of history up to the last century we have been independent. Neither Egypt nor Great Britain had any claims to sovereignty over us. In 1820 Mohammed Ali the Turkish ruler of Egypt, acting in the Turkish interest, invaded us in order to exploit us by taking our natural riches, and by selling our youth into slavery, and bondage; the response to the call by those Islamic leaders who formed the pioneers to his invading army paved the way to an easy victory for them. From that time until our liberation by the Mahdi, the Turkish flag flew over the Sudan, and under its shadow flourished one of the most oppressive, inhuman, and corrupt regimes in the whole history of mankind. In 1885 we regained our freedom and for fourteen years we were completely independent, acknowledging no master except our own rulers. These fourteen years of freedom erased any claims based on the sixty five years of misrule that had gone before. The rights based on conquest terminate when that conquest is turned into defeat. As Halleck says (International Law Ch.33) "The rights of conquest are derived from force alone. They begin with possession and they end in the loss of possession".

In 1898 the Sudan was invaded for a second time, but on this occasion the invading forces were not Turkish troops, but a joint force made up of British and Egyptians. The present existing administrative rights of the two powers in the Sudan are based on this conquest. Neither Britain nor Egypt had any rights prior to 1898. For reasons connected with the entry of another power, France, into the Sudan, an attempt was made to picture the "Reconquest" as the suppression of a rebellion in some of the outlying Egyptian Provinces, but this pretention was merely a political manoeuvre unfounded on any tenable basis in International Law. That Lord Cromer was the first to recognise this is shown by his statement in 1901, when in a speech at Khartoum he said (Translated), "Both the Egyptians and the British are strangers . . . We aim at a true Sudanese Parliamentary Representation, and it is possible for such to be created." At no time since the conquest has Great Britain claimed the Sudan as part of the British Empire; neither has Egypt treated our country as though it were part of the Kingdom of Egypt. On the contrary, the British have consistently rejected the suggestion that the Sudan should be treated in the same way as the dependencies in the Colonial Empire, and the Egyptian Government, on their part, have gone so far as to plead before the Mixed Courts in Egypt that the Sudan Government was constitutionally an autonomous Government absolutely separate from the Egyptian Government. The court upheld this plea and found that by the 1899 agreements a new state was established in the Sudan distinct from and independent of Egypt. (Bencini et Quistas contre le Gouvernement egyptien et le Gouvernement du Soudan. vide Macmichael's "Anglo–Egyptian Sudan".)[2]

---

[2] H MacMichael, *The Anglo–Egyptian Sudan* (London, 1933) pp 65–66.

It is clear, therefore, that from the beginning of the Condominium Rule, the Sudan has been treated as a separate and detached territory over which the two condominium powers separately hold administrative rights not prejudicing its sovereignty. (Vide Clause 1, Article 11 of the 1936 Anglo–Egyptian Treaty which reads "Nothing in this article prejudices the question of sovereignty over the Sudan".)

The part played by the Sudan during the recent World War represented the people's maximum possible contribution both militarily and economically. This was duly acknowledged by His Excellency the Governor-General in his message to the people of the Sudan on victory day when His Excellency said:—

> "The Sudan can look back with pride on the part she has played in this war. She has acted throughout with the courage, the orderliness and the obedience for which Sir Stewart Symes called in 1940. She has never doubted the path to victory. In 1940 her forces stood valiantly, with their British and Indian comrades, in the path of the invader and then pressed forward with them to share in the glorious victories in Abyssinia and in North Africa. Always they have brought honour to the Sudan by their valour and their discipline. At home the Sudan assisted in the vital task of guarding the African lines of communication and gave unswerving support to the military forces who used her soil. Her citizens made many generous contributions to the effort of war, and endured steadfastly the restrictions and shortages which are the inevitable accompaniment of war. Her cultivators worked with faithful persistence. Her merchants have loyally obeyed the demands made upon them. Her officials have shouldered without complaint new and heavy burdens. Her war time economy has won praise outside the borders of the Sudan. This is indeed a proud record and let us remember it with full hearts."

His Britannic Majesty King George VI also expressed his appreciation of the efforts by the people of the Sudan in his message which read:—

> "Some years have passed since you swept the enemy from your frontiers in the early stages of the conflict which has proved so disastrous for the aggressors. Now the seal has been set on African and European victory and I am deeply conscious of the great contribution in the field and at home which has been made by your country throughout the whole period of the war."

It is unnecessary to mention that the contribution by the Sudan to the war effort for the cause of Democracy which resulted in complete victory over the Axis powers, is in fact a direct contribution to the United Nations, to Great Britain and to Egypt. By stopping the forces of Italy on the East African front, the Sudan Defence Force have defended the rear of Egypt and the British lines of communication. The participation of our forces in the battle of Alamein is but another service rendered to both Egypt and Great Britain at the darkest phases of the War. Last and not least the food stuffs and livestock offered by the Sudan to help easing the food situation in Egypt. In rendering all these services we have not for a moment doubted both Great Britain and Egypt's appreciation of our efforts.

Your Excellency,

In view of the above and of the present state of advancement in the Sudan in the military, economic, cultural and social fields, a state which surpasses levels attained in a number of the Middle East Countries, the people of the Sudan feel it is high time for them to claim complete independence of their country.

The Umma Party regard it their solemn duty to ask for the cancellation of the present condominium rule and the establishment of an independent Sudan enjoying complete sovereignty over the territory lying within its present geographical limits.

The Umma Party, fully alive of your sincerity to discharge loyally those obligations to which your Government have committed themselves by International Agreements, claim an unrefutable right trusting that you will realise the people's national aspirations without their having to resort to the United Nations Organisation or to any other means,

Awaiting Your Excellency's most favourable reply,

72 FO 371/53311, no 3666 27 Aug 1946

[Anglo–Egyptian treaty negotiations: the Sudan protocol]: inward telegram no 101 from Lord Stansgate to Mr Bevin, reporting Sidqi Pasha's arguments for recognising Egyptian sovereignty over the Sudan [Extract]

[The Egyptian government's claim to sovereignty over the Sudan was embodied in their draft of the Sudan protocol, which read: 'The High Contracting Parties agree to enter immediately into negotiations in order to determine the status of the Sudan within the framework of the welfare of the Sudanese peoples, and on the basis of the unity of the Nile Valley under the Crown of Egypt' ('Sudan Protocol', FO 371/53311, no 3776). Arguments between the British and Egyptian delegations revolved around what was meant and what was implied by 'sovereignty' and 'unity'.]

... 2. On the Sudan Sidki Pasha urges a recognition of Egyptian sovereignty arguing that article 3 of the 1899 agreement providing appointment of Governor General by Khedivial decree should make it easy for us to do this. Moreover we had never denied Egyptian sovereignty. Further, the fact that our protocol provided for Sudan attaining self-government and deciding their relationship with His Highness' government implied that they were under some sovereignty at present and since we had not denied Egyptian sovereignty that sovereignty was Egyptian. Sir R. Campbell after repeating our general attitude countered with our usual arguments adding that there were conflicting views about the sovereignty amongst jurists and that anyhow we wanted to deal with the matter as a practical one. Moreover to subscribe to a formula on sovereignty in the way Egyptians wanted would inject a disturbing element into the Sudan since at this stage it would appear to them as something new. Sidki Pasha could however let him know on this point also any suggestions he had to make. Sir R. Campbell pointed out the phrase "unity of the Nile Valley" had really no meaning or with its wide geographical scope a ridiculous meaning. He did not see how two governments could subscribe to such a phrase. Sidki Pasha said that it of course meant merely the Sudan and that he thought he could devise an alternative phrase to satisfy public opinion for whom it was a slogan. . . .

73 FO 371/53255, no 3718 27 Aug 1946

[Anglo–Egyptian treaty negotiations: the Sudan protocol]: minute by Sir O Sargent to Mr Bevin, proposing alternative drafts of the Sudan protocol

Secretary of State

After discussion with the Governor-General of the Sudan we submit in an amended form the draft Sudan article put forward by you at this morning's meeting.

As you will see, the water question is now being dealt with under section 2. We are advised that the idea of a Nile Board would not appeal to the Egyptians, whose claims to the control of the Nile are almost monopolistic; but that the possible danger to Egypt's water supplies from an independent Sudan is one which must be taken into account.

We have further restored the idea of a Commission in order to consult the Sudanese, but it is to be noted that the Commission will now function at the *end* of the period of preparation for self-government and not (as when we proposed to leave the future wholly vague) in the near future.*

As regards the question of sovereignty, the Governor-General has advised us most emphatically that, whatever safeguards as regards the actual administration might be devised, an open admission by His Majesty's Government of Egyptian sovereignty would be the only point on which the Sudanese would concentrate, with results in the Sudan which would be both unsettling to the people themselves and disastrous to the British position. Such an admission would in fact be far from being the theoretical future which it is represented as being by the Egyptians, since it would weight the scales in Sudanese minds in favour of an ultimate union with Egypt rather than of independence. Furthermore, the Egyptians cannot be trusted *not* to take advantage of the concession to develop their propaganda in the Sudan so as to undermine our position in the Sudan and to advance their own.

We therefore suggest that in the first instance the Delegation should only try the first four sections on the Egyptians. But we have added two formulae the first of which (A)[1] we suggest might be given to the Delegation for their comments, and with a view to use if the Egyptians remain unresponsive.

This formulae amounts to no more than a further reservation of the position, but it does enable the Egyptian *claim* to appear in writing. It is acceptable to the Governor-General. The second formula (B)[2] in fact embodies the Egyptian proposals. We do not think it should yet be sent to the Delegation: and we only offer it as a proposal which you might feel you had to put to the Cabinet with an emphatic warning as to its dangers and disadvantages if

(a) it became evident that without something of the kind the Egyptians would run out on the Treaty itself, and/or appeal to U.N.O. or the International Court on the question of sovereignty and the validity of the 1936 Treaty, and

* Although the King has rejected our original proposal for a Commission, we felt that we should offer it again as a sign that we wish to associate the Egyptian Government in deciding the future of the Sudan.

---

[1] (A) refers to section 5 in the attached Sudan protocol.

[2] (B) refers to the alternative section 5 in the protocol.

(b) you felt that it was worthwhile paying this price to prevent either of these things happening.

Sudan protocol

(1) The High Contracting Parties agree that their primary policy in the Sudan shall continue to be the welfare of the Sudanese and the active preparation of the Sudanese for self-government.

(2) As soon as this latter objective is attained, the Sudanese people shall be free to decide their future. It is understood that if the Sudanese should decide in favour of independence, suitable agreements shall be made with regard to the development and utilisation of the waters of the Nile Valley for the greatest benefit of the Egyptian and Sudanese peoples.

(3) The High Contracting Parties will, from time to time, consult with each other with a view to accelerating the progress of the Sudanese peoples towards the goal of self-government. At a suitable time the High Contracting Parties will appoint a joint commission to report on the question whether the Sudanese are prepared for full self-government and in a position to decide upon the future of the Sudan and, if so, to recommend suitable arrangements for ascertaining what are the wishes of the Sudanese peoples and for giving effect thereto.

(4) Meanwhile, the administration of the Sudan shall continue to be exercised jointly by the United Kingdom and Egypt in accordance with the Condominium Agreements of 1899 as modified by Article 11 of the Treaty of 1936.*

(5) The Egyptian Government declare that the preceding provisions of this Protocol do not prejudice the claim of H.M. the King of Egypt to be the sovereign of the Sudan. The Government of the United Kingdom, while pointing out that it will be for the Sudanese people to decide upon their future in accordance with paragraph (2) above and declining to make any pronouncement on the question of sovereignty, declare that nothing in the preceding Protocol prejudices that question.

Alternative (5). Subject to the preceding provisions of the present Protocol, the High Contracting Parties agree that H.M. the King of Egypt is the ultimate sovereign of the Sudan.

* Article 11 of the 1936 Treaty gives the Egyptians valuable rights in the Sudan, such as the right to maintain Egyptian troops, which will lapse when the 1936 Treaty is replaced by the new one. It is therefore in the Egyptian interest to keep Article 11 of the 1936 Treaty alive in this way.

74 FO 371/53255, no 3719 29 Aug 1926

[Sovereignty and self-determination]: memorandum by Mr Bevin on the Sudan

I have to face the modern tendency that in dealing with any Colonial or Quasi-Colonial problem, the United States' Government is not satisfied unless some hope and prospect is held out of self-government.

2. It is the principle of U.N.O. that where self-government cannot be established, the method of international trusteeship should be introduced.

3. If, therefore, we were, in the Anglo–Egyptian Treaty, to recognise Egyptian sovereignty with the Sudan, it would be regarded as a retrograde step.

4. It would be wise for Egypt and ourselves to look forward and weigh carefully world opinion before taking a decision on this question.

5. I am not in favour of making the Sudan a trusteeship because I believe that, arising out of our mutual responsibility, we can settle the problem satisfactorily between ourselves without bringing extraneous powers into discussion.

6. We have no desire to prejudice the Egyptian claim for sovereignty over Egypt [sic], but for us to take the step of recognising it, would introduce problems such as:—

(a) the weakening of our own position; the King of Egypt's title is never mentioned in the Sudan and the Sudanese would think that we had sold them to Egypt;
(b) the Sudanese would look to Egypt as their ultimate master and accept union as their ultimate destiny;
(c) the Sudanese people would become restless and uncertain about their future.

7. If we agreed to what the Egyptians want without having consulted the Sudanese people themselves, we should be charged with Imperial behaviour and with overlooking the fundamental modern concept that the people themselves should be heard before a change in their status is made. There is no doubt that the Sudanese would regard as a change the measure the Egyptians are trying to get us to accept.

8. The King of Egypt said that he is convinced of the need of a Treaty, but not at any price (the price being the Sudan). Equally I cannot do what I believe to be wrong in order to get a quick Treaty of Alliance.

75 FO 371/53255, no 3707 29 Aug 1946

[Sovereignty and self-determination]: inward telegram no 608 (reply) from Mr Bevin to Sir O Sargent, on possible consequences of recognising Egyptian sovereignty over the Sudan

(1) I have been thinking about the Sudan following yesterday's meeting with the Governor-General and after receiving your minute of yesterday's date with a new draft of a Sudanese protocol.[1] As far as I can see it, three important consequences might result from unqualified recognition of Egyptian sovereignty over the Sudan:—

(A) There might be serious unsettlement in the Sudan, involving difficulties to our administration during the interim period.
(B) The recognition of Egyptian sovereignty might be viewed as a considerable sacrifice of face on our part;
(C) Recognition of Egyptian sovereignty would weight the future status of the Sudan in favour of union with Egypt.

(2) Before we decide the importance to attach to (C) we must have a clear picture in our minds of what we wish the future of the Sudan to be. I am not, for instance, convinced that independence is the best solution. It seems to me that the Sudan will have considerable difficulty in standing alone. Provided our defence interests in

[1] See 73.

Egypt are sufficiently secured and the Defence Board is working effectively, I am not sure that our interests would not best be served by the Union of the Sudan with Egypt.

(3) However, even if we accept Union as a desirable goal, I would not be prepared to agree to any wording such as that used by the Egyptians in their draft protocol recognising "the unity of the Nile Valley under the crown of Egypt". Nor do I like the formula attached to your minute under which "the high contracting parties agree that His Majesty The King of Egypt is the ultimate sovereign of the Sudan". Both these formulae are, I consider, open to grave objections under the headings (A) and (B) above.

I believe that Egyptian *amour propre* and their wish to promote the prospect of union, might be secured by a different approach. I have been considering whether it would be possible to have a form of words which would acknowledge the sovereignty of Egypt while also acknowledging the position of Great Britain as co-administrator.

4. The following formula has occurred to me. "Meanwhile the high contracting parties agree to exercise their existing rights of sovereignty in the Sudan pending a final decision as to the future of the country etc.". This draft meets King Farouk's wish that we should recognise his Sovereignty. At the same time it does not define that Sovereignty and safeguards our own position. It does not in fact do more than recognise the status quo while avoiding the difficulty of defining the respective rights of the Egyptians and ourselves in the Sudan.

(5) My immediately following telegram contains the draft text of a Sudan protocol including this alternative. As you will see I have omitted any reference to a joint commission as I do not favour the idea.

(6) I would like to have your views on my suggested formula.

(7) If you think some compromise on these lines would be workable I would like to put it to Stansgate for his views. Although we are still waiting for the Egyptians to produce their counter-drafts on Articles 2 and 3 I do not think that we will get anything further from them on the Sudan. We must not lose time, and ought to be ready to put our proposals on the Sudan to the Egyptians not later than September 1st. I shall consider how best the proposals can be presented after I have received your views on the present telegram.

76 FO 371/53255, no 3708 29 Aug 1946

[Anglo–Egyptian treaty negotiations: the Sudan protocol]: inward telegram no 609 from Mr Bevin to Sir O Sargent, forwarding a re-draft of the Sudan protocol

Following is draft of Sudan protocol referred to in my immediately preceding telegram.[1]

(1) The High Contracting Parties agree that their primary policy in the Sudan shall continue to be the welfare of the Sudanese and the active preparation of the Sudanese for self-government.

(2) As soon as this latter objective is attained, the Sudanese people shall be free to

---

[1] See 75.

decide their future. It is understood that if the Sudanese should decide in favour of independence, suitable agreements shall be made with regard to the development and utilisation of the waters of the Nile valley for the greatest benefit of the Egyptian and Sudanese peoples.

(3) Meanwhile the High Contracting Parties agree to exercise their existing rights of sovereignty in the Sudan pending a final decision as to the future of the country in accordance with paragraph 2 above.

77 FO 371/53255, no 3708 30 Aug 1946

[Anglo–Egyptian treaty negotiations: the Sudan protocol]: outward telegram no 1224 (reply) from Sir O Sargent to Mr Bevin, relaying FO and Sir H Huddleston's comments on the proposed re-draft of the Sudan protocol

We and the Governor-General feel it is as yet too early to get a clear picture of what we wish the Sudan's future to be. The treaty and therefore the Sudan protocol attached to it will have a proposed time-limit of twenty years which will only carry us to the time when the Sudanese are expected according to the speech made by Governor General last spring to be ready for self government. The essential objective therefore it [sic, is] to keep our hands free at this stage in order that when the time comes we shall not have prejudiced any of the various solutions between which we and the Sudanese shall then have to choose. Meanwhile the question of Egyptian sovereignty must primarily be considered from the point of view of the immediate effect on the Sudanese people and the Governor-General is emphatic that the effect of recognising it in any form would be very serious. For this reason we are glad that you rule out second formula (5) in draft taken by you to Paris.[1]

2. As regards paragraph 3 of formula in your telegram No. 609[2] if we say that both High Contracting Parties will continue to exercise their existing rights of sovereignty, this must mean, that both High Contracting Parties possess some rights of sovereignty and therefore that sovereignty in the Sudan at the moment is shared. Such a text is all right from the United Kingdom point of view so far as the question of sovereignty is concerned because we have never thought of contending that the whole sovereignty in the Sudan is vested in the United Kingdom. The issue has always been whether

(a) the sovereignty resides solely in Egypt, or
(b) is shared between the United Kingdom and Egypt.

Thus this text would be an affirmation of what may be said to be the extreme United Kingdom view and for this reason it could hardly be acceptable to Egypt, whose wish is to assert that sovereignty over the Sudan resides solely in Egypt. In fact your formula might be more palatable to Egypt if the words "of sovereignty" were omitted and it simply said "the High Contracting Parties agree to exercise their existing rights".

---

[1] See 73.

[2] See 76.

3. Your formula moreover might lead to practical difficulties in so far as it merely says: "their existing rights". The repeal of the Treaty of 1936 by the new Treaty might not affect the continuance of the condominium agreements of 1899, but it would certainly repeal the concessions in favour of Egypt made in 1936. (See footnote to draft protocol attached to my minute of August 28th [sic 27th]). It was for that reason that, in the draft protocol which you took to Paris, paragraph 4,[3] we proposed to say that, subject to the provisions above relating to the decision by the Sudanese people of their future, "the administration of the Sudan shall for the time being be exercised jointly by the United Kingdom and Egypt in accordance with the condominium agreements of 1899 as modified by Article 11 of the Treaty of 1936".

4. To sum up we agree that paragraph 3 in our draft protocol about the commission should be dropped, and we think that paragraph 4 is the best formula we can devise in the circumstances. We suggest that Lord Stansgate should only be instructed to put forward in the first instance paragraphs 1, 2 and 4 of our draft leaving for later consideration in the light of Egyptian reactions question of finding a formula to meet sovereignty difficulty. In this connexion we adhere to our formula 5 (a) since it mentions existence of Egyptian claim but does not prejudice the future by accepting it. Governor-General maintains the view that while it may be difficult at first to get the Sudanese to understand it this formula (a) is helpful in so far as it stresses that their future lies in their own hands.

[3] See 73.

78 FO 371/53255, no 3712 31 Aug 1946

[Anglo–Egyptian treaty negotiations: the Sudan protocol]: outward telegram no 15 from Mr Bevin to Lord Stansgate, explaining principles behind the re-draft of the protocol

I have been considering the Sudan problem in consultation with the Foreign Office and have tried to set down the principles which should guide us through this intricate problem. They are contained in the memorandum in my immediately following telegram.[1]

2. You will see that my conclusion is that for various reasons we cannot do what the Egyptians want and recognise the King of Egypt as the sovereign of the Sudan. Nor am I disposed to buy a treaty at that price. The furthest I should be prepared to go would be to include an article in the Sudan protocol allowing the Egyptian Government to put on record that the provisions of the protocol did not prejudice the claim of the King of Egypt to be the sovereign of the Sudan, accompanied by a statement that the Government of the United Kingdom decline to make any pronouncement on the question of sovereignty but declaring that nothing in the protocol prejudices this question.

3. We have also reconsidered the draft Sudan protocol as a whole and have arrived at the text contained in my telegram No. 17 as the best we can offer. You will

[1] Outward telegram 16 from Bevin to Stansgate, 31 Aug 1946, FO 371/53255, no 3713, relaying the text of 73.

see that we have introduced into Article 2 a provision regarding the Nile waters in order to meet the Egyptian anxieties about water (paragraph 8 of your telegram No. 65 to Foreign Office).[2]

4. Since the King expressed opposition to the idea (your telegram No. 94 to Foreign Office) we have omitted the idea of a Joint Commission for the purpose of making recommendations for the future of the Sudan in consultation with the Sudanese people.

5. I have not felt able to omit in Article 3, reference to the existing agreements since I am advised that unless they are specified, our position as co-administrator may be questionable. But I have attempted to make the wording more palatable to the Egyptian Government. Moreover, article 11 of the 1936 treaty gives the Egyptians valuable rights in the Sudan such as the right to maintain Egyptian troops which will lapse when the 1936 treaty is replaced by the new one. It is, therefore, in the Egyptian interest to keep Article 11 of the 1936 treaty alive in this way.

6. Article 4 represents the furthest we can go to meet the Egyptians on the question of sovereignty. I had, however, suggested to the Foreign Office that the following form of words might go some way to meet King Farouk's wish that we should recognise his sovereignty:—

> "Meanwhile the high contracting parties agree to exercise their existing rights of sovereignty in the Sudan pending a final decision as to the future of the country in accordance with paragraph (2) above."

This form of words would meet the King's wish by acknowledging in terms, his sovereignty while also acknowledging the position of Great Britain as administrator. But I am advised that it could hardly be acceptable to Egypt whose wish it is to assert that sovereignty over the Sudan resides solely in Egypt.

7. I am anxious not to lose time and feel that our latest proposals should be presented as a whole to the Egyptian Government as soon as possible. But before you do this I should like your observations on the present telegram and also the clean draft of the remaining articles less the Sudan for which I asked you in my telegram No. 13.

[2] 'Amr stresses Egypt's interest in "unity of the Nile valley" centred on two points of view: (A) long standing popular tradition (B) water. It seems we should be prepared to say we would help in securing from any future autonomous Sudan guarantees for Egypt on this subject. There are indeed such ingrained instinctive anxieties about their water amongst the Egyptians that we consider we should be prepared to meet them if they raise the matter'. Inward telegram 65 from Stansgate to Bevin, 17 Aug 1946, FO 371/53254, no 3558.

79 FO 371/53255, no 3714 31 Aug 1946

[Anglo–Egyptian treaty negotiations: the Sudan protocol]: outward telegram no 17 from Mr Bevin to Lord Stansgate, forwarding text of re-drafted Sudan protocol [Extract]

Following is text of Draft Sudan Protocol referred to in my telegram No. 15. . . .[1]

4. The Egyptian Government declare that the preceding provisions of this Protocol do not prejudice the claim of His Majesty the King of Egypt to be the Sovereign of the

[1] Articles 1–3 are as in 76.

Sudan. The Government of the United Kingdom, while pointing out that it will be for the Sudanese people to decide upon their future in accordance with paragraph 2 above and declining to make any pronouncement on the question of sovereignty, declare that nothing in the preceding Protocol prejudices that question.

80 FO 371/53255, no 3771 5 Sept 1946

[Anglo–Egyptian treaty negotiations: the Sudan protocol]: outward telegram no 21 from Mr Bevin to Lord Stansgate [Extract]

[In response to 79 Stansgate argued for the inclusion of a proposal for a joint commission on the Sudan, on the grounds that it might satisfy the Sudanese expectation that the treaty would contain something specific about their future attainment of self-government and independence and the Egyptian insistence that there should be immediate negotiations. He went on to warn that the article on sovereignty satisfied Egypt's minimum demands only and therefore was unlikely to be accepted. He also commented that Egyptian interests in the Nile valley went beyond water, and embraced economic considerations and the possibility of emigration; therefore the protocol should include some general wording concerning safeguards for Egypt's 'material rights and interests' in the Nile valley. Finally, he provided alternative drafts, which were incorporated into the following re-draft of articles 2, 3 and 5 of the protocol (inward telegrams no 111 and 112 from Stansgate to Bevin, 3 Sept 1946, FO 371/53255, nos 3749 and 3753). Bevin refused to alter the sovereignty article, instructing instead that Stansgate should argue along the lines set out in 79 above, 'in order to reach position in which you will have made it clear why His Majesty's Government cannot commit themselves to any agreed statement on Egyptian sovereignty. You will then be in a position to say that His Majesty's Government nevertheless are now prepared as a concession to allow the Egyptians to write down in the text of the Treaty that they claim themselves to be sovereigns' (outward telegram no 20 from Bevin to Stansgate, 5 Sept 1946, FO 371/53255, no 3770). In the following re-draft articles 1 and 4 remained unchanged.]

Following is redraft of Sudan Protocol (amendments to text in my telegram No. 17 are underlined). . . .[1]

(1) The high contracting parties agree that their primary policy in the Sudan shall continue to be the welfare of the Sudanese and the active preparation of the Sudanese for self-government.

(2) As soon as this latter objective is attained, the Sudanese people shall be free to decide their future. It is understood that if the Sudanese should decide in favour of independence, suitable agreements shall be made with regard to the development and utilisation of the waters of the Nile Valley for the greatest benefit of the Egyptian and Sudanese peoples *and with regard to the other material interests of Egypt in the Nile Valley*.

(3) Meanwhile the administration of the Sudan shall continue to be exercised jointly by the United Kingdom and Egypt in accordance with the condominium agreements of 1899 *and* Article 11 of the Treaty of 1936. . . .

(5) *The high contracting parties shall from time to time secure reports from the Governor General on the progress of the Sudanese people towards the goal of self-government. At a suitable time they will appoint a joint commission to report on the question whether the Sudanese are prepared for full self-government and in a position to decide on the future of the Sudan and if so, to recommend suitable arrangements for ascertaining that* [sic, what] *are the wishes of the Sudanese people and for giving effect thereto.*

---

[1] Italicised in the text reproduced here.

81 FO 371/53312, no 4066 28 Sept 1946

[Anglo–Egyptian treaty negotiations: Egyptian reply]: inward telegram no 149 from Lord Stansgate to Mr Bevin, conveying the text of the Egyptian reply to the British draft protocol [Extract]

[As the British delegation neared the completion of its draft for presentation to Egypt, Stansgate reported growing opposition to Sidqi among the members of the Egyptian delegation. He warned that acceptance of the terms of the evacuation of troops from Egypt appeared to be dependent on settling the Sudan protocol on a basis acceptable to the Egyptians. Britain's version of the Sudan protocol was unlikely to be accepted, and a breakdown in negotiations was a very real possibility (inward telegram no 120 from Stansgate to Bevin, 11 Sept 1946, FO 371/53310, no 3838). At a meeting with the entire Egyptian Delegation on 17 Sept Stansgate presented the latest draft of both the evacuation article and the Sudan protocol. Egypt's reply, objecting to the terms of evacuation[1] and rejecting the Sudan protocol, was presented on 28 Sept. Stansgate here transmits a slightly abbreviated version of the Egyptian text.]

The Sudan

In the course of negotiations it has become clear that the object of the British delegation is to settle finally the regime in the Sudan according to 1899 arrangement as at present applied by British authorities in the Sudan. For her share in Sudan campaign British Government claimed the right to share in administration (see paragraph 3 of preamble of agreement of January 1899). 1899 agreement therefore sets up a joint Anglo–Egyptian administration but Great Britain's position in Egypt, encroachment of British officials in Sudan and unilateral measures imposed by British Government by force in 1924 have reduced Egyptian share in administration of Sudan provinces to nothing.

The first draft protocol proposed by British delegation was merely a reproduction of Article 11 of 1936 Treaty with addition of a joint commission charged with the task of making recommendations on the [gp. undec. ? regime.][2] The same idea is reproduced in second draft, which departs even further from Egyptian point of view since it makes no provision for a subsequent agreement about the Sudan.

The British protocol lays down that the object of high contracting parties is actively to prepare Sudanese for self-government. This is also the sincere desire of Egypt. But Egyptian delegation are not prepared to accept this merely as a declaration of principle in execution of which Egyptian Government will have no share. On the contrary, Egyptian Government must take an effective part in elaborating democratic regime towards which Sudanese should be moving. The 1899 and 1936 agreements give Egyptian Government no means of sharing in this task. In arrangement proposed in British draft protocol it will be the Governor General who under instructions from London alone will elaborate new Sudan statute. The only

---

[1] Egyptian objections to the terms of evacuation under a new treaty with Britain were based on disagreements, not only over the length of the evacuation period but also over the terms upon which British forces would be allowed to return to Egypt in the event of an external threat either to Egypt or to neighbouring countries. These issues are extensively documented in BDEEP series B, vol, 4, John Kent, ed, *Egypt and the defence of the Middle East*, part I, chapter 1 (see especially documents 68 & 82).

[2] The undeciphered words should read 'future of Sudan' (correction from text of document 82 cited in note 1 above).

amendments protocol makes to the Egyptian Government's objections [? gp. omitted 'are that'] they will be informed from time to time by reports from Governor General of the Sudan of progress made by the Sudanese towards self-government and to make appropriate recommendations.

Sovereignty

The British draft states that the protocol does not prejudice claim of King of Egypt to be sovereign of the Sudan. Egyptian sovereignty does not need to be claimed. It exists; it has never been possible to contest it. The British Government can no longer maintain their refusal to pronounce on this question. Either Great Britain admits the right of Egyptian sovereignty, in which case she can have no objection to recognising it, or she contests it, in which case she must state the fact in order that Egyptian people may know that Great Britain is denying them the only link which still unites them with the Sudan at the very moment that she is asking them to become an ally of Great Britain and to share with her the grave responsibilities which derive from the alliance.

For all these reasons Egyptian delegation cannot accept draft protocol presented by British delegation.

82 FO 371/53326, no 4471 Oct 1946

[Anglo–Egyptian treaty negotiations: Umma Party statements]: report from SPIS no 59 for August-September [Extract]

... 522. The Umma comments on the British draft protocol were embodied in telegrams to the delegations (the British delegation has not yet confirmed receipt) which were published in the Star of September 26th and ran as follows:—

> "that the Sudanese will not suffer the present negotiations being concluded without the admission being made of the full right of Sudanese to sovereignty over their country, and their right to enter into direct negotiations with the representatives of the two Governments of the Condominium to discuss the necessary steps to the establishments of a free democratic Sudanese Government, which bears no allegiance to any country or crown".

The two Governments will, the telegram went on, "be responsible for any results that may ensue from ignoring the wishes of the Sudanese nation".

523. The Umma leaders are worried at the enforced silence of the Sudan Government since His Excellency's statement to the Advisory Council in April.

In a letter dated August 23rd (to which we have not yet replied) they deprecate the suggestion that 20 years will bring self government and not independence, ask for reference to U.N.O. if the Co-domini can't agree, and emphasise that their participation in the Sudan Administrative Conference was "with the aim of eventual independence". . . .

83 FO 371/53312, no 4117 3 Oct 1946

[Anglo–Egyptian treaty negotiations]: inward telegram no 159 from Sir R Campbell to FO reporting Sidqi's interpretation of sovereignty

[In a subsequent meeting on 3 Oct with Campbell, following Stansgate's departure, Sidqi proposed a further meeting in London and attempted to clarify his stance on the Sudan.]

My telegram No. 157, paragraph 3.

About the Sudan, Sidki Pasha said that Egypt was asking for no more than recognition of symbolic sovereignty. As he had said, she did not expect a share in the administration. I remarked that this hardly seemed to tally with claims made about the Sudan in Egyptian Delegation's preceding Note.[1] Sidki Pasha brushed this aside by saying that it was obviously not possible for the Egyptians publicly to state their disinterestedness in the administration. I understood him to say that if satisfaction were given on the sovereignty every assurance would be forthcoming about the maintenance of the present administration. He repeated the familiar theme that sovereignty existed and that the King of Egypt could at any moment declare himself to be King of the Sudan. His title as Lord of Dartew [sic, Darfur] etc. was stated in Egyptian Consular exequaturs. I pointed out that these ancient titles were far from being equivalent to Kingship of the Sudan and repeated the familiar arguments about conflicting legal opinions and the more practical consideration of opinion in the Sudan. On the latter point Sidki Pasha as usual took the line that any expression of Sudanese views contrary to the idea of Egyptian sovereignty were instigated by the Sudan Government.

2. For the rest, Sidki Pasha did not refer to the necessity of including in the Treaty provision for immediate negotiations about the Sudan, but suggested that Egypt would be perfectly satisfied if some time—say in a year or two—an Egyptian and a British Commission should visit the Sudan and make recommendations about the handling of the question of ultimate Sudanese self-Government. Such recommendations would then form the subject of subsequent negotiations between the two condominium Governments. I gathered in this conversation Sidki Pasha was mostly repeating what he had said to Lord Stansgate just before his departure.

---

[1] See 81.

84 FO 371/53314, no 4213 5 Oct 1946

'Anglo–Egyptian treaty': FO minutes of a meeting between Mr Bevin and the British treaty delegation in Paris on the Sudan [Extract]

[Following the Egyptian rejection of the British draft Stansgate and the British delegation reported back to Bevin in Paris, where he was attending the Peace Conference. Also present at the meeting were Sir O Harvey, Sir R Campbell, Sir W Smart (oriental minister, Cairo), P Dixon (Bevin's private secretary), Wood, and D M H Riches of the FO.]

. . . 3. *The Sudan*

Lord Stansgate said that, in his view, in their minds the Foreign Office had always acknowledged Egyptian sovereignty, though they had prevented the Egyptians from exercising it. The Secretary of State was also doubtful of the validity of our previous position, and it was recognised that in order to obtain a Treaty at all it was necessary that sovereignty should be conceded to the Egyptians in some form. The Secretary of State directed that the matter should be dealt with on the following basis:—

(i) A Protocol should be drafted providing for

(a) a distinction between sovereignty and administration. Thus, the preamble should re-affirm both the historical position of the King of Egypt in the Sudan, and the administrative position of His Majesty's Government;
(b) the appointment of a Joint Council of British and Sudanese, which would be a continuing but not a permanently established Body (i.e. it would not have Headquarters and a permanent Secretariat) which would not be empowered to interfere with the Governor-General's supreme authority but which would give the Egyptians an opportunity of keeping an eye on the methods adopted to promote the self-government for the Sudanese.

(ii) Sir Ronald Campbell should reply to Sidky's message asking him to elaborate what he meant by "symbolic sovereignty". . . .[1]

[1] See 83.

85 FO 371/53257, no 4334 9 Oct 1946

[Anglo–Egyptian treaty negotiations]: letter from J W Robertson to G H Hancock (acting civil secretary), relaying the governors-general's and the civil secretary's reactions to the draft Sudan protocol

I went yesterday with H.E. to the Foreign Office where we had a meeting in the morning with Sir Orme Sargent, Sir Walter Smart, Howe, and Beckett. We were told that the Treaty had come to a standstill on the Sudan question, that Lord Stansgate and Sir Ronald Campbell had gone to Paris, explained the position to the Secretary of State, and had been told by him to see whether the Treaty could not be saved by some rewording of the Sudan protocol.[1] I attach hereto copies of the various drafts. The old draft of September 5th was the one to which H.E. agreed when we were up here at the end of August;[2] there is a draft which was prepared in Paris, and which was shown there to the Secretary of State, and the third and last draft is the Paris one amended in the Foreign Office a day or two ago.[3]

H.E. was asked what his views were on this third draft, and while he agreed that Clauses 1, 2 and 4 contained a fair and reasonable statement of what the Sudan Government wants, he said that the preamble, in which "sovereign rights" of the King of Egypt are admitted, is bound to make things extremely difficult for the Sudan Government. Although "the existing system of administration" is to continue, by the insertion of this clause in the preamble we will be certainly faced by immediate rejoicings in the pro-Egyptian Sudan Press and in Egypt, by the discomfiture of our own friends, and by a swing of the moderates to the Egyptian side—it may be that if the administration continues unchanged and we are still

[1] See 84. [2] See 76 and 79. [3] See 92, Annex A.

obviously in power, that the effect of the admission of sovereignty will gradually lessen, but it is very doubtful whether the Egyptians will leave us alone: it seems much more probable that with "sovereignty" admitted they will intensify their propaganda and infiltration into the country in order to make sure that the choice given to the Sudanese under Article 2 will be for union with Egypt.

H.E. (and I) made these sort of objections and Sir Orme Sargent admitted their force, and said that no one liked this formula, but that the benefit of a Treaty with Egypt was so great from the general world viewpoint, that the Secretary of State wished to get one if possible.

The analogy of the Sultan of Turkey's sovereignty over Egypt in Cromer's time was quoted, and the Foreign Office's idea is apparently that some symbolic sovereignty of this sort will satisfy the Egyptians and that they will be content once they have this. We doubt it—and we are also sure that it will not be easy to explain this to the Sudanese.

On the other hand, it can be said that in paragraphs 1 and 2 we get an acknowledgment from Egypt that what H.E. said in the Advisory Council is agreed to, and that should be some gain.

We were asked to return in the afternoon. At 4.30 p.m. we met again; this time Lord Stansgate, Sir Ronald Campbell, Riches and Lord Stansgate's Secretary were also present.

We went over the same ground, and the delegation from Cairo emphasised that unless some acknowledgment of Egyptian sovereign rights was made in the Sudan protocol, it would be impossible to get the Treaty which was essential for British requirements in the Middle East. H.E. asked several questions: he wondered what the Governor-General's position would be if a similar case to the Desuki[4] one arose: the Foreign Office people thought that his position would be worse, that the King of Egypt would probably have the Egyptian constitution altered to make his title "King of Egypt and the Sudan"; Beckett said that he thought there would be no way of stopping him putting this title on his stamps and coins; H.E. also said that the word "historic" was being used in two ways: the Egyptians were allowed to infer a meaning "historic and continuing" and the Sudanese would be asked to read it as "historic but obsolete". I asked whether this wording did not mean a change in the status of the Sudan, because the Secretary of State had said that no change would be made in the status of the Sudan without consulting the Sudanese people through constitutional channels. I was told by Beckett that it made no alteration, and if we were asked, we should say so: I must say that this answer does not satisfy me, and that I think it *does* alter the status, in that H.M.G. thereby admit what they have never admitted before.

I am sure we shall be faced with very strong opposition from S.A.R., the Umma, and the great mass of the moderates, if this goes through, and there might easily be active revolt against it. To what lengths this might go I can't estimate, but we might have quite considerable difficulties to face. If we did, we should be placed in the

[4] Bimbashi (Major) Dassuki al-Sabbagh was an Egyptian officer stationed at Port Sudan who led his troops in cheering Faruq as 'King of Egypt and the Sudan' during the King's birthday celebrations in February 1945. He was subsequently withdrawn from the Sudan but was received by Faruq on his return to Egypt (see inward telegram no 251 from Campbell to FO, 15 Feb 1945, FO 371/53284, no 659; letter from E W Thomas (commissioner, Port Sudan) to civil secretary, 12 Feb 1946, FO 371/53287, no 1124; and letter from Campbell to Bevin, 7 May 1946, FO 371/53295, no 2116).

intolerable position of having to put down our own friends and supporters, on behalf of our opponents. I can't see S.A.R. and his people agreeing that the Egyptians have any "historic rights"—they believe that these were ended by the Mahdia, and that any sovereign rights now existing are vested in the joint Anglo–Egyptian administration, on behalf of the peoples of the Sudan.[5]

I am also not at all sure what the reaction among our British staff will be. I imagine we shall have a number of resignations, and that the question of recruitment of new staff will be more difficult than ever. No one will wish to continue under the Egyptian Crown, nor to take on a new job under such conditions. These factors have not been considered by the Foreign Office at all; or if they have, they have been brushed aside by the importance of a Treaty.

I have been trying to think what would be the result of having no Treaty on the Sudan. Our position would be difficult, and we should have trouble from the Ashigga and their following, but if we had this Treaty we should probably have just as much trouble and should be in a much weaker position than we are now, having lost the confidence of those who now support us, and having less power than now, to prevent Egyptian propaganda and infiltration.

Sidki Pasha apparently intends to come here about the 16th and stay for some days. It is not clear in what capacity he intends to come, and whether he will be able to negotiate a final Treaty or not: it looks from telegrams I have seen that he intends to come here on an exploratory mission, and to take any concession he gets back to the Egyptian Delegation in Egypt for approval. It is unlikely that the Secretary of State would agree to negotiate on these terms as he would be put in the position of playing his last card, and perhaps having it trumped by the Egyptians in Cairo, and this is now being considered. Sir Orme Sargent asked H.E. to remain on here over the time of Sidki's visit, and H.E. has said he wishes me to stay with him. So I shall not be leaving for some time yet—perhaps about the 27th.

I very much doubt whether this draft will satisfy the Egyptians, and believe that when it is offered to them they will ask for something more. How far the British will go to meet them I don't know, but the old tag comes to mind "facile est descensus averno".

I tried to get some idea from Sir Walter Smart about the Joint Council proposed in paragraph 5 of the protocol, but I don't think any clear picture has been drawn about the numbers or constitution of the Council, which is the present shape of the commission which we once suggested for discovering the views of the Sudanese.

I think you had better carry on yourself with the Administration Conference; what I intended to do was to preside over the Conference and try to get an agreement over the Sub-Committees' reports for submission to H.E. I did not intend to take an active part myself as I thought I should not better appear to be backing any recommendations, on which I should afterwards have to advise H.E. If you would take my place therefore, I shall come to the recommendations fresh, and be more impartial, than if I had presided over the conference myself.

I am sorry not to come out when I said I should, but I think it is more important to remain at this end at present.

Will you please show this to Creed.

---

[5] This position was never admitted by either the British or the early Sudan governments, who styled the occupation of the Sudan as a 'Reconquest' undertaken to restore Egyptian rule.

86 FO 371/53257, no 4373 11 Oct 1946

[Egyptian sovereignty and the Sudan]: letter from Sir R Wingate[1] to Mr Bevin

I have never had the privilege of meeting you and I can only hope to recall my existence to you as one who was for 17 years Governor-General of the Sudan and later High Commissioner in Egypt.

The interests of the Sudanese whom I knew so well, and of the Egyptians amongst whom I worked and whose servants as Sirdar of the Egyptian Army and as Governor-General under the Condominium I was, prompt me, with considerable diffidence, to put forward the following suggestion to you.

You may have something of the kind already in your mind, but I am sure that, if H.M.G. see no insuperable objection, it would work. I myself always regarded the sovereignty of Egypt over the Sudan, as modified by the Condominium of 1899, as undoubted. In fact it was I who, during the Fashoda Incident when Kitchener and myself met Marchand, persuaded Kitchener to fly only the Turkish (Egyptian) flag and to use the argument that we had reconquered the Sudan on behalf of the Khedive and not of the British Government.

Arrangements between Great Britain and Egypt after 1922 may have modified, to some extent, the working of the Condominium in Egypt's disfavour. But it is far better to give Egypt a status in the Sudan openly if we wish ourselves to retain our paramount interest there. What must undermine our position on the spot is the ability of Egypt to influence the Sudanese against us because we, if we maintain our present position, must in effect exclude their influence. Nor does the contention that we are possibly right in protecting the Sudanese against Egyptian exploitation—and no one alive can know more at first hand of what this was than myself who saw it—alter the fact that the assertion of the protection is the worst possible way of securing it. Egypt given an assured status in the Sudan is controllable there. It will depend largely upon the personality of the Governor-General. She will doubtless try to influence the Sudanese to opt for her, but she will do it openly, and it is then up to the Sudanese.

---

[1] Governor-general of the Sudan and Sirdar (commander-in-chief) of the Egyptian army, 1899–1916; high commissioner of Egypt, 1917–1919.

87 FO 371/53315, no 4389 18 Oct 1946

'Anglo–Egyptian treaty': FO record of first meeting with the Egyptian delegation [Extract]

[Following the debriefing in Paris (see 84) preparation for the meeting with Sidqi in London included an attempt to get him to clarify in advance what he meant by 'symbolic sovereignty', and the status of his delegation to England. Sidqi proposed no alteration to the current administration of the Sudan and was prepared to follow the recommendations of an Anglo–Egyptian commission on the future form government in the Sudan should take. He was not planning to come with full authority to conclude a treaty, but hoped to be accompanied by the leaders of the two principal parties in Parliament (al-Nuqrashi of the Saadist Party and Haikal of the Wafdist Party), so as to ensure ultimate parliamentary approval of any terms agreed in London (inward telegrams nos 162 & 163, Alexandria to FO, 7 Oct 1946, FO 371/53313, nos. 4161 & 4162). Bevin was willing to hear what Sidqi had to say, but would commit himself no further than that (inward telegram no 891, Paris to FO, 9 Oct 1946, FO 371/53313, no 4191). In the meantime the Egyptian embassy in London urged the importance of a sympathetic hearing of the Egyptian case concerning the Sudan, warning that neither al-Nuqrashi nor Haikal would attend if HMG was not prepared to talk "sympathetically" (outward telegram no 1840, FO to Paris, 11 Oct 1946, FO 371/53313, no 4191). In the end both al-Nuqrashi and Haikal refused to be part of the delegation, and Abd al-Hadi, the minister of foreign affairs, attended instead. Five meetings were held over the next ten days. In the following documents (87–93) those sections concerning defence aspects of the treaty have been omitted.]

The Secretary of State said difficulties were outstanding both over the Treaty of Alliance and over the Sudan. He was disappointed that the question of the Sudan was proving so difficult because he had thought that the Egyptian Government were more concerned over evacuation. He had declared in the House of Commons that he could not leave a vacuum in Egypt and he had not yet seen anything that would, in his opinion, avoid the creation of the vacuum. He invited Sidky Pasha to state what was in his mind.

Sidky Pasha said that after the war Egypt thought it right to express her aspirations which centred on two principal matters: evacuation and unity of the Nile Valley. . . .

The Sudan

Sidky Pasha said that Mr. Bevin had mentioned that Egypt had not given sufficient thought to the question of the Sudan. The truth was otherwise. Egypt had made sacrifices over the Sudan not for hundreds but for thousands of years. As Herodotus said: "Egypt was the gift of the Nile" and, in fact, Egypt only existed by the Nile. It was not possible, therefore, for Egypt to forget the Sudan. He understood that the Sudan was not the whole Valley of the Nile but that phrase had become a slogan. Egypt had always had bonds with the Valley of the Nile. But by the present use of the word "sovereignty" they did not mean the bond of the conqueror. Egyptians would be the first to say that any domination was bad. "Sovereignty" was an emblem of unity. Egypt wanted the well-being and progress of the Sudan and wished to prepare the Sudan for the day when it would be capable of self-government. Their first aim was the welfare of the Sudanese and they were prepared to make sacrifices for that object.

Egypt and the Sudan had such common interests that separation of the two could not be envisaged. A parallel was the bond between the United Kingdom and Canada who were under the same King. If the Secretary of State asked why this bond between the two countries should be symbolic only, he would reply that the Sudan must remain loyal in order to preserve the common interests of the two countries. Egypt was the continuation of the Sudan. There must never be hostility between the two and they must work harmoniously together. The question of the administration was quite secondary. Naturally the Sudanese wanted to run their own country and Egypt understood this feeling. It was in Egypt's interests that the Sudan should be well-governed. There was no question of the ideas of sixty to eighty years ago when the Sudan feared Egypt. Egypt wanted to regard the Sudan as a smaller and weaker brother.

The Secretary of State said he was still not clear on Sidky Pasha's attitude. His Excellency had said that he wanted the Sudan well and justly governed. Did he suggest that this was not the case at present?

Sidky Pasha said that the Governor-General was an Anglo–Egyptian functionary and he could not make such an accusation against him. . . .

The Secretary of State explained that he had received Sidky Pasha's message concerning the Sudan in which he asked for "symbolic" treatment. He was not clear as to the meaning of the Egyptian requirement.

Sidky Pasha explained that the word "symbolic" was designed to show the attitude of the Egyptian Government towards the question of the sovereignty of the Sudan. The Egyptians did not seek supremacy to exploit the country nor did they look for material and moral profit. There was, however, unity with the crown of Egypt and a unity of bond which had always existed between the two countries. Furthermore, an outlet was required for the Egyptian youth which emerged from the universities. The Egyptians were willing to offer to the Sudan experts and professors in an "elder brother" relationship towards the Sudan. Although Egypt had equal Treaty rights she had been completely excluded, and, indeed, almost disregarded in the administration of the Sudan. Posts in the administration had not been given to Egyptians and he complained that Egyptian influence had been consciously brushed aside. Egypt must at all times have the loyalty of the Sudan as it is from that country that her prosperity originates.

The Secretary of State replied that he had tried and failed to understand the Egyptian point of view. He, however, took exception to the statements in the Egyptian press which suggested to him that the Egyptians were determined at a later date to secure British evacuation from that area.

Sidky Pasha asked the Foreign Secretary to disregard the views of the extremists in the service of the Opposition. Egypt sought only a union with the Sudan based on the interests of the Sudanese. Immediately the union was recognised the critics of Great Britain would disappear.

The Secretary of State said that the only impression of the Egyptian point of view which he possessed was in the draft protocol at the end of the Treaty, the meaning of which was not clear to him.

After some discussion *Sidky Pasha* agreed to submit a personal note which would explain the Egyptian point of view.

The Secretary of State pointed out to Sidky Pasha that his visit to this country did not permit him to take decisions on these matters, and he was placed in a certain difficulty in putting forward suggestions.

The Secretary of State said he could not accept the position where he could come to a conclusion on his side and then someone in Egypt would make it a jumping-off board for demanding further concessions.

Sidky Pasha assured the Foreign Secretary that he and the Egyptian Foreign Minister represented the large majority in the Egyptian Parliament and they could be relied upon not to raise the demands after their return to their own country.

In conclusion, *the Secretary of State* stated that he would put forward for discussion a re-draft of Articles II and III of the Treaty and he asked Sidky Pasha in his turn to submit his personal note on the Sudan question and to reconsider the time required for the evacuation.

The terms of a communication to the press were agreed and a further meeting was fixed for 11.30 a.m. on the 19th October, 1946.

88 FO 371/53257, no 4390 19 Oct 1946

'Anglo–Egyptian treaty': FO record of second meeting with the Egyptian delegation. *Annex:* translation of a personal note by Sidky Pasha on the Sudan question [Extract]

Sidky Pasha handed the Secretary of State a note (annexed) embodying his views on the Sudan, which was read out in English by Mr. Howe.

The Secretary of State said that he was concerned with what was involved in the conception of sovereignty. He took it that Sidky Pasha would agree that until the Sudan achieved self-government the present administration should continue.

Sidky Pasha said that until Great Britain and Egypt reached an agreement on the form which self-government for the Sudan would take, the present administration should continue. There was no question of change in the currency, the stamps, or the method of the appointment of the staff of the Sudan Government.

The Secretary of State enquired why it was desired to make this change regarding sovereignty in the Sudan now.

Sidky Pasha said that the present situation was not ideal for Egypt, but it was necessary for her to reach agreement with Britain on the measures to be taken to promote self-government. Until self-government was achieved there would be no need to make drastic changes. It was Egypt's right that the Sudan should be under the same crown.

The Secretary of State said that directly the sovereignty of Egypt over the Sudan was stated, the Sudanese would think that Great Britain had surrendered her position there.

Sidky Pasha replied that there was no fear of this. The British Governor-General and the British character of the Administration would remain. The only thing that would take place would be the reaffirmation that the Sudan remained under the Egyptian Crown.

The Secretary of State said that there was agitation in the Sudan. He had received protests from Sudanese against any change.[1]

Sidky Pasha said he had received messages from Sudanese to the contrary.

The Secretary of State said that Sidky Pasha spoke about Dominion status. But if the Sudanese chose Dominion status under the Egyptian Crown the position of Great Britain would be gravely prejudiced.

Sidky Pasha said that when the time came for the Sudanese to choose, a new political situation might have arisen and matters would probably have to be re-examined. In the meantime nothing would be changed. Egypt could not wait longer for a settlement. It was not the first time that she had asked for a reaffirmation of her sovereignty over the Sudan. The position had always been provisional in the past. Now it should be made definite as part of a general settlement.

The Secretary of State asked whether he was to understand that if sovereignty were conceded to the King of Egypt this would *not* give Egypt a greater right to enter into the administration.

---

[1] One such telegram of protest had been sent from SAR to Bevin (though probably not yet received or read) that same day (see FO 371/53258, no 4468).

Sidky Pasha said that this was correct since the 1899 agreement continued. The consecration of the bond between the two countries would not of itself involve greater Egyptian intervention. The normal relationship between the Egyptian Prime Minister and the Governor-General would continue. Egypt had no wish to meddle in the affairs of the Sudan.

The Secretary of State referred to the ancient titles of the King of Egypt and asked what title King Farouk would wish to take.

Sidky Pasha said that His Majesty would be called King of Egypt and the Sudan.

The Secretary of State said it was very difficult to see how the administration would work. What period did Sidky Pasha envisage before Great Britain and Egypt dealt with self-government for the Sudan?

Sidky Pasha replied that that will emerge by agreement as a result of talks between the two countries.

The Secretary of State said that it was difficult to accept a principle until you knew what was to follow. If he accepted Egyptian sovereignty the decision of the Sudanese on their future would be prejudiced in advance.

Sidky Pasha replied that this would not be so, because no one could deny the bond between the two countries. Egyptian intervention as sovereign would only be designed for the well-being of the Sudanese and to develop their sense of responsibility. Egypt would not prejudice the position of His Majesty's Government in the Sudan.

The Secretary of State asked whether Sidky Pasha would begin the Sudan protocol by reaffirming the condominium agreement.

Sidky Pasha replied that he would reaffirm article 11 of the 1936 Treaty less the last sentence of the first paragraph.[2] Egypt had affirmed her sovereignty in the past but Great Britain had not recognised this affirmation. Egypt did not wish to continue to be faced with this negative attitude.

Sidky Pasha said that the King of Egypt had the powers indicated by the Egyptian Constitution and by becoming King of Egypt and the Sudan no new rights would be created for him.

The Secretary of State asked whether a statement to this effect might be put in the Sudan protocol.

Sidky Pasha replied that out of regard for the person of the King this could not appear, though the fact would remain that he would not have added powers.

The Secretary of State asked whether the position of the Sudan Defence Force would be affected.

Sidky Pasha replied that nothing at all would be changed in the Sudan.

The Secretary of State asked when, if Egyptian sovereignty were conceded, Egypt would wish to begin the movement for a change in the administration of the Sudan.

Sidky Pasha replied—as soon as possible. Egypt was thinking along the same lines as His Majesty's Government in regard to the promotion of self-government for the Sudanese.

The Secretary of State said that if the Sudanese opted for independence the issue was clear; if only for self-government the situation for His Majesty's Government would be very difficult. He had the impression that that was the position in which Egypt was trying to put him.

---

[2] For article 11, paragraph 1, see 6.

Sidky Pasha replied that this was not the case. It was His Majesty's Government who had first spoken of self-government for the Sudan. Egypt was willing to work on the same lines and had no interest in embarrassing His Majesty's Government.

The Secretary of State pointed out that the British proposals for self-government pre-supposed that the question of sovereignty would not arise. He was now asked to agree that before self-government was considered the Sudan should go under Egyptian sovereignty.

Sidky Pasha said that there were examples of highly developed countries such as Canada which were self-governed though under a common monarchy. Canada encountered no difficulties and was not troubled by this arrangement. The Sudan should have a normal not an abnormal status. It was in fact a country under the sovereignty of Egypt with a special régime. It was right that the Sudan should have a King. He was not anxious to go too fast about self-government. Britain and Egypt should decide together what was a propitious moment.

The Secretary of State pointed out that, should the Sudanese decide on independence, Egyptian sovereignty must necessarily go. Was it the Egyptian claim, he asked, that sovereignty would remain after self-government had been arranged and was it recognised that the right of decision would rest with the Sudanese?

Sidky Pasha replied that he thought that it would be many years before self-government was attained. Egypt could not envisage a hostile country on her borders and the Sudan must always remain a friendly neighbour.

The Secretary of State pointed out that in Great Britain we had always insisted upon the right of a dependent nation, on reaching the status of self-government, to secede if it so wished. He reminded Sidky Pasha of recent events in India.

Sidky Pasha agreed, but he pointed out that the right of secession would be a voluntary action on the part of Egypt. Furthermore he felt that it was too early to discuss these matters, as one could not foresee the distant future. There would be, in his opinion, some long time before this matter became a live question and one could not foretell the situation at that time.

The Secretary of State insisted that the situation should be made perfectly clear. He asked Sidky Pasha to say if the Sudanese were being given a chance to be free or if the Egyptians were seeking a lasting settlement of sovereignty. It must be quite clear that the Sudanese were free to renounce the sovereignty of Egypt if they so wished. Great Britain had held a position in the Sudan which she was being asked to surrender, and before she did so he must be perfectly clear on this particular point.

Sidky Pasha replied that nothing in the Sudan would be changed *vis-à-vis* England. On the question of sovereignty he felt it was impossible to speak now. No one knew what developments would be taking place over the next half-century and he felt that the question which Mr. Bevin had asked him was a matter for our children to decide. Furthermore, the United Nations Organisation was discussing all these things and seeking their solution. There was a forward movement of ideas and in his opinion it was not possible to look so far ahead.

The Secretary of State asked for provision for these difficulties to be made now and said he sought to avoid handicapping our children when the time came to seek a solution to this problem. He said frankly he must have an assurance that a situation was not created where the Sudanese could never be independent. He pointed out to Sidky Pasha that the Egyptians had sought to embody in a protocol between two Powers the future of a third party to which Great Britain and Egypt would feel committed in the future. He repeated that the position must not be brought about in which the Sudan, struggling for independence, would forever be under Egypt. He wanted to make it quite clear to the British people that nothing was being done to prejudice the right of self-determination.

Sidky Pasha replied that if the Sudanese reached a certain point of development they would surely become independent. Nothing on paper could prejudice the right of independence nor could it bind a people in search of liberty. It was a universal principle and not a matter for incorporation in a treaty. He went on to say that as the proposed treaty was based on the United Nations Charter, which affirms independence of nations, he felt it was unnecessary in any new agreement to repeat what had already been specified in the United Nations Charter.

The Secretary of State felt that the reference to the spirit of the Atlantic Charter should be incorporated in the treaty.

Sidky Pasha felt this was already covered in the preamble.

The Secretary of State asked for time to study the matter further. He stated he had received a general statement on the Sudan from Sidky Pasha which, he understood, to be a personal view only. He would like to examine how this could be shaped into a draft article of the treaty.

Sidky Pasha repeated that his draft represented his personal view only but he was certain that it came very near to the opinion of his country.

The Secretary of State stated that he would like to examine these matters further and would get in touch with Sidky Pasha again on Tuesday. . . .

Annex to 88

Egyptian sovereignty over the Sudan is a historical and juridical fact which has been solemnly recognised by the British Government both before and after the 1899 agreement.

The sole object of the 1899 agreement was to regulate the administration of the Sudan and, even though Great Britain has asked for and obtained the right of very extensive association in this administration, she has not intended to affect the principle of Egyptian sovereignty.

Quite on the contrary, Great Britain has affirmed this sovereignty on numerous occasions in her contacts with foreign Powers and has always declared that she was acting in the Sudan only to establish the authority of the Egyptian Sovereign.

In asking to-day that the new treaty of alliance with Great Britain should include a protocol reaffirming the existence of the bond uniting Egypt to the Sudan under the same crown, the Egyptian Government takes its stand as much on legal grounds as on those of vital common interests.

The spirit underlying this bond is not one of domination nor is it the instrument of a policy of expansion and exploitation.

In effect, Egypt wishes that the chief object of the policy to be followed in the Sudan should be to ensure the well-being of the Sudanese, the respect and development of their interests and their preparation to take over the direction of their own affairs at the right moment.

To take more precise examples, Sidky Pasha contemplates the future relations of Egypt and the Sudan from the viewpoint of the existing relations between Great Britain and her Dominions.

This example abundantly proves that allegiance to the same crown is in perfect accord with full independence in internal affairs and with an administrative régime entirely conducted by the inhabitants of the respective territories.

This link with the crown has, besides, allowed a very close sacred union in the last two wars.

Egypt will never be able to accept that this bond should be broken and that the Sudan, whence come the sources of the life of Egypt, should be able to fall one day under a foreign domination which could prove hostile.

Until such time as the Sudanese are in a position themselves to take over the direction of their own affairs, a time which he hopes will be not far off, Sidky Pasha would be disposed to accept the maintenance of the present régime which resulted from the 1899 agreement.

Furthermore, Sidky Pasha could not understand that the British Government could invoke the rights and the interests of the Sudanese as a reason for hesitating to accept the mention of Egyptian sovereignty in a protocol to the treaty which is to be concluded.

Such a mention could not harm any right of the Sudanese since, as Great Britain formally recognises, they have not yet reached a degree of political evolution which would permit them to express their wishes freely.

So far as the interests of the Sudanese are concerned, it must be recalled that Egyptian sovereignty over the Sudan has always manifested itself as a care for the well-being of the Sudanese and by powerful help in all spheres of Sudanese life; this help has been given by Egypt without any *quid pro quo* and with no ulterior motive.

In addition, the Sudan does not by itself form a political entity and it is clearly in the interests of the Sudanese to continue to be joined to an organised State to which they are joined by historical bonds and which has a perfect understanding of their interests by reason of the existing geographical, racial, religious and linguistic bonds.

89 FO 371/53318, no 4814 — 23 Oct 1946

'Anglo–Egyptian treaty': FO record of third meeting with the Egyptian delegation [Extract]

. . . *The Secretary of State* said that he had read Sidky's [sic] Pasha's draft Sudan protocol. It was on lines which he would find very difficult to accept. The more he looked into the question of the Sudan the more he felt that it was not right permanently and finally to decide now that the Sudan was under the sovereignty of the Egyptian Crown.

Sidky Pasha wished to make his position quite clear. It was not the intention of Egypt to impose the future régime. When the time came the Sudanese would determine their future.

The Secretary of State asked whether His Excellency meant that when it came to the question of self-government or independence, then the Sudanese would also be free to determine their own sovereignty as well?

Sidky Pasha replied that as explained in his note there was no doubt that the Sudan was vital to Egypt and must be friendly to Egypt. The note was also clear that the interests of the Sudanese should be kept in mind.

Britain was administrating the Sudan and was on the spot. Egypt had nothing to do with the administration and could not interfere with the wishes of the Sudanese. It was, therefore, unfair for the Sudanese to choose their future now.

The Secretary of State said he approached this question from a different point of view. He did not want to be unfair to Egypt when the time came or to impose British sovereignty at the expense of Egyptian.

He would like to say at the beginning of the Sudan protocol that the primary aim of the High Contracting Parties should be the welfare of the Sudanese and their preparation for self-government.

Sidky Pasha agreed.

The Secretary of State said that the best way of achieving this was not to send a Joint Commission to the Sudan on a specific date in the near future but to set up a continuing organ—a Joint Council—which would study, say, every two or three years, the development of the Sudanese towards self-government and report to the two Governments. Self-government would come in stages and even in provinces (since development was not uniform throughout the Sudan). He thought that though it was very difficult for His Majesty's Government to make a declaration on sovereignty, through such an instrument as a Joint Council, the rights of both parties would be recognised.

Sidky Pasha felt, and emphasised that the whole of Egypt felt, that there was a legitimate union between Egypt and the Sudan. He did not use the word "sovereignty" but "union under the Egyptian Crown." As regards a Joint Council, the Egyptian members would have no responsibility and would have their position prejudiced by the British administration. The present state of affairs would be perpetuated. He thought that to send a Commission now to the Sudan would stir up a great deal of trouble.

The Secretary of State said that the members of his proposed Council would be independent persons of high standing and not Government officials. Its object would be to examine what the administration was doing and to remove the Egyptians' fears that they were being kept out of the Sudan. However, he did not wish to press the matter now. The Secretary of State said that it was quite clear from Sidky Pasha's draft that the administration was to remain as at present.

Sidky Pasha agreed. He said that his draft was extremely discreet and designed to meet Mr. Bevin's point of view. Even the Sudanese could not contest it. The Egyptians were not claiming rights or recognition of something new. They only asked that something already existing should not be disturbed.

Sidky Pasha further observed that he had not fully applied his rights under article 11 of the 1936 Treaty. The moment he pressed for them he encountered difficulties and he realised that the questions were best left alone. There could not be two administrators in the Sudan.

The Secretary of State thought it was a question of the meaning of words. No international lawyer had ever defined the meaning of the word "sovereignty".

Sidky Pasha replied that he had not spoken of sovereignty in his draft but of "unity." The most important part of the Sudan was almost Egyptian in character. Arab tribes in the Sudan had their counterparts with the same names in Egypt and the tribes had the same origins.

The Secretary of State said that neither he nor Sidky Pasha was in a position to accept any draft finally as they were not plenipotentiaries. Drafts would have to be put before the Egyptian Government.

Sidky Pasha replied that naturally this was so but he knew what Egypt wanted.

The Secretary of State said that he knew what Britain wanted. The difficulty was to reconcile the two points of view.

Sidky Pasha said that the question of the Sudan was the synthesis of the whole Treaty. If Egypt undertook great responsibilities in war in Egypt or in neighbouring countries, thus making great sacrifices and freeing British troops, it was not a great thing to ask in return that their point of view on the Sudan should be accepted.

The Secretary of State suggested that officials on both sides should look into the matter in the afternoon. He would have to consult the Prime Minister and put the matter to the Cabinet, and would not be able to say anything definite in any case until he knew whether Sidky Pasha's attitude was also the official Egyptian attitude.

Sidky Pasha replied that he felt he had taken into consideration both the administration of the Sudan and the welfare of the Sudanese. He was asking for something which Britain never denied. He was confident that he could rally Egypt behind him.

The Secretary of State said that so far the discussions had only been exploratory. It was difficult to make progress until proposals came from Egypt which were known to have the Egyptian Delegation behind them.

Sidky Pasha replied that he understood this, but the object of his visit accompanied by the vice-chairman of the biggest party in Parliament was to take back the British point of view to Egypt. So far this fully met the Egyptian point of view. Immediately he returned to Egypt he would submit the British views to the King, the Cabinet and the Delegation. When he had secured general agreement he would ask the Secretary of State to ask the members of the British Delegation to go to Egypt again to take the final decision. This would not take long. He had counted on leaving the next day and hoped to have an answer for Mr. Bevin by the end of the following week.

The Secretary of State said that he still felt that a difficulty remained. The Sudanese might be consulted on the question of sovereignty.

Abdul Hadi Pasha said that if they were ripe to decide that, then they were ripe to decide their whole future. But we all agreed that they were not yet ready for such a decision.

The Secretary of State said that he would like the officials to meet that afternoon to complete a clean draft of the whole Treaty.

Sidky Pasha said that he agreed to the redraft of Articles II and III which had been jointly prepared and reiterated that he agreed to the 1st September, 1949, as the final date for evacuation.

Amr Pasha suggested that no redrafting was necessary on the Sudan protocol, but the *Secretary of State* thought there was some wording which required looking into.

The Secretary of State said that he would like one more meeting. Thursday afternoon would be possible and he would try to arrange the time later. He would do his best to meet His Excellency's wish to leave for Egypt as soon as possible.

90 PREM 8/1388/1, DO(124)46 23 Oct 1946

‘Anglo–Egyptian treaty negotiations’: memorandum by Mr Bevin for Cabinet Defence Committee [Extract]

[Bevin reported back to the Cabinet Defence Committee after the third meeting with the Egyptian delegation. An earlier draft of this memo, written by Howe immediately after the second meeting, gave greater emphasis to the governor-general’s warning of unrest in the Sudan following any recognition of Egyptian sovereignty. In that draft Bevin noted, ‘I should here record that the Governor-General of the Sudan, while prepared to accept my proposed formula in the last resort in the higher interests of Anglo–Egyptian understanding, at the present difficult juncture, has warned me most emphatically that the recognition of Egyptian sovereignty, qualified though it be, will lead to widespread political ferment in the Sudan and may be to outbreaks of disorder, for the reason that the highly excitable Sudanese will regard such recognition as weakening the position of the Sudan Government (and of this country) and strengthening that of Egypt, a situation of which the Egyptians and their supporters in the Sudan will not be slow to take advantage’ (‘Preliminary draft of memorandum on the Anglo–Egyptian treaty negotiations’, 19 Oct 1946, FO 371/53316, no 4480). With the outcome of the third meeting the danger of widespread disorder seemed to have receded, and a more optimistic, though still cautious memo was presented to Cabinet.]

. . . (d) The Egyptian Ministers have again assured me that in asking for recognition of Egyptian “sovereignty” over the Sudan they are not asking for any change in the existing status of the Sudan; and in particular it is not their intention to touch the existing system of administration until the Sudanese people themselves have decided what their ultimate future status is to be; nor the arrangements under which the military defence of the country is at present conducted. All they ask is that Egyptian Sovereignty, which certainly exists in some measure as witness the fact that the Governor-General is appointed by Egyptian decree, shall receive recognition instead of being passed over in silence. Having regard to the agreement now reached on the defence clauses of the treaty, I have authorised my Department to meet the Egyptian officials in an endeavour to reduce these assurances, and our recognition of the King of Egypt’s sovereignty, to a mutually acceptable form which shall not prejudice our present position in the territory or the ultimate freedom of the inhabitants. I wish particularly to emphasise that under the proposed arrangements the Sudan will be in the same position from the point of view of imperial defence as it is at present. At the same time, I must add that any reference to the existence of Egyptian sovereignty may create considerable political tension—even if only temporary—in the Sudan, and that the possibility of disorder cannot be excluded. In that event we must be prepared to give full support, military and political, to the Governor General.

91 PREM 8/1388/1, DO 30(46) 24 Oct 1946

[Anglo–Egyptian treaty negotiations]: Cabinet Defence Committee minutes. *Annex:* minute by Lord Jowitt (lord chancellor) to Mr Bevin on sovereignty [Extract]

The Sudan

The Foreign Secretary said that in the course of his discussions with the Egyptian Ministers, the latter had again assured him that in asking for recognition of “Egyptian sovereignty” over the Sudan they were not asking for any change in its existing status. In particular, it was not their intention to touch the existing system of administration until the Sudanese people themselves had decided what their ultimate future status was to be, nor would any of the present arrangements be altered under which the military defence of the country was at present conducted. Nevertheless, they had insisted that Egyptian severeignty, which certainly existed in some measure, for for [sic] example the Governor General was appointed by Egyptian decree, should receive recognition instead of being omitted from the Treaty. It was on this point that the main difficulty of the present negotiations occurred and the Egyptians appeared to be adamant that if no reference was included about sovereignty rights, they would not be prepared to conclude a Treaty. The point, therefore, which he had had to consider was whether, by maintaining our objection to including the reference to Egyptian sovereignty over the Sudan, we were prepared to run the risk of foregoing any defence agreement with Egypt. He had therefore examined exhaustively the present legal position of the United Kingdom on the issue of sovereignty rights from the beginning of our conquest of the Sudan under Field Marshal Kitchener, which when concluded, had led to the agreement of January, 1899, up to the Anglo–Egyptian Treaty of 1936. He had therefore asked for legal advice from the Lord Chancellor's office, in order to bring out quite clearly what would be the position of the United Kingdom if the Egyptians thought fit to refer this question to the United Nations Organisation or to an international court.

The Committee was then read a statement compiled by the Lord Chancellor giving his opinion as to the juridical position new prevailing in regard to the Sudan.

The Foreign Secretary, continuing, said that with these legal conclusions before him and having regard to the agreement now reached on the defence clauses of the Treaty, he had authorised his Department to meet the Egyptian officials in an endeavour to draft a mutually acceptable form of words which would convey a certain measure of our recognition of the King of Egypt's sovereignty over the Sudan, but which would not prejudice our position in the territory, or the ultimate freedom of the inhabitants to choose the form of status they wished. He had received a draft of the clause which the Egyptian Ministers would like to see included in the Treaty but, with the foregoing considerations in mind, he had re-drafted this clause as follows:—

> "The policy which the High Contracting Parties undertake to follow in the Sudan (within the framework of that unity between the Sudan and Egypt which results from a common Crown) will have for its essential objectives to assure the wellbeing of the Sudanese, the development of their interests and their active preparation for self-government and the exercise of the right to choose freely the future status of the Sudan. Until the High Contracting Parties can in full common agreement realise this latter objective the Agreement of 1899 will continue and Article 11 of the Treaty of 1936 together with its Annexes and paragraphs 14 to 16 of the agreed minute annexed to the same Treaty will remain in force notwithstanding the first Article of the present Treaty.
>
> Nothing in this Protocol shall affect the present status of the Sudan, nor impair the right of the Sudanese people, when deciding the future status of the Sudan, to choose in accordance with the principles of the Atlantic Charter the complete independence of their country."

The Prime Minister said he was much impressed with the legal arguments set forward by the Lord Chancellor and he felt that we should be bound to accept it as governing the position of the United Kingdom if the issue of sovereignty was referred to an international organisation for settlement. In his opinion, and remembering back to the incident of Fashoda, he had never thought that there was doubt about the rights of Egyptian sovereignty over the Sudan. There had recently been a tendency to press our claims in this connection further than was supported by the facts. He suggested that our policy in the negotiations should be based on the opinion given by the Lord Chancellor.

The Minister without Portfolio[1] said he felt we were bound to accept the legal arguments governing this question but he would ask to be assured that the form of words ultimately decided on for inclusion in the Treaty should not omit the question of consulting the Sudanese people, as to their future and that no settlement was reached with the Egyptians which might lead to a situation whereby we had not the same strategic control over the Sudan as we had at the present moment.

The Secretary of State for the Dominions[2] made a similar point in that, whatever form of agreement was finally reached, we should be quite certain that it would not invalidate our present position in the Sudan, both from the strategic and administrative aspects, and that no alteration to its present status should be made until the Sudanese people were in a position to determine their future.

The Chancellor of the Exchequer[3] said that, whilst he could not gainsay the legal opinion, he had previously thought in 1932 when he was at the Foreign Office, that the issue on the question of sovereignty had turned rather on the meaning of the word "condominium". He was apprehensive lest any admittance by us of Egyptian sovereignty over the Sudan might ultimately lead to an alteration of our strategic position. The Sudan itself was not a natural or geographical entity, but had been artificially created as such, and he suggested that some alternative might be found by splitting the country and allowing the Egyptians rights over the Northern half, whilst retaining British control over the Southern half to ensure that our strategic position in our Colonies to the South was in no way weakened.

The Prime Minister said he thought this suggestion would not satisfy the Egyptian Government nor the Sudanese and might, on examination, prove not to be of such strategic benefit as might at first be apparent. On the subject of the Treaty itself, he agreed that the rights which we obtained from it were largely dependent on the goodwill of the Egyptians. On the issue of the Sudan, he felt that, having regard to the importance of some form of agreement on defence with the Egyptian Government and of our position as legally defined by the Lord Chancellor, the Foreign Secretary should be authorised to proceed with the discussions on the basis of his draft clause. This clause, whilst admitting of a certain measure of Egyptian sovereignty over the Sudan, would guarantee that the Sudan would be in the same position from the point of view of Imperial defence, and that the administration of the country would remain as at present, until the Sudanese were in a position to say what they wanted.

---

[1] Mr A V Alexander. [2] Viscount Addison. [3] Dr H J N Dalton.

There was general agreement with this view.

The Committee:—

(a) Approved the draft wording of Articles 2 and 3 of the proposed Anglo–Egyptian Treaty.

(b) Accepted the date for the total evacuation of British Forces from Egypt as 1st September, 1949.

(c) Agreed that the question of Air Transit Rights should be discussed by the proposed Anglo–Egyptian Joint Defence Board.

(d) Authorised the Foreign Secretary to negotiate with representatives of the Egyptian Government a clause for insertion in the Treaty which, whilst recognising a measure of Egyptian Sovereignty over the Sudan would safeguard our present defence and administrative rights, and would not prejudice the rights of the Sudanese to choose the ultimate status of their country.

Annex to 91

You asked me on Tuesday evening, 22nd October, to give you an opinion as to the juridical position now prevailing in regard to the Sudan. By that I mean the conclusion to which an International Court of Lawyers would be likely to come to if the matter were referred to them.

I disregard entirely any questions of the political issues involved and give you my opinion on the bare legal question.

I should state at the outset that there is no subject on which lawyers are more divided than this question of sovereignty. No one has succeeded in defining the conception underlying sovereignty.

There are two schools of thought about it and it is therefore impossible to pronounce on the matter with any certainty, but having formed a view on what is admittedly a juridical question I proceed to give it to you.

We start with the position that prior to 1882 the Sudan was part of the undisputed possessions of the Khedive subject to the suzerainty of the Sultan. It is for those who seek to assert that the sovereignty has passed from Egypt to state when and by what means this has been brought about.

Two methods have been suggested—one, conquest; two, by the Agreement of January 1899. It is to be observed that Lord Salisbury in his speech in the House of Lords on the 7th February 1899 preferred to rest our claim on conquest, and to a consideration of that claim I now pass.

The title by conquest

It is obviously material to consider in the first instance who was the person conquered and by whom was that person conquered. A title by conquest cannot arise unless the person conquered was previously sovereign and if the previous sovereign is himself concerned in bringing about the conquest, I do not think that such a claim can be established. It is the fact that the operations undertaken were taken against rebels and by a joint force composed in part of His [sic, Her] Majesty's troops and in part of Egyptian troops. The Officer in Command was Sir Herbert Kitchener who held Her Majesty's Commission but was also Sirdar and that is to say, an officer of the Khedive. Three-quarters of the cost appear to have been borne on the Egyptian

Treasury. These considerations alone satisfy me that any claim based on conquest is untenable. Recently our forces invaded Belgium to get rid of a foreign invader; we operated there with the approval and co-operation of the lawful Government of Belgium. Is it conceivable that anyone could assert that having "reconquered" Belgium we were entitled to claim sovereignty by right of conquest?

Secondly, to establish title by conquest it is necessary to show that after conquest came an annexation. It is quite clear that there was not only no claim to annexation made on behalf of this country, but it was in the most express terms asserted that the sovereignty of Egypt was restored and the Egyptian flag at the time of Fashoda was the only flag flown by Sir Herbert Kitchener.

On both these grounds, I come to the definite conclusion that a claim based on conquest is untenable. In this I am in agreement with Mr. Headlam-Morley[4] and I think also in agreement with Sir Maurice Amos[5] who places our title upon the Agreement of 1899, which I now proceed to consider.

The claim based on the agreement

I should explain in the first place that an English lawyer would confine himself to the text of the Agreement which in his view would have exclusive authority. A continental lawyer would have regard also to contemporary facts and expositions by the chief actors. In my view, whichever system of construction is adopted, the result is the same.

I regard the Agreement as proceeding on the basis that it leaves the juristic sovereignty where it was before—that is to say, in Egypt with the suzerainty of Turkey, and deals with a system of administration and law-making for the reconquered provinces. So far as administration is concerned, it is to my mind plain that this does not involve an assertion of sovereignty—because it must surely be one of the attributes of sovereignty that any such arrangements in regard to the administration of the sovereign's territory may be made as seem fit to the sovereign. So far as law-making is concerned, I agree that this may be regarded as one of the criteria of sovereignty, but as the law-maker is to be the Governor-General of the Sudan who is to be appointed by Khedivial decree, (albeit with the consent of the British Government) I cannot see that this involves a derogation from sovereignty.

There remains the question of the flags. I do not think the fact that the flags are to be used together throughout the Sudan (except in Suakin)[6] is in any sense conclusive of the point of where the sovereignty resides. I should suppose that the American flag would fly over the American base at Bermuda even though the sovereignty in the whole of Bermuda rests in the British Crown. So far as Suakin is concerned, it is impossible to separate this from the rest of the Sudan and to say that there is one sovereignty in Suakin and another and different sovereignty over the rest of the Sudan.

I regard the Agreement as being deliberately made so as not to involve a question of sovereignty which in its turn would have raised the question of Turkish

[4] (Sir) James Headlam-Morley (1863–1929); historical adviser to FO from 1920.

[5] Sir Maurice Amos (1872–1940); judicial adviser to government of Egypt, 1919–1925.

[6] Egypt retained the Red Sea port of Suakin throughout the period of the Mahdist state in the Sudan; thus Suakin was never 'reconquered' and in fact was one of the bases from which the subsequent 'reconquest' was launched.

suzerainty. It was an Agreement by which this country secured for itself certain preferential treatment in the Sudan and the right to share in its development. It was not in my view an Agreement affecting the juridical sovereignty which had pre-existed.

I therefore come to the conclusion that:—

(1) the title was originally Egyptian
(2) that it has not been shown that this title was taken from Egypt and vested in whole or in part in this country.

I conclude by saying that I feel that this question really depends on the meaning of the word "sovereignty" which, as I have previously said, has never yet been defined. Of course, if you define sovereignty as resting in that person who has the power to govern so as to secure peace and good order it follows that we together with Egypt are sovereigns of the Sudan, but if you accept the conclusion which I prefer that the juridical sovereignty can lie exclusively in one power and that a share in administration and control can lie in two, then I think we are not the sovereign. In my view the Agreement, which is inconsistent in its terms, was a practical working agreement and was deliberately drawn so as not to involve any transfer of the sovereignty in its juridical conception.

92 FO 371/53316, no 4455 24 Oct 1946

'Anglo–Egyptian treaty': FO record of an understanding reached at the fourth meeting between Mr Bevin and the Egyptian delegation. *Annexes* [Extract]

Sudan protocol

Mr. Bevin, accompanied by Lord Stansgate and Sir R. Campbell, called on Sidky Pasha at Claridge's Hotel on the evening of 24th October for a personal discussion with His Excellency and Abdel Hadi Pasha and the Egyptian Ambassador in order to clear up outstanding points and, in particular, the question of the Sudan.

No notes were taken.

Mr. Bevin pointed out that Sidky Pasha's revise (Annex B) of the draft Sudan Protocol left with him by Sir R. Campbell earlier in the day (Annex A) presented him with certain difficulties. It was of great importance for him that it should be possible to explain clearly to the Sudanese people and to the British Parliament that nothing agreed now in the Treaty changed the status of the Sudan. He had given an undertaking that no change of status should be made until the Sudanese people had been consulted. He had therefore chosen words for his draft designed to make possible a clear explanation that no change of status was being made.

The Egyptians stated that there was in fact no change of status; all they asked was that the existing status should be affirmed.

Mr. Bevin pointed out that it was a practical question, namely, that of making this clear to the Sudanese and to Parliament. He had had conversations with the Governor-General of the Sudan, who had pointed out that the words proposed by the Egyptians would make this explanation very difficult.

Mr. Bevin, therefore, had proposed the words "within the framework of that unity between the Sudan and Egypt which results from the common Crown." Sidky Pasha had amended this to read: "within the framework of the unity between the Sudan and Egypt under a common Crown." It would help him if his own words could be retained. If, however, this was not possible for Ismail Sidky Pasha, it would help him if His Excellency would agree to insert the word "historic" or "existing" before the word "unity."

Ismail Sidky Pasha argued against this that to the Egyptians the suggested insertion would imply that the unity was a thing of the past.

Mr. Bevin agreed to omit it.

Ismail Sidky Pasha then suggested the substitution of the words "the Crown of Egypt" for "a common Crown," and after some discussion Abdel Hadi Pasha stated that the Egyptian side would agree to the words "the common Crown of Egypt."

Another point which Mr. Bevin urged that it was essential to make clear was that the Sudanese could, if they so desire, choose independence when they had reached the stage of being able to chose the future status of the territory.

With the foregoing in mind Mr. Bevin had proposed the phrase "within the framework of that unity between the Sudan and Egypt which results from a common Crown" in the draft left with Ismail Sidky Pasha in the afternoon, and he now proposed an insertion in the second sentence of the draft designed to make clear that the Sudanese would be consulted when the time came for the two High Contracting Parties to realise in full common agreement the objectives stated in the first sentence. Mr. Bevin proposed that in the sentence beginning "Until the High Contracting Parties can in full common agreement realise this latter objective the Agreement of 1899 will continue, &c." There should be inserted between the words "objective" and "the Agreement" the words "in consultation with the Sudanese."

Ismail Sidky Pasha asked whether this affected the intention of the draft that the objective should be realised in full common agreement between the two High Contracting Parties, which meant that the decision lay with these two parties.

Mr. Bevin said that this was not the intention, but that there should be consultation of the Sudanese before the two Contracting Parties reached their agreement.

Ismail Sidky Pasha took note of this and agreed to the proposed insertion with the substitution of "*after* consultation" for "*in* consultation." This would make the point clear. *Mr. Bevin* agreed.

Mr. Bevin also accepted the deletion of the final paragraph contained in the draft left with Sidky Pasha by Sir Ronald Campbell in the afternoon.

The text of the Sudan Protocol as agreed between Mr. Bevin and Ismail Sidky Pasha is at Annex C.

Mr. Bevin then said that he wished to say frankly that there was one point which it was very important to him to clear up. Would anything in the Sudan Protocol lead the Egyptians to argue that the British undertaking to withdraw their troops from Egypt applied also to the Sudan; would Great Britain now be asked to evacuate the Sudan? Now that we were withdrawn from Egypt it was very important for the whole strategic arrangement in the Middle East that Great Britain should be able to retain troops in the Sudan.

Both *Ismail Sidky Pasha* and *Abdel Hadi Pasha* immediately and most emphatically declared that there was no question of this and that there would be no question of this. It was the right of Great Britain to maintain troops in the Sudan.

Ismail Sidky Pasha added that he wished to emphasise this strongly. *Mr. Bevin* took note and stated that Great Britain might possibly wish at some time to increase the number of British forces in the Sudan slightly, perhaps a certain number of airmen. He enquired whether there would be any difficulty about this. *Ismail Sidky Pasha* and *Abdel Hadi Pasha* both declared there would be none. Once Great Britain had satisfied the Egyptian claims in the ways now proposed, she would find that the Egyptian people would not only be her friends and Allies, but would act as such, and he thought that the record of their action during the late war showed that when they acted as friends they well knew how to do so. . . .

Annex A to 92: Sudan protocol: British revise of 24 October (based on Egyptian draft of Sudan protocol received 22nd October, with no heading, date or indication of origin)

The policy which the High Contracting Parties undertake to follow in the Sudan within the framework of that unity between the Sudan and Egypt which results from a common Crown will have for its essential objectives to assure the well-being of the Sudanese, the development of their interests, and their active preparation for self-government and the exercise of the right to choose freely the future status of the Sudan. Until the High Contracting Parties can in full common agreement realise this latter objective the Agreement of 1899 will continue and Article 11 of the Treaty of 1936 together with its Annexes and paragraphs 14 to 16 of the agreed minute annexed to the same Treaty will remain in force, notwithstanding the first Article of the present Treaty.

Nothing in this Protocol shall affect the present status of the Sudan, nor impair the right of the Sudanese people, when deciding the future status of the Sudan, to choose in accordance with the principles of the Atlantic Charter the complete independence of their country.

Annex B to 92: Sidky Pasha's revise of the secretary of state's draft Sudan protocol

The policy which the High Contracting Parties undertake to follow in the Sudan (within the framework of the unity between the Sudan and Egypt under a common Crown) will have for its essential objectives to assure the well-being of the Sudanese, the development of their interests and their active preparation for self-government and consequently the exercise of the right to choose the future status of the Sudan. Until the High Contracting Parties can in full common agreement realise this latter objective the Agreement of 1899 will continue and Article 11 of the Treaty of 1936 together with its Annexes and paragraphs 14 to 16 of the agreed minute annexed to the same Treaty will remain in force notwithstanding the first Article of the present Treaty.

Annex C to 92: Sidky Pasha's revise of the secretary of state's draft Sudan protocol, 18.00 hrs, 24th October

The policy which the High Contracting Parties undertake to follow in the Sudan (within the framework of the unity between the Sudan and Egypt under the common Crown of Egypt) will have for its essential objectives to assure the well-being of the

Sudanese, the development of their interests and their active preparation for self-government and consequently the exercise of the right to choose the future status of the Sudan. Until the High Contracting Parties can in full common agreement realise this latter objective after consultation with the Sudanese the Agreement of 1899 will continue and Article 11 of the Treaty of 1936 together with its Annexes and paragraphs 14 to 16 of the agreed minute annexed to the same Treaty will remain in force notwithstanding the first Article of the present Treaty.

93 FO 371/53317, no 4634 25 Oct 1946

'Anglo–Egyptian treaty': FO record of the fifth and final meeting with the Egyptian delegation [Extract]

British troops in the Sudan

The Secretary of State said that, if he were challenged in the House of Commons on the point of the right of His Majesty's Government to maintain whatever troops were required in the Sudan in the future, he would say that the new Treaty did not impair our rights in this matter at all.

Sidky Pasha assented. . . .

The Sudan

The Secretary of State said that the Prime Minister, Mr. Attlee, had asked him whether acceptance of the unity between the Sudan and Egypt under the common crown of Egypt changed the status of the Sudan. The Secretary of State had replied that such acceptance left the status of the Sudan as it was, but made clear a situation which had been undefined hitherto.

Sidky Pasha and the Egyptian Representatives agreed that this was the position. . . .

Sudan protocol

The policy which the High Contracting Parties undertake to follow in the Sudan (within the framework of the unity between the Sudan and Egypt under the common Crown of Egypt) will have for its essential objectives to assure the wellbeing of the Sudanese, the development of their interests and their active preparation for self-government and consequently the exercise of the right to choose the future status of the Sudan. Until the High Contracting Parties can in full common agreement realise this latter objective after consultation with the Sudanese, the Agreement of 1899 will continue and Article 11 of the Treaty of 1936, together with its Annexe and paragraphs 14 to 16 of the Agreed Minute annexed to the same Treaty, will remain in force notwithstanding the first Article of the present Treaty.

94 FO 371/53259, no 4604 31 Oct 1946

[Sudan protocol]: inward telegram no 122 from Sir H Huddleston to the embassy, Cairo, with text of Huddleston's address to the nation

[Sidqi's statement to the Egyptian press on 27 Oct that he had secured sovereignty over the Sudan created an immediate reaction among pro-independence nationalist groups in Omdurman and Khartoum. Despite a denial issued by Attlee in parliament the next day, and a subsequent partial retraction by Sidqi, a number of meetings were held in the Three Towns on 27–29 Oct denouncing the British government for betraying their pledge to consult the Sudanese people prior to any change in status (see 98). Huddleston and Robertson returned to Khartoum on the evening of 29 Oct and were faced with the twin tasks of reassuring disaffected Sudanese and British administrators. Huddleston issued an address to the nation, while Robertson wrote confidentially to senior administrators (see 95). Huddleston's statement was later reported to have calmed the provinces but had satisfied neither the pro-Egyptian nor pro-independence factions of the nationalist movement (telegram no 48, Khartoum to FO, 20 Nov 1946, FO 371/53260, no 4878).]

Following is statement I have issued to-day. Begins. I returned two days ago to Khartoum from leave and have been disappointed to find here a state of uncertainty and confusion. I now call upon all classes and conditions of. . . .[1] the conclusion of the treaty negotiations between Great Britain and Egypt has been reached after inaccurate press reports. Mr. Attlee, the British Prime Minister, confirmed in the House of Commons that no change is contemplated in the administration of the Sudan, nor is anything proposed which will impede the progress of the Sudanese towards self-government or their consequent free decision concerning the future of their country. Sidky Pasha, the Prime Minister of Egypt, subsequently issued a statement saying that previous announcements about the results of the conversations in London were inadequate and inaccurate. It is only by co-operation and good feeling between all sections of the community and between all classes of government servants that self-government can be attained and I appeal therefore to all to work together towards the goal when a full self-governing Sudan can make a final choice of its future status, and violence will not bring these objectives closer; they will only lead to unnecessary disorders, resignations from Government service from the Advisory Council and other similar bodies, or failure to co-operate with the government in its progress towards these objectives; the ends of those who are working towards them can have no result except to put back the clock. I therefore call upon all good citizens to go about their business patiently and hopefully, and to political parties to refrain from jumping to conclusions, giving you my promise that the foundations of the future Sudan, which have been laid so carefully will not be (word omitted?) by these negotiations. Ends.

---

[1] Several words from this sentence were lost in transmission.

95 FO 371/53260, no 4809 31 Oct 1946

[Sudan protocol]: circular letter from J W Robertson to heads of departments and governors, explaining the current state of the treaty negotiations

His Excellency the Governor-General returned to Khartoum from the United Kingdom on the evening of Tuesday the 29th October.

He has asked me to write to you and explain the present position regarding the Treaty Negotiations.

You will have been rather confused and bewildered I am afraid by the various reports which have recently come out in the Press and Broadcasts, about the course of the negotiations. You will realise that as these matters are still highly confidential

I cannot give any clear description of the terms of the proposed treaty. The following, however, describes the present position:—

Before Sidki Pasha went to London he categorically announced in Egypt that he was going to bring back with him 'the sovereignty of the Sudan'. This statement was widely exploited by pro-Egyptian elements in the Sudan and immediately gave rise to distrust and anxiety amongst the anti-Egyptian Sudanese who feared that the fort might be sold. Rumours which followed during the course of the London talks led to telegrams being sent by Sayed Abdel Rahman and some of the Nazirs to the Foreign Secretary and to Sidki Pasha asking for assurance that the pledge given in March by Mr. Bevin that the status of the Sudan would not be changed without consulting the Sudanese, would not be forgotten. The state of doubt and distrust culminated on October 26th when Sidki Pasha was reported by the B.B.C. as saying on leaving England that he had in fact obtained the sovereignty of the Sudan for Egypt. The subsequent statement by Mr. Attlee on October 28th in the House of Commons that no change was contemplated in the administration of the Sudan and that nothing in the proposed treaty impaired the right of the Sudanese to eventual decision as to their future status did not reassure anybody. The feeling generally seems to be that the British Government has not denied Sidki Pasha's statement and the Sudanese believe that Mr. Bevin's pledge has been dishonoured and the sovereignty has been given to Egypt. Sidki Pasha has now issued a statement in Cairo stating that the reports in the press are incomplete and inaccurate but I do not think that this will convince Sudanese opinion.

Negotiations are still in progress and are highly delicate and secret; it is, therefore, impossible for me to tell you what is really taking place. The background of the treaty negotiations of the last six months has been a strong desire on both sides to obtain a new treaty: the main Egyptian object is to rid themselves of the British occupation and control, and the British object is to secure the friendship of Egypt as a basis of a bloc of friendly territories which would ensure lines of communications with the dominions and the Far East and which would present a solid face against anti-British influences in the Middle East. Such an object could in earlier days have been obtained by a sufficient show of force in support of our diplomacy but at the present time negotiations and compromise must take the place of this out-moded method. The disruption of our Eastern lines of communication and the hostility of Arab states would leave the Sudan along with other Middle Eastern territories open to exploitation and attack by anti-British powers. It is, therefore, very much in the Sudan's interest, however distasteful it may appear, to preserve British influence in the Middle East until the country can stand on its own feet.

However advantageous to the Sudanese may be the terms of the present draft and whether they are accepted or not by the negotiating powers, the announcement of the Egyptian Prime Minister has seriously damaged our relationship with the Sudanese and their confidence in His Majesty's Government and in the Sudan Government has been shaken. Sudanese are already talking of resigning from the Advisory Council, the Sudan Administration Conference and similar bodies. There may be resignations of Government officials and it is possible that local government authorities may refuse to co-operate. Our great handicap at the present moment is that we cannot come out into the open and explain what is proposed in the present draft.

Our immediate task, and I do not wish to minimise its difficulty, is to restore confidence. Lack of confidence cannot but retard our programmes of administrative, economical, and educational advance, all of which are to the future benefit of the country.

His Excellency wishes me to convey to you his personal conviction and assurance that the proposals which are at present being considered are, in his opinion, in the best long-term interest of the Sudanese and whatever may be your immediate personal feelings he is confident that you will do all in your power to restore confidence throughout the country.

96 PREM 8/1388/2 3 Nov 1946

[Sudanese reaction to the Sudan protocol]: inward telegram no 46 from Sir H Huddleston to Mr Attlee and Mr Bevin

In my recent conversations in London regarding the Anglo–Egyptian negotiations and especially concerning acknowledgement in the Sudan protocol of a common Egyptian Crown, I always stressed the difficulties which I was sure I should experience in persuading the great majority of Sudanese to accept even a symbolic Egyptian sovereignty. When I was in London I thought that by emphasising the undoubted advantages which the protocol gives to the Sudanese, such as the maintenance of the present administration, the promise of an advance towards self-government and consequent self determination of their future status, it would be possible to get them to accept the Egyptian sovereignty of the protocol.

2. During the last four days since I returned to Khartoum I have had opportunity of estimating how the above prospects have been almost totally impaired by premature leakages in Egypt, by Sidki Pasha's emphasis upon sovereignty and failure to mention balancing concessions by Egypt to the Sudan, and by the unfortunate use of the Arabic word "seyada" meaning to the Sudanese "mastery" or "domination". This word here implies relationship of a "master" to a "slave" and has aroused a fanatical feeling of opposition amongst leaders of the Independence movement.[1] Their attention is so concentrated on this aspect to the exclusion of all others that few find reassurance in Mr. Attlee's statement in the House of Commons last Monday owing to the absence of a direct denial of Egyptian sovereignty.

3. It is still too early to estimate whether these leaders will resort to violence in their opposition to an acknowledgement of Egyptian sovereignty but this is a possibility, and in any case co-operation of officials and local Government authorities with the Government is bound to be greatly prejudiced and resignations have already occurred. As 78% of the Government officials and 100% of the local authorities are Sudanese, the danger to the Administration is grave.

4. Bulk of the parties of the Independence [? grp.omtd: ? movement] are backed by Sayed Abdul Rahman El Mahdi whose followers are mainly recruited from among virile and fanatical western tribes. It is most unlikely that the Sayed would go to the

[1] When asked to comment on the meaning of 'sayada' the oriental minister replied: 'I am advised that "Sayada" is the usual Arabic translation here for "sovereignty" and that it would be unusual to use any other word. This fact does not of course weaken our case for complaints over original disclosure but discussion having arisen over Egyptian sovereignty it was inevitable that this word should be used' (inward telegram no 1642, Bowker to FO, 5 Nov 1946, FO 371/53259, no 4632).

length of calling out these tribes but many of his supporters are irresponsible and local disturbances are to be feared. The Sayed has to-day issued at my request an appeal for calm during the negotiations. He was unwilling to tie this to my own recent appeal (reference my telegram No. 40 of October 30th to Foreign Office) but informed me that in framing his appeal he relied upon Mr. Bevin's personal message to him (your telegram No. 44 of October 26th).

5. When I was in London I believed that I had a chance of putting the Sudan protocol across without too much difficulty. But the indiscretions of Sidki Pasha have caused such a deterioration in the situation here that I feel the possibility of putting across the protocol without a major breakdown no longer exist.

6. I therefore propose to return by air to England to explain the situation more fully as soon as I receive your approval to do so.

97 PREM 8/1388/2 — 5 Nov 1946

[Sudanese reaction to the Sudan protocol]: outward telegram no 52 (reply): from Mr Attlee to Sir H Huddleston

Personal from Prime Minister to Governor-General.

I am disappointed and disturbed by your admission of failure to persuade Sudanese leaders of the very real advantages of the Sudan Protocol, such as maintenance of the administration in its present form, self-government and free choice of their future status which more than counter-balance the symbolic and face-saving concession implied in the words "within the framework of the unity between the Sudan and Egypt under the common crown of Egypt".[1] I had hoped that these positive advantages plus my statement in the House of Commons about the Sudan on 28th October, if well and truly pressed home to the Sudanese leaders would have told effectively against partial disclosures from Cairo, even taking into account an admittedly exciteable [sic] race such as the Sudanese. Moreover, your telegram No. 126 of the 3rd November had given me the impression that situation might be tending to ease a little. I hope that your propaganda efforts with important Sudanese have sufficiently emphasised what the continuation of Article 11 of the 1936 Treaty implies and that they have been made to understand that their right to choose independence is not impaired in any way. We are as you know taking action to assist you in stepping up your propaganda machine. If there is anything more that we can do to help you to cope by means of publicity with the present emergency please let me know. Meanwhile I hope that you will be able to influence Sayed Abdul Rahman El Makdi [sic] and Sayed Ali Mirghani, who have been the recipients of much honour from His Majesty's Government in the past, in the direction of controlling their followers. I understand that additional troops requested by you will be sent by air on 7th November. The letter from the Foreign Secretary which you are to show to Government officials ought to reach you within the next few days.

I am not certain whether your action in returning at this moment might not by arousing Egyptian suspicions stir up feelings in Egypt which are now beginning to subside a little.

---

[1] See 96.

Unless, therefore, you consider it absolutely necessary to return, I should prefer you to remain for the present.[2]

---

[2] The Foreign Office was not keen on a return visit of the governor general but could not deny him in the face of his insistence. They took comfort in "the fact that he feels that he can leave his post at this moment would seem to indicate that the position in the Sudan is not, at any rate for the moment, so desperate as his telegram No. 46 [h]as led us to infer" (minute, Howe to Sargent, 6 Nov 1946, PREM 8/1388/2).

98 FO 371/53259, no 4740 5 Nov 1946
[Sudanese reaction to the Sudan protocol]: aide memoire by J W Robertson. *Annex*: diary of events since 12 October

1. A report on the events of the last week in Khartoum is attached. On Friday November 1st. the feeling was tense, and prolonged disorder with serious results seemed possible. The good sense shewn by the bulk of the population, the efforts by Sayed Abdel Rahman to get his wilder followers out of the towns and the strong measures taken by the Government, have restored the position considerably and for the immediate future, I do not expect anything more than isolated incidents. But while immediate danger of widespread rioting and an upset of Government authority is much smaller than it was a day or two ago, there remains the likelihood of a great deterioration if the draft Protocol goes through.

2. The political position has far from settled down but His Excellency's call to good citizens to have patience and await the outcome of the negotiations has had some effect, and the first bewildered astonishment at what everyone considered the British "betrayal", has given place to a less immediately explosive attitude; but the sense of distrust and bitterness still remains.

It is true however that whatever hopes His Excellency may have had in London of being able to persuade the Independent Front that the acknowledgment by Egypt of the Sudan's right to self Government and consequent self determination, was worth the acknowledgment of a symbolic Egyptian crown, have been wrecked by Sidki Pasha's indiscretions, and especially by the use of the word "Seyada" to denote "sovereignty" when its meaning to the Sudanese is one of "dominance" and "masters", and means the personal status of slavery as well. It is not now possible, in view of the unreasoning opposition shewn by the Independents, to get this across, and His Excellency has had all his good cards wasted. It will hardly be possible to restore this position for a considerable time.

3. *Reactions to Sidki's indiscretions*

(a) The Ashigga, and their Mirghanist supporters were astonished and surprised. The Mirghanists, who had allied themselves to the Ashigga because the Mahdists were with the Independents, were genuinely shocked and dismayed. They no more than the Independents want Egyptian rule in the Sudan. The Mahdist reactions and especially the importation of fanatical westerners into the towns, have however realigned the Mirghanists with the Ashigga. The Ashigga will be disappointed at the continuation of the present administration, and the symbolic nature of unity will not satisfy those who hoped that by a substitution of Egypt for Britain as the controlling power in the Sudan to obtain substantial personal benefits.

(b) The Independents are fanatically opposed to Egyptian sovereignty in any form.

They see in any acknowledment of it the thin end of the wedge, and the eclipse of their hopes of a Sudanese state. Sayed Abdel Rahman especially sees his hopes of founding a dynasty on the Feisul model[1] vanishing. The feeling of the Independents is very bitter, and the fanatical intensity of men, whom I have known personally for many years has struck me forcibly during the last few days.

4. *The strength of the two parties*

(a) The Ashigga are stronger in Khartoum and Omdurman, and more of the semi-educated and educated men (i.e. effendia and merchants) belong to this party: the Independents (Umma) have among them practically all the best Sudanese brains; they are strong in the Advisory Council and in both the central and local Administrations. Each party has attached to itself one of the big religious sects, and in this way together they represent most of the Northern Sudan.

The Mirghanists (i.e. the Khatmia Tarika under Sayed Ali Mirghani) are the orthodox Mohammedans. Sayed Ali was brought back to the Sudan by the Anglo–Egyptians in 1898, and for many years was the undisputed head of Sudan Mohammedans. He has always been loyal to the Anglo–Egyptian Government, and I believe still is, but his loyalty is now obsessed by fear of his upstart (as he thinks) rival Sayed Abdel Rahman, the son of the Mahdi, who from the lowliest position until 1915, has since built up great influence and wealth, and is now probably more influential than Sayed Ali. Sayed Ali's influence is now thrown on the side of the Ashigga because he fears Sayed Abdel Rahman's pretensions to Kingship, though Sayed Ali does not apart from this favour Egyptian influence increasing in the Sudan.

The Mirghanists dominate the north, Kassala Province, Khartoum and Omdurman and have pockets of influence in the Gezira and western towns. The Mahdists are probably as numerous and stronger than the Mirghanists though less sophisticated and without so much influence in the towns and the north. They are fanatically supported by the strong tribes of the west, and the Gezira. Especially by the Baggara who formed the backbone of the Khalifa's Army during the Mahdia. The whole position is affected by S.A.R's dream of a crown. This makes him quite intransigent regarding any acknowledgment of an Egyptian sovereignty, gives the support of his fanatically inclined western followers to the Independents, and makes S.A.M. side with the Ashigga. Those who care little for either camp, the steady middle class man, small Government official and shopkeeper tend to go with the orthodox Mirghanists, being afraid of Mahdist rule, and the introduction of wild western Tribesmen into the Central Sudan and its cities.

5. *If Egypt accepts the present protocol*

It will be no relief to the two political parties that the present administration will continue unchanged, though it will reassure the ordinary moderate, and non-politically minded classes and some of the outside tribal leaders.

The Ashigga leaders who have hoped for leading places in a Sudan administration under Egyptian aegis, will be disappointed. The 'Umma' leaders in their fanatical opposition to the Egyptian crown for the reasons given above, will equally be disappointed. They have always hoped for a cleavage and the continuation of the present regime is abhorrent to them after Sidki Pasha's reported statement that it is

[1] Faisal ibn Husain the Hijazi prince who, as Faisal I, founded the Hashimite dynasty in Iraq following the First World War.

in Egypt's interest for the present administration to continue a little longer, until Egyptian propaganda can have time to win over the country.

It is probable that, if Egypt accepts the protocol and it goes through, there will be failure on both sides to co-operate with the Government, then resignations from Government posts, and from the Municipal, Town and Rural District Councils. There will in all likelihood be risings and disorders in the west, which will require to be put down by force; progress towards self-government will be severely prejudiced, and the administration will return to that of a police state. Educational, economic and administrative progress will receive a severe set-back.

6. *If Egypt refuses the draft protocol* as being inadequate, the Ashigga as a party will take the Egyptian line, and will look upon the protocol as a British trick, which the Egyptians have seen through. Symbolic sovereignty without the fruits of sovereignty does not appeal to the Ashigga. The Mirghanists will be affected largely by what the Mahdists do.

The 'Independents' will see in Egyptian rejection a clear proof of Egypt's desire to dominate the Sudan, which they fear will be the result of the present protocol, and will say that they knew a symbolic sovereignty would never satisfy the Egyptians. By Sidki's indiscretions the terms of the draft protocol have been disclosed, we have lost the confidence of the Independents who say that the British and the Sudan Governments have tried to betray them to the Egyptians, and have broken our pledge to consult them before the status of the country was changed.

If no Treaty was signed it will nevertheless be a very long time before the confidence which existed can be restored, if indeed this can ever be done.

7. *Possible way out*

(a) The ideal would be for the Sudan protocol to contain a declaration by Great Britain and Egypt that sovereignty in the Sudan, which was previously held jointly by the two High Contracting Parties is now declared by them to be inherent in the Sudanese people; that the two High Contracting Parties intend to act as Trustees for the well-being and progress towards self government of the Sudanese, until self governing status has been reached, and the Sudanese can themselves decide their future and their relationship with both High Contracting Parties.

(b) It is most unlikely that such a solution will be agreed to by Egypt, and as it seems certain that the present protocol will have most serious repercussions in the Sudan, it is recommended that another way out be sought.

It is suggested that in order to save bloodshed and a possible breakdown in the administration as a result of this protocol it should be shelved, and that the two codomini should instruct H.E. the Governor-General to enter into immediate consultations with the Independents, the Ashigga, and other representatives of Sudanese opinion to work out an interim type of Government to administer the Sudan, until it is self-governing and can make its decision as to its final status. The help of constitutional experts from outside the Sudan would be appreciated by the Government and by the people.

This solution will have the advantage of redeeming the pledge to consult which it is believed by all Sudanese and a large number of British officials, has been broken. It will give a breathing space and allow present passions to subside and also show the opposing parties that they must both compromise and that one party cannot expect the Sudan Government or the Codomini to crush the other. If the Egyptians suspected that the consultation under British rule would not be fairly carried out, they should be invited to send an observer to be present: but the freedom of speech etc., which the Sudan Government has given to both Ashigga and Umma in recent months is well known to all responsible persons in Egypt (for instance no attempt to muzzle El Azhari has ever been made). If such consultations produced any result, proposals would then be submitted by H.E. to the Codomini; if no result was achieved then H.E. and the Sudan Government would submit their own proposals, after receiving assistance of experts from outside the Sudan.

It must be emphasized very strongly that continuation of the administration, in its present form, is no winning card. It is a debit rather than a credit. The Ashigga who want the end of British influence, dislike it, and the Independents now think little of an Administration which in their view has betrayed them.

Annex to 98

October 12th. In view of reports that Azhari was to accompany Sidki Pasha to London, the Umma Party decided to send Abdullah Bey Khalil there at once.

October 18th. S.A.R. decided that in view of Sidki's confidence that he would bring back from London sovreignty [sic] over the Sudan, he had better go to London himself in order to explain the position to Mr. Bevin.

October 19th. S.A.R. wired Mr. Bevin and several Nazirs followed suit. Abdullah Bey left for London.[2]

October 20th. S.A.R. wired to Sidki. Reply received from Governor General that there was little point in S.A.R. going to London.

October 23rd. Reuter contained statement from London that Sidki Pasha, "is understood to oppose the British suggestion of consulting the Sudanese people by plebiscite or otherwise *until a period of Egyptian sovreignty* [sic] *has done something to offset British influence*."

The general effect of this on Umma opinion was that it rendered it most unlikely that H.M.G. would agree to Egyptian sovreignty [sic].

October 27th. The B.B.C. on their 8 a.m. and 10 a.m. broadcasts (G.M.T. 06.00 and 08.00 hours) announced Sidki's claim to have brought back sovreignty [sic] over the Sudan. No denial or qualification of this statement was issued until 10 p.m. (G.M.T. 08.00 hours—a time when nobody in the Sudan ever listens in). It was reported at 6 a.m. on the 28th, but was dropped from subsequent broadcasts, and the first information the Sudanese had that Sidki's claim was not fully justified, was when Mr. Attlee's statement in the House was broadcast at 6 p.m. local time.

Meanwhile on the morning of the 27th the Umma Leaders asked for an official denial of Sidki's statement, and were told that this Government had every reason to believe it to be misleading, but had no information from London. They were advised to await further news. Instead they held an immediate meeting and decided to summon their supporters from outside Khartoum, boycotting the Advisory Council and the Sudan Administrative Conference, to cable a protest to Mr. Attlee, and to hold a demonstration in Omdurman that night.

[2] Abdullah Khalil and Yaqub Uthman (editor of *an-Nil*) requested a meeting with a representative of the Secretary of State on 24 Oct and were granted an interview with C P Mayhew, parliamentary under-secretary of state, on 8 Nov. Mayhew reported that 'they put their case simply & well, & I formed a good impression of them' (minute, Mayhew to Scrivener, 8 Nov 1946, FO 371/53259, no 4671).

About 3,000 persons assembled at the Umma Club that evening, and after fiery speeches denouncing the British for having sold the Sudan to Egypt, marched to the Congress Headquarters in the Graduates' Club. They were prevented by the Police from entering the Club, and after another demonstration at the Mahdi's Tomb dispersed, after throwing stones at tramcars, breaking the windscreen of a private car and injuring some of the Ashigga Leaders.

The Ashigga remained quiet.

October 28th. Early in the morning the boys of the Farouk School marched through the streets to a number of about 200 in celebration of the Unity of the Nile Valley. This demonstration was a complete fiasco. In the evening the Umma Party had a meeting with the Republicans, the Liberals and the Nationalists and they decided to join to form a new Independent Front to oppose the Unionists Front, of which the Nationalists had hitherto been nominal members.

October 29th. His Excellency and the Civil Secretary were due to arrive by air that evening, and there had been strong rumours of an Umma proposal to stage a demonstration either at the aerodrome or at the Palace on their arrival.

The Acting Governor General interviewed four of the Umma Leaders in the morning, and pointed out the dangers of provocative behaviour. They informed him of the formation of the new United Independence Front, and said that a delegation would be at the Kitchener Statue the following evening to hand over a manifesto to the representative of His Excellency. They indicated that they would probably be followed by a crowd, but did not ask permission to hold a public meeting.

Meanwhile the Gordon College Union were holding a stormy meeting prepatory to staging a demonstration that afternoon in celebration of the achievement of the Unity of the Nile Valley. The College authorities warned them that any demonstration outside the College grounds would lead to the immediate closing of the College, and representatives of the Unionists Front, who were anxious to prevent a clash, succeeded in dissuading them from their purpose. Parties of Mahdist supporters armed with sticks and whips had meanwhile assembled at strategic points to attack them should they venture out.

His Excellency arrived early in the evening and proceeded to the Palace without incident.

A big Umma Meeting was held that night in Omdurman and a demonstration arranged for Abbas Square at 4 p.m. the following evening.

October, 30th. A crowd of between 3,000 and 4,000 assembled the following evening and proceeded in good order in companies with banners, including the red, green and black tricolour of the Independent Sudan to the Kitchener Statue, led by Abdullahi Fadil el Mahdi.[3] The Umma Leaders and various Independents, including practically every prominent Sudanese in the three towns, were already in position, and handed over a written protest, "against the decision taken by Great Britain and Egypt regarding the sovereignty over the Sudan." This was signed by representatives of the four parties and by four prominent non party men, including the Sharif. The meeting then dispersed.

October 31st. His Excellency's appeal for moderation was published on the morning of the 31st, and the Umma Leaders, who had been asked by the Civil Secretary to discuss the situation with him, refused to see him on the grounds that His

---

[3] Ansar member of the Graduates' Congress Committee.

Excellency's declaration was unsatisfactory, since neither he nor Mr. Attlee had denied the vital point of sovreignty [sic].

Meanwhile the Gordon College irritated by the Umma demonstration of the previous day, absented themselves from lectures to hold another mass meeting, and since any possibility of getting any serious work done was now out of the question, the College authorities decided of their own initiative to close the College.

Meanwhile the Unionist Party had decided that it was time something was done, and asked permission to hold a demonstration on the following (Friday) morning.

It was decided to give permission for this demonstration in view of the Umma demonstration having taken place the previous day, but a request to the Independent Front to avoid any provocative action, in recognition of their having been unmolested on the previous day, was met with an evasive reply.

November 1st. The town was now filling up with bodies of fanatical Mahdists from outside, and early in the morning attempts were made to interfere with parties of Unionists on their way in to Abbas Square. One lorry was overturned and the passengers set upon with spears (15 casualties, none fatal), and there were minor incidents in Khartoum and Omdurman, but the main procession passed off with very little incident, until it returned to Abbas Square and began to disperse. Numbers of riffraff from the market then attacked the offices of the two opposition newspapers which were guarded by strong bands of Umma supporters. Stones and bricks were thrown, and amongst others the District Commissioner and Commandant of Police were hit, but after a struggle lasting for over an hour, during which a Company of Camel Corps stood by at Province Headquarters, the police succeeded in dispersing the crowd without serious casualties.

Meanwhile an exaggerated report of the attack of the newspaper offices had reached the Umma Headquarters in Omdurman, where the party responsible for the attack on the lorry in the morning had been confined by the Umma Leaders (Said Sadiq [sic, Siddiq], the son of S.A.R. had been doing very good work in dispersing the crowds in Abbas Square). These fanatics had once marched on the Graduates Club and wrecked it, the depleted Omdurman Police Force being unable to prevent them. The Camel Corps Company was then rushed to Omdurman and with this support the Police were then able to prevent any further incident that day.

November 2nd. The events of the previous day had shocked both parties. The Unionists realising for the first time the strength and fanaticism of the Umma Supporters, and having had, many of them their first experience of civil disturbances, were appealing for Police protection and denouncing the Sudan Government for their alleged failure to maintain order.

S.A.R. arrived in Khartoum during the morning and had an interview with His Excellency, and subsequently issued an appeal to his followers to be patient and return to their homes. He based his appeal upon Mr. Bevin's telegram to him of October 26th.

Meanwhile the Civil Secretary had interviewed the secretaries of the rival Fronts and directed them to send their supporters home, abstain from all public political meetings, and give similar instructions to their branches in the provinces. At the same time a ban was placed upon all public meetings throughout the country.

Since then the situation has temporarily quitened [sic] down, and attention has concentrated on trying to remove from the three towns as quickly as possible the thousands of rival supporters who had flooded in during the week.

99 FO 371/53318, no 4885 7 Nov 1946

[Sudan protocol]: translation by FO of a note prepared by Sidqi Pasha for the Egyptian treaty delegation giving the Egyptian interpretation of the Sudan protocol

[A continuing stream of Egyptian press reports left the FO uncertain about Sidqi's presentation of the treaty, and particularly whether the Egyptian government and parliament understood and would accept the Sudanese right to choose their own future status. Political rivalries within the Egyptian treaty delegation meant that Sidqi could not count on a majority there, despite the king's strong support for the new agreement, and despite the interpretation of the Sudan protocol Sidqi offered the delegation in this note. As a result he was reported considering bypassing the delegation and going directly to the Council of Ministers to get authorisation to sign the treaty (inward telegram no 1660, Bowker to FO, 9 Nov 1946, FO 371/53317, no 4679).]

The Protocol first of all consecrates the unity of Egypt and the Sudan under the Crown of Egypt.+ For the first time the sovereignty of Egypt over the Sudan is formally and expressly recognised by Great Britain in an international act. This recognition will definitely put an end to the policy of Great Britain or her representatives in the Sudan of assuring for themselves a part of the sovereignty over the Sudan by different and more or less indirect means by calling it in official documents "Anglo–Egyptian Condominium" which suggests a joint sovereignty. This policy has spread abroad even among statesmen and jurists an erroneous idea of the rights of Egypt over the Sudan. To cite only one example, a renowned author like Fauchille, in his International Public Law, cites the Sudan in a section entitled "Copropriété, Condominium, Coimperium", and speaks of the "undivided sovereignty of Egypt and of Great Britain" over the Sudan.

The Protocol will have this great advantage of making incontestable in the eyes of all the nations the exclusive right of sovereignty of Egypt over the Sudan. That is a fact which may have great importance in the future if a problem concerning the Sudan should be one day brought before U.N.O.

But there has been opposed to this consecration that part of the Protocol which defines the future policy in the Sudan of the two High Contracting Parties and which assigns as an essential object the wellbeing of the Sudanese and their active preparation for self-government and for the exercise of the right which derives from it of choosing the future status of the Sudan.

To realise the correct implications of this declaration, we must first of all define the term "self-government". Now in international law this expression is not the equivalent of independence nor of the right of sovereignty. The United Nations Charter, in the chapter on the international régime of trusteeship, has employed this term speaking precisely of the progressive evolution of the populations of the territories under trusteeship. Article 76 mentions in fact "their progressive development towards self-government or independence", translated in the official French text as "leur évolution progressive *vers la capacité à s'administrer eux-mêmes ou l'independence*".

+ In the course of the discussion on the Sudan, Mr. Bevin asked me what title the King of Egypt intended to take. I replied that the imperial firmans styled him Khedive of Egypt, Sovereign of Nubia, Darfur, Kordofan and Sennar, but that to answer the desire of his peoples, the King would take the title of "King of Egypt and the Sudan". Mr. Bevin raised no objection.

Accordingly, in the most recent and most authorised official interpretation, that accepted together by Great Britain and Egypt and with them all the signatory states of the United Nations Charter, the expression "self-government" only signifies administrative autonomy; it is distinct from independence, which is defined by the authors as being internal sovereignty.

This question did not moreover give rise to any dispute in our conversations in London. From the British as much as from the Egyptian side, a distinction was made between self-government and independence. I specified on many occasions that we wished the Sudanese to be able to assume themselves the direction of their affairs and that this was not in contradiction with the right of Egyptian sovereignty.

But Mr. Bevin was chiefly occupied with the hypothesis that the Sudanese would claim their independence. At the beginning of the conversations he thought that he had obligations towards the Sudanese and that he could not bind them indissolubly to the sovereignty of Egypt. He also would have wished to include in the treaty a text giving assurances to the Sudanese on the question of independence. In one of the drafts presented by the British, it was foreseen that the provisions of the Protocol did not hinder the Sudanese from choosing later a status carrying with it the complete independence of their country, in conformity with the principles of the Atlantic Charter. I struck out this text and I formally refused any mention in the Protocol of even an eventual renunciation of Egyptian sovereignty.

I made clear to Mr. Bevin that it was unlikely that the Sudanese would one day demand to be separated from Egypt, that this was a hypothesis that could only be admitted in the distant future, whereas the treaty between Egypt and Great Britain was only concluded for a period of 20 years, after which the two countries would resume their liberty.

On the other hand if this question came up Egypt would resolve it with the Sudan in the most friendly spirit and in conformity with the United Nations Charter. But as Mr. Bevin abandoned the idea of independence and the eventual renunciation of Egyptian sovereignty and wished to be able to give the Sudanese assurances about their future, he insisted that the protocol should mention the future status of the Sudan.

The word "status" has not the juridical precision of "self-government"; it is rather vague and open to different interpretations, depending on its context.

To avoid the inconvenience resulting from the absence of precision in the word "status", the Egyptians, after having studied carefully different formulae, stopped at that which occurs in the Protocol and which has been finally accepted by Mr. Bevin. This formula allows the Sudanese to choose their future status as a result of self-government. This text does not accordingly grant the Sudanese immediate self-government, and then something in addition outside the self-government, that is to say the right of choosing the political, international and sovereign status which would allow them the right of secession from Egypt. It specifies, on the contrary, that the right of choosing their future status is an application and a result of self-government. The latter being only administrative autonomy, the status in question cannot exceed this framework and can only be an administrative status or internal autonomy.

It must be noted in addition that if we wish to maintain that the "future status" foreseen by the Protocol is a political and international status, we will come up against a formal contradiction in the very terms of the Protocol. This specifies that the policy of the High Contracting Parties will be carried out "within the framework of the unity of the Sudan and Egypt under a common crown, the crown of Egypt." This policy is accordingly limited by the idea of the sovereignty of Egypt. It cannot bring about measures which will go beyond these limits and which will exceed the framework of the unity of the two countries under the same crown. This excludes completely the right of secession or the grant to the Sudanese of the right of breaking the bond of sovereignty which joins them to Egypt.

In addition paragraph 2 of the Protocol foresees that the future status of the Sudan will be realised by "common agreement" between the High Contracting Parties after consultation with the Sudanese. Now if the exercise of the right of choosing the status of the Sudan, deriving from self-government, brings the right of secession for the Sudanese, it is clear that the establishment of the régime of complete independence which *ex hypothesi* they would be able to choose would have to be made without the intervention of Egypt and not by common agreement between the two Contracting Parties with simple consultation of the Sudanese.

Whatever may be the interpretation to be given to the present texts, Egyptian sovereignty over the Sudan could be abandoned only by virtue of a subsequent formal renunciation by Egypt, either as a result of a revolution of the Sudanese people, of a secession by force to which Egypt submitted, or by virtue of a voluntary renunciation, by an admission of the hypothesis that the Sudanese could one day freely express their desire for independence—going outside the framework of the Protocol—and which Egypt agrees to grant them.

The Sudanese do not in fact acquire by virtue of the text of the Protocol the right to claim their secession.

It is, furthermore, not in a Protocol of this nature annexed to a bilateral Treaty that the right of Egyptian sovereignty could be ceded or abrogated, even for the future such a serious change of relations between Egypt and the Sudan could only take place by an express and solemn act, first of all directed to the people of the Sudan and accepted by them and afterwards submitted to all the United Nations. Egyptian sovereignty pre-exists the treaty and is affirmed vis à vis all the States. The Protocol only establishes the consent of Great Britain to recognise this situation as far as that country is concerned; it does not create that sovereignty.

The Protocol itself, however, does in fact in its first paragraph admit for Great Britain the obligation to modify the present régime, for the benefit not of Egypt but of the Sudanese; if the sovereignty of Egypt is permanent, the present administrative régime has, on the contrary, a temporary character since it must evolve towards self-government, that is to say towards the progressive elimination of non-Sudanese elements. The Protocol furthermore contemplates in this modification of the present system the simultaneous participation of Egypt, Great Britain and the Sudanese themselves.

Egypt has accordingly acquired the right to participate in the elaboration of the reforms to be made in the Sudan régime. She must henceforth study and put forward the modifications which she thinks necessary for the realisation of the policy that Great Britain and Egypt are pledged to follow. Furthermore, even before these reforms are decided upon, she will equally have the right to examine and see whether the régime set up by the 1899 convention takes sufficient account of the well-being of the Sudanese which is one of the goals pursued by the two High Contracting Parties and whether in its present state, it can serve as a point of departure for the establishment of a régime of self-government.

This right of intervention and examination allows Egypt to protect the interests of the Sudanese and to improve their lot. Thanks to this right and also because she will herself be freed from British occupation and influence, Egypt will be able to take back at least a part of her authority and her influence in the Sudan, as her action will be exercised in a domain which the Sudanese certainly consider more important than the day-to-day administration, since it will be a question of giving satisfaction to Sudanese national aspirations and to regulate in a permanent fashion the future of the Sudan.

There have been criticisms of the absence in the Protocol of any mention of subsequent negotiations, but the Protocol, after having recognised the unity of Egypt and the Sudan under the Crown of Egypt, has defined the future policy to be followed in the Sudan by the two High Contracting Parties; this was the aim of the contemplated negotiations.

This policy consists of granting self-government to the Sudanese and of determining the future status of the Sudan. This cannot however be immediately realised in detail, even after study and prolonged negotiation; it is a matter of a progressive evolution which will take some years. The execution of this policy of which the final aim has been inscribed in the protocol, is a long term task to be arranged by the two governments. It will involve mutual exchange of views, discussions, preparations, programmes and even, for the most important points, negotiations which will be able to be carried out in a quasi-permanent manner during the years to come.

In the course of the London conversations, Mr. Bevin showed himself to be a supporter of the institution of a permanent Sudan joint board which would study the progress of the development of the Sudanese.

It is difficult to say now what will be the best method for Egypt to intervene in Sudanese affairs. She can be interested in making investigations, either alone or in conjunction with the British; she can prepare to have a permanent High Commissioner at Khartoum or a permanent office. Finally, it is perhaps preferable for her to act through the intermediary of the Joint Board proposed by Mr. Bevin. In any case, it would be premature for her to bind herself at the present time in this connection.

It will be for the Egyptian Government of the future to exercise vigilantly and by the most appropriate means the henceforth recognised rights of Egypt to control the regime in force and to share in the elaboration of the future status of the Sudan.

100 PREM 8/1388/2 8 Nov 1946

[Sudan government]: inward telegram no 1525 from Mr Bevin (New York) to Mr Attlee, criticising the attitude of Sudan government officials

Your telegram No. 52 to Khartoum.[1]

I am not happy about the attitude and set-up of the Sudan Government. The whole position is quite different now from what it was up to the war. We cannot any longer

[1] See 97.

run the Condominium as if it existed in isolation from the rest of the world. Critical eyes are now fixed on all our Imperial arrangements and a new outlook on the part of the Sudan Government is required.

2. I hope that the letter for the Government officials will help to explain the new situation to them. But it is also necessary that I, as Foreign Secretary, should be continuously and punctually informed of the programmes and actions of the Sudan Government. In regard to the Condominium the Foreign Secretary ought to be in as close touch with the Sudan as the Colonial Secretary is with the affairs of the Colonies.

101 PREM 8/1388/2 9 Nov 1946

[Sudan government]: minute from Sir O Sargent to Mr Attlee on the changed political circumstances in which Sudan administrators will be required to work

Prime Minister

Reference Foreign Secretary's personal telegram No. 1525.[1]

I should like to say (a) that we in the Foreign Office and in Cairo have long been aware that the Sudan could not continue to be run as a model colonial administration in isolation and (b) that in fact the Foreign Office is very closely and accurately informed of the policies and actions of the Sudan Government; and that, if the Foreign Secretary feels that existing arrangements are inadequate, the reason is that we have, owing to his present immense responsibilities, brought questions of Sudan policy to his notice only when it was essential to do so.

It is very largely true that the Sudan Government have run the Sudan in isolation from the rest of the world. After the murder of General Lee Stack in 1924 we cleared most of the Egyptians out of the administration and we have in effect run the Sudan as a British colony under the supervision of the British Foreign Secretary. (The Governor-General has supreme military and civil command, under the original Anglo–Egyptian Agreement of 1899 and he has always been a British subject). It is generally acknowledged that this administration has been a model of its kind. Apart however from the day to day dealings of Sudan frontier officials with their opposite numbers in Ethiopia, French Equatorial Africa etc. there have been little or no international contacts with the Sudan. No foreign consuls have ever been allowed to function in the Sudan.

This was all very well up to the outbreak of the war. The war has provoked a great increase of interest among the Sudanese themselves in their own administration, together with Egyptian aspirations to closer unity of the Sudan with Egypt. The former development has led to a very great increase in the Sudanisation of the administration. About 80 per cent of all the lower grade posts in the administration are now held by Sudanese. The effects of the latter development have been seen in the negotiations for a new Anglo–Egyptian Treaty and these have focussed an international spotlight on this part of Africa.

---

[1] See 100.

All the posts in the higher levels of the administration are held by British officials. They have been solely concerned with the good administration of the Sudan and they have had a free hand in this on behalf of the two condominium governments for twenty-five years. This may possibly have bred a certain narrowness of outlook. Now that all forms of colonial administration are under attack in certain international quarters and in view of the growing nationalism of the Sudanese the administration will be compelled to widen its horizons. As far as the actual material administration of the welfare of the Sudanese is concerned I do not think we have much to fear from hostile criticism. But we may well be criticised, and here the Egyptians would be against us, for insulating the Sudan from the rest of the world. We shall probably want a new type of British official whose job will be to advise and assist Sudanese in the administration of their own affairs. Up till now the Sudan officials have been able to be perfectionists. This is not really possible any longer, and they will have to be content with something less than perfection.

We should begin this process with the appointment of a new Governor-General which is due in the spring. It is clear that a man of wide political experience besides administrative qualifications is required.

102 PREM 8/1388/2 — 9 Nov 1946

[Political situation in the Sudan]: letter from Sir H Huddleston to Mr Attlee. *Enclosure*: letter from T P Creed, J W E Miller and J W Robertson to Sir H Huddleston, 6 Nov 1946

My dear Prime Minister[1]

Before I left London for the Sudan a fortnight ago, I told Mr. Bevin that in spite of all the difficulties which I foresaw, I believed that I could persuade the Sudanese to accept the Protocol.

Before I reached Khartoum however, Sidki Pasha had completely destroyed whatever chance of success I may have had by his statement on the Sovereignty of the Sudan. The whole attention of the Sudanese was immediately focussed exclusively on the Sovereignty question and an "Egyptian Domination" Fear Complex developed of a far greater intensity than could possibly have been foreseen. I and my three principal advisers whose letter to me is attached having talked to several of the leading Sudanese and in particular to Sayed Abdel Rahman El Mahdi are now quite convinced that it is impossible to persuade the Independent Front, which has the support of the majority, that there are any advantages in the Protocol, which could in any way offset Egyptian Sover[e]ignty, and that the terms of the Protocol could only be carried out by force.

To use force to impose Egyptian Sovereignty on the Sudanese would be so complete a reversal of all that the Sudan Government has worked for for the past half century and would so completely destroy Sudanese faith in the good intentions of His Majesty[']s Government that I have returned at once so as to explain in person the basic change that has taken place in the situation in the last fortnight[.]

---

[1] Huddleston handed this letter personally to Attlee on 10 Nov.

I feel that it is no overstatement to say that if the Protocol has to be implemented by Force all the confidence engendered by fifty years of cooperation between British and Sudanese will vanish overnight.

I trust therefore that before the Cabinet makes its final decision full consideration may be given to these altered circumstances. If however the Cabinet decides to approve the present Protocol I must record that I am no longer in agreement with the Sovereignty clause: but nevertheless if His Majesty[']s Government wish me to continue as Governor General I am ready to do so and to carry out the terms of the Protocol in view of Paragraph 8 of attached letter—believing that my personal influence might possibly reduce the amount of Force required.

Enclosure to 102

Your Excellency,

1. In your recent consultations in London Your Excellency agreed with some hesitation to the inclusion in the proposed Sudan protocol of the reference to Egyptian sovereignty. Your Excellency believed that you had a chance of getting it accepted in the Sudan by emphasising its advantages to the Sudanese, as outweighing the concession of a symbolic sovereignty to the King of Egypt. We think that as things were then, there was a chance. We also realise that the maintenance of a strong British position in the Middle East is an essential condition of any advancement of the Sudanese.

2. Sidki Pasha's statement that he had brought back Egyptian "sovereignty" caused an instantaneous reaction in the Sudan. It has been made abundantly clear that the bulk of the Sudanese will not willingly accept the protocol as long as it gives sole sovereignty of any kind to Egypt. In their view "sovereignty" cannot be qualified and the protocol in this respect represents a breach of all British pledges.

3. The Sudan Government have taken the line that Mr. Bevin's statement of March could be trusted implicitly and to this is due the remarkable restraint shewn by the Sudanese throughout the past six months of negotiation. This government has for very many years with the encouragement of His Majesty's Government stressed the joint sovereignty of Great Britain and Egypt, adopting roughly speaking the line taken in chapter 5 of "The Anglo–Egyptian Sudan" written by Sir Harold MacMichael, a former Civil Secretary of this government and read by educated Sudanese. In unsophisticated Sudanese eyes this belief is fortified by daily visible signs of joint sovereingty [sic] with Great Britain as the predominant partner. To them any idea that Great Britain has no share in the sovereingty [sic] of the Sudan is meaningless. All Sudanese therefore consider that a change of status is involved and, whatever the legal arguments may be regarding the correct interpretation of the Condomium agreement, they believe that H.M.G. will be committing a breach of faith by making without previous consultation of the Sudanese its admission, never made in any previous negotiations, of sole Egyptian sovereignty.

4. The Prime Minister's statement in the House of Commons on October 28th, did not satisfy the Sudanese whose comment was that it did not deny the reported inclusion of Egyptian sovereignty; the advantages gained by the Sudanese were entirely ignored in view of their obsession with the sovereignty issue. When the protocol is published, Mr. Attlee's statement denying any change of status will be considered to have been misleading and will be bitterly resented.

5. On your return to Khartoum Your Excellency found that Sidki Pasha's statement had entirely altered the situation, but on the instructions Your Excellency had received in London and from the Secretary of State's telegram No. 49 of the 29th October, it was impossible to discuss the protocol publicly while it was still under consideration by the Egyptians. The many private conversations which have taken place have shewn fanatical opposition on the sovereignty issue and complete indifference to the advantages set out in Mr. Attlee's statement, which the Sudanese in any case regard as having been already promised.

6. If the protocol goes through, we believe, resignations will occur from government and local government service; there will be widespread non-cooperation from both parties, i.e. the independents who believe themselves betrayed and the "Unionists" (Wadi el Nil front) who wish to see the present administration ended. There may be risings among the tribes resulting in the loss of British lives. There will be a relapse to a police state and a consequent postponement of all the benefits to the Sudanese which it is claimed the protocol safeguards.

7. For these reasons we believe the position has been completely changed by circumstances beyond your control since Your Excellency consented in London to try to persuade the Sudanese of the real values of the protocol, and we recommend most strongly that Your Excellency should personally see the Prime Minister so that H.M.G. may reconsider the position.

8. Finally we wish to place on record that if in spite of recent events and in spite of our protest His Majesty's Government persists in acknowledging sole Egyptian sovereignty in the Sudan which we believe will result in the substitution of a government of force and repression for a government of cooperation and political development a policy repugnant to us and contrary to all the traditions of this government, we desire that Your Excellency should see the Sudan through the difficult months ahead. Your Excellency has the complete confidence of the British officials of this service and no Governor-General could rival you in your influence with all classes of Sudanse.

9. We request that this memorandum be presented to the Prime Minister on your arrival in the United Kingdom.

103 PREM 8/1388/2 11 Nov 1946

[Political situation in the Sudan]: outward telegram no 2079 (reply) from Mr Attlee to Mr Bevin, reporting and commenting upon the governor general's assessment of the political situation in the Sudan [Extract]

Your telegram No. 1525 (of November 8th: Sudan).[1]

Personal from Prime Minister to Foreign Secretary.

The Governor General of the Sudan arrived here on November 9th and he has given me his views on the situation created in the Sudan by the ill-timed and ill-

---

[1] See 100.

considered statement on Egyptian sovereignty over the Sudan attributed to Sidky. These views are as follows. . . .[2]

7. Even admitting the extreme parochial outlook of the Sudanese I find it very difficult to understand their line. In this country we have always understood that Egyptian sovereignty over the Sudan existed though not explicitly stated. This has apparently not been understood by the Sudanese. The Governor General explained that up till 1924 there was a true condominium but in that year we turned out all Egyptian troops and there was practically a complete British administration thereafter with an anti-Egyptian bias which was only slightly modified by the return of an Egyptian battalion in 1936. The fact is that the Sudanese have for the last twenty-two years shut their eyes to any Egyptian connexion and nothing was ever done to open them to the true state of affairs.[3]

8. At the best, the Governor General considers that if the protocol goes through, Sudanese officials who form 78 per cent of the administration will resign and there will be a boycott. There may be resignations among the British administration. At the worst, there will be disorders and bloodshed.

9. As regards our future policy and having balanced the situation in the Sudan as described by the Governor General with the facts in the world at large, I feel that we have no alternative but to continue the line which you have taken with Sidky. If we go back now on the Sudan Protocol there is no doubt in my mind that we lose the Treaty for Sidky's Government could no longer stand. Our relations with Egypt and all our defence arrangements in the Middle East would once more be thrown into the melting pot. We should probably be taken to United Nations Organisation by the Egyptians, on the whole issue and certainly to the International Court on the sovereignty aspect and we are advised that the Court would confirm the Egyptian case. Our position in the Sudan as a result of an adverse judgment on this point would be infinitely worse, it seems to me, than it will be under the present Sudan Protocol. Moreover, we should have gained nothing in the Sudan since the Sudanese already know that we have admitted Egyptian sovereignty.

10. There remains the question what steps we can take in the Sudan to strengthen the Sudan Government's position. It might help if the Protocol were accompanied by a joint Anglo–Egyptian declaration that the Sudanese would be free to decide their own future within a fixed period, say 10 or 15 years. In the meantime we could hurry on the process of Sudanisation by the establishment of Sudanese legislative and executive organs, the role of British officials being progressively confined to advising and assisting. When the Sudanese saw that in practice they were being put in control of their own affairs without any more interference from the

---

[2] Paras 2–6 give a near verbatim record of Huddleston's views set out in 102.

[3] In a comment on this telegram which Huddleston later sent to Bevin, with Attlee's permission, Huddleston stated: 'The Sudan Government has always believed that Egyptian sovereignty existed jointly with British sovereignty over the Sudan and has consistently brought up the Sudanese in that belief, with, as far as it was aware, the complete approval of His Majesty's Government. . . . It is not the Sudanese who have shut their eyes to the Egyptian connexion during the past 22 years; they were deliberately shut for them with his Majesty's Government's cognisance. Their violent disillusionment now through Sidqi's indiscretions without my having an opportunity to prepare them can only be regarded by them as a betrayal of the promise that there should be no change of status without consultation' (outward telegram no 2166, Huddleston to Bevin, 14 Nov 1946, PREM 8/1388/2).

Egyptian Government than in the past, we might hope for a progressive and peaceful evolution towards self-government.

11. I propose to request the Governor General to return and carry on until the future is clearer. On his way through Cairo he might call on King Farouk in order to impress on him the seriousness of the position in the Sudan and see whether the King in his speech to Parliament on the 14th could not say something to help ease the tension or at least say nothing to exacerbate it.

104 PREM 8/1388/2 12 Nov 1946

[Political situation in the Sudan]: inward telegram no 1613 (reply) from Mr Bevin to Mr Attlee

Your telegram No. 2079.[1]

Thank you for sending me this full account of your talk with the Governor General.

2. I am certain that in spite of the threat of trouble in the Sudan which the Egyptian leakages have aggravated we should stick to the line agreed with Sidky. Vacillation under the threat of force would be the worst thing for our position not only in the Sudan but throughout the Arab world.

3. In paragraph 4 of your telegram under reference you mention the Governor General's view that "if force has to be used and if what he calls a police state with censorship etc., has to be instituted all the confidence engendered by fifty years of co-operation between the British and the Sudanese will vanish overnight". This really does seem to be painting our activities in the blackest light. If we had to use force it would only be to maintain law and order nor do I see why we should be called upon to set up a "police state with censorship". As for the disappearance overnight of all the confidence in the British built up over fifty years that could only come about as a result of either malicious interpretation of the draft protocol or excessively bad presentation on our part.

4. As to your suggestions in paragraph 10, I am not in favour of a fixed date by which the future of the Sudan has to be decided. It is very difficult to tell how events will work out and at what speed. I do not believe in having to work to a hard and fast time schedule in political questions of this character. However, I am all in favour of intensifying Sudanisation. Effective action to this end together with adequate publicity on the development towards self-government emphasised in the Sudan protocol should serve to dispel any argument that we are sacrificing the Sudan to Egypt. We would review the progress of Sudanisation periodically. This was the reason for my telegram No. 1525 asking for periodic reports to the Foreign Office on the administration of the Sudan.[2] I had no knowledge that we had been acting since 1924 in the manner indicated.

---

[1] See 103.

[2] See 100.

105 FO 371/53260, no 4861 12 Nov 1946

[Political situation in the Sudan]: notes by Sir H Huddleston for and in discussion with Mr McNeil

[As Bevin was then in America, Huddleston met with McNeil at the FO. After the meeting McNeil commented: 'He is in a Messianic frame of mind, and I think he is going to resign'. He proposed that a conference of Sudanese leaders be called in London after the treaty was signed and suggested that 'this might be a straw on which Huddleston could cling, and would certainly stall his resignation' (minute, H McNeil, 12 Nov 1946, FO 371/53260, no 4861). Huddleston continued to display his 'Messianic' frame of mind in two further 'urgent' letters sent to McNeil the following day (see 106 and 107).]

1. When I tell you that the whole of the Sudanese Independents Party look upon the inclusion of the Egyptian Sovereignty clause in the Protocol as an absolute betrayal of them by H.M.G., and that in their present state of mind it is impossible for anybody to get them to change their opinion on this point in the slightest degree—Do you believe me without any reservation whatsoever?

2. Can you give me the same assurance for the Prime Minister, and for Mr. Alexander, and for Mr. Bevin when he has seen the papers?

3. If your answer to the above question is "yes"—Do you fully appreciate that the only alternative to persuasion is force, and that once force is employed, no guarantee can be given of the amount required and, in the present fanatical state of the Sudanese, very serious resistance to Government, especially in the more distant districts might easily develop which could only be put down at the cost of very considerable bloodshed?

1. We have lived on bluff for the last twenty-four years and now our bluff has been called—why should the Sudanese be punished for believing that we were honest men and not bluffers?

2. Is the matter being referred to Mr. Bevin before final decision; if so, can I go to America to see him?

3. S.A.R.—Visit of, most important. Stansgate protested against because they had been discouraged from seeing Azhari—situation entirely different—Azhari self-elected free-lance. S.A.R. acknowledged head of largest Party and group in the Sudan.

4. If I was dealing with trustworthy people, I should have no qualms—but can the Egyptians be trusted? and since when? What Ronald Weekes told me.

5. Are they counting on Egyptian Army? Is the Treaty worth while?

6. Somebody yesterday said that the Sudanese see the Egyptian flag, know the Governor-General is appointed by Egypt etc.—don't they recognise Egypt here? The answer is they saw 1924.

7. Anthony Eden.[1]

8. Written answer to my letter—I reserve the right to resign immediately. Egyptian sovereignty life and death to Sudanese but not to British—therefore my first duty to Sudanese though resignation might have serious effect on British staff.

---

[1] Anthony Eden, shadow foreign secretary, was then preparing a speech of on the Sudan, which he delivered in the House of Commons on 14 Nov. Huddleston remained in touch with him, and subsequently Eden relayed to Attlee his own, and Huddleston's disquiet over the King of Egypt's claim of sovereignty over the Sudan (PREM 8/182, Eden to Attlee, 26 Nov 1946).

106 FO 371/53260, no 4860 13 Nov 1946

[Political situation in the Sudan]: letter from Sir H Huddleston to Mr McNeil

When I gave you my written questions[1] yesterday, you very frankly admitted that I had failed to convince the members of the Cabinet, including yourself, who were at the meeting at No.10 on Monday, the 11th November, that the Sudan Independence group were, in their present state of mind, completely unmovable on the sovereignty clause. This is wishful thinking on your part, and like all wishful thinking, at base dishonest. If you don't believe me, produce only one other person with knowledge of the Sudan comparable to mine who disagrees with me; otherwise you MUST believe me. Say to me—as I said to you yesterday—"It is meet that one man die for the people" and I will agree with you.

It may be necessary for the Sudan to pay the price of the mistake of His Majesty's Government in the past. That is honest and logical. Don't avoid the issue by saying that if the Sudanese were sensible there would be no price to pay; the whole essence of our trouble is that on this particular point the Sudanese are not "sensible".

The situation is then clear and I can decide whether I can be their executioner or not.

---

[1] See 105.

107 FO 371/53260, no 4762 13 Nov 1946

[Proposed visit of SAR]: letter from Sir H Huddleston to Mr McNeil

Reference the visit of S.A.R. to this country: shortness of time prevented me yesterday from pointing out the close historical parallel to Zaghlul Pasha's[1] demand in February 1919 to go and state the case of Egypt before the Peace Conference in Paris, or at least before the Cabinet in London.

Wingate, the High Commissioner in Egypt, strongly recommended that Zaghlul should be allowed to come—but not to the point of saying "I know for certain that there will be an attempt at a general anti-British rising in Egypt if you refuse. Therefore if you will not take my advice I must resign". Zahglul's appeal was turned down—there was a general rising—a number of unarmed British scattered about Egypt were murdered—a much larger number, far larger than was known at home, of fanatically excited Egyptians were killed. I know because I helped to kill them; I was then in military command of all Upper Egypt.

Wingate was made the scapegoat; he was replaced by Allenby and was never re-employed again. But that is by the way. The point of my story is that, being wise after the event, everybody agreed that if Zaghlul had been allowed at least to come to London and unburden himself of Egypt's wrongs, there would have been no rising in

---

[1] Zaghlul Pasha, leader of the Wafd Party, pressed for Egyptian independence after the end of World War One. The rebuff of nationalist aspirations by the British Government led to demonstrations and riots in 1919. The opinion Huddleston expresses here was shared by Wingate, high commissioner for Egypt at the time (see R Wingate, *Wingate of the Sudan* (London, 1955) chapter 9).

Egypt in March 1919. Reading S.A.R. for Zaghlul and me for Wingate, is not the case the same?

I most strongly recommend that S.A.R. be allowed to come. It might be just that concession which would win him over—and would at the worst give us more time—and time is a most valuable factor in a state of general tension such as exists in the Sudan to-day. It may excite the Egyptians; but must we always dance to their tune?—must we always say "Yes, I quite agree, we ought to do so and so but it will upset the Egyptians and we must never do that"?

I enclose copies of this letter for the Prime Minister, Mr. Bevin, Sir Orme Sargent, and the members of the British Treaty Delegation.

108 PREM 8/1388/2, CM 96(46)1 14 Nov 1946

'Anglo–Egyptian treaty negotiations: Sudan protocol': Cabinet conclusions [Extract]

[In the meeting on 14 November Attlee briefed the Cabinet on the aftermath of Sidqi's disclosure, reading out Huddleston's letter (see 102), and summarising the exchange of telegrams between himself and Bevin (see 103, 104).]

. . . Discussion showed that it was the view of the Cabinet that, notwithstanding the possible reactions in the Sudan, we should not withdraw from the understandings reached with Sidky Pasha about the Sudan Protocol. There were good prospects that within the next few days the Egyptian Government would accept the latest proposals regarding the Anglo–Egyptian Treaty; and it was most important that nothing should be said or done at this stage to prejudice these prospects. At the same time, we should lose no opportunity of averting serious trouble in the Sudan. Apart from long-term measures for expediting Sudanese progress towards self-government, more immediate action could be taken to reassure the Sudanese. Thus, some of the leaders of political parties in the Sudan might be brought to this country, so that they might satisfy themselves at first hand of the desire of His Majesty's Government to enable the Sudanese to achieve self-government. Though it would be inexpedient to issue such an invitation before the Egyptian Government had reached their decision on the Treaty, preliminary arrangements could be made at once so that the invitation could be issued as soon as the decision of the Egyptian Government was known. Further, the Prime Minister could send to the Governor-General of the Sudan a letter, which he could show to some of the Sudanese leaders, assuring him that His Majesty's Government had considered his representations and were satisfied that the position of the Sudanese was fully safeguarded. This would be separate from the personal letter which the Prime Minister had already decided to send inviting the Governor-General to continue in office despite his apprehensions about the effect of the sovereignty clause in the Sudan Protocol to the Treaty.

The Cabinet:—

(1) Endorsed the Prime Minister's recommendation that, despite the possible reactions in the Sudan, we should not withdraw from our understandings with Sidky Pasha about the text of the Sudan Protocol to the new Anglo–Egyptian Treaty.

(2) Asked the Minister of State to put in hand preliminary arrangements for inviting leaders of political parties in the Sudan to visit this country.
(3) Took note that the Prime Minister would ask the Governor-General of the Sudan to continue in office[1] and that the Foreign Secretary was also sending him a letter which he could show to British Members of the Administration explaining the reasons why His Majesty's Government had recognised the Egyptian claim in regard to the Sudan and stating that the position and prospects of British officials would not be jeopardised.[2]
(4) Suggested that a further letter should be sent to the Governor General in suitable terms to be shown to the Sudanese leaders assuring him that His Majesty's Government had considered his representations and were satisfied that Sudanese interests were fully safeguarded by the proposed Sudan Protocol to the new Anglo–Egyptian Treaty.

---

[1] Attlee wrote to Huddleston the same day, informing him of the Cabinet decision, asking him to continue as governor-general, and assuring him that 'it is the considered view of His Majesty's Government that your presence in the Sudan at this moment is indispensable in British interests' (letter from Attlee to Huddleston, 14 Nov 1946, PREM 8/1388/2).
[2] See the copy of this letter in 111.

109 FO 371/53260, no 4844 15 Nov 1946

[Political propaganda in the Sudan]: note by Sir H Huddleston on measures to be taken to regain Sudanese confidence[1]

My first and principal objective on returning to the Sudan will be to recover as far as possible the confidence of the Sudanese, which has been so severely shaken by recent events, and to find some way of attracting their co-operation during the period of their training for self-government.

The only hope of achieving this will be an immediate and really substantial first instalment of self-governing institutions, something much more rapid and drastic than we have hitherto contemplated for the immediate future, which will be an earnest of the good intention of the Condominium Powers, will demonstrate the value of the protocol to the Sudanese and may offset to some extent their dismay over Egyptian sovereignty.

Speed is the essence of the matter; if there is any delay after my return to Khartoum, riots may compel me to use force and once this had happened there would be no hope of co-operation.

I therefore request that H.M.G. and the Egyptian Government shall authorise me, immediately on my return to Khartoum, to call together the leaders of all political parties and other representative persons and to invite them to formulate agreed proposals for the immediate establishment of such political and administrative institutions as they may consider necessary during the period of their training for self-government.

---

[1] This note was forwarded to Attlee with an endorsement from Sargent on 18 Nov 1946 (PREM 8/1388/2).

Their proposals would undoubtedly involve considerable alterations in the present administrative arrangements in the Sudan and I therefore request authority likewise to submit my recommendations, based on these proposals, to the Condominium Powers for approval.

110 FO 371/53260, no 4859 18 Nov 1946

[Political propaganda in the Sudan]: note by Sir H Huddleston on propaganda to be undertaken in the Sudan

[Huddleston was given approval to make the points listed in this note, with some qualifications. 'It would be desirable to connect point one very closely with point three, and indicate that the sovereignty of the King of Egypt does not mean that Egypt can directly interfere with the administration of the Sudanese, whose administration remains as it was. As regards point two there is, technically speaking, no such thing as an Egyptian "subject". The Egyptian nationality law speaks of Egyptian "nationals", and it should be put therefore that Sudanese are not Egyptian nationals. Furthermore the Sudanese remain a group *of their own* which can only be described as Sudanese or, if and when a Sudanese citizenship law is enacted, Sudanese citizens' (letter from Sargent to Huddleston, 20 Nov 1946, FO 371/53260, no 4859).]

Can I make use of the following points for propaganda purposes, as soon as I return to the Sudan?

1. The symbolic nature of Egyptian sovereignty.
2. The Sudanese will not be Egyptian subjects.
3. No change in the administrative arrangements other than those made with the consent of the Sudanese towards the objective of self-government.
4. Right of the Sudanese eventually to choose independence, including separation from the Egyptian Crown.

P.S. I do not think that this would involve any breach of confidence, as all the above have appeared in some shape or other in the newspapers.[1]

[1] Scrivener minuted (18 Nov): 'The answer in all cases appeals to be "Yes".'

111 FO 371/53318, no 4965, CP(46) 18 Nov 1946

'Anglo–Egyptian treaty': Cabinet memorandum by Mr Attlee. *Annexes* [Extract]

[In Bevin's absence in New York, this memo was drawn up in the FO for submission to the Cabinet over Attlee's signature. In fact it did not go to Cabinet, for the reasons explained in 113 and 115.]

As my colleagues will be aware, the Foreign Secretary conducted a series of conversations with the Egyptian Prime Minister in London between 17th October and 26th October with a view to removing the differences which had, until then, prevented agreement on the revision of the Anglo–Egyptian treaty of 1936. As a result, a personal agreement was reached on the basis of the texts enclosed in the present memorandum as Annexes 1, 2 and 3,[1] which are to be interpreted in the light

[1] Of the eight annexes to this memo, only nos 4 and 8 are reproduced here.

of the draft confidential letter to Sidky Pasha, which forms Annex 4.[2] It was understood that, provided the texts of Annexes 1, 2 and 3 were accepted in their entirety by the Egyptian Government, the Foreign Secretary would recommend their approval by His Majesty's Government. Having now received notification of the Egyptian Government's acceptance of these texts, I seek the Cabinet's authority to proceed to the formal signature of the treaty, and to request the British delegation to return to Egypt for that purpose.

The texts consist of:—

(1) A treaty of mutual assistance in seven articles.
(2) A Sudan Protocol.
(3) An Evacuation Protocol. . . .

(2) . . . the Defence Committee authorised the Foreign Secretary to negotiate a clause "which, while recognising a measure of Egyptian sovereignty over the Sudan, would safeguard our present defence and administrative rights, and would not prejudice the rights of the Sudanese to choose the ultimate status of the country." The Sudan Protocol annexed to the present memorandum in my opinion fulfils these conditions and, in particular, meets a desire expressed in the Committee that the Sudanese people shall be consulted before the future status of the Sudan is finally determined. The Protocol provides that until the parties, after consultation with the Sudanese, are agreed on the ultimate status of the territory, the agreements of 1899 (see Annex 5) and Article 11 of the 1936 treaty with its annex and paragraphs 14 to 16 of the agreed minute annexed to the 1936 treaty (see Annex 6) shall remain in force. Article 11 of the 1936 treaty itself reaffirms the 1899 agreement and provides that the administration of the Sudan shall be that which results from them. It confirms the exercise by the Governor-General, on the joint behalf of the British and Egyptian Governments, of the powers conferred on him by those agreements. In particular this article vests appointments and promotions of officials in the Governor-General and provides that posts "for which qualified Sudanese are not available" shall be filled by suitable Britons and Egyptians. It also provides that "in addition to Sudanese troops, both British and British [sic] and Egyptian troops shall be placed at the disposal of the Governor-General for the defence of the Sudan. The confidential letter (Annex 4) records, moreover, that the Protocol constitutes an affirmation of, and not a change in, the existing status of the Sudan; that the Sudanese shall, when the time comes, be free to choose complete independence, and that the United Kingdom has an unconditional right to maintain what troops she wishes in the territory.

The text of the Sudan Protocol was accepted by the Governor-General of the Sudan, who at the same time emphasised the difficulty of persuading the Sudanese

---

[2] As a result of Sidqi's public statements to the Egyptian press it was proposed that Sidqi give a written confirmation of the verbal undertakings he made concerning both the Sudan and Evacuation protocols. This was considered especially urgent as Sidqi was unlikely to remain in power long and it was anticipated that future Egyptian governments would not consider themselves bound by any 'Gentlemen's Agreement'. The terms of a confidential letter to be presented to Sidqi to sign at the time of the treaty signing were first drafted on 30 Oct. It originally proposed a ten year period for the continuation of the Condominium, after which the Sudanese would be consulted on whether they wanted independence, the maintenance of the Condominium, or some other status (minute, Sargent to Bevin, 30 Oct 1946, FO 371/53317, no 4549). This was changed in subsequent redrafts following comments by Bevin (see 104).

that in fact the Protocol, with its affirmation of the union between the Sudan and Egypt under a common crown, did not constitute a change of status such as would have obliged His Majesty's Government, in the light of their public undertaking of 26th March last (see Annex 7) to consult them before its acceptance. But the Governor-General was on the whole satisfied that he could succeed in this task provided that His Majesty's Government gave him their firm support. Unfortunately, as the Cabinet are aware, the Egyptian press published an interpretation of the draft protocol which stressed the affirmation of Egyptian sovereignty but concealed the provisions regarding the administration of the Sudan and the right of self-determination of the Sudanese. The results of this disclosure, which my statement in the House of Commons on 28th October unfortunately failed to efface, have been to create in the Sudan a situation of such seriousness that the Governor-General felt bound to return to London to report to me personally. It appears that the powerful Nationalist (as opposed to the pro-Egyptian) party in the Sudan, which is led by a (posthumous) son of the Mahdi, have been thrown into a mood of bitter and dangerous fanaticism, that they accuse His Majesty's Government and the Sudan Government of betraying them to Egypt, that they cannot be persuaded of the advantage of the protocol from their point of view, that force would be required to maintain public order if the protocol became an accomplished fact, and that a widespread boycott of the administration would take place. Finally, Sir H. Huddleston urged that to use force to impose Egyptian sovereignty on the Sudanese would be so complete a reversal of policy that it would destroy Sudanese faith in the good intentions of His Majesty's Government.

While I have deep sympathy with the position in which Sir H. Huddleston has been placed by the indiscretions, if not the deliberate duplicity, of the Egyptians, I am satisfied that it would be wrong to retrace our steps at this stage. If we now repudiate the Sudan Protocol we shall lose the whole treaty, for Sidky Pasha's Government would be swept away. Our relations with Egypt and our defence arrangements in the Middle East would again be in the melting pot, and we might face the international complications of an Egyptian reference to the United Nations Organisation. This might take the form of the Egyptian Government either arguing that the treaty of 1936 was out of date and its continuance a matter of dispute, or alternatively that we are violating it by maintaining a number of troops in Egypt greatly in excess of what the treaty allows. In addition there is, of course, the issue of sovereignty over the Sudan which the Egyptians might very well take to the International Court. I am therefore satisfied, after consultation with the Foreign Secretary, who is in full agreement, that we should proceed on our course. Finally, I think that my colleagues would be interested to read a letter (attached as Annex 8) which the Foreign Secretary has sent to the Governor-General explaining, for the guidance of the British officials of the Sudan Government, the implications of the Sudan Protocol....

Annex 4 to 111: draft confidential letter to Sidky Pasha

At the moment of signing the Anglo–Egyptian Treaty of Mutual Assistance, I must ask your Excellency to be so good as to confirm the following interpretations agreed upon during your recent visit to London:—

(i) It is agreed that the provisions of the Sudan Protocol involve no change in the present status of the Sudan; and that in particular the phrase regarding the unity between the Sudan and Egypt under the common crown of Egypt merely constitutes an affirmation of the existing status.

(ii) The Sudan Protocol provides that the Sudanese people shall, when they are ripe for self-government, be free to choose the future status of the Sudan. It is understood that a completely free choice is implied here, and nothing in any part of the Protocol shall limit the right of the Sudanese people to choose complete independence if that should be their wish at that time.

(iii) It is agreed that the Sudan Protocol in no way affects the unconditional right of the United Kingdom to maintain whatever troops they wish in the Sudan; and that in the exercise of this right the United Kingdom may reinforce the British contingents (more especially Royal Air Force) in the Sudan, and extend their base facilities there.

(iv) It is agreed that, until the completion of the evacuation in accordance with the provisions of the evacuation Protocol, the British forces shall continue to enjoy their present rights of transit and flight over Egypt. It is also understood that the two Governments shall, after the signature of the Treaty of Alliance, discuss, with a view to arriving at a mutual agreement, the transit rights which shall be enjoyed for their aircraft by the British forces after the evacuation of Egypt is completed. Reciprocal treatment will also be accorded to Egyptian Air Forces in British territory.

(v) It is agreed that the abrogation of the Treaty of 1936 does not affect the position of either party with regard to financial rights and liabilities which had accrued under the Treaty of 1936 at the time of the coming into force of the new Treaty of Alliance which abrogates it.

Annex 8 to 111: letter from Mr Bevin to Sir H Huddleston

The Protocol dealing with the Sudan which is to be signed at the same time as the new Anglo–Egyptian Treaty of Alliance may be perplexing to the British officials in the Sudan in that it admits "the unity between the Sudan and Egypt under the common Crown of Egypt."

It is true that, since the date of the 1899 Agreement, there has been no admission on the part of His Majesty's Government in the United Kingdom that the King of Egypt was the King of the Sudan, and that some writers have taken the view that the effect of the 1899 Agreement was to create a joint sovereignty shared between the United Kingdom and Egypt.

On the other hand, on the Egyptian side, it has been continuously claimed throughout that the Khedive (and later the King) of Egypt remained the King of the Sudan, and His Majesty's Government, though they have not admitted this title, have never expressly denied it. The attitude of His Majesty's Government throughout this period has been that, as the 1899 Agreement provided fully for the administration and settled all practical matters, the question of sovereignty was a purely academic one. Throughout the period, and particularly in connexion with the recent negotiations, the greatest value was attached by the Egyptians to obtaining a recognition by His Majesty's Government of the position of the King of Egypt as King of the Sudan.

His Majesty's Government for their part, although they continue to regard this question as an academic one, saw no objection to admitting this claim of the King of Egypt provided that such an admission did not conflict with the undertaking given by me in the House of Commons on 26th March to agree to no alteration of the status of the Sudan without consultation with the Sudanese.

Accordingly they obtained the advice of the highest legal authorities on this question of the claim of the King of Egypt, and were advised that the 1899 Agreement, while providing fully for administration, did not affect the ultimate sovereignty over the Sudan of the Crown of Egypt which did undoubtedly exist before the 1899 Agreement, and that consequently such an admission now made by His Majesty's Government would not constitute any change of status.

As you are aware, the possession by two territories of a common crown does not imply any common system of law or administration. Nor does it itself imply that the citizens of one territory which is under the common crown enjoy the rights of citizenship of the other territory which is under the common crown. The exact effects of a common crown, for which there are very many precedents both in the past and at the present time, depend in each case on both history and the exact arrangements which are made. Consequently, the exact effects of a common crown in one case do not, necessarily, afford any guide to the position in another case.

The Sudan has always been and still remains to some extent *sui generis*, and in any case the exact position of the Sudan was made plain by the 1899 Agreement and the 1936 Treaty. So far from this position being in any way changed by the new Sudan Protocol, it is expressly provided "that the Agreement of 1899 will continue and Article 11 of the Treaty of 1936 together with its annex and paragraphs 14 to 16 of the agreed minute will remain in force" notwithstanding that the new Treaty of Alliance abrogates the whole Treaty of 1936.

The only new feature contained in the recent Sudan Protocol is an explicit recognition by Egypt, as well as by the United Kingdom, that the Sudanese are to be prepared for self-government, and that as soon as they are ripe for self-government the Sudanese people are to choose the future status of the Sudan. The choice of the Sudanese is entirely unfettered. If they so desire they will be free to choose that the Sudan should become a completely independent and separate State. They may also choose, if they so desire, union with Egypt or some new régime which is neither of these things.

Further it is provided that the objective of preparing the Sudanese for self-government so as to place them in a position to make this choice is to be carried out after consultation with the Sudanese and by the United Kingdom and Egypt in common agreement.

This common objective, namely that the Sudanese should be prepared for self-government and should, at the right moment, freely choose the future of the Sudan, has not hitherto been officially admitted by the Egyptian Government, and it is the admission by both parties of the condominium of its common objective which constitutes the only new feature created by the Sudan Protocol.

In the present unsettled position of world affairs, and more especially in the need for a friendly Arab *bloc* in the Middle East, the concession which His Majesty's Government have made as regards the position of the Egyptian Crown is the more fully justified.

It is His Majesty's Government's firm intention that the present administration in the Sudan shall continue, and that the position and prospects of British officials in the country should not be jeopardised.

I hope you will pass on these assurances to your British officials by whom so much has been done in the past for the welfare of the Sudanese, and on whom the future well-being and progress of the country depends.

112 FO 371/53262, no 5267 21 Nov 1946

[Political propaganda in the Sudan]: circular letter from J W Robertson to all governors and heads of department on the presentation of treaty negotiations in the Sudan

1. I refer to my personal circular of 31.10.46 and circular to Governors No. 36.M.15 of 2.11.46.

The political situation throughout the country has improved and the unrest which was obvious in many places at the end of October has abated. There is still of course great anxiety amongst all classes of the community, and the tension among political parties and in the vernacular press is not likely to subside, until the Treaty negotiations are concluded, and forgotten.

2. I have no doubt that we shall have political manoeuvring and party conflict in Khartoum and Omdurman with us now more or less permanently, and that we cannot hope to get rid of it. But permanent extension of these symptoms to the provinces need not take place yet, and can be slowed up for the future, if we take the proper measures now.

3. It has been abundantly proved during the past month, that the chief anxiety in rural areas has been caused by reports that the "Hakuma"[1] is losing grip; that the "INGLEEZ" are going, that we are about to hand over the Government to (a) the Egyptians or (b) Sayed Abdel Rahman or (c) the Effendia. The prospect of any of these as their rulers is most heartily disliked by the rural populations and their chiefs in all parts of the country, from Darfur to Dongola, and Gedaref to Geneina. Prominent leaders of Mahdist and Khatmi groups alike have everywhere stated in no uncertain terms that it is of the utmost importance to scotch rumours that the British are about to evacuate the country. The solid mass of tribal leaders and their people, the older officials and responsible townsfolk have no sympathy with the politically-minded young men of Omdurman, and wish only to return to peaceful conditions under the present Government. Every reasonable person knows, that if the British go anarchy and chaos are inevitable.

4. You should make it known in no uncertain terms, that whatever the outcome of the present Treaty negotiations:—

(a) *there will be no change in the administration of the country*. The Union Jack will not be pulled down: British Troops will remain in the Sudan: British officials will continue at their posts.

(b) *the policy of the Sudan Government as enunciated by His Excellency the Governor-General at the Advisory Council last April will continue unchanged, i.e.—*

---

[1] *Hakuma*: government.

(i) the building up of self-governing institutions in town and rural district.
(ii) the introduction of Sudanese officials into the highest Government posts, when they are capable of doing the work.
(iii) progress towards self-government at the centre.
(iv) the consequent right of self-determination of their future status by the Sudanese.[2]

(c) *any acknowledgment of Egyptian sovereignty will not impair this policy*.
(d) *these promises* were categorically made by Mr. Attlee in the House of Commons on October 29th and they *will be carried out*.

5. You should take every opportunity of explaining the situation, and of emphasizing the firmness of the present regime's position. Personal contacts, official tours, increased fantasia and parades, big displays at King's Day, etc. will impress rural, tribal and town populations alike and should be arranged. I hope that when His Excellency the Governor-General returns, he will be able to visit provincial centres, and that Departmental officials from Khartoum will tour more than has been possible in recent years. I believe such inspections by Education, Public Works, Finance, Agricultural and other officials can be used in the provinces to show that we are still here and intend to stay until we have carried out our task.

6. The desire of the mass of the population for the continuation of the present regime is unquestioned, but they have been confused by recent reports. We must see that they are reassured, and this can be done only if we are determined and confident ourselves. It will not be so easy to win back the confidence of the politically-minded, but the first task is to restore confidence in the provinces, and to prevent uncertainties which may lead to risings and subsequent patrols.

7. This circular is marked SECRET: it can be shewn to all British officials and to Senior Sudanese at your discretion.

---

[2] In a comment to the Sudan agent Scrivener wrote: 'Will you kindly let Khartoum know that the circular to Governors of 21st November enclosed therein has struck everyone here who has read it as admirable. Our only comment is that paragraph 4(iv) might perhaps have said, "the consequent right of self-determination and the exercise by the Sudanese of the right to choose their future status"' (letter from Scrivener to Davies, 19 Dec 1946, FO 371/53262, no 5267).

113 FO 371/53319, no 4994 — 21 Nov 1946

[Egyptian treaty ratification]: letter from R J Bowker to P S Scrivener on a major crisis in the treaty negotiations

[The proposal to commit Sidqi to an exchange of letters on the Sudan protocol upon the Egyptian government's acceptance of the treaty and protocol texts had to be revised in light of information that Sidqi was intending to present his own interpretation of the protocol (see 99) to a secret session of the Egyptian parliament. Attlee and Bevin agreed that Bowker should be authorised to warn Sidqi that this interpretation was unacceptable to HMG. Attlee suggested that Sidqi be shown the text of the understanding it was proposed he sign (see 111), but Bevin asked that it be re-worded to incoroporate the wording in the minutes of his meeting with Sidqi in which he made clear his own understanding that the Sudanese had the right to choose independence (outward telegram no 2303 from Attlee to Bevin, 19 Nov 1946, and inward telegram no 16 from Bevin to Attlee, 19 Nov 1946, FO 371/53260, nos 4835 and 4856). In the meantime Sargent delivered to Amr in London a memo which reiterated that 'nothing in any part of the Protocol shall limit the right of the Sudanese people to choose complete independence if that should be their wish at that time' (note Sargent to Amr, 21 Nov 1946, FO 371/53261, no 4923). Sidqi's difficulties in persuading the Egyptian treaty delegation that his interpretation of the protocol was valid made it increasingly unlikely that the Egyptian government would accept the treaty, much less that Sidqi would agree to a secret understanding radically different in interpretation than that to which he was publicly committed. After his meeting with Amr, Sargent was convinced that they risked losing the treaty altogether if they insisted on the proposed exchange of letters (outward telegram no 2411, 22 Nov 1946, FO 371/53260, no 4884).]

We have reached a major crisis in the Treaty negotiations and the whole picture is now getting so confused that it is difficult to see any light. Sidky and the King are still straining every nerve to get the Treaty through and they are still hoping that it will be possible for Sidky to get a vote of confidence in Parliament and so short-circuit the Treaty Delegation. Meanwhile, the Liberals, as I reported by telegram today, are said to have accepted the proposals subject to conditions which would be quite inacceptable to us, and without the Liberals Sidky has no chance of getting a vote of confidance [sic] in the Chamber and far less in the Senate. According to present arrangements the interpellation will be dealt with on 26th November. It is possible that between now and then the opposing members of the Delegation may issue a statement giving their reasons for not accepting the latest proposals. Any such statement is likely to cause a fairly large commotion.

Meanwhile Sidky seems to have committed himself up to the hilt to interpretations of the Sudan Protocol, particularly on the point of the right of the Sudanese to choose their future status, which are diametrically opposed to Mr. Bevin's understanding of what was agreed with him in London and which can never be accepted by His Majesty's Government. There is no doubt that Sidky has up to now been relying on these interpretations in order to strengthen his by no means certain chances of getting a vote of confidance [sic] in Parliament.

At least Sidky has now been warned that these interpretations have no chance of acceptance by His Majesty's Government and he must realise now that it is no good his trying to get the Treaty through by using them. To that extent the position has been clarified.

Things are further complicated by Sidky's recent relapse and the fact that he is now back in bed and unable to receive visitors.

I fear the prospects are gloomy.

114 FO 371/53262, no 5130 29 Nov 1946

[SAR]: FO record of an interview between Mr Attlee and Sayyid Abd al-Rahman al-Mahdi on Nov 28, 1946

[Huddleston's proposal that SAR be allowed to visit to London (see 107) was approved, and it was agreed that it would be best for him to join the existing Umma delegation in London after the governor-general had returned to the Sudan, but before the treaty was signed. 'Time will have been gained, and if the Sayed is reassured by his visit the worst may be avoided' (minute by Sargent to Attlee, 15 Nov 1946, PREM 8/1388/2). The Sudan government was instructed to assist SAR with his air priorities, and to offer the same facilities to SAM, or any leading Ashiqqa party member (outward telegram no 8421 from Luce to Robertson, 21 Nov 1946, FO 371/53261, no 4916). In the event SAM politely declined the invitation for reasons of ill health (inward telegram no 145 from Robertson (Khartoum) to Huddleston (Cairo), 2 Dec 1946, FO 371/53262, no 5092). Bevin still being in New York, it was decided that SAR should have an audience with Attlee. Attlee commented after this meeting, 'SAR did not show any sign of understanding that the sovereignty of the King of Egypt could be anything else than absolute power' (minute by Attlee to Sargent, 30 Nov 1946, FO 371/53261, no 5067).]

After compliments, the *Prime Minister* invited the Sayed to set out his case.

The *Sayed* said that he was grateful to the Prime Minister for this opportunity to make the views of the Sudan heard. The Sudan naturally expected to continue the status it had previously held when it was a free sovereign country, and since the early days of the Sudan Government, whose duty it was to prepare them to manage their own affairs. The Sudanese people had helped in this war in the cause of democracy and freedom.

The Sudanese people had had confidence in the promises given the Sudan to have self-government. This promise had suddenly been disturbed by the declarations of Sidky Pasha in Cairo. The Sudanese people had not seen the proposed Protocol, except the version released by Sidky Pasha. This Declaration by Sidky Pasha had caused disturbance in the Sudan, and had made the Sudanese think twice of the promises which had been given to them. The Sayed had only been able to quieten his followers by the declaration by the Prime Minister that Sidky Pasha's disclosures were misleading and unimpartial. The Sudan was reassured by the Prime Minister's statement until King Farouk had said that the Egyptian Government would work towards self-government of the Sudan within the unity of the Sudan and Egypt.[1] This proved that Egypt denied to the Sudan its right to self-determination. King Farouk's declaration was inconsistent with the Governor-General's declaration that the aim of His Majesty's Government was to prepare the Sudanese for self-government and ultimately for independence and the creation of a democratic Government in the Sudan. The Sudanese knew that the aims of the Sudan Government were to start representative bodies with a view to a democratic, free Government. Egyptian sovereignty was inconsistent with the Sudanese hope of freedom and with their own sovereignty. The *Sayed* assured the Prime Minister that the Sudanese will never accept this situation, i.e., Egyptian sovereignty over the Sudan. The Sayed had not seen the Protocol, but if Egyptian sovereignty had been admitted, it meant interference with the stable administration of the Sudan.

If Egypt had any right to sovereignty over the Sudan, it was by right of conquest. This conquest was not by Egypt only. It came through British support. The Sudanese drove Egypt from the Sudan. Egypt alone could never conquer the Sudan.

The principle of the unity of the Nile was inconsistent with the right of the Sudanese to self-determination. In the 1899 Agreement, the sovereignty of the Sudan was not admitted. That Agreement concerned only administration. His Majesty's Government had objected to the title of the King of Egypt as King of the Sudan. In the 1936 Treaty Revision, Egypt had raised their claim to sovereignty, but this claim had been left in abeyance.

---

[1] In his speech from the throne, 14 Nov 1946, in which Faruq proclaimed, 'With regard to the … unity of Egypt and the Sudan under the Egyptian Crown, the Egyptian Government wished to proclaim that this unity has no other object than to safeguard the vital bonds which exist between Egypt and the Sudan. In the same way the Egyptian Government wished to affirm that Egypt looks upon the Sudan as a brother. One of her first aims would be to assure the well-being of the Sudanese, to develop their interests and prepare them effectively for self-government at the earliest possible moment' (letter from R L Speaight to Mr Bevin, 12 Dec 1946, FO 371/53321, no 5363).

The Sudanese had loyally co-operated with the present Sudan Government and they regarded the present administration as dear to them, and they wanted to preserve this and make it the foundation for their future independence.

The *Sayed* said that he would like to mention the part which the Sudan had played in this war. When the Sudan was invaded, the Sudan had defended their country alone, while Egypt, who had had troops in barracks there, did not raise a finger and even objected to the Sudan Defence Force taking any part in the war.

Self determination was admitted to all nations by the United Nations Organization and by the Atlantic Charter.

The Sudanese did not claim self-determination in the United Nations Organization except in the full confidence that His Majesty's Government would advocate the Sudan case, and that they would help the Sudan to reach independence.

Any decision regarding the political status of the Sudan without consulting the Sudanese people would provoke complications comparable to those which had arisen in Palestine. The Sayed would regret [it] if good relations which had been built up through the good work of the British administration were marred by bitterness and antagonism. The Sudanese have character, and His Majesty's Government could depend on that character.

The *Sayed* had said after the Prime Minister's declaration in Parliament that he could quieten the Sudanese, but if the Protocol were concluded, he would not be able to restrain the Sudanese people from committing excesses. His policy was continued friendship with Britain and the hope that the Sudan would gain its freedom through England. He wondered why the Sudan, who had joined the war voluntarily, while Egypt had only been a spectator, should now be suddenly handed over to Egypt. The Sudan defended her borders, helped to liberate Abyssinia, sent a force to North Africa, and had thrown all its forces and resources into the winning of the war, while Egypt never used a single soldier and sold its resources to the Allies at high prices.

The Sudan had no emnity towards Egypt and would co-operate with that country. They had told Egypt this, but the Egyptians did not believe them. Egypt was seeking the help of Great Britain in order to stay in the Sudan with British bayonets. The Sudanese were confident that Great Britain, one of the leading members of the United Nations Organization, would never help Egypt by force to separate the Sudanese from their freedom.

The Prime Minister thanked the Sayed for setting out the position so clearly. There was the deepest interest here in the welfare of the Sudan and the Sudanese people. He was very well aware of the way the Sudanese had stood fast in the difficult times of the war. He knew, too, that the Sudanese were looking forward to complete self-government and the complete right to decide their own future.

The Prime Minister said that we recognised the right of the Sudanese people to decide their own future. As the Sayed knew, with the full approval and active encouragement of His Majesty's Government, we had been pressing on with Sudanese institutions. The Governor General had the full approval of His Majesty's Government to go on to further consultations with the Sudanese leaders.

The *Sayed* said that this was very good news and he was glad to hear it. This had been his own impression in the past, but Sidky had contradicted this.

The Prime Minister said he was coming to that. The proposed Protocol does not make the slightest difference to the present status of the Sudan or to its administration. As to sovereignty, this is a legal question. Lawyers will debate for months on the exact meaning of sovereignty. There were people who thought of sovereignty as only meaning complete power of a sovereign to do as he pleases. (Here the *Sayed* interposed to say that this is what is meant in the East by Sovereignty). In Europe this word has been used to mean very different things.

The *Sayed* said that if anybody were given sovereignty, he would use it in his own way. He asked, was there any democracy in Egypt.

The Prime Minister replied that it was for the Sayed to say whether there has or has not been Egyptian sovereignty in the Sudan.

The *Sayed* replied that there had been none.

The Prime Minister said then there was none now, but lawyers might argue that there is this or that position with regard to sovereignty. The actual position, however, was that the Protocol made no change from what had existed in those years.

The *Sayed* said that he had not seen the Protocol, but Sidky Pasha and King Farouk said there was sovereignty.

The Prime Minister said that the Agreement of 1899 remained in force. The present system of administration remained except in so far as it was changed contrary to the Protocol by the Sudanese people. If there was any direct Egyptian administration, this would be resisted. The word "sovereignty" did not appear in the Protocol, so there was no need to quarrel about the word. In our view, the Protocol could not prejudice the right of the Sudanese at the proper time to achieve their complete independence if they so decided, and there was nothing in the existing situation which could in any way run counter to the right of the Sudanese people to achieve their independence if they so decided. We did not consider that the existence of a connection between the two altered the right of the Sudanese to decide their future. Therefore we should like the Sayed to collaborate with the Governor General to ensure orderly progress of the Sudanese people. Let them disregard misleading statements, because this is the position of His Majesty's Government in this matter. The Protocol recognised the existing juridical position of the Sudan. It neither added to nor subtracted from it and left the existing administration where it was. One last point. Whatever might be said by outsiders, we were in the Sudan and we and the Sudanese would control the position there. That was the position by treaties.

The *Sayed* said that the Sudanese were expecting results from his visit.

The Prime Minister replied that the Sayed would be able to tell the Sudanese that the Protocol makes no difference to the position in the Sudan.

The *Sayed* enquired what was meant by the relation between Egypt and the Sudan.

The Prime Minister replied that it meant the recognition of the fact that in our relations with Egypt, the United Kingdom and the Sudan, those three are concerned. The Governor General was appointed by the King of Egypt on the recommendation of His Majesty's Government. There was also the Egyptian flag. These things were merely the recognition of a state of affairs which has not changed by the Protocol.

The *Sayed* said that this relation was the cause of their present fear because the Egyptians were using it against the Sudanese and against His Majesty's Government in the Sudan. Was nothing to be allowed to interfere with this relation?

The Prime Minister replied that the position was unchanged in this respect.

The *Sayed* said that the danger was that King Farouk would be called the King of Egypt and the Sudan.

The Prime Minister said that he had the symbol, we had reality.

The *Sayed* said that he was faithful to the Sudanese and to the British and this made him anxious not to deceive either us or the Sudanese.

The Prime Minister said that ever since 1899 there had been a condominium. Egypt had old claims. They had never been denied. We have had the administration. The Egyptians had the symbol, and we had the reality.

The *Sayed* said that the understanding was that Egypt claimed more than she had in the past.

The Prime Minister replied that Egypt was not getting more than in the past.

The *Sayed* said that in the past the only outward sign was the Egyptian flag. Now it was intended to give other recognition which they had not had before.

The Prime Minister said that they had these things before. They do exist. If the matter were referred to an international court, the court would say that these things exist.

The *Sayed* said that under the United Nations Organization the right of the Sudanese to freedom would receive wider interpretation than under the old dispensation.

The Prime Minister said that the court would find the facts as they are. They would find sovereignty in Egypt and administration in British hands. Those are the facts.

The *Sayed* said that the rights of Egypt arose from conquest and were invalid to deprive the Sudanese of their freedom. Egypt had no greater right in the Sudan than the British had.

The Prime Minister said that whatever these rights were, they could not contradict the right of the Sudanese to do what they wished in the future.

The *Sayed* said that they still feared that Egyptian sovereignty would be used for propaganda in the Sudan. The King's name would be used in prayers in mosques.

The Prime Minister asked whether the Sudanese could not themselves look after that.

The *Sayed* replied that in the past prayers had been in the name of the Turkish Caliph up till 1914. Since 1936 Egyptian influence had increased, more troops had come into the Sudan. He was afraid for the future.

The Prime Minister said that we would work together. That was the answer.

The *Sayed* replied that they wanted this. There must be a firm foundation.

The Prime Minister said we already had this in the administration.

The *Sayed* said he could not understand the meaning of symbolic sovereignty. It would certainly take on the form of the alteration of the status quo.

The Prime Minister said that was not so. We go no further than what actually exists.

The *Sayed* said that King Farouk's statement of Egyptian desire to help the Sudanese to reach self-government meant more propaganda and interference. The Sudanese did not trust the Egyptians. Must he return to the Sudan and say that things had changed?

The Prime Minister said that he had been saying for the last half hour that nothing had been changed. The Protocol recognised the right of the Sudanese to choose their status and to do what they pleased. There was no going back.

The *Sayed* asked whether the Sudanese could decide their future.

The Prime Minister told the Sayed that he should go back and talk to the Governor General and get things moving in this direction. As soon as the Sudanese were ready they could do what they wished.

The *Sayed* said that if the Protocol is as has been published, the Sudanese would not co-operate. They wanted peace.

The Prime Minister said that the Protocol expressly provided the right of the Sudanese to choose what they wanted.

The *Sayed* said that the only thing which could create the Sudan was the Prime Minister's word.

The Prime Minister said there will be a Sudan as it is to-day, working and developing.

The *Sayed* said that he had confidence in the Prime Minister's word, but the Sudanese would say "What have you got for us?" What should be the reply?

The Prime Minister replied that he did not think that the Sayed would have any difficulty about that.

The *Sayed* said that he was staying here for several days and expected assurances from the Prime Minister.

115 PREM 8/1388/3 30 Nov 1946

[Sudanese self-determination]: letter from Mr Attlee to Sir H Huddleston reaffirming the right of the Sudanese to achieve independence

[Attlee's letter giving HMG's interpretation of the Sudan protocol (see 108 & 111) was delayed as the letter of understanding to be sent to Sidqi was also redrafted. Attlee's original letter to Huddleston authorised him to reassure the Sudanese leaders that they had "the right to separate themselves from the Egyptian Crown should they wish to do so" (letter from Attlee to Hudleston, 20 Nov 1946, FO 371/53261, no 4906; see 111). This was rescinded at Bevin's insistence, on the grounds that 'secession' had never been agreed between Sidqi and him, and that the word 'secession' was not used in relation to the dominions of the Commonwealth in the Statute of Westminster (inward telegram no 1918 from Bevin to Sargent, 23 Nov 1946, FO 371/53261, no 4936). The Sudan government, however, understood that the Sudanese 'right to secede' was guaranteed by the protocol and both the governor-general and the civil secretary pressed hard to be allowed to tell Sudanese leaders this (letter from Robertson to Bowker, 16 Nov 1946, FO 371/53261, no 4962, and inward telegram no 1746 from Bowker to FO, 25 Nov 1946, FO 371/53261, no 4944). Huddleston complained that the proposed substitution of 'independence' for 'the right to separate themselves from the Egyptian Crown', was 'quite valueless to me' in his dealing with the Sudanese (inward telegram no 1770 from Huddleston to Attlee, 27 Nov 1946, FO 371/53261, no 5026). Privately Attlee complained: 'Sir H. Huddleston is unreasonable. We cannot give the Sudanese any more rights against Egypt than already exist' (minute from Attlee to Sargent, 30 Nov 1946, FO 371/53261, no 5067). To Huddleston, who was still in Cairo, he explained that he could go no further in expressing HMG's opinion, until an agreed interpretation of the Sudan protocol had been reached with Sidqi. He had, in any case, already assured SAR that nothing prejudiced the right of the Sudanese to achieve 'complete independence' (see 114). He therefore urged the governor-general 'to do the best you can with the foregoing . . .' (outward telegram no 2038 from Attlee to Huddleston, 30 Nov 1946, FO 371/53261, no 5067). Huddleston promised to do so 'since it is clear complete independence can have no limitation and therefore must include the right to separation', and planned to return to Khartoum as soon as he received his copy of Attlee's letter (inward telegram no 1795 from Huddleston to Attlee, 1 Dec 1946, FO 371/53262, no 5076).]

In the course of your visit you have informed His Majesty's Government of the great anxiety aroused amongst large sections of the Sudanese people by the recent statements in the Egyptian press regarding the conversations in London between Sidky Pasha and the Foreign Secretary on the subject of the Sudan. You emphasised in particular the fears that had been expressed by the Sudanese that the recognition by His Majesty's Government of the existence of a union between the Sudan and Egypt represented by a common crown would prejudice their advance towards self-Government and the right, conceded to them by His Majesty's Government, to be consulted before any change was made in the status of the Sudan as a result of the Anglo–Egyptian treaty.

In reply I expressed to you my regret that the Sudanese should have been misled by partial disclosures; and I gave you an assurance which you are authorised to convey to the leaders of the Sudanese people that His Majesty's Government are for their part determined that nothing shall be permitted to deflect the Sudan Government, whose constitution and powers remain unaltered by the recent conversations, from the task to which that Government had applied themselves, viz. the preparation of the Sudanese for self-Government and for the task of choosing freely what their future status is to be. The Sudan Protocol in fact provides that the Sudanese people shall, when they are ripe for self-government, be free to choose the future status of the Sudan. His Majesty's Government consider that, in the words used by the Egyptian Prime Minister to the British Foreign Secretary, nothing in the proposed treaty can prejudice the right of the Sudanese to achieve their independence nor bind a people in search of liberty.[1] The Egyptian Prime Minister pointed out to the British Foreign Secretary that this was a universal principle and therefore not a matter for incorporation in a treaty.

His Majesty's Government are glad to learn that you intend immediately on your return to hold consultations with representative Sudanese regarding their closer association with the administration, and to submit the resulting recommendations to the condominium governments. Meanwhile the present system of administration will continue; your authority will be in no way impaired; and the agreements of 1899 and Article 11 of the Anglo–Egyptian Treaty of 1936 remain in force.

The object of the recent Anglo–Egyptian negotiations has been to conclude a treaty acceptable to both parties and to reaffirm Anglo–Egyptian friendship. The Sudanese can only benefit from harmonious relations between the British and Egyptian Governments; their interests can only suffer as a result of disagreement and strained relations between those Governments.

[1] A verbatum quotation from Sidqi (see 88).

116 FO 371/53262, no 5155 2 Dec 1946

[SAR in London]: record by Lord Stansgate of a meeting with SAR and advisers

Persons interviewed are:—
Sir Reginald Wingate, ex-Governor-General.
Mr. Udal, ex-Sudan Service, Secretary of the Atheneum.[1]
Judge Shangetti, Sudan Judge.
The Mahdi.

[1] N R Udal, SPS, 1906–1915; Education Dept, 1915–1930; warden of Gordon College, 1927–1930; at this time adviser to SAR.

Judge Shangetti is very well spoken of by the Sudanese Government. He explained to me that at one time in 1924 he was in opposition to the British Government but had now come to see that the British Government were their friends.

Mr. Udal spoke very highly of Shangetti. *Shangetti* himself seemed an accommodating man, anxious to help.

Sir Reginald Wingate's story of his mission with Rodd in 1898 to Addis Ababa, because he had heard that the Abyssinians had sent a letter to the Khalifa. He was received by Menelik and French and Russian officers. He secured a copy of the letter which had been sent to Khartoum and it was an arrangement, by which, through an Abyssinian/Dervish alliance, the French would secure themselves in the Sudan. It was part of the plan for which Marchand advanced on Fashoda.

Wingate described his long argument with Kitchener as to which flag was to be flown at Fashoda when they arrived. He convinced Kitchener that they must only fly the Turkish/Egyptian flag (red).[2] Marchand had arrived in July, 1898. The incident took place in September and Marchand retired in December when both British and Egyptian flags were flown.

Wingate also spoke of his visit to London in 1919. He had a high opinion of Zaghlul[3] who had offered a firm and permanent alliance in return for Egyptian independence. After being kept waiting a fortnight Wingate was received by Lord Curzon who looked at the clock and asked him to cut it short. Wingate said he only wanted a minute or two. The result was a "firm" declaration by Curzon and all the ensuing trouble with Zaghlul.

Wingate said that Egyptian rule was very bad. He visited an Egyptian fort, where all the women and children of the local Sudanese had been collected and were being ill-treated until the Sudanese men in the villages consented to pay their taxes. This had happened several times that year.

Wingate said that his complimentary references to Egypt in his book, "Mahdism and the Egyptian Sudan"[4] were written when he was in the Egyptian service.

Shangetti said in defence of the Mahdia that Slatin's book was only published as propaganda to get the reconquest of the Sudan started. The same could be said of Ohrwalder's book.[5]

Udal was rather inclined to glorify the Mahdi, who was a good man, whereas the Khalifa[6] was a tyrant.

The father of S.A.M. *Wingate* said was El Morghani, and S.A.M. as a boy had been brought to Cairo and placed in hospital there with an English nurse. He had fallen under the influence of the Egyptians, (but S.A.M. had signed with S.A.R., letters approving the British rule—S.)

---

[2] See 86. [3] See 107. [4] See F R Wingate, *Mahdiism and the Egyptian Sudan* (London, 1891).

[5] R Slatin, *Fire and sword in the Sudan* (London, 1896), and F R Wingate, *Ten year's captivity in the Mahdi's camp, 1882–1892* (London, 1892). Both Ohrwalder (an Austrian Catholic missionary) and Slatin (an Austrian soldier of fortune in Egyptian service) had surrendered to the Mahdi's forces prior to the fall of Khartoum (1885) and had been resident in Omdurman until enabled to escape by agents of Wingate's intelligence department. Accounts of their captivity were edited and reworked by Wingate and his intelligence staff as part of the propaganda effort to generate public support in England for the reconquest of the Sudan.

[6] The Khalifa Abdallah (1846–1899), the successor to the Mahdi and theocratic head of the Mahdist state, 1885–1898.

Shangetti in an aside said that the educated Sudanese were paying less attention to the religious leaders, S.A.M. and S.A.R. As a matter of fact S.A.M. was not really behind Ashigga. He explained also that whereas S.A.R. was merely a prophet, S.A.M. claimed to be divine.[7]

Wingate said that on S.A.M.'s return he was so popular and had received so many gifts that he, Wingate, had to put a stop to it.

Udal said that he thought the followers of S.A.R. were three quarters of the people of the Sudan. S.A.R., himself, in conversation said that 5% only were behind Ashigga.

Shangetti explained that [the Graduates'] Congress was alright as long as it was interested in social welfare but lost its influence when it went in for politics.

Other personalities were the Khalifa. Three of his sons were with S.A.R., but there were 3 who were not. One was insane and lived in Egypt and 2 were officers in the Sudan and followed Ashigga.

Immediate course of action

Shangetti of course was very much opposed to the declaration of sovereignty and *Udal* thought the Sudanese could not get over it. *Shangetti* thought that the Treaty itself should contain a statement about the necessary steps for the emancipation of the Sudan.

Wingate and *Udal* agreed that what was required was a round table conference preferably in London. The Governor-General should nominate Sudanese. The Egyptians should certainly participate with us and some immediate step was required as evidence that we meant business in Sudanese self-Government. All the Sudanese parties, including Ashigga, should be invited. This would fulfil the pledge, which Wingate emphasised, that the Sudan should be consulted. The real guarantee was the continuation of the Condominium (Wingate did not seem to realise how far opinion had moved amongst the Sudanese since his day).[8]

As regards relations with Egypt *Shangetti* told me that S.A.R. had asked Sidki to see him, but no reply had been received.

In conversation the distinction between the north and south Sudan became very clear. Shangetti boasted that the Sudanese had come from Arabia. He spoke very contemptuously of Abdel Latif (now in an insane asylum). He said his mother was a negress, his father was unknown, and that he, Latif, had at one time collected old tins from barracks.[9] *S.A.R.*, also, when the South was mentioned indicated that they, the

[7] SAM was a child of about three at the beginning of the Mahdiya (1881). His father, Shaikh Muhammad Uthman al-Mirghani (the grandson of the founder of the order), was the leader of the Khatmiya at that time and allied with the Egyptian government in opposing the claims of Muhammad Ahmad al-Mahdi. Both SAM and SAR were leaders of religious orders founded by direct ancestors, and both were considered by their followers to have inherited the *baraka* (blessing, or sanctity) of their ancestors. Neither claimed to be divine. It is unlikely that Stansgate accurately reported Shinqiti's claim that SAR was a 'prophet'. Muhammad is considered 'the Seal of the Prophets', and it is blasphemy for any Muslim to claim to be a prophet.

[8] Sir R Campbell minuted (9 Dec 1946), 'There seems to me to be a germ of utility in the 3-party conference suggestion, which is amenable to a variety of forms and could be combined with the S of S's proposal for a joint permanent council to supervise the preparation of the Sudanese for self-govt.'

[9] Ali Abd al-Latif (*c.* 1892–1948), a leader of the White Flag League which, in the 1920s, advocated the Unity of the Nile Valley and 'Sudan for the Sudanese', was a Sudanese officer of the Egyptian army. He was born in Egypt, his father being a Nuba soldier and his mother a Dinka, both of whom had been slaves in the Sudan. Shingiti is here expressing contempt not only for Ali Abd al-Latif's non-Arab origin, but for the slave status of his parents. It was only much later, following the Free Officers' coup in Egypt in 1952 and the May Revolution of 1969 in the Sudan that Ali Abd al-Latif and similar Sudanese officers of African (and slave) origin were officially honoured as nationalist heroes.

North, could deal with it very satisfactorily. The people in the south were called slaves, but *Shangetti* explained that this term was not much used now and probably his sons would never employ it at all.[10]

Through the conversation with *S.A.R.* the general theme was that the Sudan wanted the help of the world, that if the Sudanese were backed by us, they would be very willing to give us any military facilities we required. In the interview with *Wingate* and *Udal* the term the "Umma are very loyal" was continuously used. *S.A.R.* indicated that rather than be joined to Egypt he would join what he called "Africa."

Shangetti intimated that the harsh rule of the time of Macmichael,[11] of whom he spoke very critically, had been succeeded by a new regime, more in earnest in advancing the Sudanese towards self-government.

In the scheme of associating Egypt with Great Britain in settling the Sudan question, a wise step would be to persuade the Egyptians to show a little of their lavish courtesy to the Sudanese. The S.A.R. himself on his return might be treated with signal honour in Cairo. It might, perhaps, be possible to ask the Egyptian Ambassador to show him some special favour in London, but all this must be done under Egyptian auspices.

A second helpful step would be to get the Egyptians, if they would, to join in some declaration instructing the Governor-General to call a round table conference in which we should all particpate with a view to carrying out the undertakings given in the Protocol as to the welfare of the Sudanese and their advancement to self-government.

---

[10] Shingiti (who was acting as SAR's interpreter) here seems to be trying to explain away a casual reference by SAR to Southern Sudanese as *abid* (slaves).

[11] Sir H MacMichael, SPS, 1905–1933; civil secretary, 1926–1933.

117 FO 371/53262, no 5303 5 Dec 1946

[SAR on self-government]: FO record of a meeting between Mr McNeil and Sayyid Abd al-Rahman al-Mahdi

After the usual exchange of compliments the *Sayed* referred to the text of the Sudan Protocol which had been published in Egypt. He did not consider that the Protocol was in line with Mr. Bevin's declaration of March 26th.[1] He considered that it made an entire change in the situation, because neither the words "monarch" nor "unity" existed in the previous situation. He felt that the co-operation between Great Britain and the Sudan, which in the past had been based on the expectation of the fulfilment of British promises, could not continue since the declaration of the Protocol. This declaration made the position of himself and his followers impossible if they wished to continue co-operation. He asked what guarantees there were that there would be co-operation between the British and the Sudanese in the administration of the Sudan.

The *Minister of State* said that there were no guarantees other than our word and the practical operation of the administration. No further guarantees were necessary, since there had been no change in the situation.

---

[1] See 54.

The *Sayed* said that the Protocol and the statement of the King of Egypt did not accord with the interpretation that there had been no change. British administration during the past fifty years had developed the Sudan, protected the Sudanese people and led them towards self-government. What would the British now protect except the Egyptian crown? His argument was based on the documents and declarations that had been made available. Were there any other documents?

The *Minister* replied that since the opening of the Egyptian talks His Majesty's Government had always borne in mind that our policy was to develop the Sudan for self-government and had never overlooked this. We would not sign a treaty which in any way limited that high policy. Whose word did the Sudanese prefer, that of Mr. Attlee or that of Sidky Pasha? The Sudanese had 640 friends in the House of Commons who were proud of our record in the Sudan. Of course any treaty must come before the House of Commons before signature.

The *Sayed* said that he was grateful and reassured. His mission however was to make clear how people in the east understood things so that in our actions the British Government could know how their actions would be interpreted.

The *Minister of State* said that what counted were our actions in the Sudan. Sayed should not pay too much attention to newspaper reports or to what one man or another said.

The *Sayed* referred to the 1936 treaty which did not affect the position of the Sudan and said that the 1936 treaty was to stand for 20 years. It was now to be revised after 10 years.

The *Minister* replied that it was provided in the 1936 treaty that it *could* be revised after 10 years.

The *Sayed* then referred to the phrase "unity under the common crown of Egypt". Although the word "sovereignty" was not mentioned specifically the former phrase was mentioned. These words worried him and had brought him to London.

He was also concerned about King Farouk's declaration that "welfare" and "self-rule" would be his aims.[2] This was not compatible with Mr. Bevin's declaration that "self-rule" is a first step towards independence. According to the Protocol as it was released His Majesty's Government were not to consult the Sudanese about their self-rule but only the Egyptians.

The *Minister* asserted that our position and our pledges were quite unshaken.

The *Sayed* said that he wanted to proceed to self-government in the Sudan now with British support and guidance. This would be a protection against the present Egyptian Government, which was a corrupt one.

The *Minister* said that this seemed a completely new development; it had not been referred to in the Sayed's talk with the Prime Minister,[3] and he could not make any pronouncement immediately.

The *Sayed* then referred to the record of his conversation with the Prime Minister in which Mr. Attlee had said that the Governor-General had the support of the British Government to consult the Sudanese towards these aims.

The *Minister* said that this was not the same thing as giving immediate self-government.

---

[2] See 114, note 1.

[3] See 114.

The *Sayed* replied that the Sudanese had now reached the stage when they had established local self-government and an advisory council which was now developing towards a legislative assembly. This meant that the Sudanese were ready for a further step towards self-government.

The *Minister* replied that His Majesty's Government were of course anxious to take every step that would hasten self-government and it was precisely for that purpose that the Governor-General had been sent back to the Sudan. His Majesty's Government wanted to take steps to implement our policy in the Sudan and to ensure that the Sudanese could eventually be completely masters of their own destiny. They would not be parties to any treaty which impeded that policy.

The *Sayed* referred to a document which he had brought with him and which he then read out. He demanded

1. complete self-government forthwith;
2. independence in 10 years; and
3. that these conditions should be written into the treaty.

He asked for a written answer to these points before he returned to the Sudan.

The *Minister of State* said that this was a completely new departure, and he could not comment at this stage, but it appeared to him from what he had heard that there were no differences in principle between the Sayed and himself, the differences were only those of method. Negotiations for a treaty were now at a final stage, and this could not be reconciled with the Sayed's demands, but he could rest assured that in its final form the treaty would not conflict with our promises or his hopes.

The *Sayed* said that all he wanted was that the Protocol should, when it was made public, contain something of solid value for the Sudanese which the Sudanese people could seize upon and understand. He wanted to know that he could leave for the Sudan confident that his appeal would be met and that he could have something real which he could present to the Sudanese people. He would not be happy if he had to return without some assurance in his mind that the dangers which he foresaw were averted.

Egyptian propaganda was already filtering into the Sudan and would increase and have a chance of spreading ill-feeling against Great Britain unless he had the assurance for which he asked.

The *Minister of State* in conclusion said that he would examine the Sayed's statement very carefully, but he could now assure the Sayed that nothing would conflict with His Majesty's Government's policy of taking all possible steps towards self-government. He hoped that the Sayed would be convinced that no person and no country had more friends in the House of Commons than himself and the Sudanese people, and it was in fact the House of Commons, before whom the treaty must be laid, who were the masters, not the Ministers of the Government.

118 FO 371/53262, no 5219 6 Dec 1946

[Sudan protocol]: aide memoire by Sir O Sargent on the interpretation of the Sudan protocol handed to Amr Pasha. *Annex* [Extract]

[Sidqi's problems with his own treaty delegation continued. Many were unconvinced by the interpretation of the Sudan protocol which he presented to them (see 99). On 26 Nov seven members of the delegation (including the former and future prime ministers Husain Sirri and Ali Mahir) issued a public rejection of the treaty. The version of the Sudan protocol agreed between Sidqi and Bevin, they claimed, 'destroys the essential features of unity of the Nile Valley, maintains the status quo without promising negotiations for its modification, and by giving the Sudanese right to choose their future status, opens the way for the separation of the 2 parts of Nile Valley' (inward telegram no 1946 from Bowker to FO, 26 Nov 1946, FO 371/53318, no 49763). Given this opposition Sidqi could not exchange letters of interpretation which would have substantially confirmed this criticism (inward telegram no 1779 from Bowker to FO, 29 Nov 1946, FO 371/53319, no 5059). For his part Bevin in New York reasserted: 'I cannot accept Sidky's interpretation of what we agreed in London, namely that the existence of the crown of Egypt over the Sudan imposes a limiting factor upon the choice of the Sudanese as to their future status' (inward telegram no 2145 from Bevin to FO, 30 Nov 1946, FO 371/53262, no 5074). At the same time he attempted to find a formula which, while affirming the right of the Sudanese to eventually choose independence, also mentioned other possible options for continued association with Egypt. He hoped this would mollify Sidqi; yet he also felt it necessary to warn Sidqi that failure to agree to an exchange of letters could force HMG to issue a unilateral statement of interpretation (inward telegram 2326 from Bevin to FO, 5 Dec 1946, FO 371/53320, no 5165). Stansgate was critical of Bevin's proposal, minuting 'It would be interesting to know when the British Government took a decision that the Sudan should have the choice of independence. It certainly was never foreshadowed in the Agreements of 1899' (minute by Stansgate to Campbell, Sargent and Howe, 6 Dec 1946, FO 731/53321, no 5311).]

His Majesty's Government would like Sidky Pasha to be reminded of the understandings reached in London. His Majesty's Government are now in an extremely awkward position as a result of the leakages and Sidky Pasha's one-sided interpretations. They have a House of Commons and public opinion which could not agree that the Sudanese, far from being placed on the road to self-government, should be set one stage back and made subject, so far as their liberty of choice is concerned, to the Egyptian Government. His Majesty's Government therefore wish for letters of interpretation which in no way prejudice the Egyptian position, in no way go beyond what Sidky Pasha agreed in London, but which set out in more detail the purpose of the Sudan Protocol as His Majesty's Government understand it. Mr. Bevin has been trying to meet Sidky Pasha's difficulty over a letter and has worked out a wording which will, he thinks, prove acceptable to him. This text is attached.

Mr. Bevin would like Amr Pasha to understand, and explain to Sidky Pasha, that if His Majesty's Government do not get letters of interpretation he will have to make a full statement in the House of Commons at the time of ratification referring to all that Sidky Pasha had agreed in London and to His Majesty's Government's clear-cut interpretation of the meaning of the protocol. If Mr. Bevin is forced to make a statement of this kind it may prove far more difficult for Sidky Pasha than a letter of interpretation on the lines of the enclosed draft.

Mr. Bevin's statement in the House would explain what is at the back of the Sudan Protocol, namely, the preparation of the Sudanese for self-government and secondly the exercise of their right, when ripe for self-government, to choose their future status which includes independence. The House would be told how the phrase "under a common crown" had been inserted in the protocol. This was a recognition of symbolic sovereignty and was never intended as a brake on the wheel of Sudanese progress towards independence. His Majesty's Government could never in this age and with the spirit of the United Nations Charter guiding them in their foreign policy, accept the idea that the protocol had in some way imposed some check upon the Sudanese in the choice of their future status. As regards the present position in the Sudan Mr. Bevin would say in the House that the protocol involved no change but merely amounted to an affirmation of the existing status. Under the protocol His Majesty's Government would continue to secure the defence of the Sudan with all the necessary facilities.

Annex to 118: draft letter of interpretation

At the moment of signing the treaty of to-day's date I am happy to place on record my understanding of our agreement in regard to the meaning of certain parts of the Sudan protocol annexed to the treaty. We are agreed that the provisions of the Sudan protocol involve no change in the present status of the Sudan and that the protocol in fact amounts to an affirmation of the existing status. There will therefore be no changes in the present administration except in so far as this is necessary for the preparation of the Sudanese people for self government.[1] As to the future, the Sudan protocol provides that the Sudanese people shall when they are ripe for self-government be free to choose the future status of the Sudan. This future status may take several forms: the Sudanese people may choose association with the crown of Egypt similar to that of the self-governing Dominions with the British crown; they may choose some other form of self-governing association with the crown of Egypt; or they may choose independence. We are agreed that in the Sudan protocol, a completely free choice on the part of the Sudanese people is implied.

We are also agreed that the Sudan protocol in no way affects the right of the United Kingdom to secure the defence of the Sudan with whatever troops and facilities they may require. . . .[2]

---

[1] This sentence was added to Bevin's draft by Attlee (marginal note to inward telegram no 2329 from Bevin to FO, 6 Dec 1946, FO 371/53320, no 5168).

[2] Paragraphs dealing with the evacuation protocol are not printed.

119 FO 371/53320, no 5424 — 10 Dec 1946

[Sidqi's resignation]: inward telegram no 1844 from R J Bowker to FO

[The first news of Sidqi's resignation on 9 Dec gave HMG some grounds for optimism. Palace sources reported to the embassy in Cairo that the initiative for the resignation had come from King Faruq, who had concluded 'that British relations with Sidki Pasha had become too strained and Sidki Pasha was too compromised by his various statements about the treaty for any furher progress to be made. The King wants to appoint Nokrashi since he has steadfastly supported the treaty throughout and kept his mouth shut' (inward telegram no 1839 from Bowker to FO, 9 Dec 1946, FO 371/53320, no 5210). al-Nuqrashi's first statement on the treaty negotiations did not live up to British expectations.]

Press has published text of Sidky's letter of resignation; Royal Rescript No. 66 accepting Sidky's resignation; Royal Rescript No. 67 charging Nokrashi Pasha with formation of Cabinet and Nokrashi Pasha's reply thereto.

2. Sidky's letter stated that in view of his prolonged illness he considered it his duty to submit his resignation in the interest of the cause which could not be deferred and expresses appreciation of His Majesty's satisfaction and the confidence of Parliament without which there could be no constitutional Cabinet in a democratic

country. It concludes with the hope that his successor will accomplish the heavy task of realising the national aspirations of the country. Royal Rescript No. 66 expresses regret that the country should be deprived of Sidky's services in the present critical circumstances and appreciation of the tenacious efforts which Sidky has made.

3. Royal Rescript No. 67 addressed to Nokrashi refers to the need for ensuring the stability of the country by the realisation of the national aspirations. Nokrashi's reply states that the most important thing for the Government is to work for the evacuation of foreign troops from Egyptian territory and to realise the will of the people of the Nile Valley by the unity of Egypt and the Sudan. It refers to the general anxiety resulting from the prolongation of the negotiations and recent signs which increase anxiety with regard to the destiny of the Sudan. The natural bond—it continues—which unites the two parties of the Valley linguistically socially and historically cannot be damaged or broken and Egyptians are resolved to safeguard it. Egypt has undertaken to direct the Sudan towards progress in different domains of life with a view to attaining self-government within the framework of permanent unity with Egypt under King Farouk's crown. The country is unanimous on the objectives of evacuation and unity of the Nile Valley. Egypt is anxious to continue serving world peace and will always take care that her international obligations remain within the limits traced by the United Nations Charter in the letter and the spirit. As regards internal policy Nokrashi states that he will continue to apply the policy proclaimed in the speeches from the Throne of 1945 and 1946.

120 PREM 8/1338/3 — 10 Dec 1946

[Anglo–Egyptian treaty negotiations]: note by Lord Stansgate[1] to Mr Attlee on the question of Sudanese independence and the prospect of successfully concluding the treaty negotiations

The chances of getting the Egyptian Treaty are diminishing unless we can find rapidly some compromise.

Nokrashi is pig-headed, honest and very determined. When Stack was murdered, Huddleston took over and Nokrashi stood in the dock.

If the Cabinet has decided to insist on unqualified independence for the Sudan and let the Treaty go, the following points should be considered:—

(1) The bitter and long-standing anti-Egyptian feeling of the Sudan Government.
(2) The self-seeking motives of the Mahdi.
(3) Our ignorance of any but Umma opinion.
(4) The strategic implications of losing Egypt even if we dominate the Sudan.

A compromise might take the line of Dominion Status or we might suggest signing the Treaty and appointing a joint Commission to consider how to implement the Protocol.

So much was achieved by personal contact that the Foreign Secretary might think it worth while to ask Hadi, who is Nokrashi's close friend to fly to New York.

Time is very short.

---

[1] By this time Stansgate was no longer directly involved in the treaty negotiations. A note attached to this document reads 'Found on Cabinet Table; seen by PM'.

121 FO 371/53262, no 5337 14 Dec 1946
[Governor-general's statement to the Sudanese]: inward telegram no 1885 from R J Bowker to FO

[On 7 Dec, prior to Sidqi's resignation, Huddleston issued his statement based on Attlee's letter to him (see 115). Though his additional plea to 'enlightened Sudanese' came very close to meeting the demands then being pressed by the Umma Party and the Independence Front,[1] it served merely to harden Egyptian opinion, and al-Nuqrashi firmly rejected 'the right of Sudan to secede from Egypt' in his meeting with Bowker (inward telegram no 1872 from Bowker to FO, 12 Dec, FO 371/53262, no 5278, and inward telegram no 1884 from Bowker to Bevin, 13 Dec 1946, FO 371/53332, no 5330). Huddleston reiterated his call for a united effort between the Sudanese people and the Sudan government in the opening address to the Advisory Council on 1 Jan 1947, when he announced the imminent submission of the Administrative Conference's proposals 'for the expansion of the Advisory Council into a more representative and responsible assembly' (inward telegram no 2 from Huddleston to FO, 3 Jan 1947, FO 371/62939, no 52).]

Following is text of Governor-General's statement.

Begins. I have just returned from London and Cairo where I have spent nearly a month in connexion with the treaty negotiations between Great Britain and Egypt. These negotiations are still in progress but whatever the outcome may be, I am authorised in writing by Mr. Attlee, the British Prime-Minister, to give the Sudanese the following assurance.

> "That His Majesty's Government are for their part determined that nothing shall be permitted to deflect the Sudan Government, whose constitution and powers remain unaltered by the recent conversations, from the task to which that Government had applied themselves, viz, the preparation of the Sudanese for self-government and for the task of choosing freely what their future status is to be. The Sudan Protocol in fact provides that the Sudanese people shall, when they are ripe for self-government, be free to choose the future status of the Sudan. His Majesty's Government consider that, in the words used by the Egyptian Prime Minister to the British Foreign Secretary, nothing in the proposed Treaty can prejudice the right of the Sudanese to achieve their independence nor bind a people in search of liberty. The Egyptian Prime Minister pointed out to the British Foreign Secretary that this was a universal principle and therefore not a matter for incorporation in a Treaty".

There is one point on which all enlightened Sudanese are agreed, that they wish to become self-governing as soon as possible. This wish is shared by the Governments of both Great Britain and Egypt and there is no reason why the Sudan Government should not press on at once towards this goal. I am determined that nothing shall

[1] By mid-December the Umma and Independence Front delegation to London were calling for 'the immediate termination of the Anglo–Egyptian Condominium and the restoration of sovereign rights to the Sudanese people', along with 'the establishment of a Sudanese interim Government preparatory to the establishment of a free, democratic Sudanese Government in the shortest possible time. This Government, based on the will of the majority of the people, would determine the form of rule in the Sudan' (Abdallah Khalil, Yaqub Uthman, Muhammad Ahmad Mahjub, 'The Sudan case and the Anglo–Egyptian negotiations', nd, received 13 Dec 1946, PREM 8/1388/3)

hinder the establishment of a Sudanese Government and I call on all who wish to serve their country to co-operate with me and my officials in working out the next step towards this end. Only by goodwill among yourselves and by co-operation with the Government can you reach the goal of self-government which is desired by all sections and parties. I appeal to you, therefore, to lay aside your internal differences and unite in a great effort to achieve your aims. The Sudan Administrative Conference will forthwith be summoned to consider the recommendations prepared by it's [sic] Sub-Committee which dealt with the Sudanisation of the Central Government, and I wish the Conference to submit recommendation to me as soon as possible. I understand that neither the British nor the Egyptian Governments are unfavourably disposed in principle to the recommendation made by the Sub-Committee, though many points of detail require further consideration before a workable plan is evolved. I hope that those who were previously unwilling to join this Conference will now give it their support, and that any individuals who have ideas on the next steps to be taken will submit them. In conclusion, I again appeal for co-operation and unity and a determined effort to continue the work we have begun. Only if we work unfalteringly and are united can a Sudanese Government be achieved quickly and will you be able to take your free decision about the status of your country. *Ends*.

122 FO 371/53321, no 5355 17 Dec 1946

[Al-Nuqrashi's statement on the unity of the Nile Valley]: inward telegram no 1904 from R J Bowker to FO

[Despite al-Nuqrashi's initial statement (see 119) Bevin remained optimistic that he would give a favourable reply to the aide-mémoire sent to the Egyptian government shortly before Sidqi's resignation (see 118), and instructed Bowker to give a personal message to al-Nuqrashi soon after his appointment. 'Mr. Bowker might rub in that the protocol in fact commits neither His Majesty's Government nor the Egyptian Government on the nature of the future status of the Sudanese', he advised; yet he concluded: 'I cannot be put in a position where I can be accused of going against all the principles of the United Nations for it to be said that two large nations have prejudiced in a treaty the fate of a smaller one who has not been consulted in the treaty' (inward telegram no 44 from Bevin to FO, 11 Dec 1946, FO 371/53320, no 5265). Privately al-Nuqrashi appeared to want to sign the treaty (inward telegram no 1911 from Bowker to FO, 18 Dec 1946, FO 371/53263, no 5372), but partly as a result of Huddleston's statement (see 121) he adopted a more uncompromising public position.]

Following are translations of Press versions of passages in Nokrashi's two statements in the Chamber dealing specifically with the treaty situation.

2. In affirming the permanent unity of Egypt and the Sudan under the Crown of Egypt we are only expressing the will and desire of the inhabitants of this valley. It is moreover a natural desire engendered by unity of interest and language by a common existence and by bonds too ancient and too solid to be broken or loosened. We shall spare no effort to direct the Sudan towards self-Government, to prepare its inhabitants to conduct their affairs and to work for their happiness and prosperity.

3. As regards the delicate situation in which the country now finds itself I have frankly stated the point I have said that we shall follow any way likely to enable us to reach our national objectives and that is devoid of any ambiguity. I took charge of the Government at the moment when the negotiations had come to a crisis. I

immediately considered it useful to make known Egypt's opinion as regards her cause, everybody must know that when I say "unity of Egypt and the Sudan under the Egyptian Crown" I mean a permanent unity and I hope that the world knows that I express the opinion of all Egyptians. This unity derives from the will of the people of the valley, the will of the people of Egypt, and that of the people of the Sudan without distinction. Our opinion on this subject cannot be interpreted erroneously. Indeed I have clearly said that we will spare no effort to lead the Sudan to self-government. We do not want domination or colonisation but we will do our best to prepare its people to administer its affairs. Nobody should imagine that we want colonisation or domination of the Sudan. It cannot be so between two brothers but what there should be between them is independent unity bound by the Crown as by the Nile.

4. I repeat that the unity of Egypt and the Sudan will continue always and that no Egyptian could admit the separation of Egypt and the Sudan. I have also clearly said that I will follow any way capable of allowing us to attain our objectives that is negotiations or resort to the Security Council. In February 1946 I declared in the Senate that the Government would take advantage of all the methods authorised by the United Nations Charter and that Egypt had the right to refer to the Security Council which is competent, in fact the Egyptian Delegation has taken advantage of this right to follow its course and has turned it to good account.

123 FO 371/53263, no 5451 — 23 Dec 1946

[Appointment of Sudanese grand qadi]: inward telegram no 1940 from Sir R Campbell to Mr Bevin

[The position of grand qadi, who supervised the sharia, or religious courts throughout the Sudan, had been held by an Egyptian Islamic jurist since the establishment of the Condominium. A previous governor-general, Sir John Maffey, had as early as 1931 declared that the appointment of a Sudanese to the post of grand qadi could no longer be delayed. The international situation in 1940, when the appointment of a new qadi was next discussed, was such that the Sudan government agreed to appoint Shaikh Hasan Mamun for a term of three years, renewable for two years. In January 1946, his contract was extended for a further year, so as not to prejudice the forthcoming Anglo–Egyptian negotiations. With the approaching expiration of Shaikh Hasan's contract in January 1947 Huddleston proposed to appoint the Sudanese deputy grand qadi, Shaikh Ahmad al-Tahir, to replace him, and justified this as being in line with the Sudanisation policy (inward telegram no 154 from Huddleston to Campbell, 25 Dec 1946, FO 371/53263, no 5462). Al-Nuqrashi's objections, reported here, were repeated by King Faruq (inward telegram no 1954 from Campbell to Bevin, 26 Dec 1946, FO 371/53263, no 5481), and by Amr Pasha (letter from Abd al-Fattah Amr to Bevin, 28 Dec 1946, FO 371/53263, no 5529). Bevin advised that Huddleston extend Shaikh Hasan's contract, a request that Huddleston rejected on the grounds that it interfered with his constitutional authority to appoint Sudan government oficials (inward telegram no 157 from Huddleston to Campbell, 29 Dec 1946, FO 371/53263, no 5508). As the appointment of a Sudanese grand qadi had been agreed in the Sudan government's negotiations with SAR and the Umma Party leaders to resume cooperation with the government, following the demonstrations against the Sudan protocol, Huddleston felt that he could do no more than delay the formal nomination of Shaikh Hasan's successor (inward telegram no 159 from Huddleston to Campbell, 31 Dec 1946, FO 371/62958, no 8). Shaikh Ahmad was appointed acting grand qadi, and his final appointment as grand qadi was delayed until Oct 1947 (letter from Creed to Bowker, 5 Oct 1947, FO 371/62959, no 5014).]

Before I had requested interview the Prime Minister asked me to call this morning. He said that at the request of the Council of Ministers he wished to make urgent representations regarding termination of contract of Grand Kadi Sudan, report of which had appeared in this morning's press in a message from Khartoum. He had received on December 21st letter from Governor-General dated December 13th (which he showed me) reminding him that the Kadi's contract expired (gr.undec. ?in) January and stating that he (Governor General) had decided not to renew it but to appoint present deputy Grand Kadi (a Sudanese) in his stead. He said in passing that as date of expiry was January 2nd notice given was very short (Kadi had been informed on December 17th): but he wished to impress on me the effect of this decision on Egyptian opinion which at this moment would be "disastrous". Post of Kadi was the only high post in Sudan occupied by an Egyptian and to remove an Egyptian at this moment in favour of a Sudanese and thus to sever this link with Egypt would be taken as additional and clear evidence of a British policy to separate the Sudan from Egypt. The position and functions of a Grand Kadi moreover had a religious significance strongly felt in this country so much so that when a previous Egyptian incumbent had been offered the post he had required before accepting that he should receive a mandate from Mohammedan ruler and a formula for giving him mandate of King of Egypt had been issued. Since then and little by little the position in this respect had in fact been modified by policy of Governors-General to constitute themselves exclusive source of all appointments in Sudan administration without exception. I said that elimination of 1899 agreement surely gave Governor-General this position. The Prime Minister admitted it but said that sentiment here over religious significance of appointment continued strong. The matter therefore raised both political and religious feelings. He begged me to consider what he had said with a view to a modification of decision. He hoped announcement of appointment of a successor would be deferred while his representations were being considered. He had urged on Governor-General a year ago the desirability of continuing Grand Kadi in office beyond the term of contract. Sir H. Huddleston had made no commitment of any kind but as Kadi had been continued during this year and nothing had been said by Governor-General Prime Minister was surprised at this sudden decision without longer warning. He had urged on Mr. Bowker recently that there should be no more declarations interpretive [sic ?interpretative] of policy but here was something which would universally be regarded here as calculated (gr.undec.?action) in implication (sic) of policy of separation.

2. I told the Prime Minister; firstly I personally had (gr.undec.) matter of decision was clearly based on policy agreed in Article 11 of 1936 [treaty] to appoint Sudanese where qualified, to posts in Sudan administration. Implementation of this policy had become more urgent, point on which I thought Egyptian and British Governments was [sic] agreed, as witness Sudan Protocol. I assured him His Majesty's Government had no policy of separation. I contested appropriateness of regarding post of Kadi as a link between Egypt and Sudan: it was only accidental that hitherto an Egyptian in default of qualified Sudanese had held post that constituted link. Prime Minister had urged political and moral grounds against Governor-General's decision to appoint a Sudanese. But there seemed to me great difficulty in subjecting Sudanisation to considerations of a kind which were external to Sudan and according to his argument belonged to the sphere of Anglo–Egyptian relations. The Sudan must know that present Kadi's contract was due to expire and that qualified Sudanese was [sic] available for the post and failure to appoint Sudanese would raise doubts about sincerity of policy of Sudanisation as a part of programme of promoting welfare of Sudan and preparing them for self government.

3. Nokrashi Pasha emphasised Egyptians could only rejoice that a Sudanese was ready for this responsible post and that Egyptian contact had thus been shown to be beneficial, for officials of Sharia Court were pupils of Kadi. But all Egypt favoured preparation of Sudan for self government and reports again emphasise political effect at this moment of termination of Kadi's contract and religious aspect involved in matter. He wondered whether it would not be possible to maintain present Kadi in office, create post of deputy Grand Kadi to be filled by Sudan candidate and replace latter as Mufti of Sudan by another Sudanese. The Egyptian Government would if necessary be ready to shoulder expense of extra post.

4. I said I could not say that any action would be possible but I would report his representations immediately.

5. It is unfortunate that this incident should coincide with present moment in Treaty negotiations when we are trying to get Egyptian Prime Minister to help in breaking deadlock and when one of the difficulties is Egypt's fear that His Majesty's Government are aiming at permanent separation of Sudan from Egypt. If without compromising their position Sudan Government could prolong for say a year the present Grand Kadi's contract this would remove a factor likely to envenom atmosphere as regards Sudan and I would make as much capital as possible out of concession in any further discussions with Nokrashi.

124 FO 371/53263, no 5458 24 Dec 1946

[Al-Nuqrashi's position on the Sudan]: inward telegram no 1942 from Sir R Campbell to Mr Bevin

[Campbell's meeting with al-Nuqrashi on 23 Dec lasted nearly one and a half hours. After forwarding al-Nuqrashi's views on the Sudan Campbell wrote to Sargent, 'the moment is an important one as Nokrashi does need help and evidently puts his hopes in Mr. Bevin.... What he has asked in connection with the Sudan protocol, would, as far as I can see do us no harm, in itself. The possibility of doing what he requests depends obviously, on whether the S. of S. can satisfy opinion in Parliament and the Sudan if he stands on a position in which H.M.G.'s views on the unfettered freedom of choice of the Sudanese have been placed on record and not in any way retracted or modified and in which the Egyptian Government have not only failed to express agreement with those views but openly published their disagreement. Nokrashi (graciously!) does not seem to suggest or hope for any statement on our side to endorse the Egyptian point of view, but to be content that the two divergent views should remain without further re-iteration or reconciliation. It is conceivable that a willingness on our part to to [sic] the statements urged by Nokrashi might dispose and enable him to say something on his part which would help us' (letter from Campbell to Sargent, 25 Dec 1946, FO 371/53263, no 5451). Scrivener's comment on this telegram was: 'Nokrashi wants the S/S' help to get him out of a 'spot' created by his predecesor; and the S/S wants Nokrashi's help to get HMG out of a similar spot created by the same predecessor' (Scrivener, minute, 26 Dec 1946, FO 371/53263, no 5460).]

When Nokrashi had finished with subject of Grand Kadi (my telegram No. 1940)[1] conversation easily turned to Sudan issue. I expressed hope that in a general statement on Government's policy he was due to make to Senate this evening His Excellency would not say anything to make solution more difficult. He said his remarks would be on same lines as his speech in the Chamber.[2] He felt it right and

---

[1] See 123. [2] See 122.

advisable to state his position frankly and clearly. He did not think chances of solution would be prejudiced. I asked whether he was considering means of issue from impasse and had any special thoughts. He said he was and that he had indirectly and unofficially made some suggestions recently and had rather expected to hear how they struck His Majesty's Government. With very little encouragement he told me what these had been. They were that His Majesty's Government should state that (1) they had no intention of encouraging the Sudanese to separate themselves from Egypt and (2) if the Sudanese eventually chose to remain united to Egypt His Majesty's Government would place no obstacle in the way and would "be happy" to see this happen (compare paragraph 4 of Mr. Bowker's telegram No. 1911).[3] He asked whether I had seen the Egyptian Ambassador before leaving London. I said unfortunately I had not and enquired whether he had instructed Amr Pasha to put any suggestions to His Majesty's Government. He said he had and had hoped for some response. I reminded him you had only just returned: he said Amr had seen the Minister of State and he seems to have hoped for an immediate response.

2. Nokrashi Pasha urged that after the statement by the Governor General based on the Prime Minister's letter the fear of the Egyptians that His Majesty's Government were encouraging separation had been greatly intensified (the action in respect of the Grand Kadi—my telegram No. 1940—would be regarded as striking evidence of such a policy and as the first positive action in ensuring it). He could not over-emphasise the Egyptian pre-occupation with this prospect. The Sudan was Egypt's life-line. He thought he had the right to ask for a statement such as he suggested. It in no way ran counter to the British position as stated. If His Majesty's Government could realise the strength of the anxiety here he felt confident they would agree to action designed to remove it. His Majesty's Government must (he apologised for using the word) do so in the interests of breaking the deadlock. There were plenty of people here trying to sabotage a treaty and they were making full use of Egyptian fears about separation. He urged strongly his need for material with which to answer them.

3. I said you would no doubt consider his suggestions. Meanwhile certain points occurred to me. They did not appear to meet the difficulties in which you had been put by the various statements interpreting the Sudan protocol published here. You had made these difficulties clear in your personal message to Nokrashi. You would have to answer questions in Parliament about the freedom of choice of the Sudanese. Beginning with the conversations with Sidky Pasha you had consistently stated your position. You could not either on particular grounds connected with the Treaty nor on general grounds be put in position of apparently endorsing a denial of the right of self-determination. Nokrashi, I said, had told me the Egyptian Government proceeded and must proceed on the assumption that the Sudanese wished to remain united to Egypt. Even if this assumption was correct it might be disproved after the passage of years. Could he not make clear that though Egypt hoped and expected that the Sudan would choose to remain in association, should they do otherwise Egypt would not oppose? He was suggesting that you should help him to remove a

[3] In which it is reported that Nuqrashi reiterated his refusal to concede the Sudan's right to secede and said there was no question of an exchange of letters of interpretation (inward telegram no 1911 from Bowker to FO, 18 Dec 1946, FO 371/53263, no 5372).

suspicion (for which I could assure him there was no justification whatever): could he not help you on his side? (I said this because he had given no indication of an intention to make any statement at all on his side, as prognosticated by Amr—compare your telegram No. 2134.)

4. Nokrashi Pasha said that no Egyptian could say anything admitting Egyptian readiness to see the Sudanese separate themselves from Egypt. He could not say in advance he was willing for his leg to be amputated. The very life of Egypt depended on the Sudan through which the Nile flowed. I then spoke in the sense of the first part of paragraph 8 of Sir O. Sargent's memo of December 17th[4] and went on to say that it was obvious that safeguards for Egypt's water would have to be devised and established if the Sudanese should choose independence, and that this should not be too difficult. If it were done, would it not remove the Egyptian Government's difficulty? Nokrashi replied that it was not juridical or paper safeguards that Egypt required—other countries might be tempted to flirt with an independent Sudan to the detriment of Egypt's vital interest.

5. In further discussion in which he again emphasised strength of Egyptian feeling over this life-line and influence of this on Egyptian Government's attitude in present impasse, Nokrashi Pasha said he had great faith in you and that if only you could fully realise the depth of the sentiment here he felt sure you would understand and meet his point of view. You represented the new age. I said this lent point to your statement that you could not appear as going against all the principles of the United Nations Charter. When he said that His Majesty's Government had made their position clear I replied that the two Governments could hardly figure as signing a treaty which each understood differently. In giving continued thought to ways of solving the impasse (which he had promised to do) would he not take this into account? Nokrashi said we must both do our best. For the moment there seemed complete deadlock, and he hinted at possibility that only solution would be found in "a new formula" (for the protocol) even though this would mean fresh discussions from beginning and all that that involved and was therefore to be deprecated. I was discouraging on this hint (since any new formula acceptable to Egyptians must almost certainly be detrimental to our ideas).

6. At one moment His Excellency recalled that in autumn of 1945 it was he who had persuaded Council of Elder Statesmen in favour of a Treaty: many had been opposed or indifferent. He considered this a feat on his part and still believed his stand had been right. He had been surprised and hurt then at receiving a slap in the face in the shape of Mr. Attlee's letter and Governor General's statement. I said I

---

[4] 'It is suggested that we should test Noqrashi's attitude and as a first step say to Nokrashi that we note the Egyptian attitude as endorsed by his statement; that we assume that the only grounds on which the Egyptian Government can base itself in figuring before the world as desiring to deny to the Sudanese *in perpetuo* the right of all peoples to eventual self-determination is that it is so deeply anxious about Egypt's vital interest in the Nile Waters; that we well understand this anxiety and indeed our consciousness of it had prompted appropriate proposals which we put forward during the negotiations in our draft Sudan protocol; that we now wish to take the matter up with the Egyptian Government again with a view to devising safeguards and machinery for securing safeguards for Egyptian interests; that this ought surely not to be very difficult and that we anticipate that once it is accomplished the Egyptians will cease to find difficulty in admitting that a right of the Sudanese to choose their future status includes the possibility of their choosing (and being given) complete independence' (Sargent to Attlee, memo, 17 Dec 1946, FO 371/53262, no 5275).

thought you would think this a curious description of action which had only been necessitated by declarations made here. You had consistently expressed your point of view to Sidky Pasha.

7. I finally urged him to go on thinking of ways out of present difficulty and he said he would do so. I added that though Egyptians seemed unwilling to admit that there were large numbers of Sudanese who feared that their freedom of choice was being fettered, His Majesty's Government were satisfied that there were and that the fact must be taken into account. I begged him, in his deliberations, to give due weight to this factor.

8. Conversation was friendly throughout and Nokrashi Pasha more communicative than I had anticipated.

125 FO 371/53263, no 5481 28 Dec 1946

[Restatement of HMG's position on the Sudan]: outward telegram no 2170 (reply) from Mr Bevin to Sir R Campbell

[Al-Nuqrashi very quickly rejected this renewed proposal for an exchange of letters or jointly agreed statements. He instead urgently pleaded for a statement from Bevin alone, along the lines of his request in 124, as a way of relieving tension in Egypt and opening the way to 'further conversations' in which he might propose a new Sudan protocol (inward telegram no 1966 from Campbell to Bevin, 30 Dec 1946, FO 371/53262, no 5512).]

I have now studied the telegrams on Sudan issue ending with your telegram No. 1954,[1] and should like you to restate my position once again in the hope that Nokrashi will, in the discussion with you, arrive at an agreement which will solve this problem. I must reiterate that this trouble was caused by Egypt as a result of Sidky Pasha endeavouring to saddle upon me interpretations to which I had never agreed. The present Egyptian Government cannot escape from the effect in this country of Sidky's action.

2. My objective all through has been to deal with this matter on a basis of co-operation and not antagonism and finally remove the legacy left by the events of 1924. This legacy causes the Egyptian Government to see in every act of the Sudan Government an attempt to separate the Sudan from Egypt; and causes the Sudan Government likewise to view Egyptian activities in the Sudan with suspicion. We cannot be a party to a situation calculated to lead to a repetition of 1924 and therefore it was definitely understood in London that there should be no interference by Egypt with the Sudan administration, and no change in the status of the Sudan as fixed by Treaty. This position, I now understand, is accepted by the Egyptian Government. At the same time—and particularly because we take an economic as well as a political view of the question—I fully understand the danger to Egypt of a hostile Sudan and I am ready to direct British policy in a way that will not endanger Egypt's safety from this point of view. What we must do now is to live down the past and act honestly by each other and direct our own respective policies accordingly.

---

[1] Reporting King Faruq's concern that Britain was pursuing an 'opportunist policy' in the Sudan, and that Egypt 'would not contemplate the possibility of the Sudan becoming "a belligerent nation"' (inward telegram no 1954 from Campbell to Bevin, 26 Dec 1946, FO 371/53263, no 5481).

3. The wording of the Sudan Protocol was devised for this purpose, on the one hand to establish the symbolic association of Egypt and the Sudan; on the other to ensure the steady and undisturbed development of the Sudanese. No one can foresee now precisely whither this development will lead: the answer largely depends on what occurs in the interim. The essential is that both Governments should work honestly for the welfare of the Sudanese, and prepare them for self-government; then the Governments and the Sudanese will consult together and arrive at a decision in the interests of the Sudanese. At this stage the Sudanese must have this freedom of choice. They have many possible choices, and if they choose union with Egypt His Majesty's Government will be perfectly content. But I must again make it unmistakably clear that His Majesty's Government cannot directly or by implication involve themselves in a compact, in defiance of the whole spirit of the United Nations Charter, to *deny* the possibility of Sudanese free choice. At the same time His Majesty's Government will bear in mind, I repeat, the necessity of safeguarding the position of Egypt and particularly in relation to its life-line.

4. If the present difficulties can be removed by exchange of letters or by statements (which must be jointly and mutually agreed) then the way would be clear for the era of co-operation for Sudanese welfare and the removal of all antagonisms.

5. I have spoken to Amr in very general terms on these lines, and prefer to deal with Nokrashi through yourself. You should see Nokrashi and point out to him that I am willing to consider any proposals that may emerge from your discussions and which are in the spirit of the discussions which took place in London and with which you are familiar.

126 FO 371/62960, no 56 — 2 Jan 1947

[Anglo–Egyptian treaty negotiations]: inward telegram no 12 from Sir R Campbell to Mr Bevin [Extract]

[An impasse having been reached with al-Nuqrashi, the FO began considering the likely repercussions of a complete breakdown in negotiations. Sargent outlined what he thought would be the positive aspects in the Sudan: 'In the Sudan the effects of a rupture on the Sudan issue would be wholly beneficial from the point of view of the Sudan Government. Faith in His Majesty's Government would be fully restored, and the Governor-General could carry on his Sudanisation plans in a much more favourable atmosphere than at present. It is doubtful whether the Ashigga party could make much trouble, though they would certainly try' (memo from Sargent to Bevin, 1 Jan 1947, FO 371/62960, no 86). On his return to Egypt Campbell considered the wider implications.]

. . . 2. In accordance with my instructions I have on my return to Cairo explored the situation with a view to finding some compromise on the Sudan issue, of a nature to safeguard the right of the Sudan to develop towards self-government and, if they wish it, independence. The result of my explorations has been to show that there is no likelihood of the Egyptians committing themselves to any compromise on these lines, and *their intention is clearly to get control of the Sudan for themselves sooner or later.*[1] It is for this reason that, as I explained in my telegram

[1] All words in italics underlined in original by Scrivener.

under reference (tel no 11, analysing present situation and implications), I think we must now face the probable necessity of making a stand. The form of that stand should I suggest be, that His Majesty's Government should make a firm and unambiguous communication to the Egyptian Government to the effect that His Majesty's Government cannot sign any treaty which does not make clear the right of the Sudanese to opt for independence after they have reached the stage of self-government. In the statement His Majesty's Government would add that if however the Sudanese should opt for continued attachment to Egypt, His Majesty's Government would be quite agreeable thereto and that it is not their intention or policy to encourage them to separate.

3. We must realise that the results of such a statement will be at least a temporary and possibly a final breakdown of Treaty negotiations, perhaps an appeal by Egypt to U.N.O. or/and anti-British turbulencies and disorders encouraged by the Government on familiar lines e.g. Sidki Pasha's organised manifestations in Cairo and Alexandria in February and March last and perhaps worse. On past form however, if we stand firm and react strongly to any attacks on British lives and property, the situation will eventually evolve through successive crises into the form of régime which would be more sensible as far as we are concerned. An unpredictable factor would be the result of an appeal to U.N.O. Evolution during the past twelve years and appearance on the scene of Communist under-ground activity may have modified the accuracy of the last prognostication to a certain degree.

4. If owing to considerations connected with manpower or our economic position or the moral effect of physical embroilment in Egypt, we cannot afford to stand up to the Egyptians in this way, then the sooner we yield to them the better. *The present discussions have become un-real* and the longer they continue the greater the danger of more demands from the Egyptian side, in each case leading to African mass hysteria and oriental auto-suggestion. But if we are going to yield on the question of principle now at stake we should realise quite clearly what that means. It is not only a question of our losing the Sudan as a military base or passage; but our position in other parts of the Orient and Africa might be greatly affected.

127 FO 371/62939, no 128, CC 2(47)8 6 Jan 1947

[Anglo–Egyptian treaty negotiations]: Cabinet conclusions on Mr Bevin's decision to risk a breakdown in treaty negotiations over the Sudan's right to self-determination [Extract]

The Foreign Secretary informed the Cabinet that no means had yet been found of overcoming the difficulty which had arisen over the Sudan Protocol to the Anglo–Egyptian Treaty. The Egyptian Government were seeking to persuade him to agree to a proposal which would in effect deprive the Sudanese, when at some future date they were ready for self-government, of their right of self-determination. He had no alternative but to resist this, even though the result was a breakdown of the negotiations for the Treaty. . . .

128 FO 371/62939, no 10 15 Jan 1947

[Anglo–Egyptian treaty negotiations]: letter from Sir R Howe to Sir R Campbell on the distinction between 'self-government' and 'independence' in HMG's colonial policy [Extract]

[Towards the end of 1946 Campbell reported to Howe that the Egyptian Ministry of Foreign Affairs had referred to the precedent of the British delegation at San Francisco insisting on the substitution of the term 'self-government' for 'independence' in the UN charter. 'I have a feeling that what we said is true, and seem to remember that the late Government was insistent on care being had to use the word "self-government" as the object of a renewed liberal policy for the colonies, and never the word "independence". We may get this point flung at us and perhaps we should be ready with an answer both on the facts and, if they *are* correct, on the argument. . . . Perhaps you would consider this and give us ammunition' (letter from Campbell to Howe, 27 Dec 1946, FO 371/62939, no 10).]

. . . We have consulted the Colonial Office and others concerned, with the following results.

United Kingdom Delegations have always taken the line that to lay down the principle that independence was the objective of all colonial policy was misleading. While independence in the sense of control of the external as well as the internal affairs was clearly appropriate for India, it would not have been appropriate for e.g. St. Helena. It is not the intention of His Majesty's Government to dissolve the British Empire into a series of completely independent states, however small. United Kingdom Delegations have always drawn a distinction between freedom in the sense of implementing the four freedoms (or self-government) and national independence.

Consequently, it was important to avoid inclusion in the Charter of any general statement of principle which would have bound all members to promote or agree to the independence of any unit of territory however small if the members of that unit had demanded it. The United States Delegation took a similar line very strongly. The Chinese proposed the insertion of independence in the draft of the Charter, but Dr. Wellington Koo was eventually induced to take it out.

On the other hand, Article 73 (b) of the Charter lays on nations responsible for the administration of non-self-governing territories the obligation "to develop self-government, to take due account of the political aspirations of the peoples, and to assist them in the progressive development of their free political institutions according to the particular circumstances of each territory and its peoples and their varying stages of advancement".

Thus the text of the Charter itself carries our views exactly into effect. A colony etc. is to be developed to self-government etc. and according to the particular circumstances of each territory and its peoples and their varying stages of advancement. Then, as regards the future, account has to be taken of the political aspirations of the peoples and again of the particular circumstances and the stage of advancement. St. Helena could never be independent, though it might be self-governing. Another territory might be self-governing but its political aspirations might not turn towards independence but to something else. A third territory might be self-governing and its political aspirations would turn towards independence, and where this is so and where the other particular circumstances of the case do not exclude it, viz. very small size etc., it seems to us that the real meaning of the Charter is that it should become independent. This third case covers in one [? our] view the future of the Sudan.

129 FO 371/62942, no 723 8 Feb 1947

[Anglo–Egyptian treaty negotiations]: letter from Lord Stansgate to Mr Bevin, forwarding a memorandum on the current state of the Anglo–Egyptian treaty negotiations [Extract]

Minutes by D M H Riches, D Scott Fox[1] and W E Beckett

[Stansgate had been released from the treaty negotiations, partly because it was felt he had been too inclined to concede points to the Egyptians. His own feeling, expressed in this memo to Bevin, was that the terms he had earlier negotiated with Sidqi were essentially the same that Bevin eventually obtained, but that the delay caused by Bevin's intervention contributed to the hardening of the Egyptian attitude generally to the negotiations. This retrospective look at Anglo–Egyptian relations placed on record his scepticism about the government's Sudan policy.[2] The attached minutes follow the paragraph numbers of the covering letter and memo.]

. . . 3. Nokrashi wants to help, but is facing a very strong and united Egyptian opinion on the Sudan. That is the chief difficulty.

4. We might get over this obstacle by adhering to the Protocol as agreed and making a joint submission for an interpretation of the meaning of the words in dispute (choice of future status). We could promise to abide by the decision given.[3]

5. This plan would give the necessary cover to Nokrashi and might enable him to conclude the Treaty as he earnestly wishes to do.

6. As soon as Huddleston's term is up we should consult King Farouk and select a successor really congenial to the King.

7. We should remember that for many reasons Egypt and the Sudan are bound to be linked by federation, union or unity and our part should be that of honest broker in helping this consummation.

8. The alternative—a fortified British Sudan and a hostile Egypt—is strategically unsound.

Memorandum with 129

. . . 12 . . . My own view is that we have been too much inclined to think that the Prime Minister of the moment was being obdurate and that a little pressure would bring him to reason. The fact is that both Prime Ministers, and particularly Sidki, have been doing their best to persuade their public opinion to come to agreement. Sidki might have been the more helpful. We made much of his indiscretions and so discredited him and, perhaps, contributed to the King's decision to dismiss him, but in point of fact the first indiscretion, that is to say, the first declaration, in recent time, of independence for the Sudan was made by the Governor-General in his speech to the Advisory Council in April, where being a servant of both parties he declared his policy without consulting Egypt, thus going, as the Egyptians say, outside his proper function. His speech, of course, angered them and was the subject of complaint to me by the King. Sidki, who, by his indiscretions, was striving to

---

[1] Egyptian Dept (ex-Italian colonies).

[2] For an extract from the same document on the defence aspect of the treaty negotiations, see BDEEP series B, vol 4, J Kent, ed, *Egypt and the defence of the Middle East*, part I, 92.

[3] Marginal note by Bevin: 'We hope U.N.O. will do this.'

defeat his opponents and come to an agreement with us, was destroyed and Nokrashi took his place. The whole episode, for which Sidki was only partly to blame, was disastrous . . .

The Sudan

19. I feel that we have never taken the measure of the Egyptian feeling about the Sudan. In 1884 Cherif was dismissed for refusing to agree to the withdrawal; Boutros was assassinated for, among other reasons, signing the Agreement of 1899; Zaghlul never disguised the strength of his feelings. It is not entirely a question of water, although that is the main element. The Cairo Government feels about the South exactly as we felt in the days of the occupation, and you will find in the writings of Cromer, Milner and especially Churchill the strongest assertion of the essential unity of the Nile Valley.

20. The Egyptians believe that the autonomy which we have created in the Sudan is a preparation for secession. There is something to be said for their fears. We prevented the King by an ultimatum from assuming the title of "King of Egypt and the Sudan".[4] When Egypt was declared independent in 1922 we, ourselves, made plans to transfer the allegiance of the Egyptian Army in the Sudan from the King of Egypt to the Governor-General. Later on, when Sir Lee Stack was murdered we presented an ultimatum threatening to reduce their water supply (this ultimatum was much disapproved at the time and quickly abandoned); we expelled their nationals, created the S.D.F. and until the Treaty of 1936 ran the Sudan as a monopoly. This monopoly, which was greatly to the advantage of the Sudan, is the basis of the argument that we favour secession or colonisation.

21. What the Egyptians ignore is the growth of Sudanese Nationalism. On this question they are particularly pig-headed. They know little about the Sudan and they certainly have no experience of the growth of Dominion status, as understood by us or the Dutch.

22. On our side I must say I would have been glad to have more information on this subject. We do know that there are two parties, the Umma and the Ashigga, both demanding independence, but both agreed that union with Egypt in some form is ultimately desirable.[5] Their differences would appear to be those of tactics, the Umma thinking that if they can be declared independent under our guarantee they can make better terms with Egypt, and the Ashigga that if they can use Egypt to get rid of us they can then deal with the Egyptians in their own strength. The demand that, as soon as possible, the Condominium should cease and we should evacuate the Sudan, appears to be a common principle of both parties.

23. I think we made a mistake once the Sudan was determined to be heard in London, in not attempting to hear both sides. The representative of Ashigga was available, but was not received. On the other hand, it appeared that our influence was to be placed entirely behind the Mahdi and Umma, thus, again lending support to Egyptian suspicions of secession. One of the results of this will be that if the case goes to U.N.O. our right to speak for the Sudan will be challenged by a Sudanese speaker who will assert that he represents a majority in his own country.

---

[4] Marginal note by Bevin: 'We have now agreed to unity of Egypt & Sudan & common crown'.

[5] Marginal note by Bevin: 'No'.

24. Looking forward a little the situation would appear to be shaping as follows:
25. A British administration in the Sudan supported by solid elements, such as the Mahdi, a very rich man, and the sheikhs, and the subject of constant pressure by the young politicals. Any differences between Ashigga and Umma are likely to be merged in a common demand for the immediate evacuation of the British. And this demand, of course, will be supported fully by Egypt as it was in 1924 with the cry "Sudan for the Sudanese". Egypt has great advantages of common religion and language and geography and wealth. We may find in the end that we are left with only the support of an interested and influential party in opposition to what will appear to be a National Movement.
26. I have said nothing about the South Sudan, nor have I any information as to how an independent Sudan, even with British guidance, is to incorporate the South, where fears of the slavery of the Mahdia are still common.

Sudan policy
27. It may well be that for the moment we cannot reach an understanding, but the policy we should have in mind, I think is clear. The day is over when the Condominium means that the Governor-General's appointment is signed by the King of Egypt and his policy run either by himself alone or from Whitehall. We must go back to what Cromer originally intended, namely, that the Sudan policy (though not administration), should be a joint affair. I have already suggested to you, but the Egyptians have not accepted it, that there should be held a conference (as recommended by U.N.O.) to lead up to the creation of a three-party Council to watch the execution of Sudan policy. In a word the real solution of the Anglo–Egyptian-Sudanese question is regional and does not lie in the direction of the creation of a petty independent state. A good part of this the Egyptians would accept. They merely stipulate that the development of Sudan "independence" should start from the basis of the existing sovereignty, and that, in a word, is the sole issue between us.

Minutes on 129

4.[6] This evades the issue. We agreed to the Sudan protocol on our interpretation of it. If an international body gives an interpretation differing from our understanding then presumably we want the protocol changed. . . .
6. I agree that other things being equal it is obviously preferable to have a Governor-General friendly to King Farouk. But our primary objective must be to find a good administrator acceptable to the Sudanese and capable of enforcing a policy of rapid sudanization.
7. I entirely disagree. What are the reasons for this statement? If it is the common Nile then Uganda, the Belgian Congo, Kenya, Tanganyika, and Ethiopia are also bound to federate with Egypt. If a common language and religion then it applies only to the N. Sudan and Egypt will eventually be federated with all Arab states; if history and conquest, Mohammed Ali and Ibrahim's conquests extended through Palestine and Syria and the Hejaz & Somali land, as well as into the Sudan.

[6] 4–8 of Riches's minute refer to paragraphs in Stansgate's letter; 21–27 refer to paragraphs in the memo.

8. The alternative is rather an independent Sudan leaning on us for protection against an imperialist Egypt. . . .

21. This is only too true.

22. The Umma do *not* favour union with Egypt in some form though they were inveigled into something very like this when they joined, very temporarily, Azhari's delegation to Cairo when the treaty talks opened. In any case they have very much recanted since.

23. Azhari was not received in London because he did not approach the Secretary of State through the Sudan Agent as was suggested to him.

25. The young politicals at present number some 5–10,000. The only national movement likely to appear in the Sudan is a recrudescence of Mahdi-ism which would result from too much Egyptian infiltration. I agree that Egypt has great advantages of religion etc.; but she has also great disadvantages in previous history, her contemptuous attitude towards the Sudanese, and the fact that her imperialism is on the upswing while ours is very obviously on the downgrade.

26. This is a real problem which will require considerable investigation and thought in the next few years.

27. I agree that we shall probably have to bring the Egyptians more into the policy side of the government of the Sudan in future. This, like sudanization, will mean a deterioration in the administration and will have to be done in the teeth of a good many British officials who are rightly proud of what they have contributed towards building up in the Sudan . . .

D.M.H.R.
15.2.47

. . . it is difficult to see how a U.N.O. decision which went some way towards depriving the Sudanese of their right to choose freely their future status would be any more palatable to the Sudanese nationalists than would a bilateral Anglo–Egyptian decision in that sense. If we are to promise to abide by U.N.O.'s decision, it would be the logical corollary that we should warn U.N.O. that a decision in favour of the Egyptian thesis would lead to trouble in the Sudan and that U.N.O. should at least share in the responsibility for dealing with the trouble caused by their decision. Such a warning might give the U.N.O. pause before deciding against us, but the logical conclusion of such an argument would be that troops from other members of U.N.O. should help us deal with the resultant disorders and that would hardly suit us . . .

D.S.F.
17.2.47

Paragraph 12. Without in any way endorsing most of what Lord Stansgate says, I have myself felt that, in some recent cases, the Governor-General of the Sudan has made pronouncements which would better have been made by a Minister of the U.K.

Paragraph 19. The Egyptians have a way of assassinating ministers. Unless I am mistaken, the minister who agreed to the Suez Canal concession was also assassinated.

Paragraph 27. Cromer's intention that the Sudan policy should be a joint affair is, of course, rather a debating point than a real point. After all, Cromer ruled Egypt really, and therefore we know what he meant by a "joint affair".

Paragraph 27, last sentence. This is hardly right, seeing that the existing

Protocol certainly starts from the basis of an existing Egyptian sovereignty and the split came not on this point but on the question whether the Sudan could ever achieve complete independence or not.

W.E.B.
28.2.47

130 PREM 8/1388/3 3 Mar 1947

[Anglo–Egyptian treaty negotiations]: inward telegram no 557 from Sir R Campbell to Mr Bevin giving text of al-Nuqrashi's statement on the breakdown of the treaty negotiations

[In late January Bevin proposed a new draft of the Sudan protocol which pledged both Egypt and Britain to the preparation of the Sudanese for self-government, and (after consultation with the Sudanese) the free exercise of choice of future status of the Sudan 'in accordance with the principles of the charter of the United Nations concerning non-self-governing territories' (outgoing telegram no 173 from Bevin to Campbell, 23 Jan 1947, FO 371/62941, no 3781). Al-Nuqrashi objected to this, asserting that there was no need for an explicit statement about freedom to exercise choice. Failure to reach an agreement, he further warned, 'meant reference to U.N.O. and though we would no doubt both agree to go to U.N.O. in an amicable way . . . one could never be sure of what people would say in stress of discussion and he feared the possibility of heated language' (inward telegram no 226 from Campbell to Bevin, 25 Jan 1947, FO 371/62941, no 402). In expressing his own disappointment over al-Nuqrashi's response, and fully anticipating the breakdown of negotiations, Bevin instructed Campbell: 'on one point you should disabuse Nokrashi's mind at once, i.e. that we shall go to U.N.O. as friends if he decides to go there. This issue involves two parties to the chief sec, fundamental right of a third under the United Nations Charter; and this point is so vital that British opinion will compel its representatives to express themselves openly and forcefully' (outward telegram no 191 from Bevin to Campbell, 25 Jan 1947, FO 371/62941, no 402).]

At 4.30 Today the Prime Minister Nokrashy Pasha held a press conference. He issued the following statement. The negotiations between Egypt and Britain began in April 1946 and lasted ten months during which the Egyptian side earnestly tried in every way to come to an agreement. This was clearly demonstrated by the journey undertaken by the Egyptian Prime Minister to London for the purpose of personally contacting Mr. Bevin. The final breaking off of these negotiations may be attributed only to the inability of Egypt to obtain satisfaction on the following two essential points, which are claimed by the Egyptian people.

1. Evacuation of British troops from Egypt. This evacuation must be immediate, complete, and not conditioned by a treaty.

2. Maintenance of the unity of Egypt and the Sudan, self Government for the Sudanese and restoration to Egypt of her rights in the administration in the Sudan in order to further the preparation of the Sudanese for self Government. The unity of Egypt and Sudan is the will of both Egyptians and Sudanese. Whereas the British policy is directed towards inciting the Sudanese to secede from Egypt. As for self government, had Egypt not been forcibly deprived of her rights in the administration of the Sudan, the preparation of the Sudanese for self government would not be so delayed. Egypt is in a better position and is more anxious than Great Britain to prepare for self government a people of the same race, the same language, same religion and dependent for their very existence on the Nile. Egypt wants the Sudanese to be able as soon as possible to express their views freely,

which can be accomplished only when British troops have evacuated the Sudan. The two preceding points are fair application of the principles of the United Nations charter. For that reason, after exceptionally prolonged negotiations, the Egyptian Government, regretfully convinced that direct discussions held no hope of success, decided to appeal to the Security Council. This decision has received the enthusiastic endorsement of the entire Egyptian people. Egypt has abiding faith in United Nations and is absolutely confident that justice will be accorded to a small nation which has always firmly upheld the principles of the supremacy of international law.

131 FO 371/62943, no 1533 [31 Mar] 1947

[Anglo–Egyptian treaty negotiations]: minute by Sir R Howe on Mr Bevin's provisional instructions for an approach to King Faruq

[The retirement of Huddleston and his replacement by Howe as governor-general of the Sudan offered the FO the opportunity of renewing its approaches to the Egyptian government through one of their own number who had been intimately involved in the earlier stages of the treaty negotiations. Bevin was anxious to create a better atmosphere in Egypt, and while in Moscow (for a meeting of foreign ministers) he suggested that this might be achieved by allowing Egyptian administrative officers into the Sudan, and proposed that Howe raise this, and other possibilities, with King Faruq when they met on Howe's way to Khartoum (inward telegram no 325, 25 Mar 1947, from Bevin to FO, FO 371/62943, no 1409, and inward telegram no 448, 29 Mar 1947, from Bevin to FO, FO 371/62943, no 1533). Howe responded with the following criciticism. The gist of his argument was relayed to Bevin through Sargent, and Bevin eventually agreed that Howe should not 'dangle a tempting series of concessions before King Farouk. All I suggest is that the new policy in the Sudan, which we shall need to follow, not in the interests of a settlement in Egypt, but in our own world interests, should be present in Sir R. Howe's mind as the background of an exploratory talk with the King' (inward telegram no 524, 1 Apr 1947, from Bevin to Sargent, FO 371/62943, no 1553).]

The policy which the Secretary of State proposes to follow in the Sudan as set out in this telegram can be summarised as follows:—

(a) Nothing should be allowed to prejudice the right of the Sudanese to self-determination.

(b) Nothing must be done to interfere with the Sudanisation of the administration of the Sudan.

In order to give effect to this policy the Secretary of State wishes to propose to King Farouk the following measures to be taken now.

(c) The institution of a kind of Supervisory Council composed of Egyptians, British and Sudanese whose duty would be

(i) to supervise the preparations of the Sudanese for Sudanisation

(ii) to report to both British and Egyptian Governments on the progress being made in this field

(iii) to recommend measures to speed up Sudanisation.

(d) To bring more Egyptians into the Sudan administration.

(e) A special body to control the utilisation of the Nile waters.

The Secretary of State further proposes to re-affirm the unity of Egypt and the Sudan under the Egyptian crown, which previously he was only prepared to concede as the price of an agreement.

(f) A customs and currency union.

It seems to me that if I am going to propose all these things to the Egyptians we are going to do precisely what we have agreed would be the worst possible thing for us to do at this juncture. We are all agreed that it is futile to make further proposals on the question of the Sudan to the Egyptians because they will inevitably regard it as a sign of weakness on our part and as constituting further concessions to their point of view. From the tactical point of view, therefore, it seems to be all wrong.

Furthermore, as regards (a) Nokrashi has said that Egypt will insist on the permanent unity of the Sudan with Egypt and we shall only provoke this rejoinder by telling the King that nothing should be allowed to prejudice the right of the Sudanese to self-determination.

As regards (c) we have already proposed to Nokrashi the institution of this kind of body and the Egyptians have rejected it. The proposed Council would presumably sit in Cairo and there might be some advantage in having a body of this kind, whose duty would be to agree on the interpretation of the Condominium Agreement so that the co-domini could give agreed instructions to the Governor-General. On the other hand, if it is going to function in the Sudan, it seems to me that it would cut across the functions of the Governor-General. It would be contrary to the Condominium Agreement which lays down that the Governor-General is the supreme executive and legislative authority. It would be inconsistent with the new constitutional proposals of the Sudan Government which aim at setting up in the near future a legislative council for the Sudan.

As regards bringing more Egyptians into the service, this proposal needs very careful consideration in view of the 1936 Treaty which lays down that qualified Sudanese are to have the first opportunity. To give a pledge regarding more Egyptians without first seeing whether qualified Sudanese are available would prejudice our policy of Sudanisation as well as running contrary to the 1936 Treaty which says that qualified Sudanese are to have the first opportunity. It seems to me that on this point it would be necessary to examine carefully the position in the Sudan before giving a blank cheque on this score. We don't want a repetition of 1924.

As regards the control of the Nile waters, this is all provided for in the Nile Waters Agreement. It does not seem that any further special arrangements need be considered at this stage. See also S/S's proposal to Sidky in the Nile waters in the event of Sudan choosing independence.

As regards (f) there is already a customs union between Egypt and the Sudan under Article 7 of the Condominium Agreement, while the currency is the same in both countries.

I think that the line for me to take with the Egyptians in Cairo is to say that it would be my duty as Governor-General to see that Egyptian interests in the Sudan are safeguarded, that the policy of the Sudan Government shall not in any way be directed against those interests and that I shall hope to have the fullest and frankest cooperation with the Egyptians in carrying out this policy, that I shall keep them informed of all developments in the progress of the Sudanese towards self-government and that I look to them to give me their fullest support in this task.

Finally in proposing all these things to the Egyptians now we should be giving away in advance those things we might have to concede in return for a treaty, if & when negotiations are resumed.

132 FO 371/2944, no 2002 27 Apr-28 May 1947
[Southern Sudan]: minutes by D M H Riches and D W Lascelles

[The future of the Southern Sudan was still not a major concern for either HMG or the Sudan government, but there had been increasing signs that northern Sudanese nationalists were making the matter an issue, and some concerned voices were beginning to be raised in England. H M Medland (Lab MP for Drake Division of Plymouth, 1945–1950), forwarded to the FO a letter from one of his consitutents, Major P M Larken,[1] a former district commissioner in the Southern Sudan, expressing horror at the news that the South was to be 'handed over to the [northern] Sudanese', which he condemned as 'a shameful betrayal of our trust. To my mind, there is not the least doubt that they would be exploited, or at the best, neglected' (Larken to Medland, 22 Apr 1947, FO 371/2944, no 2002). The internal discussion concerning the best way to answer this letter was not part of any formulation of policy, but it reveals that the Foreign Office was still open to posibilities which had already been ruled out in Khartoum.]

It is perfectly true that the Southern Sudanese are entirely different on all counts to the northern Arab Sudanese; and that they fear exploitation by the latter.

It is a common Egyptian cry that we are seeking to accentuate & play on these differences with the object of separating the South & annexing it to Uganda.

(A) | Obviously such separation could only be effected with the consent of Egypt. Such consent would never be given. Equally obviously we must press on with Sudanization. The only ways therefore to safeguard the South are by (a)
(B) | affording equal opportunities for education etc. in the South. This the Sudan Govt are trying to do; & (b) by instilling into Sudanese Arab administrators some idea of public service & devotion to the welfare of the southerners whom they may have to administer.

I suggest that the reply to Mr Medland might be on the lines that

(a) The Sudan is a Condominium & HMG cannot take unilateral action to separate the South from the Sudan.
(b) The achievement of self government by the Sudanese will take some time in the view of H.M.G. & it is premature to speak of the south being handed over immediately to the Arabs of the north.

D.M.H.R.
27.4.47

I don't altogether agree with Mr. Riches' minute above. As regards the passage which I have marked (A), it is not true that Egypt will never consent to the separation of southern from northern Sudan. Admittedly she will never consent to this as long as the Sudan remains an Anglo–Egyptian Condominium. But it will not remain that

[1] P M Larken, SPS, 1910–1932, served exclusively in the Southern Sudan, sixteen years in the Zande districts of Tembura and Yambio alone.

indefinitely if the United Nations fulfil their role. At some stage they will be called upon to judge whether the Sudanese people have reached the stage at which they will be entitled to control their own destinies; and if their judgment is favourable, Egypt will not be able to prevent its execution.

2. Nevertheless the problem raised by Major Larken is a real and difficult one. Despite (B) of Mr. Riches' minute, the Sudan Government have not shone as promoters of education in the black and primitive South. Even if they were to go all out now, the South could never hope to catch up on the North; and consequently it would be bullied by the North in an independent Sudan, whatever the theoretical set-up might be as regards proportional representation, etc.

3. The only safeguard would seem to be for us to endeavour to take the question of Sudanese independence by stages, inducing the U.N. (which would presumably be the final arbiter) to confirm the political maturity of the North, and hence its right to chose independence, before it does the same for the South. The South would thus remain longer under the Condominium arrangement, and would have time to mature. Eventually it could be declared politically mature and given the same liberty as the North to choose its own fate. It might elect to join up with the North, or to become an independent entity. Either way, our moral obligation would be discharged.

4. Major Larken wrongly assumes that the Sudan is going to achieve independence in the immediate future. If he had not assumed this, he would probably have raised another awkward point: we are committed to a policy of Sudanisation of the administration on wide and unassailable grounds of principle, but this policy means an increasingly raw deal for the South while we are still in (co-) charge of the country. There is no escape from this.

5. The Sudan Agent's letter to me, attached at Flag A,[2] suggests a form of reply to Mr. Medland. If I were in Major Larken's position, I should regard this reply as a piece of heartless official humbug. Mr. Mayall tells me that Major Larken, though rather fanatically "pro-South", is an honest man who could be trusted not to quote or misquote us if we had a talk with him. (Obviously we cannot afford to be too frank on paper). I think this would be the best solution provided that Mr. Medland would not feel slighted or short-circuited.[3]

D.W.L. 30.4.47

I saw Major Larken to-day, and he went away quite happy.

D.W.L. 28.5.47

---

[2] The Sudan Agent had proposed as a possible answer to Larken a statement that there is no intention of handing over the peoples of the South to the Northerners, money from the North's economic growth was going to be used to develop the South, the South may be included in the administrative reorganisation being carried out in the North, and that Southerners would have an equal voice with the Northerners in choosing their political future (letter from Mayall to Lascelles, 29 Apr 1947, FO 371/62944, no 2002).

[3] McNeil sent a letter to Medland, reassuring him that the problem, while serious, was not urgent, as the Sudan would not be likely to achieve independence in the near future, but inviting Larken to meet Lascelles for a personal discussion.

133 FO 371/63053, no 2409 20 May 1947

[Egypt and the Sudan]: despatch no 440 from Sir R Campbell to Mr Bevin on the dilemma of excluding Egypt from the administration of the Sudan while admitting sovereignty

There was enclosed with Mr. Speaight's letter to Mr. Lascelles 364/67/47 of May 3rd a series of notes prepared by the Civil Secretariat at Khartoum illustrating the practical difficulties of co-operation with the Egyptians in the administration of the Sudan and, in particular, the virtual impossibility of introducing more Egyptian officials at a high level in the administration without grave danger of wrecking the whole machine. These notes, and other evidence furnished by the Sudan Government of the dangers of Egyptian influence (for example, Mr. Robertson's letter CS/SCR/97.H.6 of April 7th, a copy of which was sent to Mr. Butler) all help to emphasise one of the fundamental problems with which we are faced in the Sudan: namely the need to ensure that the welfare of the Sudanese continues to be the primary object of the administration while, at the same time, satisfying the Egyptians themselves and world opinion that the legitimate interests and rights of Egypt in the Sudan are not being ignored. In the following paragraphs I attempt to give a brief statement of the opposing points of view and my suggestion for what seems to me the best means of steering round the dilemma. The facts are of course already well-known but it may help to clear our minds at this stage if I recapitulate them.

2. If the long term interests of the Sudanese could be considered in a vacuum, the future course would be clear. Egypt has no real interest in the welfare of the Sudanese and no serious contribution to make to its future development, either in the material or spiritual sphere. In the early days of the condominium, Egyptian officials were useful at the lower level of the administration, because both they and the Egyptian Government itself were under British control. But a stage has now been reached where, with the exception of a few technical posts, the Sudanese themselves are capable of filling any post not still occupied by a British official. Their standard of efficiency may be below that of the better type of Egyptian official, but the difference is certainly not great enough to justify favouring Egyptians at the expense of the Sudanese. As regards the higher posts still in British hands, there are very few, if any, of these which could be handed over to the Egyptians without grave prejudice to the efficiency of the administration, constant friction within the administration and an out-cry from all politically conscious Sudanese, including even the Ashigga Party, whose conception of union with Egypt does not extend to direct government by Egyptian officials. It is thus easy to demonstrate that the Sudanese neither want, nor would profit by, any increase in the Egyptian share in the administration. Indeed, one can go further and maintain that, since Egypt has shown herself incapable of exercising the duties of a colonial power in accordance with the principles of the United Nations, the interests of the Sudanese would be best served by bringing the condominium to an end and placing them under British trusteeship until such time as they were able to stand on their own feet.

3. But unfortunately there is also the Egyptian side of the picture. The present Egyptian Government claim—and we must assume that any other Egyptian Government will make the same claim—that they are entitled to a greater, if not a predominant, share in the administration of the Sudan. In justification of this claim

they maintain that Egypt and the Sudan form a geographical and economic unit and that Egyptian interest in the upper waters of the Nile is vital; that the condominium agreement implies a joint Anglo–Egyptian administration which has never been realised; and that the Sudan is under Egyptian sovereignty. We can meet to some extent the first and second of these arguments but there is no getting away from the claim to sovereignty which was admitted, at least by implication (though in the more or less symbolic form of a personal union), in the Bevin/Sidky draft Sudan protocol and which the Law Officers of the Crown consider to be on the whole wellfounded. Moreover, apart from Egypt's legal claims, Egyptian political opinion has worked itself up to such an extent over the Sudan that Anglo–Egyptian relations can never run smoothly until some accommodation has been reached over this problem; and it might be said that Anglo–Egyptian relations, of great importance to His Majesty's Government, cannot fail to have an effect also on the Sudan.

4. Here then is the dilemma. If we not only insist on giving Egypt only the shadow and denying her all the substance of sovereignty, but at the same time deny her any but the most tenuous share in the administration of the Sudan, we permanently bedevil Anglo–Egyptian relations and make it easy for Egypt to prove at U.N.O. that we have gone back on our Treaty obligations by refusing her her share in the condominium. If we let more Egyptians in, we cause chaos in the administration and disillusionment amongst the Sudanese, and give the Egyptians an opportunity, which they are unlikely to neglect, of undermining our whole position in the Sudan, and bringing about a repetition of the 1924 crisis. In other words, we have got to give a semblance of reality to a condominium administration which since 1922 has never yet functioned satisfactorily on a condominium basis. Up to 1922 British influence in Egypt was sufficient to enable us effectively to control the Egyptian as well as the British side of the condominium. Between the declaration of Egyptian independence in 1922 and the murder of Sir Lee Stack in 1924, the Egyptians set themselves to wreck the joint administration and came within measurable distance of succeeding. From 1924 to 1936, we deliberately deprived the Egyptians of all share in the condominium. Since 1936 the Egyptians have again embarked on their wrecking tactics, although owing to the war it is only in the last two years that the impact of these tactics has been seriously felt.

5. There can be no quick way out of the dilemma. The only real solution is the long term one of doing everything possible to expedite the political evolution of the Sudanese so that they can dispense with the administrative supervision of both codomini. This, however, will take a number of years and during the interim period I can see no practicable alternative to attempting to continue the condominium agreement and trying to work it in such a way that the Egyptian Government can at least give the impression to the Opposition of the day and to the public that they are playing their full part, and yet are not put in a position to make mischief. Egyptian interest in the Sudan, however real in some important respects, has, in respect of the claim for participation of a greater number of Egyptians in the administration, a large element of "window-dressing" in that no Egyptian official will willingly relegate himself to such distant parts if he can find an excuse for remaining in Cairo. It may not be impossible in these circumstances to achieve an uneasy working arrangement on the lines suggested above. Our policy should, I submit, be to regularise as far as possible our (official) position under the condominium agreement (see, for example, my despatch No. 321 of 17th April, 1947) and for the Sudan

Government to be firm in the face of Egyptian provocation in the Sudan wherever their case is a good one.

6. I am sending a copy of this despatch to the Governor-General of the Sudan.

134 FO 371/63052, no 2096 29 July 1947

[Representation of the Southern Sudan]: recommendations by J W Robertson on the first report of the Sudan Administration Conference. *Annex*: resolution of the Governor-General's Council [Extract]

[The Sudan Administration Conference, under the chairmanship of the civil secretary, submitted its first report on 31 Mar 1947. The conference had been divided into two sub-committees: the central government sub-committee (sub-committee 'A'), and the local government sub-committee (sub-committee 'B'). The first report dealt entirely with the work of sub-committee 'A' on the steps to be taken for 'the closer association of the Sudanese with the Central Government' and its recommendations for the establishment of a Legislative Assembly and an Excutive Council to replace the Advisory Council for the Northern Sudan and the Governor-General's Council. On the matter of the future of the Southern Sudan the report stated: 'we are of the opinion that the future of the Sudan depends on welding together the people of the whole country. The Southern Provinces, though not Arab in origin (in common with many areas of the Northern Provinces) must look to the rest of the Sudan for economic and social development. Through the representation of the Southern Provinces on a Legislative Assembly responsible to the whole country the unification of the Sudanese peoples will more quickly be achieved and it is on this that the welfare of all Sudanese ultimately depends. We are fully aware of the relative backwardness of the peoples of the Southern Provinces and of the advances which they must make before they can reach the degree of civilisation attained by many of the peoples of the North. But at the same time a decision must be made, and made now, that the Sudan should be administered as one country. . . .' (*Sudan Administration Conference. First Report*, para 13, p 4). No Southern Sudanese had been appointed to the sub-committee, and the South was represented by B V Marwood, governor of Equatoria, who was invited to attend only the last meeting of the conference. Between the submission of the report and its presentation to the governor-general in council, Robertson convened a conference in Juba (12–13 June) which canvassed the views of a few junior Southern Sudanese officials. It was on the basis of their agreement to participate in the Legislative Assembly that Robertson made the following recommendations concerning the representation of the South. His comments on the other recommendations of the report were confined to procedural matters and minor re-wording of clauses.]

Paras. 12 & 13. Representation of the South

One of the main problems of the Report is its recommendation that the Southern Sudan should send representatives to the Legislative Assembly and for better or for worse become wedded to the Northern Sudan which on its part will have to endow the South with much of its worldly wealth. The Southern Sudan is inhabited by tribes of non-Arab origin, and owing to their primitive and pagan nature, and to the distance and inhospitable nature of the country in which they live, they have not made the same progress towards civilisation as the Northern Sudanese. Furthermore, owing to the scanty resources of the Sudan Government, it has not been possible until lately to find the money necessary to push ahead with the educational and economic development of these provinces.

It has however, been generally accepted in the last few years that the South is historically, geographically and economically connected inextricably with the Northern Sudan.

If the primitive inhabitants are to be persuaded to cooperate with the Government peaceably, it will be necessary for some time to come to protect their tribal customs and their personal laws regarding marriage, inheritance etc., from too sudden a shock by the impact of Northern ideas, and I think that they must be safe-guarded by law from too sudden interference in these matters, if they are to develop progressively along indigenous lines. This view was confirmed at a meeting which I held in Juba in June 1947 when a representative body of Southerners endorsed the view that they should not be administered separately from the Northern Sudan, but emphasised their backwardness and their fears of Northern domination and infiltration.

In my opinion the South must be administered as an integral part of a united Sudan: it must be encouraged to set up organs of local government speedily, with Province Councils, which initially until the Southerners have progressed far enough for elections to be held, should select representatives to the Legislative Assembly.

The proposed Legislative Assembly and Executive Council should administer the Sudan as a whole, but I recommend that power should be reserved to the Governor-General in cases where legislation or administrative action appears to him to have possible unfortunate results in the South to order that such legislation or administrative action should not be operative until the Southern Province Councils have been consulted about it. A further safeguard which I recommend is that a senior official with long experience of Southern tribes and customs should be summoned when necessary to advise the Executive Council on the implications of any proposed policy on the South.

I feel that the appointment of Southern members to the Legislative Assembly will have excellent results in widening the outlook of the Southern Sudanese, and will help to hasten the closer unification of the Sudan.

Fears have been expressed that too close contact with the North will lead to exploitation and domination of the South by the North. There is this danger but on the other hand it must be pointed out that progress in the South is dependent upon the Northern taxpayer, and it is surely not unjust that if the Northern Sudan is paying some L.E. 900,000 in 1947 to make up the deficit on Southern revenues it should have some say in how this money is to be spent.

The Southern semi-educated and clerical classes are keen for motives of self-interest, better pay and prospects etc., to come in to the same administrative system as the North. They are inclined to blame the Sudan Government, rather than the accidents of history and geography, for the backwardness of the South. I am convinced that should Southern representation in the Legislative Assembly be delayed, or should the Legislative Assembly not be allowed to deal with the Southern Sudan, agitation would be aroused in both North and South, and the Government would be accused of segregating the Southerners in a sort of human zoological park.

I believe it is to the ultimate welfare of the South to be opened up and have a chance of development and cohesion with the North. It will then be able to play its part in the advancement of the country as a whole. . . .

Annex to 134

The Civil Secretary submitted the first report of the Sudan Administration Conference with his recommendations regarding its implementation.

Council approved the following resolutions:—

1. That the First Report of the Sudan Administration Conference regarding the development of the Advisory Council into a Legislative Assembly and the proposed evolution of the existing Governor-General's Council into an Executive Council be noted, and that its main proposals be accepted in principle.

2. That the proposal that the Legislative Assembly should be representative of the whole Sudan and that its scope should not be limited to the Northern Sudan be accepted, but that safeguards be introduced into the legislation setting up the new constitution, which will ensure the healthy and steady development of the Southern peoples.

3. That the proposal for the appointment by the government of members of the Legislative Assembly as "Under Secretaries" in the principal departments be approved: that instructions be issued for these members to be given proper administrative responsibility in the departments concerned, and that measures be taken forthwith to work out the implications of this step: that such members should represent their department in the Assembly.

4. That the proposal to set up an Executive Council of 12 members composed of:—

(1) Three Secretaries and Kaid
(2) Six Sudanese "Under Secretaries" to be chosen by the Government from among the "Under Secretaries"
(3) Two members to be nominated by the Governor-General

be agreed to.

5. That these proposals should be submitted to the British and Egyptian Governments for their consideration.

135 FO 371/62947, no 36997 30 July 1947

[SAR]: record by the secretariat, Khartoum, of a meeting between Sir R Howe and Sayyid Abd al-Rahman al-Mahdi. *Annexes Minutes* by C Howson[1] and D M H Riches

[Howe's initial telegraphic summary of his meeting with SAR caused some disquiet in the FO. Howe reported SAR's concern about the apparent weakness of the Sudan government in relation to Egypt, the increasing pressure being exerted on him by Egyptian Muslims (including Hasan Banna, leader of Muslim Brothers) to support the unity of the Nile Valley, the independence parties' disillusionment with HMG, and the demands being raised by them for the termination of the condominium and formation of a Sudanese government (inward telegram from Howe to Bevin no 120, 30 July 1947, FO 371/62947, no 3586). Bevin commented: 'We had better look at vigorous counter-measures in this case.' The action recommended, after receipt of these minutes, was improvement of public relations in Khartoum in order to publicise British actions more widely (letter from Sargent to Howe, 8 Aug 1947, FO 371/62947, no 3586.]

After the usual opening gambits concerning the weather, etc., Sayed Abdel Rahman set the ball rolling by saying that he had asked for an interview with H.E. this evening

[1] African Dept, FO, 1947–1949.

in accordance with H.E's request at their last meeting that Sayed Abdel Rahman should always feel free to come and see him about anything that was worrying him.

Two things at the moment were uppermost in everyone's mind: the Sudan case at U.N.O. and the Legislative Assembly.

With regard to the first Sayed Abdel Rahman said he thought it had been a mistake not to consult nor to inform any Sudanese before sending the Sudan Government Delegation. He said his party were not sending representatives largely for fear that if they did so the Egyptians would encourage Azhari also to go, but as no Sudanese were going he could only hope that the British Government would carry out their duties as trustees for the Sudan to the best of their ability. In particular, he hoped, that they would make it clear to U.N.O. that the intervention by Egyptians in the administration of the Sudan had, in the past, always been to the Sudan's detriment, and that no future penetration by Egypt should be allowed.

H.E. said that Sayed Abdel Rahman had touched upon the fundamental issue now at stake. Egypt's complaint at U.N.O. was based on her claim that the Sudan Government refused to allow her to participate in the administration and development of the Sudan; Sayed Abdel Rahman was now asking us to do this very thing. There seemed to be considerable misunderstanding among many Sudanese as to the exact functions and powers of the Governor-General. He was merely the agent of the two Co-domini and was bound legally to carry out any instructions which the two powers in agreement might give him.

Sayed Abdel Rahman said he realised this, but he, and many other Sudanese, thought that the Governor-General could exercise far greater independence in internal affairs than he had in fact exercised in the past. The 1899 Treaty gave him the supreme military and civil command in the Sudan, and in the 1936 Treaty the two Co-domini had agreed that the primary aim of their administration in the Sudan must be the welfare of the Sudanese. Both Co-domini had expressed at one time or another their desire that the Sudan should have self-government. In his view, therefore, the Governor-General had full constitutional powers to take any steps leading to the grant of self-government to the Sudanese.

He then raised the second point which was worrying him—i.e. the delay in the setting up of the Legislative Assembly. This delay was responsible for implanting doubt in the minds of many of his friends and followers with regard to the real intention of the Sudan Government. His Excellency had stated that any legislation which might be passed would have to be referred to the two Co-domini. Apart, therefore, from the delay in drafting the legislation, the Government by referring it to Egypt was incurring a very grave risk of the whole project being held up. He did not see why Egypt should be consulted.

H.E. replied that the Advisory Council had only considered the proposals some two months ago; since then H.E. had been touring the South in order to formulate his views as to the part which the South should take in the Assembly. There had, therefore, been no unavoidable delay. The Government was as anxious as the Sudanese themselves to see the Assembly established. As for the question of submitting the legislation to Egypt, this was unavoidable. In the introduction to the Governor-General's Council Ordinance, 1910, the approval of the two Co-domini is specifically recorded, and as the Executive Council would be replacing the Governor-General's Council their approval would also be necessary for the two new constitutional bodies.

The Sayed accepted this, saying he was not a legal expert, but merely regarded these matters from a common sense point of view. He emphasised, however, the prime importance, during the interim period before the Legislative Assembly had got going, of consulting Sudanese opinion (and in particular himself) before taking any important action. The Government, like all alien governments, were too prone to make their decisions in vacuo. In the present difficult circumstances they could not afford to make mistakes, and the best way of avoiding these was to consult leading Sudanese of experience and judgement.

Sayed Abdel Rahman then talked about the effects of Egyptian propaganda and Egyptian pressure. He said that he had recently received messages from Ahmed Hussein and Saleh Harb[2] in which they appealed to him as a fellow Moslem to join his cause with that of Egypt. These messages had been given wide publicity throughout the Middle East. Moreover, the flood of Egyptian propaganda continued to pour into the Sudan and inevitably weakened both his own personal position and the control which he exercised over the political views of his followers. The Government seemed content to do nothing at all to stop this propaganda. The Egyptian press had a very baleful influence in the Sudan. He also instanced the Ramadan preachers, Egyptian students, etc.

H.E. replied by saying that this type of propaganda was a new thing in the Sudan. The British, however, had had long experience of it and it had been proved in the past that propaganda based on false premises always recoiled on the people who spread it. H.E. had no doubt that this would be the eventual fate of Egyptian propaganda in the Sudan.

The Sayed agreed that this might be so, but said that this was a long term view; if nothing was done soon to stop it it would have the effect of removing him and his influence from the political scene.

H.E. said that in these days of newspapers and wireless it was virtually impossible to stop this sort of propaganda; the only defence was to take a firm stand and show high moral courage.

The Sayed said that this might be so, but he felt that the Government could do more than it had been doing (e.g. it could instruct its Province officials to give the "pro-Government party" a fair wind in any matter affecting it's [sic] relations with the pro-Egyptian party). He would continue to take a firm stand, but it was becoming increasingly difficult to do so.

As an instance of the difficulty he was having in restraining his followers and in persuading them to adopt loyally a policy of co-operation with the Government, he gave H.E. a letter[3] addressed to him (Sayed Abdel Rahman) by the Independence Front, which, he said, he had just received. H.E. said that he would read it at his leisure.

Finally the Sayed said that he had taken up his present attitude in the knowledge that he had had promises by the British to support him. H.E. asked which promises he was referring to. The Sayed said that they were many, but instanced in particular his conversation with Sir Hubert Huddleston in Cairo last year when the Sayed was on his way to England to see Mr. Attlee. The Sayed asked Sir Hubert what he should

---

[2] Ahmad Husain and Salah Harb were two Khatmiya shaikhs.

[3] Reproduced here as Annex 1.

do about meeting the Egyptian authorities. He had addressed a request to Sidky Pasha for an interview but had had no reply. Sir Hubert said that he should not worry his head about the Egyptians, that the British highly appreciated his action in going to England, and that he could rely on their support. The Sayed also referred to a conversation with the late Sir Douglas Newbold in which the latter had said that although he could not prophesy what reward the Sudan would be given as a result of the allied victory, he was sure that the Sudan would get its share, and that the Sayed would have his share of that share.

H.E. replied that the Sayed had of his own choice taken up a certain position; this position must inevitably bring him into conflict with a certain party. He must, therefore, expect and accept the opposition of that party and must face it with courage. The British Government would give him what support they could, but in the nature of things they could not shield him from every attack.

The Sayed said that he gratified to know that he would have the continued support of the British, and this was what he had really come to H.E. to find out. He was going down to Aba in a week's time, but before he left he hoped to be able to issue a message to his followers.

H.E. thanked him for coming and said that he would always be glad to discuss any question with him.

Sayed Abdel Rahman then left, the interview laving [sic] lasted some two hours.

Later: note by J S Owen, deputy assistant civil secretary

Next morning Sayed Abdel Rahman rang me up to ask if I would go round and see him as he had some afterthoughts which he wished to have conveyed to H.E.

He first referred to the letter from the Independence Front which he had given H.E. He now had had time to read it and he thought that possibly the English translation given to H.E. was incorrect in certain details. He also thought that the letter could have been more happily phrased. He, therefore, asked me to retrieve it when I got back to the office, for correction.

Sayed Abdel Rahman then elaborated his point about co-operation and consultation prior to any new major decision by the Government. If the Government always consulted him before taking any important step he could ensure that his followers would support the Government's action, otherwise he could not. (I commented here that his papers were among the first to denounce the dangers of individual consultations.). He also referred to the failure of our many efforts to gain the support of Sayed Ali el Mirghani, who, he alleged, had recently received £E.15,000 from the Egyptians. He could not understand the Government's attitude to this man; they had allowed him to hold the holia[4] of Sayed el Hassan lasting 15 days, whereas they would only allow him (Sayed Abdel Rahman) two days for the opening of the Mahdi's tomb; they had even helped Sayed Ali el Mirghani to put up his tents in Abbas Square by giving him prisoners to help him. There was a certain Governor (no names, no packdrill) who declared that he was an adherent of the Khatmia. The Government must surely realise by now that Sayed Ali was its enemy and that it must withdraw any semblance of official support from him, otherwise it weakened the faith of those loyal to the Government.

[4] *Hulia*: 'joy after sadness', a religious celebration in honour of a saint.

I asked him what practical steps he could suggest the Government might take.

He said that he did not really know, but he thought that the Government should from now on studiously ignore Sayed Ali, while, at the same time, it should instruct its officials to help on the party loyal to the Government. In this connection he said that Sir Hubert Huddleston had said to him in Cairo that he was writing to Mr. Robertson, the Civil Secretary, to tell him to ensure that Province Authorities encouraged adherents to Sayed Abdel Rahman's party.

I expressed surprise at this, and said I had never seen any such letter.

The Sayed started to take up the attitude that his position was a very weak one and that unless the Government gave him its full support he was unable to do anything.

I pointed out to him that this was inconsistent with his claim that his followers constituted the majority in the country.

He admitted the inconsistency of this but said that he was worried about the outcome of the elections to the Legislative Assembly. He thought the Government should take steps to rig the elections and ensure that a pro-Government majority will be returned.

I expressed my surprise at this undemocratic suggestion, and asked him what steps he thought the Government should take.

He said that in the rural areas where indirect elections were to be held the Government should make it perfectly clear to the local authorities which candidates the Government wished to be returned. In the urban areas his candidates never had a chance because his followers were on the whole in the lower strata of society and were, therefore, disenfranchised by the Rates qualification. The Government should, therefore, lower this qualification or even introduce adult male suffrage into the towns. The Sayed appeared to be genuinely concerned about the danger of a pro-Egyptian majority in the Assembly.

Before I left I told the Sayed that though the Government knew that he felt strongly that they should take more definite action in certain directions, they had not yet received from him any concrete suggestions as to how this action should be taken practically.

The Sayed said that he would give this his consideration and let us know if he had any suggestions to make.[5]

Annex 1 to 135: copy of a translation of a letter to El Sayed Sir Abdel Rahman el Mahdi Pasha from the Independence Front, July 1947

The Sudanese have a natural right to independence supported by the role they played in the second world war for freedom and secured by the Atlantic Charter. The Sudan that asks for its sovereign right is opposed by Egypt and Great Britain who administer it on the strength of the 1899 Agreement and 1936 Treaty. Egypt denies the Sudan the right to independence and view its just demand with a hostile attitude that made understanding with it impossible. It accepts nothing short of sovereignty over the Sudan, and so-called unity is but a veiled imperialism.

As for Great Britain it promises the Sudan self-government and did not deny it the

---

[5] See Annex 2 for suggestions received in the Governor General's Office on 31 July.

right of self-determination but it does not consider that the Sudan reached a self-governing status. [It] did put forward a detailed programme for a definite time limit.

On your return from England last December you emphasised to us the point of view of the Government of Great Britain and requested us to co-operate with the Sudan Government on the basis agreed upon between the Prime Minister of Great Britain and you namely:—

(a) The Government of Great Britain supports the Governor-General of the Sudan in developing the Sudan to a self-governing country.
(b) The Sudan shall have self-determination free from any influence and may ask for independence.

On your assurances we did our part in the co-operation with the Sudan Government and brought to an end the state of unrest and disturbance which nearly wrecked everything the Sudan Government had done. But the Sudan Government did not do its part in the co-operation with us, the thing that made us to reconsider the situation. Whatever our opinion of the Sudan Government be, it is impossible for us to continue on this co-operation with it so long as it failed to fulfil the agreement on which co-operation was based. Indeed the Sudan Government gave in, in many instances, to the wish of the elements that oppose the interests of the Sudanese and let them free to prison [? poison] the thoughts of the people and retard the progress of the Sudan.

We did not co-operate with the Sudan Government to prolong the condominium rule which is opposed by everyone. But our co-operation was aimed at the setting up of the Sudanese self-government. An initial step to complete independence from both Egypt and Britain.

The steps taken by the Sudan Government in the way of realising self-government did not meet the approval of anyone. The proposed Legislation [sic] Assembly is still far from reality, and it is incomplete in itself and will not assure the setting up of self-government until it provides for the appointment of Sudanese Ministers with portfolios who will take charge of the affairs of the country. We have our potential fears. The slow policy that dominated in the past and in the present is a (danger?) to us and to our case which is now before the Security Council, while there is no recognised Sudanese to voice the point of view of the people. The dispute will be between Egypt and Britain over their rights of conquest, the important parts in the dispute is not heard. The Sudan Government in a pamphlet recently published about the progress of the Sudan stated that the Southerner shall have the rights of self-determination vis-a-vis the Northern Sudan.[6] It is a queer logic and it is just as if Wales is given the right of separation from England. A spokesman on behalf of the British Foreign Office stated that Britain will never leave the Sudan until it is ready

---

[6] *The Sudan, a Record of Progress, 1898–1947* (Sudan government, n.d.), which was prepared by the Sudan government and the Foreign Office as part of the United Kingdom's case to the UN. Referring to the the accentuation of the division between North and South, and the Northern Sudanese fear that the country would ultimately be split, it suggested that such a question might be considered by an international commission in the future. 'Meanwhile, the present Government ... is developing local government institutions on the lines which have proved successful in the north and, while doing nothing to prejudice the issue, is proposing to associate sympathetic northern Sudanese with the implementation of a policy which aims at giving the south the same chances of ultimate self-determination as have been promised to the north' (pp 13–14).

for self-government, but how and when no-one made any such statement. This means prolonging the Condominium rule indefinitely. The Premier [sic] of the British to keep the power and remain in the Sudan for the longest possible period is the source of all troubles and will lead to bad results which the country will suffer.

The situation needs urgent and decisive action to save the country. We shall not continue to co-operate with the Sudan Government except on these clear grounds:—

(a) Termination of the Condominium rule which has become unsuitable.
(b) Formation of a Sudanese Government which will have the confidence and support of the country.

The formation of the Sudanese Government is an easy matter and agreed upon by the two Co-domini, who both agreed that the Sudan shall have self-government. It need not be referred for sanction by either of them.

The way of self-government is the setting up of the Legislative Assembly at once and the appointment of Sudanese Ministers responsible to the Assembly.

(c) The Sudan Government being responsible for public security in the Sudan and for its administration should request the Security Council to postpone the Sudan question until the Sudanese self-government is set up to speak for the Sudan.

Your Excellency knows very well that a revival of Bevin/Sidky Protocol or any prolongation of the Condominium rule will mean that the British shall govern the Sudan for themselves and Egypt by force, if this time is suitable for government by force. It will be a going back by Britain to her promises and principles and the Sudan will be compelled to adopt the method fit for the realisation of its aspiration.

We rely on your wisdom and good handling of matters to find a way out from this situation.

Annex 2 to 135: Suggestions submitted by Sayed Siddik on behalf of his father, Sayed Abdel Rahman, as to the policy that should be adopted by the Sudan government

1. Permission should be granted to the followers of the Sayed and to the Umma Party to visit all parts of the Sudan.

2. The Government should change its policy which, up to the very recent past, it has adopted towards the Sayed and his followers (a policy which was laid down under the conditions existing at the time of the re-conquest) and it should openly show its support to the tribal leaders of the Sayed and the policy which he has adopted with regard to the future of the country.

3. The Government should support the Sayed and his followers on every suitable opportunity and should increase his prestige as a true patriot in the eyes of the public so that they may co-operate with the Government in her policy which she is adopting for the good of the country.

4. The Government should oppose the opponents of the Sayed in the West by means of propaganda by the Sayed. This will lead to the spreading of true knowledge about the Mahdist Creed which calls for virtue and which assists in the keeping of the public peace. This propaganda to be carried out without hurting the feelings of the non-Mahdists.

5. The Government should advise the tribal leaders and encourage them to adopt the policy of the Independence Party which is the policy of the Government and of the Sayed. It should consult the leaders of the Independence Party so as to give them the opportunity of drawing up a policy in common which can be defended by the Independence press.

6. As it is the Sayed who is financing the Independence movement, the Government should give him every possible help to improve his financial position, i.e. by enabling him to increase the areas of cultivation and also to assist him to strengthen his social position as a political leader who is supporting the Government.

7. The policy which the Government had adopted during their 50 years in the country has resulted in a creation of a certain class of persons in the towns (i.e. the supporters of Sayed Ali). In order to counter their influence and also in accordance with democracy the Rate qualification for voters in the towns should be lowered so as to increase the franchise which will increase the number of supporters of the Government.

Minutes on 135

It may perhaps be important to note that the Sayed A.R.'s followers stand less chance of success in local elections, owing to their being below the rate qualification, than those of S.A.M. who are, on the whole, wealthier. If, therefore, S.A.R's. statement is true, some widening of the franchise might be advantageous to the Umma party & indirectly to HMG.

For the rest, S.A.R. seems to be filled with a rather querulous & overt self-interest.

C.H.
7.8.47

This gives me a much more reassuring impression than did the telegraphic summary.

D.M.H.R.
7.8.47

136 FO 371/62947, no 3886 8 Aug 1947

[Condition of the Sudan]: letter from Sir R Howe to Sir O Sargent, relaying his first impressions of the Sudan [Extract]

... 2. I have been trying for some time to get off a letter to you, but the job of learning to administer this colossal country does not leave much spare time. Also it has been one of the worst summers on record. Gordon said no European could live in Khartoum in the summer. Gordon was right. In addition to temperatures running around 115 we have had some of the worst sandstorms on record.

3. There have been a lot of goings to and fro recently between the leaders of the National Front (the Ashigga plus Congress) and the Independence Front (composed chiefly, of course, of the Umma). It was strongly rumoured a couple of days ago that

agreement had been reached for a common front on the basis of (a) abolition of the Condominium and (b) immediate set-up of a Sudanese Government. The negotiations finally broke down because the National Front would not agree on the eventual right of the Sudanese Government to a free choice of their future and because the Umma party would have nothing to do with any kind of unity with Egypt. In fact Sayed Abdel Rahman was heard to say that if the Sudanese agreed to anything in the way of unity or to anything which would bring the Egyptians back to the Sudan he would declare a "Jehad". I think the old boy is quite capable of doing it. He has recently been making a lot of enquiries about the numbers of Egyptian soldiers in the Sudan and their armament. I also hear that the National Front were persuaded from agreeing to the inclusion of the Sudanese right to final self-determination in the joint programme only by the strong efforts of Abbas Bey Abdel Hamid, the Egyptian Chief Staff Officer who you will remember caused all the fuss last December over his right of entry to the Garden Party in honour of King George at the Palace.

4. Since my arrival I have had a number of talks with the higher and better types of Sudanese officials and leaders, none of whom want the end of the British connection. It is not so easy to get in touch with the Effendia among whom is a considerable ferment of half-baked ideas. They all talk about the end of Condominium rule but they have not thought of what is going to take its place. The more Sudanisation we have, and consequently the fewer British officials, the more difficult it is going to be to keep contact with this section of Sudanese opinion.

5. The approval by the Advisory Council for the Northern Sudan of the proposals for self-Government put forward by the 1946 Committee made it necessary for me to find out what the feeling was in the South on the question of union. I have only just got back from a six weeks tour of that part of the Sudan. It is an odd world and one which makes nonsense of the Egyptian claim that the Sudanese are of the same race, religion and language as the Egyptians. The desert North ends as though cut with a knife and you come into the great Nile swamps inhabited by Dinka, Nuer and Shilluk, the three big Nilotic tribal blocs. The Dinka particularly are fascinating people, most of the men stand about seven feet high and are completely naked. They made me a Dinka tribal chief with the name of Red Mouthed Fish Eagle, and presented me with an enormous bull. Fortunately I was able to hand this back and thus avoid an embarrassing commitment.

6. The South are generally agreed on the necessity of union with the North, and of sending representatives to the proposed Legislative Assembly, but since very few of them talk Arabic or anything beyond their tribal languages we shall have to insist on safeguards for the South in the new constitutional set-up. The trouble, of course, is that the South is at least a generation behind the North largely due to the fact that in 1935 it was decided to put the South on a care and maintenance basis, and it was only two years ago that the Sudan Government woke up to the necessity of getting a move on with progress and development. I think that we shall find it difficult to avoid some very hard criticism of our policy in the South at the hands of any Commission which went fact-finding on the Sudan. Union of the South is bound to mean the spread of Arabic and Islam in the South, and we shall be up against the Christian missionaries who have till now been largely responsible for education of the Southern native. In the last two or three years the Government have been taking an increased share in education, and there is a big five-year development plan for the South. As the whole

cost of the South comes out of Northern revenues it is difficult to deny the claim of the North for a unified Sudan.

7. I was appalled at the low standard of life among the Southern natives. The diseases with which man and beast are afflicted are frightful. In the native run dispensaries and in all the Sudan Medical Service hospitals cases are legion of tropical ulcer, leprosy, yaws, sleeping sickness, and horrible worms which burrow their way through the body.[1]

8. Our development schemes are running us into about two million pounds, for bush schools, elementary schools, intermediate schools, teacher training classes, more hospitals, more dispensaries, agricultural settlements, technical and trade schools.

9. I wonder what will come out of New York. I imagine that we shall find it rather difficult to resist a U.N.O. Commission. If one does come it is essential that they spend sufficient time to visit the South as well as the North. For climatic reasons they could hardly come before the end of the year, and I hope by that time we shall have got our Legislative Assembly and Executive Council going. I think that is the most important thing to get on with, and will go a long way towards keeping the political temperature down. In the absence of a constitutional advance of this kind I do not think the present position can be held much longer. Egyptian propaganda here in the Sudan is completely subversive of Condominium rule and the Sudan Government is like the child of divorced parents neither of whom can agree on the up-bringing of the infant.

10. Every Egyptian official in this country openly preaches the overthrow of "British Colonial Imperialism" in the Sudan and the Unity of the Nile Valley. Our Sudanese friends cannot understand why we do not throw these people out of the country, or at any rate give them the same facilities for their propaganda as the Ashigga get from Cairo. Sayed Abdel Rahman always harps on this whenever I see him.

11. You will remember that when I was appointed to the Sudan the Secretary of State's idea was that we should initiate unilaterally a new policy of a greater Egyptian share in the Condominium. I am quite convinced that any such policy in the present circumstances is quite out of the question. Every Egyptian official in this country is now a spearhead of Egyptian anti-British propaganda and would in fact get short shrift on his return to Egypt if he refused to play this role.

12. I am not sure how far our Egyptian friends were responsible for the strike in the Railway workshops at Atbara. I think they had a hand in it, but I am inclined to think that other causes were predominant. There has been agitation for some time now in the Railway workshops for some representation of labour, but the trouble is that the men themselves do not know what is the most suitable form of labour organisation, nor do I think the Railways administration was any better fitted to provide it. I think it might be a very good thing if we could get a good Trade Union

---

[1] Howe's first impressions of administration in the Southern Sudan were in direct contradiction with the image which had been fostered by the Sudan government and the embassy in Cairo. Earlier in the year Howe had been present when Bowker briefed Bevin on the Sudan. Bowker had assured Bevin that in the South 'there were good medical services and hospitals. Sleeping sickness had been practically eliminated' ('Record of the secretary of state's talk with His Majesty's minister at Cairo on 17th February [1947]', FO 371/62942, no 839).

leader from home to come out and advise the men on what they ought to set up and how they ought to work it.

13. Generally speaking I have the impression that not only the Governor-General but the Sudan Administration are living in ivory towers. We must break down this remoteness from the people, and as I said before increased Sudanisation only makes the problem more difficult. The proposed constitutional developments may help in this respect, and there are certain archaic social customs that I am going to do away with. What I am convinced of is that the British connection is the best possible thing for these people in their present stage of development. I cannot see any UNO trusteeship being any better.

14. This summer has nearly finished me off, and I accordingly propose to leave, UNO permitting, for England about the end of this month. I hope I shall see you in London.

137 FO 371/62947, no 3933 16 Aug 1947

[Sudan case at the UN]: record by D W Lascelles of a conversation with the Umma delegation to the Security Council

The Umma Delegation, consisting of Sayyid Siddiq, Abdullah Khalil Bey, and Messrs. Shingeti and Mahjoub, called on Sir Walter Smart and myself to-day by arrangement with the Sudan Government Delegation.

It had been explained to us that the main object of the visit was to allow the Sudanese to blow off steam. This they did. They made it quite clear that their intention was to demand from the Security Council the termination of the condominium and complete and immediate independence. The line we took was that, if they did this, they would seriously hamper the United Kingdom Delegation in the immediate and essential task of securing the defeat of the Egyptian appeal. The attention of the Council would inevitably be deflected from the present issue, namely the validity of the 1936 Treaty, and the whole business would be hopelessly fogged. The only members of the Council who would be really pleased would be the Russian and the Pole.

Mr. Mahjoub, who did most of the talking and is a lawyer obviously not very well disposed towards us, had evidently been encouraged by the Polish representative's speech, and held forth at length to the effect that the Security Council could not do otherwise than grant the Sudan immediate and complete independence since both the Egyptians and the British were in the Sudan by virtue of the obsolete right of conquest alone. He also expounded at considerable length a version of that legal theory, with which we are already familiar, according to which Egypt has no case in law for claiming sovereignty over the Sudan, even on the assumption that rights gained by conquest are still valid, since her conquest of the Sudan was during the period when she was not herself independent and at the period when she did obtain her independence from us we did not give her the Sudan. We pointed out that an argument on these lines was open to challenge and could be countered by arguments on quite different lines which the highest legal authorities of H.M.G. were inclined to regard as at least equally cogent. There was in fact at least a 50% chance that, if the whole question of sovereignty were taken before the competent international tribunal, i.e. the Hague Court, it would go in favour of Egypt. For the Umma Delegation to provoke such a development was therefore in our view extremely risky and not at all in their own interests, and if the Umma Delegation did clamour for immediate independence this would be the inescapable result. Egypt, having everything to lose if the Security Council received the Sudanese demand favourably, would obviously see to it that the sovereignty case was referred to the International Court. As regards the theory that rights acquired by conquest were no longer valid in the eyes of the United Nations, we would merely point out that, if this theory were literally upheld, the whole map of the world would undergo extensive alteration. The alteration, moreover, would to a very large extent be to the detriment of a considerable number of the members of the Security Council. In short, as we saw it, the Umma and the Sudanese people who thought like them, had the following choice before them: on the one hand, action which constituted a very serious risk of their losing all hope of future independence and being tied to Egypt for good and all; on the other, a period of waiting—which admittedly is irksome to them—followed by independence secured by the good offices of H.M.G. If the Umma were prepared to take our advice and to let us tackle one thing at a time, the immediate practical result would be that the administration in the Sudan would go on much as it had in the past, under predominently British guidance and with steady progress towards Sudanisation and self-government. If, on the contrary, the Umma put a spoke in our wheel by taking the line which they proposed to take, not only would they endanger their whole future status for the reasons given above, but the immediate and practical result would be that Nokrashi would probably not lose his case; and that would mean at the best a large influx of Egyptian officials into the Sudan administration, since one of the Egyptian grievances was the present lack of parity.

The members of the party other than Mahjoub (who continued to declare rather truculently that he did not care which side won if the claim for immediate independence was not made now) appeared to be rather shaken by what we had said, explaining that they had not realised before that we should regard the making of this claim as a spoke in our wheel. They said that they would think the whole matter over again in light of what we had told them, and would keep in touch with us.

138 FO 371/62948, no 4183 2 Sept 1947

'Egypt and the Sudan': draft Cabinet paper by Sir O Sargent to Mr Bevin, recommending action in the Sudan in anticipation of the Security Council's decision on the Anglo–Egyptian dispute[1]

The following paper has been prepared as a result of discussion between the Secretary of State and the Governor-General of the Sudan.

In spite of the farcical and inept manner in which the Anglo–Egyptian dispute has hitherto been conducted in the Security Council, it seems likely that the proceedings will shortly terminate in the passage of a resolution recommending the resumption of direct negotiations between the two parties.

---

[1] Initialled without comment by Bevin and sent to the Defence Office for distribution to the Defence Committee (10 Sept).

2. It is inevitable that such negotiations will have to cover the Sudan as well as Egypt, but is difficult to see on what basis they could be conducted. As regards Egypt, the abortive Bevin-Sidky treaty of last November represented pretty well the limit to which His Majesty's Government could go as regards mutual defence arrangements, though we might perhaps make a further concession by advancing the date of evacuation of our troops from the Canal Zone.

3. But even if there may be some slight room for manoeuvre on the purely Egyptian part of the dispute, there seems to be no possible compromise whatever over the Sudan. The Bevin-Sidky Protocol on the Sudan was the result of very hard bargaining and represented the limit to which either side would agree. But even that Protocol is no longer possible, for any revival of agreement between Egypt and Great Britain on the "unity of Egypt and the Sudan" or on the "common Crown of Egypt" would, in view of what has passed since, in all probability blow the Sudan wide open. Thus any concession in regard to the Egyptian claims over the Sudan would alienate our friends in the Independence front and enable them to turn the whole country against us.

4. If we are not careful over this we may find ourselves pushed out of *both* Egypt and the Sudan, whereas if we leave Egypt we must at all costs maintain our predominant position in the Sudan.

5. Meanwhile, Egyptian subversive propaganda in that country, which is virulent, widespread and backed by unlimited money, continues. It is the definite policy of the present Egyptian Government to subvert the Sudanese from their loyalty to the Administration and to the Condominium. Nokrashi has indeed informed the Sudanese Independence Delegation in New York that the Egyptian Government intend to continue and intensify their propaganda in the Sudan. We are rapidly approaching the situation which the Egyptian Government created in 1924 when, as a result of similar Egyptian intrigues, the Governor-General was assassinated and Sudanese troops mutinied.

6. It is necessary therefore that we should try and consolidate our position in the Sudan generally and take steps to prevent a possible disaster there. It is important also that we should do this in advance of any renewed negotiations about the Sudan so as to be able to play our hand from strength and not from weakness.

Recommendations

(i) Firm action against Egyptian intrigues in the Sudan would strengthen the Administration and the position of His Majesty's Government more than any other step. What would be desirable would be a declaration at the appropriate moment by His Majesty's Government similar to that made by Mr. Ramsay Macdonald in 1924 (text attached),[2] to the effect that they will not tolerate the continuation of these activities by the Egyptians in the Sudan.

(ii) It would be desirable to strengthen the present two British battalions by the addition of some armoured force and a few light bombers.

(iii) We should press on with the constitutional proposals and inaugurate without delay the Legislative Assembly and Executive Council. These proposals have already been submitted to the Co-Domini.

---

[2] Not printed.

(iv) In reviewing the situation in the event of our being deprived of the use of Egypt and possibly Palestine and Cyrenaica as a base for our defence arrangements in the Middle East, it should not be forgotten that the Sudan came to our help in the last war with thirty thousand first-class fighting men, and that her seven million people might be a useful reservoir of manpower, which might in part compensate for the loss of the Indian manpower on which we shall now no longer be able to draw. It is for consideration therefore whether we might not build up the Sudan Defence Forces again to war time strength.

(v) We must maintain the quality of the British recruits for the Sudan Government Service. This is being looked into. In view of the Sudanisation of Government services, which is now the policy of the Sudan Government, we shall only be able to recruit men of the requisite qualifications if we can guarantee them their pensions and a continuation of their careers in corresponding branches of service under His Majesty's Government, if and when their Sudan posts are Sudanised.

(vi) The Sudan Government should also improve the quality of its publicity among the Sudanese, and steps to achieve this are under consideration.

139 FO 371/62949, no 5234 — 29–30 Oct 1947

'Sudan constitutional reform': minutes by D H M Riches concerning the Egyptian government's rejection of the proposed changes in the Sudan's constitution [Extract]

On September 10th the Government of the Sudan presented to His Majesty's Government and to the Egyptian Government, as Codomini, the decisions of the Governor-General's Council on the report of the Sudan Administration Conference on Constitutional Reform in the Sudan. The letter to the Egyptian Government in which this was conveyed was drafted in a manner which allowed the Egyptians to comment if they wished to do so, while not inviting their comments; nor admitting specifically that the approval of the Egyptian (or British) Governments was necessary before the proposals could be implemented; and expressing the conviction that the reforms would be welcomed as in conformity with the publicly expressed policy of the Codomini to forward constitutional advance in the Sudan.

On October 14th we sent a despatch to H.M. Ambassador at Cairo informing him of our agreement with the reforms and saying that H.M.G. had no comment to make beyond welcoming them as a step in the progressive development of self-government in the Sudan. This despatch instructed Sir R. Campbell to convey this information to the acting Governor-General of the Sudan and to send a copy of his communication to the Egyptian Prime Minister.

Simultaneously with the receipt of our despatch in Cairo, the Egyptian Prime Minister replied to the acting Governor-General in a letter in which he claimed that the proposals had only reached him while he was in New York, and that the Egyptian Government had had inadequate time to comment on them. The letter made various charges that the reforms had been elaborated by the British and Sudanese only without Egyptian participation and without consulting some of the political parties in the Sudan (in fact those of Egyptian sympathy). The letter added that the Egyptian Government would need time in which to study the proposals and that their rights were not confined to approval or rejection but included the right of initiative (this presumably implies that they will make proposals of their own).

In view of this letter, Sir R. Campbell sent a despatch to the acting Governor-General in the terms of our instructions, but asked that it should not be regarded as officially delivered until we confirmed that we wished this done. The Egyptians meanwhile published Nokrashi's letter.

Whatever the future action to be taken it seems obvious that our views, which were not controversial and which we had a perfect right to put on record, should be delivered without delay. It is unfortunate indeed that we did not get them in before the Egyptians made their own comments. We have therefore telegraphed urgently to Cairo asking them to carry on with the delivery of the despatch and the communication of a copy of it to the Egyptian Government.

The question of what reply the Sudan Government should return to the Egyptian letter has been discussed with Sir R. Howe, who proposes to send us a draft on his return to Khartoum at the end of this week. Our preliminary feeling is that the reply should be restricted to acknowledging receipt and expressing the hope that any comments which the Egyptian Government wish to make will not be long delayed.

D.M.H.R.
29.10.47

This question was considered by Sir O. Sargent and the Governor-General on the 29th October. Mr. Robertson, the Civil Secretary to the Sudan Government and Mr Grey were also present. . . . Sir R. Howe said that the proposed legislation and his plans generally would not be ready until the end of the year. If the Egyptians then produced substantial counter-proposals they could be put to the Sudanese (for rejection.)

D.M.H.R.
30.10.47

140 FO 371/63047, no 5856 24 Nov 1947

[Sudan case at the UN]: report from SPIS no 5 for Aug–Oct on the Sudanese reaction to the Anglo–Egyptian dispute at the Security Council [Extract]

. . .

Introduction

140. The last review of this series carried the story up to the time when the Egyptian case was about to be discussed at the Security Council. This report deals with the period starting with the departure of the various delegations to U.N.O. and ending with their return.

Local reactions to the Anglo–Egyptian dispute at U.N.O.

141. The news that the Sudan Government was sending a "delegation" composed entirely of British, gave rise to considerable criticism in the Press and elsewhere, and

was one of the reasons which caused the Independence Front to revise their earlier decision not to send representatives to America. Their delegation, which was financed mainly by Sayed Abdel Rahman El Mahdi was composed of Mohammed Ahmed Mahjub and Abdulla Bey Khalil (the Secretaries of the Independence Front and the Umma party respectively) who left by air for New York on 9th August, to be followed shortly afterwards by Sayed Siddiq Abdel Rahman el Mahdi and Mohammed Saleh Eff. Shingeiti. The latter is a High Court Judge and his participation in a political mission of this nature has caused widespread criticism although by punctilious observance of the proprieties he avoided any specific charge of political activity; he took the line that he was merely taking his annual leave in New York as a spectator of the proceedings at the Security Council. There is, however, no question but that he provided the real brains of the delegation and that Sayed Abdel Rahman, of whom he is a personal friend, had sent him in order to keep Mahjub under control.

142. As soon as the Unionists heard that the Independents had left they arranged to send Ismail el Azhari, Ibrahim el Mufti and Dardiri Ahmed Ismail (all members of the so-called Sudan delegation in Cairo) together with Tawfiq el Bakri (a Sudanese journalist domiciled in Cairo). Hamid Bey Saleh and Sayed Omar Eff. el Khalifa, (S.D.F. Officers on pension) followed later. This delegation was apparently financed by the Egyptian Government, and appeared in New York as part and parcel of the official Egyptian delegation. Efforts to collect money inside the Sudan for their expenses produced negligible results. It is known that Nokrashi Pasha was reluctant to allow Azhari and the others to go to America as he thought their presence in the Council Chamber could do the Egyptian case little good.

143. The proceedings at Lake Success went on for almost a month before ending in deadlock. In general they evoked surprisingly little interest in the Sudan except among the small circle of politically-conscious intelligentsia in the larger towns, many of whom thought that Egypt would be enabled to increase her share in the administration of the Sudan and that the days of the British were rapidly drawing to a close. The absence of the leaders of the various parties had however a quietening effect and interest was diverted from events of purely local significance, though owing to the numerous motions, amendments and counter-amendments proposed by the members of the Security Council, and also owing to the haze of words which obscured the real points at issue, the public were quickly befogged as to what was really happening. Russian support of the Egyptian demand for the evacuation of British troops was acclaimed by the Unionists, who failed to notice that she had carefully abstained from expressing any opinion on the Sudan issue. However Russia was popular, momentarily, among the vocal sections of Egyptian public opinion and this popularity was echoed unthinkingly by the pro-Egyptians here. Pro-Russian slogans have been a feature of some recent processions and meetings.

144. When deadlock was reached and the Security Council adjourned any further consideration of the dispute sine die, the public generally interpreted this as a rebuff to Egypt whose demands had been rejected. This had the following result on public opinion:—

(a) It increased British prestige, both because of the way in which she presented her case and also because it is generally held that she "won" hands down. Many Sudanese had previously been led to believe, by the press and by the apparent supineness of the British in the face of Egyptian provocation, that Britain's power

had waned and that she was a bankrupt nation incapable of standing up for herself in international politics. This theory is now out of fashion.
(b) By the same token, Egyptian prestige slumped. She failed, and the East has little respect for failure.
(c) Sir A. Cadogan's statement in which he was quoted (not quite accurately) by the press as saying that the British would never leave the Sudan until the Sudanese were ready for self-determination has probably had, on the whole, a steadying effect, though it has upset some wishful thinkers on both sides. At all events it has helped to counter the idea sedulously put about by the pro-Egyptians during recent months that the British are about to pull out of the Sudan almost immediately.
(d) The rather naive faith of many Sudanese that international organisations were bound to give them their independence has been shattered. An increasing number of them have come to realise that their only hope of survival as a nation is to have a great power such as Britain in close and friendly relations with them.

145. The effect on particular sections of public opinion is briefly as follows:—

(a) *The Independence Front*
They were delighted at the defeat of Egypt, and although they are disappointed at their failure to achieve an independent Sudan under British tutelage they feel that solid progress has been made in that all the delegates stressed the right of the Sudanese to self-determination and that the world in general is at last more or less Sudan-conscious. They are however fearful that the continuance of the Condominium with the Co-domini at loggerheads will mean obstruction of progress to self-government and an intensification of Egyptian propaganda, and they are pressing for more power to be given to the Sudanese so that they may combat it without inhibition. Should it prove impossible for the Sudan Government to take what they consider effective steps in this direction there is a possibility that they may swing into opposition but this is not, at the moment, likely to occur.
(b) *The Unionists*
Most of these have begun to see the danger of linking themselves too closely with Egypt, in whom they have lost faith; they have also lost faith in their pro-Egyptian leaders. An influential section wish to break away from the Khatmia whom they regard as being only half-hearted in their opposition to the Sudan Government. In this connection, Sir Ali el Mirghani's wire to U.N.O. . . . with its studied omission of support for the Unionist cause has had considerable effect. The leaders are now thinking of cutting loose from direct dependence on Egypt, and of concentrating their efforts towards becoming the focus of a nationalistic anti-Government movement, for which there will always be support in a non-self governing territory.
(c) *The Khatmia* have also seen the danger of linking themselves too closely with Egypt, and many of them are now anxious to re-establish good relations with the Sudan Government and to break away from the Ashigga party for whose leaders they have little respect.
(d) *The non-vocal majority*, are longing for the Government to adopt a definite line and stick to it. They have been unable to understand the Government's inaction during the past two years, and now that the case before U.N.O. appears to be moribund they expect the Government to re-establish public tranquillity as quickly and as firmly as possible. The events of the last few weeks have done much to reassure them.

146. At the beginning of September, with the delegates still away in America, the various political parties were perplexed and undecided what to do next. His Excellency the A/Governor-General's[1] proclamation on September 13th came therefore at a time when it was most effective.

In it he stressed the determination of the Government to press on with its plans for a Legislative Assembly, to allow no interference with its policy of Sudanising the Civil Service, and to maintain law and order in the meantime. The Egyptian Press, which does not understand the difference between "Sudanisation policy" and the proposals for constitutional reform, interpreted the proclamation as a "hands-off" notice to the Egyptian Government, and took violent exception to it, although the Acting Prime Minister had sent a telegram on August 29th expressing his anxiety lest there be disturbances in the Sudan. Nokrashi himself adopted a more cautious line and contented himself with a despatch in which he "assumed" that the A/Governor-General had no intention of denying the Royal Egyptian Government's powers to approve or disapprove the proposed constitutional legislation and hinted at detailed amendments to follow.

The local effect of the proclamation was considerable. The majority of Sudanese was glad that the Government showed signs of tightening its hold on the reins, though many reserved judgment until they could determine how far it was proposing to put its words into practice. Others, particularly those holding anti-Government views, regarded the proclamation as a threat of retribution and retaliation. Subsequent events such as the appointment of a Sudanese Grand Kadi, the banning of the return of the Farouk School Headmaster, the dismissal of Hammad Tawfik and the prosecution of two newspapers and the Secretary of the Republican party have all tended to re-establish confidence in the Government's determination to continue governing. The proclamation is now generally regarded as marking the end of a chapter and the beginning of another.

---

[1] Acting governor-general.

141 FO 371/63055, no 5846 25 Nov 1947

[Sudan Administration Conference]: letter from Abd al-Fattah Amr Pasha to Mr Bevin, transmitting a note on the recommendations of the conference embodying the results of the study made by the Egyptian government [Extract]

[The governor-general conveyed the full text of the recommendations of the Sudan Administration Conference to the Egyptian government on 22 Aug 1947. On receiving this reply Lascelles minuted: 'This development, though by no means unexpected, is embarrassing. The Egyptians have made out a very able case against the Sudan Government's proposed constitutional reforms, and its cogency is not really lessened by the fact that the Egyptian Co-Dominus has never before evinced the slightest interest in the progress of the Sudanese towards self-government. The motive, viz. the desire to outbid us, is obvious enough; but it is excellent pro-Egyptian propaganda for all that' (minute by Lascelles, 29 Nov 1947, FO 371/63055, no 5846).]

These recommendations do not fulfil the objectives envisaged by them, namely closer association of the Sudanese with the Central Government. It is stated in the report prepared by the Sudan Administration Conference that "the Sudanese will not be able to govern themselves unless they have previously been trained in the art of government, and this, in turn, can be learnt only through the assumption of responsibility. This responsibility, at any given time, should be sufficiently great to extend fully the capacity of the Sudanese to shoulder it successfully, in this way their training will proceed at the greatest possible rate."

These premises are in conflict with the conclusions reached by the conference in its proposed system. The new system does not allow for the proper and full representation of the Sudanese, nor does it admit their participation, in a measure due to them, in the responsibility of self-government despite the declaration avowed in the conclusion of the report that the proposals "aim at taxing the capacity of the Sudanese to the full."

2. That the proposed system does not allow for the proper and full representation of the Sudanese is evidenced by the manner in which the Legislative Assembly is composed. It is composed of seventy members of whom ten are nominated by the Governor-General and the remainder are elected. The method of election, however, is nearer to nomination rather than to proper election. The representatives of the Southern Provinces are frankly to be appointed by the Provincial Governors. In the Northern Provinces the method of election in rural districts is not clearly defined; it may vary in different areas. No definition is given of electors nor of the various units comprising electoral areas. These were altogether left to the discretion of Provincial Governors. It can, therefore, be clearly seen that election in rural districts will, to a considerable extent, be subject to the influence of administrative authorities. If we add that civil servants may be permitted to sit as members of the Legislative Assembly while retaining their posts, we may well enquire to what extent will the Legislative Assembly—such being its composition—be removed from the influence of the executive authorities even within the bounds of its limited jurisdiction? It is essential in this fundamental question that an electoral law allowing for the full representation of the Sudanese be definitely drawn up.

3. That the proposed system does not admit the participation of the Sudanese, in a measure due to them, in the responsibility of self-government is evidenced by the limited powers vested in the Legislative Assembly and by the wide powers given to the Governor-General and his four assistants who are considered members *ex officio* of the Executive Council and who are all British.

4. The Legislative Assembly is only given limited powers. This may be seen from the following:—

(a) The Assembly has a purely consultative voice as regards legislation submitted to it. Should a legislation be rejected by the Assembly this would not necessarily entail the non-adoption of that legislation, nor even its postponement. If it be argued in this connexion that the Sudanese have not as yet been trained in governing themselves, and that they will gradually develop through this system, in the limited period, towards self-government, it could be answered that one of the first stages of development in self-government is that the rejection by the Assembly of a legislation should have a material effect on suspending that legislation. Again, if it be argued that it may be premature for the Legislative Assembly to give a decisive opinion on legislation, the least that can be done should be to postpone a rejected legislation until the next session. This power is regarded as one in the first stages of constitutional powers. It is not too much for the Sudanese to have their Legislative Assembly given that limited power. If at the end of those three years set for the new régime, the experiment proves successful, the expansion of those powers should then be proceeded with.

(b) The Legislative Assembly, though having no more than that purely consultative voice cannot examine all legislations before their being put into effect. There are those urgent legislations which cannot be considered by the Assembly until they have become effective laws. Nor is that all, they are to be dealt with not in a special session, but in the next ordinary session. If we observe that the session of the Legislative Assembly lasts for only four months in each year, we would realise that so many legislations will be labelled urgent. These are the legislations called for during the remaining eight months and they will become effective laws before being considered by the Legislative Assembly, and the time for their consideration will thus drag on. There are even ordinary unurgent legislations which are promulgated while the Assembly is in session without being considered by the Assembly. These are legislations which the Business Committee—after consultation with the Executive Council—finds that the Assembly has too short a time to consider. Thus will the principal function of the Assembly, *i.e.*, giving their opinion on legislations before their promulgation, be suspended on account of too short a session. This session should, in the opinion of the Egyptian Government, be of no less than six months' duration in each year. The Assembly should, moreover, be entitled to special sessions to be held as need may arise.

The prolongation of the session cannot be objected to by the argument that certain members of the Assembly are civil servants, and that if they are absent too long a time from their posts, Government work will inevitably be retarded in consequence. The combining of a Government post with the membership of the Assembly is, as already pointed out, inadmissable. The shortness of the session—which is an obvious defect of the system—should in no way be a justification for further defect. The conference's report, however, after stating that "as long as the sessions of the Assembly last for no more than four months in each year, a Government servant who is a member of the Assembly may still be able to retain his post," could not deny the anomaly existing in combining a Government post with the Assembly's membership, and predicted the quick elimination of this defective system by pointing out "that the time is fast approaching when the Sudanese, who have received the benefit of education, must make up their minds whether they wish to make the civil service or politics their career."

(c) As to the budget—including taxation—there is no explicit provision in the proposed system to render the Assembly's opinion decisive in matters connected therewith. We can even find in the report of the sub-committee certain explicit texts showing that the Assembly's opinion on those matters is purely consultative. As to the report of the conference, it is vague on this point. On one occasion it says that the Financial Secretary will submit the budget to the Assembly "in the same way as other Government Bills." This conveys the idea that the Assembly's opinion is just as consultative on matters pertaining to the budget as it is on other Bills. On other occasions it says that the Assembly will have authority to reduce all items of the budget, from which it may be understood that the Assembly's opinion is decisive on reduction. It may also be understood that the Assembly is competent to give an opinion on reductions in budget items to the exclusion of increases, and that the

Assembly's opinion on reductions is still as consultative as it is on all other matters. The conference's report is at any rate explicit in that the Assembly have no authority to increase any budget item even though such item be connected with so vital a subject as education. It is essential that explicit provisions giving the Assembly a decisive opinion on the approval of the budget and introducing modifications by reduction or increase, should be made. In any case, the Assembly should at least be given the authority, as from now, to approve taxation in accordance with the well-known principle of "no taxation without representation."

(d) Members of the Legislative Assembly cannot take the initiative of directly submitting to the Assembly draft laws. According to the proposed system it is necessary that these draft laws should pass through the Business Committee which, after consultation with the Executive Council, will submit to the Assembly only those laws it approves of. This constitutes an unwarranted restriction on the right of members to propose laws which they deem necessary for the development and welfare of the Sudan. Members of the Legislative Assembly should have the right to submit directly to the Assembly any draft laws of their own, and it is then incumbent upon the Assembly to consider them.

5. Too wide a power is given in the proposed system to the Governor-General. He has absolute authority to approve or reject legislation. Should he reject a legislation after being passed by both the Legislative Assembly and the Executive Council no other higher authority can control his decision. This power is unparalleled in constitutional systems. Should the Governor-General give his consent to a legislation, it has to be submitted to the Egyptian Government for approval. This is a fundamental principle in the present régime which should be clearly provided for in the text.

It should, therefore, be established in this connexion—so long as the present régime in the Sudan remains in force—that the Governor-General cannot approve or reject a legislation passed by the Legislative Assembly and the Executive Council unless the two Governments concerned have ratified its rejection or approval. Also, the Governor-General cannot promulgate a legislation on which the Executive Council and the Legislative Assembly are at variance unless the two Government's [sic] ratification has been obtained.

6. The four assistants of the Governor-General, who are considered members *ex officio* of the Executive Council, are given in the proposed system supreme authority over the Council. It is they who will have the final decision in the choice of the Sudanese Under-Secretaries from whom the six Sudanese members of the Executive Council are chosen. Thus, they will have—all of them being British—the last word in a Council in which they only form a minority. No single Sudanese member of the Executive Council assumes first-rank responsibility, since one and all of the six Sudanese members are subordinate to British chiefs. Their ostensible duty is to act as media between the British chiefs and the Legislative Assembly and to face the questions and discussions that may be raised by the Assembly. It is essential that the Sudanese should have a share of the key positions in the Executive Council and should also have all the other posts in the Sudan Government. This would afford them real training in assuming the responsibilities of government and would pave the way for their filling all key positions after the expiration of the three years set for the trial period.

7. The proposed system—despite its avowed aim being the training of the

Sudanese in self-government—lays the full responsibility on the British side. There is not a single provision to give Egypt any share in this responsibility. Without prejudicing the right of the Sudanese to share in the key positions in the Executive Council, Egypt should undertake an important part in this responsibility during the three years' trial period so that it may help the Sudanese in training in self-government.

8. The proposed system has omitted even a mere reference to constitutional freedom. This is a matter of vital importance to the Sudan. The Sudanese are on the threshold of a social and political awakening. It is essential that the régime under which they live should ensure for them respect of personal freedom, freedom of opinion, freedom of faith, freedom of meetings, freedom of the press and all other freedoms without which they cannot live free men and cannot feel secure unless they are ensured for them. These freedoms have to be regulated by law. The Sudanese should not be at the mercy of the Administration in their meetings, their press and their personal freedom in its variegated forms. It is essential that all this should be provided for in the proposed system, otherwise this system will be *no more than modifications of administrative type* dealing with but a few scores of Sudanese officials and members of the Legislative Assembly who may easily become a tool in the hands of the Central Government.

We may point out in this connexion that legislative assemblies, even though of limited powers, are instrumental in checking the arbitrary action of the Administration. This is not the case with the Sudan, where an absolute form of government exists, considering the wide powers assigned to the Governor-General and the retention by British officials of key positions without any control whatsoever. Should the proposed reforms be applied within the framework of the present autocratic régime, they will lack the importance which these constitutional laws seem to endow, and it will be difficult for nationalists wishing to voice their aspirations and those of their countrymen—unless they are given full and free exercise of public freedom—to strive against the domination of an all-powerful Administration having at its disposal all means of authority and pressure.

9. The defects already pointed out in the proposed system, which are, in our opinion, cardinal defects, are attributable to the fact that the conference which examined the question and reported thereon has lacked certain elements whose presence was essential for the satisfactory discharge of the task entrusted to it. The conference was composed of thirty members, of whom twenty-five were Government officials, and comprised not a single Egyptian among its members. It could not even be claimed that it was fully representative of the Sudanese people. Several political parties in the Sudan, including the Graduates' General Congress itself that represents the educated class, which should be the first to be consulted on constitutional reforms and for whom the road should be cleared for the assumption of the responsibilities of government, nominated no representatives on the conference.

It was not, therefore, surprising that the conference's recommendations fell short of giving a true expression of real public opinion in the Sudan.

Members of the Sudan Administration Conference themselves have realised this fact when they frankly expressed this view in the conclusion of their report: "We are very conscious of our limitation as an instrument for laying down the foundations of a new system of administration. The members of the conference are all busy men, distracted by the necessity of carrying on their normal duties, and with little or no experience of similar work in the past."

10. It was not surprising, also, that we should receive a note from the Sudan delegation which is held in high esteem by Sudanese public opinion, rejecting the conference's recommendations. This note was duly communicated to both the British and the Sudan Governments.

The Royal Egyptian Government therefore cannot agree to these recommendations unless the modifications, herein outlined, are introduced.

142 FO 371/63130, no 5878 28 Nov 1947

[Nile Waters: Lake Tsana]: despatch no 818 from D W Lascelles to Sir R Campbell on the importance to the Sudan of HMG's participation in the Lake Tsana negotiations

[The uncertainty over the strength of the Sudan's case for reopening discussions concerning its share of the Nile waters reinforced the importance of the Lake Tsana project as the most likely scheme to provide water to meet the country's anticipated needs (see 32 and 45). The disagreement between the UK and Egypt over the sovereignty issue introduced new complications into the tripartite negotiations, raising questions not only about the Sudan's participation in any talks, but HMG's negotiating status as well. Prior to the war both HMG and the Sudan government were actively involved in discussions at various levels with Ethiopia and Egypt over the cost and design of the Lake Tsana scheme, as well as the allocation of waters produced by it (see 27). After the failure of the Sidki-Bevin negotiations such arrangements could no longer be taken for granted.]

In your despatch No. 546 (445/38/47) of the 20th June, Your Excellency expressed doubts as to the expediency of approaching the Egyptian Government regarding the Lake Tsana scheme at a moment when the political atmosphere was vitiated by the preparations being made for the Egyptian appeal to the Security Council.

2. At that time I shared your view that the moment was exceptionally unpropitious, and that it would therefore be well to delay the proposed approach to the Egyptian Government at any rate until after the Egyptian case had been disposed of at Lake Success. Nevertheless I must emphasize that the legitimate interest of His Majesty's Government in the Lake Tsana scheme is considerably greater than would appear from your despatch under reference. In the first place, their status as Co-dominus gives them an indisputable right to interest themselves in any development which tends to affect the welfare of the Condominium. I can see no reason to conceal the fact that His Majesty's Government do, in virtue of that status, intend to take an equal part with Egypt in all international discussions concerning the control of a river which is in large measure the Sudan's life-blood as well as Egypt's. In any case the fact cannot be concealed even if it were desirable that it should be: so long as the administration of the Sudan remains in British hands, no-one either in Egypt or elsewhere can be expected to believe that in regard to so important a question the Sudan Government had hitherto acted otherwise than in close consultation with His Majesty's Government. Secondly, it is clear that, in respect of the next and really international phase of the negotiations, the direct participation of His Majesty's Government is not merely justified, but also legally essential if the project is to be pursued at all. The annex to Article 11 of the 1936 Treaty, which lays down the method of adherence of the Sudan to international conventions and hence by implication the general international status of the Condominium, shows that any negotiations with a foreign State must be undertaken on behalf of the Sudan by the

two Co-domini acting in concert. Thirdly, His Majesty's Government are directly concerned in any negotiations regarding the Nile waters by virtue of the veto which, under the 1902 Treaty, they have the right to exercise over the construction of any new works. In addition, His Majesty's Government have had since 1941 a special relationship with the Government of Ethiopia.[1]

3. For these reasons I do not consider that the Egyptian Government could have made during the debates before the Security Council, or could make now, any damaging capital out of such proof as we might then have provided, or may now provide, of the direct interest taken by His Majesty's Government in this matter. That is not to say, however, that the present moment is necessarily propitious for approaching the Egyptian Government. The Lake Tsana scheme would, it is true, be of considerable material benefit both to Egypt herself and to the Sudan; and consequently it would be against the Egyptian Government's true interest for them to refuse to concert with His Majesty's Government in an approach to Ethiopia. Nevertheless, so long as Nokrashi Pasha remains Prime Minister there seems some reason to fear that he would in fact subordinate his country's true interest to his doctrinaire attitude of non-cooperation with the British Co-dominus in all matters affecting the Sudan. It occurs to me that if there is any considerable likelihood of Nokrashi Pasha's being replaced in the fairly near future by another Prime Minister, it might be worth our while to await this event before making any approach to the Egyptian authorities. It would clearly be easier for the new Prime Minister to take a sensible and cooperative line with us in this matter if we had given his predecessor no opportunity to take up an official stand based on Egypt's theoretical repudiation of the Condominium Agreement. It is true that the proposed approach to the Egyptian Government, without which no progress can be made towards the realisation of the scheme, has already been much delayed. But it may be that, for the reason I have suggested above, a slight further delay in making the approach would conduce to the ultimate progress of the scheme by enabling us to overcome an obstacle which might otherwise prove insuperable.

4. I shall be glad, therefore, if Your Excellency will consider carefully, in the light of the local political factors of which you are of course the best judge, whether or not such further delay is advisable. Should you decide that it is not, the approach can now be made to the Egyptian Government in the terms of draft note "B" enclosed in your despatch under reference. (I presume that it was not your intention to include the phrase in brackets in the second paragraph of that draft.)[2]

5. I am sending copies of this despatch to the Governor-General of the Sudan, whose views on the question of timing I shall also be glad to receive by telegraph, and to His Majesty's Chargé d'Affaires at Addis Ababa.

---

[1] See 27.

[2] The draft paragraph read: 'I am now instructed to inform Your Excellency officially that H.M.G. endorse the action of the Governor-General in approving these agreements, and I shall be glad to learn whether the Egyptian Government for their part also approve them, (with the implication that they, too, endorse the action of the Governor-General), so that, if they do, arrangements may be concerted between our two governments for negotiations with the Ethiopian Government on the lines so approved. In the view of H.M.G., representatives of the Sudan Government should be present at the negotiations as technical advisers to the delegations of H.M.G. and the Egyptian Government, and the rights and requirements of the Sudan Government should be clearly specified either in a prior agreement between our two Governments or in the agreement which it is hoped will result from the propoposed negotiations with Ethiopia.'

143 FO 371/63137, no 6300 9 Dec 1947

[Sudan's borders: Ilemi Triangle]: letter from J W Robertson (Khartoum) to J D Rankine (Nairobi) on the inclusion of part of the Ilemi Triangle in the administration of Kenya. *Minute* by I W Bell[1]

[The Sudan's southeastern border with Ethiopia, agreed in 1902 and demarcated in 1903, created a permanent administrative problem for the Sudan by cutting through the eastern settlements of both the Nuer and Anuak peoples. In the aftermath of the war the Sudan government proposed to reopen the question of the transfer of the Baro salient from Ethiopia to the Sudan, last discussed with an Ethiopian government in 1932, so as to include the entire populations of both the Nuer and the Anuak under one administration. Howe considered the rectificaiton of the Baro frontier as next to the Lake Tsana project in importance in the Sudan's dealings with Ethiopia, but not worth pursuing if it would worsen the Sudan's position in the Anglo–Egyptian treaty negotiations or jeopardise agreement over the Lake Tsana scheme (inward telegram no 204 from Campbell to FO, 22 Jan 1947, FO 371/63133, no 387). In proposing that Ethiopia agree to the Sudan's incorporation of all Nuer and Anuak within a single boundary, Howe considered ceding land to Ethiopia further south along the Boma plateau (outward telegram no 8 from Howe to Addis Ababa, 4 Mar 1947, FO 371/63133, no 1115). The Sudan's negotiating position was complicated first by Egypt's assertion of its sovereignty over any adjustment of the Sudan's borders (inward telegram no 803 from Campbell to FO, 28 Mar 1947, FO 371/63134, no 1489), and then by Ethiopia's expressed interest in a rectification of the 'Ilemi Triangle' boundary in the far southeastern corner of the Sudan, affecting Kenya as well as the Sudan and Ethiopia. The official southern boundary in this area had been fixed in 1914 as a straight line. An agreement to extend Kenyan administration over Turkana grazing grounds north of this line, contained within an administrative boundary called the Red Line, was reached in 1931. For many years it was unclear whether the Red Line was meant to be a provisional administrative boundary or to become the international frontier.[2] Ethiopia's interest in advancing its own borders closer to the Triangle caused a reaction from Mitchell (governor of Kenya) who impressed upon the FO (with the full concurrence of the CO) the undesirability of even contemplating cession of any part of the Ilemi Triangle to Ethiopia (outward telegram no 1073 from FO to Cairo, 3 June 1947, FO 371/63135, no 2360). This view was reiterated in a detailed despatch from Mitchell to Creech-Jones, referred to below (Mitchell to Creech-Jones, 24 Nov 1947, FO 371/63137, no 5914). J D Rankine, chief secretary of Kenya, also proposed to the civil secretary a further expansion of Kenyan administrative responsibilities to include an area north of the Red Line contained within a new boundary called the Blue Line (letter from Rankine to Robertson, 24 Nov 1947, FO 371/63137, no 6300).]

I have the honour to acknowledge receipt of your Secret letter No.S/A.XAF.3–2/III/5 of November 25th and of the copy of Kenya Secret despatch of November 24th from the Governor of Kenya to His Britannic Majesty's Secretary of State for the Colonies which was enclosed therewith.

2. I should like first to thank you for stating the Kenya requirements so clearly and in particular for the readiness of the Kenya Government to take over the administration of the areas of the Ilemi Triangle which are necessary to them. I also express the appreciation of the Sudan Government of the Kenya Government's great help in sending Mr. Reece and Mr. Turnbull[3] here for discussions on the proposed frontier in the Ilemi Triangle. The discussions were most valuable to us, and they have saved a great deal of correspondence which would otherwise have been

---

[1] FO, 1946; first secretary, 1947.

[2] Ian Brownlie, *African boundaries: a legal and diplomatic encyclopedia* (London, 1979) pp 917–921.

[3] G Reece, provincial commissioner, Northern Province, Kenya; R G Turnbull, Kenya secretariat (former district commissioner, Turkana).

necessary. I attach a record, which was seen by Mr. Turnbull in draft, of the more formal meeting held on November 27th.[4]

3. The Sudan Government agree that the proposed Blue Line would make a very satisfactory administrative boundary between the Turkana and the Tapotha and Nyangatom.

4. During the discussions held last June in Addis Ababa with the Ethiopian Government for the rectification of the Sudan frontier in the Baro Salient, it became abundantly clear that the Sudan Government had no hope of obtaining the area required there for the proper administration of the Nuer and Anuak unless another area could be offered to the Ethiopian Government in exchange. The only area which the Sudan Government can offer in exchange is in the Ilemi Triangle; part of the triangle is however required for the Tapotha, and the remainder available for exchange is now still further reduced by the reservation of the portion south of the Blue Line for the Turkana. Furthermore the area which seems available adjacent and south of the Boma plateau is little known, and there may be good reasons why we should not dispose of it to Ethiopia, even in order to obtain the sorely needed rectification of the Baro Salient frontier, the Sudan Government cannot come to a final decision until further information has been obtained.

5. With this in mind now that the Kenya Government are willing to take over the Ilemi Appendix south of the Blue Line for the Turkana, and if the Sudan Government in fact decides to go ahead, our two Governments should co-operate in arriving at a settlement with the Ethiopians and that our respective proposals should be based on the same principle, particularly as the Ethiopians will undoubtedly regard such a settlement as a "settlement with the British", whether in fact the area under discussion affects the Sudan or Kenya. The principle on which the Sudan Government wish to rely in arriving at a settlement is that the new frontier should be satisfactory both from a geographical and from an ethnological point of view; in fact that the territory of a tribe should not be cut in half by the international frontier.

6. The discussions in Khartoum have made clear that the most difficult question in arriving at a satisfactory ethnological boundary in this area is likely to be the future of the Merille. Not only have the Merille traditional grazing rights west of the Gwynn and Maud Lines and north-west of Lake Rudolf, in the Lorienatom and Lomogol areas, but they have similar rights south of the Kenya-Ethiopian frontier and east of Lake Rudolf also. Mr. Reece undertook to investigate the possibility of making them a concession in the latter area. Mr. Reece also stated that he wished to make the new frontier with Ethiopia east of Lake Rudolf a "closed" frontier, and to make any Merille south of the frontier opt either for Ethiopia or for Kenya after which individuals would not be allowed to move from one side of the line to the other. The Sudan Government share Mr. Reece's wish for a "closed" frontier with Ethiopia, but believe that this will only be attained if the frontier is based on the principle stated in the previous paragraph.

7. The Sudan Government have experience in the Baro Salient area of an international frontier which cuts arbitrarily across tribal territories, and have found it almost impossible to administer, particularly with the Ethiopians on the other side. It is in fact to avoid this very difficulty that the Sudan Government are so

[4] Not printed.

anxious to see all Nuer and Anuak in the Baro Salient territory included within the boundaries of the Sudan. While conditions east of Lake Rudolf are obviously very different from those in the Baro Salient similar difficulties might, it is felt, result if the Merille remain divided between Kenya and Ethiopia. I therefore wish to ask that every consideration be given to the suggestion that any area over which the Merille may be found to have legitimate rights should be earmarked for surrender to Ethiopia as part of a general settlement. If, by such a surrender, a satisfactory tribal boundary, between the Merille on the one hand and the Gabra and Rendile on the other, could be arrived at, the commitments of the Kenya Government in this area might perhaps be reduced.

8. From the point of view of the Sudan Government of course this suggested concession to the Merille east of Lake Rudolf could, should you agree to it, be used as a counter in the bargaining with the Ethiopians over the Baro Salient. I therefore hope you will agree that if, after the investigation Mr. Reece has undertaken to make, it should prove that there is an area east of Lake Rudolf which could be allotted to the Merille, this area should be so used in view of the concession to the Turkana of the area which this Government has promised to earmark for them south of the Blue Line, and which you have signified the willingness of the Kenya Government to incorporate within the boundaries of Kenya.

9. The situation may I think now be described in short as follows:—

(a) The Sudan Government wish to obtain the Baro Salient from Ethiopia by exchange of territory.

(b) The Kenya Government cannot allow the area of the Ilemi Triangle South of the Blue Line from the Sudan to be transferred to Ethiopia.

(c) These requirements are both based on the necessity to settle the boundaries finally on satisfactory ethnological lines.

(d) The Sudan Government can only hope to obtain the Baro Salient by offering to Ethiopia as nearly equivalent an area of territory as possible.

(e) The only area of the Sudan available to be offered to Ethiopia is the Ilemi Triangle *less* the ethnological and tribal requirements of the Tapotha (Sudan) and of the Turkana (Kenya). This is almost certainly insufficient to satisfy the Ethiopians.

(f) There is however an area of Kenya east of Lake Rudolf over which the Merille tribe (Ethiopia) have grazing rights. If this could be offered to Ethiopia as well as the available portion of the Ilemi Triangle and were accepted, then

(i) the Merille tribal boundary would leave them and their grazing grounds in Ethiopia, in accordance with (c) above.

(ii) the combined extent of the two areas might secure Ethiopian agreement to exchange them for the Baro Salient.

(g) Therefore it will I hope be agreed by our Governments that in order to attain their respective desiderata they should act as one vis a vis the Ethiopian Government, and offer the two areas described in exchange for the Baro Salient, to ensure, so far as Kenya is concerned a final and satisfactory boundary between the Tapotha, Nyangatom and Merille tribes and the Turkana.

(h) I shall be most grateful to have your views on this.

10. Settlement of the Kenya–Sudan boundary between Zulia and Makonnen Cherosh raised by Captain King in paragraph 19 of the Record appears to be purely a

question between our two Governments;[5] but I suggest that it is advisable that the mapping and final demarcation of this part of the frontier should be undertaken sooner rather than later in view of possible political developments in the Sudan which might make a settlement more difficult in the future. I shall be grateful to know whether on this you also agree.

Minute on 143

The Sudan Govt. appear to have accepted Kenya's special position in the Ilemi Triangle and to have agreed not to offer the Ethiopians any territory south of the blue line on the map on J5914 (i.e. the new frontier proposed by the Govt. of Kenya).[6] In return, the Govt. of Kenya seems to be contemplating concessions to Ethiopia east of Lake Rudolph. This would appear to involve some modification of the new Kenya–Ethiopia frontier agreed upon on the 29th September last.

I cannot help feeling that this is unwise from Kenya's point of view since, in return for a concession to Ethiopia which may last indefinitely, they obtain the administration of an (admittedly large) area of Sudanese territory only as long as our administration of the Sudan lasts—unless we can get the Egn. govt's. agreement at some stage.

Furthermore, I can forsee considerable complications in negotiating with Ethiopia (a) jointly with Egypt on behalf of the Sudan and (b) alone on behalf of Kenya, both at the same time.

I.W.B
28.12.47

[5] G R King (district commissioner, Eastern District, Equatoria Province, Sudan), proposed only a minor adjustment in the Sudan-Kenya boundary close to the junction of the international boundaries of the Sudan, Kenya and Uganda. It was agreed at the meeting on 27 November 'that in view of possible political developments in the Sudan it was most desirable to get this cleared up as soon as possible. Egypt might easily raise difficulties and any boundary adjustments required were likely to become increasingly difficult to put through in future' ('Record of a meeting held in the civil secretary's office Khartoum, on November 27th 1947, to discuss possible frontier rectifications in the Ilemi Triangle', FO 371/63137, no 6300).

[6] See map on p vii.

144 FO 371/62949, no 6364 9 Dec 1947

'Egyptian reaction to Sudanization programme': minute by D W Lascelles to Mr Bevin on the proposed constitutional reforms[1]

[Extract]

It will be remembered that it was felt necessary for Sir R. Howe to submit to both the Codomini the decisions taken by the Governor-General's Council on the report of the Sudan Administration Conference regarding constitutional reform, the Governor-General having no power under the Condominium Agreement to introduce major constitutional changes on his own.

[1] Lascelles comments in this minute on the recommendations in 141.

2. His Majesty's Government replied briefly and without comment, concurring in the proposals; and their reply was in due course published. The Egyptian Government, on the other hand, have now sent the Governor-General a long and critical note, the gist of which is that they cannot concur in anything so half-hearted: Sudanisation must be far more radical. This reply also has been published in Egypt. . . .[2]

4. It was inevitable that the Egyptians should have reacted in this way. They do not, of course, wish to promote genuine Sudanisation (though they would no doubt like to promote self-government if they could pack the legislative body with their own adherents); but they cannot afford to estrange their supporters in the Sudan by turning down the scheme on the ground that it goes too far. Consequently they had to outbid us by saying that it does not go far enough.

5. We have asked for, and are awaiting, Sir R. Howe's comments and suggestions. Meanwhile it is clear that this Egyptian move is potentially very embarrassing. There are, indeed, a number of minor points which are open to counter-criticism, and there is one major point: item (4) above,[3] which complains of the Governor-General's retention of the power to approve or reject legislation, makes it clear that the Egyptian Government want to get this power for themselves, not to give the Sudan legislative body freedom from outside control. Nevertheless the Egyptian note, taken as a whole, will probably impress a great many Sudanese, including sections of the Umma party, as a noble document advocating complete emancipation.

6. The real answer is of course that the Sudanese are not yet ripe for anything like complete self-government and must be initiated gradually. But this answer, apart from the fact that it would estrange our own supporters in the Sudan, is largely anticipated in the Egyptian note, which emphasises that a system under which the Assembly would not have the final word in budgetary and fiscal matters, and could not even secure a delay in the rejection by the Governor-General of legislation submitted by it for his approval, can hardly be called even a beginning.

7. One obvious counter-measure would be to arrange for the Egyptian proposals to be examined by the Sudan Administration Conference and rejected by it. As, however, the Egyptian note lays great stress on the insufficiently representative nature of the Conference and the extent to which it was directly and indirectly packed and controlled by the British, this would not provide the perfect propaganda answer.

8. Another course might conceivably be to hold a referendum on the Sudan Government's proposals and the Egyptian counter-proposals, taking care to make it clear that the latter would involve an influx of Egyptians into the Administration (item (6) in para. 3 above) and Egyptian control over all Sudanese legislation (item (4), already referred to). Emphasis on these two points would no doubt be enough to ensure rejection of the Egyptian proposals in any impartially-managed referendum; but so long as the administration is British we cannot hope to convince anybody outside the Sudan that a referendum would in fact be impartially conducted.

8. [sic] The Egyptian note is careful to safeguard the position of principle adopted by the Egyptian Government in respect of the Condominium Agreement. It says in effect that although the Egyptian Government no longer regard that

[2] Paragraph 3 of Lascelles's minute summarises paras 1–10 in 141.

[3] A reference to para 5 (on the governor-general's power) in 141.

agreement as in force, they are nevertheless consenting to discuss the question as though they were merely one of two Codomini, and are doing this solely with the practical object of getting ahead with self-government for the Sudan. We cannot, in view of this explicit reservation, make capital out of the Egyptian note as a proof that Egypt still recognises the 1899 Agreement when it suits her to do so.

9. Further consideration of this awkward problem may be easier when we get Sir R. Howe's comments.

145 FO 371/62949, no 6364 14 Dec 1947

[Constitutional reform]: letter (reply) from Sir R Howe to Sir O Sargent giving the Sudan government's response to the Egyptian government's rejection of their proposed constitutional reforms[1]

In accordance with paragraph 5 of my telegram No. 240 of 11th December, 1947, I set out below my detailed comments on the points raised in the Egyptian Memorandum. The numbering of the paragraphs is that of the Memorandum.

1. The Sudan Government has accepted the principles of the Sudan Administration Conference Report, though not necessarily all its details, as a first step towards self-government, but it has to look considerably further forward if constitutional upheaval every few years is to be avoided, with the inevitable claim by the Egyptian Government to a decisive voice in these changes. To this end the new legislation which is now being drafted, in addition to setting up the Assembly and Council, is to be wide enough to allow for the progressive development of the political machinery which will be necessary in the final stage of fully responsible self-government. It will allow for the evolution of the Under-Secretary into a responsible Minister and of the Executive Council into a Cabinet, thus anticipating the Egyptian criticism that the proposals do not go far enough.

2. No decision has yet been reached as to electoral methods and so the Egyptian criticism is premature, but it is proposed to provide in the Ordinance for a wide variety of procedure in the first instance to meet the various conditions throughout the country, and to allow for future adjustments on the initiative of the Assembly itself. Full use will be made in country areas of the existing democratic Arab methods of election which it is thought will throw up more genuinely representative members than the Western ballot box.

The Sudan Government has discussed and re-discussed the question of admitting Civil Servants to the Assembly, and fully supports the principle that ideally they should take no public part in politics; but in the Sudan, at present, the vast majority of educated men experienced in administration are in Government service, and progress will be hardly possible and certainly very slow if they are all excluded from the Assembly. Their admission will be a temporary expedient.

3. The Assembly has in fact very wide powers as emphasised below under paragraph 4, but until the final stage of fully responsible self-government is reached, the ultimate power must remain where the ultimate responsibility is, with the Governor-General.

---

[1] See 141.

4. (a) It is quite wrong to say that the Assembly will be an entirely consultative body. Even though its decisions may be over-ridden, it will be a statutory legislative body to which all normal legislation will have to be presented, which legislation it will have the right to debate, amend, or reject. It will also have the right to question any acts and policy of the Government, and to pass resolutions. It will not be possible for its decisions to be lightly or frequently set aside without alienating those moderate Sudanese whose goodwill it is so essential for the Government to retain.

(b) It is not the Government's intention to lay down the length of a session, which will last as long as there is business to occupy the Assembly. Provision for the passing of urgent legislation during a recess will include the right of ratification or rejection by the Assembly when it meets. Legislation of this kind is expected to be rare, and will consist of minor amendments.

(c) The Egyptian view that the Assembly should have complete financial power cannot be accepted, but it is intended that the Assembly will have full opportunity to discuss and recommend alterations in the Budget provided its equilibrium is not thereby upset. As taxation in the Sudan is imposed by Ordinance, the Assembly will have power to impose or increase taxation when such Ordinances are laid before it.

(d) It is proposed that private members shall be given full facilities for the introduction of bills, except money bills and bills on reserved subjects, subject only to the leave of the Assembly.

5. The Governor-General's veto must be retained in order to accord with Articles III and IV of the 1899 Condominium Agreement, and to enable him to discharge his responsibilities under them.

Under Article IV of the Condominium Agreement, the Governor-General's power to make laws is specified as subject only to the condition that he shall inform the British and Egyptian Governments as soon as the law has been passed. The Egyptian Government's proposal that all laws should be approved by them is contrary to the Agreement and to the 1936 Treaty; the proposal is retrograde, unworkable, and inconsistent with their expressed desire to accelerate Sudanese self-government.

7. [sic] The appointment of four senior Civil Servants to the Executive Council is necessary at present until Ministers can be appointed. The fact that these positions are at present held by officials of British nationality does not give the British Government control over the administration of the country, for they are Sudan Government officials, and in due course the posts will be held by Sudanese.

The other points in the Memorandum, namely, paragraphs 6, 8, 9 and 10 are presumably included as political propaganda. The freedoms mentioned in paragraph 8 are at present secured by law and are more liberal than in Egypt. It was not the Sudan Government's fault that some political parties in the Sudan refused to accept an invitation to attend the Conference.

The new Ordinance to set up the Assembly and Council with the necessary standing orders and rules of procedures is now in draft and as soon as it has reached a more final stage, will be sent to you for your information.

146 FO 371/69209, no 117 6 Jan 1948

[Anglo–Egyptian negotiations]: inward telegram no 29 from E A Chapman-Andrews[1] to Sir R Campbell reporting Sir R Howe's stance on further negotiations with Egypt

[Howe's proposal to present the Advisory Council with draft legislation for approval, and the Egyptian criticisms of the Sudan Administration Conference for rejection, did not meet the threat of a possible Egyptian veto on any constitutional changes within the Sudan. Campbell suggested that such a veto could be avoided only by resuming talks with Egypt ostensibly on constitutional reform, but as a means of reopening the question of the Sudan as a whole (outward telegram no 329 from the FO to Howe, 27 Dec 1947, FO 371/63055, no 6280). Howe resisted this, and also initially declined an invitation to join Campbell in discussions at the FO early in the new year. Prior to departing for London Campbell argued: 'Neither I nor, I feel sure, the Egyptian Government can regard as of purely parochial concern, the matter of compromise constitutional reform. All major questions in regard to the Sudan, including projected constitutional reform, are now regarded by the Egyptians as in the main political arena. They substantially affect Anglo–Egyptian relations and I submit that we ought not to allow these, with their highly important strategical angle, to be perpetually vitiated, by the possibility of disorder caused by political factions in the Sudan' (inward telegram no 4 from Campbell to FO, 1 Jan 1948, FO 371/69155, no 21). Howe was persuaded to come too only when the FO suggested that in his meetings with them Campbell would no doubt raise 'the possibility of soothing Egyptian susceptibilities by, e.g., giving them a greater share (or at least a greater appearance of sharing) in the Administration' (outward telegram no 1 from FO to Howe, 1 Jan 1948, FO 371/69155, no 7). Howe stopped off at Cairo on his way to London, and Chapman-Andrews reported to Campbell (by now already at the FO) on his state of mind.]

I am afraid you will find Howe uncompromising. I had a long talk with him last night. Line he takes is that whereas Sudan Government might have just got away with Bevin/Sidki Pasha protocol at the time it was initialled they could not do so to-day. Indeed, unless existing administration in Sudan can be left alone to lead Sudan to full self-government (i.e. without any interference whatever on the part of Egypt) there will be trouble. By trouble he means complete non-cooperation of Sudanese in Government services and possibly the raising of tribes and rekindling of old Mahdia fanaticism. As Howe sees it, it is question either of leaving present administration a free hand or of "our losing the Sudan". By this he means that Sudan would be denied to us utterly for military purposes because there would be widespread and uncontrollable disorder.

2. His opinion is, therefore, that we should tell Egyptians "hands off Sudan". If as a result Egyptians cut up rusty that is too bad. Facilities in the Sudan are, he said, according to C.I.G.S.[2] more important to us than those in Egypt. C.I.G.S. told him the other day there was no reason why we should not clear out of Egypt but we must stay in Cyprus, Cyrenaica and the Sudan. Howe thought that if in time of war we had to come back, Egyptians would probably be only too thankful, treaty or no treaty and would welcome us. If, on the other hand, we had to force our way back we need not be put off by the fear we should find no (repeat no) Egyptians to co-operate with us. They would co-operate when it was question of their bread and butter. We could if it came to it, coerce Egyptians but we could never coerce Sudanese owing to the vast area of the Sudan, the fact that population was very scattered and because the

[1] Then minister in Cairo.

[2] Lord Montgomery.

fanatical Sudanese warrior was an altogether different proposition from the Egyptian. Not that it would come to coercing the Egyptians. He thought the Egyptians were now more anxious to reach agreement because they were frightened. This was not the moment to make concessions to them therefore. In fact he thought that if someone with sufficient weight and authority, for instance the C.I.G.S., were to come out and see King Farouk and explain the military needs of the situation we need not discount our getting Egyptians to agree to our retaining troops here even in peace time.

3. On subject of the 1899 agreement Howe said that though doubtless valid as a legal document it was a dead letter in the political sense. Not a single Sudanese, not even Ashigga, accepted it. It was unrealistic therefore to refer to it. Times had changed since 1899 and since 1924; for that matter even since 1936 and October 1946. A document to which Sudanese were not a party but which settled their political status nearly 50 years ago after suppression by the British of their rebellion against Egyptians was quite unacceptable to them to-day. Above all they would not concede having Egyptians, for whom they did not conceal their contempt, brought into the picture.

147 FO 371/69155, no 549 — 6 Jan 1948

[Constitutional reform]: letter from Sir R Howe to Mahmud al-Nuqrashi Pasha responding informally to the Egyptian note on the Sudan Administration Conference. *Enclosure*: 'Aide Memoire'

[Howe was instructed by the FO to pay a courtesy call on al-Nuqrashi and to give him an interim written reply to the Egyptian note, as long as it was non-controversial. Due to aircraft delays the draft of Howe's text arrived in the FO late, and contained over-conciliartory remarks in the covering letter, and apparently controversial points in the enclosure. A telegram was despatched to Howe, already in Cairo, to forestall the delivery of the text. 'This is considerably more controversial than anything we had envisaged. Enclosure, for instance, covers highly controversial question of your powers under Condominium Agreements and Egyptian claim to control all Sudanese legislation'. After requesting modifications to the letter, the FO went on to suggest, 'If it is not too late, we should much prefer that you should give Nokrashi the covering letter only' (outward telegram no 22 from FO to Howe, 5 Jan 1948, FO 371/69155, no 119). The final text, though backdated to 4 Jan in the FO copy and 5 Jan on the copy presented to the Egyptian government, was amended as requested and delivered to Nuqrashi on 6 Jan.]

I have the honour to refer to Your Excellency's despatch No. 92–3/27 of 26th November, 1947, enclosing copy of the note which Your Excellency has transmitted to the British Government about the recommendations of the Sudan Administration Conference.[1]

2. I have considered very carefully the points made in Your Excellency's despatch and Note. The general support and encouragement[2] of the Royal Egyptian Government to the proposed advance of the Sudanese towards self-government is warmly appreciated by the Sudan Government and by the great majority of the Sudanese, and I trust that Your Excellency will agree that the Ordinance which I

---

[1] See 141.

[2] This originally read 'general approval' but was changed at FO instructions.

hope shortly to submit to Your Excellency in draft will meet most of the modifications[3] suggested in Your Excellency's Note.

3. I am confident that Your Excellency will find that the main criticisms of the proposals of the Sudan Administration Conference's report have been answered in the draft Ordinance. As Your Excellency is aware, the Sudan Government accepted the Report of the Sudan Administration Conference in principle, but in preparing the Ordinance have already anticipated many of the points made in Your Excellency's Note.

4. I propose to lay the draft Ordinance before the Advisory Council for the Northern Sudan at its next meeting for their views, but it will if necessary be made clear to them that the comments of the British and Egyptian Governments upon the draft have still to be received.

5. I am sending a copy of this letter to His Britannic Majesty's Ambassador in Cairo.

I avail myself of this opportunity to renew to Your Excellency the assurance of my very high consideration.

Enclosure to 147

1. The anxiety of the Royal Egyptian Government to give greater responsibility to the Sudanese than is visualised in the Report of the Administration Conference is shared by the Sudan Government, and the new Ordinances will go substantially further than the Report. It is the wish of the Sudan Government to give the Sudanese now as much responsibility as they can undertake without imperilling good government. As stated in its Report, the Conference considered only the next steps towards self-government, but the legislation now being prepared will provide not only for these first steps, but for the progressive assumption of further responsibilities by the Sudanese as and when they are able to shoulder it.

2. The Report did not define the methods of election and criticisms of the Egyptian Government have been anticipated by the Sudan Government. A Schedule to the Ordinance will lay down electoral constituencies and define the qualifications of electors and the methods of election. It is proposed to hold direct elections in urban constituencies and, for the present, indirect elections in the rural area of the Northern Sudan. This form of election has already been tried successfully in Local Government and has been found to provide a suitable method in a sparsely populated country.

In the Southern Sudan Provincial Councils are now being set up which will elect representatives for the Assembly until the people have advanced far enough to make a more direct method of election possible.

The Sudan Government shares the desire of the Royal Egyptian Government to make the Assembly as representative as possible in the circumstances of the country, and at least sixty of the Members will be elected.

3. Under the existing constitution of the Sudan, the Governor-General has been invested by the Co-domini with very wide powers of administration, and the

[3] This originally read 'will meet the modifications' but was changed at FO instructions.

Governor-General is informed by his legal advisers that under the terms of the 1899 Agreement he cannot divest himself of them. It is legally necessary, therefore, to ensure in the new legislation that the Governor-General retains the right to exercise his constitutional powers even though it is expected that, in fact, these powers will seldom, if ever, be used.

The Sudan Government shares the dislike evinced by the Royal Egyptian Government of allowing Government Officials to be Members of the Assembly, but in the circumstances of the country to debar such a large proportion of the educated classes would delay progress. It is intended that participation by officials should be only temporary, and that judges, army and police officers, and certain administrative officials should not be eligible for membership.

4. (a) It is felt that the Royal Egyptian Government's fears that the Legislative Assembly will be no more than a consultative body are groundless. It will be the statutory legal body to which all legislation will have to be presented and which will have power to debate, pass amend or reject it. It will also have powers to question any acts or policy of the Government and to pass resolutions thereon.

(b) It is not intended to lay down the length of Sessions, which will last as long as is necessary to complete the business before the Assembly, and there is no provision in the present proposals that routine or unimportant legislations should not be submitted to the Assembly before enactment. It is only urgent measures which may have to be enacted without the prior consent of the Assembly, but, even so, these will be submitted for ratification to the Assembly at the earliest opportunity.

(c) It is proposed to allow the Assembly full powers to put forward its views before the budget is framed and to discuss the budget itself and certain alterations needed, provided that, at that stage, its equilibrium is not upset. As taxation in the Sudan is imposed by Ordinance, the Assembly will have power to impose or increase taxation when such Ordinances are set before it.

(d) Private Members will be given full facilities for the introduction of Bills subject only to a few limitations and to the leave of the Assembly being obtained for their introduction.

5. As explained in paragraph 2 above, so long as the present regime remains in force, the Governor-General cannot divest himself of the basic powers which he exercises under the 1899 Agreement. Article IV of this Agreement invests him with the power to make laws and thereafter to notify them to the British and Egyptian Governments. To introduce into the new Ordinance a provision for the previous submission of all legislation would therefore be at variance with the existing constitution. Furthermore, it would impose a serious limitation upon the self-governing powers of the Assembly which the Royal Egyptian Government is anxious to increase, and the inevitable delay in the issue of legislation would constitute a grave administrative inconvenience.

6. Until Sudanese of sufficient administrative experience have emerged, it is necessary for the good government of the country to retain seats on the Executive Council for senior members of the administration, but it is hoped that before long Sudanese Ministers will be appointed, and that the Executive Council will gradually evolve into a Council of Ministers. The Ordinance will contain provision for such evolution and in the initial stages will afford training for Sudanese in quasi

Ministerial work. The Sudan Government fully shares the desire of the Royal Egyptian Government to give Sudanese executive powers as soon as possible, and will spare no efforts in hastening the time when substantial power is in their hands.

7. It is true that at present the three Secretaries are British by nationality, but they are Sudan Government servants and in no way responsible to the British Government, and they are being appointed to the Executive Council solely in that capacity, by virtue of the official position which they have achieved through their long service in the Sudan and their knowledge of the people and its problems.

8. "Personal freedom, freedom of opinion, freedom of faith, freedom of meetings, freedom of the press, and the other freedoms without which man cannot be free", are already ensured in the Sudan by law and conditions compare very favourably with those in most other countries in the world. It will furthermore be in the Assembly's power to review the laws under which these freedoms are secured, and to amend them should they feel it necessary. It has already been emphasised in para. 4(a) above, that the Assembly will have full power to question, debate and criticise the Executive actions of the Government. The allegations made in certain quarters about the lack of freedom in the Sudan are illfounded.

9. The recommendations of the Sudan Administration Conference have generally had a favourable reception in the Sudan and it is expected that all save a small minority will take part in the elections for the Assembly. This minority, though invited to take part in the original Conference, refused to do so, and it and the so-called Sudan Delegation do not now represent real public opinion in the Sudan on this matter.

148 FO 371/69209, no 143 — 7 Jan 1948

[Anglo–Egyptian negotiations]: inward telegram no 34 from E A Chapman-Andrews to Sir R Campbell reporting on Sir R Howe's meeting with al-Nuqrashi Pasha

Following personal for Sir R. Campbell from Chapman Andrews.

After Howe had seen Foreign Office telegram No. 22[1] he fell into a more pensive mood of which I took the advantage to remind him that there was an Egyptian angle which the Egyptians were fully entitled to ask to be taken into account. We then glanced together at the preamble to the 1899 agreement,[2] I emphasising that from it we British derived the right "to share—in future working and development—of administration and legislation". I emphasised the word "share" and the ever-present evidence throughout the Sudan of the Egyptian flag flying side by side with our own to prove the continued existence of Egyptian share. I said that while it may be true that there was not a single Sudanese who to-day accepted the 1899 agreement it was also true that many if not most of the Egyptians also professed to want to do away with it in order that they might re-enter into what they regarded as their inheritance. I suggested it was in our British interests to uphold the 1899 agreement as it had been upheld in the 1936 Treaty and in the 1946 protocol. It was from this agreement that

[1] See 147, note.

[2] See Appendix, part I.

the Governor General derived the constitutional powers referred to in the memorandum accompanying his draft note to Egyptian Government on constitutional reform (to which Foreign Office telegram 22 refers). Howe took the point.

2. I ended by suggesting that it was at least doubtful whether the Sudanese were on this matter unamenable to reason and as potentially fanatical as some would have us believe and that if so the question [grp. undec.] resolved itself into a choice between "losing" either the Sudan or Egypt and it was up to us to find a way of keeping both, which I thought could be done if such form of words as we might be able to agree upon with the Egyptians were backed up with the right sort of explanatory propaganda to the Sudanese. It was not as though they were in imminent danger of being taken by Egypt as an Egyptian province. We had got over that difficulty and we knew that Egypt appeared to be now prepared to drop completely their former claim that the Sudan was and must for ever remain an integral part of Egypt. I told him of your talk with Khashaba Pasha and showed him a copy of your despatch reporting on this.[3] He described the latter as "all very unrealistic" but seemed more inclined than he was at the beginning to admit the existence of a legitimate Egyptian point of view.

3. On the following morning Howe saw Nokrashy with whom he stayed over an hour. He told me afterwards that he had presented reply amended in accordance with Foreign Office telegram No. 22 but that after discussing at some length with Nokrashy the whole problem of constitutional reforms he had left also with him memorandum amended in accordance with Foreign Office telegram No. 22 as a separate document in the form of an aide memoire of what he had actually said during conversation.[4] He told me that Nokrashy had not appeared very much concerned about the problem of constitutional reform over which he skated very lightly. What had concerned him was the Sudan Government's attitude towards Egyptian school masters. He had spent an hour trying to get the Governor General to agree to the return of former director Abdel Hadi. The Governor General however had not given way though he might have been inclined to consider it had the Prime Minister not stated that he regarded it as the sacred duty of every Egyptian in the Sudan to propagate his belief in unity of Nile Valley. I asked Howe whether it was regarded as necessarily seditious to do this in the Sudan. Surely there was a political party there whose avowed object was to achieve the unity of Egypt and Sudan. He replied that such speeches as Abdel Hadi had made caused student demonstrations (in favour of unity of the Nile Valley); that demonstrations led to strikes and disorders which it was the duty of Sudan Government to prevent. I said I thought it was most important that a clear distinction should be drawn between sedition and incitement to disorder on the one hand and free expression of political opinion however distasteful such opinion might be to the Government in power on the other hand. He said Nokrashy Pasha professed to refuse to believe there was free expression of political opinion for Egyptians in the Sudan to-day to which I replied one could hardly blame the Egyptians for not knowing what was going on in the Sudan when so

[3] In which Khashaba Pasha proposed that the text of the old Sudan protocol be retained, with a note added to interpret it, but in which he also stated that the right of the Sudanese to choose their future status 'was so obvious both on principle and from a practical point of view, and it was so comparatively far in the future that it did not seem to need mentioning' (despatch no 2 from Campbell to Bevin, 2 Jan 1948, FO 371/69209, no 66).

[4] See 147.

many obstacles were put in the way of their people going there. To this Howe replied that they had a battalion of the Egyptian army and the Director General of the Irrigation Department as well as schoolmasters, who could if they wished keep the Egyptian Government accurately informed. Nevertheless papers this morning stated that the conversation between Howe and the Egyptian Prime Minister was "cordial" and this is confirmed by Quilliam who, waiting in ante room, heard shouts of laughter constantly coming from within.

4. Meanwhile rumour here is rife to the effect that there are fundamental differences between you and Howe about the Sudan and that you were thinking of resigning. I also hear that there are rumours in Khartoum to the effect that there is to be an Egyptian Deputy Governor-General. We here have taken the line that rumour mongers are a nuisance and that for the time being and perhaps for a long time to come there will be no official announcement simply because there is nothing new to be said.

149 FO 371/69192, no 276 8 Jan 1948

[Anglo–Egyptian negotiations]: notes by G L McDermott[1] of an FO meeting to discuss the position of the Sudan in treaty negotiations [Extract]

A meeting was held in Mr. Wright's room on the 8th January, to discuss Egypt and the Sudan. Mr. Wright presided for the first half, and Mr. Lascelles when he had to leave. Sir R. Campbell, Sir R. Howe, Mr. Speaight and Mr. McDermott attended.

The Sudan Government's constitutional proposals

It was agreed that a reply should now be drafted to Nobrasky's [sic] letter enclosing the Egyptian Government's comments. We should assume in reply that their suggestion that all Sudanese legislation should be submitted to the Egyptian Government (our gloss on this should be "to the Co-Domini") could not have been intended to cover routine legislation on internal matters, and that we could not accept a complete abolition of the Governor-General's right of veto, which was his by virtue of the agreements regulating the condominium. We should however go on to say that we understood that the draft ordinance which the Governor-General was about to lay before the Advisory Council, as he had told Nobrasky [sic] Pasha, would go far to meet the Egyptian Government's proposals; and in particular that it would enumerate those subjects on which legislation could not be initiated at all by the Legislature [sic] Assembly and therefore the Governor General's right of veto did not arise—viz. questions affecting the constitution, nationality etc.—and on which the Governor-General consequently had no right of veto. Further, that we understood the Governor-General was about to lay the draft Ordinance before the Advisory Council with the explanation that it was also being submitted to the Co-domini. We would therefore suggest to Nobrasky [sic] that the draft Ordinance should form the subject of Anglo–Egyptian discussions in Cairo. (N.B. In a subsequent discussion on January 9th it was agreed to leave the venue unspecified.) Further details could be worked out in due course.

[1] First secretary, FO, 1948.

The proposed discussions
The Governor-General said that he was anxious to convene the Advisory Council very soon, as its discussion of the draft ordinance was publicly known to have been postponed for some months already. The Sudan Government were of course not bound to accept its findings. It was agreed that there would be no harm in the Advisory Council's being convened, and considering the draft ordinance, provided that His Majesty's Government's reply to Nobrasky [sic] had been sent in i.e. the proposed discussions between the Co-Domini need not actually have begun first though there would be advantage if they could have done so. It was agreed that the discussions would probably have to be merely Anglo–Egyptian, with the possible co-option of (British) experts from the Sudan Government service when required, as although Arbigga [sic: Ashigga] members might be prepared to attend and voice pro-Egyptian sentiments, respectable Independence parties representatives would probably decline to attend meetings which they would feel could only lead to an increase of Egyptian influence in the Sudan. (Sir R. Howe thought it *might* nevertheless be possible to get the Advisory Council to appoint a representative to the discussions.) But the discussions should be useful, if only as an approach to an agreement with the Egyptian Government on Sudanese questions. Unfortunately, a comprehensive agreement probably could not be reached without excessive concessions to the Egyptians.

Increased Egyptian participation in the administration of the Sudan
It was agreed that the Egyptians wanted political as well as technical posts, some of them at the top. (As a debating point, but no more, it could however be pointed out that in the Egyptian Government's comments on the Sudan Government's proposals they did not demand this but only the right to train more Sudanese. At Lake Success, however, Nobrasky [sic] had demanded increased Egyptian participation in the administration). The Governor-General was quite definite that this could not be conceded (e.g. an Egyptian deputy Governor-General, Egyptian members of the proposed Executive Council) because it would conflict with the Sudan Government's pledges regarding Sudanisation and Mr. Attlee's assurances to Saiyid [sic] Abdul-rahman el-Mahdi (and in Parliament)[2] that the present system of administration would not be altered, and would disrupt the administration. But possible concessions in this direction might be:—

(a) the notices published in the English and Egyptian press asking for experts for technical posts under the Sudan Government could in addition be communicated direct to Egyptian government departments;
(b) a joint tripartite commission—British, Egyptian, perhaps under neutral chairmanship—might be appointed by us and the Egyptians (not by UNO because this might let the Soviet bloc in), consisting of independent non-officials, to be in permanent session and render periodic reports to the co-domini on the progress of the Sudan towards self-government, as had been proposed by us in the treaty negotiations and rejected by Sidky; definition of the commission's functions would be necessary;
(c) a similar commission might watch the elections to the proposed Legislative

[2] See 114.

Assembly, so that the Egyptians could not very well claim afterwards that the Assembly was wholly unrepresentative.

The Sudanese question and the treaty
The Governor-General said that the Sudanese would not accept references to 'unity' and/or 'the common crown' at any price: their objections had been strengthened by their impressions of unanimous inter-national support at Lake Success. (Even the British members of the administration would probably resign if such references were inserted). They would not be particularly gratified by a mere cutting out of all reference to 'unity', which they had never acknowledged anyway; even less so if as a counter-concession to the Egyptians we were to cut out, say, all reference to 'self-determination' for the Sudan. But in any case the Egyptians showed no signs of readiness to abandon all reference to 'unity' and/or 'the common crown'; and this the Sudan Government could no longer accept, though H.M.G. could state publicly that they would have no objection to the Sudan's eventually uniting itself with Egypt if it wished to. The Egyptians however would retort that we should take good care that it would not wish to do so when the time came.

The Egyptian Government might agree—as they had proposed during the last negotiations—to shelve the Sudan question on the basis that the 'common crown' was acknowledged. The Governor-General said that the Sudanese would never accept this.

The Egyptian Government would no doubt refuse, as Sidky had done, to accept any arrangements similar to those made under the Statute of Westminster in connexion with Dominion status. The Egyptian government might just conceivably agree to shelve the Sudan question without any stipulation if this were part of an otherwise comprehensive treaty agreeable to them; but not, for instance, as part of an arrangement in which Article 7 of the 1936 treaty was still in force i.e. a scheme such as that recently under consideration in London for the reduction of our forces in Egypt to 1,000 on condition that re-entry rights were guaranteed, etc. We should be faced with the need of finding a way of plausibly explaining away our retreat from our comparatively more favourable attitude in 1946 (the Sidky-Bevin protocol).

There might just be a way round if a reference could be included, in any agreement reached on other matters, to the Sudan questions being already under discussion.

Other suggestions were:—

(a) Mr. Beckett should be asked to find a form of words to get round the difficulty;
(b) a form of words such as 'national community of interests between the inhabitants of the Nile Valley';
(c) a frank approach to King Farouk on the lines that if he wanted a treaty he must make a concession in connexion with the Sudan: it was thought that, although His Majesty was increasingly afraid of the U.S.S.R., he was not yet sufficiently so to give way on this;
(d) a commission of the co-domini plus a neutral to report when the Sudanese were politically mature enough to make a choice, whether the Sudanese really wanted to join Egypt or no;
(e) a UNO commission: this would let the Soviet bloc in; and although some Sudanese wanted such a commission, this was really only in the hope that it would report in favour of complete independence for the Sudan immediately. . . .

150 FO 371/69192, no 255 10 Jan 1948

'Egypt & Sudan': FO minutes of a discussion with Mr Bevin on constitutional reform [Extract]

The *S. of State* had before him the paper on the Sudan constitutional reform question and the draft reply to Amr Pasha. He said he did not disagree with the course of action suggested, but he was anxious to get ahead with the general negotiations with Egypt. If we failed to bring off a settlement before next March he felt that we should probably never bring one off at all. The political situation was boiling up in Palestine, Greece and Germany. The Egyptians were showing increased willingness to reach a settlement, and anxiety over the international situation played a part in this.

Sir O. Sargent pointed out that it was a question of what we could get in the way of a settlement and how much we should have to pay for it. These things might be clearer once the Palestine problem was out of the way and we were safely installed in Cyrenaica.

The *S. of State* did not agree that we should wait. We might not get Cyrenaica, and might lose Egypt also through waiting. He would like to have the bird in the hand *and* the bird in the bush.

Sir O. Sargent observed that the Egyptians wanted a settlement even more than we did, and had been brought to this state largely by our policy of sitting tight.

The *S. of State* repeated that the time to settle was now. Soviet policy might before long become less intolerable to the world in general, and if that happened people would begin once more to run after them. He had discussed the Egyptian problem with the Prime Minister, who agreed with him. As for the price of a settlement, there was no reason to pay anything.

As regards the Sudan, he considered that the line of approach suggested was the right one. We should confine our negotiations in regard to the Egyptian side of the problem to the question of withdrawal of troops. We could not go back to the Bevin–Sidky agreement, and in particular we could not go back to the sovereignty formula in that agreement.

Sir R. Campbell said that the Egyptians undoubtedly wanted that formula to be incorporated in any new agreement about the Sudan. That was one of their two main desiderata. The other was that they should be given at least the appearance of a share in the Administration. The second point was largely a matter of face-saving. What they had actually proposed was that there should be an Egyptian Deputy Governor-General and an increase of Egyptians in the technical branches of the Administration.

The *Secretary of State* said that the course proposed in the paper on constitutional reform was as far as we could go for the present. He was still prepared to go back to the offer he had made to Sidky Pasha, that the Sudan question should be held over while the Egyptian side of the overall settlement was negotiated and got out of the way, and that as regards the Sudan there should be a tripartite supervisory body. In its original form, this body was to have been an "occasional" one, i.e. it would have made an investigation into, and reported on, the state of progress towards self-government every three years or even every five years. He was now quite prepared that it should function continuously once Egypt had agreed to the creation of the

Legislative Assembly. The Assembly would provide the means whereby the Sudanese people could express their point of view. He was not prepared to treat the Sudanese as a subordinate people on whom the wishes of the British Co-Dominus could simply be imposed, and he did not see why the Egyptians should claim the right to do so either.

Sir R. Howe agreed.

Sir R. Campbell thought that the Egyptians might also agree, but that they would insist, in any formal treaty, on a re-statement of the formula about unity with Egypt under the common crown.

The *S. of State* said that he could not go back to that. The programme should be as follows:

First, the Legislative Assembly should be created, thus giving the Sudanese a voice in their own affairs;

Second, we should create a tripartite body (with the Sudan as a member on an equal footing) to supervise the development of the Sudan towards self-government and to report at intervals to the Co-Domini;

Third, large-scale economic development schemes for the Sudan should be set in train, again on a tripartite basis. The Egyptians were rich—the sterling balances would have to be released by gradual stages—and their money would come in useful for such schemes;

Fourth, the Sudan should be brought into the general scheme of defence for Egypt and the Middle East as a whole. (In the initial stages the member for the Sudan on the Joint Defence Board would have to be a representative of the Governor-General and British, as no Sudanese of sufficient calibre was available, but this need not be so indefinitely—the Sudan, like Ceylon, would develop gradually towards Commonwealth status). This last point in the programme would provide a guarantee of Egypt's own security and would thus give her far more than any formula about the common crown.

As regards the creation of the tripartite body mentioned in the second item above, this would place Egypt in a minority in so far as the British and Sudanese members were likely to work together, and we should have to guarantee that her interests in the Nile waters and in economic matters generally were not prejudiced.

The Secretary of State reiterated that he could not go back to the formula regarding the Sudan in the Bevin–Sidky Agreement. Egyptian misrepresentations had rendered this quite impossible. The creation of the Legislative Assembly would put the Sudan on a proper footing as regards representation, and henceforth she must be treated as an equal. Only so could he defend our policy before Parliament and the United Nations.

As regards immediate tactics –

Sir R. Campbell thought that the Egyptians might regard the exchange of views between the Co-Domini on the question of constitutional reform as providing the means of exploring the wider problem, and that, once discussions on the subsidiary question had been started, they might be prepared to negotiate an agreement on the Egyptian side of the problem, for it could then be said that negotiations concerning the Sudan "were in progress". But they would certainly try to get us committed at this point to a reaffirmation of the "common crown" formula.

The *S. of State* ruled this out: King Farouk and the Egyptian Government had better be told frankly at the outset that there could be no going back to this formula.

His plan, as outlined above, would benefit both Egypt and the Sudan. To the former it would give economic and military advantages; to the latter, an equality of status such as the Bevin-Sidky Agreement had not provided. He was anxious to get the whole matter out of the hands of the politicians and into the hands of fair-minded people.

Sir O. Sargent asked for confirmation that the Secretary of State approved the Foreign Office plan regarding the Sudan constitutional reform question, i.e. that the Governor-General should go ahead with the reform notwithstanding Egyptian objections.

The *S. of State* confirmed this. It was brought out in the discussion that, on the basis of the programme elaborated in our talks with Sir R. Campbell and Sir R. Howe we should in fact be giving the Egyptians the opportunity to comment on the draft ordinance, and that meanwhile the Governor-General would not promulgate the reform scheme. . . .

151 FO 371/69155, no 283 15 Jan 1948

[Constitutional Reform]: letter from D W Lascelles (for Mr Attlee) to Abd al-Fattah Amr, responding to Egyptian criticisms of the Sudan Administration Conference[1]

I have the honour to refer to Your Excellency's Note No. 4179/8–1/14 of the 25th November last,[2] in which you were good enough to acquaint me with the views of the Egyptian Government regarding the administrative measures which the Governor-General of the Sudan proposed to take in order to give effect to the recommendations of the Sudan Administration Conference, and with which you enclosed a memorandum enumerating the points on which your Government considered that the proposed measures should be modified.

2. With regard to the third paragraph of the Egyptian Government's communication as quoted by Your Excellency, I need only say here that the views of His Majesty's Government regarding the continued validity of the Condominium Agreements are also on record and were expounded to the Security Council.

3. Sir Robert Howe informs me that he has already explained to the Egyptian Prime Minister the views of the Sudan Government on the various points raised in the Egyptian memorandum,[3] and has assured His Excellency that a number of these points will be covered by the ordinance enacting the administrative reforms which will shortly be submitted in draft form to the two Co-Domini. I understand that the draft ordinance will also be laid before the Advisory Council for the Northern Sudan at its session next month, but that it will be made clear to the Council if necessary that the views of the Co-Domini on this ordinance are still outstanding. In order that the achievement of this eagerly-awaited step towards Sudanese self-government should not be unduly delayed, His Majesty's Government consider it important that the Co-Domini should seek to reach agreement at an early date on any amendments which they may jointly consider it desirable that the Governor-General should introduce into the ordinance so as to ensure that its provisions are truly in the

---

[1] This letter is based on a draft provided by Campbell, as amended following the discussion minuted in 150, and signed by Lascelles on Attlee's behalf.

[2] See 141.

[3] See 147.

interests of the Sudanese people and that it affords them the maximum degree of self-government consistent with their present stage of development. His Majesty's Government therefore proposes that as soon as they receive the text of the proposed ordinance the two Governments should appoint representatives to meet forthwith, in a place to be determined later, for the purpose of examining together its provisions, in consultation with technical experts of the Sudan Government and taking into consideration representative Sudanese opinion, and of thereafter making recommendations to the Co-Domini. His Majesty's Government suggest that these representatives should be non-official persons who are recognised authorities on constitutional practice. In order that no time may be lost, it is suggested that Sir Ronald Campbell should discuss with the Egyptian Government on his return to Cairo the detailed procedure for the appointment of these British and Egyptian representatives and for the hearing of evidence.

4. As the Egyptian Government are aware, His Majesty's Government have already signified to the Governor-General their approval of the general principles of the proposed reforms as notified to the Co-Domini. Pending receipt of the text of the ordinance, they do not intend to comment in detail on all the points raised in the Egyptian memorandum. They consider it expedient, nevertheless, to record their view on the contention in paragraph 5 of the memorandum that the Governor-General should obtain the prior consent of the Co-Domini before approving or rejecting the legislation passed by the Legislative Assembly and the Executive Council. His Majesty's Government assume that it is not the intention of the Egyptian Government to seek to curtail the Governor-General's executive powers for the enactment of legislation concerning only the internal affairs of the Sudan, since clearly this would so limit his authority as to make it impossible for him adequately to fulfil his obligations towards the Co-Domini for the good administration of the Sudan. On the other hand His Majesty's Government recognise that, by virtue of the terms of the Condominium Agreement of January 19th, 1899, the Governor-General cannot, without the consent of the Co-Domini, promulgate legislation materially affecting the constitution or international status of the Sudan. They understand that a definition concerning this limitation of his powers will be included in the text of the ordinance which will in fact contain a list of reserved subjects. For the rest, this question could naturally be included if necessary amongst those to be examined by the British and Egyptian representatives appointed as proposed in paragraph 3 above.

152 FO 371/69235, no 975 5 Feb 1948

'Note on Sudan railways strike January 26th–29th, 1948': note by the Civil Secretary's Office, Khartoum

[At the end of the first rail strike in August 1947 (summarised below), the civil secretary noted, 'the settlement of the Railway Strike has meant the establishment of what is virtually a Trade Union amongst good authority employees who have little or no idea of the method of running the Union. Furthermore we have no Trade Union legislation on the statute books' (inward telegram no 1688 from Robertson to the Sudan agent, London (5 Aug 1947). He requested that someone with trade union experience be sent out to advise both the Atbara workers on the running of their committee and the government in drafting its trade union legislation. Before such an adviser could be sent out, however, a further confrontation over pay began.]

Background

1. In settlement of the Railway strike in July, 1947 it was agreed between the Management and Workers that there should be set up representative Departmental Committees in each of the five departments, and a Workers' Affairs Association, composed of three elected representatives from each of the Departmental Committees. This Association would represent the whole body of railway employees and would meet from time to time jointly with the Management.

2. The first such meeting was held in October, when a number of demands were presented by the Workers' Affairs Association to the Management for transmission to the Central Government. The principal of these demands were:—

(1) A general increase in non-classified workmen's wages varying between 50% for lower categories and 25% for higher, the average increase being 40%.
(2) A general increase in the amount of annual leave for all employees.
(3) A large extension of the privilege of second class travel on railways.
(4) A reduction of working hours from 8 to 6½ hours daily.
(5) The revision of arrangements for compensation in case of accidents.
(6) The revision of scales of payment for overtime.

The Association requested that the reply of the Central Government should be given within 20 days.

3. In an interim reply the Financial Secretary pointed out that the increases of pay demanded for some 15,000 workers would cost LE.470,000 a year in the Railways alone, that similar increases to other Government employees would be inevitable and that the total additional cost might well be in the neighbourhood of LE. 1 million a year, without reckoning the possible effect on the rates of pay of classified officials. Such an increase would be beyond the financial resources of the country and could not be justified.

Full and careful consideration of the Association's demands was promised but no undertaking could be given to reply finally within the time stipulated.

4. The Workers' Affairs Association, in a further letter, challenged the argument that the financial resources were inadequate to meet the additional cost, elaborated its demands and submitted a number of individual budgets, which were, however, clearly inaccurate and inconsistent in many respects.

5. On 31st December, the Financial Secretary sent a further reply. While maintaining that the burden to the whole country of a general increase in wages could not be justified, he agreed to increase forthwith the minimum basic starting rate of wage to 180 PT. per month, which, with cost of living allowance added, ensured that no adult male worker could earn less than 306 PT. per month. He announced the setting up of an independent Committee to review, against the conditions in other types of employment, the findings of a Committee already set up by the General Manager to investigate the scales of pay of all railway employees: it was hoped that the independent Committee would complete its work by the end of February. He also undertook to give sympathetic consideration to various alleged grievances about leave, travel privileges, working hours, compensation for injuries and rates of pay for overtime.

The strike.

6. The Financial Secretary's letter of 31st December, did not satisfy the Workers' Affairs Association and the question of a strike in token of their dissatisfaction was

raised. During the first three weeks of January rumour on the subject was rife and there was great activity amongst the workers on the part of a few of the leaders. The chief of these are Suleiman Musa, the President of the Association and a chargeman in the Mechanical Department, Tayed El Hassan, a pattern maker and Gasim el Amin, an electrician, both also in the Mechanical department. The two latter are the most powerful amongst the Workers' leaders. There is reason to believe that the two religious leaders, Sayed Ali el Mirghani and Sayed Abdel Rahman el Mahdi, used their influence during this period against the proposal to strike, and there is no evidence that the political parties encouraged the workers to strike.

7. There was considerable uncertainty as to whether a strike would be called, and, if it was, to what extent the workers would respond. However, on 22nd January, the Workers' Affairs Association posted notices in Atbara and at other main railway centres calling on all employees to strike for three days from the morning of 26th January. At the same time, a letter was sent to the Governor-General giving the reasons for the strike and stating that if their demands are not met in full by the end of February, another stand will be made and "a different attitude" adopted. It was stated that copies of this letter had been sent to the Prime Ministers of Great Britain and Egypt.

The strike was almost fully effective among employees and they were joined by a number of classified staff. All railway traffic was brought to a standstill and power stations in Atbara and Port Sudan were affected.

There was no picketting [sic] and there was little evidence of any intimidation of workers, and although many of them were doubtless bewildered as to the object of the strike there can be no doubt about their solidarity with the Workers' Affairs Association.

The strike ended punctually on the morning of 29th January, and traffic was at once resumed.

9. [sic] The strike was notable for the following features:—

(a) there was no disorderliness of any kind.

(b) there was no evidence of intervention or influence on the part of the political parties.

(c) the organisation was very much more effective than would normally be expected: this suggests that the organisers may have been supported by political agencies outside the Sudan, but there is as yet no definite evidence of this.

10. The Public and the local press were restrained in their expressions of opinion. While inclined to deprecate the use of the strike weapon as a threat to the prosperity of the country, they showed some sympathy with the workers in their desire to improve their conditions. There was however little attempt to relate these demands to the general financial position of the country.

The aftermath

11. The strike has proved the present power of the leaders of the Workers' Affairs Association to influence the whole body of railway employees. The threat, mentioned in para. 7 of a further and possibly less peaceful strike at the end of February must therefore be taken seriously.

12. All classified officials who joined the strike are to be dealt with and fined under the Officials' Discipline Ordinance. All employees will lost [sic] their pay for

the days not worked. Legally all the strikers could be prosecuted under Section 143 of the Sudan Penal Code. It has, however, been decided not to take such action on this occasion, but to take steps to ensure that in future every worker will be aware of the legal position regarding strikes and of the penalties to which strikers are liable.

13. Everything possible will be done to publicise the Sudan Government's point of view in this dispute and the independent committee mentioned in para. 5 will begin work as soon as possible. Should a further strike occur early in March, the issues will thus be clear cut and there will be no doubt in the minds of the workers and their leaders as to the legal position. The Government would then have no hesitation in taking action to break the strike.

14. In the meantime, all essential preparations to meet the possibility of another strike will be made.

153 FO 371/69156, no 1247 17 Feb 1948

'Executive Council and Legislative Assembly Ordinance': explanatory note by Civil Secretary's Office, Khartoum. *Minute* by G L McDermott

The draft of the Ordinance, which will be considered at the eighth session of the Advisory Council, is submitted for the consideration of Members, together with the relevant correspondence between the British and Egyptian Governments.

In most respects the Ordinance follows fairly closely the lines recommended by the Sudan Administration Conference whose report was debated by the Council at its seventh session, but there are some important differences.

The most important difference is that whereas the Conference said (section 8 of the report) "we have tried to confine our recommendations to the next steps which should be taken in any particular function of government", the Government, in preparing the legislation, has looked much further ahead. At present there is no political machinery for working a democratic form of self-government but it must be brought into existence. The Ordinance is designed to allow for, and to encourage, the progressive development of self-governing institutions, stopping short only at the final step, which is the transfer of the ultimate responsibility from the Governor-General to the elected representatives of the people. When that stage is reached a new constitution will of course be required.

The advantages of such a method of approach are many. It enables the country to feel its way forward, to try experiments, to progress rapidly in directions where things go well undelayed because in another direction things are proving more difficult. The speed of advance is governed, not by a series of paper constitutions but by the availability of men capable of filling adequately the posts to be created, the ability of Sudanese to assume genuine, as opposed to nominal, responsibility and the degree of cooperation of all concerned. The situation will, in fact, be under continuous review and advances will not have to await the laborious preparation of fresh legislation.

It will be noticed, for instance, that the Ordinance provides for the appointment of fully responsible Ministers. It is not proposed to appoint Ministers at the outset, as it is intended that potential Ministers should first gain experience and prove themselves as Under Secretaries. It will not necessarily be that the holder of any

Under Secretaryship will himself later be appointed a Minister—in fact if he is a Government Servant he cannot be, unless he resigns to take up a political career—but experience of the working of the post will be of value when someone who is a potential Minister is available.

For this reason the Government has not accepted the recommendation of the Sudan Administration Conference that Under Secretaries should be chosen by the Assembly. If he is to develop into a Minister the Under Secretary must be appointed in the same way as a Minister, that is to say by the Government. No Prime Minister under any constitution would consent to have his Ministers chosen for him, and in practice such an arrangement could not possibly work. The Under Secretary would be in an entirely false position and the experiment would lead nowhere.

The Assembly as now proposed is rather larger than the body suggested by the Conference. The elected members have been increased from 60 to 65 in order to fit the proposed constituencies. There are still 10 nominated members but there is also provision that all members of the Council and all Under Secretaries should, if not already elected or nominated, be ex-officio members, so that the Assembly will in practice number about 90.

This virtually raises the proportion of nominated members above that recommended by the Conference, and one reason for this is the provisional decision not to allow Government Servants to stand for election. If there were no nominations apart from the Under Secretaries etc. the largest and most influential section of educated opinion would be barred from the Assembly except as holders of office.

The vexed question of the part to be played by Government Servants under this Ordinance has, subject to Administrative Regulations, been provisionally decided thus. In general they are barred from taking part, but as a temporary measure the Governor-General may make exceptions. The position will then be that a Government Servant:—

1. cannot be a Minister,
2. can be an Under Secretary, a member of the Council or a *nominated* member of the Assembly, provided that if he holds one of the offices in schedule I he shall cease to exercise the functions of that office,
3. cannot stand for *election* to the Assembly.

The electoral system is of great importance and is the subject of a separate note as it is one on which the Government wishes to take the advice of the Council.

Various criticisms have been levelled at the proposals, in particular it has been said that the over-riding power of the Governor-General reduces the Assembly to a consultative body with no more power than the Advisory Council. This is very far from being the case, as is explained in the Aide Memoire handed by the Governor-General to the President of the Council of Ministers para 4(a), and its power and responsibility in day-to-day government is virtually unaffected by the fact that an over-riding power exists. It should be noted that the provisions with regard to the budget give the Assembly considerably wider powers than were proposed by the Conference, while the provisions suggested by them for exempting from the scrutiny of the Assembly legislation of minor importance (section 32(a) of the Report) have been rejected.

With regard to the Governor-General's powers, apart altogether from the legal necessity of retaining the powers granted to him under the 1899 agreement so long as that agreement remains in force, it is essential that the ultimate power lies in the same hands as the ultimate responsibility.

The proposal as a whole provides a very real administrative advance from the beginning, with provision for steady progress on the road to self-government, a progress the speed of which depends on many unpredictable factors, but chiefly on the extent to which the members of the Assembly and Council, the office holders and the public at large cooperate wholeheartedly in working it.

Minute on 153

As is stated in the explanatory note, the draft Ordinance goes a good deal further than the proposals of the Sudan Administration conference, and this is all to the good. The draft Ordinance has been drawn up with the advice of several distinguished British experts and this is hardly the place to criticise its form in detail ... A reasonable critic would, I think, say that it is on the whole a good compromise between the autocratic system with a powerful Governor-General at its head, which will still be essential for the Sudan for some years to come, and the institution of representative government in its first stages.

G.L.M.
23.2.48

154 FO 371/69156, no 1696 11 Mar 1948

[Constitutional reform]: letter from G G Fitzmaurice[1] to Sir H Shawcross[2] asking advice on whether the Sudan government can unilaterally introduce constitutional reforms [Extract]

Minute by W E Beckett

... 2. The point at issue is, briefly, whether the Governor-General of the Sudan has, in the last resort, the power to introduce certain constitutional reforms even though one of the two condominium Powers (namely ourselves and Egypt) objects to, or anyhow refuses to give its assent to, these reforms. . . .

19. The specific points on which we should be grateful for your advice might be put as follows:—

(1) Could it, with reasonable prospects of success, be contended that even if the Condominium Agreement must be interpreted as precluding any substantial change in the powers of the Governor-General without the prior assent of the two Condominium Powers, nevertheless the present draft Ordinance is not in fact inconsistent with the powers of the Governor-General as laid down by that Agreement, and does not involve any fundamental departure from the Agreement.
(2) Assuming the answer to the first question to be in the affirmative, could the Egyptians successfully argue that the proposals are nevertheless of a

[1] 2nd legal adviser, FO. [2] Attorney-general.

constitutional character relating to the Governor-General's powers and that, in accordance with a tacitly accepted practice, such proposals must be submitted to the condominium Powers for their prior assent. It may be that, on the basis of the correspondence (see for instance enclosures 2 and 5), we ourselves are committed to that view, but it is not so certain that the Governor-General is. Could he argue that there is a practice by which constitutional proposals are submitted to the condominium Powers in advance of and not merely simultaneously with promulgation, but that the object of this is merely to enable them to comment, and that it does not in the last resort affect his power to promulgate his proposals as law after considering their comments. The nearest any Governor-General seems to have got to committing himself in this matter was a rather unfortunate statement by the Acting Governor-General in communicating the recommendations of the Sudan Administration conference to the Egyptians (vide paragraph 9 above) that the eventual legislation embodying these recommendations would be submitted to the condominium Governments "for their approval" (copy enclosed as Enclosure 8); but in fact when the Ordinance was eventually submitted it was simply "submitted" and nothing was said about assent or approval.

(3) If the answer to the first question is in the negative, could it be successfully contended that, the Condominium Agreement is to be interpreted as not forbidding or rendering *ultra vires* a divestment or delegation on the part of the Governor-General of some of his legislative powers.

(4) If the answer to the preceding question is in the negative and it has to be accepted that the Condominium Agreement, taken by itself, does not permit of such action by the Governor-General without the consent of the condominium Powers, could it be argued that the Egyptian Government *have in fact consented* at any rate to the *principle* of a delegation of powers on the part of the Governor-General, so that, although they may retain the right to comment on his proposals, they cannot in the last resort block them on the ground that they do not go far enough. Alternatively are they, as it were, now stopped from alleging that a delegation of powers is in principle inconsistent with the Condominium Agreement.

Minute on 154

This question was discussed this afternoon at the House of Commons with the Attorney-General. The Governor-General, Mr. Sandars from the Sudan, Mr. Chapman-Andrews from Cairo, Mr. Michael Wright and myself were present.

The Attorney-General stated that his view was that the Governor-General had no right to enact this ordinance without the assent of the two co-domini, but that he would reply in writing to Mr. Fitzmaurice's letter. The view expressed by the Attorney-General was the same as that I had myself tentatively expressed at an informal meeting in my room this morning. . . .

W.E.B.
16.3.48

155 FO 371/69157, no 1773 11 Mar 1948

[Constitutional reform]: letter (reply) from A Shawqi, chargé d'affaires, Egyptian embassy, to Mr Bevin, communicating the text of the Egyptian government's rejection of the Legislative Assembly and Executive Council Ordinance [Extract]

I am instructed by His Excellency the President of the Council of Ministers to make to you, on behalf of the Royal Egyptian Government, the following communication:

"1. I have received Your Excellency's letter dated 15th January, 1948[1] in which you proposed that the Egyptian and British Governments should appoint representatives to meet forthwith, in a place to be determined later, for the purpose of examining the provisions of the draft ordinance enacting the reforms proposed for the closer association of the Sudanese with the Central Administration of the Sudan.

2. Sir Robert Howe, Governor-General of the Sudan came to see me in Cairo on his way to London and handed me a letter dated 5th January, 1948,[2] in which he referred to the modifications suggested by the Egyptian Government in connection with these reforms and in which he pointed out that the Ordinance he is preparing and which he hopes to submit to me in draft "will meet most of the modifications suggested." I was therefore astonished, on receiving the project dated 17th February, 1948,[3] to find that none of the modifications suggested was included in the draft Ordinance.

3. The Egyptian Government wish to call attention to the fact that they have already explained that they consented to participate in these reforms—while fully maintaining their position which had been clearly defined before the Security Council namely the necessity of terminating the existing regime in the Sudan—only because they desired that the delay in settling the Anglo-Egyptian dispute will not retard the progress of the Sudanese on the road to self-government. The Egyptian Government, have, therefore, noted that the modifications they have asked to introduce into the proposed regime were such as to provide for the Sudanese effective steps on the road to self-government; but the project, as already pointed out, fails to achieve that purpose. . . .[4]

10. The essential object envisaged by the modifications which the Egyptian Government wished to introduce into the proposed regime is that it should constitute—both in its basic principles and objectives—a transitional regime lasting no more than three years during which the Sudanese may be trained in self-government through the assumption of certain key posts and through shouldering a part of the responsibilities of government helped along by a few Egyptians while Sudanese public opinion representing the elite of freely elected Sudanese who are truly representative of their country exercise supervision over them. Thus they will all effectively co-operate in directing government affairs until the transition period has expired, on which the Sudanese shall take over the full responsibilities of administration together with all government posts under the common Crown and within the unity of the Nile Valley.

---

[1] See 151.

[2] See 147, note.

[3] See 153.

[4] Paragraphs 4–9 restate the criticisms in 141.

We find, however, that the project fulfils none of these. Indeed, it tends, in toto and in detail, to extend the Governor-General's authority farther afield and stretch it even beyond the provisions of the 1899 Agreement; also it surrounds the Governor-General with mere formal bodies, without real power and bereft of any authority to decide on any matter. Moreover, the project has deliberately removed Egyptians from all touch with Sudanese affairs and excluded them from shouldering any responsibility as if they were complete strangers who care nothing about the Sudan. Indeed the project came to no more than to create certain posts of limited authority to be given to a number of Sudanese chosen by the Governor-General. Thus the project falls lamentably short of the desired reforms as envisaged by our proposals.

11. The Egyptian Government have, furthermore, noted that it can be elicited from the preamble of the draft Ordinance that the Governor-General of the Sudan in Council, by virtue of the powers vested in him by the 1899 Agreement, may enact the proposed regime. Doubtless this is absolutely wrong for it is obvious that the Governor-General has no authority in this respect.

In as much as it is certain that the 1899 Agreement does not create any separate international status for the Sudan as distinct from that of Egypt, it is also certain that this Agreement does not permit the Governor-General taking any measure affecting the administrative regime or legal status of the Sudan.

12. It may be seen from the above that the project in question does not fulfil the principles enunciated by the Egyptian Government and does not eliminate the defects pointed out by them, nor does it include the essential modifications without which the Egyptian Government, as clearly stated before, cannot agree to the recommendations. On the contrary the project shows a definite tendency in certain provisions towards restricting the recommendations of the Conference, small though they may have been, and aims at extending the Governor-General's authority even rendering it absolute.

13. The Egyptian Government wish to place on record in this connection that while they are anxious that the Sudanese should be accorded the maximum possible share of self-government preparatory to their assumption in the near future of full responsibility, the project submitted by the Sudan Government does not provide for the Sudanese effective steps on the road to self-government.

14. The Egyptian Government cannot therefore, find in the proposed draft a suitable basis for discussion. They cannot concede to the request made by the British Government of calling together representatives of both Governments for the purpose of examining the provisions of this project. The meeting of representatives will not be productive—as already pointed out in our communication of 1st March—unless the principles enunciated by the Egyptian Government are recognised by the British Government.

Finally the Egyptian Government wish to make it clear that their participation in drawing up this provisional regime must not be taken to mean an acceptance of the existing regime in the Sudan but on the contrary they fully maintain their viewpoint of the necessity of terminating this regime."

156 FO 371/69193, 1872 12 Mar 1948

'Egypt and Sudan': FO note of a meeting between Mr Bevin and Sir R Howe[1] [Extract]

[Other events in the Middle East (notably in Palestine) continued to press in on the FO throughout the controversy over constitutional reform in the Sudan, leading Campbell to observe, 'a fundamental difficulty which confronts us when we tackle this problem is that Egypt is affected by events throughout the Arabic speaking world including the Sudan whereas the Sudan itself remains largely unconcerned by outside happenings. From the point of view of the Sudan Government it is a comparatively simple problem of administration which has to be solved. Their purpose is to ensure that solution reached is the best from the point of view of good administration and helping the Sudan to achieve self-government. It is not their business to worry about the effect on our position in Egypt and still less about the effect elsewhere in the Middle East. His Majesty's Government however have to bear these wider considerations in mind, for what happens in the Sudan is a vital factor in Anglo–Egyptian relations and these in turn affect our relations with every other Middle Eastern State. In fact position at present seems that we cannot settle with Egypt without some agreement on Sudan and that we cannot settle our position in the Middle East (satisfactorily at least) without Egypt' (inward telegram no 315 from Campbell to FO, 5 Mar 1948, FO 371/69156, no 1618). 'We thus have the usual double deadlock: between the Co-Domini, & between Cairo & Khartoum', McDermott minuted. 'The only hope seems to me to discuss these matters personally with the Gov.-Gen. & Mr. Chapman-Andrews later this week' (minute, McDermott, 8 Mar 1948, *ibid*). Before that meeting could take place the Advisory Council accepted the draft ordinance in principle, 8 Mar, and the Egyptian note (see 155) was received.]

The Secretary of State said that he was very much concerned about the Sudan question. Whatever suggestions he put to the Egyptians they turned down and as he had told the Egyptian Ambassador, he had had enough of it. He did not see how we could make any progress with King Farouk or Nokrashy. Nokrashy was hopeless. As regards the ordinance, he would welcome information on the question of timing.

Sir R. Howe said that there was no fixed date for the promulgation of the ordinance but the Northern Advisory Council had pressed the Sudan Government to promulgate soon. He could possibly hold it up for one month. In the answer to the Secretary of State's question, he explained that the Northern Advisory Council consisted entirely of Sudanese except for the Chairman who was the Civil Secretary and the British nominated member.

Mr. Chapman-Andrews said that the Egyptians claimed that it was a packed assembly.

Sir R. Howe explained in detail how the members of the Northern Advisory Council were freely appointed by the Provincial Councils, consisting entirely of Sudanese and how in the last resort the system was based on free elections in accordance with old tribal customs except that in the towns there were direct elections of members of the Council. In the towns, everybody paying six Egyptian pounds a year in rent was qualified to vote, and this covered a very large proportion. The Egyptians appeared to want direct elections everywhere.

The Secretary of State commented that the Egyptians no doubt wanted elections as corrupt as their own.

Sir R. Howe pointed out that the Sudan Government had offered to allow a supervisory body, including Egyptians, to observe the elections.

---

[1] Those also present included: G E R Sandars, M R Wright, E A Chapman-Andrews, F K Roberts, D W Lascelles, and G L McDermott.

The Secretary of State emphasised the importance of this point.

Sir R. Howe explained that the draft ordinance had been given to the members of the Council over a fortnight before the Council meeting of March 3rd; they had discussed it for four days in assembly; and they had proposed various amendments which would be incorporated in the ordinance. He said that copies of the ordinance as amended would be sent to the codomini.

Mr. Chapman-Andrews said that the Egyptians claimed that the text of the draft ordinance which was known to be unsatisfactory to them had been deliberately withheld from them while we tried to get them to negotiate an agreement on strategic questions etc.

Sir R. Howe denied that there had been any such trickery. The memorandum which he had given to Nokrashy on January 5th[2] had explained in detail the extent to which the Egyptian suggestions would be met in the draft ordinance.

Mr. Chapman-Andrews thought that there was room for doubt as to how far the draft ordinance really went to meet the Egyptian suggestions and indeed his impression was that it did not go very far. But admittedly, many of the Egyptian points which had not been met were the more unreasonable ones such as the insistence on the prior submission of all legislation to the codomini.

Mr. Lascelles pointed out that H.M.G. too had made it clear that as a codominus they could not accept this point.

The Secretary of State pointed out the Egyptian note just received[3] again insisted on Egyptian sovereignty over the Sudan.

Mr. Chapman-Andrews admitted that this was contrary to the idea discussed with the Egyptians that this issue should be shelved.

Sir R. Howe showed the Secretary of State a detailed list of the Egyptian suggestions with an account of the extent to which each one had been met in the draft ordinance. He suggested that they had been met to a very great extent.

Mr. Chapman-Andrews said that the crux of the matter was that the Egyptians felt that they should be treated as a codominus in practice, e.g. over questions such as representation in the Executive Council, which would enable them to play a real part in guiding the Sudanese.

The Secretary of State said that matters would be different if we were dealing in Egypt with a decent government which really wanted to work with us. Three years had passed since the scheme for democratization in the Sudan had first been drafted, and this was a long time. The House of Commons would be asking him questions. The Egyptian note which had just been received was complet[e]ly unhelpful.

Mr. Roberts said that the Minister of State had asked him to make the point that any concessions to the Egyptians at the expense of the Sudanese would be badly received by the House of Commons.

The Secretary of State thought that as soon as there was a reasonable government in Egypt matters would improve. The objections raised by the present Egyptian Government were merely designed to prevent any progress. They were well aware that the Sudanese were not yet ready for self-government. On the supposition that there were a reasonable government in Egypt, what would be necessary to bring about an agreement?

---

[2] See 147.

[3] See 155.

Mr. Chapman-Andrews thought that even with the present Egyptian Government, we should try one last offer: we should put it to them that if they would accept the ordinance, two Egyptians should have places on the Executive Council. He considered that Nokrashy was bound to go if we rejected the latest Egyptian note.

The Secretary of State said that we should certainly not accept its suggestions. But was not King Farouk just as bad as Nokrashy over this question?

Mr. Chapman-Andrews thought not. He thought that King Farouk was as sick of Nokrashy as was the Secretary of State himself. He thought that for instance Abdul Hadi[4] might form a government and would be better than Nokrashy. The King's representative had told the Embassy that the sovereignty issue could be shelved provided that the Egyptians could have a share in the government of the Sudan, as was their right under the condominium. He suggested that in addition we might repeat the offer of the proposed tripartite Supervisory Commission.

Sir R. Howe agreed.

Mr. Chapman-Andrews was not hopeful that the Egyptians could be persuaded to accept this bargain.

The Secretary of State said that he was not prepared to do any persuading. The Egyptian Government had recently behaved almost like an enemy government, for instance in the influence they had exerted on the other Arab Governments in connection with treaty questions. He himself had been very patient and had even gone to the Anglo–Egyptian Society's dinner in unpleasant circumstances. If there were a chance of the Egyptians accepting the ordinance on the proposed terms, he would advise the Governor-General to agree on the two points mentioned. He did not proposed to go further than this.

Sir R. Howe said that some Sudanese in the Northern Advisory Council had expressed the view that they would not object to the inclusion in the Executive Council of Egyptians already in the Sudan service. After some discussion by the meeting as to whether this would be preferable to the inclusion of two Egyptian outsiders or not the conclusion was reached that the Governor-General might appoint, for instance, the Egyptian Director General of Irrigation (who was, on occasions, already co-opted on the Governor-General's Council) and the Egyptian Town Planning Expert.

The Secretary of State said that he was not prepared to give way to the Egyptians any more or to make any new offers. But if the Embassy, in conversation with the Egyptian authorities, could put across the proposed bargain, then the Embassy could agree to put it up to H.M.G. in the knowledge that it would be accepted by them and by the Governor-General. The Egyptian Government was one of several which appeared to think that Britain was down and out and could be harassed with impunity and the Secretary of State was not prepared to put up with this any longer.

Mr. Chapman-Andrews said that a principal Egyptian complaint was that there was a date in the ordinance (he thought, June 30th) by which certain nominations were to be made and that this looked to the Egyptians like an ultimatum. In reply to a question by the Secretary of State, he said that he thought it would take two or three weeks to see whether the new proposal would be accepted by the Egyptians.

---

[2] Foreign minister in Sidqi's government.

The Secretary of State said that this would be satisfactorily rapid, particularly if it implied that Nokrashy would be out of power by that time. He did not want to run the risk of being taken to the Security Council before we had given up the Palestine Mandate i.e. May 15th. He would like the Governor-General to fit in with this timing. Egypt would have other matters to worry about after May 15th.

Mr. Chapman-Andrews did not think that the Egyptian Government were likely to go back to the Security Council on the Sudan issue on which they had met with little success last time.

The Secretary of State said that nevertheless the Soviet Government might encourage them to do so. He did not want to delay the ordinance much beyond May 15th.

Sir R. Howe said that he might be under great pressure by the Sudanese to promulgate before that date.

The Secretary of State said that the ordinance should in any case be held up for three weeks at the end of which we could see how matters had developed in Egypt and whether for instance Nokrashy had gone. There was of course no question of reviving the offer of an Anglo–Egyptian Committee to consider the ordinance since the Egyptian Government had turned it down.

Mr. Chapman-Andrews said that the Embassy would do their best but might well fail.

The Secretary of State said that it would be a shock to him if they succeeded.

Sir R. Howe specified that the Tripartite Committee, which was to be mentioned in the new offer to the Egyptians was the one first mooted two years ago and again mentioned in the Secretary of State's Four-Point Programme.[5]

Mr. Chapman-Andrews thought that the Egyptian Government might take the question to the Hague Court though, as he had said, probably not to the Security Council. He suggested that the opinion of the Attorney General for which the Foreign Office had asked,[6] should be awaited.

The Secretary of State did not think that the Egyptian Government would take the matter to the Hague court. If they did the ordinance could still be put into force provisionally.

Mr. Lascelles suggested that the Foreign Office could help the Governor General to find reasons for delay by informing him, when they received the ordinance, that while they regarded it favourably in a general sense, they required some time to consider it in detail.

Sir R. Howe said in answer to a question by the Secretary of State that if it had been a question of going straight ahead in accordance with normal procedure he would expect to be promulgating the ordinance in about one month from now.

The Secretary of State said that the Governor General should not commit himself definitely to promulgation in a month; in about three weeks' time, we should be able to see the situation more clearly. . . .[7]

---

[5] See 150.

[6] See 154.

[7] For the remainder of the document, concerning the defence treaty, see BDEEP series B, vol 4, J Kent, ed, *Egypt and the defence of the Middle East*, part 1, 115.

157 FO 371/69157, no 1963 17 Mar 1948

[Constitutional reform]: letter (reply) from Sir H Shawcross to W E Beckett concerning restrictions on the governor-general's ability to institute constitutional reform under the condominium agreement

In the light of our consultation on Tuesday,[1] I have given further thought to the question how far the Governor General of the Sudan is entitled, under the Condominium Agreement of 1899, to introduce constitutional changes in the Sudan in spite of the objection of one of the two Condominium Powers. I regret, however, that I have not been able to reach a conclusion differing from the one I tentatively formed on Fitzmaurice's letter.

The language of Article 4 of the Condominium Agreement[2] is no doubt wide, but regard must be had to the expressed purpose of the Agreement, which was to enable the two Condominium Powers to share in the future government of the Sudan, and I think also to the general circumstances, of which one is that legal sovereignty probably still resides in Egypt.

In my view the intention and effect of the Agreement was to create a delegation of legislative functions from the Sovereign Power (Egypt), with the concurrence of the Power which had assisted in the reconquest of the territories (Great Britain), to an officer who was acceptable to both of them. There would no doubt have been strong objection to giving legislative powers to any representative assembly at the time the Condominium Agreement was entered into, and it is difficult to think that either of the Condominium Powers contemplated that the officer to whom they were delegating legislative authority would, without their concurrence, have power himself to delegate to a representative Assembly. I think the true view is that the Agreement is subject to an implied term that the Governor General may do nothing inconsistent with its own provisions, and that the Condominium Powers having provided that legislative powers should vest in him, the Governor-General has no authority to vest them in someone else, to share them or to fetter his own exercise of them.

To accord to the Governor General a power to make fundamental changes of a constitutional nature seems to me to be inconsistent with the expressed terms of the Condominium Agreement and contrary to its intention of enabling both Governments to share in the development of the Government of the Sudan. Once, however, that view is conceded, one is faced by the dilemma that either the present proposals do give some effective legislative powers to the Assembly which it is proposed to set up, in which event they derogate *pro tanto* from the powers vested in the Governor General, or they do not, in which case they are illusory and hardly justify the precipitation of a dispute with the Egyptian Government in which that Government will, indeed, contend that that is their very objection to the proposals.

I think the true view is that the proposals are not wholly illusory. Their effect is that so long as the proposed arrangements continued in operation, Government legislation will normally be initiated by the council and passed by the Assembly before coming to the Governor General for his assent. The combined result of

---

[1] See 154.

[2] See Appendix, part I.

Articles 19 and 50(6) is no doubt that the Governor General retains a power to legislate without the concurrence of either the Council or the Assembly, but this he can only exercise if and when one or other or both the two bodies have failed to pass legislation which he considers ought to be enacted. The proposed machinery does, in my view, therefore, effect a substantial delegation of powers which under the Agreement are vested in him alone to a tripartite legislature of which he is only one part, albeit the most powerful. Nor do I think that the Governor General's right under Article 63(1) to resume the exclusive exercise of legislative power greatly affects the matter. Whatever the legal position may be, the political implications of giving a share in legislative powers to a representative Assembly are considerable. Once such powers are given, they cannot easily be taken away, and their existence forms a severe fetter on the otherwise restricted discretion of the Governor General.

I do not consider that the willingness of the Egyptian Government to concur in more far reaching proposals affects the legal position. The Egyptian Government is entitled to say that, whilst rejecting the present proposals as inadequate and likely, once established, to retard the establishment of full self government, it would be prepared to concur in a more complete delegation or in the emancipation of the Sudan. The making of a more far reaching counter offer does not in law involve any acceptance of the original proposal. The maxim that half a loaf is better than no bread is not one which has any legal recognition in these circumstances.

I am fortified in my view as to the construction of the 1899 Agreement by the fact that on the 14th November, 1909, Sir Eldon Gorst,[3] in a letter to the Foreign Office which may or may not be available to the Egyptians, conceded that the prior assent of the Egyptian Government was required in respect of a less significant constitutional change then proposed, and that on the 15th January of this year the Foreign Office, in a letter to the Egyptian Ambassador about the present proposals, expressly stated that the Governor General could not promulgate them without the consent of the Condominium Powers.[4] It would be highly embarrassing if the British Government had to resile from the position taken up in these letters, to the latter of which at least the International Court would be entitled to look in arriving at a proper interpretation of the Treaty.

My conclusion on the whole matter is, therefore, that, in the event of the proposed ordinance being promulgated by the Governor General, the Egyptian Government would be entitled to raise the matter in the Security Council, and that if it were eventually referred to the International Court (as the Security Council may well recommend), the probability (although the contrary view is by no means unarguable) is that that Court would come to the conclusion that the Egyptian Government's interpretation of the powers of the Governor General under Article 4 of the Condominium Agreement was correct, in which case we should find it difficult to avoid agreeing to the termination of his appointment.

I must therefore answer the specific questions put to me in Fitzmaurice's letter as follows:—

1. I do not think that this argument would be successful.
2. I think it could be argued that, even if the Governor General had powers to make constitutional changes, a practice had arisen binding the two Condominium

---

[3] HBM's agent and consul-general to Egypt, 1907–1911.

[4] See 151.

Powers that such changes would be the subject of prior agreement between them. Although the Governor General might not himself be bound by this practice, the fact that His Majesty's Government had concurred in and supported his action, which would hardly be unknown, would involve a breach of this practice and no doubt give rise to a dispute in the Security Council.

3. I do not think that the argument in favour of the existence of power to delegate, although possible, would succeed.

4. No.

158 FO 371/69251, no 2299 21 Mar 1948
[Railway strike]: SPIS series 1948, no 2, report for Feb–Mar [Extract]

[Shortly after the January strike ended (see 152) Robertson warned that another strike was imminent and outlined the military and disciplinary measures being prepared to meet it (inward telegram no 9 from Robertson to Sudan agents, 14 Feb 1948, FO 371/69235, no 1148). He also noted confidentially: '. . . we think there is outside influence behind our labour troubles because we don't think the Sudanese could run such a show themselves: we suspect British communists [among the British railwaymen at Atbara], have no evidence, but are trying to get it' (letter from Robertson to Mayall, 14 Feb 1948, FO 371/69235, no 1227). The Foreign Office took a different line on the Sudan's labour troubles and advised: 'To be frank, it looks from here as though more rapid action to meet worker's grievances as far as possible might be well worth while in the long run even if it costs money now. Conversely, military action and prosecution of strikers might have regrettable long-term effects even if their immediate results appeared good. As you know there are many people in Egypt and elsewhere ready to misrepresent the Sudan Government's actions' (outward telegram no 53 from Lascelles to Robertson, 27 Feb 1948, FO 371/69235, no 1148). Robertson explained the delay in setting up an independent committee: 'In the absence of labour machinery we had to give management reasonable time to enquire into grievances before setting up Independent Committee' (inward telegram no 55 from Robertson to Lascelles, 2 Mar 1948, FO 371/69235, no 1519). On 1 Mar the WAA announced a strike beginning on 16 Mar if their demands were not met in full.]

. . .

General situation of the country

27. It is clear that the next six months will be as difficult as anything we have had to put up with since the end of the war. The proposed cuts in the Sudan's quota of heavy oils will hit all sections of the community, and will have a grave effect upon the economic position of the country as a whole. The main consumers of heavy oil at this time of year are the Syndicate ginning factories and mechanical ploughing machines, and any cuts made there will have an obvious effect, the first immediate and the second on the future productivity of the land. Cuts on pump scheme consumption will cause financial loss to owners and to their tenantry and labour, as well as reducing cash crops and food crops, and probably involving heavy purchase of grain for the Northern Province. In addition the closing down or reduction of output in minor industries, which has already begun, will cause unemployment and distress.

These cuts will therefore produce a situation in which public discontent is more likely to contribute to general unrest than at any previous time.

The railway strike

28. With this prospect ahead, the country has now been plunged, quite unnecessarily, into a Railway strike. There seemed at one time to be every hope that moderate counsels would prevail. The Workers' Affairs Association agreed to postpone their proposed strike in February and to co-operate with the Independent Committee which was set up to investigate their grievances. The sympathetic attitude adopted by this Committee appears, however, to have encouraged the hotheads to imagine that their grievances could be met in full without further delay, and in spite of pressure from public opinion, voiced not only in the press but by a series of unofficial delegations to Atbara, the Association decided at the eleventh hour to strike on March 16th, a fortnight before the Committee's report could be presented, after which the Government had promised its decision within 10 days. Public opinion has condemned the strike as being unnecessary and this condemnation may prove valuable as the price of food-stuffs and other necessities rises. It is a clear advantage that the blame for the hardship which is to be inflicted on the community should rest fairly and squarely upon the head of the workers and not upon the Government, who have demonstrably done everything possible to avert it.

29. In spite of this, however, sympathetic one-day and two-day strikes have been staged by workers of the Sudan Irrigation Department and the Public Works Department. The Atbara Conservancy men wished also to come out but were asked to stay at work by the Workers' Affairs Association. . . .

159 FO 371/69251, no 3106 19 Apr 1948

[Railway strike]: SPIS series 1948, no 3, report for Mar–Apr [Extract]

[The strike was not resolved until after the independent committee's report was presented and acted upon. Even though earlier allegations of communist influence among the railway workers proved unfounded, the government insisted that full blame for the strike rested with labour: 'The Government has possibly been slow off the mark in dealing with railwaymen's demands for representation. Labour here has, however, as yet no experience of conciliation machinery and present labour organisation has not yet discovered how to negotiate or even discuss their problems in a reasonable way' (inward telegram no 80 from Howe to Bevin, 30 Mar 1948, FO 371/69251, no 2228).]

. . . The Railway strike lasted for a month. Public opinion, while recognising that to strike before the Independent Committee had been able to produce its report was an act of folly, has none the less tended to put the major portion of the blame upon the central government, on the grounds that it delayed so long its investigation of the railwaymen's grievances. The Committee's report and the concessions granted have confirmed the feeling that the grievances were legitimate. This is important because the W.A.A. showed throughout the strike that they were very sensitive to public opinion, and public opinion regards the government's award as being fair on the whole. It would not therefore have countenanced a continuation of the strike, but neither would it have countenanced action on the government's part to punish those responsible, other than by routine disciplinary action for breach of administrative regulations. . . .

160 FO 371/69159, no 2682 19 Apr 1948

[Constitutional reform]: outward telegram no 506 from FO to E A Chapman-Andrews relaying the text of Abd al-Fattah Amr's letter proposing Egyptian participation in Sudanese constitutional reforms

[The attorney general's opinion (see 157) left few options open other than to play for time until May, when the ending of Britain's mandate in Palestine was likely to preoccupy Egypt and the Security Council. In early April al-Nuqrashi's government was further shaken by strikes among police cadets and junior officers and disorders in Alexandria and elsewhere, raising the possibility that al-Nuqrashi would soon resign, but also that a new initiative to resolve the Sudan issue might make some headway (inward telegram no 418 from Campbell to FO, 5 Apr 1948, FO 371/69158, no 2358). In the meantime Chapman-Andrews had taken the occasion of Amr Pasha's temporary return to Cairo to begin informal and unofficial discussions with the Egyptian ambassador, exploring a possible formula which Egypt could present to Britain as a way out of the diplomatic impasse (letter from Chapman-Andrews to Amr Pasha, 28 Mar 1948, FO 371/69158, no 2427). Both Amr and Chapman-Andrews agreed a text, and even though it was an 'unofficial' letter, Amr sought and obtained the approval of the minister of foreign affairs, the chief of the Royal Cabinet, and the rest of the council of ministers beforehand. Al-Nuqrashi alone was reported to be holding out (inward telegram no 438 from Campbell to FO, 8 Apr 1948, FO 371/69158, no 2427). The final text, which was reported to be harsher in tone than that originally read to Chapman-Andrews in Cairo (inward telegram no 493 from Campbell to FO, 22 Apr 1948, FO 371/69160, no 2768), was delivered to the FO after Amr returned to London.]

Following is text of letter from Amr Pasha to Chapman Andrews dated 17th April about the Sudan. Original is being sent to you by air bag.

Begins: I thank you for your letter of the 28th March in which you were good enough to set out your views on the present Anglo–Egyptian situation regarding the Sudan, in the light of your visit to London.

2. This letter, like yours to me, is also personal, confidential, quite unofficial and equally inspired by the same spirit of cooperation and friendship.

3. I can assure you that the Egyptian Government never meant by their last reply to close the door of understanding against the establishment of free institutions in the Sudan, to ensure the speedy progress of the Sudanese towards self-government. The Egyptian Government's policy is founded on the basis of the unity between Egypt and the Sudan under the common Crown of Egypt, with the Sudanese undertaking full self-government within that unity, and with every effort being made for their attaining that stage at the earliest possible opportunity. The Egyptian Government had no other object in view when they sent their modifications to the British Government. The Egyptian Government expected that the Governor-General's draft ordinance would meet these modifications, as already promised by him, but on finding out that he failed to meet even the most essential of these modifications, they sent their reply of 11th March,[1] not to close the door of understanding, but to put matters in their proper perspective.

4. The Egyptian Government are still of the opinion that the Anglo–Egyptian dispute on the Sudan Question should not retard the progress of the Sudanese, for any period, on the road to self-government.

5. I feel that the suggestions set down in your letter may be regarded as a step

---

[1] See 155.

forward in response to the Egyptian modifications. I have no doubt that this step from the British side will be met with due consideration on the Egyptian side.

6. This step is summed up in the following three proposals:—

(a) The Governor-General will agree to nominate two Egyptians already serving in the Sudan to the Executive Council.
(b) There should be an Anglo–Egyptian committee to supervise the elections.
(c) There should be an Anglo–Egyptian–Sudanese standing committee to supervise the development of the Sudanese towards full self-government.

7. While I do not wish to minimise the value of these proposals, I must not conceal from you that they have given rise to several remarks which I feel anxious to point out to you, personally, confidentially and unofficially.

8. The problem at the moment is that the Egyptian side does not feel that it is being permitted to play a full part in the progress of the Sudan. All those with whom I discussed this question feel that it is not sufficiently appreciated in Great Britain how vitally the Sudan Problem affects Egypt and how powerfully it influences the minds of the Egyptian people as a whole, a fact which no Egyptian Government is in a position to ignore.

9. Apropos the first proposal in your letter, I cannot but welcome the principle of Egyptians participating in the Executive Council. It is natural that they will have the same standing and number as the British on the said Council, in order to give effect to the Egyptian Government's responsibility for preparing the Sudanese for self-government. And, since they will have that standing and will be serving under the Sudan Government, I do not think that there will be any objection to their being nominated by the Governor-General who is appointed by a Royal Egyptian Decree for the Administration of the Sudan.

10. I am also in favour of the idea of setting up an Anglo–Egyptian Committee to supervise the elections. I am sure that its composition and competence will provide an adequate guarantee for the proper representation of Sudanese public opinion.

11. There is one important point which has particularly attracted my attention. It is stated in your letter that for the proposed constitutional regime in the Sudan, His Majesty's Government have in mind something nearer twenty-five years than three years. I should like to be perfectly clear on this point in order to obviate the possibility of any misunderstanding in the future. This regime is naturally meant to be a provisional regime under which the Sudanese may progressively govern themselves, not a dual regime which may be interpreted as an agreement between Egypt and Britain to govern the Sudan for as long as possible. Egypt, on her part, does not wish to govern the Sudanese but, on the contrary, she looks forward to the first opportunity of handing over the responsibilities of government to the Sudanese. She has, therefore, made it as basis of her policy to speed up the training of the Sudanese in self-government so that they may go through this stage in the shortest possible time. In the estimation of the Egyptian Government, three years are just about ample to achieve this purpose. Should the first experiment of the system agreed upon prove successful, it would be possible on the expiration of the three years period to reconsider the extension of the powers of the free institutions which are now being set up, with a view to securing fuller responsibilities of self-government for the Sudanese.

12. I do not wish, on the other hand, to conceal from you that the Egyptian

Government hope for a settlement of the Anglo–Egyptian dispute regarding the Sudan in the course of these three years, for they believe that a settlement of this dispute would be certain to drive away the clouds overshadowing the relations between the two countries.

13. I am bound to stress the point that any regime set up for the Sudan can only be a provisional one and can in no way affect the substance of the dispute between Egypt and Britain regarding the Sudan.

14. I am also of the opinion that the proposals outlined in your letter pave the way for submitting a draft ordinance of the proposed reforms for the association of the Sudanese with the Central Administration of the Sudan to the joint Committee of Egyptian and British representatives to which His Majesty's Government have referred in their note of 15th January last,[2] for considering the said draft and making recommendations in connexion therewith to the Egyptian and British Governments.

15. It would be possible when this committee is held to submit to it the question of the safeguards of public freedoms and the question of legislations enacted by the Governor-General, which of these legislations need be approved by the Egyptian Government before being promulgated and which of them need no such measure.

16. As the British Government have not as yet stated their views concerning the draft ordinance of the constitutional reforms, I believe that, should the proposals outlined by you be incorporated in His Majesty's Government's reply, it would afford the Egyptian Government an opportunity to announce their readiness to send representatives to the joint committee for the above purpose.

17. I am thoroughly convinced that, with good faith and as long as the interest of the Sudanese themselves is the object of the two Governments, nothing can stand in the way of agreement. I earnestly hope that the cloud which cast a shadow on the relations between the two countries will soon be dispelled, leaving a clear atmosphere for them to regain those happy relations which formerly prevailed, and pave the way before them to complete agreement. *Ends*.

---

[2] See 151.

161 FO 371/69160, no 2972 — 1 May 1948

[Constitutional reform]: letter (reply) from Mr Bevin to Abd al-Fattah Amr, welcoming Egyptian participation in Sudanese constitutional reform

[Prior to the receipt of Amr's letter (see 160) Campbell had advised that HMG's official reply to the 11 Mar note (see 155) should avoid giving a detailed counter-proposal (inward telegram no 418 from Campbell to FO, 5 Apr 1948, FO 371/69158, no 2358). In the knowledge that a new, and probably more favourable proposal was being drafted, even Khartoum advised that HMG's reply 'should be couched in general terms' (inward telegram no 90 from Robertson to Lascelles, 10 Apr 1948, FO 371/69159, no 2486). The text of Amr's letter, when it arrived, was a disappointment. Clutton commented: 'In short, what has happened is this. We proposed to the Egyptians that if they accepted the draft Ordinance, we would see that two Egyptians were nominated to the Executive Council, and set up an Anglo–Egyptian Committee to supervise the election to the Legislative Assembly and an Anglo–Egyptian–Sudanese Commission to supervise Sudan progress towards self-government. The Egyptians have replied to this that if these three concessions are granted to them in a manner much more favourable than we proposed (e.g. four Egyptians and not two on the Executive Council), they will agree that an

Anglo–Egyptian Committee should study the draft ordinance and such other matters as what legislation enacted by the Governor-General should be referred to the Egyptian Government for its consent' (minute by Clutton, 24 Apr 1948, FO 371/69160, no 2768). Despite British dissatisfaction with certain 'objectionable passages' in Amr's letter, Bevin's reply followed the initial advice of both Cairo and Khartoum in keeping to generalities.]

I have given most careful consideration to the views contained in the Note of the Egyptian Chargé d'Affaires in London of March 11th. It is the earnest desire of His Majesty's Government to reach an agreement with the Egyptian Government on this issue. I am happy to learn that it is not the intention of the Egyptian Government to close the door of understanding. I am writing to Your Excellency now in the same spirit, and with the confident hope that a happy solution will be reached which will be acceptable to both our governments.

I have the honour to inform Your Excellency that the Governor-General has carefully re-examined the terms of the proposed Ordinance in the light of the views expressed by the Egyptian Government. The Ordinance in its final form embodies a number of amendments specially intended to meet the criticisms by the Egyptian Government of the original proposals.

It has been suggested that the effect of the Ordinance would be to confer upon the Governor-General powers which he does not at present possess. I am able to assure Your Excellency that this is not the intention or meaning of the Ordinance. I hope that this assurance that the Ordinance does not, as had apparently been understood, involve any enlargement of the Governor-General's powers will help to bring our views closer together.

His Majesty's Government have given special thought to the desire of the Egyptian Government, as expressed in paragraph 8 of the Note of March 11th from the Egyptian Chargé d'Affaires in London, that Egypt should undertake an important part in preparing the Sudanese for self-government during the transition period. His Majesty's Government have certain suggestions to make in response to the wishes of the Egyptian Government.

His Majesty's Government are happy to learn that the Egyptian Government are in agreement that a committee should be set up forthwith, which will consist of one Egyptian and one British representative, with the object of reaching agreement on the question of the Ordinance. The committee may also talk over suggestions which, as stated in paragraph 4 above, His Majesty's Government have had it in mind to discuss. His Majesty's Government are also glad that the two governments are in agreement that the committee should conclude its work within a very short time and not later than three weeks.

162 FO 371/69166, no 3915 2 June 1948

'Anglo–Egyptian conversations on the Sudan': minute by G L Clutton on constitutional reform

[Following Amr's letter (see 160) and Bevin's reply (see 161) Campbell entered into negotiations with Khashaba Pasha to obtain Egyptian approval for the draft ordinance. The impending Arab-Israeli war, following the declaration of the state of Israel in May meant that Khashaba's time was fully occupied with the Palestine crisis and he was unable to press the Sudan case in Cabinet or overcome al-Nuqrashi's opposition. The crisis strengthened al-Nuqrashi's domestic position, at least temporarily, and Britain could no longer hope for his removal (inward telegram no 803 from Campbell to FO, 7 June 1948, FO 371/69166, no 3947). Britain kept extending its deadline to Egypt for a response, but pressure in both the Sudan and the House of Commons meant that a decision to promulgate unilaterally had to be taken. Bevin made a statement in the House on 14 June, in answer to a written question, permitting the governor-general to begin the procedure of promulgation. The ordinance was passed on 15 June and published in the Sudan Gazette on 19 June.]

Conversations have been proceeding in Cairo since May 10th between His Majesty's Ambassador and the Egyptian Minister for Foreign Affairs in an attempt to secure Egyptian approval of the draft Ordinance for constitutional reform in the Sudan. In return for Egyptian approval we were prepared to offer:—

(i) two nominated Egyptian members on the Executive Council;

(ii) an Anglo–Egyptian Committee to supervise the elections to the Legislative Assembly;

(iii) an Anglo–Egyptian–Sudanese Committee to supervise the Sudan's progress towards self-government.

In view of the agitation in the Sudan for the early introduction of the proposed constitutional reform, His Majesty's Ambassador was instructed to report success or failure by May 24th. Just before this date Sir Ronald Campbell reported that he thought agreement could be reached on all points except the number and status of the Egyptian members of the Executive Council. The Egyptians were pressing hard that the Egyptian members should have the same status as the four British members, i.e. that they should be heads of departments inside the Sudan administration. This we could not agree to because we are pledged to the Sudanese not to introduce Egyptians into the actual administration, i.e. the Civil Service. In an attempt to meet the Egyptian point of view Sir Ronald Campbell was authorised as a last resort to offer in addition to the two nominated members of the Executive Council a third seat for the senior Staff Officer of the Egyptian Forces in the Sudan who would attend meetings of the Council whenever defence matters were discussed. It was stipulated, however, that as the British members retired from the Council in measure as Sudanese replaced them, the Egyptian members, after equality of numbers had been reached, should retire pari passu with the British.

This last offer was put to the Egyptians on May 28th and on May 30th the Minister for Foreign Affairs stated that he accepted the offer and that as far as he was concerned full agreement had been reached. On the other hand, his agreement was subject to ratification by the Egyptian Cabinet.

The Egyptian Minister for Foreign Affairs has been canvassing his colleagues and we have information to show that agreement on the lines reached with Sir Ronald Campbell has the support of the majority of the Cabinet. Nokrashi Pasha, the Prime Minister, has, however, shown himself opposed to the agreement because it does not give the Egyptian members of the Executive Council identity of status with the British. We cannot meet him on this point, firstly because of our pledge to the Sudanese, and secondly because any attempt to do so would lead to the complete boycotting of the reforms by the Sudanese themselves and therefore land us in chaos.

In the meantime the Minister for Foreign Affairs has gone to Amman and Sir Ronald Campbell has been authorised to extend the time-limit for the final Egyptian reply up to 48 hours after his return to Egypt. In view of Nokrashi Pasha's opposition it is, however, quite on the cards that the Minister for Foreign Affairs will be repudiated. In this case we shall probably have to authorise the Governor-General to promulgate the Ordinance without Egyptian approval. This, in the official opinion of the Attorney-General, would be an illegal act on his part. On the other hand, our case in equity would be a strong one and in view of the importance of British friendship to Egypt at the present juncture it seems unlikely that the Egyptians would take the case to an international body, and they would most likely only register a protest.

163 FO 371/69232, no 4348 22 June 1948
[Nile Waters]: FO minutes of an inter-departmental meeting

[Following requests for clarification of Egyptian proposals for projects in the Nile headwaters (see 55, 62, 63), inter-governmental meetings were held at Nairobi, 25 Nov 1947, and Entebbe, 17 Feb 1947, to discuss Nile control and Lake Victoria. The East African governors gave preliminary consent to Egyptian proposals to raise Lake Victoria's level by three metres (letter from W G Wilson (CO) to G L McDermott (FO), 11 Mar 1948, FO 371/69231, no 1763). Uganda and Egypt were considering two projects: a hydro-electric power scheme of either 90,000 or 120,000 kilowatts at Owen Falls, and the raising of the level of Lake Albert to act as a storage reservoir for increased water from a raised Lake Victoria. Egypt was reluctant to participate in the full 120,000 kilowatt hydro-electric scheme, but had agreed to pay Uganda compensation for loss of power if it implemented the lesser scheme (minute by Allen, 'Nile Waters', 4 May 1948, FO 371/96231, no 3182). The Sudan was directly concerned with Egypt over a variety of Nile Waters issues, including proposals to construct the Jonglei Canal (see 29, 41, 45) and a dam at the source of the Blue Nile at Lake Tsana (see 24, 27, 32, 39, 45). Negotiations with Ethiopia over the latter had been stalled by Egypt's objections to the Sudan's participation (see 142). The Sudan government was particularly anxious that their satisfactory relations with the Egyptian government on technical matters not be disturbed by entangling Nile Waters negotiations (especially concerning Lake Tsana) in the existing Anglo–Egyptian dispute (Chick to Clutton, 10 May 1948, FO 371/69231, no 3308). All these proposals required Britain's mediation of conflicting needs between Uganda and the Sudan, as well as co-ordination of negotiations with Egypt and Ethiopia. Clutton commented: 'I am not wholly clear in my mind how far the Victoria-Albert project, plus the Jonglei Canal, will give the Sudan an extra water entitlement. This is a point on which we require clarification. In any case I think the days have really passed when one territory in Africa can consider its interests alone. Our policy today is to develop Africa as a unit to relieve not our but Europe's dependence on dollar imports. The Uganda Government must therefore, when necessary, subordinate her particular interests to the common good' (Clutton, minute, 17 June 1948, FO 371/69232, no 3625).]

Mr. Galsworthy[1] said that a new despatch had just been received from Uganda reporting that the Egyptians were backing out of the agreement to compensate Uganda. The Colonial Office also expected another despatch recommending that Uganda should go ahead with the full 120,000 kilowatt scheme.

Mr. Allan[2] said in reply to a question that the Sudan was closely concerned in both the Equatorial and Lake Tsana projects. The Equatorial combined scheme for storage and power would imply that, in Egypt's interests, parts of the south and central Sudan would be alternately flooded and uncovered, and that some 600,000 inhabitants and 1,000,000 cattle would have to be installed elsewhere. There would also be occasional excess floods in the Sudan. That was why she needed excess flood

---

[1] A N Galsworthy, assistant secretary, CO, head of International Relations Dept.

[2] See 39, note 1.

storage in Lake Albert up to 18.5 metres at Butiaba, which even so was only just enough but could be accepted subject to review in twenty years time. Egypt, like the Sudan, would have preferred 20 metres but Uganda could not agree. Egypt would have to pay compensation to the Sudan for the resettlement of the displaced population. The Sudan felt strongly that the Nile Waters question must be treated as a whole, or at any rate that no measures must be taken which did not safeguard the Sudan's interests (as well as Uganda's—compare paragraph 27 of the Governor of Uganda's despatch No. 2 of the 10th May). The Sudan would benefit by the long term improvement of conditions in the south Sudan, although for tactical reasons this should not be emphasised at present. Mr. Allan felt that the right tactics to follow were to base all discussions on the Nile Waters agreements and to suggest the necessary supplementary agreements rather than fresh agreements replacing the original ones. In reply to a question he said that it was possible for the Egyptians to delay all progress but they for their part could not carry out works in the Sudan without the agreement of the local authorities, and this was a bargaining point on our side. He agreed that the Lake Tsana scheme was not really of any benefit to the Sudan without extra entitlements in the wet season.

Mr. Clutton commented that the important point was that the whole question, including Lake Tsana, must be dealt with comprehensively, as the Sudan's position might otherwise be prejudiced.

Mr. Allan said that it would be physically possible for the Sudan to draw the necessary water even if no agreement with Egypt were reached on Lake Tsana, but that this would be very unsatisfactory.

Mr. Galsworthy pointed out that we must eventually get Ethiopian agreement on Lake Tsana and that the Ethiopian Government were likely to use this as a bargaining counter in connexion with the ex-Italian Colonies.[3]

Mr. Clutton agreed that this would be so, at any rate until the General Assembly of the United Nations in December, but he thought that the Ethiopian attitude would change for the better after that.

Mr. Galsworthy feared that the Ethiopian Government might continue to be obstructive as long as the question of the ex-Italian Colonies was in the balance. Although he understood why the question of the Nile Waters must be treated comprehensively, it seemed that Uganda's interests must suffer as a result.

Mr. Allan said that in practice it would be very difficult to get results on all aspects of the question at once. Our object should be to enable Uganda to go ahead soon but without prejudicing the comprehensive scheme.

This was generally *agreed*.

Mr. Allan suggested that Uganda might be able to carry out the larger, combined, scheme but only operate the smaller scheme until Egypt had agreed to come in. The difficulty was that this would cost Uganda, at a rough estimate, £200,000 extra, although Egypt would be called on to pay this eventually if she came in. Certain Egyptians opposed schemes situated very far from Egypt and proposed schemes in the Sudan instead, on the grounds that Egypt could have closer control of them, but in fact there was no satisfactory substitute for the Equatorial projects which were

---

[3] Proposals for the disposal of the Italian colonies, including Eritrea and Somaliland, were in the process of being decided by the UN. See BDEEP series A, vol 2, R Hyam, ed, *The Labour government and the end of empire 1945–1951*, part 3, 283–318.

necessary for the full development of the Nile basin. Both Egypt and the Sudan really needed the Lake Tsana scheme most.

Mr. Crawford[4] said that if His Majesty's Government or Uganda took any type of unilateral action the Egyptians would make a tremendous fuss about it.

Mr. Allan said that the smaller Uganda scheme had been discussed with the Egyptian technicians and they had never complained that it was contrary to the Nile Waters agreement.

Mr. McDermott said that Egyptian politicians might nevertheless do so on the grounds that it was obstructing or delaying the larger scheme which would be of benefit to Egypt.

Mr. Allan said in reply to a question that the Sudan would not agree that action should now be taken on the lines suggested in the Governor of Uganda's despatch of the 10th May and the Colonial Office's letter of the 18th June because adequate safeguards would not be provided for the Sudan. Khartoum would be wanting to comment.

Mr. McDermott suggested that it was necessary to await Khartoum's comments and the new Uganda despatch before making any approach to the Egyptians.

This was *agreed*.

Mr. Clutton emphasised that Uganda should not take any action liable to upset the Nile Waters arrangements as a whole either technically or politically.

Mr. McDermott said in reply to a question that it could be said that Uganda was called on to spend an extra £200,000 in order to make it easier for comprehensive Nile Waters arrangements to be made. He suggested that a case for a contribution by H.M.G. might be put to the Treasury.

Mr. Allan volunteered the personal opinion that the Sudan might contribute. He pointed out that Egypt would not benefit from the proposed new arrangements until she agreed to pay her share.

It was agreed that the Colonial Office would telegraph to the Governor of Uganda asking for his latest views.

Mr. Clutton said that the Belgian Government should be brought in at the earliest possible stage though this did not mean immediately since the present position was confused. The Foreign Office would investigate the question whether the Belgian Government had any special treaty rights to intervene in Nile Waters arrangements.

---

[4] W F Crawford, head of British Middle East Development Division, FO, 1948–1960.

164 FO 371/69233, no 6258 17 Sept 1948

[Nile Waters]: FO minutes of an inter-departmental meeting with Sir J Hall and Sir R Campbell

[The Uganda government's opposition to linking negotiations over the Equatorial Nile Project with the Lake Tsana scheme hardened, citing their fear that Egypt, having already started a quarrel over the latter, would refuse to agree to the former (record of FO meeting, 14 Sept 1948, FO 371/69233, no 6224).]

A meeting to discuss the desirability or otherwise of presenting the Equatorial Nile and the Lake Tana Projects jointly in our proposed approach to the Egyptian Government was held at the Foreign Office on the 17th September. . . .

Sir John Hall stated that the Government of Uganda and the Colonial Office considered it undesirable that the two schemes should be linked in our approach to the Egyptian Government for the following reasons:—

(a) The Egyptians had already raised the Sudan constitutional issue in connexion with the Lake Tana Project and therefore if the two schemes were considered together it was likely that the disagreement which already existed would prejudice the chances of obtaining Egyptian agreement to the Equatorial Nile Project.
(b) It was possible that agreement on the Lake Victoria hydro-electric scheme could be reached on the technical level and that the political aspect of the problem might be obscured.
(c) It was vital to the industrial development of Uganda that the schemes for the generation of electricity should go ahead and in order to synchronise the establishment of the various industrial installations the Government of Uganda required to know how much electric power would be available at any given time. It was not therefore in the interests of the people of Uganda either that Egyptian agreement to the Lake Victoria scheme should be prejudiced by political arguments or that its execution should be indefinitely delayed by an Anglo–Egyptian political wrangle.

Mr. Clutton summarised the Foreign Office point of view that both schemes should be considered together as follows:—

(a) He agreed with the Sudan Government that the development of the use of the Nile Waters could only be achieved successfully if the various schemes were treated as a whole since the water which the Sudan Government required to receive from one branch of the Nile depended on the quantity of water which it was to receive from the other.
(b) Precisely the same political difficulty existed in the Equatorial Nile Project and if the Egyptians wished to make an issue of it they would certainly do so. If on the other hand they considered that the combined scheme had practical advantages they might be prepared to submerge the political arguments and if they were prepared to do so in connexion with the Equatorial Nile Project they might be prepared to do so in connexion with the Lake Tana Project.

He then asked what the Uganda Government had to lose if we did present the schemes to the Egyptian Government as a whole. It seemed to him that the Uganda Government should go ahead now with the 90,000 kw scheme since it did not contravene the Nile Waters Agreement; if the Uganda Government wished to put the 150,000 kw scheme into operation they were faced with two alternatives. Either they could seek Egyptian agreement or they could act unilaterally and in case of need take the matter to arbitration. He realised, however, that both alternatives might involve considerable delays. He also wished to know how soon the Uganda Government would require the extra 60,000 kw if the 90,000 kw scheme were begun immediately. In his view the potential loss to the Uganda Government of the extra 60,000 kw must be balanced against the loss of water which the Sudan would incur if we did not link the schemes in our negotiations with the Egyptians.

Mr. Allan[1] said that the Sudan's desire for a comprehensive settlement was not

[1] See 39 and 163, note 2.

new having been set out in Khartoum despatch No.2 of 3rd January, 1946.[2] He estimated that the Sudan would ultimately require its 50% share in the benefit of Lake Tana, and also a share of approximately 15% in the water which would become available as a result of the Equatorial Nile project. Since it was imperative that the Egyptian Government be informed that some such share was required by the Sudan when the Equatorial Nile Project was presented to Egypt, it was inevitable that the question of the Sudan's ultimate share in Nile Waters as a whole would be raised, whether the schemes were taken together or one by one. It had to be borne in mind, moreover, that at this stage in the Sudan's development any approach on behalf of the Sudan must have the support of the Sudanese themselves. There was already a keen interest in Nile Waters amongst the Sudanese, and he thought that the whole question would almost certainly rank high on the agenda for the new Executive Council and Legislative Assembly. He inquired whether Uganda's industrial development would be limited if it were found necessary to build a series of 90,000 k.w. power stations at the various sites on the river instead of a lesser number of larger stations. If not, it would appear that the difficulty to Uganda would be largely one of cost, whereas on the Sudan side it was a matter of securing supplies of water which were vital to her economic development. He also pointed out that, of the participants in the various projects, the Sudan was the only one whose people and territories would be exposed, as a result of their development, to serious dangers and losses in periods of excessive floods, unless adequate protective and remedial measures were taken. These measures could only be properly ensured as a result of a comprehensive settlement.

Mr. Wright then asked whether the Uganda Government would be prepared to proceed with the 150,000 kw scheme at Owen Falls without financial or any other assistance from Egypt.

Sir John Hall replied that they were prepared to do so. The fact that there was no provision for water storage in the 150,000 kw scheme weakened the Uganda Government's case against the proposed scheme at Nimule.

Mr. Wright then said that the position as he saw it was that if we approached the Egyptian Government on the Equatorial Nile Project alone and they refused to co-operate, the Uganda Government would then go ahead with the 150,000 kw scheme and would be prepared if necessary to submit their right to do so to arbitration; and if on the other hand a combined scheme were put forward and the Egyptians again refused to co-operate the Uganda Government's tactics would be the same.

Sir John Hall agreed that this was so but there was the difficulty that without Egyptian agreement the Uganda Government would have no intermediate stage between the 90,000 and 150,000 kw schemes.[3]

In answer to Mr. Clutton's question as to whether the Uganda Government required the extra 60,000 kw soon or not, he said that the industrial schemes which were contemplated in Uganda were all either dollar-earners or dollar-savers and that they were therefore urgent; it was hoped that they would be in the productive stage in 1950 or 1951. In answer to Mr. Clutton's other point that the same constitutional

---

[2] See 45.

[3] The 90,000 kw scheme at Owen Falls would have used the natural flow of the river and would have required no storage. The 120,000 kw scheme did require storage, and therefore needed Egyptian agreement.

issue would arise whether the schemes were taken together or separately, he suggested that the fact that the Lake Tana Project required His Majesty's Government and the Egyptian Government to approach a third party might make this issue more apparent in the Lake Tana Project.

Mr. Poynton[4] thought that the Egyptians would have little incentive to raise the Sudan issue in the case of the 120,000 kw scheme since the Egyptians would then be wanting to receive something from Uganda.

Sir Ronald Campbell considered that it was not a case of Egypt wanting something from Uganda but of Uganda trying to avoid contravening the Nile Waters Agreement. While he saw the force of Sir John Hall's argument that the political issue in the Equatorial Nile Project might be sidestepped he considered that Egyptian ingenuity was capable of finding a means of raising the issue if it were so desired. There would be no safeguard that the matter would not be raised if the schemes were considered separately and he thought that since the Egyptian Government had already started an argument over the Lake Tana Project they were likely to do so if the Lake Victoria scheme alone were discussed. He did not think that the fact that a third party was involved in the Lake Tana Project affected the issue since Nokrashy Pasha would find a means of raising the Sudan question if the internal situation in Egypt demanded that he should.

From a general political point of view and from the point of view of the joint development of the Sudan, he thought that there was a great advantage in dealing with the Nile Waters schemes as a comprehensive whole. He was not convinced in any case that the constitutional issue had arisen permanently in connexion with the Lake Tana Project since the Egyptians were quite capable of forgetting what they had said previously if it were convenient for them to do so. He would much prefer to negotiate with the Egyptians on a comprehensive basis and considered that he would have greater chances of success if he did so.

Mr. Clutton pointed out that the Foreign Office had it in mind that preliminary soundings would be made before the note mentioning the two schemes together was communicated to the Egyptian Government; the note would in fact be the crystallization of previous discussions.

Mr. Wright then said that the Governor of Uganda had clearly stated his views and that they merited the closest attention. He pointed out, however, that Mr. Bevin wished these schemes to be linked in our approach to the Egyptians for the following reasons:

(a) Agreement with the Egyptians on an important matter such as the various Nile Waters schemes would make it easier to reach agreement on other very important matters.

(b) It was in our interest that Egypt should have more water and greater food production.

(c) It was also in our interest that the Sudan should have more water so that further development could take place.

Mr. Clutton then mentioned that there was a third way in which our approach to the Egyptian Government might be made. This would be based on an oral agreement

---

[1] A H Poynton (KCMG 1949), assistant under-secretary of state at the Colonial Office, 1946–1948; deputy under-secretary of state at the Colonial Office, 1948–1959.

with the Egyptians that the constitutional issue would not in any circumstances be raised; notes would be exchanged between the Egyptian Government, the Sudan Government, the Ethiopian Government and His Majesty's Government in such a way that the question of a representation of the Sudan's interest would not arise.

Mr. Wright then mentioned that the Egyptian Government were sending a strong delegation to attend the General Assembly of the United Nations in Paris and he considered it desirable that Mr. Bevin should be clearly briefed on this matter in case the Egyptians should raise it.

Mr. Poynton agreed but he made it clear that the Colonial Office point of view was that Uganda's interest should not be prejudiced either financially or by undue delay if the approach to Egypt were made on the basis of the two schemes.

It was agreed that the question should in the first instance be discussed by Mr. Bevin and Mr. Creech-Jones in order that Mr. Bevin could be briefed on the method in which this question should if necessary be presented to the Egyptians in Paris.

165 FO 371/69251, no 6992 20 Oct 1948

[Elections to the Legislative Assembly]: SPIS series 1948, no 8, report for Sept–Oct [Extract]

. . .

Primary elections

142. It is a pity that the first election results to be published are from the Northern Province where conditions combined to produce a very low attendance at the polls.

Jaaliin and other Gellaba[1] are disgruntled at the loss of the Black Market owing to removal of controls and therefore present a particularly easy field for propaganda by the organizers of the boycott. Nor does it appear that the people of Shendi district, in particular, are contented with their present local government set-up. Here and elsewhere, (in Nahud for instance), the public has been shown to be apathetic and bored with elections in general and a heavy poll is unlikely anywhere in the absence of keen party rivalry. Many too have taken the line that the Nazir was bound to be elected anyway so why should they bother. Others announced that they disapproved of the speed at which the Government is going and refused to vote on the grounds that they prefer the old system of direct administration. This is the line which Sayed Ali himself has taken and his influence is, of course, very strong in the Northern Province.

There can be little doubt that the various delegations of Khatmia who have been in to Khartoum North to visit the Sayed were given instructions to boycott the elections. The Sayed has denied this and it is true that in various parts of the country Khatmia have voted and are standing for elections, but in general the Sayed has been discouraging. The ostensible reasons for this go back to the Mahdist majority on the Advisory Council and the Sudan Administrative Conference, but in point of fact the

[1] *Jallaba* (Ar.), traders. The Jaaliyin from the Dongola area of Northern province provided one of the biggest networks of traders throughout the Sudan.

Sayed's true motives are: (1) his determination not to have any truck with any institution favoured by Sayed Abdal Rahman, and (2) desire to keep on good terms with Egypt. For this reason he was bound to raise objections and there is no reason to suppose that his present pretext, that there are not enough direct elections, would not have been replaced by some other objection had it been met. The Sayed was asked by the Civil Secretary last April to put down his objections to the new constitution in writing and he refused to do so. When therefore indirect approaches were made to the Government at the beginning of September, intimating that if the number of direct elections were increased from ten to fifteen, the Sayed might abandon his non-committal, or rather his obstructive attitude, it did not appear likely that any such concession would in fact produce a change of attitude. On the contrary it was clear from conversations with members of his entourage that his next step would be to ask for a postponement in order to enable him to get his electoral machine working. Any such postponement would, of course, have had disastrous results on public opinion and would have quite possibly resulted in a boycott by the Independence Front, which would have reduced the whole project to absurdity.

143. The situation in Kassala is peculiar because there the assumption by the Khatmia Sayeds of a leading role in the boycott has resulted in Sayed Ali's supporters adopting a more co-operative attitude than elsewhere. The ancient quarrel between their father Sayed Ahmed and his brother Sayed Ali has never died and in recent years Sayed El Hassan and Sayed Mohammed Osman have been persecuting Bimbashi Osman Ali Keila and others of Sayed Ali's adherents. . . .

144. The attitude of the authorities towards the organisers of the boycott has been less severe in the Three Towns, where the opposition is strong and the public innured [sic] to political activity, than in the Provinces, where a less sophisticated population is not prepared to accept with equanimity seditious attacks upon the Government's policy. Steps are however being taken to tighten up control in the Three Towns and the police throughout the country are doing their best to obtain evidence against the League of National Liberation, a body with a strong Communist tinge which has been deluging the towns with posters and circulars of a violently seditious nature.

145. In the absence of any second chamber in the new constitution, a number of Nazirs are putting themselves forward as candidates and although many of them will be valuable members of the new Assembly, their action is obviously open to objections in that it makes it very difficult for reasonable men to stand against them. El Sherif Ibrahim Yussef el Hindi is, for example, reluctant to stand as a candidate in the Butana because of the inevitable subsequent friction with the Abusin family. Elsewhere, as has already been noted, the result has been an increasing apathy amongst the electorate. . . .

166 FO 371/69233, no 7198 3 Nov 1948

[Nile Waters and the Sudan question]: minutes by G L Clutton, M R Wright and Mr Bevin

The Secretary of State recently saw the Colonial Secretary when they discussed the question of Nile waters and the development schemes for Lake Tsana (Blue Nile) and Lakes Victoria and Albert (White Nile). It is understood that the Colonial Secretary said that whenever the Colonial Office put forward a proposal for development schemes in regard to Uganda they come up against Foreign Office objections based on the existing Nile Waters Agreement. The Secretary of State feels that schemes so obviously for the social and economic benefit of the inhabitants of the Nile Valley should not be held up by Egyptian obstinacy about the Nile Waters Agreement and that even if Egypt took us to the United Nations on such an issue we could defend ourselves. He asked that a paper should be prepared for the Cabinet on the subject.

The real obstacle to progress in the plans for the development of both the Blue Nile and the White Nile is not primarily the Nile Waters Agreement but the Sudan question. Progress regarding Lake Tsana is held up because the Egyptians have refused to admit our right to join with them in negotiations with the Ethiopians or to have any voice in guaranteeing the Sudan her extra water allocation. We fear that if an approach is made to the Egyptians on the political level to put into execution the plans for the development of the White Nile the same issue will be raised. It is, however, vital from the Sudan's point of view that her rights and interests in this scheme should be safeguarded.

The Department have not despaired of finding a solution to these difficulties and have had a whole series of discussions on the matter during the past months with the Governor-General of the Sudan, His Majesty's Ambassador at Cairo, representatives of the Colonial Office and the Governor of Uganda. Further progress has however been held up by a most unfortunate interdepartmental dispute. The Department, the Governor-General of the Sudan and His Majesty's Ambassador at Cairo are in agreement in believing that the problem should be treated as a whole. Their idea is that with the Egyptians putting out feelers for a settlement with us we should seize the opportunity to point out that here was a matter the importance of which to all parties was obvious where there might be useful Anglo–Egyptian co-operation leading to co-operation in yet more important matters. We would point out further that this co-operation could be easily achieved if both sides agreed to evade the constitutional issues and that the method of doing so could be discussed around a table together with final arrangements putting into execution plans already approved on a technical level. The Governor of Uganda and the Colonial Office consider that the approach to the Egyptian Government should be confined to the scheme for the White Nile in which Uganda is interested on the grounds (which we believe to be erroneous) that this would not raise any political question. This dispute is set out in a minute which will be found at Flag C and which it was decided to postpone submitting to the Secretary of State for a few weeks owing to his absences in Paris and the pressure of work on him.

If the Secretary of State approves the lines suggested by the Department and can secure the Colonial Secretary's agreement then there would be no need to take this matter to the Cabinet and we could send Sir Ronald Campbell instructions at once. The question of the Nile Waters Agreement would only arise if our approach to the Egyptians failed. Here, however, it would be necessary to consult again His Majesty's Ambassador in Cairo and the Governor-General of the Sudan whose views when last consulted were that any action on our part violating the Nile Waters Agreement should at all costs be avoided.

If, nevertheless, the Secretary of State would like a Cabinet paper prepared the

Department would be grateful to know if he would like this done during his absence or held over until his return.

G.L.C.
3.11.48

I agree.

The recommendation is that the Secretary of State should ask the Secretary of State for the Colonies to agree (as explained in greater detail at Flag C) that H.M. Ambassador at Cairo should now approach the Egyptian Government on both the scheme for the Blue Nile and the scheme for the White Nile.

If the Egyptian Government refuse again we shall have to choose the most effective means of proceeding without their consent.

M.R.W.
3.11.48

I will see Col Sec before I leave today. I do not understand why it has been delayed by our interdepartmental disputes. These disputes should be brought to me for settlement at once.

E.B.
[nd]

167 FO 371/69195, no 7852 30 Nov 1948

[Anglo–Egyptian settlement]: letter from Sir R Campbell to M R Wright accusing the Sudan government of creating obstacles towards an Anglo–Egyptian settlement

We are agreed that in the past King Farouk has failed to show persistence in putting over on his Government even things which he felt pretty certain were needed. He has now been told by Amr and by me that if he has decided that a military arrangement with us is necessary, he will really have to be persistent and go through with it. He has told his Royal Cabinet, Amr Pasha, his Prime Minister, and also myself (on more than one occasion, of which the last was his visit to me, undertaken not least for this purpose at Amr's suggestion) that he intends to do so. He has asked that, if he does so, we should not let him down, and that we should avoid making difficulties for him.

All this is a very satisfactory development, which we could hardly have expected, and provides a glimmer of hope. But such a development of King Farouk's attitude must in any case be a delicate seedling, and you will have seen that the Secretary of State agrees with me that we shall have to do all we can to encourage its growth into a sturdy plant able to stand up to the weather.

Therefore I am really distressed over the hooroosh[1] that has arisen over the Sudan, a matter over which Egyptians are sensitive and excitable and which closely affects the King of Egypt. The hooroosh originated out of action by the Egyptians, but it is nevertheless awkward and might possibly, as I suggested in a telegram, force the King off his position, or at any rate back into his shell. So far he seems to be behaving

[1] Arabic meaning quarrel.

sensibly over it and not letting it cloud the main issue for him. I am told, though, that he considers that the Sudan Government might have managed things more cleverly and spared us and him some embarrassment. But it would be rash to bank on this mood continuing if the hooroosh should continue and grow, or be fed by further incidents, and we should not try him too highly. His present attitude to this Sudan matter makes him more vulnerable to a charge which is already being made in Wafdist quarters, namely, that if he is now turning to the British, it is merely for the sake of preserving his own position.

The difficulty is that the Sudan Government are inclined to react rapidly, and sometimes perhaps hastily, about actions of the Egyptians, without regard to repercussions in the wide political field. This is all right from their point of view, and perhaps proper, since in principle their only concern is the welfare of the Sudanese, and law and order in the Sudan. In fact their job is really a purely administrative one. This would be all right if, in the past, the Sudan Government and His Majesty's Government had really suited their policy and actions to the existence of the Condominium; but for the last twenty-four years they have not done so, while of later years the Sudan Government have almost abandoned, even in outer forms, (except the most minor ones) the pretence of doing so.

Somewhere in the late 1920's the thread of policy seems to have got broken. Cromer's idea always was that the creation of policy (not only external but even major internal administrative policy) was a matter in the first place for the two Co-domini, and its execution was the task of the Governor-General and his staff. But somewhere after the Stack murder we lost sight of this and allowed separatism to grow up unchecked in the outlook and actions of the (British) Political Service. Paradoxical as it may seem, ease of communications has accentuated a schism between the Sudan administration and Egypt, rather than acting as a binding force, for routes that avoid Egypt are now available. As I said in the Foreign Office while I was on leave, the officials no longer come to Cairo, even on their way to and from leave (that is any officials of consequence) and it is clear that they omit to do so by design, as a matter of policy. The Governor-General himself journeys direct between Khartoum and London, making only exceptional, and even then very brief, visits to Cairo. This is not the way to keep up a façade, and so to give some excuse to the Egyptians to acquiesce in the position. Nor is it the way to forestall or explain away suspicions and misunderstandings of the Sudan Government's actions and measures. It can be said that the Governor-General, within the terms of the Condominium Agreement, must act independently of both Governments, and this is right, but our policy of the last quarter-of-a-century has been such that he has acted very largely as a British official. This has not gone unnoticed here. If one puts onesself [sic] in the place of the Egyptians, one can see that it must be quite hard for them not to believe, on the record, that we really do mean to separate the Sudan from Egypt. (I hope that neither the Sudan Government nor His Majesty's Government do mean to do so, for I think it would be dishonourable, and one pays dearly for any dishonourable action. Is not the Condominium in present world circumstances the only solid ground for our presence in the Sudan?) There is not only this neglect of Egypt by Sudan officials, but the Sudan (British) Government openly backs S.A.R., the head of a fanatical movement which in its earlier form was instrumental in the ejection of Egypt from the Sudan, and which now openly advocates immediate independence. Thus the experience and events of twenty-four years have been too much probably for the

Egyptians to induce a belief that our offer in the agreement with Khashaba concealed no *arrière-pensée* and that, in view of the process which had been going on since 1924, it covered sufficiently what they feel is their due to regain. The result is that the Sudan Government, in Egyptian eyes (quite apart from the fact that the Political Service is manned by British subjects) is a British government. Everything done by the Sudan Government, therefore, is, for the Egyptians, a "British" action, to which the Egyptians attribute His Majesty's Government's instigation, or at least endorsement. We are, therefore, really reaping where we have sown, and I submit that we must accept the consequences to this extent, at least, that we insist on greater control over the Sudan Government and the Governor-General. That is what is necessary. Until lately this control, in the interest of the Egyptian co-dominus and of His Majesty's Government's Egyptian and general policy, was exerted from this mission. Now it is the job of the Foreign Office. His Majesty's Government must, it seems to me, require to be kept punctually informed of developments that may occur in the Sudan, and be given an opportunity, in the interests of their wider policy, of guiding the Governor-General in his treatment of issues that arise between him and the Egyptian Government, or matters which may raise an issue. We cannot divest ourselves in Egyptian eyes, or, if it comes to that, in fact, of responsibility for his actions. It may seem anomalous that His Majesty's Government, as one member of a partnership, should singly give instructions to a servant of both members. But we have allowed, if not encouraged, a position to develop in which this is necessary, and I see no way out of it, if worse is not to befall.

I will not say that the Sudan Government could or should have taken a different stand on the points of principle recently raised (though the reason for refusing permission to the Egyptian lawyers to plead, when it was open to the Legal Secretary to give it, did not strike me as terribly strong.[2] It seems to me that if the Governor-General had placed himself on the ground of the danger to law and order it would have been better. The danger was a real one.) I do, however, consider that with greater wisdom or awareness they might have done what they did differently, and that at any rate they should have given you time to consider matters and direct them.

I do not for a moment suggest that the Egyptians aren't quite unconscionable in Sudan matters, and no doubt recent disturbances during the Sudan elections may, as the Sudan Government claim, have been due to a measure of Egyptian instigation, or perhaps to their use of Sudanese fuel which was already lying about. But in the period preceding 1924, as in the years preceding the present time, there had no doubt been, on our side, actions which seemed to go outside the strict provisions, and even the spirit, of the Condominium Agreement, seemed to neglect the Egyptian part in the Condominium, and hurt Egyptian nationalist sentiment, without which the urge for subversive propaganda would have been considerably less, if not absent. I do wish that the Governor-General and the members of the Administration could be persuaded to pay some deference to the fact that they are half servants of the Egyptian Government, and I earnestly hope that what was discussed and decided upon as desirable at our meeting in your room with Bob Howe and Robertson will be insisted upon and put through. Is it not rash in the extreme to give colour to the

---

[2] Egyptian lawyers hired to defend Sudanese arrested and charged with sedition late in 1947 were denied entry into the Sudan.

Egyptian view that the Governor-General is first and foremost a British official (besides being a British subject) and, if at all an Egyptian official, only one secondly and lastly—and a very poor second and last, at that? A moment's reflection will, I think, show that it is extremely rash. If our intentions are honest, we must want to make the Condominium work, to prevent an issue on which we must break. What then about the choice of the next Governor-General, if we allow a situation to continue in which the Egyptians can hardly look on him as anything but an exclusively British official? There is a great fuss in the press over the latest developments in the Sudan, and some agitation amongst the students, who had been quiescent for quite a long time. If, in the face of all this, King Farouk's recent initiative as regards Anglo–Egyptian relations in general, and a military arrangement in particular, with all that this might lead to, were to prove still-born, I would regard it as a real tragedy.

Meanwhile I am telling Egyptians that all this is the result of their own futile statesmanship. His Majesty's Government had shown their desire to meet them and enhance their participation in the guidance of the Sudan. They could have had an Anglo–Egyptian–Sudanese Committee in permanent being to watch over Sudan constitutional development etc. It was not for them to cast doubt on the elections, and they are in no position to do so, not having been there; but they could have had a special Anglo–Egyptian Committee to supervise them. His Majesty's Government had agreed to all this, and the nomination of two Egyptians to the Sudan Executive Council, but they had rejected it, etc. etc. etc. I am also saying that there is no difficulty about Egyptians going to the Sudan on ordinary and legitimate business, but that by and large the only ones who seem occasionally to want to go are those whose object is a political stunt to embarrass either the Sudan Government, the British Government, the Egyptian Government or some other Egyptian political party or personage. It is indeed lamentably true that the Egyptians behaved like complete nitwits, and worse. Unfortunately that does not get us out of our difficulties and the embarrassments which this flurry has created.

As for the internal situation in the Sudan, I have not sufficient material or close acquaintance to deal with it; but from here it does not seem to me to be particularly reassuring for His Majesty's Government. I have always thought it showed a mistaken spirit to speak of S.A.R. and his followers as "our friends" and the party "loyal" to us, and of the Ashigga people as "disloyal". Moreover, the "loyalists" seem determined on complete independence almost immediately. The Sudan Government and S.A.R. himself may very much like, and no doubt rightly, the prospect of being independent of *Egypt* at once, but is it a good bargain for us that this should happen, if the price is almost immediate independence from *us* also? S.A.R. may have been told that early independence is moonshine, and we may have statements from him and his followers and from members of the less articulate masses that they will want to be in alliance with us and have British advisers; but when it comes to the aspirations of dependent peoples for independence, this sort of thing does not often work out according to schedule; and we have to remember the existence of the Legislative Assembly.

Further, is it not a bit odd, in the light of history, for us to be backing the son of the Mahdi and his party, which ultimately must mean that the Sudan Government governs on his sufferance?

The present flurry may well die down and be chased from the front page by some other event. But the incidents will have sunk into the Egyptian consciousness, and may arise later to plague us in connection with any military arrangement or any general settlement. It may force or encourage King Farouk to say later that a military arrangement must be accompanied or immediately followed by a political settlement.

I have of course painted only part of the picture. There is much that could be put in to correct the colour and make it more representative of the whole truth. But I have tried to depict the scene as the Egyptians wilfully or blindly or emotionally see it, and the causes of the degree of distortion there is in their vision. It is this distortion and the reasons for it which we have to deal with in the interests of our wider policy: and I hope they may be given mature consideration. What we need is to realise that, in our own interest, the Sudan question requires honest thinking and cool statesmanship. We must get rid of partisan feeling, and put distrust of Egypt, disapproval of the corrupt influence of Egyptians, etc. etc. in their proper perspective. However awkward to everybody the Egyptian connection may be, however ideal in some people's judgment it might be to isolate the Sudan from Egypt and give the Sudanese *complete* shelter from undesirable Egyptian influences, we must see things as they are. We must realise that Egypt, whether we like it or not, is by geographical circumstances and by diplomatic agreement, a factor which can never be ignored. Further, the Sudan cannot be isolated any longer from the winds blowing about the world, so that the idea of isolating the Sudanese children from all outside influences is no longer possible, even if such a policy had ever been wise. (Most parents have learned that it is both impossible and unwise).

Forgive this terribly long letter, but I really feel strongly that the moment has come when we cannot delay to stop, look and listen.

168 FO 371/69172, no 8064 14 Dec 1948

[Sudanese Executive Council]: minutes by G L Clutton and M R Wright

Under the proposals made during the Campbell–Khashaba conversations last summer, the Governor General of the Sudan agreed to nominate Egyptians to two out of the three nominated seats on the proposed Executive Council. The third was to be Sudanese. The Executive Council was thus to have in the first place twelve members so that there would be six Sudanese, four British and two Egyptians. A balance of fifty-fifty would thus be struck between the Sudanese and the non-Sudanese on the Council (the membership of the Executive Council on occasions of the senior Egyptian staff officer in the Sudan can be left out here).

When owing to protracted and deliberate delays on the part of the Egyptians, H.M.G. no longer felt able to stand in the way of the Governor General promulgating the Constitutional Ordinance, it was always understood that the Governor General would keep open two vacancies on the Executive Council for the Egyptians as long as he could, in the hope that the Egyptian Government would after all agree to cooperate with us on the basis of the Ordinance. This was implicit in the supplementary answers to the Parliamentary Under Secretary of State's statement of the 14th June (see flag A).[1]

---

[1] References in flags not printed.

The Sudanese elections have taken place and the Legislative Assembly is to meet on the 23rd December. On the 19th December the Governor General proposes to complete the Executive Council by nominating the Sudanese Ministers and Under-Secretaries and by filling the three nominated vacancies. He proposes to nominate one Sudanese (the Speaker of the Assembly) and two British officials whose names we do not know. By so doing he will preserve the original balance of the Executive Council where there will be six British and six Sudanese.

H.M. Ambassador at Cairo (see Cairo telegram No. 1698 of the 9th December, flag B) has urged strongly that the Governor General should reconsider his decision and the Governor General has replied in his telegram No. 295 of the 12th December (flag C) giving the reasons why he considers he should carry out his proposed action. Briefly, the arguments and counter arguments are as follows:

Case of H.M. ambassador

(1) H.M. Ambassador points out that to appoint all three Councillors in this manner is to slam the door at a critical moment in Anglo–Egyptian relations and he asks that the two seats originally allocated to the Egyptians should be kept vacant.

(2) H.M. Ambassador at Cairo considers it would be most advisable that there should be a majority of Sudanese on the Council since filling up two vacancies to create equality would make fuel for Egyptian propaganda that the whole Sudanese set-up was British rigged. He claims that the two British appointments are being made mainly because they are British.

Case of the governor general

(1) The Governor General points out that the Egyptians have been given six months since June to make up their minds whether to cooperate with us or not and that they have shown no signs of doing so but have continued to do their utmost to prevent the constitutional Ordinance coming into force. To keep the nominations open would arouse intense Sudanese opposition to no avail because his action would not ameliorate Egyptian opinion.

(2) The Governor General thinks it is unwise to allow too big a proportion of Sudanese on the Council to begin with since it would be embarrassing for him to over-ride decisions of the Council in matters of vital importance, and from an administrative point of view the Governor General does not think that a Sudanese majority on the Council would be advisable. The two Councillors are not being nominated solely because they are British but because their presence on the Council will be useful.

On balance, the Department feel that the decision in this matter must be left to the Governor General whose attention has been drawn to the desirability, in view of the proposed Anglo–Egyptian military talks, of damping down all controversial issues. Their feeling is that this is mainly an administrative matter on which the Governor General feels strongly and in which it would be difficult to intervene since the Governor General promulgated the Ordinance on his own authority as part of the measures he was taking for the good Government of the Sudan. The point he makes that in the initial stages of this experiment in self-government it would be unwise to risk a situation where he well might have to over-ride his Executive Council is very cogent, and it must be remembered that once the balance on the

Executive Council was in favour of the Sudanese that balance could not in practice be altered except in the direction of further Sudanisation. Moreover, as the Governor General points out in the last paragraph of his telegram, he is entitled to make fresh appointments to the Council at the beginning of the first session of each new Assembly, i.e. every three years. There is therefore nothing to prevent him from appointing Egyptians to replace the two British nominated members at some later stage. The two British members could also be asked to retire if need be to make place for two Egyptians.

Recommendation
The Department recommend that the Governor General should be allowed to go ahead as he proposes subject to the understanding that if the Egyptians show themselves willing to cooperate with us in the Sudan, he will be asked to nominate two Egyptians to the Council in the place of the two British nominated members.

A draft telegram is submitted.

G.L.C.
14.12.48

This is an awkward dilemma, which, as usual, comes at a particularly difficult moment. But the Governor General[']s arguments are very strong, and I do not think we should be justified in seeking to overrule him.[2]

M.R.W.
14.12.48

---

[2] Bevin commented: 'I agree'.

169 FO 371/69209, no 8221 15 Dec 1948

[Dr Muhammad Adam Adham and the Black Bloc]: note by the Civil Secretary's Office, Khartoum

[One legacy of slavery in the Sudan was the presence in northern towns of substantial numbers of ex-slaves and their descendants of non-Arab (mainly Southern Sudanese) origin. Many had served in the Egyptian army during the reconquest, and the native officer corps of Sudanese units in the Egyptian army prior to World War I was drawn almost entirely from this group. Classed as 'de-tribalised' natives by a Sudan government which administered the country increasingly on tribal lines, the old officer corps was gradually eased out of the army as new units were raised in the Northern Sudan and the old Sudanese battalions were disbanded. The White Flag League and the mutiny of 1924 confirmed to the government the dangerous divided loyalty of 'de-tribalised' officers, such as Ali Abd al-Latif, and speeded the demise of the Sudanese battalions and the further reduction of their numbers in the officer corps of the new Sudan Defence Force. But the White Flag League's nationalist slogan of 'Sudan for the Sudanese' was an ambiguous one, not only was it potentially aimed externally at the co-domini, but also internally at the displacement of the true 'Sudanese' (i.e., the black African ex-slave class) from positions in the administration and army by 'Arab' Northern Sudanese who now formed the government's main clients and allies. Dissatisfaction with their inferior status was expressed by some remaining Sudanese officers in the 1930s, and a 'Co-operative Union of Blacks' (also known as 'Hisb el Zinuj') was formed, mainly as a social organisation, in 1945 (SPIS, no 53, report for Sept 1945, FO 371/45972, no 3693). The formation of the 'Black Bloc' was reported in

Sept 1948, when it was also noted that the Ashiqqa party was trying to enlist ex-Sudanese officers married to Egyptian wives to organise pro-Egyptian counter-propaganda (SPIS no 7, report for Aug–Sept 1948, FO 371/69251, no 6523). Dr Muhammad Adam Adham was elected by direct election to represent the Omdurman South constituency in the Legislative Assembly (1948–1953).]

Dr. Mohammed Adam Adham is of negroid origin, about thirty-eight years old, and son of a retired Sudan Defence Force officer who lives at El Obeid and is himself an active member of the Black Bloc. Dr. Adham is a graduate of the Gordon Memorial College and a diplomate of the Kitchener School of Medicine. In 1936 he joined the Sudan Medical Service as a medical officer, but his career was not successful and on several occasions he was tried by a board of discipline for drunkenness and negligence in the performance of his duties. Finally, unable to mend his ways, he was compelled to resign. With financial assistance from his family he then opened a private clinic in Omdurman, gave up drinking and made a success of his new venture. His reputation both as a doctor and as a citizen now stands fairly high. He is also owner and editor of a fortnightly journal called 'Africa' which devotes itself to social and cultural subjects.

2. Dr. Adham formed the Black Bloc in September 1948 in the towns of Khartoum, Khartoum North and Omdurman. Its members, who are said to number about four thousand are of Southern Sudan origin and its aims have been defined as follows:—

(1) The strengthening of the Nation by national reforms to achieve a strong national unity.
(2) Social betterment, improvements of conditions amongst the poor, reduction of crime etc.
(3) Elimination of social distinction.[1]
(4) The institution in the Sudan of a free democratic Sudanese government which will maintain social justice and equality and develop the country in all respects.
(5) A strong army equipped with all modern weapons.

3. The Bloc has supported the setting up of the Legislative Assembly and two of its leaders have been elected members of the Assembly for constituencies in Khartoum and Omdurman.

4. Propaganda on behalf of the Bloc has been conducted at Wad Medani, El Obeid and Juba, the principal line being a demand for economic and social equality for southern Sudanese in the northern Sudan.

5. The Bloc has so far worked in harmony with the Umma Party and has thereby incurred the hostility of the Unity Parties. Some of the Umma, however, regard the movement with caution and are not yet convinced that it will not develop into a movement for separation of the southern Sudan from the North. It is expected that its leaders will try to make close contact with the representatives of the Southern Sudan in the Legislative Assembly.

---

[1] An earlier report of the Bloc's platform listed this point as the 'elimination of racial distinction' (SPIS no 7, report for Aug–Sept 1948, FO 371/69251, no 6523).

170 FO 371/73472, no 343 4 Jan 1949
[SAR]: letter from Sir R Howe to Sir O Sargent. *Enclosure*: 'Note on Sayed Abdel Rahman's interview with His Excellency at the palace, Khartoum, on Tuesday, 28th December, 1948' *Minute* by G L Clutton

[In his reply Sargent expressed sympathy for the problem of SAR alienating traditional government supporters, but he suggested a policy along the lines of Clutton's minute (letter from Sargent to Howe, 18 Feb 1949, FO 371/73472, no 343).]

I send you herewith a note of a conversation I had on the 28th December with Sayed Abdel Rahman el Mahdi, who recently asked for an interview.

2. I think you will find this record of some interest. It confirms two impressions which have been growing in my mind for some time. These are:—

(a) That S.A.R. is anxious to get the Sudan Government committed heart and soul to his side—anxious in fact to get what he described as a vote of confidence, and

(b) That he is now definitely committed to the pursuit of his ambition to set himself or his son on a Sudanese throne.

These two desires are not identical, but (b) would hardly fail to be greatly strengthened by (a).

3. During the last few years since the Sudan Government decided to go for the first step in their aim of self-government for the Sudanese, S.A.R. has thrown the whole weight of his admittedly great influence on the side of the Government. It was inevitable that he should regard himself and be regarded in the country as the Government's and H.M.G's man. The first step in self-government has now been accomplished. The Legislative Assembly has come into being and the Sayed, without doubt, is realising that the weight of the Sudan Government's support has shifted its focus from him to the Assembly.

4. Now the Assembly, it is true, contains a goodly number of S.A.R's Independence Party, viz.—the Umma, but, and it is a very important 'but', the Assembly also contains a pretty solid bloc of country members, the Nazirs, etc., who for solid reasons are loyally attached to the Government and are not interested in 'Independence', still less in Kingship. These people represent a kind of centre party, although the name has not yet appeared publicly.

5. The above of course leaves out of consideration the Khatmia who to a great extent boycotted the elections, are opposed to S.A.R. and the Umma, and have withdrawn their support of the Sudan Government over the Legislative Assembly, even though they may be still in the main loyal to the Government; simply and solely because they hate and fear the very idea of a Mahdist revival of power such as would be exemplified by King S.A.R.

6. The appointment of Ministers and Under-Secretaries who are generally recognised as being the best talent available has had a good effect and has served to reassure the Khatmia a lot. I hope that with time this effect will increase and lead the Khatmia to modify their attitude towards the Assembly and lead them to co-operate in its working. Nevertheless we are faced with a situation in which a large and solid bloc of traditional Government support is being withheld and the only way or at any rate the most effective way of restoring their confidence in Government and bring-

ing them back into the fold would be to remove their fear of S.A.R's kingly ambitions.

7. It has been suggested that this could best be done by an announcement in categorical terms by the Government that they will not lend their countenance to any attempt at planning or setting up a Sudan Kingdom, or alternatively that H.M.G. in the U.K. should make such an announcement at an appropriate moment. It is argued that such a positive step would have a good effect internally and would effectively serve to protect many people here who are at present inclined to fall victims to Egyptian propaganda which exploits the deep-seated fear of Mahdism among the Khatmia.

8. Another line of policy is to run a centre party both in the Legislative Assembly and in the country based on local notables such as the Nazirs who constitute the loyal backbone of the country. This idea is already in the air here.

9. S.A.R. fears that the centre party is already emerging in the Legislative Assembly—hence, I think, his appeal to me on the 28th December for a vote of confidence in him.

10. Any such positive steps such as those outlined above would doubtless provoke a crisis in our relations with S.A.R. and the effects of which I am not yet able to assess; they might be serious. But I have felt it desirable to let you know the currents which are stirring as we might sooner or later be compelled to act on these lines.

11. A good way out would be to induce S.A.R. to retire gracefully from public life, and announce that he was no longer concerned with politics. He did in fact mention this possibility some time ago, but his attitude when I saw him on the 28th was not at all consistent with retirement. Financially of course he has benefitted heavily from his close connection with the Government.

12. I am sending a copy of this to Ronnie Campbell.

Enclosure to 170

1. The Sayed's arguments were not always clear or consistent, but the underlying motif was as follows:—

(a) The present situation was satisfactory and he regarded it as the joint result of the efforts of H.E. and of Sir Hubert Huddleston and of his own consistent line of policy beginning with his interview with Mr. Attlee in 1946.[1] The outlook for the future was, however, anxious, and His Majesty's Government's future policy had not been made clear. If they waited until 1956 when the present Treaty expires the Egyptians might quote the Bevin–Sidky protocol and obtain from U.N.O. the grant of sovereignty over the Sudan. If H.M.G. did then succeed in obtaining for the Sudanese the right to determine their own fate there was a grave danger that in the interval Egyptian propaganda, which he admitted to be ineffective at present, would have succeeded, in some way which he did not explain, in winning over Sudanese opinion until they opted for some form of union with Egypt.

(b) To counteract this he asked for:—

---

[1] See 114.

(1) A vote of confidence from His Excellency and an assurance of support from the British Government and the Sudan Government such as H.E. had given him on a former occasion and enabled him to carry on up to the present. He also wanted some form of recognition of his status as the right-hand man of the Government. He did not mean by this any special office or decoration for himself or for his son, but the opposition were already making use of Sayed Siddik's non-appointment as Leader of the Assembly to argue that the Sayed had been rebuffed and that the Government, having used him, proposed tacitly to drop him. He had had many ups and downs since the Government first admitted him to its confidence in 1917, but he could not now afford any downs. He wanted it made clear to the Sudan that he stood at the Government's right hand.

(2) A line on the Government's policy during the next three years so that he could keep in tune with it.

(3) The fixing of an early date for independence and strong discouragement of those time-servers who profess to be loyal to the existing regime and ask for a brake on the wheels of progress, when their real object is to keep the door open for Egypt through the retention of the Condominium regime.

The Government had identified itself once and for all with the policy of swift progress towards independence and anybody who pretended to be a supporter of the Government while opposing the Government's policy could not call himself a loyal citizen. The Government must realise by now that independence as envisaged by him and his supporters did not mean the severance of the British connection or the departure of the British official on which and on whom the country would rely for years to come.

These time-servers and the supposed Centre Block of "loyal" opinion were more dangerous than the Khatmia, because the Government had learned by experience how hopeless it was to try and get Khatmia collaboration and were now toying with this new idea of a pro-Government party.

In this connection he said that he felt that by continuing to make approaches to the Khatmia leaders after so many rebuffs the Government was losing face and putting itself into a most undignified position.

2. His Excellency's reply to (a) was that there need be no fear whatever that the future of the Sudan could now be settled without the Sudanese themselves being consulted. The time for any such contingency had passed. Their present verdict was clear on the recent elections. The only considerable body of opposition to the Assembly had as its motive not a desire for union with Egypt but fear of the Sayed's own personal ambitions.

The Sayed declared that there was no real fear in the country. He was liked and respected by the vast majority of the population. What alternatives had these patriots to suggest? If Sayed Ali el Mirghani had been capable of anything he would have built up so strong a position during many decades of Government support that he, S.A.R., would never have been able to get anywhere at all. No—they wanted Egypt, and only Egypt. At the same time he belittled their strength and reverted to his fear lest it be increased in the years to come, by Egyptian propaganda. He made no attempt to deny his ambitions and implied that the Government had no alternative but to support them.

In answer to his para. (b) above His Excellency assured him that the Government would continue to support his efforts for the progress of the Sudan. It was not, however, possible to fix a date for independence or for the next step towards self-government because no-one could say how these things would work out in practice. Much—if not all—would depend on the success of the new Assembly, and it was the Government's policy to co-operate with and support that Assembly to the utmost. It also naturally hoped and would work for the inclusion in the Assembly of all other shades of opinion.

The Sayed expressed his full agreement with this last object provided that the ostensible agreement of fundamentally disloyal and pro-Egyptian elements should not be bought at the expense of the Government's true friends. He quoted a proverb of roughly the same sense as the fable of the dog with a bone in its mouth and hinted that if the Government alienated him all its efforts would come to nothing.

Minute on 170

This is not an entirely satisfactory letter but I think it is clear that Sir R. Howe is not asking for any decision on the various suggestions mentioned. He is just telling us how the winds are blowing in the Sudan.

Our "alliance" with S.A.R. always had its dangers, namely that this probably most powerful single personality and influence in the Sudan would alienate other and probably steadier influences. This has happened in the withdrawal of support from the Government of the Khatmia. It is quite easy to understand the Governor-General's reluctance to be entirely dependent on S.A.R. and I am quite certain that an administration based solely on him would be bound to run into difficulties. It is not, however, our job to tell the Governor-General precisely how he is to find the extra support he requires. We can only give him guidance in form of general principles.

It is quite obvious that any question of a Kingship of the Sudan under S.A.R. would not merely wreck our relations with Egypt, but would also split the Sudan. A Mahdist régime would be bitterly opposed by large parts of the Arabic speaking country and it would be a disaster for the non-Moslem south. Nor is there any call for the Sudan Government so to speak to pass a vote of confidence in S.A.R. It is more usual for political parties, etc. to pass votes of confidence in Governments. Moreover, I do not think S.A.R.'s position is all that strong. The Umma party do not regard him as a political but as a religious leader, and it is probably this knowledge, and the fact that it was by the will of the Umma party leaders that Sadik his son was not elected leader of the Assembly, that S.A.R. is now seeking to re-gain his position by calling in the support of the Government. It also has to be remembered that S.A.R. is very much dependent on the Government financially (cotton).

It would, moreover, it seems to me, be equally wrong to go as far as is suggested in paragraph 7 of this letter and make a public declaration either at Khartoum or here about Kingship. This would surely prejudice a free decision about the future of the Sudan, which it is our policy to keep open until such time as the Sudanese themselves are capable of making a decision. Surely our consistent policy in the Sudan should be that the Government should hold the ring while the various elements in the Sudan develop organically without help or hindrance from us until the day comes when the Sudan can decide for herself her future international status. This is the policy set out admirably in the last paragraph of the political summary (No. 1 of 1949) in J682/16.

G.L.C.
29.1.49

171 FO 371/73613, no 704 3–4 Feb 1949
[Nile Waters]: minutes by G L Clutton and Sir O Sargent

[The FO and CO having resolved their disagreement over the best strategy of approaching Egypt about the Nile waters projects (see 164 and 166), Campbell found that political conditions within Egypt were not opportune for initiating discussions. Concerned by this continued delay both the CO and Khartoum urged the FO to renew its efforts so that talks could soon begin.]

On December 8th instructions were sent to Sir R. Campbell to approach King Farouk about the Nile Waters (see J 7189/518/16 at flag B). As apparently no action had been taken on this despatch, the Department enquired just before Christmas how matters stood, and Sir R. Campbell replied that the form of the approach he had been instructed to make was a matter of great delicacy, particularly in the circumstances then prevailing when Egyptian feeling had been roused by the disturbances which accompanied the elections in the Sudan. The situation still further deteriorated with the assassination of Nokrashy and the débâcle in Palestine. Sir R. Campbell has now written to the Secretary of State (see J 786 at flag A) saying that although he is prepared to take action at once, his strong inclination is to wait at least another week or two in the hope of a turn of the tide bringing with it a real chance of success. In the meantime, the Colonial Secretary has naturally become somewhat disturbed by the delay and has written to the Secretary of State urging immediate action (see his letter of the 31st January at flag C).[1]

The Department quite understand Sir R. Campbell's difficulty and they are certain that at any rate until very recently, it would have been foolish to have tried to approach King Farouk. As the Ambassador himself has pointed out on more than one occasion, Egyptian thoughts were so pre-occupied with the question of the supply of arms that it would have been 75% certain that the approach would have been met by a request for such supplies. The situation has somewhat changed, however, and a sign of this was the friendly reception given in the Egyptian press to the Secretary of State's statement on Palestine in the House of Commons. Such a reception would not have been of any significance in any other Arab country, but it is of significance in Egypt where for years the press has been consistently hostile to anything we have done. Moreover, if we approach King Farouk about Anglo–American planning in the Mediterranean and Middle East, this occasion would be very propitious for also talking to him about the Nile Waters. The military planning contemplated represents the military measures it is intended to take against Communist infiltration into the Middle East. The development of the Nile Waters represents the social and economic measures to be taken against this danger.

The Department do not feel that there is really any alternative in this question to an approach to King Farouk either now or in the very near future. Unilateral action on our part has been considered time and time again but it represents no satisfactory solution. As far as the irrigation side of the two schemes is concerned, such action would precipitate a really first class crisis in our relations with Egypt and in any case would lead to little practical result since Egyptian participation in the schemes is essential for their success. It is a case of the uselessness of taking a horse to the water

---

[1] In which Creech Jones expressed his anxiety that the political issues concerning the Equatorial Nile project and Lake Tsana be settled quickly (Creech Jones to Bevin, 31 Jan 1949, FO 371/73613, no 1118).

if you can't make it drink. As regards the hydro-electric side of the scheme, Uganda's *immediate* needs are satisfied by the power station now being erected at Owen Falls, which does not require Egyptian consent. The subsequent stages (the 120,000 and 150,000 kilowatt stations) are later developments to take place in several years' time. The 120,000 kilowatt station would require Egyptian agreement and is an integral part of the irrigation scheme. In the case of the 150,000 kilowatt station, there is an arguable case that it does not infringe the Nile Waters Agreement and therefore require Egyptian consent.[2] If, therefore, the Egyptian Government refuse to play, it may be necessary to skip the second stage. In any case, before we can usefully even consider unilateral action, we must approach the Egyptians and be in a position to say that they have definitely refused to participate in a scheme of development for the benefit of the whole of the Nile Valley.

In his letter Sir R. Campbell makes two points. He questions the desirability of stipulating that the works at Lake Kyoga in Uganda should be entrusted to British contractors. This concession has already been agreed by the Egyptians at the technical level, and it seems a reasonable stipulation by the Uganda Government for general security reasons. Otherwise they would have no control over what was going on in their own territory. The second point is that the Egyptian Government should be allowed to take the lead in negotiations with foreign Governments regarding the schemes. This seems reasonable provided, of course, that it does not involve any sacrifice of the Sudan's interests or questions of principle about the sovereignty over the Sudan. It should be quite possible to avoid all these dangers. The Governor-General (see Khartoum telegram No. 15 to Cairo in J 704, flag D)[3] seems to be making undue objections on this point and the subject has been dealt with by the Department separately.

Recommendation

The Department recommend that Sir R. Campbell be instructed to approach King Farouk as soon as possible, preferably on the same occasion as he takes up the matter of Anglo–American planning if such a démarche is finally agreed.

Drafts are submitted.

G.L.C.
3.2.49

I agree.

It was the Colonial Office and the Governor of Uganda whose delay for several weeks meant that we lost the opportunity of taking this up with the Egyptians in November.

O.G.S.
4.2.49

---

[2] See 164, note 3.

[3] In commenting on Campbell's 14 Jan letter to Bevin, in which Campbell suggested ways to avoid constitutional issues being raised along with the Nile Waters question, Howe proposed that the pre-requisites to allowing the Egyptians to be the sole negotiators with Ethiopia (about Lake Tsana) and with Uganda and Belgium (about Equatorial Nile project) would be Egyptian ratification of the technical agreement on sharing benefits and costs of Lake Tsana project; an agreement on sharing the benefits and costs of the Equatorial Nile project; a revision of the Nile waters agreement (inward telegram no 21 from Howe to FO, 27 Jan 1949, FO 371/73613, no 704).

172 FO 371/73613, no 1130 9 Feb 1949

[Nile Waters]: despatch no 89 from E A Chapman-Andrews to Mr Bevin on the reopening of Nile Waters discussions with Egypt.[1] *Enclosure*: translation by FO of Egyptian aide-mémoire (7 Feb 1949)

I have the honour to refer to my telegram No. 212 of 8th February on the subject of the Nile waters' projects, and to transmit herewith the English translation of an aide-mémoire handed to me by the Minister for Foreign Affairs on the evening of 7th February. You will see that the position of the two committees which have been formed to study this question is not entirely clear. It appears, however, that the technical committee of senior officials of the Ministry of Public Works submitted their report with seven recommendations; subsequently a three-man committee, consisting of eminent engineers who were also ex-Ministers of Public Works, was formed and they apparently recommended that the Lake Tana dam should be constructed as a matter of urgency, and that Egypt should participate with the Uganda Government in the Owen Falls scheme. It is not clear from the aide-mémoire whether the Egyptian Government wish to participate in the construction itself or whether they intend to limit their participation to financing the work. On the other five recommendations of the technical committee the three-man committee has not yet given its views but hopes to do so within three months. There is, therefore, a small error in the third sentence of paragraph 1 of my telegram under reference, where the words "technical committee" should be substituted for "committee of three experts."

2. The next point which I think needs further elucidation is the insistence of the Minister for Foreign Affairs, which was reaffirmed by the Prime Minister, that no unilateral action should be taken by the Uganda Government on the Owen Falls project until the Egyptian Government have had time to declare their intention to co-operate in this scheme. I suspect that the reason for this insistence was that neither the Minister for Foreign Affairs nor the Prime Minister had fully understood from my note of 19th January that the plans for the construction for which orders have already been placed by the Uganda Government would not prejudice, and indeed contemplated, the larger scheme, which would benefit Egypt as well as Uganda. The Minister for Foreign Affairs told me that three or four Egyptian Ministers had expressed a desire for further review and discussion of this scheme in view of the considerable expenditure which Egypt would be asked to bear, and it seems likely that he feared that unless he could prove there would be a direct advantage to Egypt, these Ministers might oppose the whole scheme. I managed to persuade the Minister for Foreign Affairs that he had nothing to fear on this score. The Prime Minister, when I assured him in the same sense, accepted what I said but nevertheless repeated his plea for temporary suspension of action by the Uganda Government. I told his Excellency that I did not know whether a delay was possible since power was most urgently needed for the benefit of the inhabitants of Uganda. He said he wished to be able to demonstrate that the two Governments were working together from the beginning. I think he is sincere in this. It is, of course, probable that Abdul Hadi

[1] This is the ambassador's despatch, submitted by Chapman-Andrews, who was officiating in Campbell's absence.

Pasha is also afraid of missing the chance of giving a demonstration to the world that Egypt is capable of co-operating in progressive schemes for the benefit of the peoples of Uganda, Sudan and Egypt, and also of missing the opportunity to gain considerable prestige for himself and his Government by participating in these works.

3. As regards the Sudan constitutional issue, I told the Minister for Foreign Affairs that it would be the greatest pity if constitutional questions were allowed to delay or be an obstacle to agreement of works which would be of such great practical benefit to the individual ordinary man. He said that he agreed with this and pointed out that there were always people who were ready to mar beneficial projects of this sort by insistence on political points, and went on to say that they should not be allowed to do so. I told him that His Majesty's Government would be pleased to hear this. The Prime Minister, when I raised this question with him, also agreed fully that political and constitutional difficulties should be avoided.

4. As regards publicity for these projects, I fully appreciate that you do not wish to be accused of lagging behind the United States Government in a matter in which His Majesty's Government should obviously take the lead, but at the same time it would be unfortunate if we allowed it to appear that the Egyptian Government were tagging on behind the British Government in a project of this sort and the vanity of both King Farouk and Abdul Hadi Pasha might be hurt and the whole project damaged in consequence if publicity made this appear to be the case. Subject to the position of His Majesty's Government being safeguarded, I think we should do everything possible to give the Egyptians the illusion that they themselves will have their full share of responsibility if these schemes go through, and that they will earn the respect and gratitude of the outside world for farsighted statesmanship. As I stated in paragraph 5 of my telegram No. 212, I propose to take an early opportunity to speak to King Farouk on the lines of your instructions in order to emphasise to him your personal interest and the importance that you attach to the work going ahead.

I am sending copies of this despatch to the Governor-General of the Sudan, the Governor of Uganda and His Majesty's representatives at Washington, Brussels and Addis Ababa and to Sir John Troutbeck,[2] British Middle East Office.

Enclosure to 172

With reference to your Excellency's letter of 19th January, 1949, regarding the proposed dam at Owen Falls, I wish to make clear the standpoint of the Egyptian Government with regard to the major irrigation projects for the control of the River Nile necessary to cope with Egypt's water requirements in the future.

A Technical Committee of senior officers of the Ministry of Public Works was formed to study and report on these projects. They have already completed their study and submitted their comprehensive report recommending the following:

1. The participation with the Uganda Government in the construction of the dam at Owen Falls for the purpose of over-year storage and building up of a reserve in Lake Victoria; and the construction of—

[2] Sir John Troutbeck, head of BMEO, Cairo, 1947–1950.

2. A regulator at Lake Kioga exit for control of the lake.
3. A dam across the Albert Nile at or near Mutir.
4. The Sudd channels, together with the requisite masonry and constructional works.
5. A dam at the 4th or 2nd Cataract on the Main Nile between Khartum and Haifa. Either of these dams or both will play an important part in protecting the country against dangerous floods, over and above supplementing the working of the lake's reservoirs for the control of water supply in timely season.
6. The dam at the Lake Tana exit for the benefit of both Egypt and the Sudan.
7. The raising of the storage level in Gebel Aulia reservoir.

Owing to the vital importance of these major projects the Egyptian Government have thought it fit and necessary to consult three eminent engineers of ex-Ministers of Public Works.

This National Expert Committee have set to work ever since last November and are still meeting regularly with the object of completing their studies as soon as possible.

The first result of these studies is their recommendation to hasten up the construction of the Lake Tana dam. They also approve Egypt's participation with the Uganda Government in the construction of the Owen Falls dam.

I trust this committee will complete their studies of remaining projects and submit their final report to the Government in three month's time.

The Egyptian Government is keen on conveying to your Excellency the importance she attaches to the Owen Falls dam scheme being an important link in the chain of major projects on the Nile referred to above.

The Egyptian Government is, therefore, losing no time in taking the necessary constitutional steps to put the matter before the Council of Ministers and to Parliament with the object of obtaining an early decision with regard to Egypt's participation in the construction of the Owen Falls scheme.

The Egyptian Government trust that no steps be taken by the Uganda Government in the matter in order that the construction may be started on the lines of the joint scheme for the benefit of both countries.

173 FO 371/73475, no 2400 — 15 Mar 1949

[Trade union legislation and the general strike]: minutes by G L Clutton and Mr Bevin on trade union legislation in the Sudan

On the 11th March the Workers' Congress in Atbara sent an ultimatum to the Governor-General of the Sudan demanding the immediate annulment of the Trade Union Ordinance, failing which a strike will be called on the 15th March. A report has just been received from Khartoum to the effect that it is believed there will be a one-day strike of a general nature today.

The Secretary of State will recall that after the three-day railway strike[1] and the so called "indefinite strike" which took place in the Sudan a year ago,[2] the Sudan Government drew up legislation regulating the setting up of Trades Unions, the means of settling trades disputes, conditions of employment and workers' compensation. Generally speaking, this legislation was well received, but the Trade

---

[1] See 152.

[2] See 158 and 159.

Union Ordinance which was proclaimed in January last and is to become effective today has met with some criticism.

The root of this opposition lies, of course, in the Anglo–Egyptian quarrel over the status of the Sudan which has divided intelligent Sudanese into two main groups, the Umma, who favour ultimate independence, and the Ashigga, who advocate union with Egypt. The dispute between these two parties is aggravated by conflicting religious and personal loyalties. The result has been that where the Umma have supported the Government over the establishment of the Legislative Assembly, the Ashigga have opposed them, and this opposition has been carried into other spheres. Where the Umma support the new Trades Union Legislation the Ashigga oppose it. The instrument of Ashigga policy in this case is the Workers' Affairs Association which provoked the railway strike a year ago. The danger in the present situation lies in the extent to which Communists can take advantage of the rivalry between the Ashigga and the Umma parties. We know that the Trade Unions in Egypt are affiliated to the World Federation of Trade Unions which is no more than an instrument for the furtherance of Soviet Communist policy, and it is therefore highly probable that Communist elements are fostering the pro-Egyptian Ashigga party's criticism of the Ordinance, and are ultimately responsible for the present threatened strike. A report received from Mr. Cowan, the Labour Commissioner, that Communist converts have already made their appearance in the Workers' Affairs Association, tends to confirm this view. Moreover, further propaganda against the Trade Union Ordinance has been circulated by the "Sudanese Movement for National Liberation" which is closely connected with the "Democratic Movement of National Liberation", which is the principal Communist organisation in Egypt.

The Workers' Affairs Association have two principal objections to the Ordinance. In the first place it gives freedom to all to organise, and the Association's "leadership" will in due course be challenged; secondly the Association will have to account for their funds by the responsible Audit, whereas last year a substantial balance of some thousands of pounds which they received from Cairo quietly disappeared.

The Sudan Government are fully aware of the danger inherent in the present situation should they be obliged to prosecute the recalcitrants in the event of their striking, after refusing to register under the Ordinance. To meet the present emergency the Sudan Government has issued instructions that unclassified employees on strike will lose one day's pay, but no further action will be taken against them; classified officials who refuse, neglect or fail to perform their duty without reasonable excuse will be tried by a Board of Discipline, and the Sudan Government have suggested that they should be fined a few days' pay according to circumstances, with a maximum of 7 days.

The Department are being kept fully informed of the situation by the Sudan Agency in London.

Since the above was written the Department have been informed by the Sudan Agency that the strike began at 5.30 this morning. The strike has been 100% effective amongst the unclassified (non-pensionable) workers; all Post and Telegraph staffs have carried on but only 25% of the Public Works staff have refused to strike. No hospital staffs have struck. No incidents had been reported up to midday today and it is expected that the strike will end at 5.30 tomorrow morning.

G.L.C.
15.3.49

This may be a rehearsal for something later on. The Communist generally begins with one-day strikes. The Govt. should leave nothing to chance and begin now building up a counter organization. We should warn the Egyptian Govt. they may be playing with fire if they encourage the use of the industrial strike for political purposes.

E.B.
17.3.49

174 FO 371/73615, no 3034 9 Apr 1949

[Nile Waters]: inward Savingram no 76 from Sir R Campbell to FO on the participation of the Sudan in Nile Waters projects. *Minute* by D J D Maitland[1]

In paragraph 9 of my despatch No.207[2] now on its way to you, I referred to certain policy questions now confronting us.

2. These all arise from the need to protect the interests of the Sudan and appear to be as follows:—

(I) *Participation of the Sudan in the White Nile scheme*

It appears that the Sudan will eventually require a considerable quantity of water from the White Nile scheme. The summary of the scheme handed to the Egyptian Government makes no mention of this requirement nor have the Egyptians been made aware of it in any other way except informally. Their reaction is therefore not known, but is likely to be unfavourable.

It is important to consider the Sudan's claim *now* because (a) the Blue and White Nile projects when executed will practically exhaust the possibilities of increasing and regularising the flow of the Nile once and for all, and there will therefore be no other projects from which the Sudan's requirements could be satisfied later (b) although the Egyptian Government cannot in practice execute either the Blue or the White Nile scheme against the wishes of His Majesty's Government owing to the latter's influence in Ethiopia and Uganda and her position as Co-dominus of the Sudan, the bargaining weapon which this gives us will become increasingly difficult to use as the projects progress, unless we are to lay ourselves open to charges of bad faith and possibly of breaking of international law.

The tactics to be pursued are difficult to decide upon. It can be held that by allowing the Egyptian Government to participate even in the Owen Falls scheme without any commitment to share the benefits of the White Nile project with the Sudan, we have already lost bargaining strength. This contention will apply with increasing force at each stage of the White Nile scheme if no agreement is reached on the Sudan's share. It can also be held that it is wise to defer the raising of this issue until the Egyptian Government are fully committed to the Tsana scheme in which they are now taking so welcome an interest and on which a division of benefits with

[1] Egyptian Dept, FO, 1948–1950.

[2] Reporting a conversation with the Egyptian foreign minister concerning Nile Waters (FO 371/73615, no 2924).

the Sudan has already been worked out and recently endorsed in an Egyptian Aide Memoire.[3] It will be recalled that in the short term the Tsana scheme is considered to be much more important to the Sudan than the White Nile scheme.

There are many permutations of arguments in either direction.

(II) *The representation of the Sudan in the Tsana negotiations and agreement*
While an agreement between Egypt and the Sudan only on a division of cost and benefit might be honoured indefinitely by Egypt, it is generally considered to be desirable that such an agreement should somehow be consecrated in the agreement which will have to be negotiated with the Ethiopian Government and that the Sudan should somehow formally be a party to that agreement. Both Egypt and Ethiopia would in this way be bound *vis-a-vis* the Sudan by an international instrument, giving the latter proper security for her share of water and her financial commitment. But the caution which the Egyptians display towards any form of procedure which implies formal acceptance of the equal status of Co-domini or the equal status of Egypt and the Sudan, coupled with the fact that Egypt is a vitally interested party and the United Kingdom is not, makes it peculiarly difficult to find the right formula.

(III) *Revision of the Nile Waters agreement*
The execution of the Egyptian–Sudan technical agreement on division of benefits of the Tsana scheme, by altering the amounts of water to which they are entitled, *ipso facto* requires the amendment of the Nile Waters agreement. I understand that this technical agreement does not in any case provide in terms for the *year-round* entitlement of the Sudan, and an agreement regarding this will have to be negotiated before modification of the Nile Waters agreement is achieved. Similar considerations will apply in respect of the White Nile scheme. The Nile Waters agreement contains no provision for denunciation but is written in terms contemplating a review in changed circumstances. It is an open question how and when the revision of the Nile Waters agreement is to be tackled.

3. I have discussed these matters at great length with members of my staff and briefly with Mr. Allan the Irrigation Consultant to the Sudan Government during his recent visit here. I have come to the conclusion that they can only be resolved after a full discussion between representatives of the Sudan Government, your own department, and this Embassy. Mr. Allan is planning to return to London later this month and I suggest therefore that the discussion take place here on April 21st and 22nd which would enable him to attend this meeting by breaking his journey here. I have no doubt that the Sudan Government, if they agree to the meeting, will also wish to send a representative qualified to deal with the political side of the matter. On the assumption that you also agree, I venture to suggest that the representative from your department might be Mr. Donald Maitland, who I believe is well acquainted with these matters. It would not be necessary to keep him for more than two days if he could be spared only for a short period.

4. I should appreciate a very early indication of your view, and that of the Sudan Government, upon this proposal.

[3] See 172.

Minute on 174

This telegram is a supplement to the despatch in J2924/14210/16, which is submitted simultaneously.

I have discussed this with Mr. Stewart[4] and our preliminary comments are as follows:

On (I), it would be better to raise this question with the Egyptian Government sooner rather than later and on the highest level. An opportunity to do so might arise if we can offer the Egyptians a favourable solution to the tenders and contracts problem.

On II and III, a revision of the Nile Waters Agreement is of course necessary because the 1929 Agreement consisted of an Exchange of Notes covering the report of the 1925 Commission which has been superseded by the technical agreement of April 1948. The Sudan constitutional question might be avoided if the new Nile Waters Agreement were tripartite or quadripartite—i.e. signed by and binding on the Egyptian Government (*per se* and as one co-dominus), H.M.G. (as metropolitan country of Uganda and the other co-dominus), the Ethiopian Government and, possibly, the Belgian Government. During the negotiation of the Agreement the Sudan's interests could be represented by advisers at the disposal of the delegations of both co-domini; this would go some way towards satisfying Sudanese prestige. The Agreement itself would say, amongst other things, that so much of the Lake Tana water would be used in the Sudan and so much would pass on to Egypt and so on.

Mr Stewart agreed that I should express the above as personal views in Cairo and that I should ask that any recommendations arising from the discussions should be subject to further consideration in the Foreign Office.

D.J.D.M.
15.4.49

---

[4] FO, 1948–1951; assistant head of African Dept, 1950.

175 FO 371/73842, no 3261 23 Apr 1949

[Western Eritrea and the Sudan]: minutes by M N F Stewart and Sir E Beckett on proposal to incorporate the province of Western Eritrea into the Sudan.

[The future of the former Italian colonies, including Eritrea, was placed before the General Assembly of the UN. Britain was most concerned about the fate of the Italian colonists and the effect any settlement would have on its relations with Italy and Ethiopia. It was the US State Department which proposed to separate the largely Muslim Western Province from the rest of highland Eritrea, with its Christian majority, and cede it to the Sudan. Britain was at first reluctant to agree to this, for fear that it would provoke Egypt into raising constitutional questions regarding the Sudan. Egypt proved unexpectedly amenable to the proposal, however, and the text of a draft resolution was agreed between the State Department and the FO (inward telegram no 1756 from Clutton to the FO, 28 Mar 1949, FO 371/73842, no 2593). The FO was still concerned that the debate in the General Assembly would lead to some proposed interference by the UN in the Sudan as a whole. In the end the South American caucus in the General Assembly proposed that the Western Province be placed under an international trusteeship, to which both Britain and Egypt objected. By the end of 1949 the international debate on Eritrea had moved away from partition and on to only two possible options: the total cession of Eritrea to

Ethiopia, or complete independence for Eritrea (minute by H G Bower, 'Withdrawal from Eritrea', 25 Nov 1949, FO 371/73847, no 8555). Despite the Sudan government's obvious reluctance to absorb Western Eritrea, the issue revived Campbell's complaint about 'the rapidly increasing tendency of the Sudan Government to take upon itself something of the nature of the government of an independent state', with Robertson apparently assuming the role of prime minister to the governor-general's head of state, especially in external affairs, as evidenced by his alleged desire to readjust the frontier with Kenya and Ethiopia (see 143) and annex Western Eritrea without reference to Egypt. Since the ambassador had ceased to be high commissioner for the Sudan the embassy in Cairo could exercise no oversight in such matters; therefore 'I beg of you to look once more at the question of what seems to me Foreign Office responsibility to control the actions of the Sudan Government.' (letter from Campbell to Wright, 14 May 1949, FO 371/73472, no 4357).]

The Secretary of State said at a meeting held in his room on the 22nd April that he had no objection to the proposal to incorporate the Western Province of Eritrea into the Sudan provided

(a) it would not involve either a U.N. Commission of Enquiry visiting the Sudan or the Western Province.

(b) there was no form of interference by the Assembly in the affairs of the Sudan, e.g. by the former asking to hear the views of the Sudanese Delegation, or by otherwise enquiring into the affairs of the Anglo–Egyptian condominium.

He had in mind the possibility that, as apparently the Egyptian Government would make no advance, some member of the Slav bloc or even the South American states might take the opportunity of embarrassing the H.M.G., and of disturbing Anglo–Egyptian relations.

These are primarily political considerations on which the U.K. Delegation will have to advise. The Secretary of State also wished for advice on the proper form of taking the Sudan Government's views on the proposal and of securing consent.

The Governor General of the Sudan has already taken private and unofficial soundings of the Sudanese members of his Executive Council (see Khartoum telegram No. 72, Flag K)[1] who are dubious about the questions of the expense of administering the province and the possible unfriendly reactions of Ethiopia. The Governor General should be in a position to reassure them since the Secretary of State has said that he is willing to ask the Treasury to pay the cost of administration (at present calculated at between £25,000 and £30,000 a year) until such a time as the province can become self-supporting. As regards Ethiopian reaction, the Ethiopian Delegation in New York has given assurances and has asked their Government to confirm them.[2] Perhaps Sir Eric Beckett would be good enough to

---

[1] The Sudanese members of the Executive Council were concerned about administrative cost to the Sudanese tax-payers, the possibility of opposition from the inhabitants of Western Eritrea, and the probability of creating difficulties over the Lake Tsana project should Ethiopia wish to take over all of Eritrea. The last was seen as the most important consideration, and Robertson reported that the Sudanese members of the council would be unlikely to agree to the proposal if Ethiopia did not consent (inward telegram no 72 from Robertson to Stewart, 12 Apr 1949, FO 371/73842, no 3031).

[2] The Ethiopian delegation to the UN assured the UK delegation that relations between the two countries would be unaffected by the General Assembly awarding Western Eritrea to the Sudan. They even went so far as to seek authority from Addis Ababa to renounce Ethiopia's claim to the Western Province (inward telegram no 944 from Clutton (NY) to Robertson (FO), 19 Apr 1949, FO 371/73842, no 3261).

advise on the question of officially ascertaining the Sudan Government's views mentioned above.

M.N.F.S.
23.4.49

It is outside the authority of the Governor-General of the Sudan under the Condominium Agreement to accept a new province for inclusion in the Sudan. The decision on this point rests with the two co-domini but the two co-domini may think it proper, before deciding, to obtain the views of the Governor-General, and in this case an enquiry by both co-domini to the Governor-General and a reply by him to both co-domini is the right procedure, the decision on the point being conveyed to the Assembly by the two co-domini.

W.E.B.
26.4.49

176 FO 371/73406, no 4316 4 May 1949

[Political climate in the Sudan]: memorandum by E A Chapman-Andrews on a recent visit to the Sudan [Extract]

The following is not intended to be a report in the ordinary sense of the term relating more or less exactly what various people told me, but rather to be some account of my visit to the Sudan indicating the sort of people I talked things over with, the general burden of what they had to say, though not exactly in their own language, and my own impressions of the result.

I left Cairo by air on the morning of Thursday, 10th March, and returned on the morning of Thursday, 17th March. I got into action on the day of my arrival by having tea at the Governor-General's residence with the three Sudanese "Ministers" and I ended the proceedings with being entertained by them to tea the evening before I left. The only changes I made in the programme of engagements drawn up for me by the Governor-General's staff were to exclude interviews with the press and to include visits to the Officer Commanding Egyptian Troops in the Sudan, the Unionist Party Club at Omdurman and a short talk with a leading Independent who was until recently Secretary-General of the Umma Party.[1]

Among the Sudanese, in addition to my two talks with the three Ministers (Agriculture, Education and Health) I had talks with the Speaker of the Chamber, the Under-Secretaries (there are no Ministers for these Departments) of the Interior, Defence, Irrigation, Economics and Trade and Finance, the Assistant Director of Works, the Town Clerk of Omdurman (who took me round both Omdurman and Khartoum to show me what was being done in the way of town planning and housing for the Sudanese), various members of the Legislative Assembly, including a certain number from the South and tribal Nazirs and, last but not least, long talks with the two irreconcilables, El Sayed Sir Abdul Rahman El Mahdi Pasha and El Sayed Sir Aly El Mirghany Pasha. I also visited the Chamber during a Session. . . .

---

[1] Possibly Muhammad Ahmad Mahjub, nominated member to the Assembly. Abdallah Khalil had been secretary general of the Umma Party since its inception.

Of all the above, apart from the members of the Unionist Party Club and the Egyptian Army officers, who had nothing to say about politics, only four or five could be classed as in opposition to the policies of the Sudan Government and of the Umma Party. Of these the most important individual was, of course, El Sayed Aly El Mirghany. I had a three hour talk with him over tea the day after my arrival.

He took the line that as a holy man, the head of a sect that had long been established throughout the length of the Nile Valley and had its origin in Mecca, he could not also be a politician. You could not, however, altogether divorce religion from politics and he had advised his followers, who were the majority of the people of the Sudan, that they were free to adopt any attitude they wished towards political questions save only that they must not support the Umma Party. They could, for example, be for or against the Ordinance and the Legislative Assembly though it seemed clear to him that the Ordinance had been deliberately constructed to forward government policy which in its turn was to assure ascendency in the Sudan to the Umma Party. That was why most of his followers had in fact opposed the Ordinance. He had heard of people fighting and dying in order to have a Parliament, but surely never before had there been an example of the majority of people struggling against the Government and being imprisoned and losing their property in order *not to have a Parliament*. Yet such was the case in the Sudan. The reason why his followers were not free to join the Umma Party was that it was a revival of Mahdism under which the Mirghanists had suffered until the reconquest of the Sudan at the end of the last century. Mahdism was both a religion and a political creed. As a religion it was anathema to true believers. It had its origins not in the holy land of Arabia, but in the native soil of the Sudan and its first prophet claimed that he was equal to God's Prophet. The Mahdi had so declared himself (as had his successor the Khalifa) on the banners borne by the Dervish army in their first insurrection against the "Turks"[2] (by this expression he always referred indiscriminately to the members of the Sudan Political Service and their predecessors in Khedivial days whether British or Egyptian) which had led to the murder of the Turkish Governor-General, Gordon Pasha and during their resistance to the onward march of Kitchener's Army 15 years later. Those 15 years were surely the blackest period in the Sudan's history. The Mahdists claimed them as the only era of true Sudanese independence and it was by that standard that the present Umma (Independence) Party should be measured. Slavery, oppression and darkness descended on the Sudan in those days and rather than risk a return to such conditions Sayed Aly and his followers would prefer that there should be no independence for the Sudan and that the present Condominium should remain but if that were not possible they would have the Egyptian Crown or even Egyptian rule. There was nothing abhorrent about the idea of Egyptian rule as there was about a revival of Mahdism; and there was a real danger of such a revival. The Mahdists were well organised and strong. They had always been the martial element in the Sudan and once they got rid of the British and the Egyptians the towns along the Nile Valley which were the Mirghanists' strongholds, as in the past, would be at the mercy of the Mahdists. It was these towns that were the centres of

[2] Muhammad Ahmad al-Mahdi was, in fact, careful to declare his subordination to the Prophet Muhammad, even when imitating him. His flags carried the slogan, 'Muhammad Ahmad is the Khalifa (Successor) to the Prophet of God'.

commerce, international trade, cultural and religious institutions and in fact all that was most worth preserving in the Sudan. The Mahdist youth were already well organised and the uniform they wore was the patched jibba affected by the Dervish warriors. These Mahdist youth groups were even called by the very word ANSAR ("Conquerors")[3] adopted by the leaders of the Dervish armies during the Mahdia. Moreover the head of the Umma Party was a man of unbounded ambition. He wanted to be King of the Sudan. He might not admit it in so many words but such was the case. He was unscrupulous too and prepared to use his religion to advance his wordly ambitions and to take advantage of his increase in power and influence to impose his religion upon others. And it was the unmistakable policy of the Sudan Government to support the Mahdi. They had helped him to acquire land by which he had enriched himself. They had appointed his followers to government office all over the country and now they had so drafted the Ordinance as to ensure a very large Mahdist majority in the Legislative Assembly despite the fact that the other parties commanded more support throughout the country and represented the more enlightened classes. So long as this remained government policy Sayed Aly's followers would do everything in their power to oppose it.

The other three or four Mirghanists with whom I spoke held the same view (though with varying intensity) about the danger of a revival of the Mahdia but they were not against free institutions as such.

They were all (but one in particular—a man who had a son at Cambridge and who has himself refused the offer of a ministerial portfolio because he was opposed to the Ordinance in its present form) intelligent men and, as I thought, very reasonable critics. They wanted to see the Ordinance amended in order to provide for stronger representation of the towns and the representation of tribal areas by other than the Nazirs who were in fact really appointed by the Government and in a sense Government servants. These Nazirs were not only the supreme judicial, administrative and executive authorities in their districts but also represented those districts in the Assembly. Yet ordinary civil servants who stood for the Assembly had to resign. The rule should be that *both* civil servants *and* Nazirs were excluded or else that *neither* should be excluded. My interlocutors seemed to think that *both* should be excluded.

They also thought there should be some rearrangement of constituencies. . . .

El Sayed Sir Abdul Rahman El Mahdi Pasha invited me to breakfast in his house which no doubt in some ways was intended to resemble a palace. It is in fact called by this name, in competition possibly with the residence of the Governor-General which is similarly designated. There were silver-framed photographs of royalties in his drawing room and the old man himself with his little entourage has quite a regal bearing. While I was there they were working away on a very large reception room or hall on the ground floor which was being added to his residence; and the thought crossed my mind (as it has I believe that of many others) that this was to be a sort of throne room. At both my talks with him the Mahdi was accompanied by his son who had been to Gordon College and speaks quite adequate English.

The Mahdi told me he was a posthumous son of his father, the founder of the Mahdia. After his father's death the Khalifa ("Successor"), of whom he retained most affectionate memories, treated him as his own son. After the battle of Omdurman

[3] 'Ansar' means 'helper', the term the Prophet Muhammad applied to his own followers.

and the dispersal of the Khalifa's Army, Sayed Abdul Rahman was concealed for a time but finally surrendered to Sir Reginald Wingate, then Sirdar and Governor-General of the Sudan. Sir Reginald befriended him and got small grants of land for him in the provinces, but these years were a period of trial for his father's former followers. The Government in those days befriended the Mirghanists. But during the first world war the loyalty to the Government of some of these Mirghanists was called in question. Some of them followed the example of certain Egyptian officers of the Army and refused to take part in a war against Turkey because the Sultan was both Caliph and Suzerain of the Egyptian Khedive. It was at that time that the Sudan Government invited Sayed Abdul Rahman to tour the Sudan urging support of the Allies against Germany and Turkey. After the war the Sudan Government came to rely increasingly upon the support of Sayed Abdul Rahman and his followers and gave them increasing freedom to organise themselves and prepare themselves generally to serve the interests of the Sudan. In the intervening years he and his followers had prospered and there was no doubt that they now constituted the most reliable and best trained elements in the country. They had their detractors but their loyalty and gratitude to Britain should not be called in question. They fully realised that the days of colonial government were over and that people were becoming increasingly free to choose their own form of government. The Sudanese respected the British but they wanted quite naturally to run their own country. They would do this, when the time came, with British help and advice but they must hold the supreme power in their own hands. He realised that the Government of the Sudan still depended upon the Condominium Agreement, but the Sudanese had been promised that no further agreement concerning the Sudan would be entered into between the Co-Domini without the Sudanese being consulted and approving it. He was apprehensive lest in our anxiety to obtain a workable military arrangement with Egypt we should be prepared to sacrifice the Sudan or the interests of the Sudanese or come to some arrangement with Egypt affecting the future of the Sudan without the consent of the Sudanese and he warned me that any such action on our part would undoubtedly lead to widespread outbreaks of revolt. His people would not stand for it. His father had revolted against "Turkish" oppression and had achieved independence for the Sudan which would have remained independent to this day but for the British conquest. Although I asked him many questions about the period of the Mahdia, which he remembered quite well, he would not admit that it was a black interlude in the country's history and therefore best forgotten. On the contrary his whole attitude seemed to be that it was a glorious epoch in which his father's achievements set the standard for his own strivings. I asked him outright whether he contemplated ever being King of the Sudan and he replied that he did not; but this was not a matter that called even for discussion at the moment. Some of his followers indeed wanted an independent Sudan within the British Commonwealth. All of them wanted an independent Sudan run with British assistance and advice and in most friendly relations with the British Commonwealth. None of them wanted or would tolerate Egyptian control. They would welcome an arrangement with Britain that would give Britain all she required in the way of military facilities. They were grateful to Britain but was not Britain also grateful to the Sudan? Did Britain not know that she could rely on the Sudan to fight at her side whenever Britain was at war? Could Britain rely on Egypt? Was it worth alienating the Sudan to get a military arrangement with Egypt and would it not be better to let Egypt go her own way and make a military arrangement with the Sudan? The Umma Party wanted good relations with Egypt also. They realised full well that they must be on terms of intimate friendship with Egypt. Egypt and the Sudan could not get along without one another. They might be glad of help from Egypt provided they were sure that the Egyptians furnishing it and working in the Sudan were not *foci* of political unrest and spearheads of Egyptian imperialism as were without exception Egyptians working in the Sudan at the present moment notably the officer commanding the Egyptian troops and a large number of Egyptian schoolmasters. He realised (though he did not volunteer it—I had to wring it out of him) that Egyptian assent to the Ordinance was desirable. Indeed he seemed, on being pressed, apprehensive of the possible consequences of not obtaining it. He seemed ready to discuss this matter with me tentatively but, as I explained to him, as to all others, I was not briefed for negotiations but was merely enquiring about viewpoints.

So much for the Mahdi.

To compare the two men no more need be said than that the Mahdi impresses one as being undoubtedly the better man of the two. He may have ambitions but I think very few fears. He is probably a bully. The other may have no ambitions but is full of fears. Sayed Aly, I think, nurses feelings of frustration, disappointment, envy, hatred and malice and an ambition to see the Mahdi's power again destroyed. Sayed Abdul Rahman, on the other hand, is a full man and I think *could be persuaded* to compromise on practical issues if given assurances.

The Mahdi's followers struck me as a good lot and I must admit that they did not seem to me to be the sort of men who would lend themselves to or tolerate anything like a revival of the Mahdia in the old sense. They were serious minded, well educated men, trying very hard, it seemed to me, in the face of great difficulties, to run the country decently and progressively and learning how to do this through a parliamentary system. They differed considerably among themselves about the future. Some wanted full independence very soon, others later. Some wanted British dominion status and the sooner the better. All wanted the continuance of British advice and guidance, and many told me they realised that it would be some time before the Sudanese themselves could be capable of running their own show as they wanted to see it run. At the same time they felt that although the existing Sudan Political Service provided an excellent administration it was very expensive and something of a luxury. They did not think the Sudan should or could afford it. There would admittedly have to be some sacrifice of standards of efficiency. That was inevitable. They did not think the maintenance of such high standards of administration necessary but they all said they were determined to try and maintain these standards themselves. At least they would know that such standards existed and could be maintained. All this struck me as very honest. These followers of the Mahdi too were almost without exception anxious to establish good neighbourly relations with Egypt. They were afraid of the Common Crown because, for one thing, to reassert the principle of it now after that principle had lain dormant for many years would be taken by the masses as an indication of a forward Egyptian policy in the Sudan; and that they would never accept. They realised, however, that so long as the Ordinance lacked Egyptian assent it was a weak instrument and they would welcome arrangements (in the negotiation of which they claimed to have a right to take part) that would bring the boycott parties to the polling booth.

And now for a word about the British officials. They are, of course, beyond reproach as administrators and magistrates; but they are undoubtedly strongly geared in with the Mahdi's supporters and indeed the opinions some hold regarding the future status of the Sudan seemed to me to be more extreme than those of many of the Mahdists. It is my opinion that the number of British officials should be reduced fairly rapidly and that a fiat should go forth from the Governor-General that these officials must not discuss with the Sudanese such questions as the future status of the Sudan or Anglo–Egyptian relations or relations of the Sudan with Britain and Egypt. They should be reminded of their duty which is *to administer the Sudan* and they should confine themselves to the performance of that duty, difficult as it may be to reconcile it with an increasing measure of self-government by the Sudanese themselves. The power of the senior British officials in the Sudan is the real governing power of the country. It is rather like the control exercised by the heads of houses in English public schools and indeed the attitude of these senior officials towards the Ordinance struck me as being rather like that of the head of a house or even a housemaster towards, say, an experiment in school self-government. A strong team spirit is almost spontaneously engendered by contact with these people and though that is all very well as far as it goes, it ought to fall short of encouraging defiance of the board of governors.

I may be wrong but I think some importance should be attached to what was said to me by a young lawyer who, as stated above, was until recently secretary of the Umma Party. I saw him alone. He is said to be earning several thousand a year (fantastic for a Sudanese) at the Bar for he is regarded as quite the ablest native advocate in the country. Though of very humble origins (his mother is said to have been a slave) he told me he had left the Party in order to be independent in the Legislative Assembly with a view to forming a party of his own—a little later. I believe he represents Atbara (a railway junction town) and he has been concerned as a lawyer with railway workers [sic] disputes and their settlement. He is thinking of starting a sort of labour party with the support of the trade unionists and making a clean break away from the two Sayeds whose role in his opinion should be confined to religious matters. Regarding sovereignty of the Sudan he takes the view that it rests with the people of the country. He denies the existence of Condominium status. It may have existed at the time of the Condominium Agreement, but could not be substantiated now with the passage of years and the change of conditions. The Sudanese people have acquired sovereignty or perhaps re-acquired it. He thinks that insofar as this thesis could be challenged it might be challenged to some extent by the British Government who have, with the admitted consent of the Sudanese, provided a body of officials to govern the country for the past 50 years; but he does not think that it could be challenged by the Egyptian Government who 25 years ago ceased to have any real say in the way the country was governed. A day or two before I saw him he had introduced a private members [sic] bill in the Assembly something on the lines of the Egyptian Companies Law aimed at severely limiting the employment of foreign capital in the Sudan. This was defeated by what I thought was a surprisingly narrow margin. I see from the papers that since my visit he has taken a leading part in a debate about the period of time which should elapse before the Sudan should achieve full self-government. He told me that if there should ever be any question of imposing the Egyptian Crown or any increased measure of Egyptian control over the Sudan he would fight against it by every means in his power and not confine himself to the floor of the Assembly or to speech-making outside. . . .

177 FO 371/73617, no 4598 7 May 1949

[Nile Waters]: note by A L Chick on a discussion on Nile Waters by the Executive Council of the Sudan

At an informal meeting of the Executive Council on 3rd May I reported that H.B.M's Ambassador in Cairo would shortly speak to the Egyptian Prime Minister about the Equatorial Nile and Lake Tana Projects. The Ambassador would propose:—

(a) that the technical agreements of May, 1935, and the supplement of November, 1946, about the Lake Tana Project should be adopted by the Egyptian Government subject to such revision or modification by agreement as might be found necessary for the full development of the project or in order to reach a satisfactory agreement with the Ethiopian Government;
(b) that the negotiations with the Ethiopian Government should be conducted by delegations representing the British Government and the Egyptian Government, who would have at their joint disposal advisers from the Sudan. Any agreement reached with the Ethiopian Government would be signed by the Egyptian representative on behalf of Egypt and jointly by the British and Egyptian representatives on behalf of the Sudan;
(c) that the Sudan's share in the benefits of the Equatorial Nile Project and her financial contribution towards its cost should be the subject of technical discussions between Egypt and the Sudan, the results of which would be embodied in the agreements to be concluded between the interested Governments concerning the Project;
(d) that this procedure should be adopted regarding the Sudan's participation in any projects on the Nile other than the Equatorial Nile and Lake Tana Projects; and
(e) that the British and Egyptian Governments should recognize that a review and amendment of the Nile Waters Agreement would be necessary to give effect to the arrangements made and to be made regarding the distribution of Nile Waters.

2. I said that if the Egyptian Government accepted these proposals in principle we would have taken a long step towards our goal of safeguarding the Sudan's interests in Nile Waters. I remarked as regards (b) above that while we would all have liked the Sudan Government to be separately represented in any negotiations with the Ethiopian Government about Lake Tana, to press for this would raise the constitutional issue: there was no hope that the Egyptian Government would concede the claim and the only result would be yet further delay. Whether the Sudan sent representatives or advisers would, I suggested, make little practical difference since the British and Egyptian representatives would negotiate within a framework already agreed between Egypt and the Sudan. Moreover, we could rely on the British Government's representative (who would be advised by our own advisers) to protect the Sudan's interests: and both the British and Sudan Governments had the (admittedly negative) power of veto under the 1902 Treaty.

3. Considerable discussion ensued on this point. The Sudanese members of the Council who were present (Sayyeds Abdulla Khalil, Abdel Rahman Ali Taha,[1] Ibrahim

[1] Abd al-Rahman Ali Taha was an Umma Party member elected to the Legislative Assembly, and minister of education in the Executive Council.

Ahmed and Abdel Magid Ahmed) felt strongly that the Sudan should be represented; other considerations apart, the fact that she would be paying part of the cost of the Project entitled her to representation. The Sudan's non-representation would inevitably be severely criticized in the Assembly and they would feel embarrassed if they had to defend it. They would like to be able to say that the Egyptian Government had refused to agree to separate representation for the Sudan and to have a written refusal.

4. I replied that we already had such a refusal and quoted certain passages from the late Nokrashi Pasha's despatch of 10th July, 1948. While there seemed to be a welcome change in the Egyptian Government's attitude as regards the representation of the British Government in the negotiations, nothing had since happened to suggest that they would agree to separate representation for the Sudan. In support of this, I mentioned the Egyptian Government's recent objection to the Sudan sending a delegate to the International Cotton Advisory Committee's meeting in Brussels.

5. The Sudanese members argued that the situation had been changed since the Egyptian Government's refusal by the setting up of the Executive Council and the Legislative Assembly and they felt that because of this, the Egyptian Government should again be asked to agree to separate representation for the Sudan. Sir James Robertson and I both stressed that that did not constitute a relevant change, since the Council and the Assembly were set up within the framework of the 1899 Agreement and the 1936 Treaty. The Sudan Government had no right to separate representation and to ask for it would be to invite a rebuff and could only result in further delay. The Acting Legal Secretary, Mr. Lindsay, pointed out that the Sudanese members were, in effect, asking for a revision of the Agreement and Treaty.

6. The Sudanese members agreed not to press their point but they asked that their views should be recorded.

178 FO 371/73617, no 4201 16 May 1949

[Nile Waters]: minute by D J D Maitland to Mr Bevin on the Owen Falls dam and Equatorial Nile projects

[Following the decision to inform the Egyptian government of the Sudan's need to participate in the Equatorial Nile project (see 174), the Embassy in Cairo prepared drafts of notes on the Owen Falls dam, Equatorial Nile and Lake Tsana projects for discussion with the Egyptian government who, however, claimed that they were not yet in a position to exchange notes concerning comprehensive Nile Waters schemes (inward telegram no 663 from Campbell to FO, 9 May 1949, FO 371/73616, no 3343). The meeting between Bevin and Amr Pasha, for which these minutes were prepared, dealt with the related issues of the Owen Falls dam and the Equatorial Nile project.]

The Egyptian Ambassador is coming to discuss the Nile Waters schemes with the Secretary of State this afternoon.

The present position is that two questions remain to be settled:—

(a) the ownership of the Owen Falls dam, and

(b) recognition of the entitlement of the Sudan to share in the benefit of the Equatorial Nile and other projects.

(a) presents no serious difficulty since we, the Egyptian Government and the Uganda Electricity Board have agreed that no reference should be made to the question of ownership in any announcement which may be made about the Owen Falls dam. The Egyptian Prime Minister has expressed his willingness to make a declaration in the Egyptian Parliament safeguarding the freedom of action of the Uganda Electricity Board so far as the generation of hydro-electric power at Owen Falls is concerned.

As regards (b), both Sir Ronald Campbell and the Department feel that it is essential that the question of the Sudan's share in the waters of the Equatorial and Main Nile and the approach to the Ethiopian Government on the Lake Tana scheme should be settled simultaneously with the question of the Owen Falls dam. Our reasons for thinking so are:—

(i) It is important that the misconception that Egypt alone is entitled to the full benefit of the Equatorial Nile Project should not be perpetuated; in this connexion the Secretary of State will recall that no mention was made of the Sudan's share in the Equatorial Nile Project when the Summaries of the whole scheme were presented to the Egyptian Government in February last because we felt at that time that Anglo–Egyptian relations were insufficiently stable to allow us to take the risk of injecting the Sudan issue in any form into a matter such as the Nile Waters schemes, on which we were anxious to reach preliminary agreement.[1] Unless we settle the question of the Sudan's share of the waters now, it is possible that there will be another deterioration in Anglo–Egyptian relations which will make it more difficult to do so at a later date.

(ii) To come to an agreement with the Egyptian Government on the Owen Falls dam without making any mention of the Sudan's share of the waters when the whole Project has been agreed would cause great dismay in the Sudan.

(iii) The Owen Falls scheme represents only one part of the whole of the Equatorial Nile Project from which the Sudan and Egypt are both to benefit. If we settle the Owen Falls scheme alone now without making it clear to the Egyptian Government that the Sudan is also entitled to some benefit from it, it will enable the Egyptian Government at a later date, if they so wish, to protest that we are claiming benefits for the Sudan which were not made clear at the time when the agreement on the Owen Falls scheme alone was arrived at.

The Department are discussing these questions with the Egyptian Ambassador this afternoon before he calls to see the Secretary of State and will inform the Secretary of State of any developments which may occur. Meanwhile, the Department recommend:

(a) that the Secretary of State should inform the Egyptian Ambassador that he is happy to learn that there is now no serious obstacle to the settlement of the question of the ownership of the Owen Falls dam;

(b) that he should inform the Egyptian Ambassador that H.M.G. consider that it would be harmful to the interests of Egypt and of the Sudan if our two Governments do not recognise the right of the Sudan to share in the benefits of the Equatorial Nile Project at the same time as our two Governments agree on the

---

[1] See 171 and 172.

Owen Falls dam. We need do no more at present than acknowledge the fact that the Sudan's participation in the Owen Falls and other schemes, including her financial contribution, should be the subject of technical discussions to take place at some future date between Egypt and the Sudan. H.M.G. are also anxious to agree now on the method of negotiating with the Ethiopian Government on the Lake Tana scheme in order to avoid delay.

179 FO 371/73475, no 4322 16 May 1949

[Trade Union legislation]: letter from Sir J Robertson to M N F Stewart reporting outcome of conference called to discuss Trade Unions and Trade Unions Disputes Ordinances

I refer to the Secretary of State's despatch No. 288 of 29th April to the Ambassador in Cairo on which I am commenting by "under the counter" means in accordance with our normal procedure.

2. I assume that you will have seen Sudan Political Intelligence Summary No. 2 of 1949, para. 34 of which shows that after the one-day protest strike on 15th March a conference was convened by the Government to discuss the criticisms of the Labour Ordinance and to make recommendations to the Executive Council. The Sudan Government was represented by four Sudanese members together with the Commissioner of Labour and a representative of the Legal Secretary. Two neutral non-Government Sudanese accepted nomination as members. The Workers' Affairs Association appointed seven representatives and the Leader of the Legislative Assembly presided.

3. It was known before the conference opened that the W.A.A. had appointed a moderate delegation following complaints from the workers about the strike on 15th March.[1] At the outset the workers' delegation pointedly renounced the irresponsible manifesto which was issued last January denouncing the Sudan Ordinances. Instead they presented alternative Ordinances, which although less virulent, were still quite impossible. These, also, they set aside very early in the proceedings of the conference. In the course of seven lengthy sessions, the conference examined every detail of the Trades Union Ordinances, the Trades Dispute Ordinance, and the Arbitration and Inquiry Ordinance. The relevant sections of the Egyptian Laws were available for discussion but the workers' representatives made it clear that they did not wish any comparisons to be made.

4. The Conference was an outstanding success owing in large degree to the patience and unswerving support of the principles of the Ordinance on the part of the Sudanese Government members and the two neutral members. The suspicions of the W.A.A. delegates were slowly dispelled and in the end complete acceptance of the Ordinances was secured following agreement to recommend several minor amendments. These amendments in no way touch the fundamental principles of the Ordinances nor do they exceed the bounds of customary practice elsewhere. Many of them indeed are devices to save the face of the W.A.A. I enclose a copy of the

---

[1] See 173.

Conference report setting out the recommendations in detail.[2] Since the conference dispersed, the Workers' delegates are reported to have secured acceptance of the agreed recommendations, and it is expected that Trades Union registrations will be applied for within the next few months. It is hoped to have a British Trade Union Officer available shortly to advise and assist the new movement and already there are indications that his services will be welcome to the workers.

5. It is premature yet to say that we are out of the wood and much will depend on the type and political sympathies of the leaders selected by the Union branches. When Unions are registered and the Government scheme of negotiating committees has been set up, Communist elements will no doubt do their best to make their influence felt. We are fully alive to this danger and shall do all we can to combat it.

6. From the above you will see that for the time being at least the labour situation here has improved beyond our expectations and we do not think that at present there is any need to approach the Egyptian Government on the subject. But if in the future we have evidence that Communist or other sources in Egypt are attempting to stir up further labour trouble in the Sudan, we should certainly agree that the Egyptian Government be asked for their support in discouraging such action. It is note worthy, although perhaps only a coincidence that since the successful result of the Conference there has been a complete absence of Communist pamphleteering.

7. I am sending a copy of this letter to Maclean.

---

[2] Not printed.

180 FO 371/73472, no 5256 — 24 June 1949

"The state of the condominium": minute by G L Clutton on the strained relations between the embassy in Cairo and the Sudan government

[In April F Roberts from the FO visited Cairo. He reported back to Wright: 'I know too little about the Sudan to judge, but I have an uneasy feeling that we are too much at the mercy of the Sudan Civil Servant, who, with all his admirable qualities, has a rather limited and parochial public-school outlook. Nor do I like having to put our money on the Mahdist faction, which can hardly be said to represent the forces of moderation in the Sudan. As the Cairo embassy and Khartoum inevitably have opposing interests in the matter, might it not be a good thing for you or someone from the F.O. to go and see the problems on the spot?' (letter from Roberts to Wright, 18 Apr 1949, FO 371/43472, no 4358). Strang minuted that Bevin 'thinks there is a good deal of truth in the criticism of the Sudan Civil Service. He would like this question looked into', and he further suggested that there be some interchange between the FO and the CO in respect of the Sudan (minute by Strang to Wright, 17 May 1949, FO 371/74372, no 4358). There was a growing anxiety within the FO about the effect the apparent intransigence of Sudan government officials was having on Anglo–Egyptian relations. Stewart wrote: 'The Egyptian Government have at least shown some willingness to make the Condominium work. . . . If the Sudan Government continue to be suspicious of Egyptian intentions and continue to oppose Egyptian participation the general improvement in our relations with Egypt will be hindered, a settlement on strategic matters in Egypt will be delayed and an eventual solution of the Sudan problem will be made more difficult. Whatever our interests may be in the Sudan our strategic requirements in Egypt are of the utmost importance and any tendency which can hinder a satisfactory settlement of this question should be avoided' (minute on the Sudan by Stewart, 19 May 1949, FO 371/73472, no 4359).]

During the past few months there have developed strained (and in a number of cases very strained) relationships between the Foreign Office and the Embassy at Cairo on the one hand, and the Sudan Government on the other. These strained relationships were manifested in particular at the time of the International Cotton meeting at Brussels, the Owen Falls agreement, and the famine in the Sudan.[1]

I have been much worried by this situation and have given it considerable thought. The following is my analysis of the situation.

(1) There is, I think, at the Embassy in Cairo a certain lack of comprehension of the organic character of an administration. When the Sudan Legislative Assembly and the Executive Council Ordinance was promulgated this was not the end of a stage of constitutional development but the beginning of one. Political life does not march by sudden leaps and bounds, but is something progressive. There will therefore be all sorts of developments flowing from the concrete step of the promulgation of the Ordinance which are inevitable and some of which may cause us serious bother. The complaint made by Sir R. Campbell about the debate on self-government in the Legislative Assembly (see J 3610 at flag A) seems to me unreasonable. If there had been a debate on independence it would have been improper, bit [sic] the actual debate was on self-government, and I do not see how a body of men embarking on the first step in self-government could be reasonably expected not to debate self-government.

(2) The Sudan is in many respects a very isolated country, and there is undoubtedly lack of comprehension in the Sudan of what is taking place in the world as a whole. For instance, it is true that the Sudan Government were to all intents and purposes responsible for the creation of the International Cotton Organisation, the meeting of which recently took place at Brussels. The Sudan's complaint here was that although they are a foundation member of the organisation, they are now excluded from it. What the Sudan Government officials do not realise is the manner in which matters which were previously purely technical have now become political. The International Cotton Organisation started life as a technical body. It has since become a political body, ranking with a diplomatic conference. In consequence, the Sudan cannot be represented any longer as a full member. Similarly, there is certainly a lack of realisation on the part of the Sudan Government of the fact that what goes on in a non-self governing territory is no longer a purely domestic matter. When the Indonesian question first came before the United Nations it was juridically speaking undoubtedly a purely domestic matter, but politically it was no longer so, as the Dutch have since learned to their cost. So it is in the Sudan. Administrative measures to which the outside world no longer paid attention are now, whether the Sudan Government like it or not, matters of international interest.

[1] There were reports of drought and famine in the eastern Sudan by the end of the 1949 dry season (Apr–May). When the Egyptian government voted to contribute to famine relief the Sudan government disputed their right to interfere, and were accused in turn by the Egyptians of obstructing relief. The FO accepted the Sudan government's claim that reports of famine were exaggerated, but nevertheless complained that 'the irascibility of the Sudan Government in these cases is to be deprecated' (minute by R W Bailey, first secretary, FO, 16 May 1949, FO 371/73665 no 3469, and minute by Maitland, 21 May 1949, FO 371/73665 no 4264).

This situation has been complicated by a series of factors of a more or less personal nature.

(i) There is no doubt that the present governmental structure in the Sudan is not entirely satisfactory. The Governor-General is not an Administrator. Very properly he has spent much time touring his territory.

The result, however, has been that during the past year out of the 200 days odd he has been in the Sudan, he has been 90 days out of Khartoum. The result has been that a very heavy burden of responsibility has been placed on the Civil Secretary, Sir James Robertson, and he has had to act as Governor-General in times of crisis (the Governor-General has not been in Khartoum for any of the big events except the opening of the Legislative Assembly during the past year; he was absent during the election troubles and at the time of the attempted visit to the Sudan by the Wafd Delegation and the Egyptian lawyers). Sir J. Robertson's responsibilities have been further added to by the fact that his two co-equals and colleagues, the Financial Secretary (Mr. Chick) and the Legal Secretary (Mr. C. Cuming) are men of very light weight. They were both appointed by Sir R. Howe and they were probably the best men available from the Sudan Political Service. On the other hand, it is questionable whether the Governor-General should not have sought recruits from outside.

In short, the situation seems to me to be that the Governor-General has not as yet (although he may have later when he gets to know the country better) the grip on the Government owing to his absences that a Governor-General should have, and it is possible that if he had had greater grip he would have altered some of Sir James Robertson's telegrams, which at times bordered on impertinence. Sir R. Howe, as a Foreign Service man, moreover, is particularly fitted to lead the Sudan Government in questions where foreign policy is concerned.

(ii) The personal relations between certain members of the Embassy at Cairo and members of the Sudan Government are not of the happiest and often, I am afraid, Sudan questions have been covered by personal animosities. The statement in the memorandum in J 4316 at flag B[2] that the number of higher British officials in the Sudan administration could be cut down seems to be quite unwarrantable and outside the competence of the writer.

Conclusion

The situation as I have described it is difficult to handle, and I do not think direct action would help. On the other hand, in our conversations with Sir R. Howe we should certainly bear these matters in mind.

---

[2] See 176.

181 FO 371/73619, no 5927 — 19 July 1949

[Nile Waters]: minute by G L Clutton on the Lake Tsana negotiations

[In the discussion between Bevin and Amr about the Owen Falls dam on 16 May (see 178), Amr was reluctant to make public reference to the Sudan's participation in the benefits of the Nile Waters projects, as this would raise the discussion from the purely technical to the political level; thus running the risk of introducing an argument on the status of the Sudan. Bevin offered to allow Egypt to take the initiative in 'safeguarding' the Sudan's interests, and Amr agreed a formula (outlined in 178) whereby Bevin announced to the House of Commons that the Egyptian Government welcomed the participation of the Sudan in projects for the control of the Nile; and that 'the participation of the Sudan in these Projects will be the subject of technical discussions between Egypt and the Sudan, the results of which will be embodied in agreements to be concluded in connexion with these projects' (outward telegram no 991 from Bevin to Campbell, 19 May 1949, FO 371/73617, no 4212; also outward telegram no 970 from Bevin to Campbell, 17 May 1949, FO 371/73617, no 4201). The Egyptian prime minister issued a similar statement before parliament, following which notes were formally exchanged between the two governments ('Exchange of Notes regarding Nile Waters Projects', 30–31 May 1949, FO 371/73618, no 4749). It was after this that Egypt objected to the Sudan being represented in the Lake Tsana treaty negotiations.]

A difficulty has arisen in connexion with the form of the proposed agreement with Ethiopia about the Lake Tana Project.

Article 3 of the 1902 Treaty with Ethiopia states that the Ethiopian Government may not construct any works across the Blue Nile and Sobat except with the agreement of H.M. Government and the Government of the Sudan.[1] In the course of the Owen Falls negotiations in Cairo in the spring we proposed to the Egyptians (see J 3837/14210/16—Flag A) that the Lake Tana Agreement should be signed once by Ethiopia, once by the U.K. (as co-dominus of the Sudan) and twice by Egypt (as co-dominus of the Sudan and on her own behalf). This would mean in effect that the Agreement would be signed by Ethiopia, Egypt and the Sudan. Since, however, H.M. Government would sign the Agreement as a part of the process of the Sudan signing, it could not be argued that H.M. Government had not signified their agreement to the work in accordance with Article 3 of the 1902 Treaty with Ethiopia.

When Sir R. Campbell raised this question on our instructions on the 7th July, Khashaba Pasha objected to this formula on the grounds that it would raise the constitutional issue which Egypt and ourselves wished to avoid (see J 5584/14210/16—Flag B). The form of the Agreement was, therefore, reconsidered by the Embassy and by the Department and we have reached the same conclusion that the only practical alternative is an agreement signed once only by Ethiopia, Egypt and the U.K. (see the suspended draft telegram in J 5584/14210/16—Flag C and J 5753/14210/16—Flag D). This formula is legally correct. The only political objection to it is that the Sudan may resent the fact that they will not be a party to the Agreement in their own right. Khartoum have pointed out that the Executive Council would be unlikely to accept any formula which excluded the attachment of Sudanese advisers to both the Egyptian and British Delegations.[2] It has always been our intention that the burden of the negotiations with the Ethiopian Government should fall on the technical experts from Egypt and the Sudan who are in any case on very friendly terms.

The Department recommend that H.M. Chargé d'Affaires at Alexandria be instructed to discuss this new formula with the Egyptian Foreign Minister and to point out that we should, of course, like to see the Sudan represented in the negotiations by advisers at the disposal of the British and Egyptian Delegations as was so successfuly [sic] the case at the regional meetings of the World Health Organisation and the Food and Agricultural Organisation at Cairo early this year.

I submit a draft telegram.

The question of the exploratory discussions with the Ethiopian Government is being dealt with separately.

---

[1] See 27. [2] See 177.

182 FO 371/73506, no 6441 9 Aug 1949

[Anglo–Egyptian negotiations]: FO minutes of a meeting to discuss the Sudan [Extract]

[A meeting attended by Strang, Campbell, Howe, Wright, Stewart and Maitland was held at the FO to discuss a number of issues concerning the Sudan, in particular the Sudan question in relation to a treaty with Egypt.]

. . . 4. The Egyptians do not wish to see the Sudan independent. They realise that they cannot hold the Sudan themselves and that the presence of a British Administration in the Sudan safeguards their southern frontier. In this respect we are in a strong negotiating position vis-à-vis Egypt since we could threaten to leave the Sudan. We could not in fact leave the Sudan without betraying our trust in the Sudanese.

The Egyptians' chief complaint has been that, in spite of the Condominium Agreements, they have been denied a share in the administration of the Sudan, while the preparation of the Sudan for self-government has been urgently pursued. . . .

14. The meeting agreed that:—

(a) the questions of the sovereignty of the Sudan and the ultimate future of the Sudan cannot and probably need not be settled for the present;
(b) a settlement of the Sudan question on the lines of the Sudan Protocol of 1946 is no longer possible;
(c) His Majesty's Government cannot now justifiably ask the Governor-General of the Sudan to appoint Egyptians to the Executive Council;
(d) an interim settlement identifying the Egyptian Government in some way with the preparation of the Sudanese for self-government is possible and desirable.

183 FO 371/73665, no 6995 31 Aug 1949

[Sudanese famine]: letter from the Civil Secretary's Office, Khartoum to the Africa Department (FO), on Egyptian and Sudanese reactions to reports of famine in the eastern Sudan[1]

With reference to your request dated 17.8.49 (J.5869/1711/16) for observations on the telegram from the Sudan Graduates' Congress to Mr. Bevin, the text of which follows, with the various points it makes numbered for reference with the comments below:—

"We were surprised at your reply to the question submitted by Member of Parliament Mr. Gallacher Esq., as it reveals that your informers were misleading and untruthful. (1) Last April the Civil Secretary officially declared his refusal of Egyptian aid and (2) denied its necessity. By virtue of press campaigns Civil Secretary (3) confessed the facts and agreed to accept the Egyptian aid (4) on condition that the Red Crescent shall not take part in distribution lest the bitter situation might be revealed. (5) But after three months the Civil Secretary and under various impressions agreed to allow the Secretary General of the Red Crescent to tour those

---

[1] See 180, note 1.

parts which were less affected by famine. (6) Despite this the Red Crescent Secretary announced that the situation is worse than pictured by press and that the Egyptian aid (£50,000) is only a meagre start. Your statement that none died as a result of famine is at least inconsistent with official report (7) by British Governor of Kassala in May last to the effect that in one section (Abu Deleig) twenty deaths due to malnutrition. It is not true that Sudan Government took precautionary steps (8) against the famine since July 1948 because a number of chiefs in Eastern Sudan directed the attention of Beja District Commissioner in August 1948 to the noticeable drop in grain and fodder production. (9) Nothing was done until things came to a climax after six months only. (10) As to public eating houses the Sudan Government has never opened any in this country. The groundless contention of Sudan Government that matters are in hand is defeated by the fact that the famine (11) is growing acute in spite of the Egyptian aid and other national bodies including the outstanding donations and care of Sir Sayed Ali El Mirghani Pasha the Sudan Government contributed with (12) one thousand tons of dura. Official figures show that (13) one hundred and fifty thousand were affected by famine. (14) The spread of famine is primarily due to Government's gross negligence. In your capacity as Condominium partner the Graduates' General Congress asks for Parliamentary Commission to investigate and fix liability. (15) Graduates' General Congress.

1. The Civil Secretary never, officially or unofficially, refused Egyptian aid though he did point out that the Egyptian Government had clearly been misled by exaggerated reports and, in an interview with the Egyptian Minister of Supply, expressed surprise at the discourteous and irregular manner in which the "offer" had been made.

Far from making difficulties, the Government assisted the Egyptian authorities to purchase 1000 tons of millet from South Africa, made the necessary sterling available (£24,138:13:7) accepting payment in Egyptian currency, allowed it in duty free and provided free transport for it on the railway.

2. He certainly denied its necessity, as the Government had the situation well in hand as is shown by subsequent figures, and the fact that although the main bulk of the Egyptian relief was not available till August, no deaths from starvation have yet been reported.

3. The Civil Secretary has never admitted the "Facts" (sic) quoted in the press campaign.

4. It was suggested, and readily agreed by the Egyptian Government, that distribution of Egyptian aid could better be done by those who were already distributing Government and voluntary assistance, assisted by officers of the Egyptian Army, than by parties of complete strangers to the country.

5. The visit of the Secretary General of the Red Crescent was first suggested on June 16th, was welcomed by the Government whose guests he and his party were immediately invited to become, and he arrived on June 20th and proceeded straight to Sinkat and Erkowit the centre of the famine area.

6. It is not known what the Secretary General of the Red Crescent may have said on his return to Egypt, but any announcement that the situation was worse than pictured by the press is quite inconsistent with the statement he made here to the press at the conclusion of his visit.

7. No such report was made. The following are extracts from Governor Kassala's reports during April and May referring to the area in question:—

17.4.49. "Omda of Abu Zuleig (Abu Deleig area) reports death of 20 people from what sounded like an acute form of dysentery which may be partly due to malnutrition."
3.5.49 "Governor visited Abu Deleig area. Provision for further relief works on hafirs (tanks) and for free relief on a small scale to distressed persons are in hand. Condition of animals and people was better than expected. Grain from Government supplies for sale will be needed later on an increased scale as trade supplies are not sufficient."
28.5.49 "District Commissioner Gedaref has made a further inspection of the Abu Deleig area and reports that relief on an increased scale is needed there. This was foreshadowed in my recent report." Arrangements made for provision of 225 tons of millet in the area for issue in June, July and August.

The Ministry of Health confirms that no deaths from starvation or primarily due to malnutrition have yet been reported by any of their staff, which has been temporarily increased in that area.[2]

8. First warning that famine conditions might develop received from Governor Kassala in a letter dated 6.6.48. Starting in July /48 relief works in Beja area were commenced, tickets at nominal fare issued to places where work was available, and issue of grain at reduced price arranged. In August /48 relief provided for the nomads of Northern Province on a fairly large scale (650 tons of grain). Relief on a smaller scale around Kassala for the aged and infirm (100 tons of grain) also in August.

Situation was temporarily relieved by the rains though they were poor. The Government had ample reserves of grain, and though certain relief works were continued and issues of grain on a small scale were made in February and March there was little to be done till famine conditions became imminent.

9. A press statement issued 30th March, 1949 included:— "It is expected that conditions of famine will become general through the Northern part of the Beja district during the months of May, June and July and relief measures to deal with these conditions have been worked out by Governor Kassala and are now being considered by the Central Government."

At the same time proposals for the assistance of the Nomads of Northern Province were received from the Governor.

In April action on a considerable scale began, and increased as the famine became wide-spread.

10. The reference to communal kitchens in the Foreign Secretary's reply to Mr. Gallacher was misleading. In one of our reports it was mentioned that Governor Kassala had reported on 27.10.48 that D.C. Gedaref had organised relief works and a communal kitchen to tide the people over till the 1949 rains. This no doubt was the origin of the report. It is customary in this country to arrange for communal feeding for workers engaged in such works, and doubtless similar arrangements were made at other places, but this part of the reply has been seized on by those who are trying to make political capital out of this famine, as showing that S.G. and/or H.M.G. are being deliberately dishonest.

[2] A study of the Sudanese famine in Darfur in 1984 has given support to the common local explanation that famine deaths are in fact caused by disease rather than starvation, see Alex de Waal, *Famine that kills: Darfur, Sudan, 1984–1985* (Oxford, 1989).

11. The famine was bound to continue growing more acute until the rains came to provide grazing for the animals and a harvest for the cultivators. Rains started generally at the end of July.

12. Recent statement shows that 3,400 tons of free dura and over 1,400 tons at reduced price were issued by Government to end of July, apart from much relief of other kinds. Whereas Egyptian relief in same period was 400 tons maize and rice and 8,000 yds. of cloth, with a further 1,000 tons of millet to come in August. Voluntary contributions from all sources had amount [ed] to about 275 tons of grain and some £7,000 cash.

13. Free grain has been issued by Government to a considerably larger number than this.

14. The spread of famine is due entirely to Act of God. The Sudan Government is not of opinion that a parliamentary commission is required to fix His responsibility and pay.

15. The "Graduate General Congress" is now a discredited rump long since repudiated by those of the "Intelligentsia" with any claim to intelligence, which never even in its palmiest days represented the views of the great mass of the people, and which has now fallen entirely into the hands of that small but vocal party who appear to hope to gain political freedom by selling their country to Egypt.

184 FO 371/80358, no 10115 1 Dec 1949

[Umma Party]: letter from Sir R Howe to Sir W Strang evaluating the political scene. *Minute* by R H G Edmonds[1]

Since my return from leave at the beginning of November, I have had conversations with the Speaker of the Legislative Assembly and the three Sudanese Ministers in the Executive Council, and I think you should know the way their minds are moving at the present time.

As you know, these four Sudanese are leading members of the Umma Party and religious followers of Sayed Abdel Rahman. They all took much the same line with me in their talks, namely that the Condominium was all very well when one of the Co-domini was a sleeping partner, but now that Egypt is pressing its claim to share in practice in the administration of the Sudan, and in view of the Egyptian claim to sovereignty which would mean absolute Egyptian monarchical rule here, the Condominium has become not a means of progress but a stranglehold on progress. They all stated that the Condominium had outlived its usefulness; the only thing now was to pull down the two flags which were its outward and visible sign, after which the Sudanese would be free to push on with the development of their country under the advice and guidance of its present administrators. They all seemed to think that this would be quite a simple thing for me to do.

This has been a favourite theme of the Umma Party for the past two or three years, and there were indications last summer from the Speaker and the Minister of Education, when they were in England, that the Umma leaders intended to press the Sudan Government hard during this winter to take a further decisive step towards

---

[1] Foreign Service from 1946; Cairo, 1947; FO, 1949.

the dissolution of the Condominium and a declaration of self-government in the Sudan.

As was to be expected, the decision of the United Nations to grant independence to Libya in 1952 and to Somaliland in ten years has stimulated the Sudan Independence Front to an assertion of the Sudan's right to immediate independence, and has provided its leaders with a plausible excuse to pursue with renewed vigour their long cherished aim of ending the Condominium.

I have had to remind the Speaker and the Ministers that the Sudan is still a Condominium and that the Condominium powers would be unlikely to acquiesce in any such action. The Condominium had been set up by treaty and treaties were not to be set aside unilaterally. It was unthinkable that Egypt would abandon her claim for the unity of Egypt and the Sudan. In any case any demand for the abolition of the present system would have to be visibly backed by the majority of the country. At present the Khatmia, who form a very considerable part of public opinion, are hardly represented in the Legislative Assembly so that any action by that body as proposed could not be regarded as representing the view of the country as a whole. The Independents admit this and have expressed their willingness to agree to a modification of the electoral rules of the Assembly to meet the objections of the Khatmia and so permit the latter to contest the next elections. There are indications that the Khatmia would be prepared to take part in elections to the next Assembly if the electoral rules were amended in accordance with their wishes, and the Sudan Government are at present considering the matter.

The motives behind this increase of pressure from the Umma leaders are not far to seek. There is no doubt that they are sincere in their dislike of the Condominium, for it involves a continuation of the Egyptian connection, even in its present diminished form, which is abhorrent to them. Their fathers and grandfathers threw the Egyptians out bag and baggage in 1885 and they are afraid that if action is not taken to squash soon this threat from the North, Egyptian money and propaganda may undermine the morale of the Sudanese and enable the Egyptians to achieve their ends. We may think that their fears are sometimes exaggerated, but they are none the less real.

But equally there is no doubt that self-interest plays a large part in their calculations. While the Umma admit the desirability of bringing the Khatmia into the Assembly—they cannot very well do otherwise—they are by no means happy about the possible effects on their own position after the next elections. At present they have it all their own way, but they would enjoy nothing like the same degree of power in an Assembly in which the Khatmia were fully represented. It is natural therefore that they should want to take the opportunity which their present position offers them of achieving their main object by urging the Sudan Government to commit itself now to a public promise of self-government in the very near future.

The Umma raised this subject with a number of the country members of the Assembly when they returned to Khartoum in October, but they found little support for their proposal of immediate self-government. This may have the effect of damping their ardour to some extent, but nevertheless I shall not be surprised to receive soon some organised approach from the Umma and other Independents to announce either that the Sudan is now ready for self-government, or to fix a date when this desirable consummation can be stated.

I think you should know of this possibility but at the same time perhaps we need not worry too much about it. For the present we have the unasseilable [sic] reply that until the Khatmia take part in the constitutional machinery of the country it would be premature to talk of self-government, and the tribal leaders in the Assembly, who represent the views of the bulk of the population, are solidly opposed to any precipitate move in that direction.

Minute on 184

The immediate background to this interesting letter is contained in paragraphs 73 and 94 of the Sudan Political Intelligence Summaries in J7206 and J8547/1013/16 respectively, and in my minute on J9032/10114/16, all of which are attached. Sir Robert Howe's letter, however, raises the whole problem of the future of the Sudan and of its effect upon Anglo/Egyptian relations. I venture to submit a few observations which may be of some use if it is considered that his letter should be answered.

2. The egyptophobia of the Umma Party is certainly, as Sir Robert Howe remarks at the end of the sixth paragraph of his letter, real, but it is also exaggerated. In the same paragraph he points out that their attitude stems from the events of 1885. It is, however, as well to remember, first, that these events cannot, as the Umma Party would have us believe, be regarded as purely an Egypto–Sudanese affair; they are equally a part of British history, since they led to the subsequent re-conquest without which there would be no British officials in Khartoum today. Secondly, the Egyptian interest in the Sudan is not purely legalistic or prompted by motives of national vanity; it has a sound basis in Egypt's dependence upon the waters of the Nile. The end to which Egyptian propaganda in the Sudan is devoted is a matter of opinion. One thing, however, is certain, that the sort of control over the Sudan which Egyptian politicians envisage, however deleterious to the Sudan it would be, will be highly remote. Egyptian politicians find it hard enough to stay in Cairo during the summer months: I can remember no recent case of any of them visiting the Sudan except in the depth of winter. It is only the better sort of Egyptian official (for example, irrigation engineers) who is prepared to spend most of the year in the Sudan.

3. The last sentence of the 7th paragraph of Sir R. Howe's letter seems to me very pertinent. The basic issue at stake in the Sudan at the present moment is who shall control the machinery of government, and all the patronage which this involves, when we eventually hand it over. What is going on now, in my opinion, is a straightforward struggle for temporal power in a religious guise,* and as the Governor-General points out, the Umma's advantage in this conflict is now greater than it is ever likely to be in the foreseeable future. At the moment the Sudan is being governed, or partially governed, by a Legislative Assembly, in which a large proportion of the educated class is not represented. (How large it is difficult to assess, but I should say at least half, which I believe includes a large number of the officers

* (The Umma's religious guise is wearing pretty thin, except in the eyes of their illiterate followers, for Mahdism is generally regarded by Muslims of other denominations as a wholly bogus sect). [Edmonds' own insertion]

of the Sudan Defence Force). The possibility of an amendment of the Legislative Assembly Ordinance in favour of the Khatmia, designed to persuade them not to boycott the next elections, is, on balance, desirable, and I think Sir James Robertson holds this opinion.[2] Admittedly, if they stick to their pro-Egyptian line, the extreme Ashigga wing of the Khatmia representatives could make a lot of trouble in the Assembly, but on the whole it seems to me that this will be very much less dangerous than their present trouble-making capacity outside the Assembly.

4. There are two important questions which arise from this letter:—

(a) If the Umma Party decide to let the Khatmia in, would this provide an opportunity for some form of Anglo–Egyptian rapprochement as regards the Sudan?
(b) If, on the other hand, the Umma Party decide to demand immediate independence next year, what line will the Egyptian Government and the Khatmia adopt, and what should be our own attitude?

5. Whether or not we discuss the answers to these two questions with the Governor-General now, I suggest that we should at any rate send him a letter approving the line he has so far taken with the Umma Party's leaders, as reported in the 5th paragraph of his letter.

R.H.G.E.
8.12.49.

[2] Marginal note by Clutton: 'I think we are all agreed on this'.

185 FO 371/80352, no 2 15 Jan 1950

[Communism]: letter from D Maclean[1] to Sir J Robertson, on communist infiltration in Sudan

[In a report on communist infiltration in the Sudan mention was made of Russian-trained instructors in Egypt. When requested by MacLean in the Cairo embassy to elaborate on this claim the civil secretary replied: 'The reference in our recent paper on Communism to instructors in Egypt having been specially trained in Russia was based on information which came to the Commissioner of Police from a Sudanese source whose contacts had been in touch with Communist Agents in Cairo. The Commissioner had no means of checking the information but he accepted it because he knew, from his experience in Palestine, that not many years ago Muslim Arabs from that country went to Russia to be trained to disseminate Communist propaganda in Palestine' (Robertson to McLean, 29 Dec 1949, FO 371/80352, no 1). MacLean's reply (in full) is below.]

Thank you for your letter No. SCO/36.G.4/4 of the 29th December, about the reference in your recent paper on communism to some agents in Egypt having been specially trained in Russia.

We do not wish to be captious but is not this information based on rather too shaky evidence to be presented as fact? A good deal of effort is concentrated here on the question of communist activities in Egypt, and indeed this particular aspect of it. The people concerned, while in no position to say that this section of your report is definitely inaccurate, have no evidence to support it.

[1] Head of chancery at the embassy in Cairo until Nov 1950 when he returned to the FO; uncovered as a Soviet agent in 1951.

186 FO 371/80514, no 33 2 Mar 1950

[Nile Waters: Lake Tsana]: minute by R Allen on Egyptian obstruction of Nile Waters negotiations with Ethiopia

It will be recalled that the Egyptian Government have been making difficulties about the approach to be made to the Ethiopian Government in order to start the discussions on the Lake Tana project. The Egyptian Government have asked our agreement to send a purely Egyptian delegation to Addis Ababa to present the joint memorandum which has been agreed with the Sudanese experts. The main issues involved in this proposal were, first, the constitutional one, namely, that the Egyptians are not entitled to speak alone on behalf of the Sudanese and to admit their right to do so on this occasion would weaken the Condominium Agreement, and, secondly, the fact that technical negotiations in Addis Ababa would be of little practical value without Sudanese participation. After consideration of these issues, and in view of the desirability of getting the negotiations under way as soon as possible, the Secretary of State approved the suggestion that we might agree to the Egyptian delegation presenting the technical memorandum alone, but that we should safeguard our position by notifying the Ethiopian Government of our agreement, and enlisting their support in insisting that after the presentation of the memorandum, Sudanese experts should participate in the negotiations.[1]

Since then there have been two major developments. In the first place, the Governor-General of the Sudan has declared his inability to concur in the course proposed, on the grounds that it would prejudice technically the partnership between Egypt and the Sudan and that whatever reservations might be made in the early stages Egypt would be unwilling to agree to Sudanese participation in subsequent negotiations. The Governor-General has discussed the matter with his Executive Council who were unanimously and strongly of the opinion that urgent as is the Sudan's need for more water, the Sudan should accept yet more delay rather than allow herself to be elbowed out of her right and recognized position as a partner in the project. The second development is a report from the Embassy in Cairo of conversations between the Minister and the Under-Secretary at the Ministry of Foreign Affairs, and between the Ambassador and the Minister for Foreign Affairs. From these conversations it appears quite clear that the Egyptian Government are thinking in terms not only of the presentation by Egypt alone of the technical memorandum, but also of action by Egypt alone in the later or political stages of the negotiations. In fact, the Egyptian position appears to be that, Nokrashy Pasha, having said what he had at Lake Success[2] about the non-validity of the 1936 Treaty and the Sudan, the Government of Nahas Pasha cannot adopt a less advanced position. It is thus clear that the Egyptian Government are not concerned merely to discover a face-saving device with us, but that they are determined to exclude us and the Sudan from every stage of the negotiations.

The Department have considered carefully whether there is any way out of this impasse. On both legal and practical grounds we cannot give up our right, and

---

[1] See 181.

[2] During the presentation of the Egyptian case against the UK at the UN in 1947, following the breakdown of the Anglo–Egyptian treaty negotiations.

indeed our obligation, to participate in these negotiations. Not only would it be politically unwise to authorise the Egyptian Government to negotiate on our behalf (one of the suggestions put forward by the Egyptian Minister for Foreign Affairs), but under the 1902 Anglo–Ethiopian Treaty concerning (among other things) the Waters of the Blue Nile we are bound to be parties to any agreement which may be concluded in connexion with Lake Tana.

Meanwhile our Ambassador in Addis Ababa has discussed the matter with the Ethiopian Minister for Foreign Affairs, who has made it plain that the Ethiopians would accept British and Sudanese participation in the negotiations.

Recommendation. It is therefore recommended that we should instruct His Majesty's Ambassador at Cairo to return to the charge with the Egyptians, and that, subject to his views and those of the Governor-General of the Sudan, we should instruct His Majesty's Ambassador at Addis Ababa to induce the Ethiopian Government to issue invitations to both the Egyptians and ourselves to open the negotiations. To refuse such an invitation would at least put the Egyptians into an uncomfortable position tactically, and it is possible that when the Egyptian Minister for Foreign Affairs has been more fully briefed and has had time to think things over, he may be prepared to give way. If he does not, we might consider going ahead with the negotiations on a bilateral basis ourselves with the Ethiopians even though we can hardly get to the point of signing any agreement without Egyptian participation.

Telegrams to Cairo and Addis Ababa on these lines are submitted herewith.

187 FO 371/80358, no 2 8 Mar 1950

[Self-government]: letter from Sir R Howe to Sir W Strang on Umma Party proposals to accelerate self-government and government plans to expand election rules. *Minute* by R H G Edmonds

In my letter to you of the 1st December[1] last regarding self-government for the Sudanese I said that I should not be surprised to receive before long some organised approach from the Umma Party and other Independents to announce either that the Sudan is now ready for self-government or to fix a date when this could be stated.

As the date for the opening of the Second Session of the Legislative Assembly—which took place on the 6th March—approached it became evident that this question was exercising the minds of the Umma Party and particularly the Sudanese members of this party in the Executive Council, and on the 13th February, the day before I was due to leave for a tour of the southern Sudan, the Leader of the Assembly—Abdulla Bey Khalil—came to see me on this matter. He said that his party were pressing strongly for the introduction of a motion during the next session of the Legislative Assembly stating that the Sudan was now ready for self-government or for independence at a definite date within the near future, on the lines of the declarations in regard to Libya and Italian Somaliland which had been made by the United Nations. Abdulla Bey said that he himself was not in favour of another motion on these lines being debated in the Legislative Assembly but its introduction there

[1] See 184.

was being very strongly pressed by leading members of the party and that if it were introduced in the next session he thought it would without doubt be approved by a majority of the Assembly because he and other moderates would not be able to speak against it.

He and his colleagues in the government had accordingly thought to scotch the proposed motion through some other means of convincing the party that the Sudanese were in fact already exercising a measure of self-government and they had decided that the best means to do this was by an increase in the number of Sudanese Ministers in the Executive Council. Their proposals were for the promotion of the existing Sudanese members of Council who are not Ministers to be Ministers and the appointment of two additional Sudanese as Minister of the Interior and Minister Without Portfolio.

Abdulla Bey Khalil asked me if I would approve the above appointments.

I told Abdulla Bey that I had no inherent objection in principle to an increase in the number of Sudanese Ministers in the Executive Council. I myself regarded the present Ordinance as a first step only on the road to self-government for the Sudan. I would, however, prefer as the next step to widen the representation of Sudanese political parties in the Legislative Assembly as the best way of building the foundations for parliamentary government in the Sudan. It could not yet be said that the Assembly was a representative body of Sudanese opinion. The Khatmia were not represented as they should be and I would prefer, by such measures as amendments to the electoral rules, to make such representation possible. Moreover I did not at this moment want to disturb the situation here in view of the possibility of Anglo–Egyptian negotiations in the near future in regard to the Sudan and the consequent necessity for the Sudanese to present a united front so that consultations with Sudanese opinion, as promised by the British government in 1946 as a preliminary to any change in the status of the Sudan, could be secured. I asked Abdulla Bey how such consultation could be obtained in present circumstances. He said through the Assembly. I replied that if the Condominium argued, as Egypt undoubtedly would, that the Assembly is not a representative body what would be the answer? Abdulla Bey Khalil said that that could not be helped. It was their own fault if the Khatmia were not in the Assembly. He thought that they would certainly contest the next election even if the rules were not amended as I had proposed.

On my return from the South I sent for Abdulla Bey Khalil the day before yesterday. Meanwhile the Executive Council had drawn up the draft of my speech for the opening of the Assembly on March 6th with the references to the increase of Sudanese representation on the Executive Council and the ultimate political future of the Sudan about which Cairo telegraphed (Your telegram No. 45 of March 3rd) and which was subsequently amended as reported by telegram on March 5th to the Sudan Agent London.

I told Abdulla Bey that I had carefully considered the proposal for additional Ministries which he had put before me. At present the Executive Council was composed of an equal number of Sudanese and British and his proposal would mean in practice eight Sudanese members to six British. This would give a Sudanese majority in the Executive Council and would in effect be equivalent to the granting of immediate self-government to the Sudan subject to the reserved powers of the Governor-General. For such a revolutionary proposal to be justifiable from the internal point of view I should have to be satisfied that it was backed by a majority of

Sudanese opinion. I was not satisfied that such support existed and to make such a sweeping modification in the present constitutional arrangements might well defeat any prospect of that body becoming a more representative institution since the other important party might well refuse to co-operate, even if the electoral rules were modified in the way which we had in mind, and would postpone any prospect of making that body the more fully representative institution which we hoped it would be.

That, however, was not the only aspect of the matter. The Sudan was, as I had reminded him previously, still a condominium under the control of two powers, Great Britain and Egypt. It was true that the Governor-General had extensive powers under the Condominium Agreement but he did not, in my view, have the power on his own to make the radical departure from the status of the Sudan set up under the Condominium Agreement, as the proposal for four new Ministries involved. I should be obliged to submit the proposal to the Condominium Powers. It was true that His Majesty's Government in the United Kingdom had given their approval to the Ordinance and to the idea of the progressive development of the Sudan towards self-government but the other Co-dominus, Egypt, had refused to accept the Ordinance and the Governor-General as agent for both Co-domini could not assume their agreement. I asked Abdulla Bey to consider what their reaction would be on being presented with such a proposal. Undoubtedly there would be a very sharp reaction on the part of the present government in Egypt the result of which would no doubt be to harden still further their attitude regarding the unity of Egypt and the Sudan, which the new Wafd government had only recently proclaimed on coming into power. Apart from this it seemed to me absolutely essential that the proposal should manifestly have the support of the majority of the Sudanese before the Governor-General could possibly consider submitting it to the Co-domini. It was for this reason that I prefered [sic] to go ahead with the plans for making the Legislative Assembly more representative so that any such steps would be justified, although I would not rule out the creation of one or two more ministries as vacancies in the Council or other suitable opportunity occurred in the normal course of events.

Abdulla Bey said that he and his colleagues in the Independence Party had, in making their proposals, been proceeding on the assumption that the Governor-General had it in his power alone to carry them out. He confessed that they had not considered the external angle at all and he fully agreed with the arguments which I had put before him from the external aspect.

The above is the background against which the references in the speech at the opening of the new session of the Legislative Assembly must be considered. In the event the opening ceremony and the reading of the speech went off very well but the Sudanese members of the Government were obviously glum that the references to political aspirations and greater Sudanese representation on the Executive Council had been so watered down. There had been some idea previously that they might resign from the Executive Council unless their proposal for a majority of Sudanese members were accepted. This would be awkward and until the debate on the speech is finished, as it will be within the next few days, we shall not be able to gauge accurately the extent of the support which the idea of a Sudanese majority in Council commands. We may yet be faced with a withdrawal of Umma support from the government.

Minute on 187

In the last sentence of this extremely interesting letter, the Governor-General refers to the possibility of the Umma group withdrawing its support from the Sudan Government. In the event, Sir Robert Howe and Sir James Robertson seem to have been more successful in averting this possibility than they dared to hope. In the Legislative Assembly's debate on the Governor-General's Address, the amendment motion (regretting that the Sudan Government's policy regarding the Sudanese'[s] share in directing internal policy of the country was "vague and indefinite") was defeated by 57 votes to 14 on the 13th March. Almost all the "country members" and the "Southerners" voted with the Government; all Ministers and Under-Secretaries opposed the amendment. Counsels of moderation, therefore, appear to have prevailed at the last moment. So ends, for the time being, a crisis in the Sudan which might easily have led to results which would have been most embarrassing to H.M.G.

2. As regards the main issue discussed by the Governor-General in his letter to Sir William Strang, namely, his right to increase the Sudanese membership of his Executive Council, there is no doubt that under Article 10 of the Ordinance, the Governor-General would have been fully justified in taking this step without reference to the Codomini. By taking the line that he did, however, (see in particular page 3 within), the Governor-General has virtually put the Umma leaders in a position where they will be obliged to agree—as the price of an increase in Sudanese membership of the Executive Council—to making amendments to the electoral rules of the Sudan, which are the *sine qua non* of the Khatmia's participation in the next elections for the Legislative Assembly. Since no real political progress can be made in the Sudan until both the main Muslim groups are represented in the Legislative Assembly, it seems to me that Sir Robert Howe has made a very astute move.

3. For all this, the dangers inherent in the situation in the Sudan remain as before. The Legislative Assembly is not a fully representative body; a large and important section of the Muslim population has no share in the government of the country; the struggle for the eventual control of the machinery of government between the Umma and Khatmia groups continues; and there is always the risk—as was illustrated by the flirtation last month between the Umma and the Wafd—that the frustrated leaders of the Umma may be tempted to strike a bargain with the Egyptian Government behind our backs.

R.H.G.E.
15.3.50

188 FO 371/80358, no 3 11 Mar 1950

'Report on the Southern provinces': note by the Civil Secretary's Office, Khartoum

[The first biennial report on the Southern Sudan was produced in February 1948 and forwarded confidentially to the FO through the Sudan agent in London. On forwarding this report the civil secretary proposed, and the FO agreed, that its contents should not be published, and that future biennial reports should be sent unofficially to HMG alone (Robertson to Allen, 9 Mar 1950, and Allen to Robertson, 27 Mar 1950, FO 371/80358, no 3).]

(It must be noted that the period since the last report is too short to provide any definite conclusions concerning the Southern Sudanese capability to play a part in the development of the country, and that the report which follows describes what has been and is being done to assist in the progress of the Southern Sudan peoples).

Capabilities of the Southern Sudanese to play their part in the affairs of the whole country on equal and not on servile terms

The assessment of these capabilities can be made in three spheres: Central Government, Local Government, and the field of administrative careers. Important developments have taken place in all three since the last report submitted in December 1947, associating Southern Sudanese for the first time on equal terms with Northerners. In the official opening of the Legislative Assembly on the 23rd December 1948, thirteen Southerners took their places beside their fellow members from the North to share in the central government of the country. They had been elected to the Assembly by three newly constituted Province Councils. The first two warranted local government councils have been established in the Southern Provinces, and the number of provisional councils has been steadily expanding and now totals eleven. The conditions of service of classified Government staff have been amended to enable Southerners to attain the same classifications as Northern Sudanese.

In their participation in the Legislative Assembly, Southern members are now in a position to get first-hand experience of the responsibilities of government and the interests of the country as a whole. They could not be expected at so early a stage to play a prominent part in the business of the Assembly, but one or two of them have made a considerable contribution to its proceedings. They have shown that they can stand up for and maintain the particular interests of the peoples they represent, and have certainly justified the entry of Southern Sudanese into the management of the country's affairs.

The inauguration of the three Province Councils in 1948 was an important step forward in associating tribal heads with other educated Southerners in the affairs of state. These Councils are consultative bodies only, but they have two valuable aspects. Firstly, they give collective voice to many of the wisest and most experienced heads in the South, and their discussions have been of practical value in a number of issues and have helped to shape policy. Secondly, the Councils are educative institutions, introducing to the problems of the South and of the whole Sudan men whose horizon has previously been bounded by tribal or purely local affairs. The difficulty of conducting the proceedings in several languages, while preventing any real debates, has not impeded this necessary enlightenment.

Inasmuch as it is the field of training for citizenship, the spread of local government is among the most important developments. Here the language problem is a more serious hindrance, and the expansion of the local government network is necessarily conditioned by it. The establishment of new units is, however, progressing steadily, and the work so far achieved by those which have been established has given satisfactory evidence of the ability of members to make useful contributions to local administration.

The application of Northern scales of classification to Southern clerks and accountants with the appropriate educational qualifications has opened the way to equal composition with Northern officials. With the fulfilment of the new educational programme, access to secondary schools, and general teaching of Arabic, in the course of time no post open to Northern Sudanese will be closed to Southerners; and there is no reason why, if they have the merit, they should not rise to the highest appointments. It is early yet to see how far the Southerner will avail himself of these opportunities, and the still limited facilities for education above the elementary level have not produced enough educated men for any reliable assessment to be made. It may be said, however, that experience so far indicates that the Southern Sudanese make good clerks, but a large proportion fail when given positions of financial responsibility. Many of the educated Southerners reveal an instability of character and proneness to alcoholic excess which is a little disturbing. This tendency may be due to the fact that education lifts them far out of their tribal environment, and up to now has failed to provide many of them with a suitable set of alternative values. It is hoped, however, that this failing will decrease as education is extended.

To further the extent to which Southern Sudanese can fill vacancies in Government staff, and to enhance their prospects of promotion, the Ministry of Education has, during the past two years, opened a secondary school, an intermediate school, two teachers' training colleges and a training centre for better instruction in professional subjects. It has also continued the programme of elementary school expansion, in which local interest has been increasingly aroused through local education councils.

Capabilities of the Southern Sudanese to contribute to the general economic progress of the country, and so to improve social services among themselves

Under this heading progress has been slower. There are only two major fields for development in the South: agriculture and cattle. Climatic and geographical conditions, added to the Southern peasant's general lack of desire to produce any crop in excess of the family's staple needs, or to sell any available surplus, have made advances difficult. In large areas of the South an excess of water, either by rain or river floods, is the chief obstacle to agricultural expansion. The problem of food crops is therefore mainly an administrative one of opening up these regions by providing communications and storage reservoirs in the higher land suitable for rain cultivation. Considerable progress has been made in this provision in the Upper Nile Province, and mechanical reservoir excavation teams have made available much new land in which agriculture is making satisfactory headway.

The primary exploitable wealth of the South, however, on which real economic progress depends, is cattle. Here the requirements are threefold: reduction of cattle diseases, extension of grazing areas, and inducement of the Nilotics to sell their beasts. Sustained veterinary efforts with prophylactics have reduced disease and herds are increasing. In particular, it is hoped that a rapid increase will result from the recent intensive campaign against rinderpest in which attenuated goat-virus serum has been used for the first time. The expansion of good pasture land, from which herds have hitherto been excluded owing to lack of water, has been proceeding well during the last two years.

What has so far not been solved is how to overcome Nilotic conservatism, which regards cattle as a social institution and a means to the acquisition of wives instead of an economic asset. Efforts to induce them to sell their animals have met with limited success and new means of achieving this are being earnestly considered. If a large increase in the size of herds does result from the mass inoculation and immunization being pursued by the Veterinary Department, cattle owners will have more for barter and local consumption and may become less averse to releasing more beasts for disposal in the markets. Other factors which, it is hoped, will change their attitude are a surer supply of agricultural products, more educational facilities, and intensified instruction in the preparation of hides for export. Province Councils have impressed upon chiefs the importance of cattle and hide exports, not only to their Provinces but to the whole Sudan, and they have begun to co-operate in propagating this amongst the tribesmen.

Probably the most effective means of persuasion, however, would be stimulation of the demand for and supply of consumer goods. The tendency towards a cash economy would be greatly hastened if more goods were available to tempt the cattle breeder's fancy; but the general run of merchants are wedded to the system of large profits on a very restricted range of commodities, which has small attraction, and little progress has been achieved.

In this connection, the experiment in social emergence being conducted amongst the Zande tribe in Equatoria Province may be of significance.[1] The cotton crop, grown as part of the scheme and ginned locally, has been sold to the British Raw Cotton Commission. A spinning and weaving mill is in the course of erection, an oil press and soap factory are being built, and the Trading Division of the Equatoria Projects Board has managed to procure a wide variety of consumer goods for sale in the area by travelling vans. The success of this scheme, and the popularity of the broad range of goods which the people can buy with the proceeds of their work, are an encouraging sign of what may eventually be achieved throughout the whole area.

Capabilities of the Southern Sudanese to win social consideration, as equals rather than as inferior people, from the North

Little advance has so far been made in the evolution of social equality or the sincere association of Northern and Southern Sudanese. This fact must partly be laid at the door of the Southerner, who is not readily responsive or companionable outside his own immediate circle. At present the club-life so attractive to the Northerner, and encounters with different types of man, make little appeal to him. There is no open or general hostility between Arab and African, and they can work together well enough; but each tends to keep to himself, conscious of being different. Potential rancour is latent and occasionally manifests itself in a covert manner.

Participation in the Legislative Assembly and the Northern classifications of Government employment have begun to remove the Southerner's feeling of inferior or limited status. At the same time, with the awakening of political consciousness there have appeared signs of a hardening of his attitude towards the North. He is still highly suspicious of the objects of closer association with the Northern Sudan, and a directive from the Ministry of Education, explaining the proposed inclusion of Arabic

---

[1] The Zande scheme, a project begun in 1946, administered by the Equatoria Projects board, attempting self-contained and self-sufficient agro-industrial development through the cultivation of cotton and the local manufacture of textiles and other goods at factories established at Nzara. It was conceived as a social experiment, aimed to achieve 'the complete social emergence and economic stability to the Zande people' which, if successful, could be used as the model for further development in the southern provinces (see P de Schlippe, *Shifting cultivation in Africa. The Zande system of agriculture* (London, 1956), pp 20–23).

teaching in the curriculum of Southern schools, was interpreted as a deliberate attempt to stamp out vernacular languages and retard the Southerners' emergence. In the south there is therefore still little confidence that the people are "being equipped to stand up for themselves as socially and economically the equals of their partners in the North", and still less that this policy is accepted by the Northerners, whom they observe being given more and more control of the reins of government.

The fault is very largely the Northerners. While the attitude of senior Northern Sudanese Government officials to their Southern subordinates has been generally faultless, the attitude of less responsible Northerners has not usually been so good. Moreover one must not lay too much stress on the welcome accorded in Khartoum to the Southern members of the Assembly, the good impression they have made there, or the sentiments of a few high-minded and perfectly honest Northern Sudanese leaders. They have no doubt made the North aware that the Southerner has professional and social capabilities, and their Northern fellow-members have gone out of their way to show them outward respect; but there has probably been an element of political propaganda in the latter's acclamation, and a desire to impress upon the outside world that the North and South are already one. Outside the Assembly, Northerners appear tacitly if not avowedly willing to accept the Southern Sudanese as a potential equal only on their own terms, i.e. Arabicization, and there is as yet no noticeable change in the traditional Arab outlook on the South.

The interval since the last report has been too brief for an assessment of the pace at which the effects of centuries of seclusion, geographical and ethnological circumstances, and an ability to resist outside interference developed from slave-raid times, can be dispelled; but it is bound to be very slow. Until the Southerner's suspicions of Northern intentions, and apprehension of the Northerner's increasing political power, have been overcome, he will be awkward in his relations with the Northerner who will continue reluctant to consider him as an equal. His increasing participation in the affairs of the country will be the best way of dispelling these doubts, and the speed at which this is achieved will depend upon the rate of his educational development. The spread of all forms of education, including special methods of enlightenment now being tried, such as the sending of Southern schoolboys on tours of the North, the appointment by the Ministry of Education of a senior Northern Sudanese to work specially for the improvement of mutual relations through clubs and other social activities, encouragement of the Scout movement and the teaching of Arabic, is thus the prerequisite for increasing Southern capabilities to win from the North social consideration as equals.

189 FO 371/80516, no 60 22 May 1950

[Nile Waters: Lake Tsana]: letter from Sir R Campbell to M R Wright on a possible Egyptian strategy of obstructing Lake Tsana scheme in order to obtain recognition for sovereignty over the Sudan

This is by way of an interim report on the Lake Tsana position and to let you know that the Minister for Foreign Affairs asked me to call and see him on the 18th May last.

I am not in a position yet to report fully to you on our conversation because he asked to speak with me through an interpreter, as he wanted to speak in Arabic in order to be careful of his words, and I have not yet received a written translation of them as recorded by the Interpreter. I have however arranged to see the copy of what has been recorded, to which I shall add my replies, and this will be sent to you in due course. The interpreter failed to take down my remarks, except to "note one or two points".

You should know, however, that the interview went badly. I was prepared for this by two conversations which Chapman-Andrews had had one with Hakki Bey, the Under Secretary at the Ministry of Foreign Affairs, and the other with Osman Moharrem Pasha, Ministry of Public Works. These two gentlemen spoke with one voice, saying that Egypt contended that all necessary consultations with the Sudan had already taken place, and that the 1935 Agreement and the 1946 one also between Egypt and the Sudan proved this. Egypt could therefore negotiate and sign with Ethiopia alone. So far as the Sudan was concerned Egypt was bound, and would continue to be bound, by her agreement with the Sudan. Chapman-Andrews told both of them plainly that he saw no possibility of progress unless this attitude was changed. The Minister took the same line with me.

He spoke carefully, constantly referring to a document, and I was able to intervene about three times in the course of it. At the last interval I said that the original idea had been for a purely technical approach in the first instance with political negotiations to follow. I was not sure I understood His Excellency's present proposal which seemed to contemplate only one step, namely immediate negotiations with the Ethiopians; but this was impossible, as I understood it, for the technicians had not yet got all the information they required. This seemed to take him aback but after a pause he enquired whether in view of the difficulty of reconciling our points of view, we could not proceed with the purely technical step, the Sudan technical experts being associated with the Egyptian expert as members of his staff? By the time that step had been taken, who knew but that our two Governments might then be engaged in a general discussion and even have reached a conclusion and the constitution and difficulty resolved. I countered this with the usual argument of the necessity of the Sudanese to be technical colleagues of equal status, etc. and added that surely from his point of view, it would be a psychological error on the part of Egypt either to keep the Sudanese out or give their technicians an inferior status. The argument continued as I have already said for no less than an hour and a half and we got nowhere at all.

That evening Hakki Bey, at dinner, asked me how my conversation with Mohamed Salah El Dine [sic] Bey had gone. I told him we had made no progress, and gave details. He in turn argued that Egypt had full right to negotiate alone, since she enjoyed sovereignty over the Sudan as had been admitted in the Bevin/Sidky Protocol. I said that surely our object was to avoid raising the question of sovereignty and thus the constitutional issue, and declined to argue further on the point. Hakki Bey then went on to say that Egypt was fully entitled to make an agreement with whomever she liked on a question affecting herself. What could prevent her from doing this? If it were subsequently considered that a given agreement would benefit the Sudan, the Sudan could accede to it. He said that paragraph 3 (he doubtless meant paragraph 4) of the Annex to Article 11 of the 1936 Agreement laid down what was to be done. (This deals with the accession of the Sudan to international conventions, generally of a technical or humanitarian character; but it is interesting that Hakki Bey would be ready to use the analogy in the case of an agreement with Ethiopia on the question of Lake Tsana.) This idea is a variation of the one by which Egypt should negotiate alone with Ethiopia *by agreement* with His Majesty's Government; but since both procedures involve formal action by His Majesty's Government on behalf of the Sudan, it is surprising that he should think it would help Egypt whose object is obviously to figure before its public as being alone responsible in any matter concerning the Sudan's external relations. It is doubtful though whether he has thought the point out thoroughly.

I am not at all sure that all these conversations do not point to one thing, that is the possibility that Egypt's real object is to use Tsana and our anxiety to proceed rapidly and successfully with the Tsana Dam scheme, to induce us to discuss the Sudan and to concede the Egypt case.

As stated above, this should be treated as an interim communication only. I will report more fully when I have been able to agree the record of my conversation with Salah El Dine [sic].

I am copying this letter to the Governor-General, Khartoum, His Majesty's Ambassador, Addis Ababa and British Middle East Office.

190 FO 371/80387, no 13 25 Aug 1950

[Self-government]: despatch no 349 from Sir R Stevenson to Mr Bevin on Hamid Zaki's proposals for a transitional form of self-government

[By Spring 1950 the embassy in Cairo sensed a change in the thinking of Egyptian government officials concerning the Sudan, and an acceptance that ultimately the question of the future of the Sudan was a decision to be taken by Sudanese (minute on Egypt by Wright, 24 Mar 1950, and minute by Stevenson, 31 May 1950, FO 371/80382, nos 4 and 20). This appeared to be confirmed in August when Stevenson had two meetings with Dr Hamid Zaki, minister of state for foreign affairs, who was the minister chiefly concerned with the Sudan. Zaki agreed that nothing, in the end, could stop the Sudanese from deciding their own future, and the co-domini could not impose a solution on the Sudanese against their wishes. As a way of associating the Sudanese with the Anglo–Egyptian discussions he proposed the re-establishment of condominium rule in the Sudan: first by holding elections for a new Legislative Assembly which would produce a purely Sudanese Cabinet; second by attaching a British 'advisor' with some executive authority to each ministry, as in the Egyptian cabinet of 1914; and finally by replacing the governor-general with 'a prominent Sudanese as a kind of Viceroy with very narrow constitutional powers'. Sudanisation of the administration would continue at the same rate as before, and he hoped the Legislative Assembly might adopt a resolution 'recognising the Egyptian crown as the symbol of the brotherhood of the peoples of the Nile Valley' (despatch no 348 from Stevenson to Bevin, 25 Aug 1950, FO 371/80387, no 12).]

In my Despatch No. 348 (1031/4/50G) of 25th August I reported the lines along which Dr. Hamed Zaki Bey, Minister of State, appears to be thinking in his efforts to find a solution to the Sudan question acceptable to both the Egyptian and His Majesty's Governments.

2. In the practical and, on the whole, sensible nature of his ideas Zaki Bey is, of course, far in advance of his colleagues and indeed of most Egyptian thought on the Sudan; this particularly applies to his acceptance of the fact that the Sudanese are set on self-government and mean to have it.

3. But his tentative programme for the removal of the Governor-General etc. is, I think, a number of years ahead of its time. It is the sort of programme which might, at the right moment, be implemented in the normal process of evolution of the Sudan along the lines which have been set by the Sudan Government. But even if an amended Legislative Assembly Ordinance should result in producing a completely representative Legislative Assembly, I doubt whether it could reasonably be maintained that the Sudanese by then would have advanced far enough politically and administratively to run a government on the lines of the government established in Egypt in 1914. Moreover, the question of choosing a Sudanese Governor-General or Viceroy would at present pose almost insuperable difficulties, and I suggest that it could not reasonably be done until after the deaths of both Sayed Abdel Rahman and Sayed Ali el Mirghani, when the strong sectarian feelings and, particularly, the extreme personal rivalries of the two families may be expected to have lessened.

4. A somewhat similar difficulty exists in regard to the question of associating the Sudanese with Anglo–Egyptian discussions. It is clear that, when the time comes, they must participate fully in deciding how the country is to be enabled to decide its own future. But a rather different problem would be presented by the establishment now of a tripartite commission having as its object the planning of the relations of the Sudan with the two Co-domini in the period intervening *before* the Sudan's final status is considered. In the first place, there would be great difficulty at present in obtaining a representative Sudanese delegation which, in future years, would not be repudiated by one or other section of the Sudan. In the second place, if such a delegation could be selected there would probably be a great deal of friction and intrigue between the Egyptian delegation and the various elements of the Sudanese Delegation, since the Egyptians would inevitably fall to the temptation to lobby on the question of the final disposal of the Sudan. There would be a real danger that other considerations would obscure the proper issue, namely, the relations between the three parties during the interim period, without prejudice to the final decision. Nevertheless, I see even more difficulty in trying to settle even the immediate future of the Sudan over the heads of the Sudanese. It therefore seems essential, as Hamed Zaki himself admits, that Sudanese should somehow be brought into any discussion for a settlement of the immediate problem.

5. My own view is that it is no good even thinking of disrupting the present organisation of the Sudan Government unless some lasting advantage is to be obtained in the way of satisfying Egypt and establishing a foundation for a friendly and enduring relationship between Egypt and the Sudan. In the broadest terms, I suggest that our objects for the Sudan must now be:—

(a) to allow the present Administration of the Sudan to continue along the path they have set, as undisturbed as may be consistent with a regard for Egypt's legitimate interests in the Sudan;

(b) a return, as far as may be possible without prejudicing (a) above, to the proper working of the Condominium; i.e. we must achieve greater Egyptian association with the Government of the Sudan.

6. Our tactics over the last few years have been devoted to (a); we have endeavoured, and continue to endeavour, to prevent the Egyptians hampering the

day-to-day running and development of the Sudan, securing their cooperation at working level if possible but, if not, doing without it, and forming as far as possible a buffer against Egyptian interference behind which the Sudan could carry on.

7. There are two reasons why we should now go further than this:—

(i) We want a general settlement with Egypt which, in deference to the latter's views, will almost certainly have to include the Sudan;
(ii) Recent information from Khartoum suggests that the political parties there are working up for a period of increasingly bitter political strife centring round the question of the final relationship of the Sudan with Egypt. It may be that a statement this year by the two Co-domini together, laying down an agreed programme for the Sudan, would quell this strife before it became serious.

8. In an effort to reach a settlement with the Egyptians, I suggest that we might offer the following:—

(a) A statement acknowledging Egypt's legitimate interest in Nile Waters, and in maintaining close and good relations with the Sudanese, many of whom are of the Arab race.
(b) A statement that His Majesty's Government have no economic or strategic interest in the Sudan, and are quite prepared eventually to sever all connection with that country, if that proves to be the wish of the Sudan Government.
(c) A statement that His Majesty's Government have no feeling, one way or the other, about the relationship between the Sudan and Egypt once the Sudanese have reached the stage of being able to choose for themselves.
(d) An offer to revive the idea of a tripartite Anglo–Egyptian–Sudanese Supervisory Council to advise on the development of the Sudan. I believe that the Sudan Government now think that the time is past for this and that it would never be accepted in the Sudan; but I suggest that this proposal has not lately been so closely examined as to force us to discard it and that, provided it had no executive powers, such a Supervisory Council might be put across. It might be best to delay choosing the Sudanese representation on the Council until after the general election for the Legislative Assembly.
(e) Joint Anglo–Egyptian, or United Nations, observation of the next general election for the Legislative Assembly, and of any election or plebiscite that might be held to determine the constitutional status of the Sudan.
(f) Withdrawal of the British Forces from the Sudan, as soon as the Sudan Defence Force and Police can take over (which may well be now). The Officer Commanding, British Troops is also Kaid of the Sudan Defence Force, and it might be necessary to provide for the continued occupation of this post by a British Officer. The Royal Air Force should also be withdrawn except in so far as they might want a staging post at Khartoum, or be required to remain in the Sudan for "integrated air defence."

It would probably be unnecessary to demand the withdrawal at the same time of the Egyptian troops from the Sudan (this especially applies to those guarding the dams), but we ought not to concede this point at once. The Sudan Government might offer to try to step up the recruiting of Sudanese for the Egyptian Army.

9. It is probable that we should have to reject any of the following proposals that might be made:—

(1) Any statement implying recognition of Egyptian sovereignty over the Sudan, or any statement that might in any way prejudge the issue of the final determination of the country's status.
(2) Any Egyptian participation in the work of the Executive Council. This was another of the main points of the Campbell/Khashaba agreement; but it seems certain that the time has now passed when it might have been possible, without causing too much trouble in the Sudan, to have Egyptian members of the Executive Council.
(3) It is unlikely that it will be possible to arrange for greater participation by Egyptian officials in the administration of the country, but there is no reason why the Governor-General should not reiterate his undertaking to search for recruits equally in Egypt and in the United Kingdom for posts for which no Sudanese are available.
(4) The removal of British servants of the Sudan Government, except in accordance with the existing programme of Sudanisation.
(5) The appointment of an Egyptian as Governor-General.

10. Subject to your remarks, and those of the Governor-General of the Sudan, I should like in due course to discuss these suggestions informally with the Egyptian Government. I am meeting the Minister for Foreign Affairs tomorrow for a conversation on the Sudan, at which I shall confine myself if possible to listening to what he has to say and promising to pass on his remarks to you. I do not expect him to put forward anything of a practical nature.

11. Egyptian thinking had seemed to become so set in a dreary, unrealistic channel, that I have been encouraged to find a Minister with such an open mind on the subject as Zaki Bey, and I think it would be worthwhile if we could now show the Egyptian Government, by producing definite suggestions for a compromise between our differing interests, that we are not the nigger in the woodpile that the Egyptian press makes us out to be. I suggest also that it would be a good move if the Sudan Government would now invite Zaki Bey to visit the country in the course of the coming winter, either officially or informally, as he might prefer. I also think it would be most useful if he saw and was perhaps entertained by an Under-Secretary during his stay in London. He will be there from September 3rd to 7th and again for a few days after the Inter-Parliamentary Union conference in Dublin.

I am sending a copy of this despatch to the Acting Governor-General of the Sudan.

191 FO 371/80387, no 14 31 Aug 1950

[Self-government]: inward telegram no 156 from Sir R Stevenson to FO, reporting a conversation with Muhammad Salah al-Din on the future of Sudanese self-government

[Edmonds minuted that: 'The idea of a plebiscite . . . is one which we, & the Sudan Govt. might *eventually* be able to accept: but not in existing circumstances, I suggest, & certainly not until there is a fully representative Legislative Assembly in being. The need for the latter is becoming increasingly urgent'. Comparing Salah ad-Din's attitude with those of his minister of state (190), he noted that Hamid Zaki's proposal was 'a more realistic approach to the problem, which has unfortunately been made by a relatively unimportant member of the Egyptian Govt' (minute by R H G Edmonds, 4 Sept 1950, FO 371/803887, no 14).]

Minister for Foreign Affairs and I met again on 26th August. The same persons were present as at the previous meeting.

2. After discussing defence matters for some time (see my immediately following saving telegram) we embarked on an examination of the Sudan question. The Minister for Foreign Affairs gave me a lengthy historical resumé by means of which he sought to prove that Egypt and the Sudan should be left alone by Britain and that the Condominium should be brought to an end and replaced by a regime worked out by the Egyptians and Sudanese to their mutual satisfaction.

3. I did not seek to dispute the historical facts which he adduced but maintained that the inferences which he drew from them were faulty. The mere fact that Britain had been deeply concerned in the administration of the Sudan for more than fifty years laid on her a responsibility for the welfare of the peoples inhabiting the territory which she could not and would not shirk. His Majesty's Government were ready to consider any practical solution of the problem which did not involve imposing anything on the Sudanese peoples against their will or without their consent.

4. The Minister for Foreign Affairs rejected the thesis that fifty years of administration gave Britain any rights or responsibilities. She had throughout been acting on behalf of Egypt and the time had now come to hand back to Egypt the trust she had been carrying out. This claim to have some responsibility towards the Sudanese was quite new and had only been put forward when Egypt began to demand her rights. The whole course of British "imperialist" policy in the Sudan seemed to have been shaped with a view to keeping the Sudanese people in a backward state, separating them from the people of Egypt and prolonging British control. But when one came to compare the state of the Sudan's advancement with that of Libya it was obvious that the Sudan had progressed further. Yet Britain was prepared to see an independent Libya created in 1952 while she considered that the Sudan would not be capable of self-government for a long period.

5. I had no great difficulty in disposing of the charge that our claim to responsibility towards the peoples of the Sudan was a new one. I went on to say that Britain had no vital economic or strategic interest in the Sudan and had no feelings one way or the other about union between the Sudan and Egypt. It would be quite useless for us to try either to encourage or discourage such a movement. One had only to look at a map to see that the lives of the two countries were inextricably bound up together by the river Nile. No one could separate them except perhaps the Egyptians themselves by antagonising the Sudanese. It did not make sense to talk of an "Imperialist" policy on Britain's part. If she had had such a policy she would have made very sure that no situation such as the present one could arise.

6. The Minister replied to the effect that if we had no material interest in the Sudan we should leave it as we had done in the case of India. The Sudan was essential to Egypt more so even than Alexandria as Saad Zaghloul Pasha had pointed out to Mr. Ramsey MacDonald. Moreover, the Minister said, he was confident that the Sudanese people ardently desired full union with Egypt. The results of the Municipal

Elections, and the resolutions of the Graduates Conference[1] showed the feelings of the intelligentsia in this respect, as did the sympathy of the religious sects. He asked whether Britain would agree to the holding of a plebiscite in the Sudan under neutral supervision after the withdrawal of British forces and officials. He returned again to the comparison between Libya and the Sudan and maintained that the standard of education was higher in the latter and that therefore the Sudanese should also be capable of self-government and independence in two years. Finally he asked for my estimate of the time it would take the Sudanese to reach such a state of advancement.

7. In reply I drew the Minister's attention to the fact that deep feeling, whether legally and historically justified or not, existed in Britain in regard to the Sudan and could not be ignored by Egypt. On the other hand we fully appreciated the latter's vital interests. I pointed out that neither he nor I had visited the Sudan and it was difficult for either of us to speak with confidence regarding the opinions and desires of the peoples inhabiting that country. Our reports on the subject evidently differed but in speaking of the sympathy of the religious sects towards Egypt I presumed that he did not include the followers of Sayed Abdel Rahman. As regards a plebiscite I would of course put the proposal forward if he wished but I would be glad to know whether he contemplated the simultaneous withdrawal of Egyptian troops and officials, including those in the irrigation service. I pleaded ignorance of the standard of education in Libya but I understood that only 3% of Sudanese could be regarded as literate. In reply to his question of how long it would take the Sudanese to reach a state in which they could govern themselves I gave him a personal estimate of ten years and added that that was probably rather under than over the mark.

8. In reply to a question from me whether he had any concrete proposals to put forward he said that there should be a transitional period of two years during which the Sudanisation of the Administration should be pressed forward and at the end of which the British forces should be withdrawn and the Condominium should be regarded as at an end. The Sudanese would then establish their own Government under the Egyptian Crown with a common foreign policy, defence force and currency with Egypt. I asked whether he contemplated the withdrawal of all British officials on the expiry of the transitional period. He replied that the further employment of foreign officials would be a matter for the new Sudanese Government to decide. I then asked where in all this the plebiscite came in. He answered that the plebiscite must not be regarded as a definite proposal. It would be difficult for Egypt to suggest it. His aim in mentioning it was twofold: first, to demonstrate his confidence in the correctness of his views on the desires of the Sudanese and, secondly, to test the sincerity of Britain's claim that she was ready to accede to Sudanese desires. If the suggestion of a plebiscite found favour with the British Government then would be the time to consider what precise question should be put to the people of the Sudan and to decide on procedure.

---

[1] By this time the Congress was an all-Ashiqqa (pro-Egyptian) organisation. While unable to gauge its potential danger, the government had concluded earlier in the year that 'Congress is anti-Government, anti-Legislative Assembly, one hundred percent pro-Egyptian, and is backed morally and financially by Egypt, and although it does not command much respect at the moment either in the Sudan or in Egypt it is a potential menace to public security' (Civil Secretary's Office, 'Note on the Graduates' General Congress as a back ground to its potential danger to public security—(up to 31.12.1949)', 28 Feb 1950, FO 371/80358, no 5).

9. I said that I would inform you of the foregoing and that you would doubtless give it full consideration. I could not pretend, however, to regard his proposals as practical.

192 FO 371/80518, no 104 21 Sept 1950

[Nile Waters]: minute by R Allen to M R Wright on new Egyptian willingness to proceed with negotiations on Nile Waters projects

The following is the position which appears to have been reached:

Towards the end of August Moharram Pasha, the Egyptian Minister of Public Works who is at present acting as Prime Minister during the absence of Nahas, indicated that he would like to discuss the various Nile Waters projects with representatives of the Sudan Government. These projects are Lake Tana, the 4th Cataract dam and the raising of the storage level in the Sennar dam. We have been urging Khartoum to agree to this and to come to an arrangement with Moharram before Nahas gets back and the whole thing is put back on to a political plane. On the 6th September the Sudan Government representatives went to Alexandria and saw Moharram, who made it clear that he regarded all three projects as inseparably linked together. After their talk with Moharram the Sudan representatives had further discussions with the Egyptian Public Works representatives and produced draft letters which were to be exchanged between the Sudan Government and the Egyptian Government. These letters would refer to each of the three projects and would confirm that the Sudan Government agreed to the 4th Cataract project on the understanding that technical discussions between the Governments should be held at an early date with the object of reaching agreement on the Sudan's share in the benefits and cost of the project.

Meanwhile the Legal Adviser to the Egyptian Ministry of Foreign Affairs and the Embassy Legal Counsellor had drawn up a joint report agreeing on the procedure with regard to Lake Tana. This report is very satisfactory, except for the fact that it refers to the Sudan "Administration" instead of the Sudan "Government".

On the 9th September the Sudan Government representatives were informed, however, that Moharram had rejected the draft letters referring to the various projects, apparently because of the reference to the technical discussions covering the Sudan share in the benefits and costs in the 4th Cataract project. It seems that his view is that this project is purely designed to control the flood waters and is not a storage project in which the Sudan should share. If so, this view is quite incorrect. The Sudan Government have now drawn up a memorandum stating their case on this, and it has now been handed in to the Egyptian Government.

The Sudan Government are likely to object to seeing themselves described in the Legal Advisers' report as an "administration", but we have not yet had their comments on this report. Sir Ralph Stevenson has said that he proposes to request Moharram's agreement to the procedure outlined in it as soon as he has had time to study the document, but the Department considers that it would be preferable that he should not discuss it with Moharram until the Sudan Government has had an opportunity of commenting. There does not seem however to be any reason why the Ambassador should not meanwhile try to clear up the misunderstanding or difference of opinion which has arisen over the 4th Cataract project, but he should be told to say that he has had no instructions yet if Moharram refers to the Lake Tana document.

Two draft telegrams are attached:—

(i) instructing Sir R. Stevenson on the above lines;

(ii) urging the Sudan Government not to make too much fuss about the misdescription of themselves in the Lake Tana document.[1]

---

[1] Both telegrams were approved and dispatched the same day.

193 FO 371/80388, no 27 28 Sept 1950

[Self-government]: letter from Sir R Howe to Sir W Strang, responding to the Egyptian government's proposals for Sudanese self-government

[Howe set out his arguments against the Egyptian proposals in two letters: one, a full rebuttal to Strang, and another, more formal rejection to Bevin (see 194).]

I have read with interest the two despatches Nos. 348 and 349[1] from His Majesty's Ambassador in Cairo regarding his conversations with the Egyptian Minister of State, as well as the Ambassador's later telegram No. 156 on his talk with the Egyptian Minister for Foreign Affairs about the future of the Sudan.[2]

2. The Minister of State showed, as Sir Ralph Stevenson remarks, a more liberal and realistic attitude towards the Sudan problem than has hitherto been displayed by the Government of Nahas Pasha. His attitude in fact is reminiscent of that shown by that eminent Egyptian statesman, Sidky Pasha, in the conversations of 1946 in London which led up to the Sidky–Bevin protocol. That instrument was however repudiated by Egypt and there is little or no likelihood that the views of Hamid Zaki Bey, a junior minister, would prevail against those of his Minister for Foreign Affairs whose attitude as revealed in Cairo telegram 156 is quite different. Moreover, even Hamid Zaki Bey insists on the recognition of the Egyptian Crown and I see no possibility of the great majority of the Sudanese swallowing this, whatever assurances to the contrary the Minister for Foreign Affairs may have received from the Graduates' Congress in Khartoum.

3. The contrast between Hamid Zaki Bey's programme and that of the Minister for Foreign Affairs is indeed startling. Under the former the Sudanese would evolve quietly and naturally under the Condominium through self-government to their eventual status under the Egyptian Crown. Under the Minister for Foreign Affairs's programme the Sudan would be abandoned from now on by the British, the Sudanese and Egyptians would be left alone to work out in the next two years, Sudanisation having been completed, the nature of their future status under the Egyptian Crown, Foreign Office and War Office.

4. I am well aware of the vital importance attached by H.M.G. to a settlement with Egypt of the problem of the defence of the Middle East at this critical epoch in

---

[1] See 190.

[2] See 191.

international affairs and that in view of the insistence of Egypt in linking this problem to that of the Sudan, the Egyptians will demand their *quid pro quo* in the Sudan as the price of a new defence arrangement. I can only say that while I imagine there can be no likelihood of negotiations being undertaken on the basis of Hamid Zaki Bey's programme as long as it contains the provision for a common crown of Egypt, any agreement by H.M.G. to negotiate on the basis of the programme outlined by Saleh-ed-Din would be regarded by most Sudanese as a gross betrayal by H.M. Government.

5. In considering the question of the future of the Sudan, there is one very important aspect of the problem which is constantly overlooked in any projected negotiations with Egypt and that is the problem of the South. The Southern Sudan represents numerically some 30 per cent. of the total population of the country. Predominantly pagan and negroid, they are only now barely emerging from a primeval state to the appreciation of the benefits of fifty years of enlightened and Christian administration. They are already apprehensive of their future under a purely Sudanese Government. What would be their prospects under an Egyptian-dominated Sudanese Government? Given another twenty-five years of the present administration they might well be in a position to stand up against their Northern compatriots. Some even of our present Sudanese Ministers have said that when the Sudan is independent *"there is going to be no nonsense about democracy"*.

6. To return to the main problem, it is clear that there are certain fundamental matters of principle on which there cannot or should not be any compromise, such as any precipitate abandonment of our interest in the Sudan or the imposition of the Egyptian Crown. It would therefore seem that the only hope of an Anglo–Egyptian agreement must lie in agreement on matters of detail such as are outlined in Sir Ralph Stevenson's despatch No. 349 and which arise from his conversations with Hamid Zaki Bey. As regards some of the assumptions made in these two despatches, my views are as follows:—

(a) Practically all *politically-minded* Sudanese of whatever party they are, are asking for a purely Sudanese Government as soon as possible and an end of the Condominium. Some would retain as head of the state, a neutral officer, probably British; others would elect a President; others would have S.A.R. as a constitutional monarch. The Nazirs and Sheikhs, however, and the Southerners *do not wish* progress towards a Sudanese Government to be too rapid and are opposed to ending the present régime too speedily. It would be wrong in my opinion to transfer power too soon to the Effendi class against the wishes of the tribal leaders and the great mass of the Sudanese.

(b) It is our intention to discuss amendments to the Ordinance in the autumn sitting of the Assembly, and to have the amended Ordinance ready before the elections for the new Assembly in 1951/52 (probably January 1952).

(c) We aim at creating one or two more ministers shortly. This will not alter the present relative strengths of British and Sudanese on the Council (five and seven), but will give executive authority to perhaps two of those who now sit on the Council without portfolio or as Under-Secretaries.

(d) No mention is made in these despatches of the present Egyptian propaganda and money which is being poured into this country, chiefly it seems at the instance [sic] of the Palace, and no opinion is given of the likely attitude of the King of Egypt to any of these proposals. The King is personally very much interested in "his Sudanese Empire", and no proposals which do not have his blessing are likely to be successful, for in spite of alleged personal unpopularity with everyone, he still rules Egypt. The Sudanese Independents and especially Sayed Abdel Rahman are always insistent on our stopping Egyptian propaganda, which they consider is ruining the younger student classes by subversive propaganda which combines with communistic influences to undermine authority in the Sudan. Any settlement which allows this to continue, will be opposed by them.

7. I am beginning to come to the opinion that administration in the Sudan might be easier if we had a Sudanese Cabinet advised by British advisers. They would be able to take a stronger line in many things than we can and the communist approach to the people through their nationalist feelings would lose much of its appeal. On the other hand, feelings of tribal leaders and of the Southerners have to be considered, as I have already mentioned. Practically all non-politically-minded Sudanese think we should go slowly in this matter.

8. I now turn to Sir Ralph Stevenson's detailed comments on Hamid Zaki Bey's proposals in despatch No.349:—

(i) I agree generally with his views in paragraph 5 but doubt whether we can "satisfy Egypt" while maintaining the present organisation of the Sudan Government. We can obviously give Egypt assurances about her water rights, but not to the detriment of reasonable Sudanese interests. I also doubt whether we can give Egypt a closer association with the Government of the Sudan in any appreciable degree without disturbing the present organisation of the Sudan Government. Are we not deluding ourselves if we think Egypt really agrees to Sudanese self-government? Does Egypt not still wish to dominate the Sudan regardless of the wishes of the Sudanese?

(ii) Paragraph 6 seems a good description of His Majesty's Government's policy in recent years.

(iii) Paragraph 7(i) is obviously important for His Majesty's Government and it would clearly be valuable for the Sudan to have Egyptian co-operation in its future progress, if it can be obtained.

Paragraph 7(ii). I am not sure if Sir Ralph is right here. There is more unity between the Parties in the Sudan on fundamentals than ever before. They all agree in ending the present régime as soon as possible; and they all agree on a Sudanese Government with a directly-elected democratic assembly. They differ only on the ultimate political future of the country: complete independence or some link with Egypt.

Having been in close touch with these affairs for several years now, I am inclined to doubt whether the political strife is more bitter than before. On the contrary, I believe that the Ashigga Party has lost much ground, and that the new National Front, which comes closer to the Umma Party in fundamentals, is gaining ground.

9. Regarding paragraph 8:—

Sub-paragraph (a): A statement acknowledging Egypt's legitimate interest in Nile Waters

Yes—provided the Sudan's reasonable interests are also safeguarded (the Sudanese are probably more Arab than the Egyptians, among whom Arab blood is extremely diluted).

Sub-paragraph (b): A statement that H.M.G. have no economic or strategic interest in the Sudan
This is of course a matter for H.M.G., but the history of 1941–45 when the Sudan *was* important strategically comes at once to mind. I think any declaration in this respect would have to be very carefully worded.

Sub-paragraph (c): A statement that H.M.G. have no feeling one way or the other about the relationship between the Sudan and Egypt once the Sudanese have reached the stage of being able to choose for themselves
Yes. His Majesty's Government have said this before.

Sub-paragraph (d): A tripartite Anglo–Egyptian–Sudanese Supervisory Council to advise on the development of the Sudan
It is true that we agreed to this during the Campbell/Khashaba negotiations on the Executive Council and Legislative Assembly Ordinance in 1948, but the idea is no longer welcome to Sudanese Ministers, who see two dangers in it. Firstly, that its activities will undermine the authority of the Executive Council and the Ministers, who see themselves thwarted and impeded by it. As time passes and the Executive Council becomes surer of itself this difficulty will increase. Secondly, Sudanese feel that the Egyptian members of the Tripartite Council will use the opportunities of travelling in the Sudan to spread Egyptian propaganda and to work against existing institutions.

Sub-paragraph (e): Joint Anglo–Egyptian observation of next general election
I much doubt if our Independents and Umma Ministers would agree to this, although the Sudan Government did agree to it in the Campbell/Khashaba agreement. Such supervision, in the eyes of the Sudanese, implies a slight upon the whole Sudan administration, over 80 per cent. of which is now Sudanese and which is fully capable of conducting elections in a much fairer atmosphere than that in which they are conducted in Egypt, for example. The Sudanese are proud of the impartiality of their government and consider this proposal unnecessary.

Sub-paragraph (f): Withdrawal of British forces from the Sudan
I think we should oppose any withdrawal of British troops unless the Egyptians go too. For the British troops to go alone would be an enormous fillip to the pro-Egyptian Party and would indicate to all Sudanese that the British were giving up their task of leading the Sudanese to self-government and self-determination. During recent discussions among the Unity Parties about the formation of a common front this point was mentioned and some of these people even were very doubtful of not evacuating the Egyptians if the British went.

In fact neither Force plays any role in day to day maintenance of public security and we have agreed that in certain eventualities the British should be withdrawn, e.g., on the outbreak of hostilities. We have a plan for gradually withdrawing British officers from the Sudan Defence Force until the Kaid becomes Sudanese and there is a British Military Mission. This could occur in about twelve years' time.

10. Reference paragraph 9:—

(1) Yes.

(2) Yes.

(3) I agree.

(4) Yes.

(5) Yes.

11. I can see no objection to Hamid Zaki Bey coming to the Sudan either officially or unofficially. It would be most suitable if he were my guest at the Palace, and given every official assistance to see all sides of the Sudan Government's work.

12. In view of the divergence of opinion on the Sudan shown in the talks with the Minister of State and the Minister for Foreign Affairs in Cairo, it seems to me that it would be a mistake for us to offer anything at the moment. Nothing which the Sudan Government could offer would suffice to bridge the gap, and for H.M.G. to make declarations now would be to prejudice their own position in any future talks without gaining any advantage. As far as the Sudan is concerned, I believe the right policy is to go ahead with our present plans knowing that we have the great majority of Sudanese with us.

13. I am sending a copy of this letter to H.M. Ambassador in Cairo.

194 FO 371/80388, no 22 5 Oct 1950

[Self-government]: letter (reply) from Sir R Howe to Mr Bevin, responding to Salah al-Din's proposals for Sudanese self-government[1]

At the end of August His Majesty's Ambassador in Cairo had conversations with the Egyptian Minister of State for Sudan Affairs, Hamid Zaki Bey, and a few days later with Saleh ed Din, the Egyptian Minister for Foreign Affairs.

The Minister of State showed a refreshingly liberal attitude on the whole towards the Sudan question. He agreed that nothing should stop the Sudanese ultimately from deciding their own future. He thought that it was necessary that the Sudanese should be consulted in any discussion of their future status. There could be no question of imposing on the Sudanese. He hoped that the Legislative Assembly Ordinance could be amended so as to result in a more representative body. He still held, however, to the necessity for Egypt and the Sudan to be under the common Crown of Egypt.

The Minister for Foreign Affairs on the other hand showed no inclination whatever to abandon the most extreme Egyptian view as to the unity of Egypt and the Sudan and the necessity for the evacuation of all the British from both countries.

There is little doubt which of these two views would prevail in the Egyptian Government. Nevertheless Sir Ralph Stevenson thought that it was desirable to make another effort to reach a settlement with the Egyptians and to this end suggested that H.M.G. might offer the following:—

(a) A statement of Egypt's legitimate interest in Nile Waters.

(b) A statement that H.M.G. have no economic or strategic interest in the Sudan.

(c) A statement that H.M.G. have no feeling about the relationship between Egypt and the Sudan once the Sudanese have reached the stage of being able to choose for themselves.

(d) To revive the idea of an Anglo–Egyptian–Sudanese Supervisory Council to advise on the development of the Sudan.

(e) Anglo–Egyptian or United Nations observation of the next general election to

---

[1] See 191.

the Legislative Assembly and of any election or plebiscite to determine the constitutional status of the Sudan.

(f) Withdrawal of the British forces from the Sudan as soon as the Sudan Defence Force and Police can take over.

Now these proposals are, generally speaking, an attenuated version of those put forward in 1948 in the course of the Campbell/Khashaba negotiations, with a view to inducing the Egyptians to give their agreement to the Ordinance setting up the Legislative Assembly and Executive Council and at that time it was considered well worth while for the Sudan to offer them in return for Egyptian agreement to the new constitutional set-up.[2] In the event, the Egyptian Government refused its assent to the Ordinance and they should now be considered in the light of the progress which has been made in the Sudan in the direction of self-government under the Ordinance.

On the whole the new constitutional arrangements are working well. It is true that the Assembly is not a wholly representative body as yet since many of the opposing parties in the Sudan, particularly those in favour of union with Egypt, declined to take part in the elections for it. Proposals are however now under consideration in Khartoum with a view to amending the electoral rules so as to induce the opposition parties to contest the next elections and so make the Assembly more representative. In general the pattern of evolution in the Sudan would take something like the following form:—

Stage I: Steps to make the Legislative Assembly more representative: in particular to include representatives of the Khatmia. These are now under consideration.

Stage II: Sudanese members in the Executive Council to be in a majority. This has already been achieved. There are seven Sudanese and five British members.

Stage III: British members in the Executive Council to be entirely replaced by Sudanese members.

Stage IV: The Sudan to decide its own future after direct discussion with Egypt as well as the United Kingdom.

The Sudanese Ministers in the Executive Council support the above plan and the policy has been confirmed twice in the Assembly although the Nazirs, country members and the Southerners are firmly opposed to too speedy progress. It is against this background that the suggestions put forward by Sir Ralph Stevenson, as enumerated earlier on, will have to be considered.

But in addition to these internal developments in the Sudan, there are certain developments in the international field which might have a bearing on the Anglo–Egyptian problem and also on the Sudan question, viz.:—

(a) The proposals for the reform of the United Nations Assembly.

(b) The war in Korea and the consequent reactions in the United Nations and elsewhere.

(c) Developments in Commonwealth planning for the defence of the Middle East arising out of the recent visit of the South African Minister of Defence to the United Kingdom.

---

[2] See 160–162.

In view of the progress which has been made in the Sudan towards self-government in the last two years, there can be little doubt that the Sudanese will be less prepared to accept the proposals put forward by Sir Ralph Stevenson than they were before. Viewed in this light and in that of the international developments above-mentioned, together with the fact that the Egyptian Foreign Minister will not be back from Lake Success much before the end of this year, it is for consideration whether it is necessary or even advisable to make the offers to Egypt which Sir Ralph Stevenson proposes. It seems to me that it would be a mistake to offer anything at the moment. Nothing which the Sudan Government could offer now would suffice to bridge the gap between the views of His Majesty's Government and those of Egypt in regard to the Sudan, and for H.M.G. to make declarations now might be to prejudice their own position in any future talks without gaining any advantage. As far as the Sudan is concerned, I believe the right policy is to go ahead with our present plans in the knowledge that we have the great majority of Sudanese with us.[3]

[3] Marginal note by Strang, 6 Oct 1950: 'Seen by the S/S, who agreed with the views set out therein'.

195 FO 371/80388, no 28 6 Oct 1950

'The future of the Sudan': note by M N F Stewart recording a conversation between Sir R Howe and M R Wright on self-government

Sir Robert Howe and Mr. Wright met on the 3rd October to discuss the future of the Sudan in relation to the proposals set out in Alexandria despatch No. 349 of the 25th August, Alexandria telegram No. 156 and Sir Robert Howe's letter of the 28th September to Sir William Strang.[1] Mr. Allen and Mr. Stewart were also present.

2. Mr. Wright said that he thought there had been certain developments in the international field which might have a bearing on the Egyptian attitude to the Sudan question. These were:

(a) tentative proposals for the reform of the Assembly as set out in telegrams Nos. 406 and 407 (Saving) from the U.K. Delegation, New York;
(b) the war in Korea and the reaction which it had provoked in the United Nations and elsewhere;
(c) certain developments in the Commonwealth planning for the defence of the Middle East.

As regards (c) Mr. Wright said that amongst other things it had been proposed during the recent visit of the South African Minister of Defence to the U.K. that there should be a conference of certain African countries sometime in the course of 1950 to examine the defence facilities in time of war. The conference would deal primarily with technical problems such as communications, and the present idea was that it would be attended by most African countries or territories (excluding West African). Mr. Wright asked Sir R. Howe what he considered the Sudan Government's reactions

[1] See 190, 191, 193.

would be if they were invited to attend such a conference.[2] Sir R. Howe said that the question would probably be considered on party lines in the Sudan with the Independents in favour of acceptance and the Khatmia taking the same view as Egypt. He thought, however, that he could secure a majority in the Executive Council for acceptance.

3. Mr. Wright further remarked that the Egyptian Foreign Minister would probably not be back from Lake Success much before Christmas and that apart from the considerations set out in the preceding paragraph, it was perhaps doubtful how far it was necessary or advisable to discuss the Sudan with Egypt at all in the immediate future.

4. The meeting then considered the six points which Sir R. Stevenson had suggested in paragraph 8 of his despatch No. 349 might be offered to the Egyptians. Sir R. Howe said that he really had little to add to the comments he had made in his letter to Sir William Strang. Sir R. Stevenson's first three suggestions were, so far as the Sudan Government was concerned, unobjectionable, though he doubted whether H.M.G. would wish to commit themselves to the statement that H.M.G. had no strategic interest in the Sudan. He confirmed his objections to the last three points, viz:

> The revival of the Tripartite Supervisory Council; Joint Anglo–Egyptian supervision of the next Sudanese General Elections, and the withdrawal of the British forces from the Sudan.

In discussion, however, Sir R. Howe said that it might be possible to secure Sudanese acceptance of a Tripartite Advisory body provided this body had no authority to advise or to intervene in the internal affairs of the Sudan. It was suggested, and Sir R. Howe agreed, that this body might however have advisory functions in respect of Nile Waters, Defence and Foreign Affairs.

5. The discussion then turned to the next General Elections in the Sudan and the possibility of setting up a Sudanese Cabinet in substitution for the Executive Council. Sir R. Howe did not favour the dissolution of the present Legislative Assembly and the holding of new General Elections before the present Assembly had run its natural course. That is to say, the elections in the new Assembly would take place at the beginning of 1952. He considered that there was a good prospect of the Khatmia fighting the elections. It might then be possible to form a Sudanese Cabinet either on a single party or on an all party basis, with British advisers (see paragraph 7 of Sir R. Howe's letter). Mr. Wright asked, with reference to Sir R. Stevenson's suggestions for greater Egyptian association with the Government of the Sudan, whether the Sudan Government would accept Egyptian advisers. Sir R. Howe thought it doubtful whether the Umma party would ever accept this, but agreed that it was theoretically possible that if the Khatmia were returned with a majority and formed a Government, they would accept Egyptian advisers.

---

[2] In Aug 1951 Britain and South Africa jointly convened an African Defence Facilities Conference in Nairobi. The other participants were Belgium, Ethiopia, France, Italy, Portugal and Southern Rhodesia; the US sent observers. The conference dealt with the logistical problems of moving troops and supplies between Southern Africa and the Middle East in the event of war or emergency. A second conference was held in Dakar in Mar 1954. The Sudan was not represented at either, BDEEP series A, vo 3, D Goldsworthy, ed, *The Conservative government and the end of empire 1951–1957*, part I, 69.

6. On the question of the relations between the Khatmia and the Umma, Sir R. Howe said that no reconciliation was likely as long as S.A.R. and S.A.M. were alive, but thought that if both these two gentlemen were removed from the scene of active politics, there would be a move towards the centre and that a national Sudanese policy, based on independence with some form of union with Egypt and a treaty of alliance with H.M.G., might emerge. These developments, however, were still entirely a matter of speculation.

7. With particular reference to paragraph 11 of Sir R. Stevenson's despatch No. 349, Sir R. Howe said he would be glad to see Hamid Zaki Bey or another Egyptian Minister in Khartoum and to invite him to stay at the Palace.

8. In general, it was felt that there was little that Sir R. Stevenson could offer the Egyptian Government in respect of the Sudan, but that subject to Sir R. Howe's discussions with the Secretary of State on the 6th October, Sir R. Stevenson might be informed of the limit of the offers which he might at present make to the Egyptian Government, i.e.

sub-paragraphs (a) and (c) of paragraph 8 of his despatch,
a modification of sub-paragraph (b), and
sub-paragraph (d) modified as agreed in paragraph 8 above.

Sir R. Stevenson could advise whether it was worth approaching the Egyptian Government on this limited basis.

196 FO 371/80359, no 29 17 Nov 1950

[Future of the condominium]: inward telegram no 195 from Sir R Howe to Sir W Strang asking for instructions should the Egyptian government act on King Faruq's instructions to end the condominium

[In his speech from the throne to the Egyptian parliament, 16 Nov 1950, King Faruq took the first step in the eventual abrogation of the Anglo–Egyptian treaty by announcing that measures would be introduced to bring to an end the condominium agreements of 1899 on the Sudan. Britain's immediate reaction was that a unilateral renunciation by Egypt would be illegal, and its position on the Sudan remained unchanged (minute on the Sudan by Stewart, 25 Nov 1950, FO 371/80388, no 32).]

The statement in the speech from the Throne at the opening of the Egyptian Parliament on November 16th regarding termination of Anglo–Egyptian Treaty of 1936 and termination of Condominium Agreement of 1899 has caused considerable excitment here. I have not yet received the exact text of the statement and such versions of it as have reached Khartoum do not appear to indicate that it could be regarded as a formal act of termination but merely as a statement of a policy to be pursued with a view to achieving such termination by lawful means. If this is the case then I would expect the excitment here to subside but if the Egyptian Government do in fact mean it to be a formal act, or if they took any practical steps to indicate that they did regard the Condominium as having lapsed albeit unilaterally then I would anticipate a very strong reaction by political parties in the Sudan.

2. In the above eventuality I should expect a strong demand by U.M.M.A. parties for an immediate declaration by the Sudan Government of the independence of the Sudan. A further possibility and one which would be widely acceptable here would be

a demand for a declaration by His Majesty's Government of a protectorate over the Sudan for say a period of 10 years.

3. In any event however I am likely to be asked what is His Majesty's Government's attitude regarding yesterday's declaration in the Egyptian Parliament and also what would be our attitude should Egypt formally announce abrogation of the Condominium Agreement and 1936 Treaty. I presume that His Majesty's Government would take their stand on the principle of sanctity of the treaty and on the maintenance of the Condominium which is the basis of their policy in the Sudan, and it might be useful for His Majesty's Government to reiterate this publicly together with their pledge regarding the future status of the Sudan. I would welcome your views also on the legal position in the event of a unilateral abrogation of the 1899 Agreement by Egypt and on the position of the Governor General in that event. We may be faced with questions on this in the Legislative Assembly very shortly.

4. An announcement that Egypt no longer recognised the existence of the Condominium would be acclaimed by all the political parties here. The desirability of ending the Condominium Agreement is the one point on which all parties are agreed. The U.M.M.A. party would immediately demand the removal of the Egyptian flag and opposition to the removal of the British flag and we might have some disturbance of public order. We ought to see that British forces here should not be reduced below their present strength at any rate.

197 FO 371/80388, no 37 21 Nov 1950

[Self-government]: letter from Sir R Stevenson to Sir W Strang, commenting on Sir R Howe's letter on Egypt's self-government proposals. *Minute* by R H G Edmonds

I have been studying Bob Howe's letter LO/TSF/1 of the 28th September to you about the future of the Sudan.[1]

There are various small points of difference between us, but I feel that I must record that, taken as a whole, the letter makes me a little uneasy. It shows clearly the difficulty of convincing the Sudan Government of the necessity for adopting a conciliatory attitude towards Egypt if the Sudan is eventually to be launched into fairly settled waters.

I think that the letter brings out the fact that the Sudan Government are only too ready to assume in their various activities that the Condominium is at an end and that the Sudan Government themselves have rights at least equal to those of the two Co-domini. This attitude is perhaps more unconscious than conscious, but I think it exists in the minds of a number of senior officials of the Sudan Government and, unless controlled, it is liable to give force to the common Egyptian accusation that the British-controlled Sudan Government, whose executive Head is the servant of the Co-domini, is working against Egyptian interests.

As I see it, the Governor-General has the difficult task of attempting, in the absence of any joint directives from the Co-domini, to reconcile the frequently

---

[1] See 193.

conflicting interests of the Co-domini and of the Sudanese themselves. In the face of the present Egyptian attitude the danger is, I think, for the Governor-General to identify himself too closely with the expressed desires of the Sudanese which, as in any dependent territory, are often not in accordance with or at least in advance of what is considered best for the proper and orderly development of the country. Without in any way trading the rights of the Sudan against benefits for His Majesty's Government in a settlement with Egypt, I suggest that we should not allow ourselves to be deflected from a particular course just because the idea of it seems at the moment to be unwelcome to any or all sections of informed Sudanese opinion.

For the sake of the interests of either or both the Co-domini, or for the long term interests of the Sudanese (for example, by paying due regard to Egyptian interests), it may sometimes be necessary to insist on a policy being carried out to which the initial reactions of the Sudanese and even of the Sudanese Ministers have been unfavourable; in such a case, as I see it, it would then be the duty of the Governor-General and his officials (having previously represented to His Majesty's Government the disadvantages of it) to administer the policy and, by proper handling of it, to reduce objections and obstructions to the minimum.

In short, I suggest that if our long term object is to leave the Sudanese in a status of their own chosing [sic] and in good relations with Egypt, our short term object must be to seek to draw the Egyptians into a more reasonable and co-operative attitude over the Sudan, and that this may well involve "concessions" unwelcome to Sudanese opinion; it certainly involves due recognition by the Sudan Government of the fact that they are not an independent Government.

P.S. Since the above was drafted I have seen Foreign Office despatch No.505 of 15th November.[2] I agree that, at this moment, the less said about the Sudan the better, but if and when we see an improvement in the atmosphere we should be ready to take advantage of it.

Minute on 197

I regret the delay in submitting this letter: it has taken some time to assemble the relevant papers.

2. The thesis developed in Sir R. Stevenson's letter, which has often been advanced by H.M. Embassy in Cairo in recent years, can perhaps be summarised as follows:—

(a) Sudan Government officials, including the Governor-General himself, regard the Condominium as virtually at an end, and identify themselves with the independence movement in the Sudan;
(b) In so doing, they ignore the fact that ultimately, in the interests both of the U.K. and of the Sudanese themselves, some form of settlement between Egypt and the Sudan must be brought about;
(c) The Foreign Office are themselves liable to adopt the same attitude;
(d) Instead, we should adopt a policy in regard to the Sudan based on the last two paragraphs of the letter within.

---

[2] Embodying the conclusions reached in 196.

3. Opinions on this question are bound to differ, but for what they are worth, mine are as follows:—

(a) and (b). This tendency, which began after the events of 1924, has been vastly strengthened in the last five years. It is in many ways unfortunate, but it seems to me also to be historically inevitable, in view of the intransigent Egyptian attitude towards the Sudan generally and the working of the Condominium in particular. Since the war we have made two attempts to reconcile Anglo–Egyptian differences in this respect; on both occasions they were initialled by the Egyptian negotiator *ad referendum*; and both were ultimately rejected by the Egyptian Cabinet. Had the Egyptian Government ever shown any real desire to meet us half-way over the Sudan, the attitude of Sudan Government officials would be far easier to criticise. As it is, I do not think that we can do more than to try to remind them from time to time that the Sudan *is* still a Condominium and that the Governor-General is still in theory the servant not only of H.M.G. but also of the Egyptian Government (E.g.—by encouraging Sudan Govt officials to pay their respects in Cairo, on their way to & from Khartoum).

(c). There is a danger that, in view of the obstinate absurdity of the official Egyptian attitude towards the Sudan, the Foreign Office should tend to forget that the Sudanese opponents of the Independence Party represent a very large section of the Muslim population of the Sudan and that Egypt has legitimate interests in the Sudan (in particular, in Nile Waters, as was recognised by the Secretary of State in Parliament recently). On the other hand, it is—I think—a danger of which we are aware. We have—for example—during the past year done everything we could to impress upon the Sudan Government the urgency of securing Khatmi representation in the Legislative Assembly and to moderate excessive Sudanese nationalism in regard to questions affecting Nile Waters.

(d). With respect, however, it seems to me that the real answer to Cairo's thesis is that the alternative outlined in the last two paragraphs of this letter does not offer, in present circumstances, a workable alternative. As was recognised in our despatch in JE 1059/29 and recently confirmed by the Cabinet, the gap which separates British and Egyptian policy in respect of the Sudan is for the moment unbridgable. For this reason it is impossible to envisage now a situation, such as that indicated in the fifth paragraph of Sir Ralph Stevenson's letter, in which either the two Codomini would unite to impose a policy against the wishes of the majority of the Sudanese, or H.M.G. would attempt to do so alone (which they would, incidentally, not be entitled to do under the provisions of the 1948 Ordinance.)

4. It would in fact be possible to go a step further and argue that the Sudan has progressed so far towards independence that, in the present stage of African nationalism as a whole, it is impossible to imagine either Codominus imposing upon the Sudan a policy resisted by the majority of the Sudanese. This is, however, debatable ground. What seems to me certain is that there can be no chance of an agreed Anglo–Egyptian settlement of the Sudan unless the Egyptians are prepared to modify what they regard as their historic demands. In the meantime the loyalty of Sudan Government officials, and to some extent of the Governor-General himself, is bound to be directed more and more towards the Sudanese people, and what they believe to be in the latter's best interests.

R.H.G.E.
5.12.50

198 FO 371/80360, nos 46 & 47 14 Dec 1950

[Self-government]: inward telegrams nos 221 & 222 from Sir R Howe to FO on Egypt's protest at the self-government debate in the Legislative Assembly, and the Sudan government's reply

[Following Faruq's speech to the throne the Umma Party tabled a self-government motion for debate in the Legislative Assembly in Khartoum. The debate coincided with the Egyptian foreign minister's visit to Britain. In explaining to Bevin his decision to allow the debate Howe gave the reasons outlined here in his response to the Egyptian prime minister, but also added that he felt it best not to stifle open discussion in the assembly at this point, especially as he felt the motion had little chance of passing (inward telegram no 216 from Howe to Bevin, 12 Dec 1950). Bevin was sympathetic but replied: 'I earnestly hope that you will do all in your power to ensure that no action is taken in Khartoum, particularly during the next few days, which is likely to embarrass me while I am engaged in delicate conversations with the Egyptian Foreign Minister' (outward telegram no 169 from Bevin to Howe, 13 Dec 1950, both telegrams in FO 371/80359, no 39).]

[No. 221]

Following is text of a telegram I have received from Mustafa el Nahas: "We have learnt that you have decided to table to discussion by the Legislative Assembly the proposition presented to Your Excellency by some members of that Assembly concerning the demand to grant the Sudan self-government. Egypt who is keen on the Sudanese enjoying self-government within the unity of Egypt and Sudan under the Egyptian Crown, considers that this is a purely political matter and does not fall within the jurisdication of Sudan Government. Your Excellency, as representative of the two countries administering the Sudan, should not deal with or discuss this matter which is at present the object of political discussions taking place in London. As for the letter sent to you by el Sayed Saddik el Mahdy and his colleagues of el Umma party, we resent its contents.[1] This party does not represent the Sudan people. Please inform me with the immediate measures you have taken to stop this planned campaign meant to challenge the people of Egypt and Sudan. I would like to inform you that a copy of the above mentioned text was communicated on the 9th December to the Agent of the Sudan Government".

[No. 222]

Following is text of my reply.

1. "I have received Your Excellency's telegram about a motion concerning self-government which I have allowed to be debated in the Legislative Assembly. Your Excellency's telegram only arrived here on December 13th at 16.27 hours i.e. after the debate had started.

2. The motion which I have allowed to be debated reads as follows "that an address be presented to His Excellency in the following terms:—

We the members of the Legislative Assembly of the Sudan are of opinion that the Sudan has now reached the stage at which self-government could be granted, and request Your Excellency to approach the Condominium Powers with a request that a

---

[1] This was a reaction to Faruq's speech from the throne, reiterating the Umma party's rejection of Egyptian claims to the unity of the Nile valley, and repeating its demand for immediate self-government (Siddiq al-Mahdi to Howe, 20 Nov 1950, FO 371/80360, no 53).]

joint declaration of the grant of self-government be made before the end of the third session of the first Assembly, so that the next elections may be held on this basis".

3. To this an amendment has been moved to delete all the words after the words "that the Sudan" in the third line and to substitute the following words "has made good progress towards the stage at which full self-government can be granted, and request Your Excellency to press on urgently with such measures which, while consistent with the maintenance of good government throughout the country, will ensure not only that such self-government shall be full and complete, but also that in working towards that end, all sections of the community and all parties may cooperate in developing the institutions of government so as to hasten the day when this goal is attained".

4. Your Excellency will see that this motion requests me to approach the Condominium Powers and in no way derogates from their ultimate authority. Even if the motion is passed by the Assembly, the only action which I would propose to take is to refer the matter to the British and Egyptian Governments.

5. There is in my opinion no planned campaign against either the Egyptian or Sudan people and I am confident that Your Excellency would not wish me to interfere with the exercise by the Sudanese of their right to free speech inherent both in the laws now in force in the Sudan and throughout the world.

6. I very much regret that Your Excellency has been misinformed about the terms of this motion, and I can assure you that I have no intention of acting outside my jurisdiction as representative of the Powers administering the Sudan".

199 FO 371/90129, no 1 15 Dec 1950

[Statement on the Sudan]: FO note of a statement made by Mr Bevin at a meeting with Salah al-Din

At our meeting here on 9th December, as your Excellency will remember, I undertook to study your statement about Egyptian policy regarding the Sudan and to refer it to my colleagues in the Government. I have not yet been able to put it before the Cabinet, who have been greatly preoccupied with other matters, but your Excellency may like to have a short account of my own reactions to your statement now.

In the first place, I have been struck by the gap which separates us, not so much about policy, but about our interpretation of the facts about the Sudan. Without going into the remote past, I should like to take three examples from the more recent history of the Sudan, to which you referred.

First, I cannot accept the contention that, taking advantage of the presence of our forces in Egypt, we *compelled* the Egyptian Government to withdraw from the Sudan in 1885.

Secondly, there is no evidence, of which I am aware, that it was under *compulsion* that the Khedive allowed British forces to assist in the re-conquest of the Sudan.

Finally, if the 1899 Agreement was indeed concluded under duress, it seems surprising that your present Prime Minister, as recently as 1936, should have signed a further Treaty, containing an Article which specifically provides that the administration of the Sudan should continue to be that resulting from the 1899 Agreement.

Then there is the question, which we have already discussed at our previous meeting, of the interpretation of the protocol which the late Sidky Pasha and I initialled in London four years ago. I have nothing further to say about this, except that I did not agree then—and I do not agree now—with the interpretation which Sidky Pasha placed upon this protocol. Moreover, it is important to remember that we have had certain actions in the Sudan, which I believe are in the spirit of my agreement with Sidky Pasha, and that as a result the political development of the Sudan in the intervening years has been so rapid, that that protocol has been overtaken by events.

Your Excellency suggested at one point in your statement that, for reasons of self-interest, my Government were deliberately encouraging separatism in the Sudan, in order to split the country from Egypt. I assure you categorically that the primary interest of my Government in the Sudan is simply the welfare of the Sudanese people and their progress towards self-government and self-determination. I have, however, consistently emphasised the economic facts of the Nile, and that nothing must be done to jeopardise the security of Egypt's water supplies and their development to the maximum extent possible. My Government are willing to associate themselves with any rational policy designed to achieve this end. Equally, we expect of Egypt that she, for her part, will do nothing to prejudice the water interests of the Sudan.

But again it is clear, from the four points which you listed in your statement, that our two Governments do hold different views on the facts of the political situation in the Sudan, both past and present. I shall take these four points one by one.

The first concerned the Graduates' Congress. I understand that they have said they are in favour of a union between Egypt and the Sudan. But the Congress does not even represent the majority of Sudanese intelligentsia, and it has in recent years come under the domination of an extremist clique, which represents only a very small proportion of the Sudanese people.

As regards the municipal elections I really do not believe that the facts support your Excellency's view that there is something approaching unanimity in favour of union. In fact the unionists are in a minority in Khartoum. In Omdurman they have a majority of only one. I give there [sic, these] as examples.

As regards the percentages of the electors taking part in the Legislative Assembly's election the facts are that this election was held both by direct and indirect election. Ten seats were filled by the former means, and 55 by the latter. In the direct elections it is estimated that 18 per cent. of the electorate voted. (Incidentally, I believe that in the last Egyptian general election, which returned the Government of which your Excellency is a member, only some 15 per cent. of the Cairo electorate voted.) In the indirect elections in the Sudan no figure at all can be given, since the primary elections on which they were based were mainly decided by acclamation.

As regards your fourth point, concerning the views of the religious sects in the Sudan, I think I should say that, on my information, those Sudanese who profess to favour union with Egypt are not more than about one-fifth of the total population of the country.

I now turn to another question raised by your Excellency which, although it appears relevant to the future of the Sudan at first sight, does not in my opinion affect the issue; namely, the decisions recently taken by the United Nations about the future of Libya and Eritrea.

In the first place I must make it clear that these are decisions taken by the United

Nations with which, as a loyal member of that organisation, my Government was bound to comply. Neither decision represents what, in our opinion, would have been the *ideal* solution, and great care will have to be exercised in their execution.

As regards Libya, we agree to independence within two years, since the United Nations were in favour of it. Having done so, our first consideration, as in the case of the Sudan, is that the Libyan people shall be allowed to determine their own future.

As regards Eritrea, it was our view that that part of the territory where the overwhelming majority of the inhabitants wished to be reunited with Ethiopia, should be united with that country.[1] In the event a different solution—federation—has been adopted. Here again we have complied, because in the circumstances there was no alternative.

But circumstances in the Sudan are quite different, and as I said in the House of Commons, it would be tragic if anything were to disturb the progress which has been made in the political and material fields.

I should now like to say a few words about what my Government considers the real core of the Sudan problem, namely, how soon the country should attain complete self-government and determine its own future. It is my object to persuade your Government to work with mine, towards this end. Predeclared policies of both our Goverments in regard to the Sudan are the same. What we must solve, therefore, is the practical problem, namely, how to assemble the elements necessary for a stable Government in the Sudan, and how to guide the Sudanese people towards self-government. Before I discuss this, however, I should like to refute one suggestion made in your Excellency's statement. I mean your suggestion that the Sudan Government, with my Government's approval, has deliberately kept the Southern Sudan "in a primitive condition and complete segregation from the North" and has not allowed Northern Sudanese to enter the South.

Frankly, if you study the Southern Sudan, you will find that this is not correct. History has shown over and over again that if primitive, indigenous cultures are to be preserved from extinction when they first come into contact with more advanced peoples, they must be treated with the greatest care. This the Sudan Government have successfully done.

The difference in development between the Northern and Southern Sudan presents a serious problem. In recent years, however, the Southern Sudanese have reached a stage where closer contact has become possible. To-day their representatives sit in the Sudan Legislative Assembly, where they debate on equal terms with their fellow-members from the North; Southern Sudanese civil servants, like Northern Sudanese, serve in any part of the Sudan; and I would commend to Your Excellency's study the Sudan Government's education plan for the South, which contains, among other things, provisions for the increased use of Arabic in all schools in the Southern Sudan, including those directed by Christian missionaries. If there is one sphere of the Sudan Government's administration which is beyond reproach, an impartial and unprejudiced body of observers would undoubtedly agree that it is their administration of the Southern provinces.

To return to what I described as the "core" of the Sudan problem: the granting of self-government to the Sudanese is, in my opinion, largely a matter of timing. Both

---

[1] See 175.

our Governments have a duty to discharge in this matter. If, setting aside mutual suspicion, we can work together to solve this problem, we shall have achieved a great work. The Governor-General's Executive Council now has a Sudanese majority. As I have already said, the Sudan Government hope to broaden the electoral basis of the Legislative Assembly before the next elections. There are two important steps in the right direction.

A further step would be the Unionists' participation in the next elections for the Sudan Legislative Assembly. If they do so, the Sudan people will for the first time be represented by a body not only democratically elected, but one whose members will be drawn from *all* classes and creeds. This would be a tremendous step towards a Sudan settlement.

At the moment, however, I feel bound to point out to Your Excellency that the principal obstacle to the election of a fully representative Legislative Assembly in the Sudan is the rigid attitude adopted by the Egyptian Government towards the future of the Sudan. Compromises may have to be made. The United Kingdom have a long experience of the successful guidance of other peoples, in Asia, in Africa, and elsewhere, towards self-government. So long, however, as the Egyptian Government refuse to modify their insistence on the unity of Egypt and the Sudan, their supporters in the Sudan must naturally find it hard to achieve a compromise with those Sudanese who sincerely believe that the best interest of their country lies in independence.

Meanwhile, the policy of my Government remains as before—that we shall do everything in our power to ensure that the choice which the Sudanese people finally make about the way in which their country is to be governed—is a free one.

In conclusion, I should like to say that I believe that our two Governments are agreed in principle about the future of the Sudan. I was glad to see that, at the end of your statement about the Sudan, Your Excellency made it clear that both our Governments are agreed that our aim in the Sudan is to give the Sudanese self-government as quickly as possible.

Unfortunately, we still differ about the means whereby this end should be achieved. Can we agree to create the conditions necessary for Sudanese self-government? Can we agree, forgetting mutual suspicion, to shepherd the Sudanese people and to do all in our power to assist them to achieve this end? If so, the problem of the Sudan can be solved.

200 FO 371/80360, no 60 17 Dec 1950

[Self-government]: letter from Sir R Howe to Sir W Strang on the self-government debate in the Legislative Assembly. *Enclosures*

[Following the narrow passage of the self-government motion in the Legislative Assembly (see 198) Howe forwarded background material on the debate and the motion itself. In his reply Strang agreed that the Umma party memo required no further action and added: 'We also agree that the future of the Southern Sudan is a matter of the highest importance, and that the South should not be placed under the administration of a wholly Sudanese Government in the near future. We therefore think it would be useful if you could follow up the suggestion, made in the last sentence of your memorandum, that you should find out from the Sudanese Ministers, and indeed from any Sudanese of political importance, including those belonging to the Opposition parties, what guarantees they would propose for the South in the event of the Sudanese assuming the whole responsibility for the administration of their country at any time within the next ten years' (letter from Strang to Howe, 13 Jan 1950, FO 371/80360, no 60).]

I am sending you herewith a memo. on the political future of the Sudan which was sent to me at the end of last month by Abdulla Bey Khalil, the Leader of the Legislative Assembly and Secretary-General of the Umma Party.

2. This memo. which alleges that it expresses the opinions of the Sudanese members of the Executive Council and Legislative Assembly summarises their views as:—

(1) The *immediate* setting up of a Sudanese Cabinet.

(2) The *next elections* at the end of 1951 to be declared to be on the basis of self-government.

(1) is considered to be within my powers as Governor-General, (2) must, it is admitted, be referred to the Co-domini.

3. Since this memo. was received, there has been tabled to the Assembly the motion on self-government which formed the subject of my telegram No.217 of 12th December. At the same time as the request for my consent to the debate on the motion was received I had a letter from 32 Members of the Legislative Assembly, a copy of which is attached, asking that self-government should be gradual. The Assembly have also approved a further motion to set up a Commission to examine the workings of the Executive Council and Legislative Assembly Ordinance and to suggest improvements within the present constitutional framework.

4. You will note that the memo. is said to represent the views of all the Sudanese members of the Executive Council and Legislative Assembly. One of the reasons which induced me to give my consent to the motion on self-government in the Assembly was to test whether this statement was indeed a true one. I will refer to this point later on.

5. I have discussed this memo. with Abdulla Bey Khalil and I asked him to define precisely what he and his party (for it is of course an Umma party document) mean by this term. I pointed out that full self-government seemed to me to be pretty much the same as independence and that the Sudan already enjoyed a very large measure of self-government by reason of the fact that the Executive Council had a majority of Sudanese members while the Legislative Assembly was wholly Sudanese except for five British members only among a total of ninety-two. Abdulla Bey replied that, for him, self-government meant Sudanese ministers for most of the departments of the Government, the present British officials to be advisers in those departments. Apart from that there would be no change in the administration. Sudanisation would proceed according to the programmes already drawn up and approved. There would be representatives of the Tribal Areas and the South in the Executive Council. As far as the South itself was concerned its present administration must continue down to the most junior British District Commissioner until the South was equipped to stand by itself. Abdulla Bey was prepared to say all this to the Legislative Assembly. The ultimate aim of the Independence Party was Dominion Status within the British Commonwealth.

6. I told Abdulla Bey that while I thought it was possible to increase the number of Sudanese Ministers and I was in fact considering at the moment promoting one or two of the present Sudanese on the Executive Council to be Ministers the

achievement of the other aims set out in the memo. was another matter. I was sure that they would only be considered by the Co-domini if they could be shown to be backed by a majority of the country. This could only be done by some device such as a plebiscite or through a more fully representative Legislative Assembly. The device of the plebiscite seemed to be ruled out in present circumstances. The Legislative Assembly is not yet wholly or even predominantly representative. The Khatmia are almost unrepresented. The South has 14 members representing some 2½ million people as compared with the North who have 73 representatives for 5 million people. I have developed this theme more fully in the attached memo. (B).

7. During the days preceding the debate in the Assembly the Umma Party began to exert considerable pressure on the members of the Assembly to vote in favour of it. S.A.R. himself came up from Aba Island and telegrams poured in from Umma organisations to Members of the Legislative Assembly who were considered to be opposed to immediate self-government. The debate was lengthy and spirited and the result was that the motion was passed by 39 votes to 38, the barest possible majority.

8. The result must be a hard blow to the Umma and to S.A.R's ambitions. The motion which obtained only a majority of one in a house which is supposed to be predominantly Umma is a proof that self-government as envisaged by the Umma commands no majority in the country as a whole; this however is no sign that if the House was reconstituted in such a way as to attract those who now oppose it to come in, there would not be a much larger vote in favour of self-government. It would no doubt depend largely on whether any motion for self-government were sponsered [sic] by the Umma. The vote is certainly not a vote for unity of the Sudan and Egypt; every Sudanese member who spoke against the motion made this clear but it is quite clearly the reflection of the general attitude outside Khartoum that the country does not want the present British administration to go, that the country does not want to be governed by the politically minded townsmen and half-baked effendia and that the South should be given more time under its present rulers.

9. I do not propose to send this memo. to the Co-domini or in fact to take any further action on it.

Enclosure A to 200: memorandum by Abdallah Khalil, 28 Nov 1950

His Excellency the governor general of the Sudan

I beg to submit to your Excellency the following memorandum which, in my opinion, expresses the views and aspirations of the Sudanese members of the Legislative Assembly and the Executive Council in regard to the political future of their country. These views may be summarised as follows:—

(1) The immediate setting up of a Sudanese Cabinet.

(2) The declaration of the next elections on the basis of Self-Government to be established immediately after the end of the 3rd Session of the present Assembly—that is before the end of 1951.

How to achieve these two aims will call for a detailed explanation of many points. The following is an attempt to explain briefly these points.

The present condominium rule

While we admit the useful services which the Condominium Rule has been able to render to this country during the last fifty years, we believe that if it is allowed to continue for any longer period it will seriously affect the political, economic & social development of this country; and the following are a few examples to show how this rule is becoming unsuitable:—

(1) The difference of opinion between the two Condominium powers in regard to the future political status of the Sudan. While England believes in and works for the Sudan's ultimate goal of freedom and independence, Egypt is doing all it can to obstruct and check this movement towards freedom, because it looks upon an independent Sudan as nothing but a real danger and threat to her interests as regards the Nile waters; but Egypt conceals her imperialistic aims under the usual claim that the Sudan forms an integral part of her territory and as such has no right to set up a separate constitution.

(2) The disapproval of Egypt of the present political set up and her determined attemps [sic] to encourage as many Sudanese as it can and persuade them to boycott the Legislative Assembly and other progressive institutions.

(3) The unanimous agreement of *all* Sudanese political parties that the Condominium Rule is no longer suitable and therefore must be terminated without delay.

The examples we have given are sufficient to illustrate the unsuitability of this rule and show the necessity for its termination as quickly as possible so that we can govern our own country as other free peoples do. We cannot tolerate in this age of freedom that we should remain in this anomalous situation and that we should not be self-governing and that the interests of our country should continue to progress slowly merely out of regard for the alleged interests of Egypt. While we can understand Egypt's imperialistic attitude, we can hardly believe that England—with its long democratic traditions—will support it, especially after having recognised and declared the Sudanese right to self-determination and having approved the establishment of the present political institutions.

We were and are still asking for the termination of this rule. We were already looking for the first suitable opportunity to get rid of it until the second World War broke out when we voluntarily came to the side of the democracies and contributed as much as we could at a time when Egypt refused to participate in it. Neither her partnership nor her alleged sovereignty could induce her to defend us. On the other hand we, the ruled, never thought of securing her permission to enter the war or appealed to her for any kind of help. We ought to have proclaimed our Independence at that time but unfortunately we missed the opportunity through a belief that England after having tried both of us during that decisive war would not hesitate to grant us our independence after the end of the war. But instead of coming out of the war as an independent nation the sovereignty of Egypt was about to be imposed on the Sudan as a result of the 1946 Anglo–Egyptian negotiations had it not been for the firm stand of the Independence Front, the great efforts of the late Sir Hubert Huddleston and the personal contact made by Sayed Abdel Rahman el Mahdi with the British Government. We are sure that your Excellency is fully aware of the details of these transactions and of the advice which Mr. Attlee gave to Sayed Abdel Rahman to return to the Sudan and work in full cooperation with the Governor General towards the realisation of the Sudanese national aspirations.[1] The Independence Front proceeded to cooperate with His Excellency until the first steps towards Independence were realised by the setting up of the Legislative Assembly and the Executive Council.

Egypt resorted to the Security Council after the breakdown of the negotiations with Great Britain and after her failure to impose her Sovereignty over the Sudan. At Lake Success she tried to make a case but failed. She gained nothing from her denunciation of British policy in the Sudan, nor from abandoning her earlier claim based on the right of conquest and introducing a new formula that the Sudan was part of Egypt. She came back from America with one result—the recognition by the Security Council of the right of the Sudanese to self-determination.

Your Excellency is fully aware of Egypt's attitude towards these two institutions—she repudiated them and circulated false rumours about them. She incited her supporters to boycott the election for the Assembly and to stage demonstrations in protest against its creation; she undertook to give money to any one who would work against the Independence movement. Nevertheless the majority of the Sudanese who were and are still firm believers in their rights to self-determination, accepted the two institutions as a first practical step towards independence. The Independence Front stood for the elections and succeeded in winning them. Subsequently the Assembly was formed from the majority party and continued to work for the well-being and progress of the Sudan in a manner which was commended by Your Excellency early this year. It was gratifying to see that as a result of Your Excellency's satisfaction with the achievements of the Assembly the Sudanese obtained a majority in the Executive Council.

But we are anxious that a big and decisive step forward should be taken as soon as possible. There are factors which urge us to request that such a step should take place without delay. The following are some of them:—

(1) It is right that we ask for freedom in order to Govern our country like other free peoples—this is a universally accepted principle.

(2) We see around us peoples who are smaller in numbers and less well prepared for freedom in many respects and yet they have enjoyed or are about to enjoy their right to self-determination.

(3) That if we adopt in our progress the policy of caution and slowness, we shall expose the country to dangers, the consequences of which cannot be contemplated by any true citizen of the Sudan.

In the hope of increasing the number of its supporters in the Sudan, Egypt has intensified its propaganda using all visible and invisible means—offering attractive educational facilities, building mosques, attempting to open schools and start hospitals etc. etc.

As a partner, Egypt refuses to see the Sudan represented in any international organization or any World conference so that the Sudan should not have a separate voice. She is determined to spend considerable sums of money on propaganda in the Sudan—a former prime minister of Egypt is alleged to have made a declaration to this effect. The objective behind this intention as he put it was to release the Egyptian piastre so that it reaches every house in the Sudan as a result of which Egypt's name will be on every tongue—but the real objective is obvious.

---

[1] See 114.

From the above it will appear that slowness is obviously in the interest of Egypt because the time factor will help her to achieve her ambitions through increasing her supporters in the Sudan and the country's future will be exposed to grave dangers if we follow the policy of caution and slowness. A continuation of this Egyptian propaganda will lead to moral chaos, internal dissension and corruption in social life. Egypt's continued and varied methods of propaganda are bound to have their effect on the masses and are also bound to weaken the morale of the at present cooperating majority which in order to prove that it is a majority, is calling for a plebisite [sic].

But the danger to the Sudan comes not only from Egyptian propaganda but from the potential struggle of World Powers for the control of strategic points. Such a state of affairs if it arises—as it may well do—may force statesmen to ignore, even temporarily, the rights of small nations on the assumption that World peace is at stake. Although we are confident of England's promises and do not believe for a moment that she will betray the Sudan or bargain with Egypt at our expense in case of a third World War, yet we believe at the same time that such a war will at least expose our claim to independence to the danger of postponement.

We therefore request that our problem be solved without any further delay and recommend that it be solved on the following basis:—

Anyone who reads this note and anyone who sees the plight of the Sudan as a result of this exceptional status would not hesitate to ask for complete Independence; but we realise that such a recommendation must be preceded by other steps which will enable your Excellency to approach the Co-domini and recommend to them the termination of the present situation.

We, therefore, venture to put before your Excellency the following recommendations:—

(1) The immediate setting up of a Sudanese Cabinet,

(2) The declaration of the next elections on the basis of Self-Government to be established immediately after the end of the 3rd Session of the present Assembly—that is before the end of 1951

We realise that Your Excellency as a representative of the Co-Domini must refer to them the question of Self-Government, but we also realise that the setting up of a Sudanese Cabinet is within your powers.

We therefore consider that the immediate setting up of a Sudanese Cabinet will have two advantages, namely,

(a) it will strengthen the recommendation for Self-Government, and

(b) it will allow your Excellency ample time for necessary correspondence and perhaps personal contact.

Your Excellency is well aware of the benefits that will acrue [sic] to this country from declaraing [sic] the next elections on the basis of Self-Government. Such declaration will, in our opinion, lessen Egyptian propaganda, will bring the Sudanese together and will consolidate the position of all men of good will.

In submitting these recommendations we feel we must explain briefly such points as:—

(1) the composition of the Sudanese Cabinet.
(2) what is meant by Self-Government.
(3) the future as we see it.

Here is an attempt to do so:—

Composition of a Sudanese Cabinet

Your Excellency will probably agree with us that most departments could be converted straight away to Ministries with Sudanese Ministers, but the following points in regard to the composition of the cabinet should be made clear:—

(a) British Directors of Departments should have the status of advisers.

(b) that the Ministry of Finance and the Ministry responsible for Foreign Affairs should have Sudanese Ministers only when technically qualified Sudanese are available for appointment.

(c) that this cabinet should have on it representatives for the South and for tribal areas—perhaps without portfolio at the present time.

What is meant by self-government

We realise that the declaration of Self-Government would neither terminate the present condominium rule, nor would it cause a change in the position of the head of the state but it will no doubt bring the country nearer its final goal—that is self-determination and decision on the form of Government which the citizens of this country may like to choose for themselves.

But here we must answer a question which will be in the minds of all who read this document, namely, what would be the fate of the present admirable administration while the Sudan is achieving Self-Government and later complete independence?

It is unquestionable that the Sudan enjoys at present a very high standard of administration which every wise Sudanese is determined to maintain.

We therefore feel it imperative that all British executive officers should remain in their posts until such posts are Sudanised in accordance with the principles laid down in the Sudanisation Scheme and in accordance with existing obligations as regards contracts and pensions.

The future

The immediate setting up of a Sudanese Cabinet on the lines suggested elsewhere in this notice will, without any shadow of doubt, be backed and supported by almost all the Sudanese and will thus enable both the internal and external affairs of this country to be established on a sound basis. It is this Cabinet which will be able to see the urgent need for the Sudan to make treaties with a powerful nation which will come to its aid in time of peace or war.

Conclusion

These, in our belief are the minimum recommendations which we can put forward to your Excellency. They have been dictated by our anxiety about the future of our country, by the present anomalous situation and by Egypt's determined efforts to deprive us of a universally accepted right to Self-determination—a fact which has been closely defined in the recent crown speech.

We sincerely hope that the realisation of these recommendations will be met by a quick response from Great Britain which has for so long inherited the ideals of freedom, fraternity and equality.

Enclosure 1A to 200: petition by tribal chiefs and notables

His Excellency, The Governor-General of the Sudan, Thro' Civil Secretary

(1) We, tribal chiefs and notables, representing the majority of the Sudanese people in the Assembly, have noticed a proposal by some members of the Assembly demanding self-government before the end of 1951.
(2) Although we agree to this in principle, yet we want to [sic] progress of our country to be gradual and steady.
(3) We also want to give a chance to our fellow countrymen to participate in this Assembly by their taking part in the new elections. They could then have a share in deciding on the interests of their country.[2]

Enclosure B to 200: memorandum by Sir R Howe, 29 Nov 1950

A number of members of the Legislative Assembly are asking to have a motion and a debate on self-government in the Assembly. The reason for this sudden demand is doubtless the statement in the Egyptian Speech from the Throne that the Sudan and Egypt are one. It does not yet appear what form the motion would take but probably it would be to the effect that the Sudan is fit for the immediate grant of self-government or for a further step towards it. If the motion were approved the next step would presumably be pressure by the Umma Party for a *wholly Sudanese cabinet*.

An entirely Sudanese Cabinet could maintain itself in power and function successfully in two ways:—

(a) if it had the backing of a majority of a freely elected Legislative Assembly representative of the country as a whole,
(b) if it were backed by force (presumably British)

Now the present Legislative Assembly is not representative of the whole country. The Khatmia, probably numerically as strong as the Ansar, are almost unrepresented. The South have 13 members representing some 2½ million people compared with the North who have some 75 representatives for 5 million people.

A wholly Sudanese Cabinet now, even if it were backed by the present Assembly, would not necessarily be supported by the people in general and in fact would be bitterly opposed by many of the educated and townspeople, notably the Khatmia.

The consequences might be incalculable. For example would such a Cabinet be able to command the absolute allegiance of the S.D.F. and the Police and would not the whole machinery of Egyptian propaganda, the Khatmia, the Ashigga and other opposition political parties, the labour unions and the students try to block it at every turn, and make the administration difficult if not impossible? We have recently seen S.A.M's influence powerfully exerted in the W.A.C. (Workers' Affairs Congress) [sic WAA].

---

[1] Thirty-two signatures follow, the first being that of Sharif Ibrahim al-Hindi, the leader of a small religious order with less influence than either the Ansar or the Khatmiya. Signatures 2–20 were shaikhs and notables from the rural areas of the northern Sudan; 21–31 were southern Sudanese, including James Tembura (a Zande chief), Cier Rehan (a Dinka chief), Buth Diu, Edward Odhok Dedigo and Siricio Iro who, along with Surur Muhammad Ramli (a Jaali Shaikh and signature 32) had all been delegates to the 1947 Juba conference.

The Governor-General's position as representative of the Co-domini would be difficult.

Any demand for self-government for a country to be receivable must have the approval of the majority of the people. That approval can only be expressed manifestly by some device such as a plebiscite or through a representative Assembly. The first device is out of the question in the Sudan as most people will admit and the question has been pretty well ventilated recently.

There remains the Assembly. It is not representative and if it is to be the mainspring for a demand for self-government, a necessary preliminary step must be to try to make it a nationally representative body. This means new elections in the north which will be not boycotted by the more important and numerical opposition parties and a more equitable representation for the south, who, on the same basis as the north should have about 30 members—a very difficult target to achieve at present.

It seems to me therefore in view of the present high degree of self-government we should discourage the Umma ministers from pressing these motions, or else ensure that they fail in the Assembly. We must endeavour to persuade them that the way of further self-government lies through the Assembly and not through pressure by individual political groups. If, as it may well be, their reply to this is that they must do something to counter the blast from Egypt about the unity of Egypt and the Sudan, we can say that we have forwarded their protest to the Co-domini. They have moreover the pledge of H.M.G. and the opinion of the U.N. They might of course resort to other forms of pressure such as resignation from the Executive Council or Assembly but this would be to play straight into the hands of their political opponents and I would be surprised if they were to commit such an error of judgment.

There is no reason why we should not say now that the Sudan has self-government. The facts of the situation fully warrant it, i.e. Sudanese majorities in both the Executive Council and Legislative Assembly.

My chief motive in coming to the opinions expressed above is largely anxiety as to the fate of the Southern Sudan. I could not contemplate with any peace of mind placing the south under the control of a Sudanese Government at the present time. If adequate safeguards for the south could be worked out or if it were agreed as a condition of self-government that the south should not be under the administration of a wholly Sudanese Government, my views as regards hastening self-government might possibly be modified. But it might be interesting to find out from our Sudanese ministers who are pressing the question of an immediate grant of full self-government what guarantees they would propose for the south, for I am certain that H.M.G. at any rate, would have to be satisfied on this matter.

Appendix to Part I

The Anglo–Egyptian Agreement of 1899

AGREEMENT between Her Britannic Majesty's Government and the Government of His Highness the Khedive of Egypt relative to the future administration of the Sudan.

WHEREAS certain provinces in the Sudan which were in rebellion against the authority of His Highness the Khedive have now been reconquered by the joint military and financial efforts of Her Britannic Majesty's Government and the Government of His Highness the Khedive;

AND whereas it has become necessary to decide upon a system for the administration of and for the making of laws for the said reconquered provinces, under which due allowance may be made for the backward and unsettled condition of large portions thereof, and for the varying requirements of different localities;

AND whereas it is desired to give effect to the claims which have accrued to Her Britannic Majesty's Government, by right of conquest, to share in the present settlement and future working and development of the said system of administration and legislation;

AND whereas it is conceived that for many purposes Wadi Halfa and Suakin may be most effectively administered in conjunction with the reconquered provinces to which they are respectively adjacent;

Now it is hereby agreed and declared by and between the undersigned, duly authorized for that purpose, as follows:

ARTICLE I.

The word "Sudan" in this Agreement means all the territories South of the 22nd parallel of latitude, which:

1. Have never been evacuated by Egyptian troops since the year 1882; or
2. Which having before the late rebellion in the Sudan been administered by the Government of His Highness the Khedive, were temporarily lost to Egypt, and have been reconquered by Her Majesty's Government and the Egyptian Government, acting in concert; or
3. Which may be hereafter reconquered by the two Governments acting in concert.

ARTICLE II.

The British and Egyptian flags shall be used together, both on land and water, throughout the Sudan, except in the town of Suakin, in which locality the Egyptian flag alone shall be used.

ARTICLE III.

The supreme military and civil command of the Sudan shall be vested in one officer, termed the "Governor-General of the Sudan." He shall be appointed by Khedivial

Decree on the recommendation of Her Britannic Majesty's Government, and shall be removed only by Khedivial Decree, with the consent of Her Britannic Majesty's Government.

ARTICLE IV.

Laws, as also Orders and Regulations with the full force of law, for the good government of the Sudan, and for regulating the holding, disposal, and devolution of property of every kind therein situate, may from time to time be made, altered, or abrogated by Proclamation of the Governor-General. Such Laws, Orders, and Regulations may apply to the whole or any named part of the Sudan, and may, either explicitly or by necessary implication, alter or abrogate any existing Law or Regulation.

All such Proclamations shall be forthwith notified to Her Britannic Majesty's Agent and Consul-General in Cairo, and to the President of the Council of Ministers of His Highness the Khedive.

ARTICLE V.

No Egyptian Law, Decree, Ministerial Arrêté, or other enactment hereafter to be made or promulgated shall apply to the Sudan or any part thereof save in so far as the same shall be applied by Proclamation of the Governor-General in manner hereinbefore provided.

ARTICLE VI.

In the definition by Proclamation of the conditions under which Europeans, of whatever nationality, shall be at liberty to trade with or reside in the Sudan, or to hold property, within its limits, no special privileges shall be accorded to the subjects of any one or more Power.

ARTICLE VII.

Import duties on entering the Sudan shall not be payable on goods coming from Egyptian territory. Such duties may, however, be levied on goods coming from elsewhere than Egyptian territory, but in the case of goods entering the Sudan at Suakin, or any other port on the Red Sea littoral, they shall not exceed the corresponding duties for the time being leviable on goods entering Egypt from abroad. Duties may be levied on goods leaving the Sudan, at such rates as may from time to time be prescribed by Proclamation.

ARTICLE VIII.

The jurisdiction of the Mixed Tribunals shall not extend, nor be recognised for any purpose whatsoever, in any part of the Sudan, except in the town of Suakin.

ARTICLE IX.

Until, and save so far as it shall be otherwise determined by Proclamation, the Sudan, with the exception of the town of Suakin, shall be and remain under martial law.

ARTICLE X.

No Consuls, Vice-Consuls, or Consular Agents shall be accredited in respect of nor allowed to reside in the Sudan, without the previous consent of Her Britannic Majesty's Government.

ARTICLE XI.

The importation of slaves into the Sudan, as also their exportation, is absolutely prohibited. Provision shall be made by Proclamation for the enforcement of this Regulation.

ARTICLE XII.

It is agreed between the two Governments that special attention shall be paid to the enforcement of the Brussels Act of the 2nd July, 1890, in respect of the import, sale, and manufacture of fire-arms and their munitions, and distilled or spirituous liquors.

Done in Cairo, the 19th January, 1899.

Signed: { BOUTROS GHALI
CROMER

Index of Main Subjects and Persons

This is a consolidated index for both parts of the volume. It is not a comprehensive index, but a simplified and straightforward index to document numbers, together with page references to the Introduction in part I, the latter being given at the beginning of the entry in lower case roman numerals. The index is designed to be used in conjunction with the summary lists of the preliminary pages to both parts of the volume. A preceding asterisk indicates inclusion in the Biographical Notes at the end of Part II.

Three British officials—Bevin, Sir R Howe and Sir J Robertson—and three Sudanese personalities—Ismail al-Azhari, Abd al-Rahman al-Mahdi and Ali al-Mirghani—appear prominently in both parts of the volume. In these cases the index provides, in addition to page references to the Introduction, the first document reference only; subsequent references can be identified from the summary lists. In the case of Sir A Eden, references are provided up to the point at which he became foreign secretary in 1951; thereafter references can be identified from the summary list in Part II.

The names of Egyptian and Sudanese personalities are listed under the spelling used in the introduction and editorial apparatus, with the most common spellings appearing in the documents given inside round brackets. Arabic names are alphebetised according to the English convention of listing the last name first.

The following abbreviations are used:

A – annex, appendix or enclosure
N – editor's link note (before main text of document)
n – footnote

Documents are divided between the two parts of the volume as follows:

nos 1–200 (+ Appendix) Part I
nos 201–440 (+ Appendix) Part II

The Volume Editor

DOUGLAS H JOHNSON is an historian, publisher and former regional archivist in the Sudan. He is the author of *Nuer Prophets* (1994) and *The Root Causes of Sudan's Civil Wars* (forthcoming, 1999). His edited collections of documents include *Governing the Nuer: Documents in Nuer History and Ethnography, 1922–31* (1993), *The Upper Nile Province Handbook: A Report on Peoples and Government in the Southern Sudan, 1931* (1995) and *Juan Maria Schuver's Travels in North East Africa, 1880–1883* (with Wendy James and Gerd Baumann, 1996).

Part two, covering the period between January 1951 and October 1956, begins with the crisis of Egypt's unilateral abrogation of the Anglo-Egyptian agreement, which stimulated a further acceleration towards self-government in the Sudan. The 1952 Free Officer's coup in Egypt was followed by Egypt's renunciation of its claims to sovereignty over the Sudan, but a continuation of its drive for the unification of the two countries, now fought out in the elections leading to the first all-Sudanese government. With access to power, followed by the rapid Sudanisation of the administration, police and army, and facing the possible disintegration of the country during the 1955 rising in the South, a previously pro-Egyptian Sudanese government (prompted by Britain) opted for complete independence, which was granted, in haste, on 1 January 1956.

Based on the records of the Foreign, Colonial and Prime Minister's Offices, and the Cabinet and its committees, these documents reveal a previously unappreciated complexity in this early episode of decolonisation. Bringing forth the Foreign Office's perspective on dwindling imperial power and colonial affairs, they throw new light on debates surrounding decolonisation within the first post-war Labour and Conservative governments. They also, in their attempts to foresee a future for so divided a country as the Sudan, show a prescient concern for the troubled place of the Southern Sudan, the role of sectarian Muslim politics in the nation at large and the enduring importance of that long subterranean stream, the Nile Waters question.